797,885 Books
are available to read at

Forgotten Books

www.ForgottenBooks.com

Forgotten Books' App
Available for mobile, tablet & eReader

ISBN 978-1-330-30866-0
PIBN 10021933

This book is a reproduction of an important historical work. Forgotten Books uses
state-of-the-art technology to digitally reconstruct the work, preserving the original format
whilst repairing imperfections present in the aged copy. In rare cases, an imperfection in
the original, such as a blemish or missing page, may be replicated in our edition. We do,
however, repair the vast majority of imperfections successfully; any imperfections that
remain are intentionally left to preserve the state of such historical works.

Forgotten Books is a registered trademark of FB &c Ltd.
Copyright © 2017 FB &c Ltd.
FB &c Ltd, Dalton House, 60 Windsor Avenue, London, SW19 2RR.
Company number 08720141. Registered in England and Wales.

For support please visit www.forgottenbooks.com

1 MONTH OF FREE READING

at

www.ForgottenBooks.com

By purchasing this book you are eligible for one month membership to ForgottenBooks.com, giving you unlimited access to our entire collection of over 700,000 titles via our web site and mobile apps.

To claim your free month visit: www.forgottenbooks.com/free21933

* Offer is valid for 45 days from date of purchase. Terms and conditions apply.

English
Français
Deutsche
Italiano
Español
Português

www.forgottenbooks.com

Mythology Photography **Fiction** Fishing Christianity **Art** Cooking Essays Buddhism Freemasonry Medicine **Biology** Music **Ancient Egypt** Evolution Carpentry Physics Dance Geology **Mathematics** Fitness Shakespeare **Folklore** Yoga Marketing **Confidence** Immortality Biographies Poetry **Psychology** Witchcraft Electronics Chemistry History **Law** Accounting **Philosophy** Anthropology Alchemy Drama Quantum Mechanics Atheism Sexual Health **Ancient History** **Entrepreneurship** Languages Sport Paleontology Needlework Islam **Metaphysics** Investment Archaeology Parenting Statistics Criminology **Motivational**

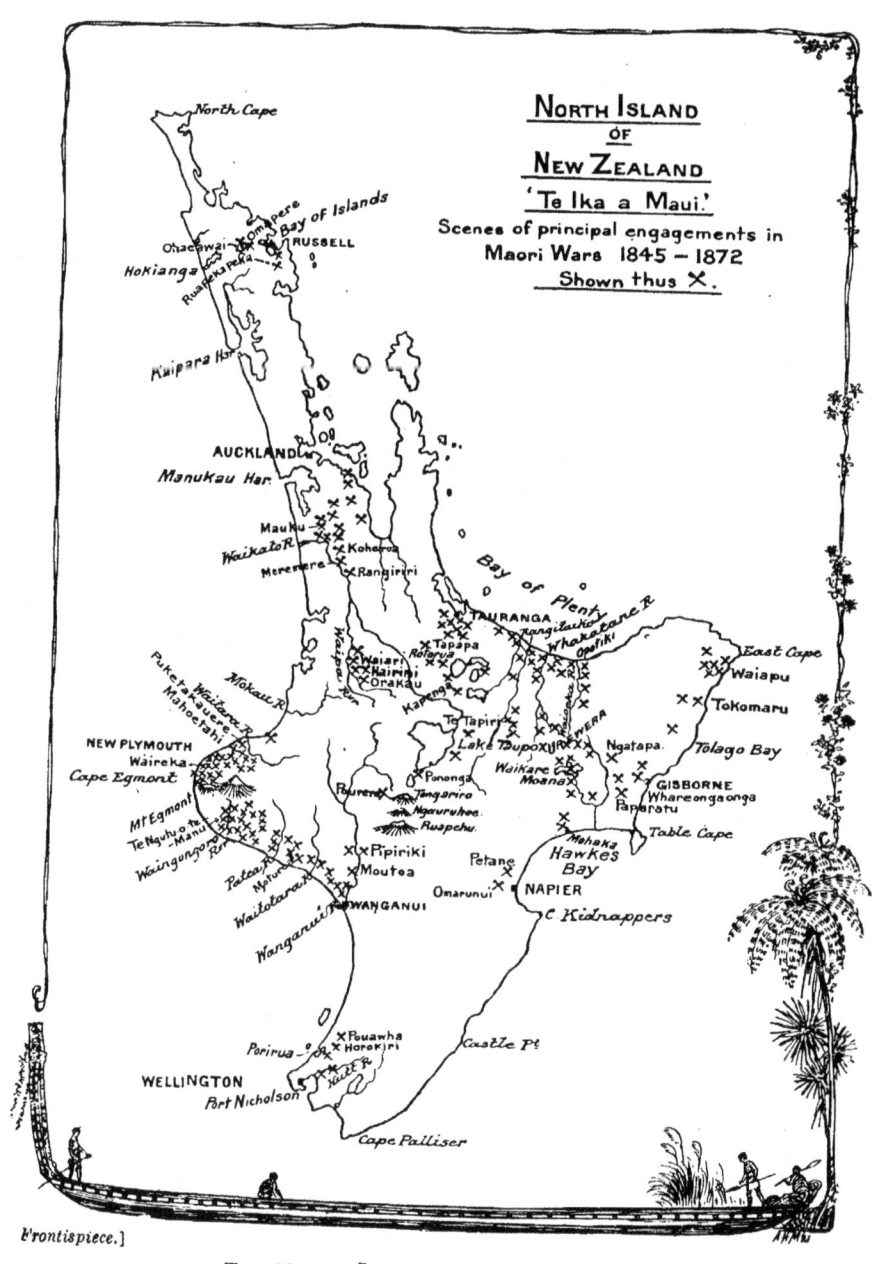

THE NORTH ISLAND OF NEW ZEALAND,
Showing sites of engagements in the Maori campaigns

THE
NEW ZEALAND WARS.

A HISTORY OF THE MAORI CAMPAIGNS AND THE PIONEERING PERIOD.

BY

JAMES COWAN, F.R.G.S.

VOL. I (1845-1864).

WITH ILLUSTRATIONS AND PLANS.

By Authority of the Hon. the Minister of Internal Affairs.

WELLINGTON.
W. A. G. SKINNER, GOVERNMENT PRINTER.
1922.

THE PIONEERS.

I

Shall not forget. I hold a trust.
They are a part of my existence. When
Adown the shining iron track
You sweep, and fields of corn flash back,
And herds of lowing steers move by,
I turn to other days, to men
Who made a pathway with their dust.

—" The Ship in the Desert " (JOAQUIN MILLER).

PREFACE.

THE increasing interest in the study of New Zealand's past emphasizes the need for a history of the wars with the Maoris since the establishment of British sovereignty and of the era of pioneering settlement and adventure, which was practically conterminous with those campaigns. Although there is in existence a considerable body of war-time literature written by participants in the conflicts, it is not possible to gather in any of the works on the subject a connected account of the successive outbreaks and campaigns which troubled the colony from 1845 to the beginning of 1872. Most of the printed narratives deal chiefly with events which came within the soldier-writers' own experience, and other contributions to the story of the campaigns are scarcely written in the impartial spirit of the historian. Some of the earlier works, and even the blue-books, contain many statements which careful inquiries and a better understanding of the Maori side of the struggle have now demolished. Most of the useful books, moreover, are out of print, and the student who wishes to make a complete survey of the field of contact between *pakeha* and Maori is compelled to work through many volumes, pamphlets, and newspaper-files in the public libraries. The fragmentary and scattered nature of our war-time literature therefore necessitates this endeavour to provide a standard history in convenient compass.

The present is probably the most favourable moment for the historian of New Zealand's wars and the adventure-teeming life of the pioneer colonists. A sufficient time has elapsed for the episodes of our nation-making to be viewed in their correct perspective ; there is a very large amount of printed matter and manuscript at the writer's hand ; and at the same time there are still with us many eye-witnesses of some of the most important events in New Zealand's history. Oral witness has its historical value, as Mr. George Macaulay Trevelyan has explained in his history "Garibaldi and the Thousand": "You cannot cross-examine a book or manuscript: that is the weakness of written evidence, which the presence of oral evidence rectifies to some degree." To this it may be added that an historian cannot thoroughly grip the spirit in which wars were waged, or appreciate to the full the motives and feelings of the contending forces, unless he has had some personal knowledge of the combatants, and has mingled with members of the warring parties. The psychology of the struggle will elude the writer who delays his work until the last veteran, the last pioneer, and the last Maori of the old school have gone from among us.

The foundation for this work of history-gathering was laid, unconsciously enough, in the writer's boyhood on a farthest-out farm on the King Country frontier. Since those youthful days on the battlefield of Orakau, where the shawl-kilted tattooed Maoris who had fought in the wars were familiar figures, and when the *pakeha* stalwarts who had carried rifle on many a bush war-path garrisoned the blockhouses and redoubts which still studded the Waikato border, the task of collecting the tales of old has been an often-renewed pleasure.

In the course of writing this History it was necessary to examine a very large amount of material in book form, in official documents, and in newspaper-files. It was necessary also to explore battlefields and sites of fortifications throughout the North Island. Veterans of the wars, European and Maori, were sought out, sometimes in the most remote places, and the field notes made on the scenes of engagements and sieges were often enhanced in value by the presence of soldiers, settlers, or natives who had fought there and who were able to describe the actions on the spot.

I take pleasure in recording here the names of those who gave valuable co-operation in this work. The History is due largely to the initiative of Dr. Thomson W. Leys, for many years editor of the *Auckland Star* and principal author of Brett's

"Early History of New Zealand," and also to the hearty assistance of the late Colonel T. W. Porter, C.B. The Hon. Sir Maui Pomare, M.P., gave much kind help in the native side of the narrative. With the guidance of Captain Gilbert Mair, N.Z.C., of Tauranga, many old fighting-trails were followed up and battle-grounds explored in the Rotorua, Bay of Plenty, and Urewera districts. In the Taranaki country Mr. William Wallace, of Meremere, and the late Colonel W. B. Messenger, of New Plymouth, gave similar assistance. Captain G. A. Preece, N.Z.C., contributed a very full and excellent diary account of the last military expeditions in the Urewera country, 1870-72; and the late Mr. S. Percy Smith, F.R.G.S., ex-Surveyor-General, lent his private journal from 1854 to 1869 and numerous Taranaki field-sketches and maps.

The following colonial soldiers, some of whom have since passed away, also assisted with narratives, diaries, plans, and other documents :—

Colonel J. M. Roberts, N.Z.C.; Colonel Stuart Newall, C.B.; Lieut.-Colonel A. Morrow; Lieut.-Colonel H. Parker; Major William G. Mair; Major D. H. Lusk; Major J. T. Large; Captain H. Northcroft, N.Z.C.; Captain C. Maling, N.Z.C.; Captain F. Mace, N.Z.C.; Captain J. R. Rushton; Captain Joseph Scott; Captain J. Stichbury; and numerous others.

The use of many historic pictures not hitherto published was given by Mr. Justice Chapman and Mr. H. Fildes, Wellington; Mr. H. E. Partridge, Auckland; Dr. P. Marshall, Mr. H. D. Bates, and Mr. T. W. Downes, Wanganui; Mrs. B. A. Crispe, Mauku; Mr. W. H. Skinner, New Plymouth; and others.

The late Mr. Alexander Turnbull, of Wellington, who bequeathed his library to the nation, was keenly interested in the compilation of this History, and in his kindly way placed all the material in his collection at my disposal, and searched out documents which threw additional light on events in New Zealand's " breaking-in " period.

I desire also to record the names of my principal Maori authorities, most of them veterans of the wars from 1845 onwards, who at various times gave information :—

Ngapuhi Tribe: Ruatara Tauramoko; Ngakuru Pana, Rihara Kou; Rawiri te Ruru; Hone Heke, M.P.

Waikato tribes: Patara te Tuhi; Honana Maioha; Mahutu te Toko; Te Aho-o-te-Rangi; Hori Kukutai.

Ngati-Paoa (Hauraki): Hori Ngakapa te Whanaunga.

Ngati-Maniapoto (King Country): Tupotahi; Te Huia Raureti and his son Raureti te Huia; Pou-patate; Peita Kotuku; Te Rohu (Rewi Maniapoto's widow); Taniora Wharauroa.

Ngati-Raukawa: Hitiri te Paerata.

Ngai-tē-Rangi (Tauranga): Hori Ngatai.

Te Arawa (Rotorua-Maketu district): Kiharoa; Te Araki te Pohu; Taua Tutanekai; Heeni Pore (Te Kiri-Karamu); Te Rangituakoha; Hohapeta te Whanarere; Te Matehaere; Rangiriri.

Ngati-Tuwharetoa (Taupo district): Te Heuheu Tukino, M.L.C.; Tokena te Kerehi; Waaka Tamaira; Wairehu.

Urewera: Eria Raukura (Te Kooti's chief priest); Netana Whakaari; Te Whiu Maraki; Tupara Kaho; Te Kauru.

Whakatohea (Opotiki): Hira te Okioki.

Ngati-Porou: Tuta Nihoniho.

Taranaki: Te Whiti o Rongomai (the prophet of Parihaka); Hori Teira.

Ngati-Ruanui (Taranaki): Tauke; Te Kahu-Pukoro; Pou-Whareumu Toi; Whareaitu.

Pakakohi (Patea): Tutange Waionui; Tu-Patea te Rongo.

Most of those mentioned were warriors who fought either against or for the Government; in a number of instances they explained on the battle-ground the details of engagements; few of them survive to recall the conditions and events of a life which has vanished for ever.

A great deal of trouble has been taken to obtain original illustrations, and Mr. A. H. Messenger, draughtsman in the New Zealand Forest Service, himself a member of a pioneer Taranaki family, has drawn for the History many pictures in line and wash from authentic material.

To the Hon. the Minister of Internal Affairs, and to the Under-Secretary of that Department, my gratitude is due for the liberal arrangements which made the writing and publication of this work possible.

The principal campaigns and expeditions dealt with in the History are as follows:—

(1.) Hone Heke's War in the north, 1845–46.
(2.) The campaign in the Wellington district, 1846
(3.) The war at Wanganui, 1847.
(4.) The first Taranaki War, 1860–61.
(5.) The second Taranaki War, 1863.
(6.) The Waikato War, 1863–64.
(7.) The Tauranga campaign, 1864.
(8.) The first Hauhau War, Taranaki, 1864–66.
(9.) The Opotiki and Matata operations, 1865.
(10.) The East Coast War, 1865.
(11.) Fighting in Tauranga and Rotorua districts, 1867.
(12.) Titokowaru's War, West Coast, 1868–69.
(13.) The campaigns against Te Kooti (East Coast, Taupo, and Urewera country), 1868–72.

The period covered in the present volume is from the outbreak of Heke's War in 1845 to the end of the Kingite wars in Taranaki, Waikato, and the Bay of Plenty, 1864. The second volume is devoted to the Hauhau campaigns, 1864–72.

Wellington, New Zealand, J. COWAN.
June, 1922.

CONTENTS.

CHAPTER I.—THE OLD RACE AND THE NEW.   PAGE

New Zealand's pioneering story—Likeness to North American frontier history—The contact between *pakeha* and Maori—Test of battle arouses mutual respect—The romance and adventure of New Zealand history—The native-born and the patriotism of the soil—Difficulties of the bush campaigns—Military qualities of the Maori underestimated by early British commanders—Maori population in the "forties" 1

CHAPTER II.—THE BEACH AT KORORAREKA.

A bay of adventure — The old landmarks — The whaleships of the "forties"—Scenes on Kororareka Beach—The whalemen and the Maoris—The old trading-stores—Aboard a New Bedford whaling-barque—The days of oil and bone 6

CHAPTER III.—HEKE AND THE FLAGSTAFF.

"God made this country for us"—Hone Heke's character—His fears for the future of his race—Early traffic with the whaleships—British Customs dues cause a decrease in Bay of Islands trade—Heke's raid on Kororareka—The Maiki flagstaff cut down—Governor Fitzroy meets the Maoris—Heke and the American flag—Troops sent to the bay—The flagstaff cut down again .. 13

CHAPTER IV.—THE FALL OF KORORAREKA.

Heke's ambush on Signal Hill—An attack at dawn—The flagstaff cut down a fourth time—Kawiti attacks the town—Encounter with a naval force—Captain Robertson's heroic fight—Sailors, soldiers, and settlers defend the town—Gallant work of Hector's gunners—The beach stockade blown up—A mismanaged defence—Evacuation of Kororareka 23

CHAPTER V.—THE FIRST BRITISH MARCH INLAND.

Operations against the Ngapuhi — Pomare's village destroyed — The friendly Maori tribes—Tamati Waka Nene's loyalty to the British—Pene Taui, and the consequences of a pun—Lieut.-Colonel Hulme's march inland 32

CHAPTER VI.—THE FIGHTING AT OMAPERE.

The Taiamai country and the plains of Omapere—Skirmishes between Heke's warriors and Tamati Waka's force—White free-lances in the fray—John Webster and F. E. Maning—Jackey Marmon, the white cannibal—Heke's stockade at Puketutu—British attack on the *pa* — Kawiti's desperate courage — Heavy skirmishing and bayonet fighting—British withdraw to the Bay of Islands—The Kapotai *pa* destroyed 37

CONTENTS.

Chapter VII.—The Attack on Ohaeawai.

The campaign renewed—Maori battle at Te Ahuahu—Heke severely wounded—Colonel Despard's expedition to Ohaeawai—A midwinter march—The heart of the Ngapuhi country—The camp before Ohaeawai—Pene Taui's strong stockade—The Maori artillery—Scenes in the stronghold—The British bombardment begins—Defects of the artillery—Failure of the "stench-balls" 47

Chapter VIII.—The Storming-party at Ohaeawai.

The bombardment—Despard's fatal blunder—Orders to storm the *pa*—The forlorn hope—The bayonet charge on the stockade—A survivor's narrative—Repulse of the storming-parties—The *pa* evacuated—Return of the troops—Ohaeawai to-day 57

Chapter IX.—The Capture of Rua-pekapeka.

Arrival of the new Governor, Captain George Grey—Another expedition prepared—Kawiti's mountain stronghold, "The Cave of the Bats"—Arduous march of the British troops—The camp before Rua-pekapeka—A general bombardment—Accuracy of the gunnery—A Sunday-morning surprise—British forces enter the fort—The Maoris driven into the bush—Peace in the north 70

Chapter X.—Wellington Settlement and the War at the Hutt.

Colonel Wakefield's purchases—Trouble in the Hutt Valley—"Dog's Ear" declines to quit—Fort-building in Wellington—Fort Arthur, at Nelson—Stockade and blockhouses at the Lower Hutt—American frontier forts the model for New Zealand stockades—Fortified posts built at Karori and Johnsonville—Troops arrive from Auckland—H.M.S. "Driver," the first steamship in Port Nicholson—Maoris evicted from Hutt settlements—Retaliatory raids on the settlers—The first skirmishes—British camp established at Porirua .. 85

Chapter XI.—The Fight at Boulcott's Farm.

A clearing in the Hutt forest—The British post at Boulcott's Farm—An early-morning surprise attack—Maoris overwhelm the picket—The gallant bugler's death—Troops' desperate battle with the natives—A commissariat carter's plucky drive—Major Last's reinforcements to the rescue—Skirmish near Taita—A hard afternoon's fighting 101

Chapter XII.—Operations at Porirua.

The British camp at Paremata—McKillop's naval patrol—Skirmish with Rangihaeata on the shore of Paua-taha-nui—A war-party from Wanganui—Despatch to Governor Grey—Surprise visit to Taupo *pa*—The capture of Te Rauparaha 109

Chapter XIII.—Paua-taha-nui and Horokiri.

Te Rangihaeata's stockade—Its site to-day—Government expedition from the Hutt—Capture of Paua-taha-nui—Te Rangihaeata's mountain camp—British expedition to Horokiri—Shelling the Maori position—British forces withdraw to Porirua—Remains of Horokiri defences—Pursuit of the fugitives 120

CONTENTS. XIII

CHAPTER XIV.—THE WAR AT WANGANUI.

An unfortunate settlement — The New Zealand Company's defective purchase—An accident and its sequel—Massacre of the Gilfillans—Wanganui besieged by the river tribes—The Rutland Stockade and blockhouses—Natives attack the town—British reinforcements arrive—The Battle of St. John's Wood—A skirmish in the swamp—Withdrawal of the Maoris, and return of peace 131

CHAPTER XV.—TARANAKI AND THE LAND LEAGUE.

New Plymouth and early land disputes—Purchases of settlement blocks—Wiremu Kingi's return to the Waitara—Formation of the Maori Land League—Intertribal fighting 140

CHAPTER XVI.—THE MAORI KING.

Movement for union of the Maori tribes—The selection of a King—The Arawa decline to join the Kingite cause—Great meeting at Pukawa, Lake Taupo—Te Heuheu's picturesque symbolism—Tongariro the centre of the Maori union—Potatau te Wherowhero chosen as King—Wiremu Tamehana's patriotic argument 145

CHAPTER XVII.—THE WAITARA PURCHASE.

Government bargain with Teira—Wiremu Kingi's protests disregarded—Maori objections to sale of the Waitara Block—The settlers' need of land 150

CHAPTER XVIII.—THE FIRST TARANAKI WAR.

Survey of the Waitara Block resisted—Martial law proclaimed—The Imperial and colonial troops—Defences of New Plymouth—The first shot—Capture of the L *pa* (Te Kohia)—Settlers build outposts for defence—The Bell Block and Omata stockades 154

CHAPTER XIX.—THE BATTLE OF WAIREKA.

Southern tribes fortify Waireka—Settlers killed at Omata—Expedition despatched to Waireka—A hot afternoon's fighting—Volunteers and Militia outnumbered and surrounded—The defence of Jury's Farmhouse—The " Niger " bluejackets capture Kaipopo *pa*—A Victoria Cross won—Return of the civilian force—Imperial officers' mismanagement—Reinforcements reach New Plymouth 166

CHAPTER XX.—PUKE-TA-KAUERE AND OTHER OPERATIONS.

A winter campaign—British attack *pas* on the Waitara—Maori fortifications at Puke-ta-kauere and Onuku-kaitara—Kingite reinforcements from the Upper Waikato—A Ngati-Maniapoto account—Rewi Maniapoto and his war-party—Major Nelson's unfortunate expedition—Hand-to-hand fighting—Heavy losses of the 40th Regiment—The slaughter in the swamp—Skirmishes near New Plymouth—The expedition to Kaihihi—Three Maori forts captured 178

CHAPTER XXI.—THE ENGAGEMENT AT MAHOETAHI.

Ngati-Haua enter the war—Wetini Taiporutu's challenge to the British—The Battle of Mahoetahi—Imperial and colonial storming-parties—Maoris make a desperate resistance—Close-quarters fighting—Defeat of the natives and death of Wetini—Song of lamentation for the slain 188

CONTENTS.

Chapter XXII.—Operations at Kairau and Huirangi.

Major-General Pratt's Waitara campaign—Maori fortifications at Kairau, Huirangi, and Te Arei—The British troops advance—Field-engineering work—Stockades and redoubts built—Skirmishing on the plain of Kairau—Sapping towards Te Arei *pa* 196

Chapter XXIII.—The Fight at No. 3 Redoubt.

Maori surprise attack—Attempt to storm No. 3 Redoubt, Huirangi—A desperate morning's work—Native forlorn hope destroyed—A British officer's graphic story 200

Chapter XXIV.—Pratt's Long Sap.

The sap towards Te Arei—Trench-digging and redoubt-building—A tedious advance—Details of the field-engineering work—Heavy skirmishing—Hapurona's stronghold heavily bombarded—Terms of peace agreed upon—End of the first Taranaki War—Heavy losses of the settlers 206

Chapter XXV.—The Second Taranaki Campaign.

Governor Grey's Maori policy—Tataraimaka Block reoccupied—The Waitara purchase abandoned—An ambush at Wairau and its consequences—Hori Teira's adventure—War renewed in Taranaki —Settlers' forest-ranging corps formed—The storming of Katikara —The Maori toll-gate—Expeditions and skirmishes—The fight at Allan's Hill—Maori stronghold at Kaitake attacked—Its final capture 215

Chapter XXVI.—The Waikato War and its Causes.

The Maori sentiment of nationalism—Growing friction with the Administration—Native demand for self-government—The Government institution at Te Awamutu—The *Hokioi* and the *Pihoihoi Mokemoke*—Ngati-Maniapoto evict Mr. Gorst—The Maori plan of campaign—Proposed attack on frontier settlements—Maori ammunition supplies—Invitations to the southern tribes—Wiremu Tamehana's warning.. 225

Chapter XXVII.—Military Forces and Frontier Defences.

The Government's war resources—Strength of the British and colonial forces—Universal military service—The Auckland Militia—Fort Britomart—Military posts south of Auckland—Redoubts and stockades in frontier settlements—Posts along the Great South Road—Churches fortified for defence—The road to the Waikato .. 236

Chapter XXVIII.—The First Engagements.

Maoris required to take the oath of allegiance—Government Proclamation to the Kingites—Eviction of natives on the Auckland frontier —A settler and his son tomahawked—General Cameron crosses the Manga-tawhiri River—The gathering of the Waikato clans—Te Huirama's trenches at Koheroa—British attack the position—Defeat of the Kingites—An ambush at Martin's Farm, Great South Road—Forest skirmish at Kirikiri—War-parties in the Wairoa and Hunua Ranges—Attacks on settlers—The Koheriki raiders—A Wairoa scouting expedition—Felling the forest, Great South Road —British party surprised at Williamson's Clearing, Pukewhau—Skirmishes at Pokeno and Razorback—Kingites kill Mr. Armitage at Camerontown—British expedition from Tuakau 244

CONTENTS.

CHAPTER XXIX.—THE FOREST RANGERS.

A special corps necessary for guerilla fighting in the bush—Formation of the Forest Rangers—Jackson's first company—Arms and equipment for forest fighting—The bowie-knife—Varied character of the Rangers—Settlers, bushmen, gold-diggers, and sailors—Arduous work in the roadless bush—Von Tempsky joins the Rangers—A daring reconnaissance—The two scouts at Paparata 257

CHAPTER XXX.—THE DEFENCE OF PUKEKOHE CHURCH STOCKADE.

Presbyterian church at Pukekohe East fortified by the settlers—Description of the stockade—The post attacked by a Kingite war-party—Gallant defence by seventeen men—Maori charge repulsed—Heavy fighting at close range—Arrival of reinforcements—A British bayonet charge—Maoris driven off with heavy loss—An attack on a farmhouse (Burtt's Farm) 265

CHAPTER XXXI.—OPERATIONS AT THE WAIROA.

Kingites in the Wairoa Ranges—Auckland reinforcements for the settlement—Engagements with the Maoris at Otau—An early-morning surprise attack—Native raids on the settlers—Homestead attacked at Mangemangeroa—Two boys killed—The Forest Rangers' expeditions—Jackson's company surprises a Koheriki camp—Seven Maoris killed 281

CHAPTER XXXII.—MAUKU AND PATUMAHOE.

Mauku Settlement in 1863—The village church fortified—Lusk's Forest Rifle Volunteers—Skirmish at the "Big Clearing," Patumahoe—Mauku Rifles and Forest Rangers in bush warfare—The Titi Hill Farm, Mauku—Invasion by a Kingite war-party—A desperate fight at close quarters—Skirmishing from log to log—Lieutenants Perceval and Norman killed—Lieutenant Lusk withdraws to the stockade—Arrival of British reinforcements 288

CHAPTER XXXIII.—THE RIVER WAR FLEET.

Colonial gunboats for the Waikato River—Arrival of the "Avon," the first steamboat on the Waikato—Reconnaissances under fire—Gunboat "Pioneer" built at Sydney for the river campaign—Four small armoured gunboats placed on the Waikato—The "Koheroa" and "Rangiriri"—The Waikato a strategic highway into the Maori country—The Royal Navy ships—The coast and harbour patrols 300

CHAPTER XXXIV.—THE TRENCHES AT MEREMERE.

Kingite entrenchments on the Meremere ridge—The Maori artillery—River reconnaissances in the gunboats—The "Avon" and "Pioneer" under fire—General Cameron reconnoitres the stronghold—Meremere outflanked and evacuated—The Miranda expedition—A chain of redoubts built—Operations of the Auckland Naval Volunteers 308

Chapter XXXV.—The Battle of Rangiriri.

Maori fortifications on Rangiriri Hill—Trenches from lake to river—Position attacked by General Cameron—Land forces and river flotilla—Artillery preparation, and assaulting-parties—The outer trenches carried—Maori central redoubt remains impregnable—Royal Artillery and Royal Navy storming-parties repulsed—Heavy British losses—Surrender of the *pa*—Prisoners sent to Auckland—The escape from Kawau Island 318

Chapter XXXVI.—The Advance on the Waipa.

The Upper Waikato invaded—Advance of Cameron's army—Scenes on the Waikato River—The Water Transport Corps flotilla—Ngaruawahia occupied—Strong fortifications at Paterangi, Pikopiko, and Rangiatea—Native genius in military engineering—The approaches to Rangiaowhia blocked—Maori artillery at Paterangi—Te Retimana the gunner—The bathing-party at Waiari—A skirmish on the Mangapiko banks—Forest Rangers' sharp fighting—How Captain Heaphy won the V.C.—Heavy losses of the Maoris 327

Chapter XXXVII.—The Invasion of Rangiaowhia.

A night march from Te Rore—Paterangi and Rangiatea outflanked—British column invades Rangiaowhia—An early-morning surprise visit—Skirmishing in the Kingite village—Colonel Nixon shot—Huts burned and defenders killed—Dramatic death of a Maori warrior—" Spare him, spare him ! "—Skirmishing at the Catholic church—Paterangi garrison hasten to defend Rangiaowhia—Hairini Hill entrenched—Position attacked by British force—Trenches stormed at the point of the bayonet—A cavalry charge—Defeat of the Kingites—British advance up the Horotiu River—Field force enters Kihikihi, Rewi's headquarters—Maoris retreat across the Puniu River 341

Chapter XXXVIII.—The Siege of Orakau.

The peach-groves and wheat-fields of Orakau—War-council of the Kingites—Decision to continue the war—Site for a fort selected at Orakau—Rewi's pessimism and the Urewera's insistence—Unsuitable position of the *pa*—Brigadier-General Carey's advance—The *pa* surrounded—British assaults repulsed—A sap commenced—Maori reinforcements appear—Scenes and war-councils in the redoubt—The heroic three hundred—Proposal to abandon the *pa* rejected—Short of water and ammunition—Firing wooden bullets—End of second day's siege 355

Chapter XXXIX.—The Siege of Orakau (continued).

The Last Day.

Dawn of the third day—" Let us charge out before it is light "—Tupotahi's advice rejected—Heavy fire concentrated on the redoubt—Sufferings of the defenders—The sap approaching the outworks—Shell-fire and hand-grenades—General Cameron's summons to surrender—Mair's interview with the Maoris—Rewi's council of war—The Maoris defiant ultimatum, " Peace shall never be made—never, never, never ! "—The fighting renewed—Hand-grenades thrown into the *pa*—The defenders retreat fighting—The flight through the swamp—Pursuit by infantry and cavalry—Incidents of the chase—Splendid heroism of the Kingites—Half the garrison killed—The bayoneting of Hine-i-turama 377

CONTENTS. XVII

Chapter XL.—The End of the Waikato War.   page
Ngati-Maniapoto entrenchments south of the Puniu—Fortified positions at Haurua, Te Roto-marama, and Paratui—British advance terminates at the Puniu—Army headquarters at Te Awamutu—Ngati-Haua fortifications at Te Tiki-o-te-Ihingarangi—The position evacuated—The last shots in the Waikato War: A skirmish at Ara-titaha—Settlement of the conquered country 398

Chapter XLI.—The Arawa Defeat of the East Coast Tribes.
Tai-Rawhiti tribes organize an expedition to Waikato—The loyal Arawa's resistance—East Coast Kingites march for Rotorua—Arawa block the way at Rotoiti—Skirmishing on the lake-side—Invaders compelled to return to the coast—An advance on Maketu—Kingite trenches at Te Whare-o-te-Rangi-marere—The invaders driven back Shelled by the warships—A running fight along the beach—The Battle of Kaokaoroa—Repulse of the East Coast tribes 404

Chapter XLII.—The Gate Pa and Te Ranga.
British expedition to Tauranga—Redoubts built at Te Papa—Ngai-te-Rangi erect fortifications—Rawiri Puhirake's challenge—The forts at Waoku and Tawhiti-nui—Construction of the Gate *Pa*—The British attack—A heavy cannonade—General Cameron orders an assault—Panic-stricken troops—Chivalry of the *pa* garrison—A half-caste heroine—Relieving the wounded under fire—Heavy losses of the British—The trenches at Te Ranga—Attack by Colonel Greer's column — British charge with the bayonet — The Maori works carried with heavy slaughter — Desperate hand-to-hand fighting—End of the Tauranga campaign 411

APPENDICES.

Supplementary Notes to Chapters	.. 431
Forest Fighting, Patumahoe (1863)	.. 445
The Wreck of H.M.S. "Orpheus"	.. 447
Militia Duty in the Waikato War	.. 448
List of Engagements and Casualties	.. 452
Index	.. 454

ii—N.Z. Wars.

LIST OF ILLUSTRATIONS.

	PAGE
Kororareka, Bay of Islands	8
Hone Heke	14
Tamati Waka Nene	17
Hone Heke, Hariata, and Kawiti	21
The Flagstaff, Russell, Bay of Islands	24
The English Church, Russell	27
Memorial to Sailors, Russell	30
Destruction of Pomare's *Pa*, Otuihu	33
The Battle of Puketutu, 1845	41
Riwhitete Pokai	43
British Attack on the Kapotai *Pa*	45
The Ohaeawai Stockade	54
Rihara Kou, of Kaikohe	56
Repulse of the Storming-parties at Ohaeawai	61
Colonel Cyprian Bridge	62
W. H. Free, a Veteran of Ohaeawai	63
Hare Puataata	64
Native Church at Ohaeawai	69
Sections of Rua-pekapeka *Pa*	74
The Bombardment of Rua-pekapeka	77
The Capture of Rua-pekapeka	79
Ruatara Tauramoko	81
Maihi Faraone Kawiti	82
The British Frigate "Castor"	83
Fort Arthur, Nelson, 1843	91
Fort Richmond and the Hutt Bridge	93
An Early Colonial Home (Karori)	95
H.M.S. "Driver"	97
Boulcott's Farm Stockade, Hutt	104
Ruins of Fort Paremata, Porirua	112
Te Rangihaeata	114
Te Rauparaha	117
Paua-taha-nui Stockade	123
The Church at Paua-taha-nui	124
Attack on Rangihaeata's Position, Horokiri	126
Summit of the Ridge, Horokiri	128
The Rear of Rangihaeata's Position	128
Front of Rangihaeata's Entrenchment	130
Rutland Stockade, Wanganui	133
Topine te Mamaku	135
The Skirmish at St. John's Wood, Wanganui	138
Wiremu Tamehana	146
Marsland Hill, New Plymouth	157
Bell Block Stockade, Taranaki	161
The Omata Stockade, Taranaki	163
Proclamations under Martial Law, Taranaki	165
Sir Harry Atkinson	168
Charles Wilson Hursthouse	170
The Battle of Waireka	171

LIST OF ILLUSTRATIONS.

	PAGE
Colonel W. B. Messenger	172
Captain Cracroft, R.N.	174
The War-steamer "Victoria"	177
British Positions at the Waitara	186
The Battlefield of Mahoetahi	190
The Mata-rikoriko Stockade	198
British Positions at Huirangi, 1861	207
The Attack on Te Arei, 1861	210
Sir George Grey	228
Tawhiao, the Maori King	230
Sir John E. Gorst	231
Patara te Tuhi	233
Fort Britomart, Auckland	238
St. John's Redoubt, Papatoetoe	239
The Queen's Redoubt, Pokeno	241
The Bluff Stockade, Havelock, Waikato River	243
Hori Ngakapa te Whanaunga	249
The Alexandra Redoubt, Tuakau	256
Major William Jackson	259
Major Von Tempsky	261
Pukekohe East Presbyterian Church	268
Attack on Pukekohe East Church Stockade	270
Captain Joseph Scott	272
Paerata Bluff and Burtt's Farm	275
Burtt's Farm Homestead, Present Day	276
Attack on Burtt's Farmhouse, Paerata	277
Camp of Movable Column, near Papatoetoe	281
Galloway Redoubt, Wairoa South	282
Maori Flag captured in the Wairoa Ranges	285
Stockade at Wairoa South	287
Mauku Church and Stockade, 1863	290
Mauku Church, Present Day	293
Major D. H. Lusk	295
The River Gunboat "Pioneer"	302
The River Gunboat "Koheroa"	303
Putataka, Waikato Heads	304
British Screw Corvettes "Miranda" and "Fawn"	305
The Gun-schooner "Caroline"	305
H.M.S. "Eclipse"	306
British Troopship "Himalaya"	307
Gunboat "Pioneer" shelling Meremere	311
The Esk Redoubt	314
British Storming-party at Rangiriri	323
Entrenchments at Rangiriri	325
Ngaruawahia, the Maori Capital	328
Maori Redoubt at Paterangi	335
The Forest Rangers at Waiari	338
Waiari, Mangapiko River	339
Maori Mission Church, Rangiaowhia	344
The Fighting at Rangiaowhia	345
Wahanui Huatare	349
The Mission Church, Te Awamutu	353
The Battlefield of Orakau, Present Day	357
Rewi Maniapoto	368
Te Huia Raureti	372
Major William G. Mair	380
Hitiri te Paerata	386
Tupotahi	390
Ahumai te Paerata	393

xx   LIST OF ILLUSTRATIONS.

	PAGE
After Fifty Years : Ngati-Maniapoto Survivors at Orakau	395
Kingite Chiefs, Ngati-Maniapoto Tribe	401
The Gate *Pa* Entrenchments	420
Hori Ngatai	422
The British Encampment at Tauranga	424
Henare Taratoa	427
Surrender of the Ngai-te-Rangi Tribe	428

PLANS AND SKETCH-MAPS.

North Island of New Zealand, showing Scenes of Engagements
                                                                Frontispiece.

Bay of Islands District	38
Ohaeawai *Pa* (Ground Plan and Sections)	51
Rua-pekapeka *Pa*	72
Cross-section of Rua-pekapeka	73
Valley of the Hutt, Wellington	87
The Pekapeka Block, Waitara	151
New Plymouth, showing Entrenchments, 1860-61	156
Marsland Hill Fortification	158
The Omata Stockade	163
The Seat of War, North Taranaki	181
The Battlefield of Mahoetahi	190
No. 3 Redoubt, Huirangi, Waitara	201
The Sap towards Te Arei *Pa*	212
Operations at Katikara, Tataraimaka	219
The Attack on Kaitake *Pa*, Taranaki	223
The Queen's Redoubt, Pokeno	242
The Engagement at Koheroa, Waikato	247
Ring's Redoubt, Kirikiri	251
Pukekohe East Church Stockade	266
Mauku Church, showing Rifle Loopholes	291
Map of South Auckland District, 1863	299
The Entrenchments at Meremere	309
The Entrenchments at Rangiriri	320
Cross-section of Maori Redoubt, Rangiriri	321
The Waikato-Waipa Delta, showing Fortifications	331
Paterangi *Pa*	333
Entrenchments at Pikopiko (Puketoki)	336
Rangiaowhia and Hairini	342
Locality Plan of Orakau	356
The Orakau Battlefield	362
The Orakau *Pa*	364
Orakau *Pa* (another Plan)	365
Fortifications at Te Tiki-o-te-Ihingarangi	400
Waiari, Mangapiko River	403
Battle-grounds, Lake Rotoiti, Maketu, and Kaokaoroa	406
The Monmouth Redoubt, Tauranga	412
Attack on the Gate *Pa*, Tauranga	414
Sketch-plans of the Gate *Pa*	417
The Attack on Te Ranga	426

CHAPTER I.

THE OLD RACE AND THE NEW.

THE story of New Zealand is rich beyond that of most young countries in episodes of adventure and romance. Australia's pioneering-work was of a different quality from ours, mainly because the nation-makers of our neighbour encountered no powerful military race of indigenes to dispute the right of way. The student of New Zealand history seeking for foreign parallels and analogies must turn to the story of the white conquest in America for the record of human endeavour that most closely approaches the early annals of these Islands. There certainly is a remarkable similarity, in all but landscape, between the old frontier life in British North America and the United States and the broad features of the violent contact between European and Maori in our country. The New England backwoodsman and the far-out plainsman were faced with many of the life-and-death problems which confronted our New Zealand settlers on the Taranaki and Waikato and East Coast borders. In reading such fascinating books as "The Conspiracy of Pontiac," "French Pioneers in the New World," or "The Winning of the West," the family likeness of the adventures of the pathfinder and the forest fighter to the New Zealand life of the "sixties" is irresistibly forced upon the mind. There was the same dual combat with wild nature and with untamed man; there was the necessity in each land for soldierly skill; the same display of all grades of human courage; much of the same tale of raid and foray, siege, trail-hunting, and ambuscade. There was as wide a difference in frontier and forest fighting-ability between the Imperial troops of the "forties" and early "sixties" and the soldier-settlers who scoured the bush after Titokowaru and Te Kooti as there was between General Braddock's unfortunate regular troops of 1755 and the provincial scouts and hunters who learned how to beat the Red Indian at his own game, and later to defy British armies. It is to the pages of Francis Parkman, Theodore Roosevelt, and Henry Cabot Lodge that the New-Zealander must turn for historic parallels in the story of the nations, rather than to those of Macaulay, Green, or Freeman.

The inevitable shock of battle between the tribesman of Aotea-roa and the white man who coveted and needed his surplus lands is a feature of our history which has had no small influence upon our national existence and national type. It coloured our story as no other element could; tragic as it was, it at least redeemed our history from the commonplaces of a sleek commercialism. The white adventurer let go his anchor on these shores with the Briton's characteristic assertion of superiority over the brown races of mankind; the white settler of our beginnings too often exhibited an ignorant contempt for the mat-girt or blanket-swathed aboriginal. The Maori, for his part, swaggering through the settlements with double-barrel gun and tomahawk, ready to fight to the death for a punctilio and avenge in blood some absurd breach of personal *tapu*, did not trouble to conceal his scorn for the *pakeha* whose only concern was huckstering and profit-making. Early Governments truckled to savage insolence for the sake of peace; the Maori, sometimes for the same reason, shrugged off the insults and swindlings of the coarser grade of white with a contemptuous "*Hei aha!*"—"What does it matter!" But it was in the last and unavoidable test, when bayonet met long-handled tomahawk and when British artillery battered Maori stockades, that the two races came to gauge each other's manly calibre, and came, finally, to respect each other for the capital virtues that only trial of war can bring to mutual view. For all the reverses that befell the ill-planned and unskilfully conducted British efforts in the field in the early campaigns, the shrewd Maori soon divested himself of his illusions of military superiority; he came to realize that he had at last met his match, and henceforth his concern was deep lest the incoming shiploads of whites should wipe him off the face of his ancestral lands. On the European's side the conceit which found expression in the declared opinion that a company of British grenadiers could march from end to end of New Zealand and carry all before them was quickly exchanged for an admission that the naked Maori was a better warrior than the heavily armed British soldier, man for man, in the forest environment in which he had been schooled to arms and the trail from his infancy. Each admitted the other's pre-eminence under certain conditions, and each protagonist came to admire the primal quality of valour in his opponent. The Ngapuhi who—to their own amazement—hurled back assaulting columns of the finest British infantry at Ohaeawai had secret tremors at the spectacle of the forlorn hope's desperate courage; well they knew that in the end they could not hope to prevail over men of such mettle. And the soldier who saw women and even children facing death in a beleaguered redoubt of sod walls, choosing to die with their men rather than surrender, first marvelled at the devotion of such a race and then came to love them for their savage chivalry. The wars ended with a strong mutual respect, tinged with a real affection, which would never have existed but for this ordeal by battle.

From the days when venturesome trading brigs and schooners lay at uneasy anchor in New Zealand bays, with boarding nettings triced up and carronades loaded, down to the firing of the last shot against Te Kooti in the Urewera Ranges, the story of contact between European and Maori is full of episodes of the quality which makes the true romance. Those episodes, whether isolated adventures or protracted campaigns, may not have presented themselves to the participants in precisely that light; it remains for the present generation, bred up in peaceful occupation of the Maori islands, to appreciate what may be called the poetry of the last century's work and endeavour in New Zealand, as opposed to the more prosaic story of industrial evolution.

In examining these tales of other days and in testing the historical knowledge of the average New-Zealander the fact is too apparent that the young generation would be the better for a more systematic schooling in the facts of national pioneer life and achievements which are a necessary foundation for the larger patriotism. Yet the passionate affection with which the Maori clung to his tribal lands is a quality which undeniably tinges the mind and outlook of the farm-bred, country-loving, white New-Zealander to-day. The native-born has unconsciously assimilated something of the peculiar patriotism that belongs to the soil; the *genius loci* of the old frontiers has not entirely vanished from the hills and streams. Not only the tribespeople of Hone Heke and Wiremu Tamehana and Wahanui, but the New-Zealander of British descent, may feel the truth which the Sage expressed in "Past and Present": "The Hill I first saw the sun rise over, when the sun and all things were in their auroral hour, who can divorce me from it? Mystic, deep as the world's centre, are the roots I have struck into my native soil; no tree that grows is rooted so." And the native-born whose eyes in childhood are daily lifted to Taranaki's high snow-cap, who watches from the farmhouse the morning mists trailing up like the smoke of fairies' camp-fires from the gullies of Pirongia, or who sees from afar Ruapehu's icy heliograph flash back the sunrise—this son of New Zealand cannot but come to love the landscape saliencies of his native place with something of the Maori adoration for "my parent the Mountain."

Regarding these old wars in the light of the ordeal of battle from which the civilized world has lately emerged, the *pakeha-Maori* conflicts seem chivalrous tournaments. The formidable character of the country in most of the operations, while it increased the hardships of the campaigns, went to keep the casualties low. As in the wars of British and French in the Canadian forests, described by Parkman in "Montcalm and Wolfe," "the problem was less how to fight the enemy than how to get at him." And exasperated Imperial commanders, from Despard down to Cameron and Chute, realized as their columns toiled ponderously and painfully over unmapped country in search of a too-mobile foe, through unroaded swamps, bush, and ranges, and unbridged rivers, the truth of the dictum that geography is two-thirds of military science.

It is curious to discover in the early records how little the military commanders and officials realized the military quality of the Maori. We find, even before New Zealand became a British colony, the Resident at the Bay of Islands, Mr. Busby, declaring in a letter to the Colonial Secretary of New South Wales urging the despatch of a detachment of soldiers to uphold the authority of the Resident and the Ngapuhi confederation of native chiefs, "With regard to the number of troops which it might be necessary to maintain, it would, I think, require little knowledge of military tactics to satisfy one who has witnessed the warfare of the native that one hundred English soldiers would be an overmatch for the united forces of the whole Islands. But in fact there is little risk of even two tribes uniting to oppose them."*

Equally fatuous was the debate in the Legislative Council at Auckland, in 1842, upon the question of arresting the cannibal chief Taraia for his attack upon the Katikati Maoris at Ongare; it was actually suggested that the old warrior should be served with a summons by a constable in his fortified *pa*. In 1844, after the tragic blunder of the Wairau, Governor Fitzroy reported of the Wellington and Nelson officials and settlers, "No one appeared disposed to give the natives credit for courage or skill in warfare; no one seemed to doubt but that they would fly before a very small detachment of military; the prevailing feeling appeared to be for a collision." That collision, when it came in the North, revealed the unsuspected capacity of the natives to meet and defeat — given their own conditions of fighting — the best British troops. While Hone Heke and Kawiti were building their stockades and moulding their bullets for their "fighting friends," the redcoats, the Polynesian cousins of the Maori, the Tahitians, were fearlessly withstanding the French; and, just as the Ngapuhi speedily undeceived the too-confident Despard, the warriors of the Society Islands falsified the boast of the officer who, previous to an encounter in rear of Papeete, was heard to declare, "Give me fifty men and I'll march through Tahiti."

In Hone Heke's day the Maori population so greatly outnumbered the whites, who were here on sufferance, that the confidence of such commanders as Despard and some of the officials and administrators of the hour is inexplicable except on the theory of an overweening faith in the white man's military invincibility. A Government return of the native population of New Zealand, laid before the Legislative Council at Auckland in 1845, gave an aggregate of 109,550, being the estimate of the

---

* From manuscript letter, 8th June, 1837, in Mr. Busby's letter-book, New Zealand archives.

Chief Protector of Aborigines. Of this number 40,000 were put down as proselytes of the Anglican Church missionaries, about 16,000 under the Wesleyans, and about 5,000 were Roman Catholics; all the rest were termed "Pagans." The Ngapuhi Tribe was estimated to number 12,000, and the Rarawa 4,000; Ngati-Whatua, 2,000; Ngati-Maru (under the famous chief Taraia), 4,000; making in all 22,000 in the North Auckland districts and on the shores of the Hauraki Gulf and about the Thames River. The East Coast population, from Tauranga round to Hawke's Bay, was estimated at 30,000. Waikato, under the great Te Wherowhero, numbered 18,400. In Taranaki proper there were only 2,000 people; there were in South Taranaki 3,000 of the Ngati-Ruanui and other tribes. The Rotorua people mustered 9,000 all told, and the Taupo clans 1,500 (a curiously small estimate). From Wanganui along the west coast of the Wellington Province and round to the country of the Ngati-Kahungunu at Ahuriri (now Napier) there were 21,950 people, of whom Te Rauparaha headed 5,000 in the Otaki and adjacent districts. In the South Island there were 4,700 Maoris, consisting of 1,000 Ngati-Toa (Rauparaha's tribe), chiefly at Cloudy Bay (Wairau), 100 of the vanquished Rangitane, and 3,600 Ngai-Tahu, whose principal chief was Taiaroa, of Otago.

The New-Zealander of the 2nd August, 1845, commenting upon these figures, said that the return showed there were nearly 70,000 natives within three hundred miles of Auckland. "This most important fact," it added, "should awake vigilance as well as stimulate firmness and decision in the present crisis."

In 1847 Lieutenant W. Servantes, interpreter to the Forces, estimated the Maoris numbers at 90,000. Bishop Selwyn's calculation of the total was 60,000. But Governor Grey, in 1849, estimated the native population at 120,000; and Dr. Shortland, in 1851, agreed with the Governor's figures.

Even taking the lowest estimate, it is apparent that a combined effort by the natives in the "forties" or early "fifties" could have driven the *pakeha* population into the sea. Had the "Land League" or the Pai-Marire fanaticism been born ten years earlier, or had a military genius like Te Kooti led the Maori tribes against the whites in 1845 and 1846, the story of New Zealand would read very differently. Certainly, had the Maoris but realized their strength, had they then possessed any political organization beyond the tribal, it was in their power to have kept these Islands indefinitely in the semi-savage condition of 1840, tolerating only the missionaries and a few coast-trading *pakeha-Maoris*. Let it not be forgotten that had it not been for the true benevolence, the hospitality, and the continued friendship of such men as Tamati Waka and Patuone, Te Kawau, Te Wherowhero, and Te Puni, the British flag might not be flying in New Zealand to-day.

CHAPTER II.

THE BEACH AT KORORAREKA.

There are some bays in the South Pacific on whose shores wild history has been made—strands saturate with a hundred romantic, adventurous, and tragic memories. Pre-eminently one of these is the beach of Apia, in Samoa; another, steeped almost as deeply in early-days legend and war-time history, is Kororareka, Bay of Islands. From the dawn of civilized enterprise on our coasts we hear of Kororareka and its fleets of whalers at anchor, its Maori "ship-girls," its gun-play between quarrelsome native *hapus*, and its all-pervading flavour of license and lawlessness; this period of pagan freedom followed by an unwilling reformation under the influence of reputable settlers and the British flag, a brief day of importance as the capital of the new-made colony, and the final debacle when the flagstaff on its sentry hill was laid in dust and the blockhouses and grog-shops alike went up in flames. Kororareka—the modern Russell—remains to-day a place apart, curiously little advanced, at any rate in population, by the passage of three-quarters of a century, and shorn of its ancient commercial glory; a sedate, pretty seaside township where the round of life in a delicious climate is seldom disturbed by intrusive shipping. The pervading air, a half-regretful recollection of a red-blooded past, is reminiscent of some of the old gold-digging towns on the coast of Westland.

The old landmarks are readily to be picked out. A modern flagstaff stands on the exact spot on Maiki Hill, 300 feet above us yonder, where Hone Heke, Haratua, and their kin four times felled the British signal-mast. The steep hills behind the little town are still clothed for the most part in *manuka* and fern as they were in Heke's day, with an immigrant admixture of gorse and sweetbrier. The old English church, with its marks of cannon-shot, still stands in the burying-ground around whose fence Kawiti fought the British bluejackets in 1845.

Let us picture something of the aspect of Kororareka Beach in the war-brewing "forties." This straggling town, its single street fitting itself closely to the rim of the gravelly beach, is a mingling of *pakeha* and Maori architecture. One- and two-storied weatherboard stores and publichouses have for close neighbours thatched *whares* of slab and fern, tree-trunk and raupo. Near the southern end of the beach is a Maori village enclosed by a palisade of split trees and *manuka* stakes. There is no jetty; the boats of men-o'-war whalers, and trading craft alike are hauled up on the beach. Over in the north cove by Waipara Spring two boats' crews from an American whaleship are towing off a string of water-casks roped together. Out in the bay lie half a dozen deep-sea vessels, most of them New Bedford whale-hunters; nearer the beach sundry fore-and-afters, schooner- or cutter-rigged, swing to an anchor; one or two of these are owned and sailed by Maoris, for the East Coast native is not only a first-rate sailor, but is beginning to taste the pleasures and profits of shipowning. Natives in their blankets and mats lounge on the beach-edge, dozing, smoking, or arguing in the vociferous manner of the Maori. Ngapuhi girls, barefooted and bareheaded, well plumped-out of figure, swing up and down the roadway flaunting the print gowns and the brightly coloured " roundabouts " and the glittering ear-rings bought with the dollars of the sailormen. Some of them are lately from the mission stations, maybe, but the temptations of Kororareka and the whaleships are irresistible. Many a native wears a little metal cross or a crucifix about his neck, or a figure of the Virgin hung by a black ribbon or tape from one ear, balancing a shark's tooth or a greenstone in the other—for the Catholic religion, newly come to the Bay, is highly popular, and Bishop Pompallier numbers his converts by the hundred. Most of the able-bodied men, tall athletes with tattooed faces, are armed. You see a party of young bloods spring ashore from a canoe, in from one of Pomare's, Heke's, or Kawiti's *pas* up the harbour, and observe that every man has his short-handled tomahawk, brightly polished of blade, thrust through his flax girdle just over the hip or at the small of the back; he would no more stir from home without it than a Far West plainsman of the old days would move abroad without his six-shooter. Many also carry their flint-lock guns, which they call *ngutu-parera* (" duckbill "—from the shape of the hammer); and note, too, the new percussion-cap gun, double-barrelled, which the Maori is able to obtain from Sydney trading craft, while his antagonist soon-to-be, the British soldier, must for some years yet be content with the ancient musket.

Whaleship watches on shore leave make lively business in the bar-rooms over their rum and ale. The captains have the parlours, sacred to the quarter-deck, and there they sit over their Scotch whisky or their cognac or squareface exchanging the news of all the seas, and relating their whale-fishing successes and misadventures from the Aleutians to Foveaux Strait and from the Japan coast to the Kermadecs. Hard old tyrants some of these whaling skippers, from Nantucket, or New Bedford, or Martha's Vineyard, or Boston, Mass.; of all sailors they are the monarchs absolute; their cruises last for years, and their crews they hold by the strong hand, and good rewards to the natives for the capture of deserters

KORORAREKA, BAY OF ISLANDS.

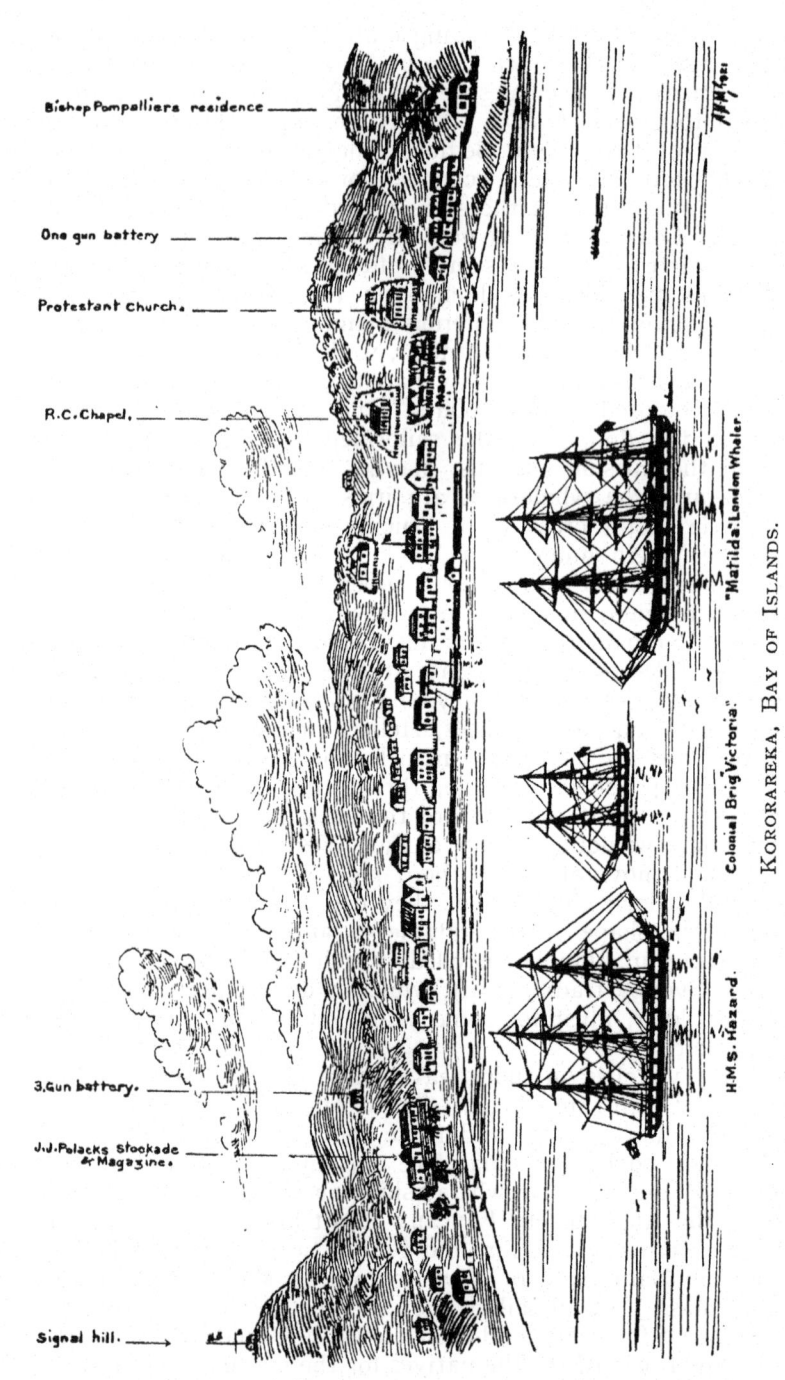

This drawing, from a sketch by Captain Clayton, of Kororareka, 10th March, 1845, shows the town as it was on the day before its destruction by Hone Heke and Kawiti.

Raffish-looking crews they captain. No two men wear clothes alike; some have blue monkey-jackets and duck trousers, some are in the dungarees of shipboard work; their headgear is a study in the variety of forecastle-made caps of canvas, Scotch caps, tarpaulins, and shapeless hats of patched cloth. Lean, hard-worked hunters of the world's biggest game; harpooneers, and oarsmen, and blubber-flenchers from all the seafaring countries of the world: long-limbed, drawling men of the New England States; coal-black darkies from Jamaica; half-breed Indians from the State of Maine; piratical ear-ringed Portuguese-negroid nondescripts from the Azores and Cape de Verde Islands; brisk Irish lads unmistakable; and here and there a sturdy man of Kent or Devon who has run perhaps from a British man-of-war with a flogging captain and found worse than the "cat" in the oil-soaked whaler.

Follow the stores-buying captain or chief officer of the "Levi Starbuck", into one of the weatherboard trading-houses, blue with strong tobacco and thick with the tang of tarred rope. This interior is a typical South Sea warehouse; the proprietor is ship-chandler, sea-stock dealer, ironmonger and gunsmith, grog-seller, gunpowder-purveyor, and a dozen other trades. He can provide a ship with anchor and cable, or set the Maoris on the track of Captain Ephraim J. Nye's runaway boat-steerer with admirable despatch; provide a 300-ton barque with a complete new set of sails or sufficient muskets and ammunition to conquer a cannibal island. There are blankets, prints, red sealing-wax, tomahawks, bullet-moulds, iron pots, tobacco by the cask, for the Maori trade; sugar and molasses and rum from the West Indies; salt beef and pork and adamant biscuit for sea-fare; sou'-westers, cutting-in spades, harpoon-line by the hundred fathom, lance-heads, charts, binnacle lanterns, spy-glasses, and boat-compasses; pistols and knuckle-dusters for the afterguard, holystones and squeejees and coal-tar to keep the fists of the 'foremast hands out of mischief.

Now board one of those whaleships lying out yonder at an easy anchor—the ships that made this Bay of Islands famous—and you shall see the most conservative of all craft afloat. While every other phase of sea-life and every other kind of ship has changed out of all likeness to the olden type, the sailing whaler does not alter. Step into the stern-sheets of one of those beautifully modelled carvel-built whaleboats with the tobacco-chewing New England mate standing at the 22-foot steer-oar. See how the crew of five stretch back to it with their ash oars—the long, full stroke of the true whaleman, who will have none of your quick and jerky Navy oarsmanship. A few of those long strokes and we are clambering up a rope ladder on to the white-scrubbed decks of a ship as clean as a yacht for all her greasy trade. The pervading but not unpleasant smell of oil, the stuff that permeates her every timber and fills half the casks in her hold; the rows of sharp-ended 30-foot boats at her cranes and davits; the leather- or canvas-covered harpoons and lances whose long shafts project from each boat; the barrel slung as a crow's-nest at her maintopgallant-masthead—these all proclaim her calling. But there is something more about her that tokens her a ship apart from all others, this barque " Narwhal," or " Levi Starbuck," " Canton Packet," " Pocahontas," or " Charles W. Morgan," or however she may be named. The bluff-bowed square-sterned craft, with her sides all hung with boats painted light blue like the sea, has an indescribable air of having been out of the world for years and years. The whale-hunter under canvas seems almost part of the sea, so long are the absences from port, so habituated the crews to the ways of the great deep.

In such a craft as this Herman Melville sails sperm-whale chasing at the time of our narrative; it is from just such a barque as the " Charles W. Morgan " or the " Awashonks " that he deserts to find the beautiful valley of Taipi and to give the world an undying true romance of the South Seas. The " Little Jule " of his Marquesan and Tahitian adventures, or the ivory-garnished " Pequod " of " Moby Dick," may veritably be one of these far-roving barques that ride at the quiet anchorages of Kororareka and Wahapu this year 1845.

If you are privileged to explore the wrinkled canvas-backed charts or look into the captain's log-book you will see curious symbols that belong to the whale-fishing trade alone. The pen-cilled zigzag lines of the vessel's cruising course across the Pacific are punctuated every here and there with rough drawings of a whale's flukes, or the head of a great sperm bull, or maybe a school of porpoises. Each pictograph tells a tale of oil-getting, or of " drawn irons " and a lost whale; perhaps now and again a boat lost. Each emblem of a " kill " is figured with the number of barrels obtained. " Dirty work for clean money ": sperm-oil these years of 1840–50 rises steadily until it is worth a dollar a gallon, and bone from the " right " whale is quoted at £200 per ton in New York.

Observe that all these merchant ships are armed, some with a single iron carronade or a brass gun on each side, some with whole broadsides of four or six guns, 9-pounders and 12-pounders. Yonder taunt-masted brig, a trader from Hobart Town, has a swivel gun on her poop as well as a whole battery on her main deck; she is lately in from a sandalwooding cruise to the New Hebrides and New Caledonia and a voyage to China, and she has used her guns against Western Pacific cannibals and Canton pirates. The merchant sailor of 1845 had to be gunner too; and it is aboard these traders and whalers that some of our young Ngapuhi, making a voyage for the love of adventure and the open sea-road, have learned to load, lay, and fire artillery, a science that is to be of use presently to their war-chief Heke.

Such were some of the distinguishing features of Kororareka Bay in the early years of British sovereignty. The visits of whaleships were all-important, for it was almost solely with them that the business of the white dealers and the Maori barterers lay. In 1845 there were more than six hundred American ships and barques engaged in whale-fishing, and of these a considerable number visited New Zealand annually; and English, French, Sydney, and Hobart whalers also frequented the coast. Mr. John Webster, of Hokianga, related in his reminiscences that when he landed at Russell Town from Sydney on the 1st May, 1841, there were over twenty whaling-vessels in the Bay, and the beach was alive with seamen and their officers. It was the season when all the whalers put in for provisions and to fit out for another year's chase of the sperm and the "right" whale. But the number of visitors quickly lessened when the Governor in Council imposed a Customs tariff on the staple articles of trade, thus making the port highly expensive for the whalemen; and, as will be shown, this falling-off in trade created annoyance and resentment in the Maori mind.

The white population of Kororareka in its days of prosperity was about a thousand; by 1845 this number had fallen to some four hundred. In 1842 the town even supported a newspaper, the *Bay of Islands Observer*, a four-page weekly sold for a shilling. Traders' advertisements in this paper give us an insight into the commercial life of the place, and enable us to picture scenes in the 'longshore stores, with their curious variety of goods stocked for maritime and Maori customers. Thomas Spicer, "Kororareka Beach," announced that he had for sale such articles as "duck frocks and trousers, muslin dresses, assorted prints, fine Congo tea, fine French capers, iron pots, tobacco, salt, shovels and spades, tomahawks, cartouche-boxes, superfine beaver hats, and crockery." C. J. Cook and Co. informed the public that they dealt in ironmongery, blankets, tea, sugar, tobacco, policemen's lanterns, umbrellas, spittoons, sealing-wax, escutcheons, solar lamps, shot, powder, tinder-boxes, salt pork, "and all other necessary commodities." At Wahapu an American, Captain William Mayhew—one of the foreign residents from whom Hone Heke received political inspiration—conducted a large store in which he stocked, among other necessaries of life, gunpowder in casks and canisters, flour, tar, anchors, butter, cheese, shot, dungaree, sealskin caps, silk hats, French bedsteads, double-barrelled flint-lock guns, single- and double-barrelled percussion guns, ploughs, pit-saws, blankets, slop clothes, and sarsaparilla.

There was a "Kororareka Observatory." William Robertson, who owned this establishment. advertised repairs to timekeepers, and added: "Commanders of vessels may have their chronometers rated by transit observations and an astronomical clock kept at Greenwich mean time."

In 1842 the falling-off in maritime trade was already marked; nevertheless, many ship-commanders preferred Kororareka to more populous ports. Small fleets of square-riggers made for the bay in the off-season; for example, in two days (4th and 5th May) in 1842 four American whaleships—the "Triad," "Caledonia," "Washington," and "Fanny"—arrived at Kororareka, bringing in their holds, as the result of their cruises in the Pacific, takes totalling 6,550 barrels of oil and 51,000 lb. of bone. The *New Zealand Gazette and Wellington Spectator* of September, 1844, said: "The receipts at the Bay of Islands from furnishing supplies to whalers averaged for several years about £45,000 annually, and now this trade is nearly extinct." Up to the date of Heke's War, however, the number of whaling-vessels using Russell and Wahapu as ports of refitting and refreshing was still considerable. Captain McKeever, of the United States warship "St. Louis," writing from the Bay of Islands, 13th March, 1845, to the Secretary of the Navy at Washington, said: "Of the high importance of the Bay of Islands to our whalesmen, and of the great value of American interests involved here (there being no less than seventy or eighty of the whalers touching and refitting annually), I presume you are well aware, and I am safe probably in saying that no other port or harbour in the world competes with it in its importance to the American whaling interests." The Bay of Islands, indeed, was regularly visited for water, wood, and stores, and for the shipping of oil, until, in the final days of the American Civil War, the Confederate commerce-destroying cruiser "Shenandoah" left a trail of burning New England whaleships across the Pacific; and even in the "nineties" I have seen an occasional whaling-barque, such as the "Gayhead," of New Bedford, lying at anchor at Russell, boating off her water-casks, as in the early days, from the perennial spring of Waipara.

CHAPTER III.

HEKE AND THE FLAGSTAFF.

" . . . God made this country for us. It cannot be sliced ; if it were a whale it might be sliced. Do you return to your own country, which was made by God for you. God made this land for us ; it is not for any stranger or foreign nation to meddle with this sacred country."—*Hone Heke's letter to the Governor, 1845.*

Robert Louis Stevenson described the town on Apia beach as the seat of the political sickness of Samoa. Cosmopolitan Kororareka was the seat of the troubles of north New Zealand; its flagstaff was the *putake o te riri*, in Maori phrase—the root and fount of the wars. And Hone Heke, one-time mission pupil, malcontent, and rebel general, played as bold a part in the drama of our early days as ever the patriotic Mataafa enacted in his little world under Upolu's palms in the last two decades of the nineteenth century.

Hone Heke's character was curiously composite—a mingling of passionate patriotism, ambition, bravado, vanity, and a shrewdness sharpened by his partial civilization. Heke foresaw more clearly than most of his countrymen the fatal consequences to the Maori of white colonization and the flooding of the country with an alien population who would regard the native New-Zealander with none of the sympathy entertained for him by the long-settled missionaries. For the mission people, of whatever denomination, Ngapuhi, like most other tribes in 1840, cherished feelings of deep regard ; they knew that those devoted men and women had not come to the Maori islands to make profit out of the natives' ignorance of trade values. Many a coast trader, timber-miller, and settler, too, were held in high estimation by the tribes of the North ; they had won the affections of the chiefs and people by their fair methods of business, and by kindly services in times of sickness and sorrow. But the numerous speculators and land-seekers who landed in north New Zealand by every vessel after the hoisting of the British flag furnished them with an argument for a policy of exclusion, for it seemed even then to keen-visioned men like Heke that the wholesale immigration of so strong a race must in years to come inundate the chieftainship of the Maori.

At the same time, there were whites whom Ngapuhi and Te Rarawa and their kin desired strongly to encourage for reasons of self-interest. These were the captains and crews of the whale-ships—the men who were chiefly responsible at once for the material prosperity and the moral deterioration of the northern tribes. The whaleships supplied practically the whole of the trade of the Bay of Islands and Mangonui, as the *kauri* timber ships did that of Hokianga; and the decrease in this trade directly following the establishment of British sovereignty went far to convince Heke and Pomare, and the many others who lived to a large extent on the profits accruing from the visits of shipping, that the old regime, when every man made his own laws, was preferable to the new order.

Hone Heke was nephew to Hongi Hika, and married that chief's daughter, Hariata Rongo. He died without issue; but

From a pencil drawing by J. A. Gilfillan.]

HONE HEKE.

his elder brother, Tuhirangi, of Kaikohe, begat Hone Ngapua, who married Niu, who gave birth in 1869 to Hone Heke the Second, who came while yet a very young man to represent the Northern Maori Electorate in the New Zealand House of Representatives. Hone Heke the First engaged in the intertribal wars of the North while still a youth, and in 1830 he displayed energy and skill in a battle at Kororareka. Three years later he was one of the Ngapuhi men, under Titore, who sailed their war-canoes down the coast to Tauranga, where they attacked Otumoetai and other *pas*. Heke was wounded in the neck in this expedition. In 1837 he took a leading part in the fighting against Pomare and Te Mau-Paraoa, whose stockaded *pa* (destroyed by the British troops in 1845) stood on Otuihu, a prominent place on the cliffs above the entrance to the Waikare and Kawakawa arms of Tokerau, and about six miles from Kororareka Town.

In an interval of peace in the "thirties" young Heke lived at Paihia in the establishment of the Rev. Henry Williams (afterwards Archdeacon of Waimate), and the respect and affection for the missionaries then engendered in his mind remained a distinguishing feature of his otherwise turbulent character. It was at Paihia that he learned something of the history of the outer world — a smattering of knowledge which he turned to shrewd account in his arguments with the Government a few years later.

The portrait of Hone Heke is an index to his character. His nose, though not the predatory *ihu-kaka*, or strong hook-nose, that distinguished some great Maori leaders, was prominent and well-shapen; his prominent jaws and chin denoted firmness and resolution. The old Kaikohe natives of to-day speak of Heke's *kauae-roa*, his long chin, as the salient character of his face. He was tattooed, but not with the full design of *moko*, such as that borne by his great kinsman and antagonist, Tamati Waka Nene.

Heke's dissatisfaction with the state of maritime trade after 1840 is scarcely to be wondered at, seeing that in addition to the returns from the sale of food-supplies to the whalemen he had collected a kind of Customs dues from visiting ships. Before the British flag was hoisted he and his cousin Titore divided a levy of £5 on each ship entering the Bay. They collected their dues from the ships outside the anchorage, boarding them in their canoes before Tapeka Point was rounded. Many ships sailed up to the anchorages off Wahapu and Otuihu, in the passage to the Kawakawa and Waikare, and here Pomare collected his toll from each ship, for he was the paramount chief of the inner waters Pomare also was the principal agent in the disreputable but profitable business of supplying girls as temporary wives to the crews of the whaleships during their stay in port This was a leading line of Maori traffic with the shipping in unscrupulous old Kororareka and Otuihu, which not even the strong mission influence could extirpate.

In 1841, in a Government Ordinance, Customs duties were set forth in a brief schedule. All spirits, British, paid 4s. per gallon to the Customs; all other spirits, foreign, 5s. Tobacco, after the 1st January, 1842, was to pay 1s. per pound on the manufactured article and 9d. per pound on the unmanufactured; snuff and cigars, 2s. per pound. Tea, sugar, flour, and grain were taxed £5 on every £100 of value; wine, £15 per £100; all other foreign goods, £5 per £100. In 1844 firearms were taxed 30 per cent. And when the storekeeper had passed on the increases to his customers, with no doubt a considerable extra margin of profit for the Maori trade, the warrior who came in to renew his supply of *whiri*, or twist tobacco, to purchase a new blanket or a musket, or to lay by a store of lead for moulding into bullets, received the clearest proof that the Treaty which he had signed had not improved his condition of life.

To this concrete evidence of trade depression was added a vague but widely diffused belief that the Treaty of Waitangi was merely a ruse of the *pakeha*, and that it was the secret intention of the whites, so soon as they became strong enough, to seize upon the lands of the Maori. In 1844 the news reached New Zealand that the House of Commons Committee on New Zealand Affairs had resolved that the Treaty of Waitangi was a part of a series of injudicious proceedings, and that "the acknowledgment by the local authorities of a right of property on the part of the natives of New Zealand in all wild land in these islands, after the sovereignty had been assumed by Her Majesty, was not essential to the true construction of the Treaty, and was an error which had been productive of very injurious consequences." In other words, the Committee thought the Government should seize upon all native land not actually occupied, and devote it to the use of white settlers. This report, the news of French aggression in Tahiti and Raiatea, Fitzroy's vacillating land policy, and simmering resentment over the execution of Maketu in 1842 for the murder of the Robertson family on Motu-arohia Island, all went to fan a war feeling among the Ngapuhi.

It was in 1844 that Heke came to the decision to use the setting-up of the flagstaff and the driving-away of the whalers as a *take*, or pretext. Shortly, he made a raid upon Kororareka with a strong war-party, on a *taua muru*, or punitive plundering expedition. This excursion seems to have been devised chiefly with a view to testing the temper of the whites and ascertaining what resistance he was likely to meet with in his campaign against the *kara*, the colours on Maiki Hill. The *taua* was by way of retaliation for an insult, serious in Maori eyes, offered by a woman in the township. This woman was Kotiro, a native of Taranaki, who had been led away captive by Ngapuhi fifteen years previously. She had been given to Heke as a slave. When she had been for some years at the Bay of Islands she married a Scottish blacksmith named Gray : one of her children was Sophia Hinerangi, the celebrated guide at Te Wairoa and Whakarewarewa, Rotorua, in after-years. When Gray died, Kotiro became the wife of another white man, Lord, who kept a store, lodginghouse, and butcher's shop on Kororareka beach. One day she was bathing in the bay with a number of other women when an altercation occurred. The name of Hone Heke was mentioned, whereon Kotiro contemptuously called him an "*upoko poaka*" ("pig's head"). This was a *kanga*, or curse, in Maori notion ; and the women promptly sent word thereof to

Heke. The *taua muru* was the sequel. Heke began to plunder Lord's store; the trader compromised by offering a cask of twist tobacco as compensation for the insult. This offer being accepted, Lord asked for time to procure a cask of tobacco from the rear of the store; but this time he employed in cutting the cask into halves—it was the only one he had in stock. He then endeavoured to pass the half-cask on to the Maoris as a whole one, whereupon there was furious uproar. Heke and his men partly looted the store; the woman Kotiro they carried off.

This was on Friday, 5th July, 1844. For the next three days the war-party remained in the town, the young bloods

From a photo.]

TAMATI WAKA NENE.

swaggering into stores and private houses alike, seizing whatever they fancied. On the 8th July the flagstaff on Maiki Hill was cut down. (Mr. Hugh Carleton, in his "Life of Henry Williams," states that on this first occasion the flagstaff was not cut down by Heke, but by Haratua, the chief of Pakaraka. Archdeacon William Williams, he says, dissuaded Heke from the deed, which his followers, however, resolved to carry out. "Heke remained in his canoe, alleging that he had pledged his word to Archdeacon William Williams and would keep it. Whereupon Haratua jumped up, axe in hand, ran up the hill with a few followers, and cut the flagstaff down.")

Governor Fitzroy's troubles were now approaching their climax. The news of Ngapuhi's deed prompted an urgent appeal to headquarters in Sydney for troops; there were only ninety men, a company of the 80th, in Auckland, and none at the Bay of Islands. In the second week of August the barque "Sydney" arrived at the Bay of Islands from New South Wales with 160 officers and men of the 99th Regiment. On the 24th of the month H.M.S. "Hazard" dropped anchor off Kororareka, bringing from Auckland the Governor; the Government brig "Victoria" arrived in company with the frigate, and the vessels landed a detachment of the 96th under Lieut.-Colonel Hulme; two light guns were also brought ashore. Heke had gone inland, to Kaikohe. The Governor and Hulme were for immediate hostilities. However, a meeting was arranged at the mission station at Waimate between Fitzroy and the chiefs of Ngapuhi. At this meeting (2nd September, 1844) the Governor was accompanied by the commander of the "Hazard" and Lieut.-Colonel Hulme. Tamati Waka besought the Governor to remove the troops and redress the native grievances in respect of the Customs duties, which had caused the trouble; he and the other chiefs on their part undertook to keep Heke in check and to protect the Europeans in the district. To these requests Fitzroy agreed. He perceived the uselessness of aggressive action with his available force, and ordered the troops back to their headquarters—the 99th to Sydney and the 80th to Auckland—and he promised that the Bay would be declared a free port.

This promise was carried out, after Ngapuhi had surrendered a few muskets in token of submission and Heke had offered to erect another mast. Customs duties were abolished throughout the colony, and a property-tax substituted.

In October trouble was renewed at the Bay. Depredations on outlying settlers were begun by the restless young men. On the 10th January, 1845, the flagstaff was cut down a second time. On the preceding day Heke had visited the Acting-Consul for the United States, a storekeeper named Henry Green Smith, at Wahapu; this trader had recently replaced one Captain William Mayhew, who had been Acting-Consul since 1840. Mayhew had helped to instil into the minds of Pomare and Heke a dislike to the British flag, consequent on the imposition of Customs duties. From him and other Americans the discontented chief had heard of the successful revolt of the American colonies against England, and the lesson was not forgotten; he burned to do likewise. From Smith he obtained an American ensign, and paddled on to Kororareka; and when the flagstaff fell to a Ngapuhi axe for a second time up went the foreign colour on the carved sternpost of Heke's war-canoe. The warrior crew paraded the harbour, their *kai-hautu*, or fugleman, yelling a battle-song, Heke at the steering-paddle, the American flag over his head.*

Excitement and apprehension now possessed the Bay settlements. The "Victoria," the Government brig, sailed into Koro-

---

* There is a curious discrepancy between the original despatches from the Bay of Islands regarding this incident and the correspondence printed in the official publications of the day. Governor Fitzroy, or his Colonial Secretary, appears to have considered it undesirable, for reasons of international policy, to make any public reference to the American share in Heke's rebellion, hence all allusions to the United States Consul and his flag at the Bay are omitted, with the result that a hiatus in one of the blue-book despatches makes it unintelligible. In the Grey Collection of documents in the Auckland Municipal Library there are manuscript copies of a number of letters from Mr. Thomas Beckham, Police Magistrate, to Governor Fitzroy, detailing the events of January, 1845. The first of these letters, dated Russell, 10th January, 1845, is as follows :—

"It is with regret I have to inform Your Excellency that John Heke and his tribe cut down the flagstaff soon after daylight this morning, but without doing any violence to the Europeans or even entering the town. The reason for his again offering this insult seems to be a general dislike to the British Government ; and it is worthy of remark that Heke was at the American Consul's yesterday, when the merits of the Treaty of Waitangi, and other political subjects connected with this colony, were discussed, after which he obtained an American ensign, which was hoisted on board his canoe immediately after our flagstaff was destroyed. Under what circumstances this flag was given I am now unable to say, but at this present crisis it looks suspicious, and is at the least very ill-judged. It is reported, but with what truth I cannot affirm, that Heke's ultimate intention is to pull down the gaol and public offices. This bad disposition does not appear to be prevalent amongst the natives generally."

In the printed despatches, however, the words between "British Government" and "Under what circumstances" are omitted ; and we are left to conclude that the mutilation, or suppression, was prompted by a desire not to implicate or offend the Americans.

In a further letter marked "Private," dated Russell, 16th January, 1845, Mr. Beckham wrote to the Governor :—

"Heke still carries the American ensign in his canoe, and I was sorry to observe it hoisted at the Consul's this morning, as also on board the United States ships, which is quite unusual, except on the arrival or departure of American vessels, which was not the case. This circumstance confirms the suspicions mentioned in my letter of the 10th instant, and I am fearful that these disturbances in opposition to the Government have been fostered by the Americans, and I beg to suggest for Your Excellency's consideration the propriety of causing the Consul's flagstaff to be removed (if practicable), as it now stands in a very conspicuous position."

The manuscripts in the Grey Collection show that on the 24th January Mr. Beckham, under instructions from the Governor, visited Henry Green Smith, of Wahapu, "the person at whose residence the American ensign has been so conspicuously exhibited lately," and informed him that he (the Magistrate) was directed to prohibit the hoisting of any national flag on shore at the Bay of Islands except that of Great Britain.

Apparently Mr. Smith made a pertinent inquiry as to Mr. Beckham's authority, for on the 25th January the Magistrate wrote to him as follows :—

"In reply to your letter of this date, referring to my communication of the 24th instant relative to the prohibition of any national flag being hoisted on shore except that of Great Britain, I now do myself the honour to inform you that I did so by the directions of His Excellency the Governor, and to state that the United States flag is included in the interdiction, there being no Consul at this port."

rareka Bay on the 17th January, and landed a small detachment of troops—a subaltern and thirty men of the 96th Regiment—who re-erected the flagstaff. The Rev. Henry Williams, at Paihia, consulted on the 18th by the Colonial Secretary and the Magistrate, advised that the flag should not be flaunted in the face of the natives, at any rate not until it could be guarded efficiently, otherwise the Maoris would have it down again. While they were speaking, Heke and his canoe flotilla, with American and other flags flying, passed close to the Paihia landing. Before it was full daylight next morning the staff was cut down for the third time and the topmast carried away; the flag itself remained in the possession of the friendly natives who were in charge of the station. Heke and his men fired a triumphant volley on the beach and danced a war-dance.

Thoroughly alarmed by this determined resistance to the establishment of British rule, Fitzroy wrote to Sir George Gipps, Governor of New South Wales, making urgent application for further military assistance. He declared that he must prepare for operations "in a woody country, at Whangarei, if not at the Bay of Islands" (there had been robberies with violence at the homes of settlers at Matakana by natives from Whangarei), and he must also take precautions for the safety of Auckland.

In compliance with this request (which did not reach Sydney till the 17th February) two companies of the 58th Regiment, the famous "Black Cuffs," numbering 207 of all ranks, received orders to embark for Auckland, but by the time they reached the Bay of Islands (28th April, 1845) the flagstaff was down again, Kororareka Town was in ashes, and war had begun.

The opening shots were fired on the 3rd March, 1845, eight days before the final disaster. Heke had given assurances to the friendly chiefs that he would not molest the white settlers, except in retaliation for hostile measures by the Government; but the old warrior Kawiti did not exercise similar forbearance. His Ngati-Hine and allied *hapus* from the Kawakawa and Waiomio carried out a series of raids on isolated settlers in some of the small bays a few miles from Kororareka. On the 28th February four large war-canoes crowded with armed natives from the Kawakawa swept down the Bay and landed in front of the house occupied by Captain Wright. The marauders plundered and burned the place. Several other houses in the vicinity of the town were similarly looted and destroyed. On the 3rd March a message reached the Police Magistrate that a party of Kawiti's men, who had come down in two canoes, were plundering the house of Benjamin Turner, an old resident; his home was at the Uruti, a deep, narrow bay about two miles in rear of Kororareka. Beckham sent off to H.M.S. "Hazard" (which had arrived from Wellington on the 15th February) for assistance, and the Acting-Commander, Lieutenant Robertson, went ashore with a party of

From a drawing, 1846.] HONE HEKE, HIS WIFE (HARIATA), AND KAWITI.

sailors armed with muskets and cutlasses. The force marched overland to Uruti, while the frigate's pinnace, carrying light guns, was sent round the coast for the purpose of cutting off the retreat of Kawiti's canoes. Both arrived too late; Turner's house and wheat-stacks were in ashes. Two horses had been taken away by a native track over the hills to Otuihu, and, with the object of recapturing these as they were being swum across the sea-arm leading to the Kawakawa River and Waikare Inlet, the pinnace, under Lieutenant Morgan, was sent in chase. Pomare's *pa* at Otuihu was passed, but off Opua it was seen that further pursuit was useless, and the boat put about to return to the ship. A fire was opened on the pinnace from both sides of the channel. The naval lieutenant returned the fire with grape-shot from his boat-guns and musketry. Two slight skirmishes in rear of the town followed during March.

By this time Kororareka had been placed in a condition of defence, though by no means an efficient condition; the chief thing lacking was a competent leader of the military and the white inhabitants. A timber stockade was built around Mr. Polack's house near the northern end of the beach; this was to be the refuge-place for white women and children. A blockhouse was erected on a small hill in the rear of the stockade and the town, close to the track leading to the Maiki flagstaff. Here were mounted three ship's guns. A gun was taken up to the other end of the town, at the entrance to the valley leading through to Mata-uhi Bay, in rear of Kororareka, the most likely avenue of attack. Mr. C. Hector, a solicitor by profession, a man of much spirit and resolution, had charge of the blockhouse battery. For the Mata-uhi gun a crew of bluejackets and marines was sent ashore from H.M.S. "Hazard." The civilians of the town were organized and drilled under the superintendence of Lieutenant Phillpotts, of the "Hazard." The Government brig "Victoria" brought from Auckland forty stand of arms and a thousand rounds of ball cartridge for the Militia. As a regular garrison, there were about fifty rank and file of the 96th Regiment from Auckland, under two young officers, Lieutenant E. Barclay and Ensign J. Campbell, neither of whom, as events developed, possessed the experience needful in such a situation. Twenty of these, under the junior subaltern, were detailed as signal-station guard; the others were quartered in the barracks built on the flat, below the three-gun blockhouse. A detachment of bluejackets and marines from the "Hazard" was also stationed in the barracks. The new flagstaff had been safeguarded by the construction of a blockhouse around the foot of the mast, which had been sheathed with iron to a height of about 10 feet as a protection against the Maori tomahawk. A trench, crossed by a plank, surrounded the blockhouse, which accommodated the garrison of twenty men, besides the signalman, an old man-of-war's-man named Tapper, and his native family.

CHAPTER IV.

THE FALL OF KORORAREKA.

Midnight on Maiki Hill. A rattle of arms at the blockhouse gateway came sharply through the tenebrous stillness; the guard was relieved—the soldier whose tedious duty was ended retired to his blankets, and the only half-awake relief, with musket and fixed bayonet, began his watch. Here, 300 feet above the sleeping town, the silence was intense; it was a windless night, with raw fog obscuring the gullies and floating upward in thin wafts. Not a sound but the footfall of the sentry and the "Kou-kou" of the *ruru*, or night-owl. Those owl-calls were unusually frequent was the thought, perhaps, that crossed the mind of the solitary soldier. Had he possessed the scout instinct he might have noticed that the bird-calls all came from the brushwood on the east and south-east slopes of the range, the aspect towards Oneroa Bay and the lower blockhouse. Owl called to owl, and the regularly repeated cries grew nearer until they formed a semi-cordon of melancholy notes about the flagstaff hill. Then, too, was heard the screech call, plain as spoken words to the Maori; it sounded to him like "*Kia toa!*" ("Be brave!")

It was a fatal cordon, for the *rurus* were the pickets of Heke's war-party announcing their positions to each other and keeping in touch as they crept towards the little fort that guarded their objective, the flagstaff. Two hundred Ngapuhi warriors, under Heke and Pokai, had landed in their canoes at Oneroa, in rear of Kororareka, late at night, and were now working their way up to surprise the hill post at the first streak of dawn. Some of them crept up until they crouched in the scrub a few yards from where the sentry stood. Most of them lay in a wooded gully close to the hilltop. They carried gun and tomahawk, and belts with heavy leather or wooden cartouche-boxes were strapped about them. The tomahawk was the weapon most favoured for such tasks as this: short-handled with wood or whalebone, thrust through the girdle at the hip or at the small of the back, as the olden Scots and the Borderers carried the "lyttel batayle axe" mentioned in Froissart's story of the Battle of Otterburne.

Grey dawn; a damp fog-laden break of day. The *ruru* calls have ceased; the dark hills are steeped in utter silence. The hidden warriors, gripping their loaded flint-lock and percussion-cap guns, are ready to spring from their cramped couches in the brushwood at the chief's first call. Some of them have cut *manuka* bushes with their tomahawks; these are to provide a moving cover for themselves as they creep up on the *pakehas*.

24   NEW ZEALAND WARS.

Now the door of the little blockhouse on Maiki hilltop opens; the plank bridge is thrown across the trench, and half a dozen men, all armed, and five of them carrying spades, come out into the misty morning. The youthful officer in charge of the post,

From a photo, 1903.]

THE FLAGSTAFF, RUSSELL, BAY OF ISLANDS.

This signal-mast occupied the site of that cut down by Hone Heke The remains of the olden trench which surrounded the small blockhouse of 1845 are seen at the foot of the flagstaff.

Ensign Campbell, takes his men along the hill-slopes to the edge of the range overlooking Oneroa Bay; here they set to work to dig a trench, intended as a protection against any attack from that direction.

Scarcely have the soldiers commenced their spade-work in the dim light than the morning silence is shattered by sudden shots, then rolling volleys. The firing comes from the south end of the town below, apparently from the direction of Mata-uhi Bay. Campbell orders his men back to the blockhouse ; and the issue of the morning's work might be very different had he the prudence to remain there with them and make secure his post. But in his curiosity to learn what is going on below he leads eight or nine men out to the brow of the hill overlooking Kororareka, nearly 200 yards from the blockhouse. The rest of the garrison, twenty men, are aroused, and, taking their arms, are putting on their belts outside the ditch facing the town.

Now is Heke's and Pokai's opportunity. Little by little the war-party creeps up, some daring fellows crawling across the open with *manuka* bushes and branches held in front of them. With a yell from their leaders, they are up and charging into the blockhouse ; it is nearly empty of its garrison.

Ensign Campbell is for charging back to the stockade, but Ngapuhi are too quick for him. They are already in the stockaded enclosure and its trench, and, while some open fire on the soldiers outside, others dash into the blockhouse, killing the four soldiers who remain to defend it. They shoot, too, but unintentionally, a little half-caste girl, the daughter of Tapper the signalman.

The surviving soldiers, confused by the surprise attack, contrive to give the Maoris a volley, but before another round can be fired it is seen that a second party of warriors is doubling up from a gully to cut off the soldiers from the lower blockhouse. Campbell, therefore, in order to escape being nipped between the two bodies, must fall back on the lower blockhouse, having lost his own. This he and his men do, and at their utmost speed ; while the triumphant Ngapuhi, not without much labour—because of the iron sheathing, which necessitates digging as well as chopping—fell the flagstaff for the fourth time.*

---

* A story of the fourth flagstaff imparts an element of comedy to the history of blunders and tragedy associated with the Maiki signal-hill. It is said that after the mast had been cut down for the third time and another pole had been procured from the forest the new stick vanished mysteriously one night, to the consternation of the military detachment sent to set it in position. It was discovered that it had been hauled away by an old chief of a neighbouring village, who declared that he had been born underneath it when it was a living tree ; he was afraid that trouble or death would befall him if Heke carried out his customary threat and felled the mast. It would be an *aitua*, or forerunner of disaster, in Maori eyes. The staff having disappeared, there was nothing for it but to obtain one to which the exasperating Maori was not likely to lay claim. The Government went to the shipping for its next spar ; the officials bought the mizzen-mast of a foreign vessel in the harbour, " being morally certain," says the *New Zealand Spectator's* narrative (22nd March, 1845), " that no Maori could have been born under it." This mast, the fifth, stood for nearly two months before Heke's axe laid it low and bereaved Kororareka of a signal-station for eight years.

Meanwhile a battle, attended with more credit for the whites than the inglorious affair on the flagstaff hill, was waged in the town below.

At 4 o'clock that morning (11th March, 1845) a force of forty-five small-arms men, composed of bluejackets and marines from H.M.S. "Hazard," under the Acting-Commander, David Robertson (who had succeeded Commander Bell, recently drowned), marched from the beach to the heights overlooking Mata-uhi Bay for the purpose of throwing up a breastwork on the face of the hill. They had just reached the spot when the sentry at the one-gun battery on the hill on the opposite or southern side of the little valley which led to Mata-uhi Bay challenged and fired; he had spied a party of Maoris creeping up on his position. This was old Kawiti's division, comprising Ngati-Hine and Roroa men; a leading brave was Pumuka. Kawiti's share of the day's work was to make an attack on the town in order to divert attention from the main task, Heke's assault on the flagstaff.

In the half-light of that hazy morning a hand-to-hand combat was fought around the enclosure of the English church as Robertson and his men fell back toward the town. The Maoris numbered about two hundred. These the forty-five "Hazards" charged. Musket and *tupara* blazed; British cutlass clashed on Maori long-handled tomahawk. The frigate's men cut their way into Kawiti's party, and steadily forced them back towards Mata-uhi. The gun, served by the sailors, was used at point-blank range against the dark warriors. Captain Robertson, wielding his sword like some hero of old romance, killed Pumuka with one blow, and felled several others of his foes in the combat at the churchyard fence. He fell at last severely wounded; he was shot through both legs, his right thigh-bone was smashed, his right arm was shot through close to the elbow, and his temple was grazed by a pistol-shot. The "Hazards" pursued the retreating Maoris, who took to the scrub on the hills and joined in the firing on the town at long range. Four seamen and a sergeant and private of Royal Marines were killed in the half-hour skirmish; besides Captain Robertson, dangerously wounded, and Acting-Lieutenant E. Morgan, slightly, six men were wounded. The command of the naval party devolved upon Acting-Lieutenant Morgan. After charging the Maoris and completing their repulse in the Mata-uhi gully, he engaged in a musketry battle with Kawiti, who from the hills opened a steady fire.

Now the detachment of the 96th Regiment, under Lieutenant E. Barclay, whose quarters were in the barracks between the beach and the lower blockhouse, entered the battle. Barclay had seen the naval force march out towards Mata-uhi, and turned out his men. Their first shots were directed on parties of Maoris who appeared on the hills to the left of the barracks.

towards Oneroa Bay. They checked the advance of these musketeers. Then enemy bullets began to drop around the soldiers from the steep hills behind; and, on facing about, it was for the first time seen that the Maoris had captured the flagstaff hill.

A message now arrived from Acting-Lieutenant Morgan informing the 96th officer that a party of the enemy held the ground at the back of the English church, nearly half a mile from the barracks. The military detachment, numbering about thirty, thereupon quickly advanced in skirmishing order, firing as they advanced. Another messenger came from Morgan; the "Hazard's"

THE ENGLISH CHURCH, RUSSELL, BAY OF ISLANDS.

This church was built prior to the war, and the engagement of the 11th March, 1845, between the sailors of H.M.S. "Hazard" and the Ngapuhi warriors under Kawiti was fought around the churchyard fence in the foreground. On the seaward side of the church there is a weatherboard cut by a round shot from the "Hazard," fired after the evacuation of Kororareka.

little force had nearly expended its ammunition, and Lieutenant Barclay turned back towards the beach to join the sailors. The one-gun battery had been abandoned, but not before the gun had been spiked by a gallant seaman, William Lovell, who next moment was shot dead. The sailors retired along the waterfront to Polack's stockade. After engaging scattered parties of natives from the flat, who drew off in the direction of Mata-uhi, the Maoris carrying away their dead and wounded as they retired, the soldiers turned about and marched to the lower blockhouse in rear of the stockade. Ensign Campbell and his dispossessed flagstaff-party were already there checking the advance of the enemy who swarmed along the heights and in the gullies in rear of the town.

The Kapotai Tribe, from the Waikare, the third division of the assailants, were now into the fray, firing at the blockhouse, the barracks, and the stockade from the half-circle of hills that rimmed the town. The troops replied from the blockhouse windows and loopholes and the sloping ground on each side. The ship's guns, on a platform outside, were worked by the volunteer artillerymen — civilians and one or two old soldiers, under Mr. Hector.

Heke on his hilltop station stood fast, watching the combat below; he had taken the key of Kororareka, which was all, indeed, that he had intended or expected.

There was no proper co-ordination of operations in the defence; the naval authority, the military, and the Police Magistrate each gave orders and acted as they thought fit, independently of the others. The "Hazard's" captain being out of action, Lieutenant Phillpotts took command of the ship. He directed the abandoned barracks (behind which some of the enemy were in cover) and the captured signal-station to be shelled. Round shot and grape-shot were thrown at the natives on the hills, and for several hours the hills of the Bay echoed and re-echoed the roar of the frigate's artillery.

It was now between 10 and 11 o'clock in the forenoon. There was a brief lull in the fighting; then, about 11 o'clock, skirmishing again commenced. There were a hundred armed civilians in Polack's stockade—a hastily drilled militia; a party of these men was sent to drive off some Maoris who were firing at the defenders of the lower blockhouse from the hill above the barracks. This was done, and the Maoris contented themselves with sniping from their *manuka* cover on the heights.

All that Heke wished for had been accomplished; but now a kind of panic seemed to have overtaken some of those in authority. Heke had no intention of attacking the civilian population; he had hoisted a white flag, and sent down under its protection the wife and daughter of the signalman Tapper, who was now employed at the guns of the lower blockhouse. About noon the white women and children, who had all been gathered with their menfolk in Polack's stockade, were sent aboard the ships in harbour—the "Hazard," the United States warship "St. Louis," the "Matilda" (English whaleship), the Government brig, and Bishop Selwyn's schooner. This was a rightful measure of prudence as it developed, but there was scarcely adequate reason for the evacuation of the town by the able-bodied men, in spite of an accident which occurred soon after the non-combatants had been removed to the shipping. A careless fellow smoked his pipe as he worked among the kegs of gunpowder in the stockade magazine. Loose powder on the floor; a dropped spark; the next moment a flash, and with a terrifying roar up went the magazine and the greater part of the buildings in fragments. The whole of the reserve ammunition in store was destroyed. That fateful pipe of tobacco decided the fortunes of Kororareka.

Lieutenant Phillpotts, the senior combatant officer, after consultation with Mr. Beckham, the Magistrate, now determined upon the complete evacuation of the place. He gave orders that the troops and the civilian population should go aboard the ships. All this time the battery on the mound in the rear of the stockade had been steadily held by Hector's civilian gunners and Barclay's redcoats. The round shot probably inflicted little harm upon the Maoris, who swarmed on the scrub-matted slopes of Titore's Mount and the minor hills around, but the gunnery and the small-arms fire at least prevented the Kapotai and their allies from descending into the town. With Mr. Hector were his two plucky sons, young boys, who gallantly carried up ammunition from the stockade under heavy fire. Tapper, the signalman, was wounded while serving one of the guns.

Hector's disgust was extreme when he was informed of the decision arrived at by the senior naval officer and the Magistrate. He went down to the beach and offered to retake the flagstaff hill if he were given fifty volunteers. The request was refused. Lieutenant Barclay also went down for ammunition; when he returned he found that the guns had been spiked—by whose orders was not clear. Nothing could have been finer than Mr. Hector's work as battery commander, and it certainly was not his fault that the post had to be abandoned. A review of the day's fighting and the day's blunders after the brave Robertson's fall at the head of his men prompts the conclusion that had the conduct of operations been in this amateur gunner's hands instead of those of the too-impulsive Phillpotts and the over-cautious Beckham, the town, in spite of the destruction of the stockade, need not have been abandoned to Ngapuhi.

Riwhitete Pokai, of Kaikohe, recounting half a century after the war his share in the fall of Kororareka, described the annoyance of the Ngapuhi at Phillpotts' indiscriminate shelling. "We treated the women and children kindly," the veteran said, "and took those of them who remained late off to the ships in our canoes. But as soon as all the refugees were on board—and even before that—the man-of-war set to and opened fire on our people on the beach. It was an act of treachery to shell us after the town had been given up to us by the whites. When the firing began some of us were sorry we had not tomahawked all the *pakehas* we could find." Such was the Maori viewpoint.

The heavy day closed with occasional shots from the frigate, little regarded by the Maoris, who were now absorbed in the joy of looting, drinking the grog in the publichouses, seizing blankets, clothes, tobacco, preserved foods, and all the varied stock of the stores. Some employed themselves loading their canoes that had been hastily paddled round from the bay in the rear of the town. The Hectors and a number of other families were in Bishop Selwyn's schooner, the "Flying Fish"; the English whaleship received over a hundred, the American frigate "St. Louis" took 125 on board, and the rest found quarters in the "Hazard" with the

MEMORIAL TO THE FALLEN SAILORS, RUSSELL CHURCHYARD.

troops. Captain McKeever, the commander of the "St. Louis," won praise from the British for his courage and humanity. Considerations of neutrality debarred him from a share in the fighting, but he sent his unarmed boats ashore, and himself frequently went under fire, like Bishop Selwyn, to bring off the women and children.

The Maori casualties of the day were heavier than those of the British, but they weighed lightly against the completeness of the victory. The British lost ten seamen and marines and privates of the 96th killed; in addition two people died from injuries received in the explosion of the magazine. The wounded numbered twenty-three. The Maori division which suffered most was Kawiti's, which in the fight near the church and on the Mata-uhi track lost at least twenty killed, and more than twice as many wounded. The total native losses in the day were reported to Governor Fitzroy as thirty-four killed and sixty-eight wounded. The united forces of the attackers numbered about six hundred. Lieutenant Phillpotts reported them at double that figure.

Some of the more determined spirits went ashore next morning intent on salvage, but the "Hazard" again opened fire on the town. The Maoris continued the work of looting, filling their canoes with goods from the stores; then they set fire to one after another of the buildings. The English and Roman Catholic churches and mission-houses, including Bishop Pompallier's home, were scrupulously protected from harm. By the afternoon all the rest of the town was burning. Fifty thousand pounds' worth of property went up in flames and smoke. Early on the following day (13th March) the fleet of five sailed for Auckland, and as the sorrowful refugees looked back they saw, long after they had rounded Tapeka Point, the black mass of smoke that lay high and unmoving above the bay, the funeral cloud of Kororareka.

CHAPTER V.

THE FIRST BRITISH MARCH INLAND.

Fears of invasion by Ngapuhi seized many of the inhabitants of the young capital when, two days after the sailing of the fleet from the Bay, the five shiploads of refugees landed at Auckland and the distressed people of Kororareka spread their story. A Militia was enrolled, and the Auckland citizen soldiery were drilled daily by instructors from the Regulars. The defences of the town were hastily set in order. Major Bunbury and his company of the 80th had already (1840–41) partly fortified Britomart Point by constructing stone barracks. These barracks formed two sides of a square; one side was loopholed; the buildings were capable of accommodating two hundred men, besides stores. Fort Britomart, as it was now called, had been an ancient *pa* of the Maoris, a tonguelike promontory, protected on the land side by a broad, deep ditch and parapet. The military utilized part of these defences; a portion of the parapet was thrown down to fill up the ditch at the entrance. On one side of the interior, where of old the warriors had built their low-eaved *whares* and kept lookout for enemy canoe flotillas, an octagonal loopholed guard-room was erected. A hospital was also built. The 96th and, later, the 58th completed the fortification, and several guns were mounted. The windows of St. Paul's Church, a brick building near by, were planked and loopholed for musketry.

H.M.S. "North Star" (Captain Sir Everard Home), a twenty-six-gun frigate, arrived at Auckland on the 22nd March. She brought from Sydney 162 officers and men of the 58th Regiment. Two days afterwards the schooner "Velocity" arrived from Sydney with fifty-five officers and men of the same regiment, and ordnance stores. In April the barque "Slains Castle" sailed in from Sydney, bringing the remainder of the 58th—more than two hundred rank and file—under Major Cyprian Bridge. On the 27th April an expedition totalling 470 officers and men under Lieut.-Colonel Hulme, of the 96th Regiment, and Major Bridge sailed from Auckland in the "Slains Castle," the "Velocity," and the schooner "Aurora," with the object of re-establishing the Queen's sovereignty at Kororareka and carrying the war into the enemy's country. Besides the 58th and 96th, there were on board about fifty volunteers, most of them late inhabitants of Kororareka, under the courageous civilian Mr. Hector. A small force was left in Auckland, which was not now considered in danger, as Te Wherowhero, the great chief of Waikato, had offered to protect the capital from attack by Ngapuhi — his hereditary enemies—or any other foe. Old Apihai te Kawau, of Orakei, and his people of Ngati-Whatua, who had sold the site of Auckland to Governor Hobson in 1840, could also be relied upon as friends of the whites.

After hoisting the British flag on Kororareka Beach, Hulme's force destroyed Pomare's *pa* at Otuihu, overlooking the channel to Opua and the Waikare. The "North Star" was anchored

THE DESTRUCTION OF POMARE'S PA, OTUIHU.

H.M.S. "North Star" in the foreground. Pomare was detained as a prisoner on board this ship. The destruction of the fortified village was carried out by detachments of the 58th and 96th Regiments.

off Otuihu, and Pomare himself was secured as a prisoner by stratagem. It was then arranged that an expedition should be directed against Heke's stronghold lately built near the shore of Lake Omapere.

The chiefs who with their tribes and *hapus* definitely ranged themselves upon the side of the Government were Tamati Waka Nene (Ngati-Hao Tribe); Mohi Tawhai (Mahurehure Tribe), of Waima, Hokianga; Makoare Tainui (Te Popoto); Wiremu Repa (Ngati-Hao); Paratene Kekeao (Ngapuhi); Tamati Pukututu (Uri-o-Ngonga), of the Kawakawa; Arama Karaka (Mahurehure);

Rangatira (Ngati-Korokoro); Moehau (Hikutu); Nopera Pana-Kareao (Te Rarawa). Some of the celebrated chiefs, such as the gigantic cannibal Tareha, Waikato (who had visited England in 1820 with Hongi Hika), and the Hokianga leader Papahia, remained neutral; and Pomare, although his *pa* was destroyed and he himself taken prisoner by Lieut.-Colonel Hulme, did not take any active share in Heke's work. Several chiefs of the Kapotai, Ngati-Wai, Ngati-Hau, Uri-Kapana, and Uri-o-Hau brought their *hapus* to Heke's assistance.

Tamati Waka Nene was allied by blood with the Hongi and Heke families. He had been Hongi's comrade on the war-path, and he had carried his musket and tomahawk as far south as Cook Strait in a great cannibal campaign twenty years before the coming of the British flag. Wise in knowledge of men and of military science as the Maori had developed it, endowed with a keen intellect and well-balanced reasoning-powers, he was the most able of all the Ngapuhi chiefs, and the best qualified, by natural gifts and by his tribal standing, to offer resistance to the disaffected sections of Ngapuhi. His brother Patuone, a man of high character and a warrior of fame, also took up the British cause, steadfastly declining to have any part in rebellion against the Queen whose right of eminent domain he had accepted in the Treaty of Waitangi.

One of the chiefs at first friendly to the British Government but ultimately found fighting in the cause of Maori independence was Pene Taui, of Waimate and Ohaeawai. A curious story is told of Pene's defection, illustrative of the serious consequences often entailed by trivial incidents among the Maoris. In 1844, when the war feeling was developing throughout the north, Pene Taui was authorized to convene a meeting of Ngapuhi to consider the political situation. The assembled chiefs resolved to plant large quantities of food (potatoes, *kumara*, *taro*, and maize) in order to provide for a general gathering of the northern tribes in the Taiamai district, the heart of the Ngapuhi country, embracing the beautiful lands from Waimate to Ohaeawai. The meeting having concluded, Pene Taui sent a messenger to Tamati Waka Nene, at Hokianga, with the somewhat peremptory words, "*Koia he kai*" ("Plant food"). When the herald delivered this message in public, as was the Maori way, Tamati Waka, resentful of its wording, immediately said, *sotto voce* but not so low that the messenger could not hear, "*Ko ia he kai.*" It was a quick play upon Pene's message; the point lay in the accenting of "*ia*" ("him") instead of "*ko*" ("plant"). Waka's utterance meant "Let him be food," or "He shall be the food." The messenger heard; he returned to Taiamai, and reported Waka's words to Pene Taui. That chief was so enraged at Waka's punning *kanga*, or curse, likening a high chief to food—cannibal fashion—that he at once made common cause with Hone Heke, taking with him all his tribe. It was Pene who built the stockade at Ohaeawai which Despard a few months later found impregnable.*

H.M.S. "Hazard" having arrived from Auckland, the fleet hove up and sailed across the Bay to Kent's Passage, where the ships anchored under shelter of the island of Moturoa. On the following morning a force of four hundred men, including about a hundred seamen and marines from the frigates, was disembarked on the beach of Onewhero. On that day (3rd May, 1845) was begun the first march inland of British troops in New Zealand.

Imperfectly informed as to the route of march, without transport arrangements, without artillery, inefficiently rationed, and without tents or camp equipage, Hulme set out into an unknown country against an enemy of unknown strength, sustained apparently by the hope of somehow worrying through, or fortified by the popular belief that one British soldier was equal to any half-dozen savages. Neither Hulme nor his officers knew anything of the real strength of Maori fortifications skilfully defended. The report on native strongholds prepared by Lieutenant Bennett of the Royal Engineers in 1843, after a visit to Tauranga, was unknown to them. Fortunate it was for them and their men that the chivalrous enemy laid no ambuscades on the track; the Maori was not so considerate in the wars twenty years later. Doubly fortunate for them was the fact that Tamati Waka Nene was their ally and helper. He was the salvation of Hulme on that May expedition, as he was of the Maori-despising Despard a few weeks later.

The opening blunder was the awkward route taken. Instead of transporting the force by boat up a good tidal river, the Kerikeri, to the mission station at the landing, only fifteen miles from Kororareka, whence a cart-road led to the Waimate, fourteen miles, the commander marched his force along a rough native track south of the river for nine miles, bivouacked in the fern, and broke off to the right next morning, marching through torrents of rain to the Kerikeri mission station. The result was that the five days' biscuit ration and two-thirds of the reserve ammunition were spoiled by the rain.

From Kerikeri the combined naval and military column moved out on the inland trail on the morning of the 6th May. The clay road, reduced to a glue-like mire by the rain, made difficult marching. Waka's and Rewa's barefooted warriors watched with pity and some amusement the efforts of the troops to march in fours and keep their dressing on this unkindly highway; they wondered how men so heavily beswagged, so tightly fastened

---

* This incident is narrated in a note sent to me by Captain Gilbert Mair, who adds, " Puns are of rare occurrence among the Maoris."

with belts and straps and leather stocks, could march and fight. The bluejackets, more handily equipped and comfortably clothed, made easier work of it; they carried with them a war-rocket tube from the "North Star" and a dozen rockets, which it was imagined would help to demolish any Maori stockade encountered. Acting-Commander George Johnson, of the "North Star," was in command of this naval brigade. The cart-road to Waimate was followed for some miles, then the column struck in a direct line across country for Waka's armed camp between Lake Omapere and Okaihau, twenty miles from Kerikeri. The march could have been simplified had the force passed through Waimate, but the members of the Church Mission there, the Revs. R. Burrows and R. Davis, had made strong efforts to keep the mission station *tapu* from armed men and to preserve an attitude of strict neutrality. After passing the Waimate at a distance, the force entered a tract of forest, chiefly *puriri;* now the troops had their first taste of New Zealand bush work. A detachment of Pioneers of the 50th had been thrown ahead with Waka's natives. With their axes they improved the difficult Maori pad-track, only a few inches wide, for the passage of the main body. Unbridged creeks in flood were waded, small swamps were crossed, hills were breasted, and at last, at sundown, the bugles called a halt, and the weary soldiers and sailors loosened their packs under the stockade of Tamati Waka's fortified camp, a mile from the Omapere Lake.

Heke's *pa*, named Puketutu, was two miles from Nene's fort, and quite close to Lake Omapere. The fort is usually but erroneously referred to as "Okaihau" by writers on the northern war. Okaihau is about three miles to the west. Half-way between the two *pas* was the small hill Taumata-Karamu, the scene of many skirmishes between Heke and Nene in April. Now and again a man was killed. By mutual arrangement no ambuscades were laid, and the fighting was only in daylight.

CHAPTER VI.

THE FIGHTING AT OMAPERE.

"No one knew, though there were many who were wise after the event, that these tribesmen (the Mamunds) were as well armed as the troops, or that they were the brave and formidable enemies they proved themselves to be. 'Never despise your enemies,' is an old lesson, but it has to be learnt afresh, year after year, by every nation that is warlike and brave."—"The Story of the Malakand Field Force," by Winston Churchill.

"We expected to make short work of Johnny Heke," said an old soldier of the 58th describing to me his march to Lake Omapere. But the difficulties of the undertaking so confidently essayed increased as the objective was approached and the military character of the Maori loomed formidably in the British warrior's vision. The unpropitious season heightened the troubles of the commander, whose deficiencies in artillery and commissariat were fatal to any chances of success. The greatest blunder of all, the failure to bring even the lightest of ship's guns, although there was a cart-road for the greater part of the way from Kerikeri to the lake, condemned the expedition to failure. This became fully apparent to the sanguine Hulme on the second day after his arrival on the terrain which Heke had selected as the battle-ground.

The country in which the rival armed bands of Heke and Waka Nene had pitched their fortified camps was an ideal region for military operations. Towards Lake Omapere the land was a gently undulating plain covered with *manuka* shrubbery, fern, flax, and *tutu* bushes, and adorned with numerous groves of the hardwood *puriri*, oak-like in the spread of its branches. To the east lay the plains and hills of Taiamai, the delectable land of the central Ngapuhi tribes. What swamps there existed were not large and could readily be avoided; streams were numerous but small. Many of these little rivers issued from fissures in the volcanic hillside, welling down cold and crystal-clear through the Maori cultivations that alternated with the wilderness of fern and *tutu*. The landscape was diversified with many a bold volcanic cone. Most conspicuous of these was Te Ahuahu ("Heaped Up"), otherwise known as Puke-nui ("Big Hill"), a long-extinct volcano now grassed to its saucer-shaped summit. It rises from the levels near the northern shore of the lake; its height

38 NEW ZEALAND WARS.

is over 1,200 feet. In the fighting which immediately preceded the arrival of the troops in May, 1845, Tamati Waka Nene fortified a position on this hill. To the west lay Okaihau, with its dense woods of *puriri;* to the south-west the Utakura Stream, issuing from the lake, coursed swiftly down to the harbour of Hokianga. Tamati Waka's first palisaded *pa*, before he shifted to the Ahuahu Hill, was built near Okaihau Forest, in order to check Heke's progress westward to the Hokianga headwaters.

There had been considerable fighting in the month of April between Heke's warriors and the *hapus* friendly to the whites, extending over this open country between Okaihau and Te Ahuahu. Heke's force numbered about three hundred men; his ally Kawiti joined in with another hundred and fifty towards the

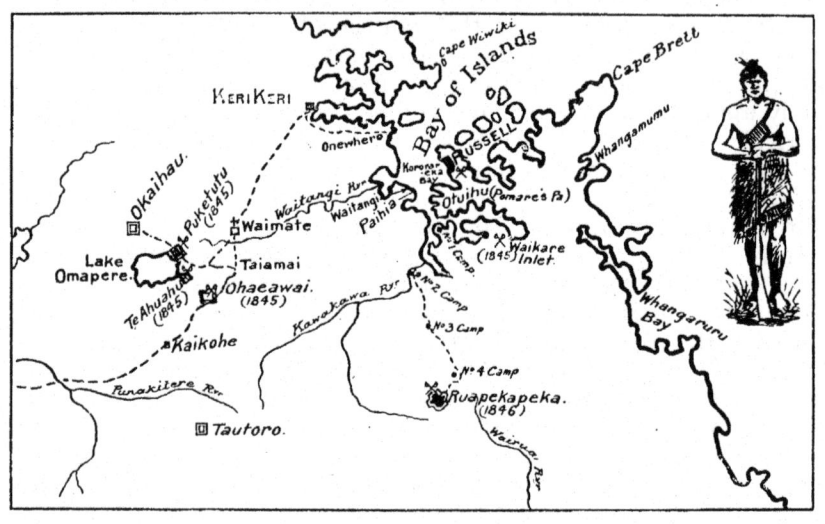

SCENES OF ENGAGEMENTS, BAY OF ISLANDS DISTRICT, 1845-46.

end of April. To these combined war-parties were opposed about four hundred men under Tamati Waka, Mohi Tawhai, and Arama Karaka Pi, from Hokianga; Taonui, Nopera Para-kareao, and other chiefs loyal to the Treaty. Besides Waka's fortified camp, two stockades were built by Taonui and his tribe from Utakura, Hokianga, and by Mohi Tawhai and his Mahurehure *hapu* from Waima. All these three forts were close together for mutual support. Two or three white men joined Waka Nene in the field as volunteers. One of these was the afterwards celebrated Judge F. E. Maning, the author of "Old New Zealand." He was a tall athletic man, whom nothing delighted so much as this opportunity of free-lance fighting. A comrade of Maning's was John Webster, of Opononi, Hokianga—a settler who had already seen much of wild life in Australia, where he fought the blacks and drove cattle on long overland journeys; in after-years he cruised with Ben Boyd in the schooner-yacht "Wanderer." Webster brought to Waka's help a rifle (a novel weapon in those days) and two hundred home-made cartridges; and when shooting began he took his place in the rifle-pits with the warriors of Hokianga. In the fighting at Ohaeawai a little later both he and Maning shared. And another white warrior came in with his gun. This was Jackey Marmon, a wild figure and the chief actor in many a bloody episode of old New Zealand. He was an ex-convict from the chain gangs of Sydney; he had settled among the Maoris in the days when New Zealand was a "No-man's Land," fought in their wars, and even shared in their cannibal feasts; his fondness for human flesh was notorious among both Maori and *pakeha* in the "thirties" and early "forties." In his war-paint of red ochre, with bare chest and arms tattooed, his shaggy head decked out with feathers, musket slung across his back, cartouche-box belts buckled around him, a long-handled tomahawk in his hand, he looked the perfect picture of a savage warrior.

The intertribal skirmishing went on until the arrival of the troops on the evening of the 6th May. Heke's *pa*, Puketutu (sometimes spoken of as "Te Mawhe," although the hill of that name is some distance to the north-east), was now the immediate objective of attack; hitherto the fighting had been in open country between the opposing camps.

Very little remains to-day to mark Puketutu *pa*, the scene of the first British attack upon an inland Maori fort; the scene, too, of the first regular British charge with the bayonet against a Maori foe. The main road from the Bay of Islands, via Ohaeawai, to Te Horeke, Hokianga, cuts through the site of the northern part of Heke's *pa*, about three miles before Okaihau Township is reached. The fortification measured about 120 yards each way; it was a rectangle, with several salients or flanking bastions, of varied outline; from these each side of the *pa* could be completely enfiladed. There appear to have been three lines of palisading along part of the defences. The stockades were constructed of stout *puriri* trunks and saplings; the outer posts were from 5 inches to 10 inches in diameter, and carefully loopholed. A high breastwork was thrown up inside the inner fence; the trench from which the earth was dug was about 5 feet in depth; it separated the inner and middle lines of palisade. The foot of the *pekerangi*, about 15 feet high, was strengthened with a facing of rocks and stones gathered from the volcanic-lava debris which lay thickly around; this was a variation from the usual Maori method of leaving the foot of the *pekerangi* open for the garrison's fire. Another innovation—used at Ohaeawai also—was the coating of the outer wall with green flax. A large portion of the face of the palisade was reinforced in this way : large quantities of the native *harakeke*, or flax, were cut and tied in bundles ; these bundles were closely and tightly lashed along the face of the timbers just above the roughly piled stone buttress. Thus fastened, the flax formed a padding or fender more than man-high along the stockade, and the smooth, thick leaves so tightly packed prevented any bullets from entering through crevices in the war-fence. The *pa*, however, was not quite finished when it was attacked, and had it been reconnoitred carefully it would probably have been found comparatively vulnerable in the rear and on the eastern flank.

On the morning of the 8th May Lieut.-Colonel Hulme advanced his force. By 9 a.m. he had placed his redcoat reserve behind a low ridge within 300 yards of Heke's *pa*, and ordered three parties of assault to take up their positions. The first of these parties consisted of the seamen of the frigates " Hazard " and " North Star," under the command of Acting-Commander George Johnson, formerly of the " North Star " and at this time in temporary command of the " Hazard " (in place of Captain Robertson, disabled at Kororareka). The second party was the Light Company of the 58th Regiment, under Captain Denny ; the third was composed of a detachment of Royal Marines and some men of the 96th Regiment, under Lieutenant and Adjutant McLerie (58th Regiment).

As the troops moved forward with fixed bayonets fire was opened upon them from two faces of the *pa*. One party, taking the *pa* in rear, marched between it and the lake, and reached a gentle rise within 200 yards of the fort and just above the lake. The rocket-tube from which so much was expected was now placed in position on the north-west side of the *pa*, at a distance of about 150 yards. Twelve rockets were fired by Lieutenant Egerton (" North Star ") and his bluejackets without any effect.

Kawiti, who had hastened to Heke's aid with a body of about three hundred men, had halted less than a quarter of a mile from the eastern side of the *pa*, where he lay in ambush under the brow of a low undulation. An advanced party of his men held a small breastwork. The troops on the hill advanced their right flank and drove the Maoris from the shelter, which was then manned by a detachment of soldiers. About noon Hone Ropiha (John Hobbs, named after the Wesleyan missionary at Hokianga), a friendly scout and guide, who had led the 58th and the sailors round the edge of the lake in rear of the *pa* to the small hill overlooking Omapere, detected Kawiti's war-party lying in ambush within 50 yards of the troops. The soldiers turned and fired a volley, and then charged with the bayonet, inflicting severe loss on Ngati-Hine.

THE FIGHTING AT OMAPERE. 41

From a drawing by Sergeant J. Williams (58th Regt.).

THE BATTLE OF PUKETUTU (8th May, 1845.)

A British ensign was hoisted on a tall flagstaff in the stockade, then up went Heke's red fighting-flag. This colour was hoisted and hauled down several times, evidently as a signal to Kawiti outside the *pa*.

The meaning soon was made clear. The chorus of a war-song came across the battlefield, accompanied by the clash of firearms and the thud of hundreds of feet. Heke's warriors were stimulating themselves for the charge by a preliminary *tutu-ngarahu*. Forming up within the walls, unseen by their foes, they leaped into the action of the dance, led by Heke himself, and this was the chant they yelled (as given by the old man Rawiri te Ruru, of Te Ahuahu) :—

> *Ka eke i te wiwi;*
> *Ka eke i te wawa;*
> *Ka eke i te papara hu-ai;*
> *Rangi-tumu huia.*
> *A ha—ha!*

This song was used in ancient days before charging up to the assault of an enemy's fortification. Its meaning was: "We'll reach the outer palisade; we'll storm the inner defence; then we'll storm the citadel; ah! then the chiefs will fall before us!"

The war-song was repeated with enormous vigour: "*E—e! Ka eke i te wiwi!*" Then the warriors chanted all together as they leaped this way and that, with upthrust guns, this centuries-old battle-song :—

> *U-uhi mai te waero,*
> *Ko roto ki taku puta.*
> *He puta nui te puta,*
> *He puta roa te puta.*
> *U—u! Weku, weku!*
> *Weku mai te hiore!*

And out through an opening in the rear of the stockade charged a hundred and fifty Ngapuhi with double-barrel guns and long-handled tomahawks. Their leader was Haratua, of Pakaraka. Kawiti was ready, and with his whole body, numbering probably three hundred, he joined Heke in an assault upon the British.

Captain Denny, commanding the Light Company of the 58th, who were in skirmishing order on the south-east of the *pa* and were now cut off from the main body by Heke's *kokiri*, gave the order to his men to close on the centre; then, "Fix bayonets—Charge!" The British dash was irresistible; the Maoris were forced back to the cover in the low bush. The force in reserve fired on Heke's men as they advanced to take the troops in the rear, and checked their rush towards the rise above the lake; those who reached that spot were shot or bayoneted. Brave old Kawiti, charging at the head of his warriors, striving to drive the troops into the lake, was forced back with heavy loss; one of his sons was killed (one had fallen at Kororareka); many other men

THE FIGHTING AT OMAPERE. 43

were killed or wounded. Kawiti himself was slightly wounded, was run over by the soldiers, and narrowly missed death. Nor did the troops escape; several were killed and many wounded. Kawiti's men tomahawked some of the wounded. The British, on their side, gave no quarter.

The "Retire" was sounded. Kawiti once more came to the charge, dashing upon the troops with desperate courage. Heke

From a portrait at Kaikohe by S. Stuart.]
RIWHITETE POKAI.

in the meantime had withdrawn his men to the *pa*. It could end only in one way when the British got to work with the bayonet in the open field. But even now, though repeatedly driven back, the warriors outside the *pa* did not entirely relinquish the battle. They skirmished from cover until the soldiers were at last withdrawn by sound of bugle.

It was now 4 o'clock in the afternoon. The skirmishing, alternating with heavy bayonet fighting, had lasted for more than four hours. Firing was maintained from the *pa*, and replied to by the troops on the western and north-west sides, till about sunset.

In the British retirement to the camp at Tamati Waka's *pa* the killed were left behind. Heavy rain came on; it was nearly dark by the time the fight ended. The bodies of thirteen soldiers and sailors strewed the ferny levels about the *pa* and the slopes above the lake; another man, a seaman of the "Hazard," died later from his wounds. The wounded numbered forty-four; they were carried off by their comrades along the edge of the lake through heavy fire.

Night was now approaching, and when the fatigued, wet, and famishing troops left the field their foes were already at their evening prayers; and the last sound the soldiers and sailors heard as they marched off was a hymn chanted by hundreds of voices rising through the air still pungent with gunpowder smoke. So ended the Battle of Puketutu—a virtual victory for the Maoris, for they retained possession of their *pa*.

The Maori loss was severe. The exact casualties were not ascertained, but at least thirty must have been killed and many wounded. For weeks after that day's fighting the Ngapuhi women and bush-doctors were busy tending men suffering from severe bayonet and gunshot wounds. A favourite method of treating such injuries was to bathe the wound with the boiled juice of flax-root and then plug it up with a dressing of clay. Such rough-and-ready surgical treatment would probably have killed the average white man, but the Maori usually made a quick recovery. Many of the best warriors of the north fell that day. One who received two bayonet-thrusts but survived to fight again was Riwhitete Pokai, of Kaikohe, Heke's relative and lieutenant. Even in his old age Pokai was a splendid specimen of the warriors of Ngapuhi.

Hulme found it impossible to resume hostilities on the following day. His commissariat was exhausted; there were no accommodation and comforts for the wounded; men were falling sick from wet, cold, and want of food; heavy rain soaked the ground, made travelling difficult, and depressed the spirits of all. The Colonel therefore decided upon a retreat as soon as litters could be made for the wounded.

On the day following the fight the Rev. R. Burrows rode in to Puketutu from Waimate—he had viewed the operations the previous day from the mountain. Pukenui—and in the drenching rain, at Heke's request, he carried out the duty of collecting and burying the dead soldiers. Heke's men assisted him. Eleven bodies were brought from the spots where they fell, and were buried in the trench which Kawiti's warriors had dug on the eastern slope of the battlefield. The other two soldiers were buried about a third of a mile away, near the shore of the lake and not far from the *pa* Hulme returned to Kerikeri and the Bay, and landed his wounded at Auckland on the 14th May.

Major Cyprian Bridge (58th), who had been left in command at the Bay, organized a boat expedition, and early on the 15th May attacked the *pa* of the Kapotai Tribe on one of the head creeks of the Waikare Inlet. He burned the *pa* while the friendly Maoris, under Tamati Waka, fought the Kapotai in the bush

From a water-colour drawing by Colonel Cyprian Bridge.]

THE BRITISH ATTACK ON THE KAPOTAI PA, WAIKARE INLET, BAY OF ISLANDS.

(15th May, 1845.)

Hauraki, a young Hokianga chief on Waka's side, brother-in-law to F. E. Maning, was mortally wounded in this skirmish.

NOTES.

The site of Puketutu *pa* is perfectly level land, and is intersected by the main road at three miles from Ohaeawai, where the highway closely approaches the rushy margin of Omapere Lake, here not more than 150 yards distant. When I visited the place (1919) the historic spot might have been passed unnoticed had it not been for the guidance of the old man Rawiri te Ruru, of Te Ahuahu. Rawiri stopped when we had reached the place where the road nears a little bay of the lake, and said, " This is where the *pa* stood.' On the right-hand side of the road we saw the ruined rifle-pits and earth parapets that formed part of the defences of the northern bastion, with scattered stones that once were heaped against the *pekerangi* to strengthen its face. The large trenches are still 4 to 5 feet deep. The main portion of the trench still traceable is fourteen paces in length, extending at right angles to the road in a northerly direction, and is 5 feet wide ; a mound or parapet separates it from two inner pits of lesser size ; from the bottom of these trenches to the top of the parapet the height is 6 feet. The stones of the outer work are scattered about in the bottom of the ditches and among the stunted furze. In the fern and grass on the left-hand side of the road, too, we find some of these ancient stones that helped to stop the big-bore round balls of the Tower musket era. In the paddock that gently slopes from the road down to the lake cattle are grazing over the old battle-ground, where there are faint indications of trenches ; the field, though ploughed over many times, retains the slight undulation that marks the war-ditches dug by Heke's warriors. The hill of Puketutu, from which the *pa* takes its name, is a gentle rise about half a mile distant, in the direction of Ohaeawai. A little farther to the north-east is Mawhe, a rounded hill, still in part covered with *puriri* groves ; this, too, was a fighting-ground contested by Tamati Waka and Heke.

Riwhitete Pokai died at Kaikohe in 1903, aged about eighty-five years. He was in charge of one of the war-parties detailed for the final attack on the flagstaff at Kororareka in 1845. To his last days he retained the warrior instinct and the alert wariness of his youth, and was fond of instructing the young men of Ngapuhi in the art of war as he had practised it. His rifle and muskets were always kept ready for use. His kinsmen tell of a characteristic trait of the veteran. He slept " with one ear awake," and kept beside him an ancient sword-stick, which King William IV had sent to Titore. At any unusual noise in or near his room he would leap from his bed and lunge out fiercely with this weapon in the darkness at his imaginary enemy.

CHAPTER VII.

THE ATTACK ON OHAEAWAI.

Lieut.-Colonel Hulme's expedition to Omapere was criticized in severe terms by professional men and lay observers alike. These criticisms were directed not so much against the officer commanding or the troops, whose courage and discipline could not have been higher, but against the ill-considered policy which had hurried an imperfectly equipped force into the wilds against an enemy of unknown strength.

It was now approaching midwinter, and the rains which make camp life in the north uncomfortable and reduce the tracks to bogs had set in heavily. The weather would not be favourable for campaigning for several months. Nevertheless, Governor Fitzroy and the military authorities resolved to recommence operations against Heke, fearing that the longer he was left unmolested the stronger would grow his forces.

Heke employed his respite in recruiting his war-parties and gathering in supplies of ammunition and food. He was not, however, left in peace, for the ever-active Waka Nene, with three or four hundred men at his command, was encamped between Okaihau and Ohaeawai, and intermittent fighting occurred early in June. In the heaviest engagement Heke received a severe gunshot wound in the thigh, and was rescued by a party led by the *tohunga* Te Atua Wera (whose *atua*, or familiar spirit, was the Nakahi, according to Ngapuhi stories). Each side lost five or six killed in this fight (12th June).

Early in June Fitzroy received reinforcements; the barque "British Sovereign" arrived at Auckland from Sydney with the headquarters of the 99th Regiment, numbering 209 officers and men, under Colonel Despard, who had seen some service in the East Indies. Colonel Despard took charge of all the troops in the colony and organized a new expedition. In the middle of June the transport fleet sailed from the Waitemata for the Bay of Islands. Disembarking at Onewhero Beach, Despard marched his force to Kerikeri mission station; the guns and stores were boated up the Kerikeri River by the "Hazard's" bluejackets. Thence the route was through Waimate to Ohaeawai; the objective was a fort which Heke and Pene Taui were reported to have built.

The strength of the column, including seventy-five volunteers from the Auckland Militia and eighteen seamen and marines from H.M.S. "Hazard," was 596 rank and file. Major Cyprian Bridge, commanding the 58th, had about 270 men under him, the largest unit in the column. Major Macpherson commanded two companies of the 99th Regiment, and Lieut.-Colonel Hulme a company of the 96th. Acting-Captain George Johnson, of the "Hazard," with him Lieutenant George Phillpotts (the "Topi" of the Maoris), brought up the naval party to work the guns. These pieces of artillery were two 6-pounder brass guns and two 12-pounder carronades.

On the morning of the 23rd June the force marched from Waimate for Ohaeawai, seven miles away. This stage of the march was much impeded by the bad roads (or, rather, bullock-tracks), the unbridged creeks, and a deep swamp.

Waka's advance guard of Hokianga Maoris was the first to come under fire. The Ohaeawai garrison had sent out parties of skirmishers, and firing began when the forces had passed the *tino* of Taiamai (the remarkable rock from which the district takes its name) about a mile, and were ascending a gentle rise in the direction of Ohaeawai. Despard heard the sound of musketry on his right front, and moved rapidly forward with his advance guard (No. 9 Company of the 58th Regiment, under Lieutenant Balneavis). Some of the friendly natives accompanied the white skirmishers; with them marched Jackey Marmon, the white cannibal warrior. Volleys of musketry saluted Balneavis and his men. The advance was over rather rough ground, covered with high fern and *manuka*, with here and there a native cultivation. A tall stockade came in sight. At about 500 yards from the north face of the Maori fort the bugles sounded the halt. Here, on gently rising ground, within musket-range of the *pa*, Despard encamped.

Next morning (24th June), after reconnoitring his enemy's position, Despard prepared for a regular siege, and opened fire from his field-pieces. In the meantime we may leave him anxiously scanning the stockade with his spy-glass after each shot, and see for ourselves what manner of fortress this was that the followers of Kawiti and Heke now held in defiance of British musket, bayonet, and artillery.

Ohaeawai *pa* in its original form was the headquarters of the chief Pene Taui. He strengthened it after the fighting at Kororareka, realizing that his own district might before long become a theatre of war. After the Battle of Puketutu, Kawiti and Heke united with Pene Taui in converting Ohaeawai into a formidable fort, proof against artillery as well as musketry. Old Kawiti, wise in all matters of warfare, marked out the lines of the new fortification, which when completed more than doubled the size of the original stockade, and in Heke's absence he superintended the labour of hauling the *puriri* palisade timbers from the forest and setting them in position. The *pa* stood on elevated ground, a terrain well adapted for defence, except in one important detail: it was commanded by a conical hill about a third of a mile away on the north-west, a knoll about 300 feet higher than the site of the stockade. This hill, Puketapu, on the northern flank of a wooded range which rose immediately west of Ohaeawai, was partly covered with *puriri* groves. The ground fell quickly away from the *pa* on all flanks but the north; the track from Waimate to Kaikohe passed under its eastern front, where the main road runs to-day. The ground sloped very gradually on the north, and it was that side, facing the quarter from which attack was expected, that the garrison made particularly strong. Eastward was the forest. Through the valley which half-encircled the *pa* hill on the west and north-west sides flowed a small stream, intersecting the Kaikohe track. Beyond this stream on the west swelled the ranges in a cloud of forest. On the partly cleared land to the north, where the British camp was pitched, stood many a large *puriri*. One of those *puriri*, still standing, could tell us, had it a tongue like Jason's talking-oak, of Despard's council of war held beneath its boughs, and of the shells and round shot which the guns of 1845 sent over its head. One of those shots fell short—there was many a defective charge —and smashed off the old tree's top branch.

The fort was oblong in form, with salients on each face and at two of the angles (south-east and south-west), giving the garrison an enfilading fire in every direction. The greatest axis was east and west; the distance from the eastern to the westernmost palisade was a little over 100 yards. The shortest flank, the western, measured 40 yards; the eastern 43 yards. The original and the newer sections of the *pa* did not run on a continuous alignment; Kawiti's portion was constructed slightly *en echelon*, projecting a few yards on the south beyond the eastern division of the *pa*. The palisades and trench, however, made an uninterrupted defence, and the numerous projections gave an admirably complete flanking fire; therein shone the innate military engineering genius of the Maori. Part of the lines was defended by three lines of stockade timbers; on two faces the palisade was double. The outer wall, the *pekerangi*, or curtain, was formed of stout timbers, most of them whole trees, sunk deeply in the ground at short intervals, with saplings and split timbers closely set between the larger posts, all bound firmly together with cross-rails and *torotoro*, or bush-vines. The smaller timbers did not quite reach the ground; it was through the spaces left that the defenders fired from their shelter in the trench behind the second palisade. The outer defence was completed by the masking of the timber wall with green flax, as at Puketutu. The stockading was 10 to 15 feet in height; it was covered from a foot above the ground to the height of 8 or 10 feet with a thick mantlet of green flax-leaves tightly bound to the palisades. This padding of *harakeke* not only afforded considerable protection by deadening the impact of bullets, but masked the real strength of the stockade.

The second line of stockade, the *kiri-tangata* ("the warrior's skin"), was stronger than even the well-constructed *pekerangi;* every timber was set in the ground to a depth of about 5 feet, and rose above ground to a height corresponding with that of the outer line. Many of the palisades so planted, set close together, were whole *puriri* trees a foot or 15 inches in diameter—some were even larger—and some when cut and hauled from the fores must have been quite 20 feet in length. This line of stockade was loopholed; the apertures for the Maori musketry fire were formed by taking a V scarf with the axe out of the two contiguous timbers. These loopholes were on the ground-level; and the Maori musketeer, pointing his gun through the aperture, was thus able to deliver his fire under the foot of the *pekerangi* without in the least exposing himself. The distance between the two fences was 3 feet. The trench in which the musketeer squatted was 5 to 6 feet deep and 4 or 5 feet wide, with earth banquette on which the defenders stood to fire, and traverses at intervals of about 2 yards, with narrow communicating-trench between each, admitting of only one man passing at a time. The venerable Rihara Kou, of Kaikohe, describing it, said: "We could travel right round the *pa* in the trench, winding in and out " (" *haere kopikopiko ana* ").

Within the double stockade and the firing-trench again, on a portion of the front at least, there was a third line of timbers, a palisade about 10 feet high, against the outer side of which the earth thrown from the ditch was heaped. Inside all these defences were the living-quarters of the garrison—the warriors, and the wives and daughters who had come to cook for them and make their cartridges. These quarters were all underground, and were made shell-proof by being covered with heavy timbers, branches of trees, and earth. The roofs of some were built with the slope of the usual low *whare*, and the soil from the excavations was heaped up against them and over their tops until they seemed mere mounds of earth. These subterranean chambers (*ruas*, or pits, the Maoris called them) were usually 6 feet deep; some were as large as a good-sized *wharepuni*, about 30 feet long and 20 feet wide. The garrison were completely sheltered here, as in the trench, until Despard's guns were mounted on the hill to the north-west, and even then few of the Maoris were hit by the plunging fire.

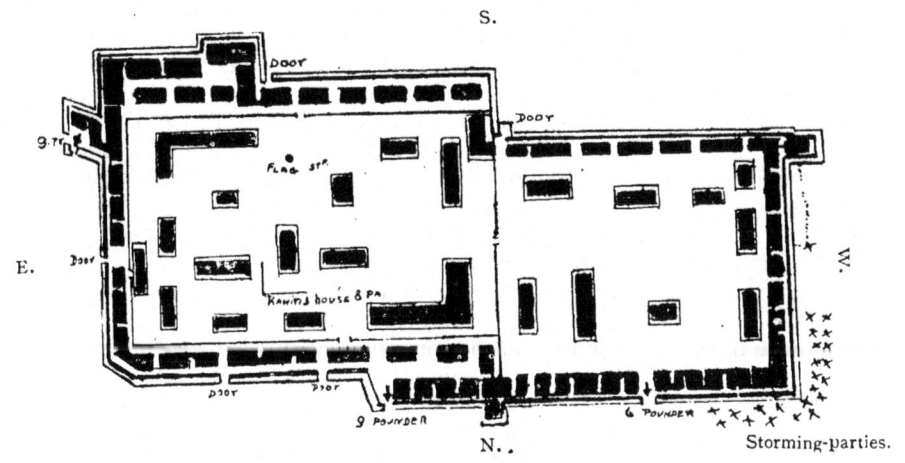

GROUND PLAN OF OHAEAWAI PA,

Showing north-west angle attacked by British storming-parties
(1st July, 1845).

SECTION OF STOCKADE AND TRENCHES.

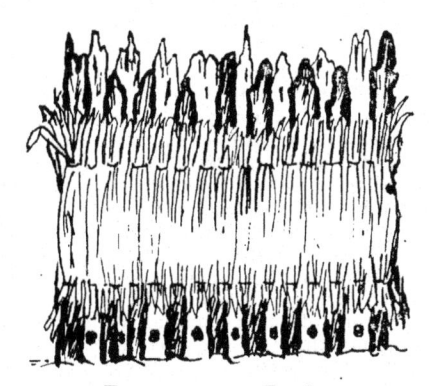

FLAX-MASKED PALISADE.

To these skilfully planned defences, evolved out of the Maori's brain, ever resourceful in devices to combat new weapons, there was added a battery of artillery. To be sure, it was a scrap-iron battery: it consisted of four old ship's guns gathered from one quarter and another, but it gave a finishing touch to the fortress. Two of the pieces were iron 9-pounders; the others were smaller iron guns, a 4-pounder and a 2-pounder swivel. The two smaller guns had been brought in bullock-drays by Heke and his friends from the Bay of Islands. One of the weapons had been taken as spoils of war from Kororareka after the fight of the 11th March. One of the 9-pounders had a curious history: it was one of two which the Maoris commandeered from the Waimate mission station. The history goes back to the year 1823, when the ship "Brampton," which had brought out the Rev. Henry Williams and his family, went to pieces on a reef, which now bears her name, outside Kororareka Bay. After the ship had been abandoned, two of the guns with which she was armed were brought to Paihia, the mission station opposite Russell, and were used there for firing salutes; afterwards they were taken to Waimate.

One of the 9-pounders found after the siege stood in a square bastion facing the east, close to the south-east angle of the *pa*. Another was mounted at an angle on the northern front, facing the encampment of the troops. One of the smaller pieces stood in an embrasure on the same front, about 70 feet from the north-west angle. The other gun, so far as can be gathered, was mounted in the small bastion at the south-west angle.*

The Maori garrison of the *pa* was considerably outnumbered by the troops. The strength of the defenders varied from time to time, as men were continually passing between the stockade and Kaikohe, five or six miles in the rear. A strong bodyguard had been sent with the wounded Heke to Tautoro,

---

* In comparing the Maori fortresses with the contemporary defensive works of other primitive races we find the closest resemblance to the New Zealand *pa* in the stockades of two far-severed peoples—the Burmese and the Indians of some of the western States in North America. In the first Burmese War (1824) the British soldiers were confronted by immense jungle stockades, built sometimes of very large tree-trunks, and defended also by an abbatis of pointed stakes and felled trees. It was found necessary to breach these stockades with artillery. In Catlin's "North American Indians" a Mandan village on the Upper Missouri is described. This fort was built on a precipitous cliff 40 or 50 feet high. The stockade was built of timbers a foot or more in diameter and 18 feet high, set firmly in the ground at a sufficient distance apart to admit of guns being fired between them. "The ditch, unlike that of civilized modes of fortification,' Catlin wrote, "is inside of the picquet, in which the warriors screen their bodies from the view and weapons of their enemies whilst they are reloading and discharging their weapons through the picquets." Exactly this plan of defence was adopted by the Maoris in the New Zealand wars.

a safe place of retreat some fourteen miles away, close to the beautiful mounta n lake of Tauanui, or Kereru, with its sacred islet. The natives say that when Despard delivered his assault on the 1st July there were not more than a hundred men in the *pa*. The principal *hapus* composing the garrison were: Ngati-Rangi, under Pene Taui; Ngati-Tautahi, of Kaikohe, under Tuhirangi (elder brother of Heke); Ngati-Whakaeke, Ngati-te-Rehu, and Ngati-te-Rangi, all Heke's *hapus;* Ngati-Kawa, of Oromahoe; and Te Uri-Taniwha, of Te Ahuahu; also Ngati-Hine, led by Kawiti.

Picture the interior of Ohaeawai stockade that midwinter of 1845. The northerly gale brings a thin but searching rain; squalls sometimes obscure the battlefield in a driving mist. The troops in their leaky tents and their roughly made *manuka* shelters are uncomfortably damp; in the securely roofed dug-outs within the stockade the Maoris are snug and dry. The floors of the *ruas* are thickly spread with soft fern and flax mats. In the store-pits are heaps of potatoes and *kumara*, baskets of dried eels, preserved pigeons, shell-fish from the Kawakawa. In the larger of the semi-subterranean huts are fires burning, fed with *manuka* branches and heaps of *kapia,** or kauri-gum. At some of these fires women and boys are roasting potatoes; at others men are cleaning and polishing their flint-lock muskets and percussion-cap guns. In the safety of the deeper dugouts groups are busy making cartridges, filling the thick paper holders from small kegs of gunpowder; others are melting lead into bullets, using moulds either bought from the trading-houses before the war or looted last March from the stores at Kororareka. There is no lack of powder or of bullets; even after hostilities had begun and after a blockade of the Bay of Islands had been established the Maoris had little difficulty in finding white traders and captains of coasting-vessels or timber-ships (chiefly at Hokianga) ready to supply ammunition at war prices.

Observe these half-stripped fort-builders and gun-fighters of Ngapuhi, the pick of Maori manhood. Tall fellows, with the shoulders and chests of athletes and the straight backs of soldiers; quick darting eyes, always on the alert; clean-shaven faces thickly scrolled with the blue-black tattoo lines of the *moko*. Some of the veterans have scarcely an inch of skin on cheeks and nose and brow and chin clear of the deeply cut lines of tattoo; their *tapu* heads are a marvel of savage carving. There are boys here only just entering their teens. Yonder is a youngster of twelve proudly handling a *hakimana;* a single-barrel percussion-cap musket; it is his first gun, and he is waiting with mingled impatience and excitement for his share of ammunition that will enable him to take his place in the fire-trenches. (The Maori took to the war-path young; so, indeed, did most people living a primitive or semi-primitive life. In the American backwoods

54 NEW ZEALAND WARS.

From a water-colour drawing by Colonel Cyprian Bridge.] THE OHAEAWAI STOCKADE.

in the old Indian fighting-days the settler's son often was already a veteran at an age when most boys are at school. "A boy of the wilderness," Sir George Otto Trevelyan wrote in "The American Revolution," "so soon as he had passed his twelfth birthday, was recognized as part of the garrison of the farm, and was allotted his loophole in the stockade which encircled it." In G. M. Trevelyan's "Garibaldi and the Making of Italy" mention is made of a Sicilian boy of twelve who behaved with such admirable courage in the Battle of Milazzo (1860) that Garibaldi made him a sergeant on the field.)

Here is dour old Kawiti, hero of many fights, burning to avenge the death of his son on the battlefield of Puketutu. Here is that most daring of Ngapuhi tomahawk-men, young Riwhitete Pokai, his two bayonet-wounds received at Puketutu scarcely healed yet. Here is Ruatara Tauramoko, of the blue-blooded clan known as the Uri-Taniwha ("Children of Sea-monsters"); clean-limbed, square-shouldered, symmetrically tattooed, he looks the perfect type of a New Zealand warrior. One of his comrades, Wi te Parihi, or Pirihonga, is a man of an alien tribe, the Arawa; he was brought here as a captive long ago, but his merits have won for him a high place among his captor's people; he and Pokai are spoken of to this day with admiration as Heke's two greatest *toas*, or braves. And in the trenches also you may see one or two young musketeers whose skin is curiously light in contrast with the dark curves of the tattoo; they are half-castes.*

The first British battery, protected by a breastwork, was placed about 100 yards in front of Despard's camp, on gently rising ground, and the first gun was fired at 8 a.m. on the 24th June. The fire was kept up from the four guns during the greater part of the day, but with little effect upon the stockade.

New emplacements were made; one battery was not more than 100 yards from the stockade. The guns made no impression on the stockade, and the only casualties were those suffered by the troops. Despard at last wrote to Acting-Captain George

---

* Ruatara, like his comrade Pokai, showed the warrior spirit to the last. In his old age, at Tautoro, he preserved with pride his armoury of seven guns—of all makes and periods, from flint-locks to modern rifles—which he kept carefully cleaned and polished, always in readiness for use if needed. Like Pokai, too, he took delight in teaching the younger generation the use of arms. In 1901 he was one of the northern chiefs in the great Maori gathering at Rotorua to welcome King George V (then Duke of Cornwall and York). The tall old tattooed warrior made a picturesque figure of the past as bareheaded and barefooted he marched up and laid his most treasured heirloom, a whalebone *hoeroa* or broadsword, at Royalty's feet.

Rihara Kou, of Kaikohe, now about ninety years of age, was in the trenches at Ohaeawai, using his first gun; he would then be about twelve years of age. Rihara is the last survivor of the defenders of Ohaeawai and Rua-pekapeka. He is a good type of the Ngapuhi, with a fine, intelligent, shrewd face and long snowy hair and beard.

Johnson, of H.M.S. "Hazard," which was anchored in the mouth of the Kerikeri River, requesting him to send up one of his 32-pounders.

Meanwhile some ingenious artilleryman, racking his wits for means of more effective attack, bethought him of the empty shell-cases. Could they be converted into stench bombs or balls, with short time-fuses, and fired from the mortars? Colour-Sergeant R. Hattaway, of the 58th, narrated the incident. Two old soldiers were sent to assist in the manufacture of the balls or shells; the experiment was regarded with high hopes by the artillery officers. "The shells," wrote Hattaway, "contained some poisonous substance the effect of which was expected to deprive the rebels of all animation, and leave them a prey to

From a photo, April, 1922.]

RIHARA KOU, OF KAIKOHE.

Last survivor of the defenders of Ohaeawai.

the European victors. As day by day passed away and nothing occurred to disturb the natives in their stronghold it was concluded that the project had been a failure."

This curious experiment, the first and only instance of the use of poison-gas in New Zealand, was attended with no better success than the other means adopted for the capture of the *pa*. The composition of the "stench-balls" remains a mystery; unknown also is the number of these shells delivered to the Maoris by vertical fire. The expectation was that the mortars, with their 45° angle of fire, would land the poison-shells within the trenches or the dugouts, where their explosion would produce stupefaction as well as consternation. Wherever they exploded, they failed to produce any noticeable ill effect upon the Maoris

CHAPTER VIII.

THE STORMING-PARTY AT OHAEAWAI.

Pene Taui's stockade was commanded at a range of less than one-third of a mile by the hill Puketapu, upon which Despard's Maori allies flew the British ensign. A modern field-gun at that distance would quickly have reduced the palisade to splinters. But what little impression was made by gun-fire upon the flax-masked defences was repaired by the garrison each night; and even when the 32-pounder arrived from the frigate "Hazard" its projectiles failed to breach the stockade. On the 30th June the gun was mounted on a platform, with strong timber slides, constructed on the lower slope of Puketapu; two of the smaller guns had been placed higher up. On the forenoon of the 1st July the 32-pounder opened fire obliquely at the front stockade.

Every one was absorbed in watching the effect of the gun-fire. Suddenly there came the noise of musket-fire in the rear, on the summit of Tamati Waka Nene's hill, and as the troops turned about in astonishment they saw the friendly Maoris, men and women, flying down the steep slope in confusion, and with them the picket (a sergeant and twelve men of the 58th) posted on the hill for the protection of the 6-pounder. They had been taken in reverse by a sortie-party of Maoris from the *pa*, advancing under cover of the forest on the right front and flank. The natives shot one soldier, seized the gun, and hauled down Waka's flag, which they carried off. Major Bridge and his 58th charged up and recaptured the hill. A few minutes later Despard's alarm and disgust turned to fury when he saw the captured British ensign run up on the flax-halliards of the Maori flagstaff in the *pa*, below the rebel flag—a *kakahu Maori*, as one of my Maori informants describes it—a native garment. Then it was that the Colonel made up his mind to storm the *pa* that day. He imagined that the few 32 lb. shot—which were soon expended—would so loosen the stockades as to enable the troops to cut and pull them down. Those who ventured to remonstrate were snubbed or insulted. Lieutenant Phillpotts, of the "Hazard," was roused to such indignation by the Colonel's retort to his protest against a senseless attack that he threw away every vestige of military attire he happened to be wearing, and in his blue sailor shirt and underclothes rushed to his death. A protest from the free-lance allies met with a similar reception. John Webster tells the story:—

"Maning, myself, and Nene went to interview Despard. We knew well the strength of the *pa* and its construction. Maning was the spokesman, and commenced with, ' Sir, we heard that you intend assaulting the *pa*, and we have come to say that unless a breach is made it will cause great loss of life and will fail.'

"'What do you civilians know of the matter?' replied Despard.

"'Sir,' said Maning, 'we may not know much, but there is one that apparently knows less, and that is yourself.'

"Despard got very angry and threatened to arrest us. Nene now inquired what the chief of the soldiers was saying. Maning told him.

"'*He tangata kuware tenci tangata*,' said Nene.

"'What does the chief say?' Despard inquired of his interpreter. (I think Meurant was the interpreter's name.) He scratched his head and said, ' It is not complimentary.'

"'But I order you, sir,' said Despard.

"'The chief says you are a very stupid person,' then replied Meurant.

"It was impossible to make any impression on the man who had so many fine young fellows' lives in his hands, and he was prepared to sacrifice them through mere obstinacy."

Tamati Waka Nene offered to make a feint attack on the stockade in the rear, in order to divert attention from the soldiers' assault, but this suggestion, like all others, met with a refusal.

The Colonel ordered a storming-party to parade at 3 o'clock in the afternoon, and instructions were issued by his brigade-major (Lieutenant and Adjutant Deering) for the guidance of the officers commanding the various divisions. The troops were ordered to get their dinners. For many of them that meal was their last. Forebodings of disaster possessed some of the more thoughtful, but in spite of the doubtful character of the enterprise there was a distinct element of elation and relief among the rank and file at the prospect of an attack at close quarters. There was also a strong desire among the troops to avenge the death of a young soldier of the 99th who had been caught by the enemy while foraging for potatoes. The men on outpost duty had heard, as they believed, his cries of agony; and a story, palpably absurd, was circulated after the fight that he had been tortured to death by burning with kauri-gum. In their ignorance of Maori ways they credited their foes with the practices of Red Indians on the war-path.

THE STORMING-PARTY AT OHAEAWAI.

At 3 o'clock the bugles sounded the assembly. Volunteers were called upon for the forlorn hope. The whole of the men of the 58th stepped forward. The right-hand man, front and rear rank, of each section was ordered to the front; a similar procedure was followed in the 99th Regiment. Two assaulting columns were composed of men of the two regiments, with a number of seamen and Pioneers. When the selection had been completed the storming-parties formed up in the little valley on the west and north-west side of the *pa*, about 100 yards from the stockade. This was the composition of the force: Advance-party, or forlorn hope—Lieutenant Beattie (99th Regiment), two sergeants, and twenty men. Assaulting column—Major Macpherson (99th Regiment), forty grenadiers from the 58th and forty from the 99th, with a small party of seamen from H.M.S. "Hazard" and thirty Pioneers (to carry axes, scaling-ladders, and ropes) from the Auckland Volunteer Militia: total, about one hundred and twenty men. Second assaulting column — Major Bridge (58th), with the remainder of the grenadiers of the 58th, made up to sixty rank and file from a battalion of that regiment, and forty rank and file from the Light Company of the 99th: total, one hundred men.

Lieut.-Colonel Hulme was posted in the valley west of the *pa* with a supporting-party consisting of a hundred men of the two regiments and some naval men. Major Bridge's party, in rear of the forlorn hope, took up a position exactly north-west of the nearest angle of the stockade (the Maoris' left front); Major Macpherson was posted due north of the same angle, under cover of a grove of *puriri* trees. The north-west angle of the *pa* was the principal objective of attack—this despite the fact that it was enfiladed by loopholed bastions on either flank.

There came now an awful interval of waiting. The storming-parties stood ready in their appointed places, while the guns in rear of them threw shot and shell into the stockade. The glinting lines of bayonets caught the fitful sunshine of a wintry afternoon; the campaign-stained red tunics and white cross-belts, too, were brightened by those gleams of gold beneath the drifting clouds. Tattered was many a uniform; coats and trousers torn and roughly patched; some of the men barefooted, some with battered boots tied on their feet with strips of flax-leaves.

Half an hour of such waiting, then out blared the bugle. It was the "Advance.". There was a quick fire of orders from commanders of columns—"Prepare to charge"; "Charge"; and with a "Hurrah!" up the ferny slope dashed the advance-party. Major Macpherson's column quickly followed; then up came Major Bridge's party of bearded campaigners in four ranks, their commander leading, sword in hand.

From a drawing by Colonel Cyprian Bridge.]

REPULSE OF THE BRITISH STORMING-PARTIES AT OHAEAWAI.

That charge up the bullet-swept glacis of Ohaeawai was described to me with graphic word and action by the last survivor of the stormers, Lieutenant W. H. Free, of New Plymouth, who was a corporal in the 58th under Major Bridge. Free was a County Wicklow lad of twenty; he had enlisted three years previously, and one of his recent memories was a voyage from England to Hobart Town as a private in the military guard in a convict ship, the "Anson."

"We formed up in close order," Free said, "elbows touching when we crooked them; four ranks, only the regulation 23 inches between each rank. There we waited in the little hollow before the *pa*, sheltered by the fall of the ground and some tree cover. We got the orders, 'Prepare to charge'; then 'Charge.' Up the rise we went at a steady double, the first two ranks at the charge with the bayonet; the second rank had room to put their bayonets in between the front-rank men; the third and fourth ranks with muskets and fixed bayonets at the slope. We were within 100 yards of the *pa* when the advance began; when we were within about fifty paces of the stockade-front we cheered and went at it with a rush, our best speed and 'divil take the hindmost.' The whole front of the *pa* flashed fire, and in a moment we were in the one-sided fight—gun-flashes from the foot of the stockade and from loopholes higher up, smoke half-hiding the *pa* from us, yells and cheers, and men falling all round.

"Not a single Maori could we see. They were all safely hidden in their trenches and pits, poking the muzzles of their guns under the foot of the outer palisade. What could we do? We tore at the fence, but it was a hopeless business. The Pioneer party left all the axes and tomahawks behind; the sailors had their cutlasses, but they could do little more than slash at the lashings of the fence. Only one scaling-ladder was carried up. The man who brought it stood it against the outer stockade. 'Here it is,' he said, 'for any one who'll go up it.' But who'd climb the ladder? It would be certain death. If any one did try it he didn't live many moments.

"We were in front of the stockade, firing through it, thrusting our bayonets in, or trying to pull a part of it down, for, I suppose, not more than two minutes and a half. From the time we got the order to charge until we got back to the hollow again it was only five to seven minutes.

"In our Light Company alone we had twenty-one men shot in the charge. As we rushed at the *pa* a man was shot in front of me, and another was hit behind me. When the bugle sounded the retreat I picked up a wounded man, and was carrying him off on my back when he was shot dead. Then I picked up a second wounded comrade, a soldier named Smith, and carried him out safely. Our captain, Grant, an officer for whom we had a great liking, was shot dead close to the stockade. Nothing was explained to us before we charged. We just brought our bayonets to the charge when we got the word, and went at it hell-for-leather."

Free narrated that he and his comrades of the 58th carried their full packs even in the charge—like King George the Third's troops in the first assault on Bunker's Hill.

Some of the garrison, appalled by the valour of the redcoats rushing with their front of steel upon the palisades, took fright and made for the rear of the *pa*, but the greater number stood

[From a portrait about 1860.]

COLONEL CYPRIAN BRIDGE.

Major (afterwards Colonel) Cyprian Bridge, of the 58th Regiment, was uncle to Admiral Sir Cyprian Bridge, G.C.B., who commanded H.M.S. "Espiegle" in the Pacific, 1882–85, and was Admiral in command of the Australian Station, 1895–97. When the 58th returned to England from New Zealand Major Bridge was appointed to the command of the regiment. Mr. H. E. Bridge, of Oriental Bay, Wellington, is a son of the Colonel. Five sons of Mr. Bridge volunteered for the Great War and wore khaki; four served abroad; one was mortally wounded on Gallipoli, and one was killed in action in France.

fast in their trenches, reserving their fire until the stormers were within 25 or 20 yards. When the few faint-hearts among the Maoris saw that the stockade was impregnable they returned to

THE STORMING-PARTY AT OHAEAWAI. 63

their posts, and assisted in the final repulse. There were probably not more than a hundred natives in the *pa* when the assault was delivered.

The Maori enfilading fire completely commanded the angle which was the centre of attack, and many men fell on the western flank, where bullets were poured into them from a small bastion. Those on the northern face became targets for the Maori gun-men in the rectangular salient midway on that flank. In one of these bastions there was a carronade which the Maoris had loaded with a bullock-chain, and this projectile, fired at

W. H. FREE, A VETERAN OF OHAEAWAI.

Corporal Free (58th) was the last survivor in New Zealand of the stormers at Ohaeawai. He fought in the Taranaki War, and was given a commission as Lieutenant. He died at New Plymouth in 1919, aged 93 years.

close quarters, killed or wounded several soldiers. Captain W. E. Grant (58th) fell shot through the head in one of the first volleys. Lieutenant Edward Beattie (96th) was mortally wounded. The impulsive naval lieutenant, Phillpotts, ran along the stockade to the right (the west flank), seeking a place to enter; the outer fence had suffered most damage there. He actually climbed the *pekerangi*, a small portion of which had been loosened by sword-cuts delivered against the *torotoro* lashings and partly pulled down. There he fell, shot through the body. A young sailor who ran up the solitary ladder which Lieutenant Free mentioned was shot dead and fell inside the stockade. Brevet-Major Macpherson was wounded severely; as he was a very heavy man it was only with difficulty that he was carried off the field. Ensign O'Reilly (99th) received a bullet which shattered his right arm at the elbow. "The soldiers fell on this side and on that," said the venerable Rihara Kou—the whitebeard made an expressive

HARE PUATAATA (PUHIKURA), OF KAIKOHE.
One of the defenders of Ohaeawai.

gesture with his hands—"they fell right and left like that, like so many sticks thrown down."

Through the din of musketry and yelling the notes of a bugle were heard. It was the "Retire." Major Bridge and many of his men thought the call had been sounded in mistake. However, the retreat was repeated, and the summons was obeyed. The

Maoris' independent firing increased, and more were killed and wounded in the withdrawal. In that five minutes nearly forty men had been killed and seventy wounded, some mortally.

One-third of the troops engaged fell before the Maori fire. The large-calibre bullets inflicted smashing wounds; in many cases the combat was at such close quarters that the clothing of the soldiers was scorched by the gunpowder-flash. Not all the wounded were carried off; all the dead were left where they fell.

Many a deed of gallantry and devotion illumined the tragedy of that retreat. Several men returned again and again through a hot fire to carry off wounded comrades. One private of the 58th, Whitethread, rescued in this way at least five men of his own regiment and the 99th; he and another man, J. Pallett, carried Major Macpherson into camp. Two Scots of the 58th lay dead together on the field; the one, McKinnon, was carrying off his dying or dead corporal, Stewart, on his back when he was shot. Corporal Free was another of those who brought away wounded comrades from the bullet-spitting *pekerangi*.

Now out upon the heels of the rescuers who are heroically bearing off the wounded there charge the victorious Maoris, naked, powder-grimed, yelling, shaking their guns and their long-handled tomahawks. A white-headed tattooed warrior, astonishingly agile in spite of his age, dashes along the palisade front; he is seeking the body of the sailor-chief " Topi.' He bends over Phillpotts's body; with his tomahawk he cuts off a portion of the scalp, and bursts into a pagan chant. It is the incantation of the *whangaihau*, offering the first of the battle-trophies to the supreme war-god of the Maori, Tu-of-the-Angry-Face. And there, amid the bodies of dead and dying whites strewn about the field, the warriors throw themselves into the movements of the *tutu-ngarahu*. This is the song they shout, with uptossed guns and tomahawks:—

> *E tama te uaua e,*
> *E tama te uaua e,*
> *E tama te maroro,*
> *Inahoki ra te tohu a te uaua na,*
> *Kei taku ringa e mau ana,*
> *Te upoko o te kawau tataki*
> *Hi—he—ha!*

[TRANSLATION.]

> O sons of strenuous might,
> O sons of warrior strength,
> Behold the trophy in my hand,
> Fruit of the battle strife—
> The head of the greedy cormorant
> That haunts the ocean shore!

A moment's breathing-space, and then the warriors chant all together this song that reverberates among the hills ; the words are those of a *mata*, or prophecy :—

> Ka whawhai, ka whawhai!
>   E he!
> Ka whawhai, ka whawhai!
>   E ha!
> Ka whawhai, ki roto ki te awa
> Puare katoa ake nei.
> E ha whawhai, ka whawhai!
> Kihai koe i mau atu ki te kainga ki Oropi,
> E te ainga mai a Wharewhare.

[TRANSLATION.]

> To battle, to battle !
>   E he!
> To battle, to battle !
>   E ha!
> We shall fight in the valley
> Spread open before us ;
> We shall fight, we shall fight !
> Ah ! You did not remain
> In your home-land in Europe.
> There you lie overwhelmed
> By the swift driving wave of the battle.

And late into the wintry night, while the surgeons in the British camp are dressing wounds and amputating shattered limbs, the choruses of battle-songs and the cries of a *tohunga* in an ecstatic fit of prophesying are borne across the battlefield. The dispirited soldiers, hearing that eerie sorcerer-voice, imagine it, in their ignorance of the Maori, to be the screams of one of their captured comrades under torture by fire.

* * * * *

For the defeat Colonel Despard blamed the seamen from H.M.S. "Hazard" under Lieutenant Phillpotts, and the party of Auckland Militia who accompanied the force as a Pioneer detachment. "The forlorn hope," he wrote, "had been provided with well-sharpened axes and hatchets for cutting away the *torotoro* vines which fastened the stockade, as well as with several scaling-ladders and ropes with grappling-irons for the purpose of pulling down the stockade." All these articles, except one scaling-ladder, were left behind by the Pioneers as unnecessary encumbrances.

In spite of Despard's excuses for his failure, it is extremely doubtful whether even scaling-ladders, grappling-irons, axes, and other apparatus of attack would have enabled the storming-parties to carry the stockade. Indeed, it was fortunate that the *pekerangi* so stoutly resisted the assault except at one point, for had the troops succeeded in demolishing it they would have been faced by the inner fence of deeply set *puriri* timbers, which could not be hauled down. And had they carried this main line of defence there would still have been the trenches and pitted interior of the stockade, subdivided by barriers and thick with underground shelters, from which every white could have been shot down.

Colonel Despard contemplated an immediate retreat upon Waimate, and orders to that end were issued on the morning of the 2nd July, but were countermanded as the result of remonstrances by the friendly chiefs, who condemned the Colonel's proposal to abandon the field leaving the dead unburied, and to destroy surplus stores. The wounded were sent off in carts and litters to Waimate, and the force remained encamped before the *pa* for another ten days. Additional ammunition had been brought up for the guns, and the 32-pounder and the smaller pieces kept up an intermittent bombardment.

The dead were not buried until the afternoon of the 3rd July, when, through the efforts of Archdeacon Henry Williams and the Rev. R. Burrows—who had been eye-witnesses of the battle—the natives permitted the bodies of the fallen soldiers to be collected. Thirty-two bodies were placed in one grave and eight in another. Several bodies were found later lying among the fern, and were buried near the others.

It was the Maori custom to abandon a fighting *pa* after blood had been spilt within it, and it was not surprising, therefore, to the missionaries and other spectators, and to the friendly natives, that the stockade was found early on the morning of the 11th July to have been evacuated during the night. Two dead bodies were found; the total Ngapuhi loss was never exactly known, but, so far as can be ascertained, it did not exceed ten killed.

The garrison retired on Kaikohe and Tautoro, to the south. At those places they prepared for further resistance in the event of being followed up; but the exhausted and famished troops were in no condition to renew the campaign immediately, and it was considered advisable to withdraw to the mission station at the Waimate.

The *pa* was destroyed—a task by no means easy. Some of the posts of *puriri* defied all efforts to pull them down. One was so large, as W. H. Free narrated, that Captain Matson, who was engaged in the demolition of the palisades, was unable to span it with his outstretched arms. "The enemy was unable to carry off his guns," Colonel Despard reported, "and we have taken three iron ones on ship-carriages, and one more was found disabled in the fortress." (Hohaia Tango, of Ohaeawai, stated that this fourth gun was mounted near the north-west angle of the *pa;* it was smashed by a shot from the British cannon, which struck it in the muzzle.) A search was made for the body of

Captain Grant, who was known to have been shot close to the palisades. It was exhumed from a light covering of earth, which had been laid over it by the Maoris. W. H. Free, who saw it unearthed, stated that portions of the posterior parts and also the calves of the legs had been cut off by the Ngapuhi; presumably the flesh was eaten as a battlefield rite, with the double object of absorbing something of the dead officer's virtue of bravery, and of weakening—as the pagan Maori believed—the arms and *mana* of the white troops. Ceremonial cannibalism, of which this Ohaeawai incident was the solitary instance in Heke's War, was revived as a sequel to battle in the Hauhau Wars of 1865–69; Titokowaru countenanced it in his Taranaki campaign as a means of fortifying the resolution of his followers and of terrifying his white enemies.

On the 14th July the British struck camp and marched to the Waimate, where the troops settled themselves in the quarters they had occupied on the march inland.

Notes.

The site of the Ohaeawai *pa* is now occupied by a Maori church and burying-ground. The scene of the battle is five miles from Kaikohe and two miles from the Township of Ohaeawai. A Maori church of old-fashioned design is seen on the left as one travels from Kaikohe; it stands on a gentle rise a short distance west of the main road. The locality is usually called Ngawha, from the hot springs in the neighbourhood, but it is the true Ohaeawai; the European township which has appropriated the name should properly be known as Taiamai. The church occupies the centre of the olden fortification, and a scoria-stone wall, 7 ft. high, encloses the sacred ground. Tukaru Tango and Hohaia Tango, two elderly men of Ngapuhi, with whom I visited the place (March, 1919), said that this fence marked almost exactly the outer line of the stockade. The churchyard is entered between great posts that might well have served as palisade *himus*. On the east crest is a stone memorial cross bearing this Maori inscription: "*Ko te Tohu Tapu tenei o nga Hoia me nga Heremana o te Kuini i hinga i te whawhai ki konei ki Ohaeawai, i te tau o to tatou Ariki 1845 Ko tenei Urupa na nga Maori i whakatakoto i muri iho o te maunga rongo.*"

The translation of this legend is: "This is a Sacred Memorial to the Soldiers and Sailors of the Queen who fell in battle here at Ohaeawai in the year of Our Lord 1845. This burying-place was laid out by the Maoris after the making of peace."

The *pa* site, viewed from the east and south, is a commanding position; on the north the land is level for some distance and then slopes very gradually. The high range beyond the valley on the west is still well wooded; and in the vicinity of the stockade-site much of the ancient forest vegetation remains, the *puriri* predominating. About 100 yards to the west of the *pa* is a hollow through which runs a small stream from the slopes of Puketapu: it was here that the storming-parties formed up.

"Topi," as the natives called Phillpotts, was the Maorified form of "Toby," the lieutenant's nickname. On the 17th March, 1919, standing by the grave of the three officers who fell at Ohaeawai, in the churchyard of Waimate, Rawiri te Ruru, of Te Ahuahu, asked me, " Is this where Topi is buried ? " When shown George Phillpotts's name on the memorial stone he told the story of the sailor's death as preserved in his family of the Ngati-Rangi Tribe. "It was my uncle Horotai who killed Topi," he said. " Horotai was a great fighter ; Topi also was a *toa* (a hero), and very much liked by the Maoris. He ran up to the *pekerangi* and got inside that outer fence. Horotai was inside the second or main stockade, the *kiri-tangata*. He thrust the barrel of his gun through a loophole in the *kiri-tangata* until it touched Topi here"—and Rawiri put his hand on his breast—" then Horotai fired and Topi fell dead."

From a sketch. J. C., 1919.]

THE NATIVE CHURCH AT OHAEAWAI.

CHAPTER IX.

THE CAPTURE OF RUA-PEKAPEKA.

For three months the sound of the bugle and all the stir of a military camp enlivened the mission station at Waimate. Employment was found for the redcoats in surrounding the buildings with a trench and parapets as a precaution against attack—much to the disgust of the mission people, who lamented to see the neutral station transformed into a fortified encampment. It was not until the middle of October that the troops, after destroying Haratua's *pa* at Pakaraka, removed to Kororareka, where they awaited the next movement in the campaign.

In October it became known that Lord Stanley, the Secretary of State for the Colonies, had recalled Captain Fitzroy, and that Captain George Grey, then Governor of South Australia, had been appointed as the new Governor of this colony. Captain Grey landed at Auckland from the East India Company's armed ship "Elphinstone" on the 14th November, and a few days later he arrived at Kororareka. He gave the insurgent leaders a final opportunity for acceptance of ex-Governor Fitzroy's terms of peace, which stipulated that the Treaty of Waitangi should be binding, that the British flag should be respected, that plunder taken from the Europeans should be restored, and that certain lands should be given up to the Crown. Old Kawiti had already replied to Fitzroy, refusing the demand for territory: " . . . You shall not have my land—no, never! Sir, if you are very desirous to get my land, I shall be equally desirous to retain it for myself." The missionary Burrows was asked to convey Grey's letter to Heke. "Let the Governor and his soldiers return to England, to the land that God has given them," replied Heke, "and leave New Zealand to us, to whom God has given it. No; we will not give up our lands. If the white man wants our country he will have to fight for it, for we will die upon our lands."

Governor Grey sent to Auckland for all available forces. Ships-of-war and battalions of soldiers were concentrated in the Bay. The latest addition to the fleet of British ships in New Zealand waters was H.M.S. "Castor," a frigate from the China Station. A transport, the barque "British Sovereign," had brought over another two hundred men of the 58th Regiment from Sydney, besides some artillery.

It had been ascertained that the enemy were gathered to the number of several hundreds in the new *pa* at Rua-pekapeka, which was reported by the friendly Maoris to be stronger even than Ohaeawai. On the 8th December, 1845, the British advance upon Kawiti's bush fortress began with more than 1,100 rank and file under Colonel Despard, besides friendly Maoris. The route of march was over more difficult country than that traversed by the Ohaeawai expedition. The ships sailed up to the entrance of the Kawakawa River, thence transport was by boat for several miles; from the head of navigation the way lay through fifteen miles of roadless hills, forests, swamps, and streams to Kawiti's mountain fort.

The following troops were engaged in the attack on Rua-pekapeka under Lieut.-Colonel Despard:—

	Officers.	Men.
Seamen of H.M.S. "Castor," "North Star," "Racehorse," and H.E.I.C. "Elphinstone," under Captain Graham and Commander Hay, R.N.	33	280
Lieutenant Wilmot, R.A., and Captain Marlow, R.E.	2	..
Royal Marines (Captain Langford)	4	80
58th Regiment (Lieut.-Colonel Wynyard)	20	543
99th Regiment (Captain Reed)	7	150
H.E.I.C. Artillery (Lieutenant Leeds)	1	15
Volunteers from Auckland (Captain Atkyns)	1	42
	68	1,110
Native allies under Tamati Waka Nene, Patuone, Tawhai, Repa, and Nopera Pana-kareao		450

Ordnance: Three naval 32-pounders, one 18-pounder, two 12-pounder howitzers, one 6-pounder brass gun, four mortars, and two rocket-tubes.

The modern road from the Township of Kawakawa to Rua-pekapeka runs closely parallel to Despard's line of march; in fact, the two routes are identical as the site of Kawiti's stronghold is approached. At the head of boat-navigation on the Kawakawa River a fortified camp was established in the *pa* of a friendly chief, Tamati Pukututu. Here troops, guns, and stores were landed, and Commander Johnson, of the "North Star," was given charge of the post with seventy men. Captain Graham, of the frigate "Castor," was senior naval officer at the seat of war, and his bluejackets and those of the "North Star," "Racehorse," and "Elphinstone," were useful in the heavy work of transporting the artillery. The march of the combined naval and military force was a fine feat of pioneering, for it was necessary to make roads, fell bush, roughly bridge streams, and to use block and tackle in hauling the guns over rough ground and up steep hills. The men were compelled to carry, in addition to their arms and equipment, boxes each containing a 24 lb. or 32 lb. shell. The way in places led over fern hills and ridges; in places it plunged into patches of heavy timber.

Before narrating the events of that midsummer of 1845–46, let us view "The Cave of the Bats" as it exists to-day, and observe how the soldierly genius of Ngapuhi selected and fortified a position of strategic value—commanding, remote, and difficult of approach.

Passing a lonely little schoolhouse perched on a hilltop, eleven miles by the present road from Kawakawa, the traveller descends

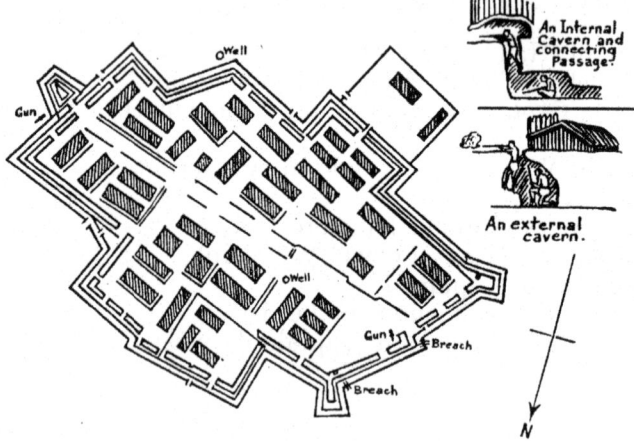

PLAN OF RUA-PEKAPEKA FORTIFICATION.

into a gully, with a flat-topped hill, some 800 feet in altitude, above him on his left. It was on this level ridge that the British column in 1845 obtained the first sight of the Ngapuhi stronghold, and here the batteries were planted and began to shell the *pa* at 1,200 yards—long range for the artillery of those days. Climbing the opposite side of the valley we find ourselves on a level stretch of ground, which the army chroniclers of Heke's day described as a "small plain." It is of very inconsiderable extent, and falls steeply away on either hand into the valley. Here the final British camp was pitched, and the guns advanced for the bombardment of the hill-fort, at a range of about a quarter of a mile. On this ridge, fringed and dotted with *puriri* trees, is an isolated farmhouse. Just before it is reached the fern-grown remains of the British entrenchments are passed; the main road, in fact, goes through the centre of the position. Somewhere here, too, are the unmarked graves of the Imperial men who fell in the attack. The exact place is forgotten ; maybe one rides over the spot where the bones of the redcoats and bluejackets lie. In the yard under the great twisted *puriri*, whose boughs trembled before the reverberations of Despard's guns, the farmer's children are playing a game of bowls of their own devising with four cannon-balls — rusty old round shot that were hurled from British 6-pounders and 12-pounders.

Beyond the farmhouse the road dips into a little hollow, flanked by thick forest on the left and a grass paddock on the right. We halt on the other side of the valley, beneath a grove at the intersection of two roads, and there, before us and above us, in the fork of the roads, is Rua-pekapeka *pa*—its palisades long demolished except for charred posts here and there, its crumbling

From *Royal Navy Officers' Survey, 1846.*]

CROSS-SECTION OF RUA-PEKAPEKA PA.

(W. to E.)

parapets clothed with fern and flax and *koromiko*. This spot is very nearly 1,000 feet above sea-level ; it is the northern face of the Tapuaeharuru (" Rumbling Footsteps ") Range. On either hand the ground slants steeply down into forested depths ; this narrow neck on which we stand was the only route by which the *pa* could be approached. Ascending the hillside we soon come to the ruined ramparts. Half-burned *puriri* logs, almost imperishable, lie about the hillside ; there are the stumps of trees felled by the Maoris when clearing the glacis of the *pa*. Three or four stockade-posts, roughly trimmed *puriri* trunks, stand on the line of the double stockade ; they resist age and weather to-day as they did the British round shot and fire-stick long ago. One of these stockade-posts stands at the lower end of the fort, near the north-west angle. It leans over the track, a tree-trunk of irregular

74   NEW ZEALAND WARS.

shape, with a rough elbow where the main branch had been lopped off; it stands 12 feet high, and is about 14 inches in diameter in the butt. White and spectral with age, it is still charred in places with the fire of 1846. This part of the work must have presented a formidable face to the attacking force; even now the height from the bottom of the outer ditch to the top of the fern-grown *maioro*, or earth wall, at the north-western bastion is 15 feet. On the south side of the *pa* a post standing 8 feet above the ground, with a diameter of 1 foot by 8 inches, a mossy old *puriri* trunk, still bears the marks of the axe. A fern-hung pit proves to be

Detail of north-west angle, Rua-pekapeka.

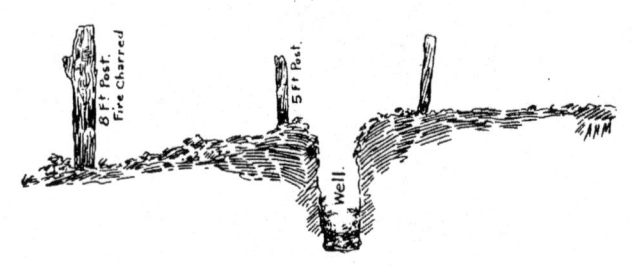

From sketches by J. Cowan, 18th March, 1919.]
Remains of palisade and well, south side of fortification.
SECTIONS OF RUA-PEKAPEKA PA.

one of the Maori wells marked on the British naval officers' plan of the *pa* drawn in 1846; at its bottom is a pile of posts and battered saplings from the demolished stockade. There is another well on the sketch-plan; this we presently discover inside the *pa*. From this side, the south and west, the ridge drops quickly to the valley lying 500 or 600 feet below and spreading away into the distances of bush and smoky-blue ranges.

At the rear (the east end) of the *pa* is another lichen-crusted stockade-post, standing on the edge of the track which trends out through the olden gateway. At another part of the outer

THE CAPTURE OF RUA-PEKAPEKA.

entrenchment we find a squared post, mossy with age, lying on the ground ; it is between 4 feet and 5 feet in length ; its butt is sharpened to a point in order to enable it to be driven into the ground—one of the line of smaller stakes between the whole-tree *himu*.

The *pa* slopes to the west and north, inclined towards the ridge by which the troops advanced, and therefore its interior lay exposed to artillery fire from the far side of the little valley intervening between the batteries and the range-face ; but the system of shot-proof and bomb-proof *ruas*, or underground shelters, protected the garrison from the guns of those days. We descend into one of these *ruas* near the centre of the *pa*. Its mossy floor is 6 feet below the surface of the ground ; it has a narrow entrance or shaft, and then it opens out fanwise underneath into a comparatively wide chamber. The interior is partly blocked up with the fallen debris of seventy-six years, but sufficient of its original shape and dimensions remain to convince us of its convenience and safety in the siege-days, when its top was roofed over with logs and earth, and when subterranean ways connected it with the neighbouring *ruas* and the main trench. The whole place is pitted with these burrow-like *ruas*. The parapets and trenches are in the most perfect state of preservation on the western and south-western aspects. Here the trench is 5 feet deep, and from the ditch-bottom to the top of the parapet the height is 8 or 10 feet. The trench system would still conceal a little army.

KAWITI'S CARRONADE.

A broken 12-pounder lying in rear of Rua-pekapeka *pa*, 18th March, 1919.

Due north, blue-shimmering in the haze, is Russell Bay, with the islands of the outer bay sleeping on its breast ; beyond again, the ocean. The Maoris from here could see the ships lying at anchor twenty miles away, could mark every daylight movement in their direction, and could even see the flagstaff hill, the root of all these troubles.

The *pa* was about 100 yards in length and 70 yards in width, with flanking bastions of earthwork and palisade. A plan drawn by the master of H.M.S. " Racehorse " shows that in the small bastion on the east face, the highest part of the *pa*, a double ditch and an earthed-over bell-shaped shelter separated the two outer rows of palisade (the *pekerangi* and *kiri-tangata*) from a high inner stockade. To-day there are indications that on a portion at least of the west end also a row of palisades stood on the inner side of the ditch. The work was much broken into flanks for enfilading-fire, and the trench was cut with traverses protecting the musketeers against a raking fire or a *ricochet* from a cannon-shot.

The advance from Kororareka occupied the troops from the 8th until the 31st December, by which time the column pitched the last camp and threw up field-works on the level space described. Mohi Tawhai with his Mahurehure friendlies had pushed on ahead and quickly constructed a stockade on this small plateau 600 to 700 yards from the *pa*. The guns were brought up by horses and bullock teams, with the assistance of man-power at many a hill and watercourse. It was the 1st January, 1846, before Kawiti's garrison made any attempt to bar the slow but certain progress of the British troops towards their mountain fort. On that day a small party of the *pa* defenders made a sortie from the *pa* and engaged a number of the friendly Maoris in the bush. The chief Wi Repa, one of the best fighters in the native auxiliary force, was severely wounded. The enemy cut off and killed one white man, a volunteer Pioneer from Auckland. On the same day Colonel Despard sent a strong body of infantry into the forest on the narrow plateau that separated him from his antagonists, and this force took up a position on a partly cleared space within a quarter of a mile of the stockade. Here, under cover of the timber which screened the troops from the view of the Maoris, a palisade and earthwork were commenced, and by nightfall the position was ready for a battery. A large body of Maoris sallied out from the *pa* and made an attempt to turn the flank of the advanced party. They were engaged by Tamati Waka and his brother Wi Waka Turau, Nopera Pana-kareao, and Mohi Tawhai with two hundred men. It was a tree-to-tree fight in which only Maoris could well be engaged. Kawiti's men were driven back with a loss of several men killed and nearly a score wounded. On the Government side five Maoris were wounded.

Another stockade was built considerably in advance and more to the right, facing the south-western angle of the *pa*. This position was not more than 160 yards from the front of Kawiti's position. An 18-pounder and a 12-pounder howitzer were mounted here. In the larger stockade, about 350 yards from the *pa*, there were mounted two 32-pounders and four mortars. Despard's main camp on the 5th January was about 750 yards from the *pa*. Mounted in front of this position, with thick woods in its front and rear, were three guns — a 32-pounder, a 12-pounder howitzer, and a light 6-pounder, besides rocket-tubes.

The Pioneer axemen attacked the heavy timber immediately in front of the advanced gun-positions, and the greater part of the Maori stockade soon lay exposed to cannon-fire. The small battery in the valley below the *pa* commanded a range along

THE CAPTURE OF RUA-PEKAPEKA. 77

The Bombardment of Rua-pekaPeka Pa.
[From a drawing, 10th January, 1846.]

both west and south flanks, and concentrated its fire on the south-west angle.

It was the morning of the 10th January before the grand bombardment began. All the batteries were complete, and sufficient supplies of ammunition were brought up, the Maoris of the friendly contingent assisting. Every gun spoke, the three naval pieces hurling their 32 lb. round shot against the palisade-front, the 18-pounder and 12-pounder in the advanced stockade throwing their metal against the south-west timber bastion, and the smaller guns and the rocket-tubes attending to the interior defences and searching the huts and *ruas*. There were two pieces of artillery in the *pa*, a 12-pounder carronade and a 4-pounder; one of these Kawiti had placed in position at the east, or rear, end; the other in an emplacement just inside and above the trench on the western face. There were gunners among the Maoris able to lay and fire these pieces, but, as at Ohaeawai, there was a shortage of projectiles. The 12-pounder came to grief early in the bombardment; an 18 lb. shot from the advanced battery in the hollow struck it in the muzzle and smashed it.

The storm of shot and shell, kept up with little intermission all day, soon began to make impression on Kawiti's *puriri* war-fence. Some of the palisade-posts, nearly 20 feet high and more than 1 foot in thickness, were battered to pieces by the impact of the 32 lb. and 18 lb. balls, and some of the less deeply set were knocked out of the ground. By the afternoon a breach had been made in the stockade at the north-western bastion, and at a point midway between that salient and the south-west angle. This face was the lower end of the *pa*, and the efforts of the artillerists were centred on demolishing the palisade here and widening the breaches sufficiently for a general assault, for which the impatient Despard longed. The Colonel had, indeed, intended launching a storming-party against the *pa* when the first breach was made, but the Governor, Captain Grey, vetoed the proposal, which would simply have resulted in another Ohaeawai. Mohi Tawhai, too, had entered a protest immediately upon learning of Despard's intention.

Governor Grey was an eye-witness of the whole of the operations; indeed, he was more than a mere spectator, for he sighted one of the guns, and he had reconnoitred the *pa* under fire more than once. Sergeant Jesse Sage (58th) recounted that the young Governor frequently walked through the bush to a position well within musket-range from the *pa*; he would take a sergeant or corporal of an advanced picket with him, and, bidding the non-commissioned officer take cover, would stand with his telescope examining the stockade, shots flying around him—"fearlessly doing his duty," said Sage, "as brave a man as ever walked."

[From a water-colour drawing by Colonel Cyprian Bridge (58th Regt.).]

THE CAPTURE OF RUA-PEKAPEKA. (11th January, 1846.)

Nightfall brought no cessation of the cannonade, for each gun was fired every half-hour, and rockets were frequently thrown into the *pa*, to prevent the garrison from repairing the damage to the stockade. The guns were laid with great accuracy throughout the firing; the directing officers were Lieutenant Bland (H.M.S. " Racehorse ") and Lieutenant Leeds (H.E.I.C.S. " Elphinstone "); Lieutenant Egerton (H.M.S. " North Star ") was in charge of the war-rocket tube.

It was discovered afterwards that the shelling had effectually swept the *pa*, so much so that some of the projectiles had gone right through several stockade-lines; holes were found ripped in the rear palisades. " We were safe underground when the big guns began to hurl their *mata-purepo* at us," says old Rihara Kou, of Kaikohe. " What had we to fear there ? " But the persistent showering of cannon-balls by night as well as day made life in the *pa* so uncomfortable that the garrison now began to fear that the place could not be defended much longer.

Hone Heke, recovered from his wound, had only arrived in the *pa* on the night before the bombardment, with a body of his tribesmen from Tautoro and Kaikohe. His contingent brought the forces in the Rua-pekapeka up to about five hundred men. That day under the artillery fire convinced him that the *pa* must be evacuated, and he counselled Kawiti to take to the forest and fight the soldiers there, where they could not haul their heavy guns. But Kawiti determined to fight his fort to the end.

The following morning, 11th January, was Sunday. The artillery fire was continued from all the batteries. There was no answering fire of musketry from the *pa* loopholes. A dozen Maori scouts, under Wi Waka Turau, worked up to the stockade near the south-west angle and crept in through one of the breaches made by the guns. Wi Waka signalled to his brother Tamati Waka, who was with Captain Denny and a hundred men of the 58th awaiting the result of the reconnaissance. The troops came up with a rush and were inside the double palisade and trench, and pushing up over the hut-and-fence-cumbered ground towards the higher end, before their presence was detected and the yell of alarm raised, " The soldiers are in the *pa*."

The garrison had nearly all left the *pa* by the hidden ways that morning, and were sheltering behind the rear earthworks and stockade in a dip of the ground—some for sleep undisturbed by rockets and shells, some to cook food, the majority for religious worship. Kawiti himself, sturdy old pagan, remained in his trenched shelter with some of his immediate followers.

The alarm given, the astonished Kawiti and his Maoris gave the troops a volley. Running out to the east end, they joined Heke and his men. A determined effort was made to regain the stronghold, but the stockade now became the troops' defence.

Meanwhile Colonel Despard had rushed up strong reinforcements, and presently hundreds of soldiers were within the *pa*, pouring a heavy fire from the east and south-east faces upon the Maoris, who took cover behind trees and breastworks of logs, and maintained a fire upon the *pa*. A crowd of soldiers and sailors rushed out through the rear gateway and attacked the Maoris on the edge of the bush. A number of the " Castor's " bluejackets dashed into the bush and became easy targets for Kawiti's musketeers, who shot several of them dead. The 58th and 99th, more seasoned to native tactics, took advantage of all the cover that offered, and killed and wounded a number of their foes. The skirmish developed into an ambush, skilfully laid by Kawiti, who directed Ruatara Tauramoko to feign a retreat with a party of men in order to draw the soldiers and sailors into the forest, while he lay in wait on either side behind the logs and trees. This piece of Maori strategy proved successful. Surprise volleys were delivered from cover, and a number of whites fell; the others discreetly retreated, taking advantage of the plentiful cover. In this bush battle some hundreds of men were engaged, and Kawiti certainly made a stout fight to retrieve his fallen fortunes. Every tree concealed a Maori sniper; every mass of fallen logs was a bush redoubt. Corporal Free saw a Maori shot in a *puriri*. " He had been potting away at us from the branches," said the veteran, " and shot two or three of our men. At last we noticed the bullets striking the ground and raising little showers of dust and twigs, and looking up we discovered the sniper. Several of us had a shot; one of my comrades got him, and he came tumbling to the ground, crashing through the branches and turning round and round as he fell."

RUATARA TAURAMOKO.

(Uri-Taniwha *hapu*, Ngapuhi Tribe.

The forest engagement lasted until 2 o'clock in the afternoon. Before that time Kawiti and Heke had determined to withdraw all their people to the inaccessible back country; the fight in the rear of the *pa* was prolonged in order to give time for the wounded to be carried off. As in old Maori warfare, the picked men, the young *toas*, such as Ruatara, fought a hard rearguard action, then vanished into the bush to rejoin the main body. They lost heavily; behind one log where the troops had been held up for more than half an hour Mr. George Clarke found nine stalwart young men lying side by side.

Thus fell Rua-pekapeka. The British loss was twelve killed —seven of whom were "Castor" men—and thirty wounded, including Mr. Murray, a midshipman of the "North Star."

Colonel Despard, who had by this time come to admit the Maori's originality and skill in fort-building, declared in his despatches that "the extraordinary strength of this place, particularly in the interior defence, far exceeded any idea that could have been formed of it." Every hut, he found, was a little fortress in itself, strongly stockaded all round with heavy timbers sunk deeply in the ground and placed close to each other, with a strong earthwork thrown up behind them.

It was apparent that the garrison had been in straits for food-supplies. Little was found in the *pa* except fern-root.

The troops set fire to the huts and stockading, but the earth-works and the trench system were of such dimensions that Despard decided to leave them undemolished and march his troops back to the Bay of Islands.

This success ended the Northern War.

MAIHI PARAONE KAWITI.
(Son of Kawiti, the defender of Rua-pekapeka.)

Brave old Kawiti, while candidly confessing at a meeting at Pomare's *pa* that he had had enough of war as waged by his "fighting friends" the British, consoled himself with the knowledge of having acted a valiant part: "Peace, peace—that is all I have to say. I did not commence the war, but I have had the whole brunt of the fighting. Recollect, it is not from fear, for I did not feel fear when the shot and shell were flying around me in the *pa*." And there was a very proper warrior pride in Kawiti's declaration to a chief after the meeting: "I am satisfied; I intend making peace, but not from fear. Whatever happens to me hereafter, I have one consolation—I am not in irons, nor am I in Auckland

Gaol. I have stood five successive engagements with the soldiers belonging to the greatest white nation in the world, the soldiers that we have been told would fight until every man was killed. But I am now perfectly satisfied they are men, not gods [*atua*], and had they nothing but muskets, the same as ourselves, I should be in my *pa* at the present time."

At this meeting it was stated by Heke's and Kawiti's Maoris that the casualties on their side since the taking of Kororareka were sixty killed and about eighty wounded.

Drawing by A. H. Messenger, after a sketch, 1852.]

THE BRITISH FRIGATE "CASTOR."

H.M.S. "Castor" was an oak frigate of 1,293 tons, built in 1832. She took part in the Syrian campaign of 1840, and shared in the bombardment of St. Jean d'Acre. After cruising on the coast of Ireland she was sent out to the East Indies Station and New Zealand. Seven of her men were killed in the fighting at Rua-pekapeka *pa*, 11th January, 1846. H.M.S. "Dido" arrived at Auckland from the East Indies on the 2nd June, 1847, and relieved the "Castor," which sailed for England three days later. In 1852 the "Castor" was Commodore Wyvill's ship on the Cape Station, and her commander was sent to the scene of the wreck of the transport "Birkenhead" to render help. The frigate remained afloat for seventy years. For many years she was employed at South Shields as drill-ship for the Royal Naval Reserve.

A Proclamation by the Governor permitting those who had been concerned in the war to return peaceably to their homes was received with relief by Ngapuhi and their allies. Proclamations raised the blockade of the east coast from Whangarei to Mangonui and Doubtless Bay, and also relieved the Bay of Islands district within a circle of sixty miles in any direction from Russell from the operation of martial law, which had existed since the 26th April, 1845. So peace came, a peace unembittered by confiscation of land or by vendettas provocative of future wars.

Heke lost the war, but carried his point. In 1848 he declared that the *tupapaku* (the corpse) of the flagstaff at Kororareka should not be roused to life, because those who had died in cutting it down could not be restored to the land of the living. This attitude he maintained to the day of his death (1850). While he lived, and while Kawiti lived, the signal-mast was not re-erected on Maiki Hill. This was the chief point in dispute, and tactfully the new Governor did not insist upon the restoration of the *tupapaku*. The Port of Russell carried on without a shipping signal-station until 1853, when Maihi Paraone Kawiti —son of Heke's ally—and his kinsmen set up a new mast in token of the friendship between the two races. Governor Grey's wisdom in refraining from confiscation of land was justified by results, for Ngapuhi have ever since 1846 been loyal friends of the whites. The forfeiture of lands would have bred not only intertribal feuds but long resentment against the Government. That Ngapuhi were given no opportunity of cherishing such memories is something for which we have reason to be thankful to-day, for it was this tribe and its neighbours, with the loyal Ngati-Porou of the East Coast, that made the strongest contribution to the Maori battalion in the Great War. Ngapuhi, Te Rarawa, and kindred tribes of the north of Auckland sent over six hundred of their young men to join the contingent which fought so well on Gallipoli in 1915, and later did good work as Pioneers in France.

CHAPTER X.

WELLINGTON SETTLEMENT AND THE WAR AT THE HUTT.

The north pacified, Governor Grey turned his attention to the Cook Strait settlements, where the position for the last year had verged upon war. The New Zealand Company's loose methods in the purchase of native lands had been followed by the repudiation of bargains, the estrangement of the two races, and the blocking of settlement. But the warriors who insisted upon muskets, gunpowder, and shot as the chief portion of the payment for the land upon which Wellington now stands were not at all dissatisfied in 1840 with the bargain they had made. They had secured arms, without which their tenure of the district in those days of almost constant intertribal jealousy and conflict would have been precarious, and they had given nothing of great value in exchange; for they were mentally resolved, if it had not been openly stated, that they would not suffer their existing cultivations and other grounds valuable as food-producing places, such as the portions of the forest richest in birds—the *kaka*, pigeon, and *tui*—to pass away for ever out of their hands.

Colonel Wakefield and his coadjutors in the first work of settlement suffered to a considerable extent from their want of knowledge of Maori laws and customs with respect to land, and also from their inability to make the natives understand the precise tenor of their questions and their documents. Richard Barrett, the whaler and trader, upon whom they placed reliance as interpreter and go-between, was illiterate, and his knowledge of the Maori tongue scarcely extended beyond colloquial phrases. Wakefield does not appear to have given close attention to the validity of the native vendor's title; so long as he found a chief or gathering of chiefs willing to sell such-and-such an area of bush, mountain and plain, he was satisfied. He was presently to gain by tragic experience a knowledge of the time and care necessary to complete a really safe and satisfactory purchase of land from the Maori. Doubtless there was at the back of Wakefield's mind a feeling that once the lands were settled by a strong body of British settlers, ready and able to hold their farms against all comers, the native population would quickly diminish in importance, if not in numbers.

Mr. Spain, the Land Claims Commissioner, in 1845 awarded the New Zealand Company 71,900 acres of land in Wellington and vicinity, excepting the villages and the lands that were actually occupied by the natives and thirty-nine native reserves. At the same time the Commissioner disallowed the Company's claims to the Wairau and Porirua lands, and in the end it was arranged (1847) that the sum of £2,000 should be paid to Ngati-Toa and their kindred for the disputed territory at Porirua, and £3,000 for the Wairau.

There seems to have been considerable uncertainty among settlers and Maoris alike as to the exact situation and boundaries of some of the reserves, more especially those in the Hutt Valley, and to this lack of precise information much of the trouble with the discontented tribes was due. In 1846 we find even the consistently friendly chief Te Puni complaining that the Ngati-Awa reserves at the Taita were occupied by European settlers. As the result of the failure to inform the Maoris of the position and bounds of the areas reserved for them, the natives in some instances cleared tracts of land outside the reserves, and in other cases occupied and cleared bush land that had been sold to settlers: disputes and suspicion were thus engendered.

The principal opposition to the white occupation of Hutt lands came in the first case from a chief named Taringa-Kuri ("Dog's Ear"), otherwise known as Kaeaea ("Sparrowhawk"). He derived his first name from his preternatural keenness of hearing; when out scouting, say the Maoris, he would put his ear to the ground and detect the approach of an enemy at a great distance. "Dog's Ear" headed the Ngati-Tama Tribe, connected both with Ngati-Awa and with Ngati-Maniapoto. The clan had fought its way down the west coast as allies of Te Rauparaha and Te Rangihaeata in the "twenties." He and his people received a sixth part of the goods first given by Colonel Wakefield in payment for the Wellington lands. When the disputes arose as to the ownership of the Hutt Valley, "Dog's Ear" and his people cut a line through the bush as a boundary dividing the lower valley from the Upper Hutt, contending that the upper part should be reserved for Ngati-Tama* and their friends Ngati-Rangatahi. In 1842 he

---

* Not many of the Ngati-Tama Tribe were engaged in the war in the Hutt Valley. The majority had gone with Pomare Ngatata to the Chatham Islands. Later, a number of Ngati-Tama, as the result of quarrels with Ngati-Mutunga at the Chathams, migrated to the Auckland Islands in a French whaler. To their disgust they found that the climate of the Aucklands was so wet and cold that their potatoes would not grow. They were removed a few years later and returned to the Chatham Islands.

built a village called Makahi-nuku, fortified with palisades, on the banks of the Hutt about two miles above the present Lower Hutt Bridge, and cleared and cultivated part of a section purchased

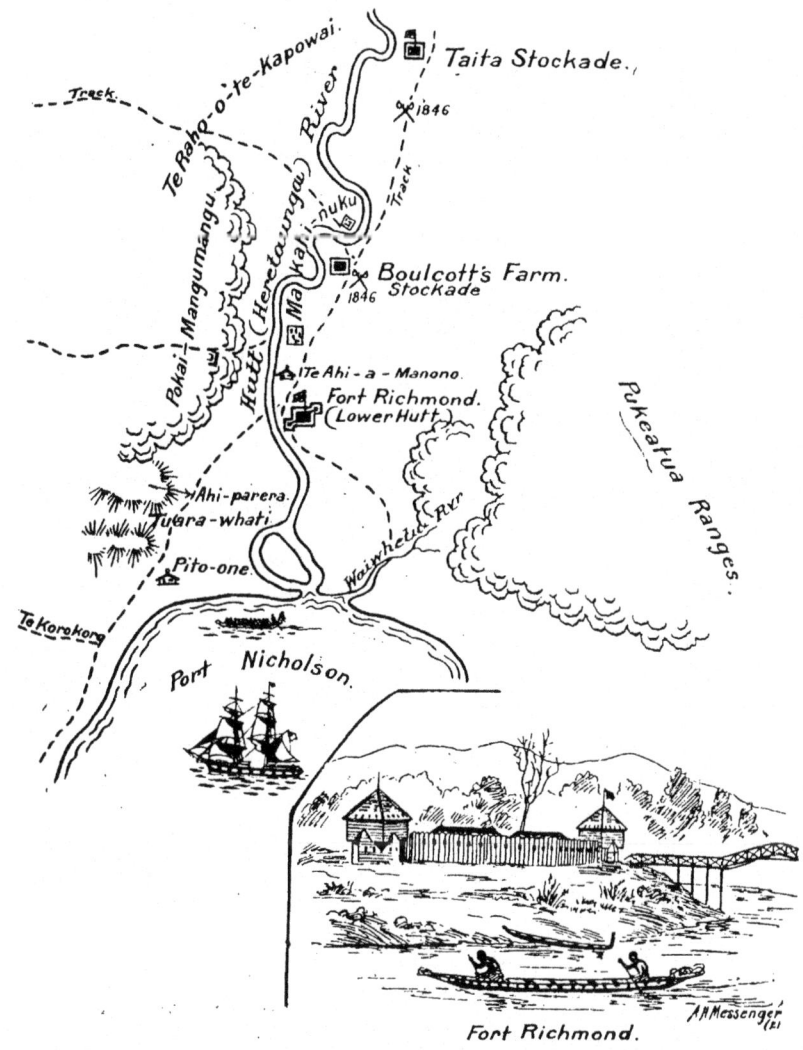

THE VALLEY OF THE HUTT, WELLINGTON,
Showing stockades and scenes of engagements, 1846.

from the Company by Mr. Swainson. This section became the chief centre of contention between the whites and the natives. In this action "Dog's Ear" was supported by the direct instructions of Te Rauparaha and Te Rangihaeata. But he had stated in his evidence before Mr. Spain's Court that Ngati-Awa and Ngati-Rangatahi sold the Hutt lest they would be invaded by Te Rauparaha with his Ngati-Toa, and Te Whatanui with his Ngati-Raukawa, from Otaki and the Manawatu. Those leaders were much offended at Ngati-Awa having taken possession of and sold the lands in the Hutt Valley. The Ngati-Rangatahi came originally to Porirua from the upper part of the Wanganui River; their leading men in the war-time migration were Kapara-te-hau, Te Oro, Te Kohera, and Kaka-herea; the last-named died in 1844. Ngati-Rangatahi shared in the Wairau affair in 1843, and soon afterwards occupied land on the banks of the Hutt under Te Rangihaeata's encouragement. The sum of £400 was paid to Te Rauparaha and Te Rangihaeata by the Government on behalf of the New Zealand Company, by way of second purchase of the Hutt Valley; nevertheless the actual occupants of the land did not benefit by this payment, and they declined to remove.

By the end of 1845 the New Zealand Government had the support of five British ships-of-war and nearly a thousand Regular troops. These forces, with the exception of some men of the 58th stationed at the Bay of Islands and two companies left in Auckland as a garrison, and the frigate "Racehorse" and the brig "Osprey," left at the Bay, were now available for the restoration of order in the Wellington settlements. There was also available a considerable and already fairly well-trained body of Militia, organized under the Militia Ordinance passed at Auckland on the 5th March, 1845. Under this enactment a citizen force was constituted for military service, composed of all able-bodied men between the ages of eighteen and sixty. Militiamen were liable for service within twenty-five miles of the post-offices in their towns, and their period of drill was twenty-eight days in the year. In Wellington the news of the war in the north and the disputes in the Hutt Valley had stimulated a volunteer spirit independently of the conscription measure, and in April, 1845, the daily musters of townsmen for military drill on Thorndon Flat and at Te Aro totalled 220 of all ranks. These drills were held at 5 o'clock in the evening; in addition there was a morning daily drill for the more enthusiastic held alternately on the parade-ground at either end of the town. The Militia drilled with the old Tower flint-lock muskets imported by the New Zealand Company for bartering with the Maoris; they were exactly the same make as the guns with which the Company had purchased the Wellington lands from the Ngati-Toa and Ngati-Awa. Later, percussion-cap guns were served out. The uniform was not elaborate or showy, but it was more suitable for campaigning than the tight red tunics, high stocks, and awkward headgear of the Regulars. The oldest surviving pioneer of the Hutt recalled that it consisted of a blue shirt, a cap similar to that worn by sailors, and "any kind of trousers."

A redoubt was built on Mr. Clifford's property on Thorndon Flat, very close to where the Normal School now stands (Hobson Crescent). It has sometimes been described as a stockade, but it was simply a square earthwork with a surrounding trench. The parapet of sods and earth was reinforced with timbers at intervals inside. All round the parapet were wood-framed loopholes for musket-fire; the timbers forming them not only kept them clear of earth but strengthened the parapet. In 1846, when the troops were on field service, a Militia guard of a sergeant, a corporal, and twelve men did duty daily at the fort.

A more extensive work was that constructed at the southern, or Te Aro, end of the town, as a place of refuge for the citizens. This was a large earthwork forming two sides of a redoubt; the other two sides were left open, but the houses which stood there were capable of defence. A pioneer resident of Wellington, Mr. John Waters, who landed in Port Nicholson in 1841, describes this Te Aro fortification as follows:—

"The earthwork consisted of a ditch and a strong parapet. The trench was 6 feet deep, and the sod wall was about 6 feet high. The area enclosed was the ground between Manners Street and the sea, which then flowed to the ground on which the Town Hall now stands. The longer side of the earthwork was that which ran from Manners Street a short distance westward or inland of what is now Lower Cuba Street. There was an acre of land fronting Manners Street between the Bank of New Zealand (present Te Aro branch) and the angle of the work. The length of this side of the fortification was about 330 feet. The other flank, which was considerably shorter, ran at right angles inland along the north side of Manners Street towards its present intersection with Willis Street. The Wesleyan Chapel in Manners Street was just on the opposite side of the street to the earthworks. The trench and parapet enclosed several large buildings, including Bethune and Hunter's and other brick stores, the bank, and some houses. There was a boatbuilding yard, besides jetties and store buildings, down on the beach inside the wall. I do not recollect any guns in this fortification.

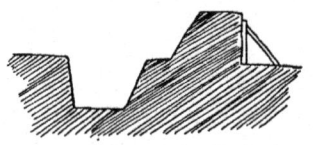

From a sketch by Judge H. S. Chapman in letter, 1845.]

CROSS-SECTION OF FIELDWORK AT TE ARO, WELLINGTON.

"On the eastern side of Lower Cuba Street, close to what is now Smith's corner, was a stockade enclosure in which the Government commissariat-stores building stood. This stockade was constructed somewhat after the manner of a Maori palisaded *pa*. It consisted of large split *totara* posts sunk in the ground at intervals, the space between them closely fenced with high slabs or pickets with pointed tops, and fastened with horizontal rails inside."

These defences of 1845 were not the first field-works constructed in Wellington for protection against the Maoris. After the Wairau tragedy in 1843 measures were taken by the New Zealand Company and the townspeople, independently of the Government, to fortify the northern and southern ends of the settlement, and guns were mounted in the works. These were 18-pounders which had originally been mounted on Somes Island, which the New Zealand Company in 1840 regarded as a suitable site for a fort. One of the fortifications of 1843 was in Thorndon; one was a small battery constructed on Clay Point, in the southern part of the settlement. "It was on the seaward extremity of the flat above Pipitea," says the pioneer settler already quoted, Mr. John Waters, "that the first Thorndon redoubt was built, or rather commenced. I remember that very well, because I saw it being built by the volunteers of the town in 1843, just after the Wairau fight, and, in fact, assisted in the work as a boy. It stood very close to the cliff above Pipitea, between the present steps at the foot of Pipitea Street and the English Church of St. Paul's, but much nearer Pipitea Street than the church. Just below it on the beach-front, now Thorndon Quay, was the police-station, a long *whare* thatched with *raupo*. We boys were given a holiday one day to help the men by carrying the sods which had been cut close by to the workers, who placed them in position on the parapet. The earthwork was not completed; the rear was left open. It consisted of three sides of an oblong, the longer side facing the sea, and the flanks extending back a short distance westward. It was not of any great size. The redoubt ditch was about 5 feet in depth and the same in width. We boys used to amuse ourselves by helping to deepen it. The earth parapet was about 6 feet high. The later redoubt was built in a different place altogether, further in on Thorndon, towards what is now Fitzherbert Terrace." The southern fortification was the battery on Clay Point, Clay Hill, or Flagstaff Hill, as the spot was variously named; after the construction of the work it was named "Waterloo Redoubt." Clay Point (now demolished) was the abrupt termination of a ridge which trended down to the sea at the place which is now the junction of Lambton Quay and Lower Willis Street. The sea then flowed and ebbed where the Bank of New Zealand now stands, and the cliff jutted out steep-to above the narrow beach, then the only thoroughfare. After Wairau, the townspeople formed a working-party, cut a track to the flat top of the hill, and dragged up three of the New Zealand Company's guns—ship's howitzers (18-pounders) on wooden carriages. The work was not an enclosed redoubt, but a parapet facing the sea—an emplacement and protection for the guns, with a trench 9 feet wide. The work was completed in one day.

The infant Town of Nelson also had its fortification in 1843, when the episode of the Wairau and reports of coming Maori raids stimulated the people to vigorous measures, with the result that the place was provided with the strongest fort south of Auckland. The resident agent of the New Zealand Company, Mr. Fox (afterwards Sir William Fox), agreed to advance the necessary funds for the work, protesting at the same time that the provision of means of public safety was the duty of the Government. Nelson's fort, named after Captain Arthur Wakefield, who fell at Wairau, occupied the most conspicuous place in the middle of the settlement, the hill at the top of Trafalgar Street on which Nelson Cathedral now stands. The following

Drawn from a sketch by the late Hon. J. W. Barnicoat, M.L.C.]

FORT ARTHUR, NELSON, IN 1843.

(Nelson Cathedral now occupies the site of this fortification.)

description of the redoubt and stockade was given in the *Nelson Examiner* of the 23rd December, 1843:—

"Fort Arthur enclosed the hill forming part of Trafalgar Square. It was built from the design and under the superintendence of Mr. J. S. Spooner. It covers rather more than an acre of ground. It is built in the form of an oblong hexagon, with bastions at each angle. The embankments, or ramparts, and the bastions are of earth, faced with sods, squared and laid in courses. It is surrounded by a moat, 8 feet deep and 12 feet wide, over which is placed a drawbridge at the north end. Inside the rampart is a trench, 5 feet deep, for musketry. On an inner and level elevation, and enclosing the church and Survey Office, is a stockade, 7 feet high, built of 2-inch planking, double, with a space between of 2 inches filled with earth, making it ball-proof, and surmounted with a *cheveaux de frise*. It is in the shape of an oblong square, 156 feet by 48 feet, with flanking towers at the corners 10 feet high; pierced throughout with loopholes for rifles and musketry, and ports for the great guns (long 18-pounder carronades)."

Nelson was not the only place in the South Island in which it was considered necessary in 1843 to erect fortified posts. The English and French residents of Akaroa resolved that three small blockhouses should be erected as a provision for the safety of the settlers and their families. One of these blockhouses was built at the eastern end of Akaroa Town, near the beach at the mouth of the Oinaka Stream; the Bruce Hotel now occupies the site. Another was placed midway along the bay, on the waterfront, near the spot where the police-station now stands. The third was erected in Otakamatua Bay, near the head of the harbour. These buildings were the first posts of the true blockhouse type, with overlapping upper storeys, built in New Zealand.

The settlers of the Hutt Valley acutely realized their defenceless state, and early in the year 1845 they decided to assure some measure of protection by building a stockaded fort in some central position, a garrison station to which they might hurry their families in the event of a conflict. The site selected was the left (east) bank of the Heretaunga, at the bridge; the exact spot is now a bed of gravel in the middle of the river, about 100 yards below the present Lower Hutt Bridge. The fortification was designed by a settler who was officer in command of the Hutt Militia, Captain George Compton; he had lived in the backwoods of North America, and he planned the stockade upon the pattern of the forts built by the United States pioneers for defence against the Indians. Fort Richmond, as it came to be called, in compliment to Major Richmond, the Superintendent of the Southern District, was a square work 95 feet each way, with flanking bastions at two diagonally opposite angles, commanding the bridge and the river on both sides. The walls were built of large slabs of timber, 9 feet 6 inches in height above the ground and 5 to 6 inches in thickness. The flanking bastions were small two-storeyed blockhouses, one 15 feet and the other 12 feet square; the upper storey was not set square with the lower, but diagonally across it (as shown in Mr. Swainson's sketch in the Wellington Art Gallery collection). This design, an idea originating on the American frontier, enabled a fire to be directed from above upon any attack on the base of the bastion. A better method of construction, however, was generally adopted in the blockhouses on the New Zealand frontiers in the "sixties," in which the upper storey projected over the lower by 2 or 3 feet all round. The Fort Richmond stockade was loopholed on each side, and the blockhouses in each storey; these apertures for musket-fire were about 4 feet apart. The one-armed veteran John Cudby (in 1919 ninety years of age) informed the writer that he helped to cart the timber for the fort. Most of the timber was cut in the forest which then covered the flat a little to the south of the present Lower Hutt Railway-station, the Pito-one side. The stockade

WELLINGTON SETTLEMENT AND THE WAR AT THE HUTT.

slabs were chiefly *pukatea*, a light but tough and strong wood; *totara* and *kahikatea* pine were mostly used for the blockhouses. The cost of the construction of the fort was set down at £124; this was exclusive of the value of the timber, which was given free by Captain Compton, and voluntary labour by settlers estimated at a value of £54 10s. The stockade was completed in April, 1845, and the Militia company of the Hutt occupied it until a redcoat garrison, a detachment of the 58th Regiment, marched in on the 24th April.

That little fort in the forest-clearing, guarding the Hutt bridge-head, and embodying the spirit of adventure and peril that entered into the life of frontier settlement, was in essentials a replica of the border posts in the American Indian country. It was the first of scores of stockades and blockhouses on the

From a drawing by W. Swainson.]
FORT RICHMOND AND THE HUTT BRIDGE (1847).

Maori border-line throughout this North Island, the advanced settler's refuge and protection, many of them garrisoned until the early "eighties." The sketches and descriptions that remain of Fort Richmond, and many a post of military settlers or Armed Constabulary in the later wars, recall like scenes in the American woods pictured for us in Whittier's poem, "The Truce of Piscataqua":—

>Once more the forest, dusk and dread,
>With here and there a clearing cut
>From the walled shadows round it shut;
>Each with its farmhouse builded rude,
>By English yeomen squared and hewed,
>And the grim flankered blockhouse bound
>With bristling palisades around.

Not only the New England and Kentucky stockades but the forts of the Hudson Bay Company, scattered over the northern continent from the Atlantic to Vancouver, were in design the prototypes of our New Zealand stockades. Their walls were built of slabs and solid tree-trunks, as high as 20 feet, with bastioned angles for enfilading-fire. Fort Douglas, which stood on the Red River a hundred years ago, an illustration of which is given in Bryce's work on the history of the Hudson Bay Company, was very similar to Fort Richmond. It had a close-set palisade of slabs and tree-trunks facing the river; at the corners were tower-like timber flanking bastions.

The Karori settlers followed the example of those at the Hutt in the construction of a small fortified post, in order to guard against an attack from Ohariu. This place of defence, built in May and June, 1846, was surrounded by a ditch, and the site chosen for it was on rising ground in the oldest settled part of Karori, a clearing walled in by a dense and lofty forest, 600 feet above sea-level. It was built exactly on the crown of the gentle rise of ground in Karori Township, on the right-hand side of the deep cutting in Lancaster Street as one walks up from the main road, and only a few yards from the electric-car line. This was the most central and commanding spot in the Karori clearings of 1846; the ground about it was still encumbered with half-burned logs and stumps. The forest had been felled for about 100 yards from the stockade on the south and west sides, but there was standing timber in the little valley alongside which the main road runs to-day. The stockade was small, measuring about 28 or 30 feet in length by 20 feet in width; its greatest axis ran about north-east and south-west. Around it was dug a trench, 3 feet in width and 4 feet in depth; this ditch filled with water in the winter soon after it was excavated. The stockade was constructed of heavy timbers, chiefly *rimu* (red-pine) and *miro*. The logs were split, squared up with the axe, and roughly trimmed into points at the top; these timbers measured 6 or 7 inches in thickness, and when firmly sunk in the ground close alongside each other formed a solid wall 10 feet high. Loopholes for musket-fire were made by cutting away with saw and tomahawk a piece in the sides of a number of the timbers before they were set in the ground; the apertures so formed were shoulder-height from the ground, between 2 and 3 feet apart, and measured about 5 inches in length vertically by 3 inches in width. Between the foot of the stockade and the surrounding small trench there was a space of 3 to 4 feet; the earth from the trench was packed firmly against the base of the timbers. The space thus left enabled the sentries on duty at night to walk around the post between trench and wall. The doorway in the stockade faced the south; the door was of thick slabs, and for want of iron hinges it was pivoted on timber sockets, after the manner still seen in some remote settlements. Within the stockade the settlers built a small house of sawn *rimu*, roofed with *kahikatea* shingles; this house measured about 16 feet by 12 feet, and was divided into two rooms. One of these rooms was for the men of the Militia garrison, and the other for the women and children of the settlement in the event

From an oil-painting by C. D. Barraud.]

AN EARLY COLONIAL HOME.

Judge H. S. Chapman's residence, "Homewood," Karori, Wellington, in 1849. The site of this pioneer dwelling, in the *rata* and *rimu* forest. is now the heart of the suburban Township of Karori. The Hon. F. R. Chapman, son of the first Judge of the Southern District of New Zealand, was born in "Homewood." The place was temporarily abandoned during the war of 1846.

of a Maori attack. In one corner was a fireplace with chimney of clay. The floor was the bare earth. There was a clear space of 10 feet all round between this house and the stockade-wall.*

---

* This description of the Karori stockade is. the first yet published. The details were given chiefly by Mr. George Shotter, one of the earliest settlers at Karori (died 1920).

The Karori Militiamen who built the stockade, assisted by a party of bluejackets from H.M.S. "Calliope" and by a detachment of the armed police from Wellington under Mr. A. C. Strode, numbered thirty or forty small farmers, sawyers, and bullock-team drivers. The post was designed chiefly as a protection against possible attack from the natives at Ohariu Bay and the mouth of the Makara Stream, and in the nights of alarm a good lookout was kept in that direction. Some of the settlers worked on their holdings with cartridge-belts over their shoulders and a "Brown Bess" lying close by. However, most of the Ohariu Maoris left by canoe for Porirua and places higher up the coast. There was greater danger from *kokiris*, or small raiding-parties, of Rangihaeata's force. The armed settlers formed sections each of eight or nine men for garrison duty, and these detachments in turn occupied the stockade-house at night. The Militia mustered for drill three times a week—two hours' drill on each muster-day.

On a commanding position on the Wellington–Porirua Road a stockade was built on Mr. Johnson's land, Section 11/181, now the heart of the Township of Johnsonville. The stockade was a structure of thick slabs, with slits for musket-fire. There was a small loft, to which access was given by a ladder.

On Sunday, the 20th April, 1845, a report reached Wellington that a strong body of natives "all painted and feathered" had descended on the Lower Hutt Valley, and had given notice of their intention to attack the whites' stockaded *pa* next day. Major Richmond ordered fifty men of the 58th Regiment to the Hutt. The quickest means of reaching the scene of trouble was by water. The brig "Bee" was lying at anchor off the town ready for sea, and the soldiers were boated aboard her. Making sail for Pito-one, the brig landed her troops on the beach. At 3 o'clock in the morning of the 21st the detachment marched into the stockade, relieving the little garrison of Militia and forestalling the native plan. A few days later two 18-pounder guns belonging to the New Zealand Company were sent out from town and mounted on the bastion blockhouses.

During 1845 two companies of Regulars had been stationed in Wellington. As soon as it was possible to withdraw troops from the Bay of Islands preparations were made for a transfer of the military forces to Wellington, and on the 3rd February, 1846, a body of nearly six hundred men under Lieut.-Colonel Hulme embarked at Auckland for the south. The fleet which transported them consisted of the British frigates "Castor" and "Calliope," the war-steamer "Driver"—which had just arrived from the China Station—the Government brig "Victoria," and the barque "Slains Castle." Inclusive of a detachment of the 99th Regiment, lately arrived from Sydney in the barque "Lloyds," the following was the detail of the force: 58th Regiment—one field

H.M.S. "DRIVER," THE FIRST STEAMSHIP IN NEW ZEALAND WATERS.

This drawing is the first picture of H.M.S. "Driver" yet published in New Zealand. It is drawn from a sketch by Captain M. T. Clayton, of Auckland, who was in Wellington in July, 1846, as an apprentice in the barque "London," and is also based on a blue-print of the hull-details received from the Secretary to the officer, two captains, four subalterns, and 202 non-commissioned officers and privates; 99th Regiment — one field officer, two captains, six subalterns, and 250 non-commissioned officers and privates; 96th Regiment — one captain, four subalterns, and seventy-three non-commissioned officers and privates; also a detachment of Royal Artillery.

The excitement created by the opportune arrival of so large a body of British soldiers, bringing the total force of redcoats in Wellington up to nearly eight hundred men, was heightened by the novel spectacle of a steam-vessel. H.M.S. "Driver" was the first steamship to visit the port; she was a wonderful craft to many a colonist, and amazing to the Maoris, who congregated to watch the strange *pakeha* ship, driven by fires in her interior, moving easily and rapidly against wind and tide. The "Driver" was a paddle-steamer of 1,058 tons, with engines of 280 horse-power; she was rigged as a brig. She was armed with six guns. Her crew, under Commander C. O. Hayes, numbered 175 officers and men. The vessel had recently been engaged in the suppression of piracy in the East Indies. Her figurehead attracted much attention: it represented an old-time English mail-coach driver with many-caped greatcoat and whip.

On the 27th February some of the troops marched to the principal village occupied by the Maoris on the Hutt banks and destroyed it. The natives had abandoned their homes on the advance of the soldiers, and were camped in the forest above Makahi-nuku. The Governor sent a missionary, the Rev. Richard Taylor, as a messenger to the Ngati-Tama and Ngati-Rangatahi, promising that if they left the place peaceably he would see they were given compensation for their crops. The destruction of the village appears to have been rather hasty, for Kapara-te-Hau, the principal chief, had agreed to the terms, and promised to leave the following day.

In retaliation for the destruction of their villages and cultivations on the banks of the Hutt the Maoris on the 1st and 3rd March, easily eluding the troops who were in camp, carried out systematic raids of plunder and destruction on the farms of the white settlers. Dividing into small armed parties and moving with rapidity and secrecy upon the Hutt and the Waiwhetu, they visited each home separately, stripped the unfortunate people of all their property but the clothes they were wearing, destroyed furniture, smashed windows, killed pigs, and threatened the settlers with death if they gave the alarm. They took away such goods as they could carry, and destroyed the rest, but did not burn the houses. Little bands of distressed settlers and their families, robbed of nearly all they had in the world, and temporarily without means of livelihood, trudged into Wellington. By order of Governor Grey the plundered people were supplied with rations.

The numbers of persons to whom rations were served out on the 5th March were: Adults, 79; children, 140; infants, 17: total, 236.

The troops remained inactive on the day of the principal raid (1st March), greatly to the indignation of the civilians. Then it became known that the Governor was undecided whether or not to proceed with hostile measures against the natives. He had been advised by the Crown law authority that he was acting illegally in evicting the Maoris, inasmuch as the grants issued by Governor Fitzroy after the purchase of the valley had excepted all native cultivations and homes. The legal adviser, further, was of the opinion that the natives were justified in resisting such eviction by force of arms.

Captain Grey, however, was not long influenced by this opinion. He quickly made up his mind to protect the settlers at all hazards, and on the 3rd March he issued a Proclamation declaring the establishment of martial law in the Wellington District, bounded on the north by a line drawn from Wainui (near Pae-kakariki) on the west coast to Castle Point on the east.

The first shots in the campaign were fired on the morning of Tuesday, the 3rd March, 1846. A party of natives under cover of the bush and felled trees fired on Captain Eyton's company of the 96th, who were stationed some distance in advance of the camp at Boulcott's Farm, two miles above Fort Richmond. Several volleys were fired into the camp. The fire was returned effectively, and the Maoris were obliged to retreat. When the news of the definite outbreak of war reached the Governor in Wellington he ordered H.M.S. "Driver" to weigh anchor and steam to Pito-one with troops. The soldiers embarked were Captain Russell's company of the 58th, twenty men of the 99th, and thirty of the 96th, under Lieutenant Barclay. A party of men of the three regiments was also despatched to the Hutt.

On the 2nd April a Lower Hutt settler named Andrew Gillespie and his young son Andrew were attacked and so terribly tomahawked that they both died. Gillespie was the first settler placed in possession of the land at the Hutt from which the natives had been evicted in the previous month. Te Pau, of Ngati-Rangatahi, was the leader of the raiding-party. The Gillespie tragedy stirred Governor Grey to speedy action. A police party set out for Porirua, as the result of a message received by the Rev. O. Hadfield from Rauparaha, who gave a hint that the slayers might be found in his district. Then, for the first time, it was discovered that the hostile *hapus* had built a stockaded and entrenched stronghold at the head of the Paua-taha-nui arm of the Porirua Harbour, five miles from the open sea. Porirua, the Governor perceived, was practically the key of the west coast; a military station there would keep communications open, and would also directly menace

Rangihaeata and his insurgents, and strike at the rear of any force attacking the Hutt. A body of 250 men of the 58th and 99th Regiments, under Major Last, embarked in the warships " Driver " and " Calliope " and the barque " Slains Castle "; on the 9th April the three vessels sailed up the coast to Porirua, where the troops were landed. The force encamped on the low sandy point near Toms' whaling-station, just within the mouth of the harbour, and presently their tents gave place to a barracks of stone, surrounded by a stockade. At the same time the Governor took measures for the construction of a good road from Wellington to Porirua by the military, under Captain Russell (58th Regiment).* Another useful step was the formation of an armed police force of fifty men, under the command of Major Durie as inspector, with Mr. Chetham Strode sub-inspector. The police company was divided into four sections, each consisting of ten whites and one Maori, under a sergeant; small detachments were stationed at the outposts at the Hutt, Porirua, and Ohariu. At the end of April H.M.S. " Calliope " was despatched to Porirua, and then began a boat patrol of the shallow inner waters, which the warship could not enter.

---

* Mr. Kilminster, of Karori Road, Wellington, who arrived from London in the ship " Lady Nugent " in 1841 and landed at Pipitea, gives the following information (1920) regarding the military stockades which in 1846 protected the Wellington Porirua Road :—

" When I was a boy I frequently went out along the Porirua Road with my father, who was engaged in transport work for the troops, and I remember the old stockaded posts very well. First of all, as one went out from Wellington there was a small outpost at Khandallah, not fortified; this was popularly known as ' Mount Misery,' and officially as ' Sentry-box Hill,' now abbreviated to ' Box Hill.' The present road over Box Hill, Khandallah, passing close to the little church, goes almost exactly over the spot where the outpost was quartered. This was a kind of midway lookout place between Wellington and Johnsonville, and was garrisoned by a few men from Johnsonville. At Johnsonville—then known as ' Johnson's Clearing '—there was a stockade, strongly built of roughly squared timbers. Then there were stockades at intervals down to Porirua Harbour —Middleton's, Leigh's, and Elliott's. Leigh's stockade stood on Tawa Flat. Fort Elliott stood near the head of the harbour. From Porirua there was a ferry service in large boats down the harbour to Fort Paremata. These places of defence along the road between Johnson's and Porirua were built in this way : A trench was dug, and large split trees and small whole trees were set in close together, and the earth firmly filled in round them ; this palisade was loopholed for musket-fire."

CHAPTER XI.

THE FIGHT AT BOULCOTT'S FARM.

Two miles above the stockade at the Hutt Bridge a pioneer settler, Mr. Boulcott, had hewn a home out of the forest. His clearing bordered the left bank of the river; most of it was in grass; the rough edges of the farm were cumbered with half-burned logs and stumps, and on three sides was heavy timber; the fourth side faced the river and the fringing thickets on the other bank; beyond were the wooded steep hills that hemmed in the Hutt Valley on the west. A rough and narrow bush road, " corduroyed " with fern-tree trunks in the marshy portions, wound through the forest from the bridge at the fort; it was little more than a track, and in many places the branches of the *rimu* and *rata* met overhead and kept the road in dampness and shadow. Here and there were settlers' clearings, with houses of sawn timber and shingled roofs, or of slabs and *nikau* palm or *raupo* reed thatch; crops of wheat, oats, and potatoes were grown in these oases in the desert of bush. Where rows of shops, cottages, and bungalows, with beautiful orchards and gardens, cover the floor of the Hutt Valley to-day, there were but these roughly trimmed forest homes.

The most advanced post of the Regular troops in May, 1846, was on Boulcott's Farm, where fifty men of the 58th Regiment were stationed under Lieutenant G. H. Page. Some little distance higher up the valley, at the Taita, an outpost was established near Mr. Mason's section, where a small detachment of the Hutt Militia was stationed. Half the force of soldiers at Boulcott's were quartered in a large barn, around which a stockade of slabs and small logs had been erected and loopholed for musket-fire. The rest of the troops were accommodated in small slab outhouses near the barn and in tents. Lieutenant Page and his soldier servant occupied Mr. Boulcott's cottage; the owner of the place and his two men servants used a small house adjoining. It was upon this post that the Maoris, under Rangihaeata's orders, and led by Topine te Mamaku (otherwise Te Karamu), of the Ngati-Haua-te-Rangi, Upper Wanganui, made a desperate assault at daybreak on the morning of the 16th May, 1846.

During the week preceding this attack a general opinion was entertained at the Hutt that some sudden movement was contemplated by Rangihaeata. A naval reconnoitring-party had been fired upon by the hostiles at Paua-taha-nui, and the failure of the authorities to retaliate had, as it proved, emboldened Rangihaeata and his fellow-warriors to launch one of those lightning blows in which the Maori bush fighter delighted. Te Puni's warning and offers of help were disregarded, and even a word of caution from Rauparaha did not seem to stir the Superintendent from his indifference. The Governor was now absent at Auckland (the troublesome Taringa-Kuri had gone with him in the " Driver "). Rauparaha, in a letter received in Wellington some days before the attack, stated that when Major Richmond and Major Last were at Porirua during the previous week he said to them, in bidding them to be on their guard against a sudden attack, "*Kei Heretaunga te huaki ai; kia mohio; huihuia atu nga pakeha*" ("At Heretaunga the assault will be made. Be wary; concentrate the white men"). As if that were not enough, a chief of the Pipitea *pa*, Wellington, called on Major Richmond on Friday, the 15th May (the day before the attack), to warn him of the danger and to offer the assistance of his people. But no extra precautions were taken. Maori and settler alike knew that Rangihaeata would strike; the civil and military heads alone seemed blind or indifferent. For economy's sake Major Richmond disbanded the Militia in Wellington, and reduced the company at the Hutt to twenty-five men; this was a few days before the blow fell.*

The fog of early morning enveloped bush and clearing that dawn of Saturday, 16th May; a white band of denser vapour coiling down the valley above the tree-tops showed the course of the silent river. The sentry near the river-bank, in front of the inlying picket's tent, shivered with the chilly touch of the hour that precedes daybreak. As he turned to pace his beat, with musket and fixed bayonet at the slope, his glance fell upon some low bushes seen obscurely through the curling mist a few yards to his front. They seemed nearer, he thought, than they had been a few moments before. Next instant he caught a glimpse of a

---

* The Hon. Dr. Pomare, M.P., narrates an incident illustrative of the insurgents' strategy. His informant was old Tungia, of Ngati-Toa. A day or two before the attack on Boulcott's Farm either Rangihaeata or Te Mamaku sent a scout up to the Tinakori Range, near the present wireless station. Here the man lit a large fire, and he employed the earlier part of the night in walking round and round this fire with the idea of giving any watchers below the impression that a large force of warriors was gathered there to descend on Wellington, and so diverting attention from the Hutt. A considerable part of the British force at the Hutt was presently ordered into the town, and was in Thorndon barracks when Te Mamaku descended on the post at Boulcott's.

shaggy head and a gun-barrel above one of those bushes. The Maoris were creeping up on the camp, with bushes and branches of scrub held before them as screens. "Maoris!" he yelled as he levelled his "Brown Bess" and fired, then snatched another cartridge from his pouch and ran to the picket tent, trying to reload as he ran, but was overtaken and tomahawked.

A volley was delivered from fifty Maori guns. The Maoris fired low, to rake the floor of the tents. A second volley; another from a different flank; then on came the enemy with the tomahawk. Not a soldier of the picket escaped. Those who were not killed by the volley fell to the short-handled *patiti*. In and about the picket tent four soldiers lay dead. One of these was William Allen, whose name will be remembered so long as the story of Boulcott's Farm is told. Allen was a tall, young soldier; he was bugler to his company. When the sentry's shot was heard he leaped up, seized his bugle, and, running outside the tent, he put the bugle to his lips to blow the alarm. In the act of sounding the call he was attacked by a Maori, who tomahawked him in the right shoulder, nearly severing his arm, and felled him to the ground. Struggling to rise, the brave lad seized the bugle with his left hand and again attempted to warn his comrades, but a second blow with the tomahawk, this time in the head, killed him. The bugler's call was not needed, however, for the whole camp had been awakened by the sentry's shot and the answering volleys.

The garrison of Boulcott's, now reduced to forty-four or forty-five men, was confronted by quite two hundred warriors—Rangihaeata's band and Te Mamaku's musketeers from the Upper Wanganui. Lieutenant Page's house was surrounded by the Maoris in a very few moments after the destruction of the picket. Page, on the first alarm, had snatched up his sword and loaded pistol, and rushed out with two men, but was confronted by scores of the natives. Driven back into the cottage, the three sallied out again, and, joined by several soldiers from one of the sheds, they fought their way to the barn, firing at close quarters at their foes, who attempted to charge in upon them with the tomahawk. The party of men in the barn, three sections, each under a sergeant, fought their post well and successfully, taking turns in firing through the light stockade and in returning to the shelter of the building to reload.

The Maoris evidently had calculated on completely surprising the troops; but what they did not accurately estimate was the steadiness of disciplined Regular troops. Lieutenant Page, having hacked and shot his way to the stockade, assembled his men, and, leaving a small party to hold the fort, came out into the open again and boldly attacked his antagonists. Extending the men in skirmishing order, with fixed bayonets, he advanced. In the

BOULCOTT'S FARM STOCKADE, ON THE HUTT.

From a water-colour drawing by Lieutenant G. H. Page (58th Regt.), 1846.

The graves of the soldiers killed here are shown in the foreground. The stockade was enlarged and the buildings grouped as shown here after the fight.

height of the engagement a party of seven of the Hutt Militia, who had been disbanded on the previous Monday, but who fortunately retained their arms, came gallantly to the assistance of the hard-pressed troops, and fought side by side with the redcoats. Their arrival was the turning-point in the fight. The rebels, seeing these Militia men dash into the battle, began to retire, and at last were driven across the Hutt, after an engagement lasting about an hour and a half. The Maoris formed up on the west side and danced a war-dance. Page estimated their numbers at about two hundred.

A little later that morning John Cudby, then a youth of seventeen, who was engaged in carting commissariat from Wellington to the troops at Boulcott's Farm (for Mr. W. B. Rhodes, the contractor for supplying rations), harnessed up in the yard of the "Aglionby Arms," Burcham's Hotel, near the bridge stockade, and drove out into the bush for the front, unaware of the fight which had just been waged a short two miles away. In this duty it was the practice of Cudby and the other carters to bring out their loads along the beach road as far as Burcham's in the afternoon, stay there that night, and go on to Boulcott's Farm or the Taita in the morning. Cudby had previously had the protection of an escort of fifteen men under a non-commissioned officer, but, to use his own words, " the poor fellows at the stockade were worked to death, and so I said I'd do without them in the future." His sole companion henceforth was a clerk, the military issuer. A double-barrel gun loaded with slugs was carried in the cart, but it never became necessary to use it. (This gun was the means of depriving Cudby of his left arm a few months later in Wellington; one of the barrels accidentally exploded, the charge shattering the lad's hand and necessitating amputation of the arm at the elbow.) The carter and his companion were in the middle of the bush, jolting over the boggy "corduroy" patches of road, when they were met by two men in a cart driving furiously from the camp. One of them shouted: "Go back, boy, go back! The Maoris have attacked the camp!"

But Cudby did not turn his team. "I dursen't go back," he cried in his broad English dialect, "I dursen't go back; I've got the rations to deliver."

The two carters whipped up their horse and hurried on toward Fort Richmond, while Cudby, in fear every moment of receiving a volley from ambush in the dark timber that almost overhung him, but resolved to fulfil his duty, drove on to Boulcott's. When he arrived at the camp he saw laid out in the barn six dead bodies, the soldiers who had fallen; one of them was Bugler Allen, whom he knew. It was Cudby who, later in the day, took the bodies in his cart to a spot on the river-bank where they were temporarily buried—a place since washed away by floods.

Meanwhile bodies of troops despatched by Major Last—who had been informed of the attack by messenger from the front—were on the march out from Thorndon barracks and the Hutt stockade to reinforce the camp. These troops reinforcing Page drove the Maoris into the bush and silenced them.

Six whites lay dead, and four were severely wounded. Two of the wounded, Sergeant E. Ingram and a civilian named Thomas Hoseman, an employee of Mr. Boulcott, died some days later. The losses of the Maoris were not accurately known, for all who fell were carried off, but two were seen shot dead, and ten or more were wounded, some of them severely.

Now the authorities, civil and military, were compelled by the pressure of public opinion to accept Te Puni's generous offer to arm his Ngati-Awa men for the campaign. A hundred stand of arms were supplied to the *hapus* at Pito-one, and the men at the town *pas* were also given muskets. Mr. David Scott, a colonist who understood the Maoris and their ways, was appointed to act as the European staff officer of the native contingent, co-operating with the chiefs Te Puni, Wi Tako Ngatata, and other tribal heads. The quality of the arms supplied the natives for their guerilla work was poor — so poor that many of the guns were unfit for use, and the ammunition had become wet and unserviceable. These friendly Maoris, however, made no delay in taking the field. Their total numbers were about two hundred and fifty; most of these assembled at Pito-one two or three days after the fight, and then marched out to a position between Fort Richmond and Boulcott's, where they built a temporary *kainga*.

The olden battle-ground is now the golfers' links. Boulcott's homestead of 1846 (Section 46/III) was close to the spot where the Lower Hutt Golf Club's house now stands. The frequent floods and the repeated changes of the river's course have considerably altered the original contour of the place, and the actual site of the stockade has been transformed to a gorse-covered waste of gravel.

The citizens appealed for arms. Muskets, accoutrements, and ammunition were served out to a large number of men, who were sworn in as Volunteers. The residents of Te Aro formed a Volunteer Corps a hundred and fifty strong, under Mr. Edward Daniell as captain, Mr. Kenneth Bethune as lieutenant, and Mr. G. D. Monteith as ensign. Nightly patrols were established to guard against an expected attack on the town, and strong lines of pickets of the Regulars, Volunteers, and Militia encircled the town and patrolled the outskirts. Captain Stanley landed seventy " Calliope " sailors to assist in the event of a hostile visit.

On the 15th June the Maoris killed with the tomahawk another settler, Richard Rush, near the present Lower Hutt Railway-station.

On the 16th June a composite force marched out from Boulcott's Farm on a reconnaissance towards the Taita district and the stretch of the Hutt River near that post. The object of Captain Reed, in command, was to acquaint himself with the tracks in the neighbourhood of the Taita and the fords across the river, and also to ascertain the position of the Maoris, who were believed to be in the vicinity. The force consisted of about fifty Regular troops, nine of the Hutt Militia, and fifteen Ngati-Awa Maoris. The main body of the Ngati-Awa, under Te Puni, meanwhile remained in their camp near the stockade. The track to the Taita was narrow and wet; the high jungly bush was on both flanks. When within about half a mile of the outpost at the Taita (which was two miles from Boulcott's Farm) the advance-guard emerged upon a new clearing, most of it a mass of fallen trees, forming perfect cover for an ambush. As the clearing was entered one of the Ngati-Awa men in the advance mounted a log to obtain a view of the surrounding felled timber and the track ahead. Just below him he saw some armed natives crouching. Firing his musket and shouting an alarm, he leaped down from the log and threw himself flat on his face on the ground. A volley followed instantly, delivered at about fifteen paces from behind the logs on the left flank of the road. The Ngati-Awa scouts and advance-guard, from cover on the same side of the track as the enemy, returned the fire; and the white troops, extending in skirmishing order, held the cover on the right flank of the road. Presently it was discovered that they were being outflanked, and a retirement was found necessary. The column fell back in good order on Boulcott's, carrying several wounded men.

Lieutenant Herbert was wounded. Half-way to the stockade the force was met by a relieving body headed by the subaltern in charge of the post and by Te Puni with a hundred men. The senior officer directed the subaltern to form an advance-guard in the direction of Boulcott's, and the stockade was reached at dark. The combined Ngati-Awa force, after seeing their white comrades into camp in safety, doubled back towards the scene of the action. Some of the enemy had gone; the others were busying themselves in digging up potatoes from one end of the clearing—it was partly for this purpose that they had crossed the river that day. Te Puni and his active fellows engaged those still on the ground, and the skirmish resulted in the withdrawal of the rebels, who recrossed the river near the Taita and took to the safety of the bush on the western hills.

In the meantime the Hutt Militiamen stationed at the Taita post—a small blockhouse surrounded by a stockade—had heard the sound of the battle in the bush, and had engaged in a brisk little skirmish of their own. Ensign White left the stockade with a sergeant and twelve men, and advanced in the direction of the firing. The little party of Militia came under fire very soon after they had entered the bush. They replied to the Maoris with coolness and skill, taking cover behind trees and fallen timber, and continued the engagement for more than an hour. At last, realizing that his detachment was in danger of being outflanked and surrounded by a superior force of the enemy—many of whom were armed with double-barrel guns—Mr. White withdrew to the stockade.

Notes.

Mr. Peter Speedy, of Belmont, Lower Hutt, who was born in Wellington in 1842, informs me that the Belmont Creek, which runs out through his property, was an old war-track of the Maoris between the Heretaunga and the Porirua districts. The trail led up the rocky bed of the creek for about half a mile to a place where the stream forked; thence there was an ascent up a steep and narrow forested spur. The natives had cleared a part of this ridge, which was only a few yards wide, and when Speedy was bushfelling there many years after the war he found the remains of huts which had been roofed with *totara* bark, also stones used in the earth-ovens, a rusted bayonet, a musket-barrel, and other relics of 1846. The lofty ridge was an excellent position for defence, and it had evidently been used as a temporary *pa* in the war-days. The ground falls precipitously away for several hundreds of feet on either side into the cañon-like valleys. It was no doubt by this route that the war-party descended on Boulcott's Farm in May, 1846; and it was this track also that the Militia and friendly natives took in the march to Paua-taha-nui. The track entered the gorge very close to the spot where the Belmont Railway-station now stands. The Maori name of the range in rear of Belmont is Te Raho-o-te-Kapowai.

Another Porirua war-track ascended the hills on the west side of the Hutt about a mile lower down the valley, not far from the present railway-station of Melling; it trended across the hills on the northern side of the peak called Pokai-mangumangu. When the Hon. Dr. Maui Pomare was clearing the site for his present home overlooking the Hutt he discovered the remains of an old Maori camp on a wooded terrace commanding a wide view over the valley. The track was up the adjacent spur near Mr. B. M. Wilson's house.

CHAPTER XII.

OPERATIONS AT PORIRUA.

To the relief alike of Wellington townsmen, outlying settlers, and Ngati-Awa friendlies, Governor Grey returned to Port Nicholson from Auckland on the 1st July in H.M.S. "Driver," and immediately infused energy into the lagging campaign against Te Rangihaeata. He revisited the military posts, made arrangements for the more speedy construction of the Wellington–Porirua Road and the road up the Hutt towards the Wairarapa, and had mutually satisfactory interviews with Te Puni and his leading chiefs. On the 12th July the "Calliope" landed at Paremata Point Major Last and a small reinforcement of twenty men of the 58th and forty-two of the 99th, under Lieutenants Page and De Winton and Ensign Blackburn. The frigate also took to Porirua a boat intended to be used as a gunboat in patrolling the inner shallow waters of Porirua and the Paua-taha-nui arm. The little craft was the longboat of the barque "Tyne," which had been wrecked on the Rimurapa rocks at Sinclair Head. An energetic midshipman of the "Calliope," Mr. H. F. McKillop, soon afterwards promoted to a lieutenancy, was given charge of the gunboat, which proved highly useful in the task of reconnoitring the upper waters and in occasional skirmishes with Rangihaeata's men. Mr. McKillop had already made a reconnaissance of Rangihaeata's position in a light four-oared boat, and had discovered that the rebel *pa*, although apparently not formidable in construction, was strategically strong in situation, being at the extreme head of Paua-taha-nui Inlet, partly surrounded by water, swamp, and bush, and difficult of approach either by land or by sea. This expedition (10th May) was a lively morning's adventure, in which McKillop and his comrades narrowly escaped being cut off.

McKillop's patrol would have been outmatched in a contest with the war-canoes which made a barbaric parade on the lake-like waters of Paua-taha-nui. A naval boat several times ventured up near the head of the arm, and on two occasions was compelled to retreat before these craft packed with Maoris. Two or three of the largest canoes were each manned by about fifty warriors, most of them armed with double-barrel guns. When, however, the longboat of the barque "Tyne" was procured and converted into a gunboat (oars and sail) with a 12-pounder carronade mounted in the bows, besides a small brass gun lent by Captain Stanley of the "Calliope" frigate, the scales were more evenly balanced. McKillop felt, with these two pieces of artillery and the addition of six bluejackets to his crew, that his little man-of-war was fit match for the whole of Rangihaeata's canoe flotilla.

On the morning of the 17th July the young naval officer, scanning the wooded coasts and the placid waters of the sea-lake,

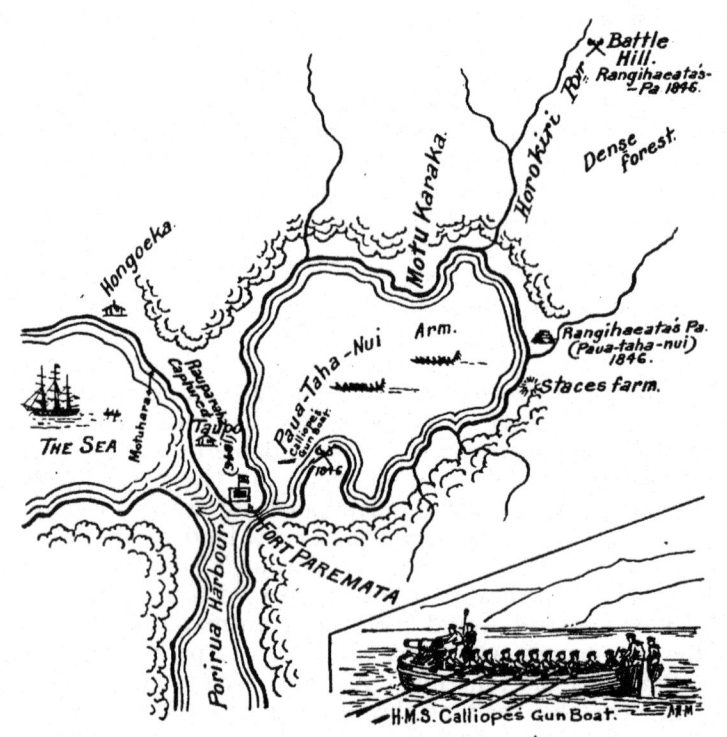

PORIRUA AND PAUA-TAHA-NUI (1846).

observed a large number of dark figures on the cleared part of a long point of hilly land which formed the largest promontory on the southern side of the Paua-taha-nui, and distant a little over a mile from Paremata camp. Through the narrow sea-passage where the railway-bridge now crosses the water near the Paremata fishing village McKillop followed the main channel of the tidal basin north-eastward until he was abreast of the promontory (to-day known as Long Point). Nothing was stirring on shore; every figure had vanished; but the officer ordered his crew to pull close in to the shore, and when within a few yards of the rocks fired a charge of canister into the *manuka* and small *ngaio* trees. Yells of mingled pain, fright, and rage arose, and from the bushes leaped a horde of shaggy-headed figures with flashing gun-barrels. It was only for a few seconds that their dusky faces were seen; they quickly took cover and opened a hot fire on the bluejackets. The gunners again raked the foliage with canister, and this fire brought out the Maoris. Firing as they came, they rushed into the open, and, seeing that the boat was within a few yards of the shore, many of them dashed into the shallow water on the edge of the main creek, attempting to board the boat. The men's beds and blankets had been lashed up in their hammocks and fastened round the top-sides and gunwale of the boat, forming a bullet-proof inner breastwork. The encounter was at such close quarters that it was almost impossible for the warriors to miss. Nearly every bullet struck the boat, and although she was coppered almost up to the gunwale many balls passed through, to be stopped by the sailors' bedding parapet.

The Maoris, it was now seen, were led by Te Rangihaeata himself. For the first time in the campaign he personally headed his men in a charge against the whites. The warriors made an attempt to board the boat, imagining that she was aground, so close was she to the point. One party made an attack upon the quarter, and, as the carronade in the bows did not bear upon these men, McKillop slewed his brass gun, which was on a swivel, and fired at them. The gun burst; the midshipman was knocked down, his eyebrows were singed off, and for some moments he was blinded by the explosion, and the flying lock cut his head. Fortunately, no other harm was done, and when McKillop had recovered from the shock and had washed the powder out of his eyes he was relieved to find that the Maoris had been beaten back from the boat's side, and that a charge of canister had checked the main party of assailants. Again the warriors came on, led by Rangihaeata, dashing out through the shallow water, some firing one barrel as they came and reserving the other for the boarding rush. The continued fire of canister from the carronade and McKillop's accurate use of his double-barrel gun finally beat back the assailants.

The crew completed their victory by firing several 12 lb. solid shot into the bushes where the Maoris had taken cover, and returned to Paremata.

By Proclamation dated the 18th June, signed by Captain George Grey, Lieutenant-Governor, the operation of martial law in the "Island of New Ulster," as the North Island was officially styled, was extended from Wainui to Wanganui. The district under martial.law was now the whole of that part of the Island to the southward of a line drawn from Wanganui on the west to Castle Point on the east coast; the Town of Wellington itself was excluded. Reinforcements were hurried round the coast to Porirua. This was the result of alarming news received from the north. A large war-party of Upper Wanganui natives was on the march down the coast to reinforce Te Rangihaeata and Te Mamaku; the main body had by this time reached Rangitikei, while an advance-party was at Waikawa, near Otaki. The expedition was headed by the fighting chiefs Ngapara (who was a near relative of Te Rangihaeata) and Maketu, two of the most turbulent warriors of the Wanganui country. This news was brought by a young Wanganui settler, Richard Deighton, who had chanced

Photo, J. C., 1918.]

RUINS OF FORT PAREMATA, PORIRUA.

to obtain sight of a letter bearing Te Rauparaha's signature, addressed to the inland and up-river natives of the Wanganui tribes, urgently inviting them to join their chief Te Mamaku and his ally Te Rangihaeata in the campaign against the European settlements. Mr. Deighton went to Mr. Samuel King, the Police Magistrate in Wanganui, and told him the substance of the letter, informing him also that he believed a war-party was being organized up the river with the object of joining the rebels in the Wellington district. In confirmation of this, the residents of Wanganui a few days later were startled by the appearance in the town of a body of over two hundred Maori warriors. Deighton, knowing this to be a subterfuge, induced the Magistrate to write a despatch to the Governor at Wellington, undertaking to deliver it into Captain Grey's hands in time to prevent the Wanganui war-party's coalition with the rebels at Porirua and the Hutt. The letter was written on very thin paper in Indian ink, and one of Deighton's sisters sewed it in the collar of his coat. On the following day the war-party left the Wanganui bank and set out on the march, accompanied, as was the Maori way, by a number of women, who carried food and cooked for their lords on the journey. Some of these women had their young children with them. The *pakeha* despatch-bearer joined them and marched with them, telling the leader Maketu that he was anxious to reach Wellington as soon as possible, as there was a box of goods awaiting him there from his father in England. After a series of adventures Deighton reached Wellington just in time to catch Governor Grey as he was about to leave for Auckland, and delivered to him not only the Wanganui despatch but also a letter to Rauparaha which Maketu had confidingly entrusted to him. He had left the Maoris at Rangitikei.

Grey acted quickly after assuring himself of Rauparaha's duplicity. He ordered a force of troops and armed police aboard the warship "Driver," with some bluejackets from the "Calliope." The "Driver" next morning anchored off Waikanae, in the strait between Kapiti Island and the long beach where the Waikanae River issues from its sand-dunes. Here Captain Grey went ashore and visited the Ngati-Awa Tribe; they were gathered in their *pa*, under Wiremu Kingi te Rangitaake, who afterwards fought the British troops in the Taranaki War. To Wiremu Kingi and his chief men the Governor explained the danger which existed of a coalition between the Wanganui war-party and Rangihaeata's force, and requested the assistance of the Waikanae people in preventing a junction. Kingi promised that if Maketu brought his *taua* along the beach through Ngati-Awa territory they would intercept and attack him, but told Grey that they could not take the tribe into the bush if the expedition left the coast route and travelled through the ranges to the head of Paua-taha-nui or the Hutt. With this attitude the Governor was satisfied; he satisfied himself also, from what he heard at Waikanae, that Rauparaha was playing the Government false. This fully decided him in his decision to strike swiftly. Rowing off again to the "Driver," Grey requested the commander to get under way and steam down past Porirua, as if going to Wellington, and then return after dark and anchor off the entrance to the harbour. This stratagem lulled any suspicions the Ngati-Toa and their wary chief might have entertained when they observed the warship on the coast.

The Ngati-Toa village of Taupo, where Te Rauparaha dwelt in fancied security with his wives, tribesmen, and slaves, stood on the northern side of the entrance to Porirua Harbour; the thatched, low-eaved huts, fenced in with palisading, occupied the sandy foreshore exactly where the seaside Township of Plimmerton stands to-day. A small stream flowed into the bay on the Paremata side of the settlement; the other or seaward side was bounded by a little knoll of a cape, the *wahi-tapu*, or holy place of the *pa;* it remains the only bit of Taupo held inviolate by the modern remnant of Ngati-Toa. The British military encampment

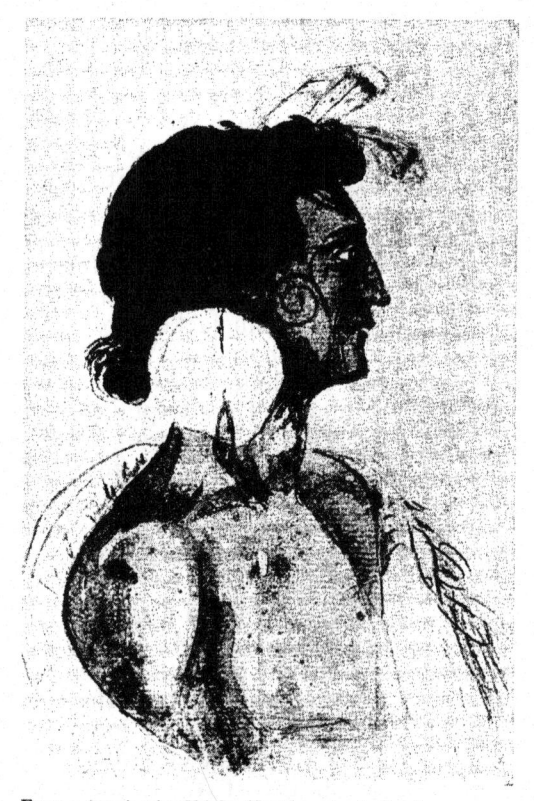

From a drawing by Charles Heaphy, about 1840.]

TE RANGIHAEATA.

("The Dawn of Day.")

on the Paremata sandy flat in the inner bay was about three-quarters of a mile distant from the *pa*.

In spite of the naval patrol on the waters of the inner harbour the hostile Maoris maintained their communication with Rauparaha and his people at Taupo, either by canoe at night or by the bush tracks on the northern side of the Paua-taha-nui arm. Gunpowder and other supplies for Rangihaeata's men were carried through the bush by these tracks from Pae-kakariki and Taupo. Unknown to the British, Rangihaeata himself was in Taupo *pa* about a week before the "Driver" made her surprise visit. He spent a night in Rauparaha's house. In the morning his mind was filled with forebodings. He said to his kinsman, "O Rau, last night I dreamed a dream, a dream of evil to come. It will be well if you come away with me. Leave this place; it is full of danger."

He strongly counselled Rauparaha to leave the sea-coast and go with him to Paua-taha-nui, where he would be safe. But Rauparaha, although uneasy, declined to leave Taupo. His wife Te Akau was ill and unable to travel. Te Akau was his chief wife; she had come down the west coast with him from Kawhia in the great migration of Ngāti-Toa a quarter of a century previously, and he was not willing to leave her now, when she was unable to move. Despite his nephew's premonition and warning, therefore, he decided to remain at Taupo for the present. Rangihaeata himself returned at once by the bush track to his *pa* at the head of the harbour.

It was towards midnight on the 22nd July that the "Driver" with her force of special-service men anchored off the bay. The Governor and Captain Stanley sent for Mr. McKillop, the midshipman of the "Calliope" who had distinguished himself on the Paua-taha-nui patrol. To the young officer the Governor unfolded his scheme. Te Rauparaha was to be arrested on a charge of treason; the chief Te Kanae and several other Maoris of Taupo were also to be captured. It was necessary to take the wily old man by surprise, and McKillop was chosen for the task, as he was acquainted with the Maoris and their village. Major Durie, the officer in charge of the Wellington armed police, was requested to capture Te Kanae and the other men. Mr. Deighton was instructed to go ashore with the party and interpret the charge of treason to Rauparaha and assist in making him a prisoner.

With the first glimmering of day McKillop and his boat's crew landed on the rocks about a quarter of a mile eastward of the *pa*. The other boats were busily employed landing the two hundred redcoats and bluejackets and the police.

"If the natives come out of their *pa* take no notice of them, but follow me silently," said the interpreter to McKillop; "I know where the old man's house is." Wading the small stream near the *pa*, the little party ran as quietly as they could up to the middle of the village, and Deighton pointed out Rauparaha's *whare*. It was now fully daylight. The arresting-party hastened on to the chief's house, and there they came upon Rauparaha; the suspicious old warrior had just crawled out through the low doorway into the thatched porch. His wife Te Akau was by his side ; she called the customary greeting, "*Haere mai, haere mai!*" Deighton informed Rauparaha that the force had come by the Governor's order to take him on board the man-of-war to be tried for having given the arms, ammunition, and provisions with which he had been supplied by the Government to Te Rangihaeata, then in open rebellion against the Government.

The interpreter had scarcely spoken the words before the old savage, who was seated immediately in front of the low doorway, threw himself back with an extraordinarily active movement for a man of his age, and in an instant seized a *taiaha*, with which he made a blow at his wife's head, realizing that she had been the indirect cause of his arrest. McKillop, who had been standing on the alert within arm's reach of Rauparaha, jumped forward and warded off the blow with his pistol. At the top of his voice the chief shouted, "*Ngati-Toa e! Ngati-Toa e!*" It was a call to his tribe for rescue. Out from the *whares* rushed the Maoris, but their chieftain was already in the grip of the sailormen. McKillop had him by the throat, while his four men secured him by legs and arms, and held him in spite of his desperate struggles and the fact that his naked body was as slippery as an eel's, coated with a mixture of *kokowai*, or red ochre and shark-oil. The coxswain of McKillop's boat, an old sailor named Bob Brenchley, was the first of the men to grip an arm of the prisoner. Rauparaha savagely fixed his teeth in Brenchley's bare arm. The bluejacket laughingly shook his arm free, and with his open hand lightly smacked Rauparaha's face, exclaiming, "Why, ye damned old cannibal, d'ye want to eat a fellow up alive?" Rauparaha, in spite of his struggles, was carried down to McKillop's pinnace, which had been rowed along to the beach in front of the *pa*. The village was by this time surrounded by the force from the "Driver," and any attempts at rescue were useless. Captain Stanley, of the "Calliope," who had just come ashore from the "Driver," called out, "Here, you, Mr. Deighton, it was you who discovered the old devil's treachery; you shall, if you like, have the honour of taking him off."

The interpreter thanked the naval captain, and jumped into the boat. Mr. McKillop remained ashore to complete his work, and the captive was quickly rowed off to the war-steamer. As the crew pulled out they passed Motuhara, a small beach settlement where some of the Ngati-Toa lived. Rauparaha again lifted up his voice in a cry to his tribe for rescue : "*Ngati-Toa e! Ngati-Toa e!*" The interpreter told the chief that if a canoe did put off to the rescue it would only take back a dead man, for he (Deighton) would certainly shoot him first. The old man, looking the interpreter directly in the eyes, said bitterly, "Shoot now ; it would be better I were dead among my own tribe than alive as a prisoner and slave in the hands of an enemy."

OPERATIONS AT PORIRUA.

Major Durie and his police had little trouble in arresting the minor chiefs, Wiremu te Kanae, Hohepa Tamaihengia, and two or three others. Every *whare* in Taupo and in the villages out westward of the point, Motuhara and Hongoeka, was searched for

From a drawing by John Bambridge, at St. John's College, Tamaki, Auckland, 16th June, 1847.]

TE RAUPARAHA.

guns and ammunition. Over thirty muskets, many tomahawks, a quantity of ball cartridge, eight casks and kegs of gunpowder, cartouche-boxes, and a small 4-pounder cannon were seized.

While the sailors and police were transferr'ng the captured arms to the boats the word came that a large party of Rangihaeata's men was putting off in canoes to assist Rauparaha, the alarm of an attack on Taupo *pa* having reached the stronghold at Paua-taha-nui. McKillop and his bluejackets were quickly aboard their gunboat and pulling up towards Paua-taha-nui to meet the Maoris. There were fifty men in a war-canoe paddling down the arm, but they put about and retreated at their utmost speed. The naval boat rowed up in pursuit until the shallows at the harbour-head were reached, opening fire with the bow carronade. The Maoris were chased back into their *pa* with McKillop's round shot flying about them; then five or six shots were fired into the stockade on the hill where the midshipman had enjoyed his morning's reconnaissance some weeks previously.

A few hours later Wellington was astonished by the news of the Governor's well-planned *coup*. The chiefs were transferred to the "Calliope," and in that frigate they were detained as prisoners of war. No charge was formulated against them, but it was undesirable that they should be at large, and the cause of peace was certainly advanced by their capture. Te Rauparaha was well treated; he was a guest rather than a prisoner. He was taken to Auckland in the frigate, and was permitted to visit his son, Tamehana te Rauparaha, at St. John's College, Selwyn's establishment at the Tamaki; he was given numerous presents, and entertained with the consideration to which his rank in the Maori nation entitled him. It was his delight to appear in a naval captain's epauletted uniform; our sketch—the best drawing of Te Rauparaha in existence—shows him attired in this costume on his visit to St. John's College in 1847. He was not permitted to return to his tribe until January, 1848, when he was landed at Otaki by H.M.S. "Inflexible." By that time his power for strife had passed. Possibly he was a more dignified figure as a captive than in his olden home at Otaki, shorn of its ancient savage glory. In Tamehana te Rauparaha's manuscript narrative of his father's life (Grey Collection, Auckland Public Library) there is a poetic speech delivered by the old man to his son when in detention aboard the "Calliope" in Port Nicholson after Tamehana's return from the North: "*Kei mea mai te tangata tenei au te noho pouri nei ia au e noho taurekareka atu nei i runga i taku kaipuke manuao nei i a 'Karaipi'; kaore rawa aku pouri, kaore au e mohio ana e noho taurekareka ana au. Ki taku whakaaro e noho rangatira ana au, he whare rangatira i a aku korero e korero atu.*" ("Let not men think that I abide in grief as I now remain in slavery aboard my warship the 'Calliope'; no, it is not so. I know not any grief, though I so remain a prisoner. In my mind I am abiding here as a chief, and my abode is an abode of a chief.")

The son in his manuscript likens these words to those of the Apostle Paul, who declared that his prison-house was a royal dwelling. A *pakeha* poet had expressed very much the same sentiment when he wrote, long before Rauparaha's day—-

> Stone walls do not a prison make,
> Nor iron bars a cage.

NOTES.

The incident of Rangihaeata's dream (*moemoea*) and his warning to Rauparaha, and the old chief's attack upon his wife, was related to me by the nearest surviving relative of Rangihaeata, Heni te Whiwhi (died 1921), of Otaki. She said the reason Rauparaha made a blow at Te Akau when he was informed that he was under arrest was that he instantly remembered that had it not been for her illness he would have been in a safe retreat inland. McKillop and the other Europeans imagined erroneously that Rauparaha struck at his wife because he believed she had betrayed him.

After the war a block of land on the coast at Hongoeka, near Plimmerton, was made over by Rangihaeata to some members of the Ngati-Mutunga Tribe in return for their services in carrying gunpowder from the coast to his *pa* at Paua-taha-nui. These Ngati-Mutunga, some of them old men, made up small casks of powder in flax-basket *pikaus* or back-loads, and transported them through the forests and ranges of Pukerua and along the northern shore of the bay.

CHAPTER XIII.

PAUA-TAHA-NUI AND HOROKIRI.

A traveller taking the main road north from Wellington City and driving round the head of the Paua-taha-nui Inlet will pass within a few yards of the spot where Te Rangihaeata and his men built their palisaded and rifle-pitted stronghold in 1846. The exact site of the *pa* can readily be identified. The spot is occupied to-day by a steepled church of old-fashioned design, crowning as in a picture the green hill above the one-street village of Paua-taha-nui — now misspelled Pahautanui. The salt water once flowed at high tide nearly to the foot of that rounded hill; the land was raised several feet by the earthquake of 1855, and now the one-time flats of sand and mud are covered with grass, and the beach where Maori war-canoes and *pakeha* boats lay long ago has become a sheep-paddock. A little stream comes down from the hills around the eastern and southern foot of the mound, and joins the sea 200 yards below the place where our main road crosses on a wooden bridge. The hill is small-wooded like a park; white grave-stones gleam among the shrubs and trees on its seaward face. It is a slumberous pretty spot—

> This old churchyard on the hill
> That keeps the green graves of the dead.

Transformed as the place is by the lapse of nearly three-quarters of a century, one still may reconstruct in imagination the hilltop as it was in Rangihaeata's year of war. It was a cleverly chosen retreat, convenient to the canoe-stream and the harbour, yet sufficiently removed from deep water to be unapproachable by heavily gunned war-vessels, and beyond effective musket-range from any but the smallest boats. It was protected on three sides by water and marshes. On the south and south-east there was a cliff, at its highest about 30 feet, now thickly covered with trees, dropping to a backwater of the little river. On the scarped front—the west—were the curving stream, with its swampy borders, and the salt water; on the north and north-west were swamps and small streams. The stream on the south was navigable for good-sized boats and canoes, which could be brought close up under the walls of the *pa*. The grass- and shrub-grown scarps in the English churchyard appear to mark the line of olden ditch-work on the south and south-west faces of the *pa*. In the paddock in rear of the church there are shallow trench and potato-pit excavations and levelled spaces indicating the sites of houses.

Rangihaeata's stronghold, on the spot where the church now stands, was in the form of a parallelogram, with two rows of palisades, a ditch within the second row, 6 feet wide and 5 feet deep, and *whares* with underground communication. The outer stockade was a weak curtain, but the inner palisades were heavy timbers up to 10 inches or a foot in thickness and about 15 feet high. The fort was about eighty paces in length and half that in width; there were flanking defences, and there were

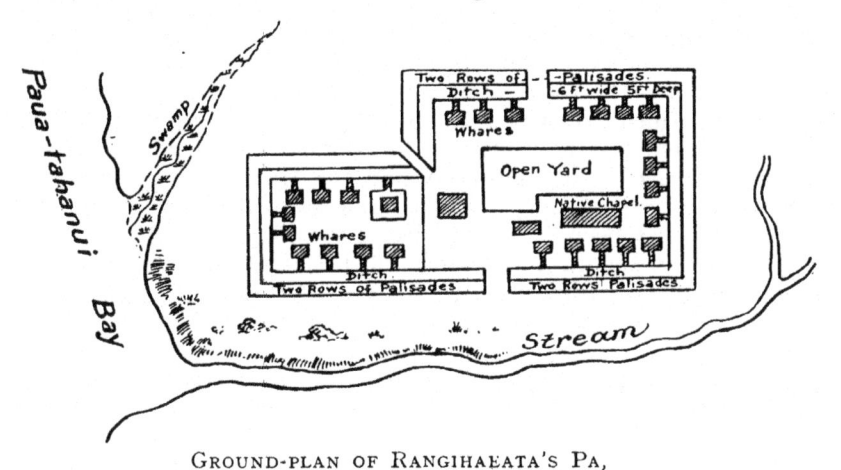

GROUND-PLAN OF RANGIHAEATA'S PA,

At the head of Paua-taha-nui Inlet, 1846.

intricate interior passage-ways, some on the surface fenced with *manuka* stakes, so narrow that only one man could pass at a time, and some underground. Shell-proof shelters covered with slabs and tree-trunks and earth were connected with the main trench by covered ways, and the main trench itself was cut with traverses protective against an enfilading fire down the ditch. The rear, as usual in Maori *pas*, was the weakest in defence; but the problem would have been to reach this part, naturally guarded as it was by water, swamp, and bush.

Captain Grey decided to approach the *pa* from the rear. He ordered a body of Militia, police, and Ngati-Awa friendlies to march across the hills from the Hutt and endeavour to carry the place by surprise. The Regular soldiers were excluded from the expedition, not being suitable troops for bush-work. On the afternoon of the 31st July this force, consisting of fifty men of the Hutt Militia, thirteen of the armed police, and 150 Ngati-Awa Maoris, left the Hutt Valley on their march over the hills. The Militia were under the command of Captain McDonogh and Lieutenant White, and the police under Mr. Chetham Strode. One Imperial officer, Ensign Middleton, of the 58th Regiment, accompanied the expedition, and Mr. Ludlam and Mr. Stilling joined as volunteers. The native friendlies were under the charge of Mr. D. Scott. The column ascended the hills on the western side of the Hutt River nearly opposite Boulcott's Farm stockade, and followed a native track over the ranges to the upper valley of the Paua-taha-nui; this track was the route used by the enemy in their raids from the Porirua district upon the Hutt. Next morning (1st August) the two foremost guides encountered a scout of the enemy, a minor Upper Wanganui chief named Whare-aitu, otherwise known grotesquely as "Martin Luther." He was captured. (In September he was court-martialled for rebellion and hanged at Paremata.) The capture was made within half a mile of the *pa*, and the incident was seen by some women from the hill stockade, which was now visible. Screaming out an alarm, they ran off to the *pa*. The main body and the Militia and police now came doubling up, and the whole force moved quickly forward. The *pa* had just been evacuated when the force rushed it.

The next stage in the history of Paua-taha-nui *pa* was its conversion into an Imperial military post. It was garrisoned by detachments of Regular regiments, and for a considerable period after hostilities had ceased it was occupied as an advanced post covering the construction of the main road northward to Pae-kakariki and Waikanae by a company of the 65th, who had arrived in Wellington on the 22nd July, 1846, by the barque "Levant" from Sydney—the first of that regiment to reach New Zealand. The force landed by the "Levant" consisted of Captain O'Connell, Captain Newenham, Lieutenant McCoy, Lieutenant Turner, and Assistant-Surgeon White (65th); Ensign Barker (58th); eight sergeants, seven corporals, and 162 rank and file of the 58th and 65th Regiments.

Our illustration showing the Paua-taha-nui post as it was at this period, with the main Maori stockading retained, is from a water-colour drawing by Lieut.-Colonel W. A. McCleverty, who was sent to Wellington from Sydney at the end of 1846 as Land Claims Commissioner, and was afterwards given command of the military operations at Wanganui.

The scene of hostilities now shifted northward. Te Rangi-haeata, it was discovered, had taken post in the wooded ranges high up above the Horokiri (now usually known as Horokiwi), a small river which has its source in the broken country immediately east of Pae-kakariki. The Government forces were strengthened—in numbers, at any rate—by the addition of over a hundred Ngati-Toa men from the Porirua villages, under their chief Rawiri Puaha. On the 3rd August, 1846, a forward movement was commenced. The forces assembled at Rangihaeata's lately abandoned quarters totalled 250 bayonets — Regulars of the 58th, 65th, and 99th, the Hutt Militia, and the Wellington armed police—and the highly useful Ngati-Awa friendlies, numbering 150. On Monday, 3rd August, the force began the march up the thickly wooded valley of the Horokiri, the natives in the advance. Puaha led his tribe ; Mr. D. Scott and Mr. Swainson

From a drawing by Colonel W. A. McCleverty, 1849.]

PAUA-TAHA-NUI STOCKADE.

were in command of the Ngati-Awa. The troops were commanded by Major Last, with Major Arney second in command. Captain Stanley, of the "Calliope," accompanied the expedition. A number of bluejackets from the frigate came up on the following day, under Mr. McKillop. A recent camp of Rangihaeata, in the unroaded woods three miles from the harbour, was occupied for the night. Suspended from the roof of one of the *whares* the Militia found the bugle which had been taken from the gallant bugler William Allen, killed in the fight at Boulcott's Farm.

The Maori party in the advance continued the march early next day (4th August), leaving the rest of the expedition to await their report. The natives wore blue-serge blouses, with "V.R." in large white letters front and back, a precaution necessary in bush warfare, where it was otherwise difficult to distinguish between friendly and hostile Maoris. The Maori scouts followed the trail until they found that the enemy's position was on the summit of the high steep range to the right (east) of the narrow gorge, where the flooded Horokiri came pouring down into the valley.

Early on the 6th August Major Last gave orders for the advance up this range to the east of the gorge. The white force was in two divisions. The first consisted of seven officers and 127 rank and file of the seamen from the "Calliope," the Regular soldiers, the Militia, and the armed police, under Major Arney (58th). The second division, of five officers and 117 men of similar detail, was under the command of Captain Armstrong (99th). The Maori allies under their white officers and tribal chiefs led the way, feeling for the enemy; then came a detachment of Pioneers with axes and other tools to cut a way through the bush. These Pioneers were troops who had been employed on the Porirua roadworks; they were under the command of Lieutenant Elliott (99th). The troops began to advance at 9 a.m., and struggled up through the wet bush that choked the mountain-side. The steep lower slopes surmounted, the column worked up along a narrow ridge, which proved to be that selected by Rangihaeata for his temporary fortification.

THE ENGLISH CHURCH AT PAUA-TAHA-NUI,

On the site of Rangihaeata's fortification.

The crest of the range was toilsomely approached; the axes of the Pioneers made the forest ring. It was a curious method of advancing to attack, for every tree felled ahead of the troops made their position more vulnerable. An old colonial officer, describing to the writer his bush-fighting experiences in the "sixties," expressed the basic principle of forest warfare exactly when he said, "We very soon learned to look on a tree as a friend." The Imperial soldier had not gripped that useful lesson in the "forties." Major Last's idea of skilful tactics was to "cut away the wood," as he expressed it in his despatch, in his advance upon the bush-entrenched foe.

The friendly natives now reported that Te Rangihaeata's position was right ahead on the crown of the ridge. At a point where it narrowed to a few yards, above a very steep slope, they had dug a trench and constructed a *parepare*, or breastwork of tree-trunks and earth; in front of this a fairly clear glacis had been made by felling the bush for a short distance, so that no sheltered frontal attack could be made. Major Last, after reconnoitring the place, came to the conclusion that the fortification was "very strong," composed, as he believed, of logs of timber placed horizontally one over another, with loopholes for musketry fire. In reality the breastwork was not a formidable affair, but the enemy held a naturally very strong position, only assailable with success by turning the flanks, an operation for which the Regular troops could not be used in such country.

A party of about twenty, consisting of soldiers, bluejackets, and Militia, under Lieutenant G. H. Page (58th), Ensign H. M. Blackburn (99th), Mr. McKillop, and Lieutenant McDonogh, advanced to within about 50 yards of the enemy's position. The main body of the troops was halted in close formation about 100 yards below the crest of the ridge. The customary method of the frontal rush so much favoured by British officers of that day was suggested, but now Major Last, warned by the experience of his fellow-soldiers in Heke's War, declined to expose his force to so great a risk. As it was, the charge thus far proved fatal to three of the British. Ensign Blackburn, who was acting-brigade-major, was killed by a Maori concealed in a tree. The troops fell back a few yards, and most of them took cover behind a large tree which had been felled across the ridge some 80 yards below the *pa*, and under a breastwork thrown up at this spot by the Pioneers.

For several hours an irregular but heavy fire was maintained by the troops and their native allies, and some thousands of rounds were expended for very little result. Firing lasted until about dark, when Major Last, fearing that the enemy would attack the troops in this position, very unfavourable for defence against a night raid, marched the greater number of the soldiers down the hill to the camp on the flat. The bluejackets meanwhile were despatched back through the bush to their boats at Paua-taha-nui, with orders to go to the Paremata fort and bring up two mortars.

McKillop and his sailors, with a number of Royal Artillery men, returned on the following day (7th August), bringing two small mortars and ammunition. It was a wearisome march from the Paua-taha-nui to the camp at the foot of the range, for everything had to be carried on the back over the narrow and slippery bush trail. The pieces were mounted on a terrace close to the right bank of the Horokiri Stream, and served by a detachment of a dozen Royal Artillery men under Captain Henderson. The shelling occupied most of the day on the 8th August, at a range of about three-quarters of a mile; about eighty shells were fired.

126   NEW ZEALAND WARS.

At the same time the Militia, armed police, and friendly natives, joined by a number of the more energetic Regular officers, skirmished with the enemy in the bush near the *pa*. The artillerymen soon found the range, and many shells fell in and around the rebel position.

Major Last by this time had come to the conclusion that it was not desirable either to advance his Regulars farther or to remain in his present camp. On the 10th August the troops were marched

Drawn by A. H. Messenger, from a water-colour sketch by Lieutenant G. H. Page (58th Regt.), 1846.]

THE ATTACK ON RANGIHAEATA'S POSITION, HOROKIRI.

back to Paua-taha-nui, whence the majority were boated down the harbour to the main camp. The natives remained on the range for a week longer, working at their palisades and occasionally skirmishing with the foe. On the 13th it was discovered that Te Rangihaeata and his whole force had quietly abandoned the place under cover of darkness and rain. The weather was now exceedingly wet and stormy, and the friendlies were unable to take up the chase until the 17th. The enemy had retired northward along the narrow forested ridges east of Horokiri and Paekakariki. The Ngati-Awa Maoris took the lead, under their chiefs Te Puni and Wi Tako Ngatata; the white officers with them were Mr. Servantes, of the 99th Regiment, interpreter to the forces, and Mr. D. Scott.

The scene of the engagement of the 6th August, 1846, is the summit of a steep and lofty range on Mr. N. Abbott's sheep-run at Horokiri. Mr. Abbott's homestead, near the foot of the range and just at the entrance of the Horokiri Gorge (through which the main north road runs to Pae-kakariki), is on or very close to the site of the main camp of the troops, under Major Last, on their expedition to Rangihaeata's mountain stronghold. The summit of the steep and narrow ridge on which the rebels made their stand is about three-quarters of a mile north of the homestead, and probably between 700 and 800 feet above sea-level. Far below it on the west runs the main road, winding through a deep and narrow wooded gorge; the bottom of the ravine is occupied by the Horokiri Stream. We take a leading spur which leads to the main ridge, and we find that we are following the same route as that taken by the troops when all this region was blanketed with unroaded bush. A little distance up the spur there is a trench or long rifle-pit, now more than half filled in and softly grassed; it does not run across the spur but almost parallel with it. Several hundred feet higher up we climb on to the knife-back which leads to the knoll on the sky-line where the Maoris lay behind their *parepare*, or breastworks of earth and logs. Fire-charred logs lie about the hillside, and the slopes are black-pencilled with the stumps of the *wheki*, a fern-tree whose butt is as hard as ironbark and almost indestructible. It was this fern-tree that the Maoris largely used in building up their *parepare* of horizontal timbers. In a slight dip in the ridge a line of depression in the turf running partly across the narrow saddle is readily recognized as the trench cut by the Government forces on the 6th August, after the encounter in which Lieutenant Blackburn was killed. The spot is about 100 yards below the fortified summit of the ridge. A few yards onward the ridge rises into a small knoll; passing over this there is a rather steep ascent to the crest of Battle Hill, as the site of the *pa* is locally called. The advance is not in a direct line; the sharp main spur, running roughly north and south, now twists to the north-east, until the narrow crest of the range is reached, when it again trends due northward. From east to west the top of the hill is only ten paces in width, and forty paces on its greater axis north and south. The face of the Maori breastwork was

SUMMIT OF THE RIDGE, HOROKIRI, HELD BY RANGIHAEATA, 1846.

Photos by F. G. Layton, 1920.]

THE REAR OF RANGIHAEATA'S POSITION, HOROKIRI, 1846.

immediately on the south end of the crest, completely commanding the troops' line of approach from the south and south-west. All traces of logwork have long since disappeared, but the trench and the shelter-pit dug immediately in rear of the *parepare* are readily traced. The ruined trench, after the lapse of three-quarters of a century, is still about 3 feet deep, and its ditch-like terminal on the verge of the precipitous slope on the south-east side is well marked. The trench extends across the ridge a distance of 26 paces; it is roughly zigzag in outline, and about its centre there is an advanced rifle-pit; the breastwork in front of this would have formed a bastion for enfilading the front of the work on right and left. Four paces in rear of the line of trench, at the north end, there is a grassy *rua*, a pit 9 feet long and 3 feet deep, occupying half the width of the ridge-crown. It was originally roofed over with earth and timber as a shell-proof shelter.

The Regular troops and the Militia having been withdrawn from the field, the operations in the forest chase were left entirely to the Ngati-Awa allies, with their white officers, and the Ngati-Toa, under Rawiri Puaha. The scene of the pursuit was the roughest imaginable terrain for campaigning. Te Rangihaeata's refuge was the broken country a few miles east of the coast between Pae-kakariki and Waikanae. Here the forested ranges slant steeply to the narrow belt of coastal flats; inland the landscape is a confusion of sharp and lofty ridges and narrow cañon-like valleys each discharging a rocky-bedded rapid stream. Into this wild bit of New Zealand range and wood Te Rangihaeata and his band were driven, more than half-starved, short of ammunition, but determined to make no submission. They could move but slowly because of the number of women and children, and this consideration impelled them to construct temporary fortifications at suitable places, similar to that at Horokiri, where they could make a stand and give the non-combatants time to move ahead. It would have been a simple matter to have descended to the level country on the sea-coast north of Pae-kakariki, but here retreat would have been barred by Wiremu Kingi and his branch of Ngati-Awa, who had promised Governor Grey to block the progress of rebel war-parties either north or south along the beach.

There was one sharp skirmish in the pursuit; this was on the seaward side of the Pouawha Range, inland of Wainui. A volley killed three of the Ngati-Awa friendlies; in the fight which followed their antagonists lost four shot dead, including Te Pau, a chief of Ngati-Rangatahi, who had led the party that killed the Gillespies at the Hutt. The fugitives made good their retreat along the ranges inland of Waikanae and into the Manawatu country. Te Mamaku and his men returned to Wanganui. The second Wanganui war-party, whose intentions had been frustrated by Mr. Deighton's march with a despatch to the Governor, had abandoned the expedition on hearing of the arrest of Te Rauparaha. Te Rangihaeata entrenched himself with about a hundred men on a mound called Paeroa, which rose like an island from the swamps between Horowhenua and the Manawatu. Here he declared the soldiers would never get him. The *pa* was named Poroutawhao; the site is now a native farm, between Levin and Foxton. The low hill upon which the palisaded stronghold was built was all but surrounded by miles of deep flax-swamps, threaded with slow-running watercourses, and dotted with lagoons swarming with wild ducks. Here, like Hereward the Wake on the mound that was

THE SITE OF RANGIHAEATA'S ENTRENCHMENT, HOROKIRI RIDGE.

his last stand amidst the fens of Ely, Te Rangihaeata and his company of fight-loving patriots lived in barbaric independence, and feasted on the eels that teemed in the swamps and the wild-fowl they snared on the lagoons and rushy runways.

Te Rangihaeata died at Otaki in 1856, from measles aggravated by a cold bath in a river. He was buried at his *pa* in Poroutawhao. So passed a type of the old pagan order, a true irreconcilable, averse to anything of the white man's but his weapons of war. He was seldom seen in any dress but the picturesque native garments of flax; and a commanding figure he was, tomahawk in hand, standing 2 inches over 6 feet, draped in a finely woven and beautifully patterned *parawai* or *kaitaka* cloak.

CHAPTER XIV.

THE WAR AT WANGANUI.

The New Zealand Company's settlement at Wanganui — or Petre, as it was officially named in compliment to Lord Petre, one of the directors of the Company—was the most unfortunate of all the colonies planted by the Wakefields. The first settlers under the Company took up their land there in 1841, but the natives very soon disputed their title to many of the sections, declaring that they had never sold the land. "Our case is indeed a hard one," Dr. Wilson, of Wanganui, wrote in his diary in 1846. "Up to the commencement of our present war state we had waited more than six years for the proprietorship of land here which we paid for in London upwards of seven years ago; but that promised land has never yet been delivered up to us." When some of the unfortunate settlers, despairing of ever being established in secure occupation of their farm sections outside the Town of Wanganui, applied to the Company for land elsewhere in New Zealand they were informed that only in the Wanganui district had they a claim for land. Those who left Wanganui were compelled to purchase afresh elsewhere, and those who remained presently found themselves compelled to arm for defence against the Maoris with whom they had hoped to live in neighbourly peace. The Company blamed the Government for preventing selection according to the conditions of sale, but Governor Hobson declared that nothing contained in the agreement between the Government and the Company had any such reference to their engagements with private parties, and held that the Company was bound to fulfil the conditions it had entered into for the disposal of their lands. Neither Hobson nor Fitzroy, however, was able to improve the unhappy position. Not until a campaign had been fought and Wanganui relieved from a state of siege, and the troubles adjusted by Governor Grey and Mr. (afterwards Sir Donald) McLean, was the peaceful progress of the district assured.

In 1845 there were not many more than two hundred Europeans in Wanganui; there were about sixty houses. This little outpost of colonization was practically surrounded by Maoris. The native population along the Wanganui River was estimated in 1846 at four thousand, most of whom were on very friendly terms with the settlers themselves, though they had no love for the New Zealand Company. Living was rough and primitive, but food was abundant; the Maoris of the numerous villages from Wanganui Heads inland plied a diligent canoe-paddle, bringing in their cargoes of pigs, potatoes, *kumara*, vegetable marrows, and pumpkins for sale by barter. Governor Grey in 1846 investigated the condition of the settlement, and made arrangements for the completion of the purchase of 40,000 acres. Major Richmond, the Superintendent of the Southern District, was deputed to settle the details. It was not until 1848, however, that the sale was finally closed. The area of purchase was increased to 80,000 acres, extending to the Kai-iwi River.

In December of 1846 the frigate "Calliope" and the Government brig "Victoria" brought up from Wellington and landed at Wanganui 180 men of the 58th Regiment, under Captain Laye and Lieutenant Balneavis, four Royal Artillery men with two 12-pounder guns, Lieutenant (afterwards Captain) T. B. Collinson, R.E., and Mr. Tyrone Power, D.A.C.G. These troops set about the work of fortifying the town. The warship also brought up the small gunboat which had been used in the Porirua patrols. Lieutenant Holmes, R.N., was detailed to command the gunboat-crew; with him was a young midshipman of the "Calliope." On the 16th April, 1847, a minor chief of the Wanganui people, by name Ngarangi, went to the midshipman's quarters to receive payment for some work done. The juvenile officer, by way of a joke, presented a pistol at him; the charge exploded, and Ngarangi received a wound in the head. He was well tended, and soon began to recover. He told his people that the wound was accidental; nevertheless a small party determined to exact *utu* for the blood-letting, and so precipitate war. Six of them attacked the home of Mr. J. A. Gilfillan, in the Mataraua Valley, severely wounded Gilfillan, and killed his wife and three children with the tomahawk; a daughter of sixteen was wounded. Five of the murderers were captured by a party of friendly natives, under Hone Wiremu Hipango, and four of them were court-martialled in Wanganui and hanged on the Rutland Stockade hill.

The natives attached to the Europeans by ties of friendship or by the teachings of their missionary, Richard Taylor, agreed that the execution of the tomahawk-party was a proper punishment. By far the greater number of the Wanganui warriors, however, resolved to take up arms to avenge the deaths of the four. The execution of Whare-aitu by the military at Paremata in the previous year was also a provocative factor.

The fortification which came to be called the Rutland Stockade was constructed on a sandy hill about 70 feet above the level of the river, near the northern end of the then small settlement of Wanganui. This height, the most commanding ground in the town, was known to the Maoris as Puke-namu (Sandfly Hill). It was the terminal of a gentle ridge which extended westward to the long hill whose forested slopes were given the name of St. John's Wood. The space enclosed by the stockade on the level summit of the hill measured 60 yards by 30 yards. The palisading consisted of rough timbers and whole trees, 9 inches or more in thickness, set closely together, sunk 3 or 4 feet in the sandy soil, and standing 8 feet high above ground. The tops of the logs were pointed ; this shed the water off and prevented decay. These uprights were braced by two inner horizontal rails, and loopholes for musket-fire were cut in the stockade all round. The two 12-pounder guns landed by the "Calliope"

RUTLAND STOCKADE AND BLOCKHOUSES, WANGANUI.

This photograph, taken in the early "eighties," shows in the foreground the monument to the friendly Maoris killed in the battle with the Hauhaus on Moutoa Island, Wanganui River, in 1864.

were mounted in the stockade, one at each end. Within the enclosure were built two strong wooden blockhouses, the first blockhouses with overhanging upper storeys built in the North Island. Upon the plan of these structures were modelled most of the frontier blockhouses built during the wars of the "sixties." The larger of the two, designed for the accommodation of eighty soldiers, consisted of two buildings, one 60 feet by 20 feet, on the ground-floor plan, and one, at right angles to it, measuring 20 feet by 20 feet. The smaller blockhouse, with a ground floor of 40 feet by 20 feet, was occupied by twenty soldiers.

These blockhouses were of two storeys, the upper floor projecting 3 feet over the lower building. The lower storey was 10-feet high and the upper one 8 feet. The lower walls were built of heavy and thick timbers, proof against all projectiles likely to be used by the Maoris. The main uprights, 6 feet apart, were 12 inches square; the intervening spaces were filled in with horizontal pieces 6 inches square, and the whole was lined inside with 1-inch boards. Smaller scantlings, bullet-proof, were used in the upper storey. The flooring of the upper storey was 2½ inches thick. The projecting part of the upper floor could be raised on hinges between each girder, for musketry fire. Both storeys were loopholed with horizontal slits, 4 feet in length and 6 inches in width, filled in with glass and shuttered outside.

This well-planned and solidly constructed fort, frowning over the little town and inspiring confidence in the settlers, cost between £3,000 and £4,000. For many a year it stood there on Puke-namu Hill, garrisoned by Imperial soldiers until well on toward the end of the " sixties," and was afterwards used by the Armed Constabulary. When the 57th Regiment arrived the original palisading was replaced by sawn timbers. So well-built were the stockade and the blockhouses that they would have stood to this day, a memorial to the troubled days of Wanganui's infancy, had not an unsentimental municipality demolished them in the " eighties," greatly to the disgust of patriotic colonists.

On a smaller mound, Patu-puhou (or Patu-puwhao), southward of Puke-namu, the military erected another fortification, a stout stockade enclosing barracks. This post was named the York Stockade. The business heart of modern Wanganui occupies the space between these two fortress hills, now converted into public parks.

In May H.M.S. "Inflexible," a paddle-steamer like the "Driver," landed at Wanganui the Grenadier Company of the 65th Regiment, a hundred strong, from Auckland. This reinforcement brought the garrison up to a strength sufficient to hold their positions, but insufficient to make any active aggressive move.

In the meantime the natives from many of the up-river settlements, from Tunuhaere as far up as Taumarunui, had united in a strong expedition against the white settlement, and came sweeping down the river in their war-canoes, chanting their paddling time-songs and their war-cries, gathering in fresh parties at each village. When the combined *taua* halted a few miles above the town its strength was five or six hundred, armed with muskets or double-barrel guns and well provided with ammunition. The principal chiefs were Topine te Mamaku, with his warriors of the Ngati-Haua-te-Rangi Tribe; Pehi Turoa; Mawae, with the Ngati-Ruaka; Tahana, with Patu-tokotoko; Ngapara, and Maketu. For some days the hostiles remained out of sight of the town, plundering and burning settlers' houses, killing cattle, and lying in wait for stragglers. A soldier of the 58th, who had gone out a mile or two into the country contrary to orders, was caught and tomahawked. His mutilated body was brought into town on the 14th May.

Captain Laye, fearing a night attack on the town, advised all the residents to leave their homes each night and spend the hours of darkness in the partly fortified houses of three of the

From an oil-painting by G. Lindauer, in the Municipal Art Gallery, Auckland.]

TOPINE TE MAMAKU.

This old warrior was prominent in the fighting at the Hutt (1846) and Wanganui (1847). He was the principal chief of the Ngati-Haua-te-Rangi Tribe, of the Upper Wanganui. One of his honorific names was " Te Ika nui o roto o te Kupenga " (" The Great Fish in the Net "). A celebrated tribal proverbial saying in reference to Te Mamaku was: *Ka unuunu te puru o Tuhua, ka maringiringi te wai o puta,*" meaning, " If you withdraw the plug of Tuhua you will be overwhelmed by the flooding hordes of the north," in allusion to this chieftain's strategic position, holding the passage of the Upper Wanganui. Te Mamaku died at Tawhata in 1887.

principal settlers, named Rees, Nixon, and Smith. This practice was observed throughout the investment of the town by the natives.

Next day (19th May) an attack in some force was delivered against the town. The armed Maoris first appeared from the seaward and western sides of the town, and as there were others on the north the settlement was practically invested on all sides but the river. The besiegers were extended in parties along the sandhills, and a large number took up a position on the southern side of Patu-puhou Hill. When the action began a party of fifteen armed civilians held the crown of this hill, but they were soon ordered to retire, and the enemy, sheltered by the ridge from the fire of the Puke-namu stockade, plundered the houses of several residents in the southern part of the town. The houses raided and sacked were those of Messrs. Allison, Campbell, Churton, Deighton, Day, Small, and Wilson. Some of these dwellings, near the riverside, were within short musket-range of the lower stockade (which enclosed the Commercial Hotel on the flat), and the troops in that post, numbering about sixty, opened fire on the raiders. The soldiers were not permitted to leave either of the stockades. Lieutenant Holmes brought his gunboat down the river from her usual anchorage under Shakespeare Cliff and fired several rounds of canister from the bow gun. The chief Maketu—he who had headed the reinforcements for Rangihaeata in the previous year—was mortally wounded, and Tatua, of Ngati-Rangatahi, also fell.

Some arrangements were made by Captain Laye and Lieutenant Holmes for the better defence of the place; a small howitzer was brought down from the Rutland Stockade to the lower fortified post, and the carronade mounted in the gunboat was hoisted on to the deck of the topsail schooner "Governor Grey," where it would be of greater use, and would enable the naval officer in command to protect vessels and troops arriving.

Governor Grey landed from H.M.S. "Inflexible" on the 24th May; with him came the old hero of the northern war, Tamati Waka Nene, the Waikato chief Potatau te Wherowhero (afterwards the first Maori King), and several other chiefs from Auckland. The *rangatiras* accompanied Captain Grey to the friendlies' village at Putiki, where Waka endeavoured to stimulate the missionary party to a decided course of action against the hostiles. Next day the Governor, with over three hundred soldiers (58th and 65th) and a number of armed settlers, made a reconnaissance in force of the ground occupied by the enemy; the limit of the march was a point about three miles above the town. Simultaneously the gun-schooner and two armed boats went up the river covering the military's right flank. A few rockets were thrown in among distant groups of Maoris.

June of 1847 was a month of harassing blockade for the whites cooped up in the narrow limits of Wanganui Town, unable to venture in safety beyond musket-shot of the stockades. One or two skirmishes enlivened the futile weeks. Reinforcements under Lieut.-Colonel McCleverty having arrived from Wellington by the war-steamer "Inflexible" and the frigate "Calliope," further reconnaissances in force were made up the valley of the Wanganui. The natives' position was six or seven miles above the town; they had fortified temporary *pas*, and immediately in their rear was the forest, where they could not be followed with any chance of success for British arms. The extremely cautious tactics of the British commander excited the impatience of the civilians, who candidly criticized the careful defensive attitude maintained by the troops. There were between five and six hundred soldiers in the garrison, now outnumbering the Maoris, but their commander, McCleverty, had no intention of attempting any bold movement. The only enterprise displayed was on the part of the armed settlers, who now and then scouted out in small parties to the abandoned farms and drove in such cattle as had not been killed by the raiders.

Even the enemy by this time had been dissatisfied with this inconclusive kind of warfare. The soldiers would not come out and attack them on the ground that suited the native manner of fighting, and they could not touch the soldiers in the stockades. The potato-planting season was approaching, and it would soon be necessary for the warriors to return to their homes up the river and attend to their crops. Before they took to their canoes, however, they resolved to make an attack upon the town with their full force and endeavour to draw the troops out from the forts. This decision produced the most important action in the tedious campaign.

On the 20th July the Maoris, numbering about four hundred, appeared on the low hills inland of the town, moving down towards it in skirmishing order. The larger number occupied the level ridge above the bush known as St. John's Wood, a little over a mile south of the town stockade; at the southern end of this ridge was a gully cutting off the terminal of the height from the main ridge; on each side of this pass they had dug trenches and rifle-pits and thrown up breastworks. In these entrenchments and in the cover of the bush on the hill-slopes the main body awaited the issue of the preliminary skirmishing, hoping that the soldiers would be induced to come out and meet them on the ground where the lightly equipped and mobile Maori would hold the advantage. Small parties of warriors were scattered over the ground between the ridge and the town and on the hills to the north. The bush and height of St. John's Wood were difficult to approach, for a large *raupo* swamp then stretched along the eastern foot of the ridge; this marsh contained a lagoon.

The only convenient approach from the town was along a narrow strip of low ground, with the pools and bogs of the swamp on either side. Two daring fellows of the enemy *opé*, skirmishing close up to the town and attempting to cut off a settler who was driving in his cattle, provoked Lieut.-Colonel McCleverty into action. He despatched two detachments of troops from the stockades in pursuit; these parties were under Lieutenant Pedder (58th) and Ensign Thelwall (65th); after them was sent a reinforcement from the 58th under Ensign Middleton. These troops, eager to meet the enemy at last with the bayonet, chased the two Maoris, who

[*From a sketch by Lieutenant G. H. Page (58th Regt.), 1847.*]

THE SKIRMISH AT ST. JOHN'S WOOD, WANGANUI.

retired across the swamp and up through the trench-flanked gully.

The first parties were soon in action, and reinforcements were despatched from the stockades, until at last four hundred soldiers were engaged in the skirmishing. In the meantime Lieutenant Holmes and Midshipman Carnegie, of the "Calliope," manned the river gunboat, and with the 12-pounder carronade and muskets checked a party of Maoris advancing along the right bank of the Wanganui. The Royal Artillery detachment, under Captain Henderson, advanced towards the edge of the swamp with two field-guns, a brass 3-pounder and a $4\frac{2}{5}$-inch howitzer, and opened fire. The Colonel now shifted his guns with a view to drawing the enemy down into the open, and the troops in the advance began to retire across the swamp. The Maoris leaped from their cover and followed closely on the troops, some firing, some dashing in with their long-handled tomahawks. The line of withdrawal was along the natural causeway through the swamp. The little rearguard faced about when the foremost of the enemy were within about 15 yards and charged. Several Maoris were bayoneted in the mêlée. Other detachments coming to the help of the rearguard, the further advance of the Maoris was stopped, and the main body of the enemy reoccupied the trenches and breastworks and the slopes of the hill south of the gully. From these positions they continued to fire on the troops so long as the latter were within range. So indecisively ended the day's engagement. The Maoris held their position under musketry and field-gun fire, but they had had a taste of the British bayonet. Two British soldiers were killed, and one died of his wounds. Ten soldiers and one Ngati-Toa Maori were wounded. Of the enemy three were killed and ten or a dozen wounded. The natives carried off and buried the body of one of the soldiers—Private Weller, of the 58th—who was killed in the bayonet charge.

The scene of this action, known in local history as the Battle of St. John's Wood, has been transformed completely. The olden lagoons and rushy swamps have long been drained, ploughed, and planted; part of the battle-ground is now occupied by the buildings of the Wanganui Collegiate School and beautiful homes and gardens. But the contour of the ridge is unaltered, and the gap separating the southernmost hill from the once-wooded land to the right, as one views it from the College grounds, is easily recognized to-day as the pass each side of which was trenched and rifle-pitted.

The 23rd July saw the Maoris' final appearance in force before the town. Some occupied the heights above St. John's Bush and the fortified hill commanding the pass from the swamp; on this knoll they planted a red flag. From these positions small parties skirmished out on the hills towards Puke-namu stockade and were saluted with a few rounds of shot and shell. Next day there was a general retirement up-river.

Early in 1848 the Governor concluded an amicable arrangement with the lately hostile chiefs. Their rebellion was condoned on condition that the stock driven off from the settlers' farms was restored. A few cattle were returned; the rest had gone into the rebels' stomachs. The settlers whose cattle had disappeared were ordered — with an unconscious humour which did not appeal to the unfortunate farmers—to pay 1s. 6d. per head to the natives who drove back any of their stock and delivered them in the town. The peace now established on the Wanganui River remained unbroken until the first Hauhau War 1864–65.

CHAPTER XV.

TARANAKI AND THE LAND LEAGUE.

Land disputes troubled the Settlement of New Plymouth almost from the day of its foundation. Commissioner Spain, who in 1844 investigated the New Zealand Company's claims, awarded 60,000 acres to the Company on payment of £200; but Governor Fitzroy set aside this award, considering that it would be an injustice to a very large number of Te Atiawa (Ngati-Awa) who were absent at the time their land was said to have been sold. Later, various blocks of land were purchased to satisfy the demands of the settlers. The principal transactions of this nature were carried out by Mr. F. Dillon Bell (afterwards Sir Dillon), who was sent in 1847 from Nelson by the New Zealand Company to supersede Mr Wicksteed as the Company's agent in New Plymouth. Mr. Dillon Bell had joined the New Zealand Company in England in 1839, and was sent to Nelson in 1843. His excellent work in Nelson led to his selection for the delicate task of satisfying the mutually antagonistic elements in Taranaki. His chief purchases were the Omata Block, of 12,000 acres, and the Hua territory, of 1,500 acres (from the Puketapu Tribe), which was named the "Bell Block." Both these settlement areas were to become famous in after-years, when the settlers built fortifications thereon and prepared by force of arms to maintain their rights to the land upon which they had made their homes. Katatore, a tragic figure in Taranaki history, stoutly opposed the sale of the Bell Block by Rawiri Waiaua and others in 1848, and he had a singular pole carved and erected on the right bank of the Wai-whakaiho River, alongside the track, as a symbol of protest against the encroachment of the *pakeha*. This post, a *puriri* spar about 30 feet high, was named by the Maoris "Pou-tutaki," and came to be known by the Europeans as the "Fitzroy pole" from its proximity to the Fitzroy Village, now a suburb of New Plymouth. It had two life-sized figures in bold relief, representing the *pakeha* cowering beneath a Maori warrior; the native figure was intended as a presentment of a chief of Puketapu, one Parata te Huia. The post was intended to mark the limit of European settlement; no *pakeha*, according to the

Maoris, was to own any land between that spot and the Auckland District. It was 1853 before the natives would permit settlements on the Bell Block. The return to Waitara from Waikanae in 1848 of the greater part of the Atiawa (or Ngati-Awa) Tribe further complicated the progress of the white settlement in Taranaki. These people, sections of whom had sold much of the land about Wellington to the New Zealand Company—they had conquered those lands from the original holders—conceived a desire to return to their ancestral homes on the Waitara, and, in spite of the opposition and even threats of Governor Grey, carried out their undertaking successfully. Grey eventually withdrew his opposition in consideration of the help afforded to the Government by the Atiawa at Waikanae and Wellington in crushing Rangihaeata's rising in 1846. Wiremu Kingi te Rangitaake, the head chief of the Waikanae people, had given valuable protection to the Wellington Settlement at a very critical period. The Governor could not very well ignore this. Crying their farewells to their lands and the few people whom they left at Waikanae and Otaki, the Atiawa emigrants set sail up the coast in April, 1848. The flotilla consisted of forty-four canoes of large size, four open boats, and a small sailing-craft. A few people also travelled overland on horseback. The total number of the Atiawa who thus returned and landed joyfully on the shore of their ancient home-land was 587, consisting of 273 men, 195 women, and 119 children. These were the people who in 1860 came into conflict with the Administration over the purchase of the 600-acre block on which the Town of Waitara now stands.

Wiremu Kingi and his tribe set to work industriously to cultivate their lands on the left (or west) side of the Waitara River mouth, and in a few years had a number of comfortable settlements near the river, with large crops of wheat, maize, and potatoes, and a considerable number of horses and cattle, besides ploughs and other agricultural implements. In 1856 they sent to market about £8,000 worth of produce, and spent the proceeds on goods in New Plymouth. Their desirable lands inevitably excited the envy of the *pakeha* settlers, who presently moved the authorities to extend their purchases towards the Waitara.

In the meantime the growing native jealousy of the *pakeha* took formidable form in a combination to prevent further land-sales. This powerful movement, to which was conjoined an effort to found a Maori kingdom, was initiated shortly after New Zealand received its Constitution Act bestowing representative government upon the colony. The connection between these most important political developments may be rather difficult to trace exactly, but the coincidence is certainly remarkable. The Maori was not to be behind the white in his struggle for national power, and while the settlers had been successful in their agitation for self-determination, he was determined that the newcomers should be restrained in their race for Maori lands.*

The anti-*pakeha* crusade was given its first expression in a great conference of the west-coast tribes held in 1854 at Manawa-pou, a large settlement of the Ngati-Ruanui, at the mouth of the Ingahape River, on the South Taranaki coast. The site of this celebrated meeting is still plainly to be traced, although it is now part of the farm of a white settler. Manawa-pou is a beautiful terrace overlooking the sea, on the south side of the mouth of the Ingahape River, where the stream comes curving out of a deep grassy valley. On the hill 300 feet above are the earth-works of the Imperial redoubt of Manawa-pou, dating back to General Cameron's campaign. Here in the "fifties" was the home of a section of the Ngati-Ruanui, notable for the large stature of its men. The tribe built an unusually large meeting-house for the gathering; it was 120 feet long and 35 feet wide. "Taiporohenui," the name given to the assembly-house, was originally that of a sacred house of instruction in Hawaiki, according to Taranaki tradition. A great patriotic song was chanted by the people at the opening of "Taiporohenui." It began :—

> *E kore Taranaki e makere atu!*
> *E kore Taranaki e makere atu!*
> *Kei marea mai—kei marea mai!*
> *Tika tonu mai ki a Piata-kai-manawa,*
> *I Piata-kai-manawa.*
> *Ka turu*
> *Ko te whakamutunga,*
> *E kapa-ti, kapa-ti!*
> *E—i—e!*

In this chant the spirit of determination to hold fast to the ancestral lands was made manifest—"Taranaki shall not be lost, shall not be abandoned to the stranger." The conference of the tribes determined that no more land should be sold to the Europeans without the general consent of the federation, and that Maori disputes should not be submitted to European juris-

---

* "If Englishmen could occasionally be brought to face the fact that since the institution of their nationality and language no permanent English community has ever passed under a foreign yoke, they would be better able to understand how impossible it is for a dominant race to do complete justice to a subject people, and how hollow is the pretence that impartial justice is rendered to such people. The strong natural sense of justice which animates Englishmen, and their intense respect for the rights of property, have doubtless helped to a vast degree to counteract the evils of domination and disparity; but if we could view the question from a national Maori point of view we should find much to approve of in the principle of the League."—Mr. Justice Chapman, in his "History of New Zealand" (Dunedin).

diction but should be settled by tribal *runanga* (councils). At this meeting, too, the idea of a Maori king for the Maori people was discussed and fervently approved.

The differences between the adherents of the Land League and those who wished to sell developed into murderous intertribal feuds. On the 3rd August, 1854, Rawiri Waiaua, who offered the Government a disputed area at Taruru-tangi, in the Puketapu Block, was fatally shot, with several of his followers, by Katatore and a party of twenty-eight men representing the non-sellers. The Government professed itself powerless to interfere. The quarrelling factions fortified themselves in their *pas*, and an intermittent skirmishing warfare prevailed for many months. The rival parties often selected the vicinity of the white settlements for their guerilla warfare. The Administration was appealed to for troops for the protection of New Plymouth, and on the 19th August, 1855, the first British garrison of the province arrived. This was a portion of the 58th Regiment, numbering about 270 men and officers, under Captain Seymour, with some Royal Artillery men and several field-guns, and some sappers and miners. In September the force was increased by the arrival from Wellington of some two hundred of the 65th Regiment.

The native-land vendetta was resumed in August, 1857, when Ihaia te Kiri-Kumara, who was very friendly to the Government and had sold some land, laid an ambush for his enemy Katatore on the road through the Bell Block Settlement. The settlers heard the firing in the morning early as Katatore was shot down. In the intertribal war thus renewed Katatore's slayer was driven out of his *pa*, which was sacked and burned. All north Taranaki, or at any rate the native portion of the population, was almost continually under arms.

The period 1858–59 was one of continual internecine strife in the district between the Bell Block and the Waitara. Ihaia's *pa*, Ika-moana, near Puketapu, was evacuated and destroyed in February, 1858. Ihaia and his party, the land-sellers, were then besieged at the Karaka, on the Waitara. On the 10th March, 1858, Mr. S. Percy Smith (afterwards Surveyor-General) rode down to the Waitara with Mr. Parris, Civil Commissioner, who was in charge of native affairs in Taranaki, and made sketches under fire of the *pas* occupied by Ihaia and Wiremu Kingi. "Plenty of bullets flying over my head while sketching," wrote Mr. Smith in his diary.

The following description of the fighting at the Bell Block arising out of the Puketapu feud over the sale of lands to the Government is from the pen of Mr. A. H. Messenger, son of the late Colonel W. B. Messenger, of New Plymouth :—

"Some curious incidents occurred in the native war waged over the newly made farms of the settlers from Devon and

Cornwall. As a boy living in one of the Taranaki frontier posts, I heard the story of those stirring times recounted by my father. The opposing tribes fought back and forth with varying fortune over the undulating country of the Waiwhakaiho River, and out on to what was later known as the Bell Block. The settlers in 1857–58 were witnesses of many thrilling incidents, and it was a frequent occurrence to have to stop work in the middle of a fencing or ploughing job and retire to the security of the farmhouse while a fierce skirmish took place in which numerous casualties occurred on both sides. Though bullets were flying in all directions, the white settlers were never molested, and their stock also was under strict *tapu*, and was not interfered with. An episode typical of those thrilling days was described by a Devonshire settler who in the midst of ploughing operations suddenly found himself in a Maori battle. The opposing war-parties had skirmished up towards one another through the high fern surrounding the little farm, and finished up with a charge and close hand-to-hand fighting with tomahawk and *mere* over the newly ploughed ground. For a moment the settler thought that his end had come, but the brown warriors took no notice of his presence, and as the battle passed on he found himself still standing, hand on plough, gazing in bewilderment at several stark figures that lay sprawled in the attitude of sudden death amid the newly turned furrows. As night fell groups of warriors, many of whom bore fresh wounds from musket-ball or blow of tomahawk, gathered round the nearest farmhouse and deposited their guns with the white settlers, telling them that they would call for them on the morrow, when fighting was resumed in the same manner.

"In another case a settler received a message from each of the opposing forces to the effect that a fight would take place on his farm in the morning, and that it would be well for him to remain in his house until the tide of war had passed by. Taking due heed of this warning, the settler was witness on the following morning of a battle in his pastures. Many bullets struck the house, and one random shot killed a sheep; otherwise no damage was done to his property. The nervous tension brought on by these conditions of life proved too much for several of the settlers, who finally left the district in search of more peaceful surroundings."

CHAPTER XVI.

THE MAORI KING.

It was Tamehana te Rauparaha, the son of the great Ngati-Toa conquistador, who first suggested the establishment of a king or high chief for the union of Maori tribes. Tamehana had made a voyage to England, and, being an exceedingly shrewd and observant man, he returned with many ideas for the betterment of his countrymen. The principal reform he felt impelled to propose was the setting-up of a king under whose control the people should live in harmony with each other and with their *pakeha* neighbours. His kinsman Matene te Whiwhi, of Otaki, seized upon the notion with patriotic enthusiasm, and travelled among the tribes advocating union and the election of some high *rangatira* as head of the Maori nation.

The members of the confederation of the anti-land-selling chiefs and people found considerable difficulty in the selection of a head for the union of the tribes. Many men of high pedigree were approached, but one after another declined the troublesome office of king. One of the chiefs whom Matene te Whiwhi and his fellow-leaguers urged to accept the kingship was Whitikau, of the Nga-Rauru Tribe, Waitotara. He refused; so did Tamati Hone, the man of highest standing in Ngati-Ruanui. A deputation of chiefs went to Wanganui and placed the position before Pehi Turoa, who refused. Te Heuheu Iwikau, of Taupo, similarly declined the offer.

The Waikato tribes held a very large meeting in 1857 at Paetai, on the Waikato River, at which the question was debated by delegates from all the tribes of the confederation, as well as others outside the league. The Arawa people of Rotorua and Maketu were represented at this gathering by Temuera te Amohau. Eloquent efforts were made to induce the Arawa to join the Kingites. Temuera refused, saying, "One of our chiefs, Timoti, was the only man of the Arawa people who signed the Treaty of Waitangi, but we shall not depart from the pledge he then gave. We will not join the king tribes. My king is Queen Victoria." ("*Taku kingi ko Kuini Wikitoria.*")

From a photo about 1865.]

WIREMU TAMEHANA TARAPIPIPI TE WAHAROA.

Temuera was taunted by some of the Waikato chiefs with the defeat Te Waharoa had inflicted on the Arawa twenty years previously at Mataipuku, near Ohinemutu. He retorted with an allusion to Te Waharoa having been taken prisoner and spared by the Arawa in his infancy. "As for us Arawa," he said, "we shall stand as firmly as a rock in the ocean. Upon that rock shall be shattered the waves of your kingdom." ("*Ka tu a te Arawa hai toka tu moana, e pakaru ai nga ngaru o to Kingitanga.*") Temuera concluded by telling the Waikato that if they wished to set up a Maori king they should apply to the highest chief in New Zealand, Te Kani-a-Takirau, of the East Cape.

This suggestion is said to have led to an offer to the chief named to become king of the federated tribes, but here again the leaguers met with a refusal. Te Kani, in any case, was not a suitable selection. He was a very high-born *rangatira*, but a man of no force of character, and his territory was remote from the chief seats of agitation.

A conference was also held in 1857 at Pukawa, Lake Taupo, and was attended by chiefs from all over the Island. The chiefs finally selected Potatau te Wherowhero, who had no desire for the honour. He was a very old and feeble man, but his warrior reputation, his exalted lineage, and his widespread tribal connections qualified him as the necessary figurehead behind whom Wiremu Tamehana and his fellow-reformers might carry out their schemes of self-government.

The late Te Heuheu Tukino, the head chief of the Ngati-Tuwharetoa Tribe, described to the writer as follows the highly ceremonious manner in which the chiefs of the various tribes assembled at Pukawa in 1857 centralized their *mana* and bestowed it upon Potatau te Wherowhero, who was then chosen as the king of the confederated tribes:—

"Te Heuheu Iwikau, who was head of our tribe since the death of my grandfather, Te Heuheu Mana-nui, in the landslip at Te Rapa (1846), caused a high flagstaff to be erected on the *marae*, the meeting-ground, at Pukawa. At the masthead he hoisted a national flag; the pattern was that of the flag given by King William IV of England to the northern Maori tribes at the Bay of Islands some years before the signing of the Treaty of Waitangi. Beneath this flag at intervals down the mast he had long ropes of plaited flax attached. The flagstaff symbolized Tongariro, the sacred mountain of our tribe. The Maoris were assembled in divisions grouped around the foot. Te Heuheu arose and said, indicating a rope, 'This is Ngongotaha' (the mountain near Rotorua Lake). 'Where is the chief of Ngongotaha who shall attach this mountain to Tongariro?' The leading chief of the Arawa Tribe, of Rotorua, rose from his place in the assemblage, and taking the end of the rope fastened it to a *manuka* peg, which he drove into the ground in front of his company. The next rope indicated by the Taupo head chief symbolized Pu-tauaki (Mount Edgecumbe), the sacred mountain of Ngati-Awa, of the Bay of Plenty. The next was Tawhiuau, the mountain belonging to Ngati-Manawa, on the western border of the Urewera country. Each tribe giving its adherence to the king movement had its rope allotted to it, representative of a mountain dear to the people. Hikurangi, near the East Cape, was for the Ngati-Porou Tribe, Maunga-pohatu for the Tuhoe (Urewera), Titi-o-kura for the Ngati-Kahungunu Tribe, Kapiti Island for the Ngati-Toa, and Otairi for the Ngati-Apa.

"The great mountains of the South Island also were named. Each had its symbolic rope—Tapuae-nuku and Kaikoura, and the greatest of all, Aorangi. Those were for the Ngai-Tahu Tribe, whose representative at the meeting was Taiaroa. Returning to the North Island mountains, our *ariki* took in turn the ropes emblematic of the west coast and the Waikato, and called upon the chiefs from those parts to secure them to the soil. These mountains were Para-te-tai-tonga (the southern peak of Ruapehu), for the Whanganui tribes; Taranaki (Mount Egmont), for Taranaki, Te Atiawa, and Ngati-Ruanui tribes; Pirongia and Taupiri, for the Waikato clans; Kakepuku, for the Ngati-Maniapoto; Rangitoto, for Ngati-Matakore and Ngati-Whakatere; Wharepuhunga, for Ngati-Raukawa; Maunga-tautari, for Ngati-Haua and Ngati-Koroki; Maunganui (at Tauranga), for Ngai-te-Rangi; Te Aroha, for Ngati-Tama-te-ra; and finally Moehau (Cape Colville Range), for the Ngati-Maru Tribe.

"Each of the ropes representing these sacred mountains of the tribes was hauled taut and staked down. So in the middle stood Tongariro, the central mountain, supported and stayed by all these tribal cords, which joined the soil of New Zealand to the central authority. Above floated the flag, emblem of Maori nationality. Thus was the union of the tribes demonstrated so that all might see, and then did Te Heuheu and his fellow-chiefs transfer to Potatau all the *mana-tapu* of the soil and acclaim him as the king of the native tribes of New Zealand."

While the scheme for a king for the Maori people originated with the two chiefs of the Ngati-Toa at Otaki, it was not long before the leading *rangatira* of the Ngati-Haua, in the Waikato-Waihou country, emerged as the great advocate of the doctrine of Maori self-government. Wiremu Tamehana was a master of logical argument expressed in plain words, and his deep knowledge of the Scripture enabled him to give point to his addresses and his letters with quotations from the Testament. Governors and Ministers were indeed hard put to it to confute his reasoning or demolish his pleas for Maori rights. Sir John Gorst, his friendly antagonist in Waikato politics, told me in 1906 that he considered Tamehana one of the most able debaters and keenest thinkers he had ever met. The kingmaker's appeals to the *pakeha* Administration read pathetically. With all the powers of a well-balanced brain he contended for the right of the Maoris to administer their own affairs within their own boundaries. He quoted the sales of native land for very small prices, only to be cut up and sold for much greater sums. "Have we not better right to this advanced price than the *pakeha*?" The land, always the land, was the theme of his earnest argument. "Surely that it is unoccupied now is no reason why it should always remain so. I hope the day will come when our descendants will not have more than they really require. As to a king, why should not every race have a king of its own? Is not the Queen (English), Nicholas (Russian), Bonaparte (French), Pomare (Tahitian), each for his own people? If all the countries were united the aloofness of the Maori might be reprehensible, but they are not."

"My friends," he wrote, "do you grudge us a king, as if it were a name greater than that of God? If it were so that God forbade us, then we would give it up; but he forbids not, and while only our fellow-men are angry we will not relinquish it." In another letter to the Government he defined the reasons for the appointment of a Maori king: "to put an end to land feuds, to put down troubles, to hold the land of the slaves, and to judge the offences of the chiefs." And this desire for a high chief for the Maori was not inconsistent with loyalty to the accepted principle of British eminent domain. He had seen the evils of disunion among the tribes, the failure of the white Government to stop bloodshed over land disputes. His ideal was peaceful union and civilization for the Maori, under the benevolent control of Christianized chiefs. "*Te Whakapono, te Aroha, me te Ture*" ("Religion, Love, and the Law") was the watchword of his political faith. But the altruistic king-maker was in advance of his contemporaries in the colony, Maori and *pakeha*. Had Sir George Grey been Governor in 1857 both the Waitara blunder and the Waikato War would probably have been avoided. But the mischief was done by Governor Gore Browne and his advisers, and when Grey returned to New Zealand in 1861 he found upon his hands the legacy of folly of the war in Taranaki and an inevitable outbreak in Waikato. In its beginning the king movement might have been turned to a blessing to the Maori people. Grey, indeed, did endeavour to meet the crisis by an offer of a semi-independent provincial government for the Maori people; but the antagonism of the more violent sections of Waikato and their co-clans had by then reached a stage at which compromise was impossible.

CHAPTER XVII.

THE WAITARA PURCHASE.

The complicated history of the Waitara purchase may be reduced to a simple summary. Teira, a minor chief of the Atiawa, living with his fellow-tribesmen on the ancestral lands on the Waitara, was persuaded to offer 600 acres of the land to the Government, at a price of £1 per acre. This block was on the left side of the Waitara, near the mouth, and included the ground on which the present Town of Waitara stands. A number of Teira's people supported him, but the majority of the Atiawa, headed by Wiremu Kingi te Rangitaåke, opposed the transaction, and made vehement and repeated protest. It was acknowledged that Teira was the occupier of a portion of the land, and the Government contention—on the advice of Mr. Parris, its local native agent—was that a native had a right to dispose of his individual interests in land. But this was long before the establishment of the Native Land Court. Titles in native land had not been individualized; it was practically impossible to determine the precise extent of Teira's interests. The case for the opponents of the sale was that while individual cultivation rights existed no one had a right to part with the tribal estate without general consent. The land was the common property of the people, and it was against accepted tribal policy to permit a wedge to be driven into the estate by deed of sale without the acquiescence of all concerned. While the whole tribe might be called upon to fight to maintain any or every member of the tribe in possession, so no member was justified in parting with the joint property of the clan. This land had always been thickly populated, and was the property of a great many families, and Wiremu Kingi, as the paramount chief, undoubtedly exercised his right in vetoing the sale. Moreover, it is known that Wiremu Kingi was the victim of a private feud. He and Teira had quarrelled, and Teira, in order to obtain revenge, deliberately proposed the sale in order to bring trouble upon his antagonist and the tribe. This was a common mode of action among the Maoris. The determined opposition of Wiremu Kingi—who was no fire-

THE WAITARA PURCHASE. 151

brand, but a well-wisher of the whites and a man of high intelligence and cool reasoning—should have been sufficient warning to the authorities, at any rate, to treat the matter delicately and

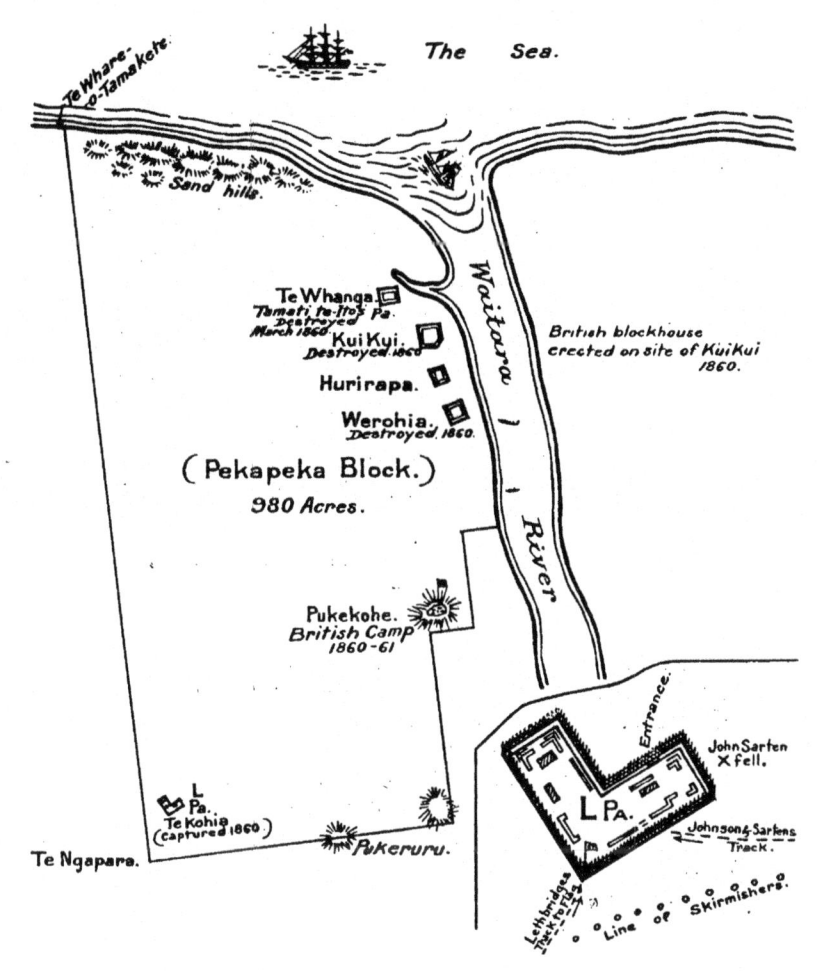

PLAN OF THE PEKAPEKA BLOCK, WAITARA.

(Inset, Te Kohia *pa*, called the "L" *pa* from its shape.)

It was the dispute over the defective purchase of this land by the Government that caused the Taranaki War. Waitara Town now occupies part of the block.

to submit the dispute to a competent tribunal. Possibly a proposal to rent the land would have been more favourably received by the Atiawa. But in the existing tension of feeling among the natives, the Waitara, with its fairly numerous population and its highly complicated system of ownership, was the worst possible spot that Governor Gore Browne's advisers could have selected for a demonstration of their announced intention to bargain with individual owners.

As was often the case in native disputes, a quarrel over a woman was one of the roots of dissension. The following is a statement by a Kingite survivor of the wars:—

"Our troubles which led to war began when our people lived in their *pa* called Karaponia (California), on the left (west) side of the Waitara River, at the mouth. A woman, Hariata, was the cause. She was the wife of Ihaia te Kiri-kumara, and because of her unfaithfulness Ihaia had her seducer, Rimene, killed. The man's body was buried in the *pa*. Because of the wrong done to him Ihaia sought for further revenge and sought compensation in land. The tribe would not agree to this, inasmuch as the offence had already been paid for sufficiently by the death of the man Rimene. Ihaia, however, would not listen to this agreement, and he joined with Teira and sold some of the land of Te Rangitaake to the Government in order to obtain compensation for the adultery of his wife. Hence this *haka* song of the Atiawa:—

> "The land was seized upon because of the woman,
> At Karaponia it all began.
> *E Mau na wa!*"

The case for the European settlers of Taranaki lay in the necessity for obtaining more land for the extension of the settlements. With thousands upon thousands of acres of beautiful and fertile but unused territory around them, it was very natural that they should urge the Administration to purchase new blocks for farms. Immigration was increasing, and the large families of the original settlers made obvious the need for more land. The vigorous men of Cornwall and Devon, who formed the larger proportion of the settlement-founders, were not disposed to permit a few hundreds of natives to bar the way to the good acres lying waste under fern and *tutu*. Hemmed in as they were between the mountains and the sea and between the domains of the Maori tribes, they were impatient for expansion of their landed possessions. The Maori, on the other hand, had become very uneasy at the steady incoming of immigrant ships, and feared that the *pakeha*, with whom at one time he would have been content to live in friendship, would presently outnumber and overrun the native people. Wise statesmanship might have averted a clash, but, unfortunately, the one man who could have devised a method of conciliating the antagonistic factions was absent from the colony.

Thoughtful men such as Sir William Martin vigorously condemned the Waitara blunder. Many years later Dr. Edward Shortland made the following comment on the land dispute and its causes in his book "Maori Religion and Mythology": "It is a recognized mode of action among the Maoris, if a chief has been treated with indignity by others of the tribe and no reasonable means of redress can be obtained, for the former to do some act which will bring trouble on the whole tribe. This mode of obtaining redress is termed *whakahe*, and means putting the other in the wrong. There appears little reason to doubt," Shortland concluded (p. 104), "that Teira's proposal to sell Waitara was prompted by a vindictive feeling towards Wi Kingi, for he knew well that by such mode of proceeding he would embroil those who would not consent with their European neighbours. At the same time it is a rather mortifying reflection that the astute policy of a Maori chief should have prevailed to drag the colony and Her Majesty's Government into a long and expensive war to avenge his own private quarrel."*

---

* See Appendices for Sir George Grey's memoranda on the Waitara question.

CHAPTER XVIII.

THE FIRST TARANAKI WAR.

The completion of the Waitara purchase, in spite of Wiremu Kingi's repeated protests, was resolved upon by the Governor in Council at Auckland early in 1860. It was decided to have the block surveyed, and to protect the survey-party with an adequate military force if obstruction were offered, and if necessary to call out the Taranaki Militia and Volunteers for active service and proclaim martial law. The Auckland Militia, it was further decided by Governor Gore Browne and his Executive Council (the Stafford Ministry), should be enrolled and armed; all males between the ages of sixteen and fifty-five were liable for service. The fateful decision to proceed with the survey was communicated to Lieut.-Colonel Murray, temporarily commanding in New Plymouth, who immediately had the country between the town and the Waitara reconnoitred for the purpose of selecting suitable places for camps and redoubts on the disputed block and along the road. On the 20th February, 1860, the title to the block was put to the test. Mr. Octavius Carrington, Chief Surveyor, and Mr. Charles Wilson Hursthouse (afterwards District Surveyor and later Chief Engineer of Roads and Bridges) and a party of chainmen went to the Waitara to commence the survey of the land. Mr. Parris, the Government's principal instrument in the purchase, accompanied them. The Maoris obstructed the surveyors and prevented them beginning their work. The party returned to New Plymouth. Lieut.-Colonel Murray gave Wiremu Kingi twenty-four hours to apologize and withdraw his opposition. The old chief replied that he did not desire war, that he loved the white people very much, but that he intended to hold the land. Thereupon (22nd February) Murray proclaimed martial law in the Taranaki District. The Militia and the Taranaki Rifle Volunteers were called out for active service, and a small mounted corps was organized and armed with carbines, revolvers, and swords. The country settlers began their migration to the town, abandoning their homes, which presently were to go up in flames.

New Plymouth in 1860 had a white population of about two thousand five hundred, of whom between five and six hundred were men and youths of fighting-age. They could have claimed, as Nelson wrote of his "Agamemnons" in 1794, "We are few, but the right sort." Nearly twenty years of Taranaki life had developed many a settler into an expert bushman, familiar with the forest tracks, and fairly well able to meet the Maori on level terms. Such families as the Atkinsons, the Smiths and Hursthouses, the Bayleys, Messengers, and Northcrofts produced ideal frontiersmen, schooled in the rough work of settlement, trained to act upon their own initiative, and quick to adapt themselves to the special conditions of Maori warfare in a country admirably fitted for guerilla fighting. From this material was formed, besides a useful body of Militia and a small cavalry corps, a Volunteer rifle force which will live in history as the first British Volunteer corps to engage an enemy in the field. This body, the Taranaki Rifle Volunteer Company, a hundred strong, was formed in New Plymouth towards the end of 1858. The first commander was Captain I. N. Watt; but when the war began the corps was divided into two companies—No. 1 Company under Captain Watt, and No. 2 Company under Captain Harry Atkinson (afterwards Premier of New Zealand). Major C. Herbert was in general command of the Taranaki Volunteers and Militia. The Rifles distinguished themselves at the outset by their gallantry and efficiency in the Battle of Waireka, and a little later at Mahoetahi. Unfortunately, during the first war they did not always receive due credit for their work from the Imperial officers, who underrated not only the military genius of the Maori but the soldiering capacity of the settler Volunteers. But as the war developed it was found that the quickly trained civilian element was better fitted to deal with certain emergencies in the field than the slow-moving and often badly led Regulars; and Atkinson and his picked men became increasingly useful as scouts and forest rangers.

Shortly after the war began the effective garrison of New Plymouth and its outposts numbered about twelve hundred men, of whom the 65th Regiment made up about half. Marsland Hill, the ancient Maori *pa* Pukaka, was an excellent headquarters site and place of refuge in case of emergency. It overlooked the town and the country for many miles, and its position just in the rear of the central settlement made it a suitable citadel. As the war went on and the out-settlers were driven in, and New Plymouth was reduced practically to a state of siege, it was deemed necessary to constrict the occupied area and to entrench the town. The accompanying plan shows the line of ditch and parapet, roughly triangular in figure. The sea-beach formed the base, and Marsland Hill citadel the apex; one side of the triangle was along the line of Liardet Street and the other along Queen Street. There were gates on the Devon Road line where this entrenchment intersected it. There were several outposts, some of which were

156   NEW ZEALAND WARS.

earthwork redoubts, others timber blockhouses. The British warships sent to the aid of Taranaki, besides the "Niger," were the "Iris," a 26-gun sailing-frigate, the "Cordelia," and the "Pelorus," both steam-corvettes; and later in the year the Victorian Government's fine barque-rigged war-steamer "Victoria" arrived from

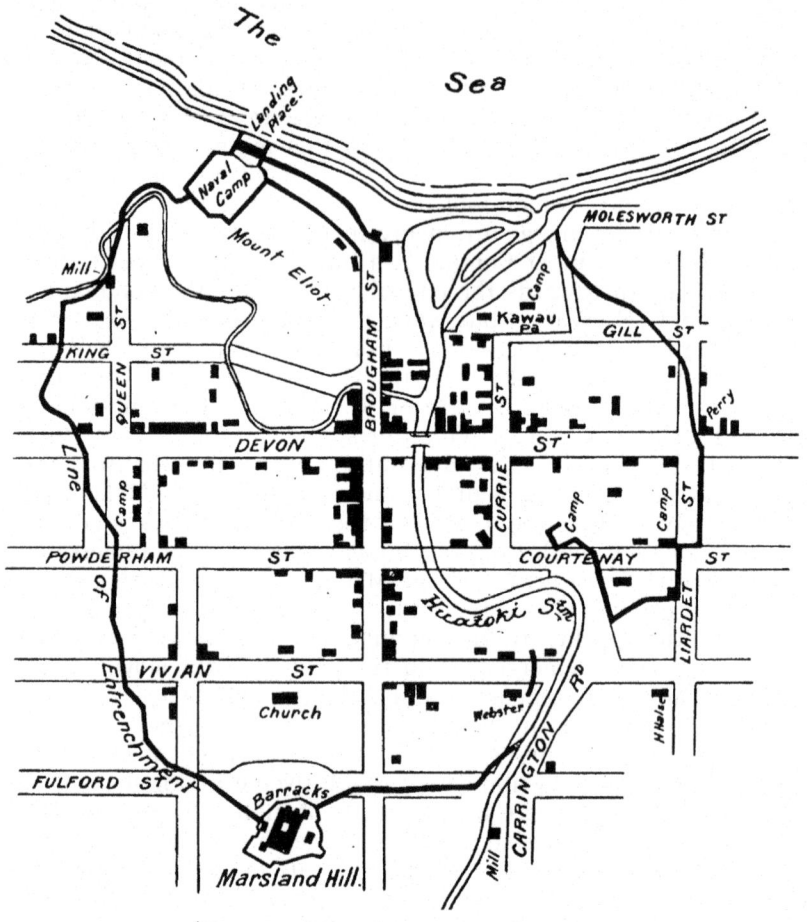

PLAN OF NEW PLYMOUTH, 1860–61,

Showing the line of entrenchment surrounding the town, with Marsland Hill as the citadel.

Melbourne, having generously been lent for the assistance of the colonists.

New Plymouth Town, crowded to excess, was now lively with all the business of preparation for war. Governor Gore Browne came down from Auckland. With him in the "Airedale" came

THE FIRST TARANAKI WAR. 157

Colonel Gold, who took over the Taranaki command until Major-General Pratt arrived. The garrison was reinforced at the same time by the headquarters and three companies of the 65th, a splendid regiment of stalwart bearded men, mostly Irishmen, young in years, but already veterans in service. H.M.S. "Niger," a barque-rigged screw-corvette under the command of Captain Cracroft, arrived on the same day (1st March), bringing a very able young Royal Artillery officer, Lieutenant MacNaghten, and some gunners. The "Niger" had a few Auckland lads in her crew; they had joined her in January. Her armament consisted

From a drawing by W. Strutt, 1858.]

MARSLAND HILL, NEW PLYMOUTH.

of twelve 32-pounder broadside guns, ten of which were slide-guns with elevating-screws; the two after-guns were the old Nelson type. Mounted forward was a 68-pounder gun (95 cwt.) working on brass slides; it could fire either to port or to starboard, and was a first-class gun for those times. The "Niger" also carried a 12-pounder brass field-piece for Naval Brigade work ashore. This gun was landed, and a body of fifty bluejackets and marines entrenched themselves on a hill on the east side of New Plymouth, which became known as "Fort Niger."

158   NEW ZEALAND WARS.

On the 5th March Colonel Gold moved upon the Waitara with a force of four hundred officers and men of the 65th Regiment, some artillery, and the newly formed Mounted Rifles (Captain Des Veaux), and a long baggage-train of wagons and carts. Camp was pitched on the disputed land, on ground overlooking the mouth of the Waitara. Here a large redoubt was built, and it became the main camp for operations which lasted just twelve months.

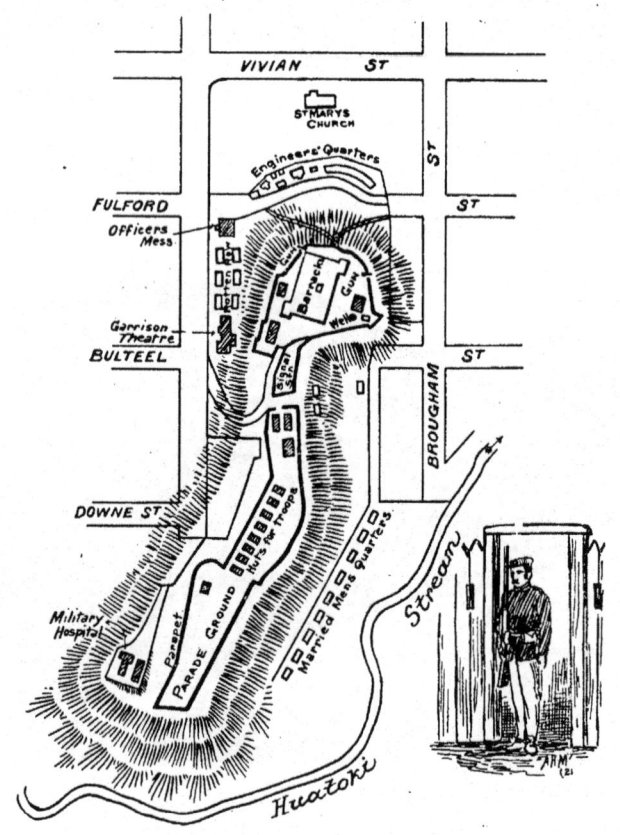

PLAN OF MARSLAND HILL, NEW PLYMOUTH,

Showing British fortifications and barracks, 1860. The hill was formerly a Maori stronghold, called Pukaka.

The Maori forces opposed to the troops were not numerous until the war had been some time in progress, when many fighting-men of Ngati-Maniapoto, Waikato, Ngati-Haua, and the south Taranaki tribes as far as the Waitotara, with some of the Whanganui, came to Wiremu Kingi's aid. They did not at any time outnumber or even equal the whites under arms, but man for man

THE FIRST TARANAKI WAR.

they were better campaigners so long as they were able to choose the ground of battle. In the bush they were only outmatched, later on, by the picked forest rangers of Atkinson's Volunteers. They were fairly well provided with ammunition when the war began, thanks to a Government Proclamation of 1858 relaxing the restriction on the purchase of guns, powder, lead, and percussion caps, but they had no regular means of renewing their supplies.

The first shot was fired on the 17th March, 1860. Wiremu Kingi and his Atiawa followers, with the fiery chief Hapurona as the war-leader, determined to maintain their right to their tribal lands. They quickly constructed a strongly entrenched and stockaded fort just within the boundary of the disputed block at Te Kohia, close to the Devon Road (seaward side), at about nine miles from New Plymouth and a little under two miles from the Waitara River. (The site is a few chains from the present road, just before the road crosses the railway-line to Waitara.) This *pa* Te Kohia, more generally known as the L *pa* from its shape, was 110 feet in length and 33 feet in width on each of its two arms, and within the double row of palisading was a series of rifle trenches and pits, most of which were roofed over with timbers, fern, and earth. The place was well provisioned with potatoes, maize, fish, and fruit. The garrison consisted of about a hundred men of Te Atiawa. Early in the afternoon of the 17th Colonel Gold attacked the *pa* with a force composed of three companies of the 65th Regiment and a few sailors from H.M.S. "Niger" (which had anchored off the mouth of the river) with a rocket-tube, twenty of the Royal Artillery with a 12-pounder and two 24-pounder field-guns, ten sappers and miners, and twenty of the Volunteer cavalry.

The artillery and the rocket-tube first opened fire at a range of 750 yards, and later were moved to within 400 yards of the *pa*. The guns made better practice at the reduced range, and many shells burst in the fortification. As the artillery range was shortened the hidden Maori musketeers opened a sharp fire, which was replied to by the infantry skirmishers. The Maori fire presently ceasing, some of the Volunteer cavalry rode up very close to the *pa* and fired their revolvers off, and two of them seized and carried away the war-flag (a red colour, bearing the name "Waitaha"); the staff had broken and was hanging down outside the stockade. A sudden volley from the *pa* mortally wounded a young cavalryman named J. Sarten, and he dropped from his horse, the first man to fall in the Taranaki War. A sailor of the "Niger" and a private of the 65th Regiment gallantly carried Sarten off under fire.

The troops spent the night entrenched behind a low breastwork in the form of a half-moon, with the guns and wagons in the rear. A fire was kept up by the Maoris for some time after dark

Their palisading had been battered considerably by the shells and solid shot, and, recognizing that they could not hope to hold the position much longer, they prudently evacuated it before daylight on the morning of the 18th.

At dawn the guns moved up close and again opened fire, and a breach was made at the south end of the stockade, through which Lieutenant MacNaghten, R.A., and some of his gunners and a portion of the 65th rushed, only to find the place empty. It is said that MacNaghten had informed Gold on the previous evening that a practicable breach had been made, but although the 65th soldiers were greatly excited and eager to rush the *pa* the cautious commander would not give the word to assault. The British casualties were slight; besides Sarten, a soldier of the 65th was mortally wounded, and a cavalryman and an infantryman each wounded, but not severely. The Maori losses were about the same as those of the attackers.

The next encounter was a much sharper affair—the engagement at Waireka, in which for the first time in New Zealand Volunteers bore the most conspicuous part. By this time the stout-hearted settlers of Omata and the Bell Block had constructed substantial little forts on commanding hills in their districts, and these two outposts, one on either side of New Plymouth, were held continuously throughout the war, even when New Plymouth was closely hemmed in by the Maoris. They were not of a uniform type: each owed its design to the sound sense and native military instinct of the local farmers.

The Bell Block stockade was built on a grassy hill, flat on top, with a rather steep face towards the principal part of the settlement. Traces of the olden trenches are still to be seen on this hill, which is close to the seaward side of the Devon Line, as the main road to Waitara is known, four miles and a half from New Plymouth. Below, on the flat near where the dairy factory now stands, is the spot where Katatore, the leader of the anti-land-sellers, was ambushed and shot in 1857. The settlers of the district, numbering about seventy men, held a meeting, when martial law was proclaimed, and appointed a committee to design a suitable place of defence to enable them to hold fast to their lands. Every able-bodied man was speedily at work felling, splitting, and carting timber, and soon a hundred bullock-cart loads of timber were on the spot selected for the post. The Imperial military authorities in New Plymouth, with an ineptitude unfortunately characteristic of headquarters in the first Taranaki War, stopped the work for a time, but after the Militia and Volunteers were called out it was resumed. The buildings and entrenchments were completed by Ensign (afterwards Colonel) W. B. Messenger, a member of one of the pioneer families of Omata, and a party of Militia. It consisted of a strong blockhouse, 62 feet long, 22 feet

THE BELL BLOCK STOCKADE, TARANAKI.

From drawings by Frank Arden, 1863.]

BLOCKHOUSE AND TOWERS, BELL BLOCK STOCKADE.

wide, and 11 feet high, with two flanking towers each 22 feet high at the diagonally opposite angles, all loopholed, with a surrounding ditch enfiladed by the towers. Later, the position was enlarged by the construction of a timber stockade and a trench close to the blockhouse, and enclosing a considerable space, which was for some time occupied by a hundred and fifty Imperial troops with a couple of field-guns. In the fort there was a flagstaff for semaphore communications with Marsland Hill in New Plymouth, and when Mata-rikoriko and other stockades were erected near the Waitara it was doubly useful as a half-way post for signalling with the town. In those days a column of two hundred or two hundred and fifty men, with a howitzer (drawn by bullocks), was required to escort the provision-carts from New Plymouth to the Bell Block.

The Omata stockade, three miles and a half south of New Plymouth, was built early in 1860 entirely by the settlers of the district without any assistance from the Imperial troops. Travelling along the south road through a beautiful and closely settled farming district, with Taranaki's snow peak soaring aloft on the left and the green valleys dipping to the blue ocean on the right, we pass on the inland side, just above the road, a symmetrical grassy mound, about 60 feet high, and perfectly rounded as though artificially formed, with a ring of trench indenting its summit. This is the Omata fort hill, once known among the Maoris as Ngaturi. It was the site of an ancient *pa*. The entrenched crown of the mound measures 25 paces by 13 paces; the ditch which encloses it is about 10 feet wide, and 12 feet deep from the top of the parapet. The stockade which surmounted the hill—all traces of the timber-work have long since disappeared—owed its construction in the first place to two settlers of the district, Mr. T. Good and Mr. G. R. Burton, both of whom received commissions in the Militia. Mr. Good, the first planner of the stockade, was often seen working alone upon the fortification before others took up the task, but sixty or seventy settlers, the pioneers of Omata, joined in and toiled vigorously to provide themselves with a place of refuge and a fort to command the settlements.

This Omata post was so skilfully designed, so serviceable, and withal so picturesque a little fort, set sentrywise there on its round hill, that it is worthy of a detailed description. The figure of the post was oblong. The stockade was constructed of heavy timbers, some of which were as large as could be hauled up by a team of bullocks. They were either whole trunks of small trees or split parts of large ones, and were sunk 3 feet to 4 feet in the ground all round. The height of the solid timber wall so formed was 10 feet. The timbers were roughly trimmed with the axe to bring them as close together as possible and to

J. E. A. From a Sketch by T. Good, Ens. T.M.

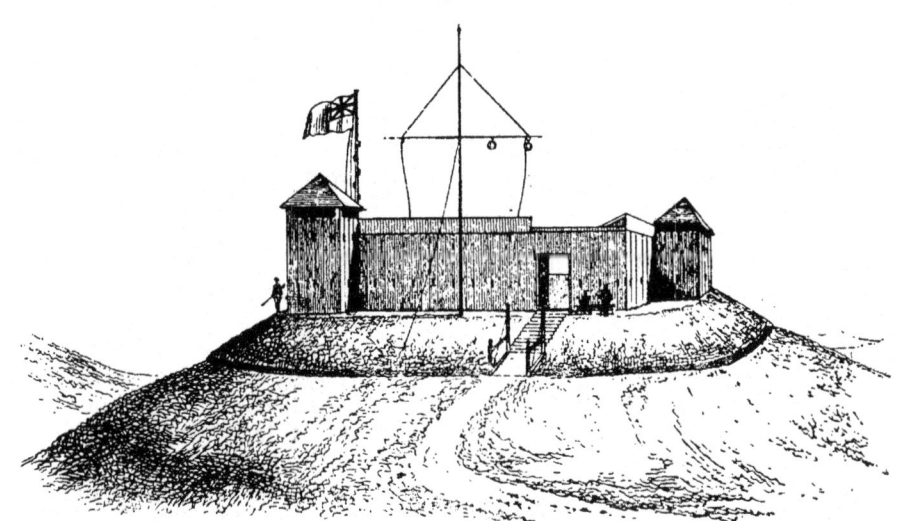

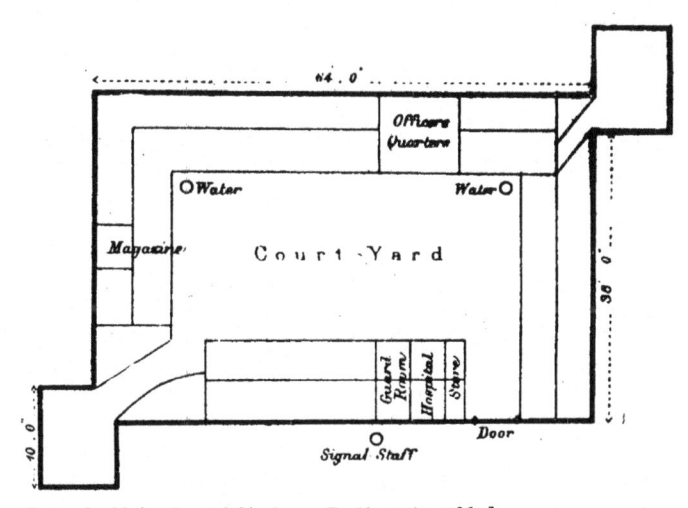

Drawn by Major-General Sir James E. Alexander, 1861.]

Ground Plan.

THE OMATA STOCKADE, TARANAKI.

remove any knots outside which might assist an enemy to scale the stockade. The small spaces left between the logs were covered inside with an upright row of thick slabs. The tops of the timbers were sawn off straight, and sawn battens, 6 inches broad by 3 inches thick, were laid along the top and fastened to the stockade with 7-inch spike nails. The average thickness of the heavy timbers was about 12 inches, and the whole was proof against musket-balls, and against rifle-balls except at very close range. A row of loopholes was cut all round about 5 feet above the inside floor, and there was a double row in the two small flanking bastions. These bastions were of two storeys each, loopholed on all four sides. The lower part was a sleeping-apartment; the upper was a post for sentries at night and in bad weather. The roof of each bastion was clear of the wall-plate, and was made to project about a foot beyond the wall of the building. This arrangement admitted of the sentries keeping a good lookout all round, and at the same time protected them from the weather. It also allowed of firing through the spaces between the roof and the wall-plate when more convenient to do so (as was often the case at long range) than through the loopholes. The roof of the sides and end of the main building within the walls projected about a foot beyond the stockade so as to make it practically impossible to scale. The deep and wide ditch was crossed by a drawbridge which had a span of 10 feet and worked on strong hinges; by ropes fastened to its front edge and running through blocks on top of the inner posts it was lifted up perpendicularly at night. The entrance-gate was made of two thicknesses of timber, each $2\frac{1}{2}$ inches thick, the outer timbers running up and down, the inner diagonally, and strongly fastened with spike nails riveted. This formed a solid door 5 inches thick. Around the inner walls were built the garrison's quarters, leaving an open courtyard in the middle of the stockade. The loopholes were cut at such an elevation as enabled the men to use their rifles clear of the roof, and also to cover any object down to the bottom of the ditch; as well as from the outer edge of the ditch down the glacis, and everywhere around the stockade. There was no "dead ground" around the little fort; and, whatever the weather, the men were firing under cover. Outside, on the inner edge of the trench, stood the signal-staff, worked from within the building. It was a single tree, 60 feet long, sunk 6 feet in the ground, and secured by stays and guys.

Mr. G. R. Burton, who designed the interior arrangements, was Captain in the Militia, and he received high praise for his amateur military engineering-work from so competent an authority as Colonel (afterwards Major-General) Sir James E. Alexander, 14th Regiment, who wrote in 1860 a report on the Omata stockade for the technical papers of the Royal Engineers' Institute, England.

PROCLAMATION.

The inhabitants will in future be required to have a candle or lamp at their front windows at night ready to light in case of alarm, and are desired to secure their doors and lower windows. The Police to see to this.

C. E. GOLD,
Colonel Commanding the Forces
New Zealand.

New Plymouth, 20th April, 1860.

PROCLAMATION.

All families numbering five children or upwards drawing rations will hold themselves in readiness to proceed to Port Cooper by the first opportunity. Passages will be provided, and every attention shall be paid to their comforts. Lads over 16 may be excepted.

(Signed) C. E. GOLD,
Colonel Commanding the Forces
New Zealand.

Friday, 27th July, 1860.

Proclamations under Martial Law, New Plymouth.

CHAPTER XIX.

THE BATTLE OF WAIREKA.

The gully-riven littoral of Waireka, five miles south-west of New Plymouth, was the theatre of an engagement (28th March, 1860) which proved the fighting-capacity of Taranaki's newly trained Volunteers and Militia, and saved the town from direct attack by the united strength of the southern tribes. The encounter was doubly memorable because it was the first occasion on which a British Volunteer corps engaged an enemy on the battlefield.

The British move upon the Waitara was quickly followed by the decision of Taranaki, Ngati-Ruanui, and Nga-Rauru, the three principal tribes of the coast curving round from Ngamotu to the Waitotara, to come to Wiremu's Kingi's aid. Ten days after the taking of the L *pa* five hundred warriors of these people, the best fighting-blood on the whole west coast south of New Plymouth, had arrived within six miles of the town. After ceremonious welcomes at Ratapihipihi and other settlements they gathered in a strongly entrenched and stockaded *pa* at Kaipopo, the most commanding part of the hills at Waireka. The fortification was alongside the road from Omata, and about a mile and a half south of the stockade commanding that settlement; the surf-beaten shore was less than three-quarters of a mile away. The district was already partially settled by Europeans, and farmhouses were scattered over the much-dissected coastland between the ranges and the sea. Clear streams, rock-bedded, coursed down through the numerous narrow wooded valleys. One of these was the Waireka ("Sweet Water"); it was joined just at the beach by a smaller hill-brook, the Waireka-iti. This broken terrain, with its spurs, knolls, and ravines giving abundance of cover, was an admirable country for the Maori's skirmishing tactics. The natives who composed the fighting force on this side of New Plymouth were chiefly Taranaki, composed of Ngamahanga, Patukai, Ngati-Haumia, Ngarangi, and other *hapus*, under Kingi Parengarenga (afterwards killed at Sentry Hill), Hori Kingi, the celebrated Wiremu Kingi te Matakaatea (not to be confused with Wiremu Kingi te Rangitaake, of Waitara), and Arama Karaka.

A war-party of Ngati-Ruanui, chiefly the Ngaruahine *hapu* of the Waimate Plains, arrived just in time for the battle; their principal *rangatira* was Te Hanataua. The men were armed with double-barrel shot-guns, and were well supplied with powder and lead; several carried rifles.

On the 27th the first blood was shed in the Omata district. Two farmers (S. Shaw and H. Passmore) and a New Plymouth business man (Samuel Ford) were shot and tomahawked by ambush-parties on the roadside near the Primitive Methodist Chapel; next day the bodies of two boys (Pote and Parker), similarly killed, were found. On the morning of the 28th, when New Plymouth was in a state of intense excitement over the news of these murders, the military authorities decided to despatch an expedition to Omata for the purpose of rescuing the Rev. H. H. Brown and his family, and several other settlers who had remained on their farms. The chiefs, however, had made proclamation that Mr. Brown would be protected, and a notice in Maori was posted at Omata declaring that the road to his place and to his neighbours' must not be trodden by war-parties. The minister was *tapu* because of his sacred office; as for the others enumerated, one settler was Portuguese and one French; the war was only with the British. The force detailed for the expedition consisted of three officers and twenty-five men of the Royal Navy (H.M.S. " Niger "), four officers and eighty-four rank and file of the 65th Regiment, with 103 officers and men of the Taranaki Rifle Volunteers and fifty-six Taranaki Militia. Lieut.-Colonel Murray was in command. Lieutenant Blake was in charge of the bluejackets (who were to be followed, if necessary, by a larger force from the " Niger "). The colonial force was under the command of Captain Charles Brown, who had with him the following officers :- Militia—Captain and Adjutant Stapp, Lieutenants McKechney and McKellar, Ensign W. B. Messenger; Volunteers—Captain Harry A. Atkinson, Lieutenants Hirst, Hamerton, Webster, and Jonas.

The first blunder made by the Imperial officers was the division of this small force despatched into hostile territory. Captain Brown, in command of the settlers, was ordered to march by the sea-coast, keeping along the beach until he reached the rear of the Maori positions at Waireka. The Regulars, under Lieut.-Colonel Murray, marched by the main road for the announced purpose of dislodging a war-party reported to be at the spot known as the " Whalers' Gate," about three-quarters of a mile on the town side of the Omata stockade. The Volunteers and Militia were expected to recover the out-settlers supposed to be in danger, and to march back by the road, joining Murray at the " Whalers' Gate." The force was not sent from town until after 1 p.m. (the colonials starting first), yet the order was given by Colonel Gold that it must be back by dark. Lieut.-Colonel Murray's implicit but unintelligent obedience to this order involved, as it developed, the desertion of the settlers' column at a critical juncture in the combat of the Waireka.

Murray did not meet with any opposition at the "Whalers' Gate," where there was no trace of Maoris. He moved leisurely along the south road until, near the Omata stockade, the sound of rapid firing about two miles off, near the sea, indicated that the civilian force was hotly engaged. He despatched the naval detachment and some of the 65th, under Lieutenant Urquhart, to Brown's assistance, while he took the main body along the road

SIR HARRY ATKINSON, MAJOR, N.Z.M.

Captain Harry Atkinson commanded No. 2 Company, Taranaki Rifle Volunteers, in the Battle of Waireka. He fought at Mahoetahi and in many other engagements, and commanded a company of Bush Rangers, 1863–64. He was promoted to be Major in 1864. He was Premier of New Zealand, 1876–77, 1883–84, and 1887–91; was knighted in 1888, and was Speaker of the Legislative Council when he died in Wellington in 1892.

and down a lane which turned off on the right to the sea. Some distance down the lane he turned into a grass paddock, entrenched his men, and opened fire on the Maori skirmishers at long range. He had a rocket-tube, and fired some rockets into a wooded gully on his left front, up which some of the Maoris were moving to cut him off from the main road, as he thought. Accordingly he took up a position in the lane so as to secure the main road, and confined himself to firing rockets at the distant *pa* and any groups of Maoris observed, and rifle-fire on the native skirmishers over the spurs and in the ravines, until he considered it time to sound the " Retire."

Meanwhile the Volunteers and the Militia were fighting a desperate battle on the slopes above the beach. Captain Brown, who had not had any previous experience of soldiering, had wisely requested his adjutant, Captain Stapp, to take command, and that veteran of the " Black Cuffs " conducted the afternoon's operations with the coolness characteristic of the well-skilled regular soldier. He had an old comrade with him who put good stiffening into the civilian ranks, Colour-Sergeant (afterwards Lieutenant) W. H. Free; both had been corporals in the 58th in Heke's War. The Volunteers were armed with medium Enfield rifles (muzzle-loading); the Militia had the old smooth-bore muskets (percussion cap), such as were first served out in the late " forties." Of ammunition there were only thirty rounds per man; no reserve supply was brought.

When the Waireka was reached where it runs down on the ironsand beach the advanced guard under Colour-Sergeant Free caught sight of a large number of armed Maoris coming down at a run from their *pa* on the Kaipopo ridge nearly a mile away. Free fired the first shot in the engagement, and Volunteer Charles Wilson Hursthouse (the surveyor) the second, at 400 yards range. Free and his party doubled forward and took cover behind a furze hedge and rail fence to prevent the Maoris seizing it. Resting his Minie rifle on the lowest rail of the fence, Free sighted for 300 yards and drilled a conspicuous warrior through his cap-band as was afterwards discovered. " Good for you, Free," shouted one of the veteran's comrades. Captain Atkinson rushed up the leading company (comprised of half the column, Volunteers and Militia mixed) in support, and took post on high ground on the south side of the Waireka, where his accurate fire kept the Maoris back for a time. However, as the number of the assailants was increased every minute by reinforcements from the *pa*, and as he was in danger of being outflanked, Captain Stapp ordered a retreat on Mr. John Jury's farmhouse, a small building on a terrace above the beach. Captain Atkinson, on his own suggestion, was sent to an excellent strategic position above the Waireka Stream and on the edge of the cliff overlooking the sea; from here he could command the flanks and rear of Jury's homestead and the mouth of the Waireka. Holding this position until the battle ceased, Atkinson and his men inflicted numerous casualties on Ngati-Ruanui. Captain Brown, with the second company of the Volunteers and Militia, occupied some rising ground immediately on the other side of the Waireka, and devoted his attention to a large number of Maoris who were firing from the cover of the bush and flax in the lower part of the river-gully. Here he was joined presently by Lieutenant Urquhart and about twenty-five men of the 65th, several of Lieutenant Blake's bluejackets (Blake had been rather badly wounded on the plateau above while endeavouring to clear the natives out of the gully), and twenty-five Militia and Volunteers under Lieutenant Armstrong from the Omata stockade, also Lieutenant MacNaghten, R.A.

The Maoris were gradually forced back into an upper gully, but, as Captain Brown perceived an attempt on their part, under cover of the high flax-bushes, to cut off the way of retreat to the

CHARLES WILSON HURSTHOUSE.

The late Mr. Hursthouse, who was Captain in the New Zealand Militia, carried out pioneer survey-work in Taranaki and the King Country under adventurous conditions. In 1860, at the age of nineteen, he surveyed the disputed Pekapeka Block, Waitara. He served in the Taranaki Rifle Volunteers at Waireka and Mahoetahi and in numerous other engagements and skirmishes, and later was an officer in the Military Settlers Force and Volunteer Militia Scouts. He became Chief Engineer of Roads and Bridges for New Zealand.

Omata stockade, he sent Urquhart to hold the commanding ground on the opposite (north) side of the Waireka-iti Stream, and so place the natives between two fires. The 65th lieutenant was doing good work here in an excellent position when he was recalled

THE BATTLE OF WAIREKA.

From a drawing by A. H. Messenger.

THE BATTLE OF WAIREKA.
Defence of Jury's Farmhouse by the Taranaki Volunteers and Militia.

by Lieut.-Colonel Murray. "I must go," he told a Volunteer regretfully; "the 'Retire' has sounded three times." With great reluctance he moved off at last, and the colonials now found themselves without support from the Regulars, save for three bluejackets and eight 65th men who had been left with Brown and Stapp.

Murray, oblivious to everything but the duty of obeying his superior officer's order to be back in New Plymouth by dark,

CAPTAIN (AFTERWARDS COLONEL) W. B. MESSENGER, N.Z.M.

(Died, 1922.)

As Ensign of Militia, William B. Messenger fought at Waireka and Mahoetahi and in other engagements. He became Captain in 1863, and served in the Military Settlers, and later in the Armed Constabulary as Sub-Inspector. For some years he was in command of the frontier redoubt at Pukearuhe, White Cliffs. In 1885 he was appointed to the command of the Permanent Artillery at Wellington, and in 1902 he went to South Africa in command of the 10th New Zealand Contingent. His military service extended over forty-three years.

marched his force along the main road homeward, and left the hard-pressed settlers to extricate themselves in the best way they could. It was now nearly dark, and the Maoris were swarming over the broken ground above the positions of the Volunteers and Militia, although many were picked off by Atkinson's company. The little force had suffered several casualties: a sergeant of Militia (Fahey) and a corporal of marines from the "Niger" had been killed and eight men wounded, including Lieutenant Hamerton and Private W. Messenger (father of Ensign Messenger). The latter had his right elbow shattered. Atkinson stood fast in his position, while the rest of the force concentrated on Stapp's post, Jury's farmhouse. Hurriedly they put the place in a state of defence, throwing together a breastwork of all sorts of material —firewood, fence posts and rails, and even sheaves of oats from stacks near the house.

The settlers were in a serious state, for their ammunition was almost done, and they believed that the Maoris would rush them when night fell. The utmost care was exercised in firing, and Ensign Messenger, at Captain Stapp's request, went round and saw that each man had a cartridge for the expected rush; there would then be only the bayonet.

Suddenly, just at dusk, the distant sound of firing and then loud cheering was heard from the direction of Kaipopo *pa*. What did it mean? Had Murray returned and attacked the *pa* after all? Some of the Volunteers went up the spur to see what it was, and found the natives falling back in great haste upon their fort. It was not considered wise, however, to march the force up towards the *pa*, ammunition being so short, and the wounded needing removal to Omata. The moon was near its setting, and as soon as it was down Captain Stapp gave the order to march, and the little force commenced its return over the hills and gullies, Atkinson's men forming the rearguard with the eight soldiers of the 65th who had remained with the settlers. Bearing their dead and wounded, the two companies retired on the Omata stockade, and half an hour after midnight reached the town, escorted in the last stage of the tramp by a body of soldiers and Volunteers who had gone out to look for them.

Turn now to the Kaipopo *pa*. The shouting and firing which had puzzled the beleaguered force at the Waireka, and the sudden withdrawal of the Maoris, were explained when the Omata stockade was reached. The diversion that saved the settlers from a rush and perhaps annihilation was due to the energy and courage of Captain Peter Cracroft, the commander of H.M.S. "Niger." At the sound of alarm guns from Marsland Hill, fired early in the afternoon to warn the women and children to take refuge in the fort, Cracroft landed a party of bluejackets and marines with their officers, numbering sixty in all. Colonel Gold had heard that the town was to be attacked by the Atiawa from the north, aided by some Waikato and other natives, hence his signal for another landing-party. With the reluctant consent of Colonel Gold, who was nervous for the safety of the town, the naval column set out for the Waireka. The sound of heavy firing was plainly heard in New Plymouth. Cracroft was guided out by a young mounted Volunteer, Frank Mace (afterwards Captain and a New Zealand Cross hero), who had ridden from the battlefield with a message for assistance, and narrowly escaped being shot by some Maoris whose intended ambush he had detected, and who fired on him as he was cutting across some paddocks to avoid them. At the Omata stockade two more young Volunteers, C. and E. Messenger, joined as guides, and led the "Nigers" by the nearest road to the Maori *pa*. Cracroft communicated with Murray, who was on his right and just about to fall back, and, regardless of messages to retire, he proceeded in his direct sailor fashion to attack. It was now about half past 5, and nearly dark. After sending some rockets into the Maori position at a range of 700 yards, he rapidly led his men against the *pa*, turning its right flank, and stormed it most gallantly. The bluejackets did their work in the traditional Navy manner, mostly with the cutlass. Charging up the hill and making little account of the fire from the rifle-pits, they dashed at the stockade with a tremendous cheer. Three flags bearing Maori war-devices were seen waving above the smoke-hazed palisades. "Ten pounds to the man who pulls down those flags!" shouted Cracroft. Yelling, shooting, and slashing, the Navy lads were over the stockade in a few moments, "like a pack of schoolboys," in the phrase of a survivor of Waireka. The first man in was William Odgers, the Captain's coxswain. He charged through to the flagstaff and hauled down the Maori ensigns. One was a flag with the patriotic emblems of Mount Egmont rising above the blue, the Sugarloaf Island (Ngamotu), and a bleeding heart. For this exploit Odgers received the first V.C. awarded in the New Zealand Wars.

Drawn from a photo.]
CAPTAIN PETER CRACROFT, R.N.

"We made good quick work of it," says a veteran of the "Niger" party (Mr. R. B. Craven, of Parakai, Helensville). "Our loss was light, but we laid out about a hundred of the Maoris. They slashed at us with their long-handled tomahawks from their fire-trenches inside, and a few of our boys were cut about the legs in this way, but we soon disposed of all opposition."

Cracroft attributed his small casualties (four men wounded) to the rapidity of the attack and to the semi-darkness, which favoured the small party and spoiled the aim of the *pa* defenders. Sixteen Maoris were killed in the trenches and several others outside. The majority of the garrison made a quick retreat into the cover of the bush and the ravines below. Such was the dashing Royal Navy way. It might not have been so successful earlier in the day, and it could not have been carried out effectively in the darkness. The attack came just at the right moment, and in the right manner to divert the natives' attention from the settlers' force and upset the usual Maori tactics.

New Plymouth was frantic with mingled excitement and alarm that 28th March. The women and children, hurrying to Marsland Hill citadel at the sound of the guns, awaited in intense anxiety the news from the scene of battle, where the settlers and townspeople, young and old, were fighting on the Waireka banks. Like the Maoris, fathers and sons and brothers and cousins fought together that day. Four of the Messengers were on the field, and several Bayleys, and members of many other pioneer Taranaki families. When Lieut.-Colonel Murray returned after nightfall, and it became known that he had left the civilian force fighting against heavy odds, indignation ran high; and on the arrival later of Cracroft's force, with the bluejackets displaying the captured flags but unaccompanied by the Volunteers and Militia, the tension and fears increased. At last, at 11 o'clock at night, a relief force of soldiers and citizens marched out to the rescue under Major Herbert, but they had not gone far down the south road before they met Brown's weary force tramping in. The scenes of rejoicing in the town must have gladdened the hearts of Cracroft and his sailor lads, but for whom it would indeed have been a disastrous night for the settler families of Taranaki.

The European casualties totalled only fourteen killed and wounded. The Maoris lost heavily through the accurate fire of Stapp's and Atkinson's men and the quick attack of Cracroft. Their killed amounted probably to fifty, with as many wounded.

The tribes concerned dispersed southward, removing their casualties in bullock-carts, and the combined movement on New Plymouth was abandoned. The Rev. H. H. Brown and his family and several other settlers came into town safely the day after the fight under Volunteer escort.

The popular opinion of Colonel Gold's methods of command and the failure of Lieut.-Colonel Murray to temper his rigid obedience to orders with some intelligence or initiative was expressed in strongly condemnatory terms. A Court of inquiry sat to consider Murray's conduct; the president was Colonel Chute (afterwards General), of the 70th Regiment; the evidence was sent to England. Captain Charles Brown and Captain Stapp were promoted Majors for their efficient work at Waireka. Captain Harry Atkinson received his majority in 1864.*

On the day after Waireka the "Niger" flew the three captured Maori flags at her mainmast-head. Next day she steamed down the coast and anchored off the reef-fringed shore at Warea, where there was a large Maori *pa* occupied by several hundred Maoris. The ship opened fire with shells and rockets, but owing to the long range not much damage was done.

In April considerable British reinforcements and large supplies of warlike stores arrived at New Plymouth from Australia. H.M. steam-corvettes "Cordelia" and "Pelorus," and the steamers "City of Sydney," "City of Hobart," and "Wongawonga," brought several hundred men of the 13th and 40th Regiments and some Royal Artillery. The warships landed some parties of sailors and marines, and there was now a Naval Brigade of about three hundred men on shore, under command of Commodore Beauchamp-Seymour (afterwards Lord Alcester), of the "Pelorus." The first Australian warship, the "Victoria," a beautiful auxiliary-screw barque, lent by the Government of Victoria, arrived soon afterwards and landed sixty men, who helped to garrison Fort Niger, the sailors' redoubt, on a hill which is now a recreation reserve, on the eastern side of the town. Others garrisoned a redoubt erected on the small hill called Mount Eliot, close to the beach and adjoining the signal-staff and surf-boats.

A four-days expedition along the coast southward as far as Warea was the principal military operation during April, 1860. The movement was directed against the Taranaki and Ngati-Ruanui Tribes who had fought at Waireka. The column consisted of 180 Royal Navy seamen and marines, 280 of the 65th, eighty Volunteers and Militia, forty Royal Artillery with two 24-pounder and four 6-pounder field-pieces, and twenty Royal Engineers. Colonel Gold was in command, and Commodore Beauchamp-Seymour accompanied him. It was a rough march across numerous ravines and unbridged rivers, and through bush and scrub. Wareatea, Mokotura, Warea, and other settlements

---

* Colonel W. B. Messenger, who was Ensign of Militia at Waireka, related the following incident of this inquiry :—

"When Colonel Chute came to hold an inquiry into Lieut.-Colonel Murray's action he visited Waireka and stood on the hill studying the lay of the battlefield. I was sent for to give information about the engagement. Chute asked me, ' Do I understand that that gully down there on your right and that one on your left were filled with Maoris, and that the troops under Colonel Murray were up there on the north side above the Maoris ? '

"' Yes, sir,' I said, ' that is so.'

"' Then,' said the Colonel, ' you ' [meaning the troops] ' ought to have killed every damned one of them !'

"' That is what I thought, sir,' I replied.

"The Colonel waved me away, saying, ' That will do, sir.' "

were entered; several *pas* were demolished, wheat-stacks were burned, a flour-mill rendered useless, and cattle and horses looted. On the return journey a force of two hundred men was left in an entrenched position on the Tataraimaka Block as an advanced outpost for the settlements. This force was withdrawn later. It was in retaliation for the destruction of villages and other property on this expedition that the Taranaki Maoris presently devastated the whole of the abandoned *pakeha* settlements, and systematically pillaged and burned nearly every house outside New Plymouth.

The War-steamer "Victoria."

The steam-corvette "Victoria," which was lent to the New Zealand Government by the authorities of Victoria for use in the Maori War in 1860, was the first ship-of-war built for an Australasian colony. She was launched at Limehouse Dockyard, London, in 1855, from the yards of Messrs. Young, Son, and Magnay. She was a beautifully modelled screw-steamer of 580 tons, built of mahogany, and was barque-rigged to royals. Her armament, supplied from the Royal Arsenal at Woolwich, consisted of one long 32-pounder swivel gun (56 cwt.) and six medium 32-pounder (25 cwt.) broadside guns. Her engines gave her a speed of twelve knots.

CHAPTER XX.

PUKE-TA-KAUERE AND OTHER OPERATIONS.

The winter of 1860 drew on with its heavy rains, which converted the roads and tracks, cut up by the continuous military traffic, into mud-channels, and the difficulties of campaigning were correspondingly increased. The rivers were often in a state of high flood, and the swamps became almost impassable. Under these conditions the Imperial forces fought an action which developed into the most disastrous affair for the British in the first Taranaki War.

Half a mile south-east of Te Kohia (the L *pa*) the native belligerents constructed two forts close together and supporting each other, on small mounds called Puke-ta-kauere and Onuku-kaitara. Outside these strongholds were numerous rifle-pits and trenches, well masked by the high fern and *tutu* bushes. The double fortification was on considerably higher ground than the British main camp at Pukekohe, on the Waitara, and its situation was admirably chosen for defence. The spur on which the twin knolls were embossed lay between two small swampy watercourses which joined a short distance to the north-east and ran through a deep morass of flax and *toetoe* to the Waitara River, half a mile distant from Puke-ta-kauere, the northernmost *pa*. The forts thus were situated in a kind of V, with the apex towards the river. The ferny plateau south of the swamps and extending to the cliffs of the Waitara offered suitable ground from which a flanking fire could be poured on any attacking-party. The Onuku-kaitara *pa* was the larger of the two. The other was notable for its strong earthwork defences; it was surrounded with two trenches; the scarp of one of these ditches presented a face nearly 20 feet high. To all intent the places were impregnable to assault. Unfortunately for the British, the commander at the Waitara neglected to have the approach to the *pas* properly scouted, and lack of knowledge of the ground, conjoined to an ignorance of Maori field-engineering genius and skill in skirmishing tactics, was responsible for a defeat which enormously heartened up the *pakeha's* antagonists, and deepened the dissatisfaction of the Taranaki settlers with the Imperial command. The

British main camp was only a mile away, and the building of the *pas* was carried on in plain view of the soldiers. From the Onuku-kaitara *pa* flagstaff flew a Maori ensign, white with a black cross. A reconnaissance-party from the camp was fired on. The senior officer, Major T. Nelson (40th Regiment), a veteran of the Indian and Afghan wars, then determined to attack.

The garrison of the double fort was much better fighting-material than the purely Atiawa force which had built and evacuated Te Kohia at the beginning of the war. Reinforcements of warriors had arrived from the Upper Waikato and the district afterwards known as the King Country, and from the southern parts of the west coast. The tribes which confronted Nelson and his 40th, besides Te Atiawa and Taranaki, were Ngati Maniapoto and Ngati-Raukawa, Nga-Rauru (Patea and Waitotara), and Whanganui. Waikato as a tribe did not come, but some of their eager young men (such as Mahutu te Toko, a near relative of the Maori King) had joined Ngati-Maniapoto.

Te Huia Raureti, of Ngati-Maniapoto, one of the few survivors of the Orakau defence, gave me an account of his tribe's first participation in the Waitara war. He said that when the news of the quarrel over the Waitara reached the Upper Waikato the *runanga* (council of chiefs) of Ngati-Maniapoto discussed the question of assisting Wiremu Kingi. This *runanga* consisted of Rewi Maniapoto (the *tumuaki*, or head of the council), his cousins Te Winitana Tupotahi and Raureti te Huia Paiaka, Epiha Tokohihi, Hopa te Rangianini, Pahata te Kiore, Matena te Reoreo (the clerk), and several other chiefs. Kihikihi Village was at that time the headquarters of Ngati-Maniapoto, and the *runanga* met in a large house which bore the famous old Hawaikian name "Hui-te-rangiora." This house of assembly was destroyed by the troops when Kihikihi was invaded in February, 1864. The conclave of chiefs did not act hastily. Two delegates, Raureti te Huia Paiaka (father of the narrator) and Pahata te Kiore, were despatched to Taranaki by the *runanga* to investigate the dispute and its causes. Their inquiries satisfied them that Wiremu Kingi's cause was just. "My father and Pahata," said Te Huia Raureti, "came to a decision adverse to Ihaia te Kiri-kumara, the Government adherent, because he had taken sufficient *utu* for his personal wrongs (the seduction of his wife) by killing the offender, and there was no just cause (*takē*) for parting with tribal lands in order further to involve Wiremu Kingi's people. On the return of this deputation to Kihikihi the *runanga* considered their report, and Rewi Maniapoto then went down to Ngaruawahia to lay the matter before King Potatau and his council. He requested the King to consent to a war-party of Ngati-Maniapoto marching to Taranaki in order to assist the Atiawa. The proposal was assented to. The old King delivered his command to the assembly of chiefs in these words: '*Ngati-Maniapoto, haere hei kai ma nga manu o te rangi. Ko koe, e Waikato, ko Pekehawani taku rohe, kaua e takahia.*' ('Ngati-Maniapoto, go you as food for the birds of the air. As for you, Waikato, Pekehawani is my boundary, do not trespass upon it!')"

Pekehawani, an ancient Hawaikian name, was here used by Potatau as an honorific term for the Puniu River, the boundary between the Waikato and the territory of Ngati-Maniapoto. Rewi Maniapoto's tribe only he released for the war, but in all probability the fiery Rewi would have gone in spite of a royal prohibition. Waikato and Ngati-Haua were restrained for the present, but after the news of the Maori victory at Puke-ta-kauere arrived they could no longer be held back from the war. The usual route taken by the Ngati-Maniapoto and the Waikato on their journeys to Taranaki was down the Mokau River by canoe from Totoro to Mokau Heads, thence along the beach by Tonga-porutu and the White Cliffs to Waitara. War-canoe expeditions down the rapid-whitened Mokau frequently covered the distance from Totoro to the Heads (forty-five miles) in one day, and by a forced march the warriors often reached Urenui or the Waitara at the close of the second day.

It was scarcely daylight on the morning of the 27th June when Major Nelson moved out from Waitara camp to the attack. He was accompanied by Captain Beauchamp-Seymour, commanding the Naval Brigade of H.M.S. "Pelorus." The force, totalling about three hundred and fifty, was divided into three. The main body, under Nelson, crossed the Devon Road and marched across the fern plain. A detachment of sixty men of he 40th Regiment, under Captain Bowdler, marched to the left, with orders to occupy a mound south-east of the camp, in order to prevent the natives escaping along the left flank of the main body and attacking the camp. If this was not attempted, Bowdler was to double up to the support of his Major. The other division, 125 strong, consisting chiefly of the Grenadier Company of the 40th, under Captain Messenger (a cousin of Ensign W. B. Messenger, of the Taranaki Militia), was detailed to get possession of Puke-ta-kauere mound, to cut off the retreat from the other *pa*, and to bar the way to Maori reinforcements. The main body (Naval Brigade numbering sixty-five, Royal Artillery with two 24-pounder howitzers, Royal Engineers, and the Light Company of the 40th) moved in extended order towards the south-west side of the fortifications, and was soon engaged by the Maoris in large force.

The artillery opened fire at 7 a.m. from level ground north-west of Onuku-kaitara, but failed to make a large-enough breach in the stockade—in the Major's view—to justify an order for the assault. The Maoris, however, did not wait to be attacked in

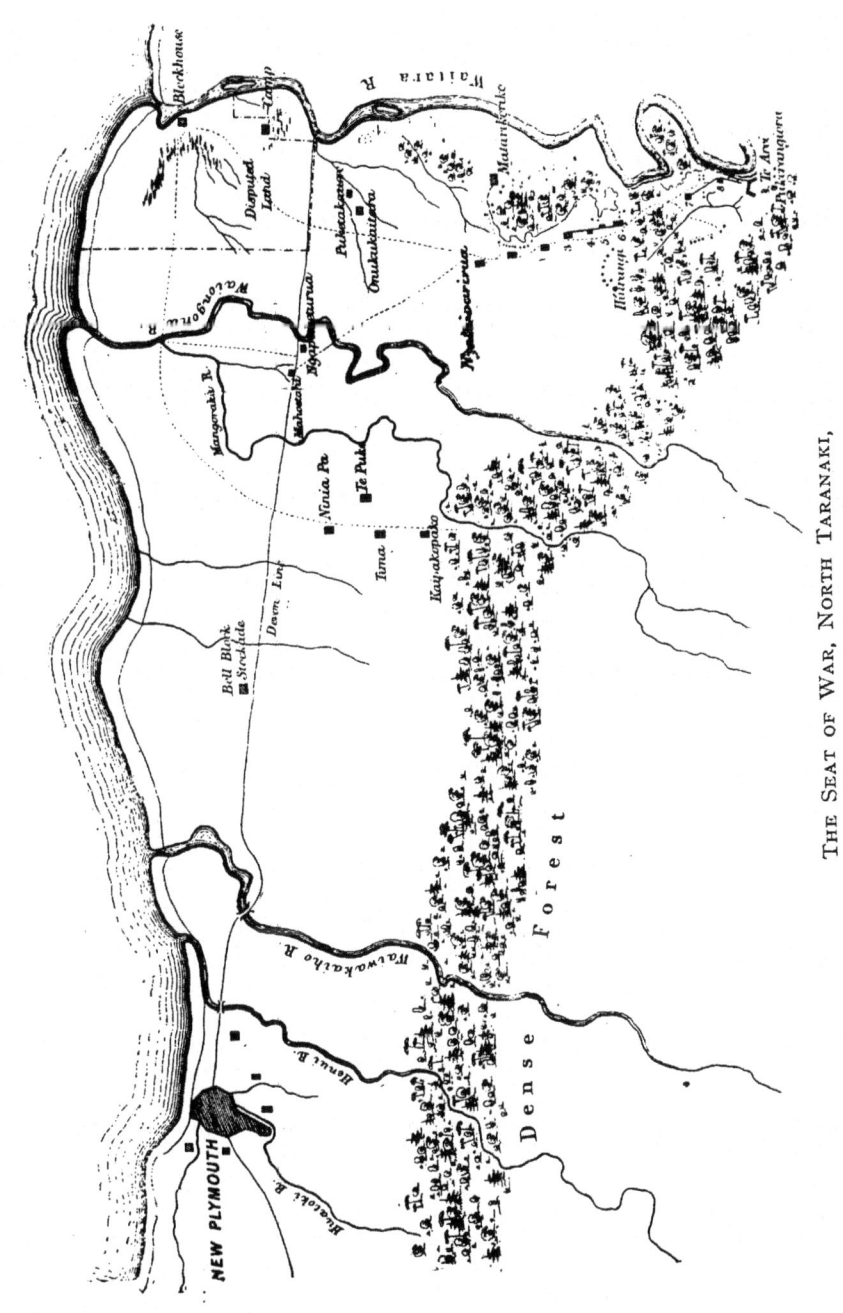

The Seat of War, North Taranaki,
Showing redoubts and line of sap to Te Arei, on the Waitara.

their forts, but came out into the fern and manned their outlying trenches. Their first fire was directed upon Captain Messenger, who was struggling around to the rear of the position on the Waitara side; but Nelson and Beauchamp-Seymour were soon in the thick of it. Large Maori reinforcements hurried down from the Kairau and other settlements in the rear, and quickly worked round the British right flank. Captain Bowdler now brought his division up at the double, but the combined strength was not sufficient to deal with the foe, who were fighting with the utmost fearlessness and determination. The bluejackets and marines, led on by their captain and supported by the Light Company of the 40th, carried a long trench on the right front, but were held up by a deep gully and two more entrenchments dug on the slopes in the fern, and found themselves under a destructive fire from the Maori double-barrel guns, loaded and discharged with lightning-like rapidity. Some survivors declared the fire encountered was hotter than anything in the great Indian battles or in the attack on the Redan in the Crimea. The British right flank came under what was described as a terrible fire from a series of trenches on the sides of the gullies.

In this tight corner Major Nelson looked anxiously, but in vain, for expected reinforcements from New Plymouth. He had arranged with Colonel Gold, Officer Commanding, who had left the time of attack to him, that he would signal with ship's rockets on the night before the movement against the *pas*, Gold undertaking to march at daylight with four hundred men and two guns and take the Maoris on their left flank. Through an artillery non-commissioned officer's default this signal—which would have been seen at the Bell Block stockade and repeated to Marsland Hill— was not sent up. The sergeant forgot to use the rockets, and Gold was unaware of Nelson's attack until the heavy firing was heard in New Plymouth. The force which was then hastily marched to the relief only got as far as the Waiongana. The river was in flood, and, as the firing had ceased, Gold considered there was no need for assistance, and marched his men back to town.

Meanwhile Major Nelson's force and the division under Captain Messenger had desperate work, and the 40th suffered a heavy defeat at the hands of the Maori musketeers. Nelson's regiment and the " Pelorus " men fought well, but they were no match for their active opponents, who came at them with the long-handled tomahawk when the commander began the heavy task of withdrawing his force from the field. It was with great reluctance that he gave the order to sound the " Retire," but there were many casualties, the obstacles in his front were great, there was no sign of reinforcements, and ammunition was running short. With the utmost difficulty the force was extricated; the Light Company was the rearguard. There was ferocious fighting in the fern at close quarters. The killed and many of the wounded were left behind. Captain Beauchamp-Seymour was shot in the leg, and had to be carried off the field. The howitzers, under Lieutenant MacNaghten, R.A., covered the retreat with a steady fire of case shot.

Captain Messenger's division of the 40th, which was given a difficult task, suffered most of all. Messenger, whose subalterns were Lieutenants C. F. Brooke and Jackson, took his men along a flat near the Waitara, and up towards the right rear of the Maori entrenchments. The route was full of obstructions—swamps, gullies, and high fern and scrub—and the Regulars were soon in trouble. It was unfortunate for them that none of Stapp's or Atkinson's settler riflemen were on the field that day. Approaching the double-ditched Puke-ta-kauere *pa* from the rear, Messenger was assailed in great force by Ngati-Maniapoto and Te Atiawa. The high fern and heavy fire caused confusion, and the 40th were soon scattered in groups, fighting a hopeless fight against a skilfully directed enemy. Messenger got some thirty men together and worked his way on in rear of the *pas* until he passed over the ground from which the main body had retreated, and caught up to Major Nelson, who sent him back to bring in the rest of his men. He found Jackson and many of his party fighting their way out. Lieutenant Brooke had been killed in the deep swamp on the Waitara side of the Maori position. Some accounts say that Brooke surrendered, offering his sword, hilt first, to his captor, but in the heat of the battle it was impossible to spare him. He, like some of his men, was waist-deep in the swamp, which few but the half-stripped Maoris could cross. "We killed them in the swamp," says a Maori who fought there. "We used chiefly the tomahawk. Such was the slaughter of the soldiers in that swamp that it came to be called by us Te Wai-Kotero [meaning a pool in which maize and potatoes are steeped until they become putrid]; this was because of the many corpses which lay there after the battle."

In small groups or one by one the survivors floundered through the morass and broke their way through the fern, and were picked up by Messenger and Jackson. Others hid in the fern and crawled out cautiously to the camp. There were many desperate hand-to-hand encounters. A curious report, given currency by Major Nelson in his official report, was that a European, supposed to be a military deserter, was shot dead while leading on a party of Maori skirmishers. Four members of the Taranaki Rifles were on the field that day and under a heavy fire. George Hoby was mounted orderly to Captain Beauchamp-Seymour; George F. Robinson, Oliver Hoby, and Isaiah Freeman drove transport teams hauling ammunition and the howitzers, and taking the wounded off the battle-ground.

The British casualties were thirty killed and thirty-four wounded, or about 18 per cent. of the force engaged. The heaviest losses fell upon the Grenadier Company of the 40th. The Maori casualties were relatively much lighter. Among the killed were two chiefs of Ngati-Maniapoto, Pahata te Kiore (one of Rewi's first delegates to Wiremu Kingi) and Wereta. One of the leaders of this tribe's war-party was Epiha Tokohihi, a member of the Kingite *runanga* at Kihikihi. Hapurona directed the skirmishers of his tribe, Te Atiawa.

The defeat at Puke-ta-kauere and the increasing confidence of the Maoris made it dangerous for the hemmed-in citizens of New

PROCLAMATION.

Much irregularity, delay and inconvenience to the public service being caused by families, ordered to embark on board the steamers provided for their conveyance, disobeying the orders they receive. The Major-General directs it to be notified that he will be compelled to employ the power with which he is invested to enforce the embarkation of such persons But he trusts that the good sense of the inhabitants will render unnecessary his having recourse to a measure so repugnant to his feelings.

By Command,
R. CAREY,
Lieut.-Colonel,
Deputy Adjutant-General.

Head-Quarters,
New Plymouth, 3rd September, 1860.

PROCLAMATION UNDER MARTIAL LAW, NEW PLYMOUTH.

Plymouth to venture out beyond the precincts of the town. It was now that the central portion of the settlement was entrenched, and it was considered necessary to remove the women and children. A proclamation calling upon the families to prepare for departure by sea was issued by Colonel Gold. Steamers were sent to take the women and children to more peaceful homes until the war was over, and most of them went to Nelson, where they were treated with great hospitality; but there were some stouthearted wives and mothers who steadfastly refused to leave their husbands and sons, defied the authorities to shift them, and remained to share the alarms and privations of a state of siege.

Reinforcements of men and artillery came in from Auckland; the principal addition to the garrison was the headquarters of the 40th Regiment (Colonel Leslie), nearly two hundred and fifty strong. Major-General Pratt arrived from Melbourne (3rd August) in the Victorian Government's warship "Victoria," with his Deputy Adjutant-General, Lieut.-Colonel Carey.

During August, 1860, the Taranaki and their southern allies became particularly daring, and numerous skirmishes occurred close to the town. Fort Carrington blockhouse and Fort Niger were fired on, and a lively skirmish occurred on the 20th August within half a mile of the barracks on Marsland Hill. Lieut.-Colonel Murray led out three companies of the 65th and a detachment of "Iris" bluejackets against a body of Maoris estimated at over two hundred. The natives, who left several dead on the field, were driven back into the bush. In a previous skirmish Captain Harry Atkinson, with his Volunteers and Militia, when out on an expedition to bring in settlers' property, fell in with a Maori marauding-party, whom, after a sharp engagement in the open, he followed into the bush, inflicting loss on them. In August two naval 32-pounders were emplaced on the end of the spur in the rear of Marsland Hill fort, in order to sweep the ground to the south of the town.

By night the blaze of fires, and by day columns of dark smoke, announced the destruction of many a settler's deserted home. The Village of Henui, only a mile from the town, was burned. The Maoris, however, invariably respected the churches in the abandoned settlements, and those at Henui, Bell Block, and Omata were found untouched at the end of the war. The town defences were reorganized by Major-General Pratt, and every Volunteer and Militiaman knew his place in the trenches in case of an attack.

The Taranaki Maoris, with some Ngati-Ruanui, laboured with enormous energy at the construction of a system of field-works on the south side of the town. They dug trenches and rifle-pits on the Waireka hills to menace Major Hutchins, who was in charge of a redoubt erected on the site of the Kaipopo *pa*. Tataraimaka was thick with well-designed entrenchments, representing a great amount of spade-work. There were frequent skirmishes about the Omata and the Waireka; at the latter place the Taranakis were shelled from the redoubt.

On the Waitara Major Nelson was busy. He took a column of the 40th and a Naval Brigade across the river and destroyed the large Atiawa villages Manu-korihi ("The Singing Bird") and Tikorangi. He also cleared the country near the road between the Waitara and the Bell Block, and demolished the fortified villages at Ninia and Tima.

On the 4th September a large composite force in three divisions, under Major-General Pratt, marched out to Burton's Hill. four miles south of the town, near Waireka. This place had been entrenched by the southern tribes, but was found deserted, the Maoris having gone home to plant their crops. The roughest work was performed by the division of Rifle Volunteers and Militia under Major Herbert; it penetrated into the bush on the march round to the rear of Burton's Hill, and burned the *pa* at Ratapihipihi on the return journey. The night and day march covered twenty miles under very wintry conditions.

On the 9th September Major-General Pratt, with the largest force yet taken into the field in New Zealand—it numbered fourteen hundred men, including a Naval Brigade, detachments of the 12th, 40th, and 65th Regiments, Rifle Volunteers, and artillery—marched out to Kairau and Huirangi, on the plateau above the left bank of the Waitara. The force burned four

BRITISH POSITIONS AT THE MOUTH OF THE WAITARA.

entrenched villages and looted many horses and cattle—some of which had, no doubt, previously been looted from the settlers. There was a sharp engagement near a large grove of peach-trees at Huirangi with some of the Atiawa under Hapurona, and the bush and trenches which sheltered the Maori *tupara* men were raked with grape and canister shot from the field-guns. A stockaded blockhouse was erected at Onuku-kaitara, on the site of the palisaded *pa* which had been evacuated by the Maoris soon after their victory in June.

On the 19th September a force of six hundred men under Major Hutchins (13th Regiment) marched for the southern settlements, and went as far as the Kaihihi River, where three occupied *pas* close together were discovered. It was found that twenty-six settlers' homes had been burned on the Tataraimaka Block, and about a hundred in the Omata and Waireka districts. The loss in stock driven off from the Tataraimaka was a hundred head of cattle, between two and three thousand sheep, and many horses.

On the 9th October a composite column numbering over a thousand—bluejackets, Royal Artillery and Royal Engineers, 12th, 40th, and 65th detachments, Volunteers, and Militia—marched from New Plymouth along the south road with the object of reducing the fortifications on the Kaihihi River. Major-General Pratt was in command. The Taranaki Rifles, Mounted Rifles, and Militia numbered 105, and there were 150 friendly natives of Te Atiawa under the charge of Mr. Parris, of the Native Department. After a march of twenty miles across difficult country for the large cart-train which accompanied the column, the force entrenched itself on the north side of the Kaihihi River and within three-quarters of a mile of the principal *pa*, Orongomaihangi. On the 11th October a sap was commenced towards the fortification by Colonel Mould, R.E. (Pratt believed in approaching such positions by means of a sap in order to avoid loss of life, and his extraordinarily long advance upon Te Arei later in the campaign remains a classic example of slowness and caution in warfare.) The outer palisade of the *pa* was covered with green flax (as at Ohaeawai in 1845), and the artillery—a naval 68-pounder, two 24-pounder howitzers, and a Coehorn mortar—failed to breach it until next morning (12th October), when a small opening was made. Preparations were being made to blow up part of the stockade with a bag of powder, and an assaulting-party was ready, when the garrison of the fort rushed out at the rear, and the place was taken. The Kaihihi River was crossed, and the Mataiaio *pa*, a square fort, was rushed by the 65th and found empty. The remaining *pa* was Puke-kakariki, a fort on the edge of the river-cliff, about 300 yards from the first *pa* taken; after a short bombardment it was captured without opposition by Captain Stapp's Rifle Volunteers and the friendly natives. All three *pas* were double-palisaded and well rifle-pitted, with shell-proof dugouts. Ropes of plaited flax hanging from the cliff-top at the first *pa* taken showed the way by which the Maoris escaped into the bed of the Kaihihi. All three *pas* were destroyed. Orongomaihangi was a particularly interesting example of Maori military engineering. Its front, with a prominent sharp salient, resembled the figure of a Vauban trace, familiar to students of the science of fortification.

CHAPTER XXI.

THE ENGAGEMENT AT MAHOETAHI.

The Upper Waikato contingent had gone home after Puke-ta-kauere to tell of their victory over the *pakeha*, exhibit their trophies of battle, and plant their crops. The news of their prowess in the field, and the sight of the soldiers' caps and red coats in which some of them paraded, their newly gotten rifles, bayonets, and cartridge-pouches, aroused at once the admiration and the jealousy of their neighbours. Ngati-Maniapoto's exploits fired all the Waikato tribes with ardour for the field. Ngati-Haua's war-fever could no longer be allayed even by the peace-loving Wiremu Tamchana. The stalwart men of Matamata, Tamahere, and Maunga-tautari had reluctantly remained in their *kaingas* when Potatau forbade Waikato and Ngati-Haua to cross the Puniu River and released only Ngati-Maniapoto for the war on the Waitara. But now the old King was dead, and his *runanga* at Ngaruawahia had little control over Ngati-Haua of the plains. Why should Ngati-Maniapoto have all the joy and glory of killing the *pakeha*? Were not Ngati-Haua the kin of the great Waharoa, the most renowned warrior of the Island? So spake Te Wetini Taiporutu and other fiery blades. In vain Wiremu Tamehana urged prudence and foretold disaster. Wetini and his war-party must off to Waitara to kill soldiers themselves. The new season's potatoes planted, the Waikato-Waipa basin and the plains of Matamata were alive with parties of young musketeers marching off for the summer's shooting in Taranaki. Nearly every village from Ngaruawahia southward sent its squad to join the war-parties in reinforcement of Wiremu Kingi. Ngati-Maniapoto provided the larger part of the force; but Ngati-Haua sent a company about eighty strong of the finest fighting-men that ever carried *tupara* and tomahawk. They were the flower of the tribe—tall athletes, fit successors of the invincible warriors whom Waharoa had led against many a stockade. Wetini Taiporutu ("The Surging Sea") was at their head. The other tribes which swelled the strength of the columns marching southward were Ngati-Raukawa and Ngati-Koroki, and these subtribes of Waikato: Ngati-Apakura (from Rangiaowhia), Ngati-Ruru (Te

Awamutu), Ngati-Koura (Orakau), Ngati-Kahukura, and Ngati-Mahuta. Rewi Maniapoto (or Manga, as he was more usually known by his own people) was the leader of the numerous *hapus* which mustered at Kihikihi; with him were Epiha Tokohihi, Te Paetai te Mahia, Mokau (of Ngati-Raukawa, at Orakau), and several other chiefs. Rewi was a veteran of the Waitara trail; as a boy of twelve he had marched on his first war expedition in 1832, when a Waikato army made one of its periodical raids on Puke-rangiora. Wetini's war-party marched apart from the others, eager to reach the scene of war and uphold the name of Ngati-Haua. From Mokau Heads they made a forced march along the beach, and, crossing the Waitara, met their allies on the strongly fortified plain at Kairau. Anxious to distinguish themselves in a battle of their own, they stayed not long at the Kairau, where they were joined by other Waikato tribes, but pushed on to Mahoetahi, an old practically unfortified *pa* on a gentle mound of a hill alongside the Devon Road, two miles and a half from Waitara and seven miles and a half from New Plymouth. Wetini took up this position as a deliberate challenge to the British General. He had sent an invitation to combat quite in the manner of the knights of old. The gage was thrown down in a letter to Mr. Parris, the Assistant Native Secretary in Taranaki: " Come inland and let us meet each other. Fish fight at sea! Come inland and tread on our feet. Make haste! make haste!"

This metaphorical trailing of Ngati-Haua's blanket was taken up by the *pakeha* with spirited alacrity. It was on the evening of the 5th November that Major-General Pratt was informed that Wetini's contingent had crossed the Waitara, and that possibly next morning they would be in the vicinity of Mahoetahi. It was thought that they were marching on New Plymouth. Their numbers were greatly exaggerated. Pratt immediately issued orders for a British column to march from New Plymouth, and another from Waitara, to meet at Mahoetahi next forenoon, and so take the Maoris between two fires. At dawn of day a young Militia officer, Lieutenant F. Standish, with a friendly Maori chief named Mahau, reconnoitred in the direction of Mahoetahi, and saw the Ngati-Haua and Waikato enter an old village on the hilltop. At 5 o'clock on a beautiful clear morning the General's column left the town. It was composed chiefly of the 65th, 40th, and 12th Regiments, with some Royal Artillery manning two 24-pounder howitzers, a few sappers and miners, and two companies of the Taranaki Rifle Volunteers and Militia, with twenty of the Volunteer cavalry. The total strength of the force was 670; of this force the Volunteers made up about 130. Some friendly Maoris also went out, but took no part in the assault. On the march out the advance-guard, in extended order, consisted of a company of the 65th Regiment, under Captain Turner, with a company of Volunteers and Militia as a flank guard on the left, and another company of the 65th flanking the advance on the right. The colonial officers who took part in the expedition were Major Herbert (late 58th Regiment), Captains C. Brown, Harry A. Atkinson, and W. S. Atkinson (the last-named in charge of the

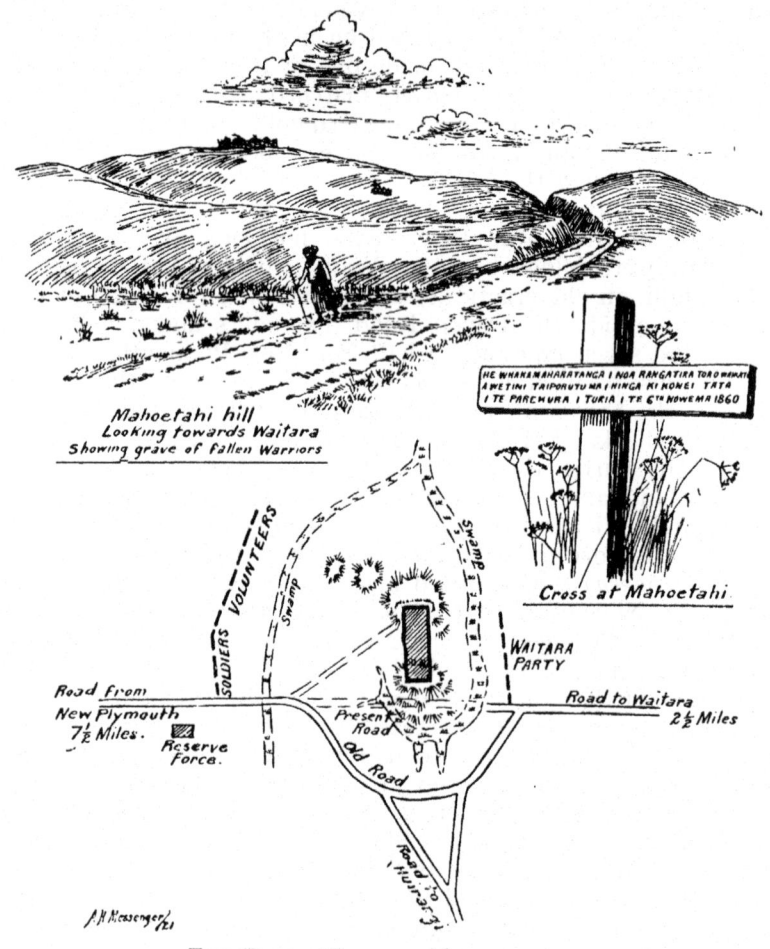

THE BATTLEFIELD OF MAHOETAHI,

Showing site of Maori position stormed by the Imperial and Colonial troops, 6th November, 1860.

Maori contingent), Lieutenants Hamerton, Morrison, Webster, and Standish, and Ensign W. B. Messenger. Mr. R. Parris, who accompanied the force, also had a captain's commission, and later was promoted to major.

Soon after crossing the Mangaoraka the firing commenced, the Maori skirmishers falling back upon the Mahoetahi Hill as the troops advanced. The advance-guard formed a line of skirmishers and moved quickly towards the Maori position, which was visible on the high ground across a narrow swamp directly in front, and just to the left of the main road where it curved inland to avoid the Mahoetahi ridge. Several casualties occurred among the 65th before the swamp was crossed.

The advance-guard halted and lay down on the low ground close to the swamp. "Fix bayonets and prepare to charge" was the next order. Meanwhile the two howitzers, under Captain Strover, R.A., opened fire on the position. The mounted scouts had just reported to the General that the British column from the Waitara was near at hand, moving towards the Maori left rear. The order to cross the swamp was given, and the troops dashed through the muddy water or jumped from tussock to tussock. Re-forming on the other side, they saw before them two low mounds, beyond which was the level top of the Mahoetahi Hill, with no stockade or regular entrenchment showing. The Taranaki Rifles and Militia were to the north-west of the *pa* (the sea side), with two companies of the 65th, facing the west flank of the hill, and another company continuing the line inland, covering the Maori left front. In the rear of the 65th were the reserves, consisting of the 12th and 40th, under Lieut.-Colonel Carey, Deputy Adjutant-General.

"Charge!" was the next order, and then there was a desperate race for the top of the mound. Volunteers and Militia were determined that no Regulars should deprive them of the honour of being first in the *pa*. The front line of the 65th received a heavy volley from the hill and was stayed for a moment or two, but the supporting company came up, and the hilltop was gained. The Taranaki men, led on by Major Herbert, sword in hand, were just breasting the upper slope when the Maoris gave them the next volley. But a moment before it was delivered Major Herbert shouted "Down!" and dropped flat on the ground, and every man followed his example on the instant. The bullets went over their heads. Leaping up, the men were into the Maori position, bayonet and bayonet with the big Irishmen of the 65th on their right. No Maori, however brave, could stand in the open before that line of steel. Most of Wetini's men, after the first volley, took cover behind an old parapet, the remains of the ancient fortification which had enclosed the centre of the hilltop, and in a number of excavations, *whare* sites, besides some dilapidated huts and fern, and masked potato-pits, which made good rifle-pits. Having only taken post in the old *pa* that morning, they had not had time to entrench themselves properly. From such cover as there was Ngati-Haua fired heavily, inflicting several casualties on the 65th and the Volunteers. Charging across the *pa*, Herbert's settler soldiers received a heavy volley delivered by the Maoris just under the crest on the reverse slope of the hill; but the fire was too high, and there were no casualties. Meanwhile the 65th had cleared the centre of the hill with the bayonet.

The Maoris retreated to the edge of the swamp on the Waitara side, and Regulars and Volunteers and Militia charged down the slope after them. Now came the most desperate work of the day. Ngati-Haua and their kin of Waikato and Maniapoto turned on the troops like lions. When there was no time to reload their *tuparas* or their rifles they threw down the now-useless weapons and countered bayonet with tomahawk. There were not more than a hundred and fifty Maoris, but, outnumbered as they were, they fought with a splendid heroism. If they were rebels they were glorious rebels. Their one thought now was to *hapai-ingoa* —to uplift the tribal name and fame.

By this time the column from the Waitara side, commanded by Colonel Mould, R.E., had crossed the Waiongana River, and had deployed into line on the inland side of the *pa*, and when the Maoris were driven into the swamp they found their right flank assailed by this force. Mould's column consisted of several companies of the 40th under Major Nelson, a company of the 65th, and a party with a 24-pounder howitzer. A few shells were thrown into the Maoris (narrowly missing the troops), and then the Regulars joined in the attack pursuit.

On the fern flat below the swamp many of the Maoris took cover in old potato-pits and fired upon their foes on the other side. But the weight of the combined advance was irresistible. Fighting yard by yard the gallant Ngati-Haua were forced back. At last they turned and fled, leaving more than a score lying dead among the tufts of tussocks and flax and in the reddened pools of water. Rifles, double-barrel guns, and cartridge-belts strewed the ground of the retreat. With the bursting shells of the howitzers and six hundred Enfields and bayonets compelling their flight, they retreated across the Waiongana towards Huirangi. Wetini Taiporutu himself was killed early in the retreat. His chivalrous challenge won him undying fame, but cost Ngati-Haua two score men. The chase across the Waiongana was carried as far as Nga-tai-pari-rua and Puke-ta-kauere; thence the pursuers returned to the captured hill and marched back to quarters. Colonel Mould was left at Mahoetahi with a force to hold the hill. The friendly Maoris searched the swamp and the hillside for the slain, and collected thirty-seven slain Maoris, most of whom were buried in a large grave dug on the western slope of Mahoetahi. The bodies of Wetini Taiporutu and two other chiefs, identified by the captured Maoris, were taken into New Plymouth and buried in St. Mary's Churchyard. More bodies were discovered on the line of retreat, and the total loss of the Maoris was estimated at about fifty killed and as many more wounded, out of not more than a hundred and fifty engaged. In spite of shell and bullet, they carried away many of their wounded to Huirangi.

The British casualties were four killed and seventeen wounded. The Rifle Volunteers, who shared the honours of the day with the Regulars, divided with them the losses; two of their number were killed (Privates F. Brown and H. Edgecombe), and four were wounded.

New Plymouth rang with stories of the combat in the swamp. An Irish private of the 65th, the moment after shooting a Maori, brained another with the butt of his rifle. "There was some good bayonet-work at Mahoetahi," said a veteran of the Taranaki Rifles, Sergeant W. H. Free (ex 58th), to the writer. "One of our men, W. Marshall, had an encounter in the swamp with a powerful Maori, who tried to wrest his rifle from him. Marshall at last got his arms free, and sent his bayonet clean through his opponent's body up to the locking-ring." A Maori got a soldier of the 65th face downwards in the muddy swamp-water, and would have drowned him but for a bullet from a fellow-soldier which stretched the Ngati-Haua dead. A soldier of the same regiment bayoneted a Maori through the chest, but the amazing warrior gripped the barrel of the rifle with his left hand and tomahawked his opponent on the arm before he fell.

Wiremu Kingi and his Atiawa held aloof from their brave allies on the battle-day, although they could have altered the fortunes of the day in some degree by coming up in the rear and checking the British attack. But Wetini and his men were afire with a desire to fight for their own hands that day, and the Atiawa contented themselves with the part of distant spectators.

Many a village of the Waipa and the Matamata plains resounded with the *tangi* of grief for the men when the wounded remnant of Wetini's contingent made their painful way home. There were some ghastly wounds among the warriors. The venerable half-caste chief Pou-patate Huihi, of Te Kopua, who fought at Mahoetahi and saw Wetini Taiporutu shot, says, "One of our men, Te Whitu, had his lower jaw carried away by a bullet. We bound it up with a cloth round his head, and he came home with us, recovered, and lived for many years afterwards." Besides Wetini, a number of chiefs of importance fell at Mahoetahi. The principal man of Ngati-Maniapoto killed was Te Paetai te Mahia, from Kihikihi. Ngati-Ruru (Te Awamutu) lost Hakopa, and Ngati-Raukawa the chief Mokau te Matapuna, of Orakau. "When the survivors returned to the Waikato," says Te Huia Raureti, of Ngati-Maniapoto, "the grief of our people at this disaster was intense, and it was felt that the defeat could never be avenged in full." The survivors did not return, however, without an effort to obtain *utu* for the loss of so many comrades. It was not many weeks after Mahoetahi before Ngati-Maniapoto and Waikato made a most determined attack upon No. 3 Redoubt at Huirangi, and only drew off after losing more than fifty men. The cumulative effect of these disasters was to heighten the war feeling throughout the Waikato and hasten the outbreak in the Auckland Province.

To this day a song of lamentation, composed by a woman named Hokepera for those killed at Mahoetahi, is heard among the people of Ngati-Maniapoto. This *waiata* (chanted to the writer by the two old comrades Te Huia Raureti and Pou-patate) is as follows:—

> *Kaore taku huhi, taku raru, ki a koutou,*
> *E pa ma, e haupu mai ra!*
> *Ka hua hoki au ki a Epiha ma e hui nei ki te runanga,*
> *He kawe pai i te tika.*
> *Kaore he mahi nui i nga maunga a Whiro kua wareware.*
>
> *Hare ra, e Tima, i te riri kaihoro a Ngati-Haua;*
> *Kaore i whakaaro ko te kupu pai a Haapurona.*
> *Ko te aha, e Rau (Raureti), e Rewi, ma korua nei?*
> *Heoi ano ra ma koutou he kawe tangata ki te Po,*
> *Aue i te mamae ra—i!*
>
> *Anea kau ana te whenua, tangi kotokoto ai te tai o Puniu.*
> *E whakahakiri ana nga tohu o te rangi, e—e.*
> *Kanapa kau ana te uira i runga o 'Tautari, te hiwi ki Rangitoto;*
> *Ko te tohu o te mate ra—i!*
>
> *Ka riro Paetai, Mokau, Tainui, Te Arawa, Raukawa, Motai—i!*
> *E koa ra e rau tangata ka takoto kau to moni!*
> *Tenei taku poho e tuwhera kau nei, he wai kokiringa mo*
> *Kiri-kumara, te tangata whakanoho i te riri.*
> *Te kino, e—e—i!*

[TRANSLATION.]

Alas! my grief, my woe! Alas, for you, my chieftains, lying in heaps on yonder mound of death! Ah! once I listened to Epiha and his chiefs in council; then I thought their words were laden with goodness and with truth. On the dark hills of Death their plans were brought to naught.

Farewell O Tima, overwhelmed in the flood of battle. 'Twas the fatal deed of Ngati-Haua, they who heeded not the wise counsel of Hapurona. What of your words, O Raureti, O Rewi? 'Tis enough that you have borne warriors down to the black night of Death. Ah me! the sorrow of it!

The land is swept by war's red tide. Mournfully roll the waters of Puniu; the waters sob as they flow. I heard the thunder's distant mutter, the rumbling omen of the sky. I saw the lightning's downward flash, the fire of portent, on Tautari's peak, on Rangitoto's mountain height—the finger of Death to the tribes!

Thou'rt gone, O Paetai! Thou'rt gone, O Mokau! Swept away are the heroes of Tainui, Te Arawa, Raukawa, Motai. Our foes in multitudes rejoice; the treasure is laid bare and desolate. See now my unprotected breast, naked to the spear of Kiri-kumara. 'Twas he who raised this storm of war. Alas! the evil of it!

NOTES.

The composer of this song of lamentation over the dead refers to the Maori belief that the passing of the spirits of chieftains was accompanied by thunder and lightning, and that the rumble of thunder along certain mountain-peaks was a portent of disaster or death to the people. The downward play of lightning upon sacred mountains was regarded as a sign that death would strike or had stricken members of the tribe. Thus Maungatautari was a *maunga-hikonga-uira* (lightning peak) of the Ngati-Raukawa Tribe; Rangitoto was the lightning mountain of the Ngati-Mıniapoto.

Major-General Sir James Alexander narrates this story of Mokau te Matapuna's end: " Mokau, retreating, saw at the edge of it [the swamp] a friend lying mortally wounded. He stopped, and, though the avengers were close behind, he seized the hand of the dying man and stooped to say farewell and to press noses in the native fashion. Raising himself up, he himself was shot through the heart, and fell across the body of his friend. His noble act of friendship had thus a fatal result."

The site of the Battle of Mahoetahi is easily identified to-day. The main road (Devon Road) from New Plymouth to Waitara cuts through the inland (south-east) end of the *pa* hill at seven miles and a half from New Plymouth. On the seaward end of the hill, which is about 60 feet high, trending at right angles to the road, there is a wire-fenced enclosure, with numerous large boulders scattered about, and the turf is uneven with the remains of olden trenches, rifle-pits, and sites of dug-in *whares*. This was the position stormed by the troops. On the slope of the hill facing New Plymouth is a smaller enclosure, with a large timber cross, lichen-crusted. This is the sacred spot where nearly forty of the Maori defenders were buried. The inscription on the cross reads :—

" *He whakamaharatanga i nga Rangatira toa o Waikato a Wetini Taiporutu ma, i hinga ki konei tata i te Parekura i turia i te 6th Nowema, 1860.*"

The meaning of this legend is :—

" In remembrance of the brave chiefs of Waikato, of Wetini Taiporutu and his comrades, who fell close to this spot in the battle fought on the 6th November, 1860."

On the reverse side of the hill, which presents a steeper slope than the western side, the ground falls to a narrow swamp, the place where so many of the Ngati-Haua made their last stand. The Devon Road intersects this part of the battlefield, and passes on the right the ancient settlement Ngapuke-tu-rua, with its two tree-grown mounds, on one of which a British stockade was built shortly after the engagement at Mahoetahi.

CHAPTER XXII.

OPERATIONS AT KAIRAU AND HUIRANGI.

The defeat at Mahoetahi, so far from crushing the Maori spirit, hardened up the fighting-fibre of Wiremu Kingi's northern allies. Reinforcements from Ngati-Maniapoto and Waikato came marching down the coast, and the story of the losses in the Mahoetahi marsh set the warrior soul athirst for revenge. Those who had lost relatives sallied out on scouting expeditions, laying ambuscades and cutting off European stragglers. Several *pakeha* settlers out seeking cattle or horses were shot and tomahawked within a short distance of New Plymouth during the summer of 1860–61. At this time the garrison of Taranaki had been reduced by several hundreds of Imperial troops, who were considered necessary for the protection of Auckland, owing to an alarm of coming hostilities with Waikato. By December, 1860, the Maori belligerents had constructed a series of field fortifications on the plateau bounding the Waitara River on the south (left bank), and garrisoned these works with considerably over a thousand men. Kairau and Huirangi were the principal defences—skilfully engineered lines of rifle-pits, trenches, and covered ways, their flanks resting on the thickly wooded gullies that dissected the edges of the tableland. These works barred the way inland to the historic hill *pa*, Puke-rangiora, high above the Waitara. A new system of fortifications on the front of this ancient stronghold was named Te Arei (" The Barrier "), and was designed as the citadel of the Atiawa.

Major-General Pratt took the field once more towards the end of December, when he concentrated a force of a thousand strong on the Waitara. Heavy artillery suitable for siege operations had been obtained from Auckland and from several of the ships of war, and with this battering-train Pratt moved from Waitara towards the Kairau forts on the 29th December. The first operation was the reduction of the stockaded trenched *pa* at Mata-rikoriko ("Winking Eyes"), a short distance inland of Puke-ta-kauere and somewhat nearer the Waitara River. The column numbered nine hundred men of all arms, with four guns. When the force reached the site of the old Kairau *pa* (destroyed on the 11th September), about 1,100 yards from Mata-rikoriko, a large redoubt was commenced for the accommodation of five hundred men. This redoubt was intended as a depot for the attack on the *pa*, and also for a movement against Huirangi. Working-parties of one hundred and fifty men were employed, under a brisk fire nearly all day from well-masked rifle-pits on the edge of a deep wooded gully about 150 yards from the redoubt. The garrison had a sleepless night, for the natives kept up a fire, with little intermission, until daylight next morning. On the 30th December the Royal Engineers and the rest of the working-parties raised and improved the parapets, formed firing-steps, and made barbettes and platforms for the guns. Two 8-inch guns were mounted on the left face of the redoubt, pointing towards Mata-rikoriko. The firing on both sides was exceedingly heavy. It was estimated that the British troops expended 70,000 rounds of rifle ammunition in less than twenty-four hours, besides about 120 rounds of shot and shell. On the morning of the 31st the *pa* was found to have been evacuated during the night, and it was quickly occupied by two companies of the 65th under Colonel Wyatt. The British lost three killed and twenty wounded. The Maoris, so far as is known, had six killed. A number of the 56th Regiment remained in occupation of Mata-rikoriko.

This episode was soon followed by a general advance upon the Huirangi works and Te Arei. The operations now developed into the most extensive field-engineering works ever undertaken by British troops in New Zealand. Major-General Pratt was a disciple of the slow, sure, and safe method of warfare; he did not believe in wasting lives in dashing assaults when the objective could be obtained less swiftly, but with less expenditure of man-power, by means of pick and shovel and artillery. Pratt exposed himself to much criticism, and his leisurely approach even excited the ridicule of his antagonists in Te Arei, who, however, came at last to realize the certainty of defeat by the inexorable sap, the covering redoubts, and the pounding artillery. The advance upon Huirangi and then upon Te Arei was enlivened by many skirmishes, which at times became sharp engagements involving hundreds of rifles. The work of the Royal Engineers, with the troops of the line pressed into the role of sappers and miners, was, however, the great feature of the move across the plains of Kairau and Huirangi. These operations were directed by Colonel T. R. Mould, R.E., the designer of numerous redoubts and block-houses in Taranaki and Waikato.

Colonel Mould's fort-building in the Waitara campaign had begun with the construction of a strong stockade on the ridge on which the Puke-ta-kauere and Onuku-kaitara *pas* had stood. The work was erected on the centre of the site of Onuku-kaitara, and was arranged to accommodate fifty men. The rough split timbers of the stockade, hauled in carts from the Waitara camp, averaged 8 inches in diameter and were 14 feet in length; they were sunk 4 feet in the ground, touching each other. A working-party of sixty men was employed, with fifty men thrown out as a covering-party. A ditch was dug around the palisades. The banks of the Puke-ta-kauere *pa* were levelled, and the ditches were filled in. After Mahoetahi a stockade was built on one of the two knolls at the ancient settlement of Nga-puke-tu-rua ("The Two Hillocks"), 800 yards on the Waitara side of Mahoetahi. Forty men were left here as a garrison. The next post built was a stockade with blockhouses on the site of the captured *pa* at Mata-rikoriko. This compact little fort (see illustration) was

From a drawing by Lieutenant H. S. Bates (65th Regt.), 1861.]

THE MATA-RIKORIKO STOCKADE.

similar in construction and arrangement to that at Onuku-kaitara. It was garrisoned by sixty men, with a howitzer. When the Maori flanking entrenchments outside the *pa* at Mata-rikoriko were examined by the Engineers it was found that one fire-trench was 178 paces in length, and another 104 paces; others measured 74, 73, and 32 paces.

On the 14th January Major-General Pratt with a force of between six hundred and seven hundred men—12th, 14th, 40th, and 65th detachments, and a Naval Brigade—marched from Waitara towards Huirangi, and came under a heavy fire from the Maoris, who had manned their rifle-pits and trenches between

Kairau and Huirangi. The guns from the Kairau (No. 1 Redoubt) and the rifles of the troops replied briskly, and under fire the Royal Engineers, with working-details, commenced the construction of a redoubt (No. 2) about 500 yards on the right front of the Kairau Redoubt. This work was 26 yards square inside the parapet, which was 7 feet high and averaged 6 feet in thickness. Banquettes were formed and a barbette raised for the howitzer on the right-front salient angle. The redoubt, finished in eleven hours, was garrisoned by one hundred and twenty men, with artillery.

On the 18th January the General moved out again to the front with a force a thousand strong, and under an all-day fire from the Maori rifle-pits a third redoubt was begun to cover the British advance towards Huirangi. This field-work, soon to become celebrated for a daring attack made by the Kingites, was built about 400 yards to the left front of No. 2. It consisted when complete of three squares closely placed *en echelon ;* the middle redoubt was 30 yards each way inside the parapet. The parapets of all these works were made with earth and fern in alternate layers, after the Maori manner. Two howitzers were mounted in the main redoubt, and an 8-inch gun on the front face of the right wing. A garrison of about three hundred men, including the headquarters of the 40th Regiment under Colonel Leslie, was placed in No. 3.

While the General was steadily making his way across the Kairau plateau, the Taranaki and Ngati-Ruanui Tribes on the southern section of the coast dug themselves in very strongly on the hills at Waireka, and completely barred the roads by a remarkably skilful system of trenches, rifle-pits, and stockaded *pas*. Several expeditions from New Plymouth during the summer of 1861 engaged the natives at Waireka Hill, Burton's Hill, and the vicinity of Omata, but without serious casualties on either side. The Rifle Volunteers and Militia, under Herbert, Stapp, and Atkinson, were conspicuously useful in the trying work of patrols and reconnaissances until the end of the war. One affair, though not an official expedition, demonstrated the pluck and coolness of the Volunteers. Fourteen young men, under Sergeant E. Hollis, were gathering peaches one Sunday morning (3rd March, 1861) at Brooklands (now Mr. Newton King's property), near the town, when they were ambuscaded by about double their number of Maoris, who gave them a volley from the cover of a ditch and hedge at very close range. Volunteer Edward Messenger, brother of Ensign W. B. Messenger, was shot dead, and a comrade, W. Smart, severely wounded. The lads returned the fire, recovered their comrade's body and arms, and kept off the Maoris until assistance arrived from the town.

CHAPTER XXIII.

THE FIGHT AT No. 3 REDOUBT.

It was the practice of the troops to stand to their arms an hour before daybreak as a precaution against surprise. In the raw and chilly early morning of the 23rd January, 1861, the Regulars in the Kairau and Huirangi redoubts turned out as usual and stood in silence awaiting the sunrise. Suddenly a single gunshot came from the fern 100 yards to the right of No. 1 Redoubt. This was a Maori signal-gun. The next instant the fringes of the murky plain were a blaze of fire, and the roar of musketry ran along the fern on the right and left flanks of the British posts. The soldiers replied with their Enfields—though there was nothing but the flashes at which to fire—and the gloomy morning, so quiet a few moments before, was thunderous with the bellow and crackle of musketry. Presently the firing near No. 1 Redoubt and No. 2 Redoubt ceased : it was a Maori feint to divert attention from the real attack. No. 3 (400 yards in advance of No. 2) was the objective, and as the excited soldiers in the rear field-works peered through the darkness they saw the advanced redoubt, which had only been completed by the 40th Regiment the previous evening, all at once encircled by a darting ring of flame that lit up the darkness like a blaze of tropical lightning, followed by an incessant roll of small-arms fire and presently the explosion of hand-grenades.

The garrison of No. 3 Redoubt (the headquarters of the 40th, under Colonel Leslie) had a crowded half-hour of fighting before dawn that morning. While the natives in the rifle-pits and the British trenches that flanked the line of advance were making ready to open their feint attack, a picked party of a hundred and forty warriors—Ngati-Haua, Ngati-Maniapoto, Waikato, and Te Atiawa—crept up to the redoubt, and about half of them silently entered the ditches on the left and right faces of the redoubt—the two unflanked sides. Their leaders were Manga (Rewi Maniapoto) and Epiha Tokohihi, from Kihikihi, and Hapurona. Some were armed with double-barrel guns or with rifles; others carried only long-handled tomahawks for close-quarters combat. They were supported by some hundreds of tribesmen in firing-trenches within close range of the redoubt.

The storming-party stealthily began to cut steps with their tomahawks in the earth of the newly scarped parapet. When they were about to attempt the assault a sentry of the 40th fired at a Maori just outside the trench. A return shot killed the soldier, and the next moment the 40th were at grips with their determined foes. The ditch was crowded with Maoris, some firing at the line of heads above them, some furiously springing up the scarp and slashing at the soldiers with their tomahawks. The men fired into the trench as fast as they could load their Enfields, and others threw short-fuse shells into the ditch. Lieutenant Jackson, of the 40th, was leaning over the parapet firing his revolver into the mass of Maoris when he was shot through the forehead. The

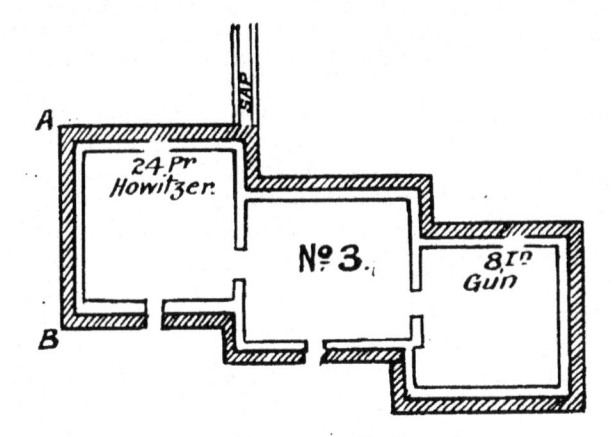

No. 3 Redoubt, Huirangi.

The flank A—B was the one first attacked by the Maoris.

attackers (including the supports in the fern) and the garrison were nearly equal in numbers.

Although the British musketry and the exploding shells and hand-grenades spread death and wounds among the warriors in the trench, the Maori forlorn hope stuck to their work tenaciously. Again and again those daring spirits essayed to scale the straight-cut scarp, only to be shot down or bayoneted by the soldiers. So the struggle went on until reinforcements came doubling up and cleared the ditch of all but the dead and dying.

A vivid account of the morning's fight is contained in an unpublished manuscript written by Colonel H. Stretton Bates, then a young ensign, who was an eye-witness of the combat. Colonel Bates was in No. 1 Redoubt with his regiment, the 65th—the "Royal Tigers"—nearly all stalwart Irishmen with experience of more than one combat. His story, after narrating the beginning of the attack, describes the despatch of reinforcements and the final scenes :—*

"It was evident to us in No. 1 that the surprise had failed, but the defenders of No. 3 were hard pressed. The heavy firing continued, and the cheers of the gallant 40th mingled with the wailing cries of the attackers as they adjured each other to be brave ('*Kia toa*') and to slay the soldiers. But hark to the clear notes of a bugle ringing out in the morning air from the advanced post! We recognize the regimental call of the 'Royal Tigers,' followed by the advance. 'Whew!' muttered our Colonel Wyatt, 'the 40th are calling for trumps'; and he ordered two companies of the 'Tigers' and one of the 12th, a detachment of which corps was with us in No. 1, to proceed at once to the help of the defenders of No. 3 Redoubt. The great bearded fellows, looking more like bushrangers than soldiers, fell in without a moment's delay, and ere the bugle had sounded a third appeal for help the column of fours was out of the redoubt and, under command of the senior captain, who was destined to receive a brevet majority for his morning's work, was making its way over the plain at a steady double. The remainder of the 'Tigers,' leaning over the parapet, watched the drama which was being enacted in front. As the three companies passed No. 2 Redoubt the occupants gave them a loud cheer, and in a few minutes more the advanced redoubt was reached.

"Day was now breaking; the fire was not so continuous as before, and what there was came mostly from the front face. Loud cheers rose from the 40th, and they called out to the reinforcers that the ditch in front of the redoubt was crammed with natives, but that the thickness of the parapet and want of flanking defence prevented their rifles being sufficiently depressed so as to reach the Maoris. There was a hasty consultation, and then the 'Tigers' descended into the wide ditch on the right of the work, and the company of the 12th Regiment into the ditch on the left, and both parties made their way towards the front of the redoubt.

"The ditch in front was crowded with the attackers. Poor fellows! they had felt confident of surprising the soldiers, and had evidently come to stay, for they had brought provision of Indian corn with them. Better that they had brought ladders or bundles of faggots to enable them to scale the parapet. One of their number was a native catechist, who repeated prayers

---

* Manuscript narrative by the late Colonel H. S. Bates, of England, lent by his son, Mr. H. D. Bates, of Wanganui. Colonel Bates served with the 65th Regiment in New Zealand for several years, and was a staff interpreter under General Cameron in the Waikato in 1863.

incessantly from the Church of England prayer-book all through the struggle. His blood-stained prayer-book was found on his body. Though the warriors were comparatively sheltered from musketry fire as they huddled together in the ditch, still ghastly wounds were being inflicted, as the soldiers lighted and flung over hand-grenades amongst the crowded mass, while some of the artillerymen, finding it impossible to depress the muzzles of the guns sufficiently, got shells and, having cut short the fuses, ignited them and rolled them over the parapet, so that falling they exploded, spreading havoc around them. In vain the doomed wretches tried to pick up the spluttering hand-grenades and fling them back; the natives were packed too closely together, and the horrid things exploded amongst them with grim result. The Maoris feared to quit the ditch and endeavour to retire, as to do this would have exposed them to the fire of the rifles which lined the parapet; besides, amongst the warriors were many of the warlike Ngati-Maniapoto and other Waikato tribes, whose motto was 'Death before dishonour.' On came the 'Tigers' along the side ditch. It was evident that a volley would greet the head of the little column as it turned the corner to make its way into the front ditch which the attackers occupied.

"Half a dozen guns ring out and down goes our leading man with a bullet through his forehead. A comrade staggers against the counterscarp, for a ball has struck him in the face and carried away part of his upper lip and some of his teeth. But on go the 'Tigers' with a wild shout. For a moment the leading files cross bayonet with tomahawk. Ugly wounds are inflicted by the whirling tomahawks and thrusting bayonets, and then the dusky warriors turn and scramble as best they can out of the ditch, endeavouring to gain the shelter of the fern and the forest. The occupants of the redoubt fire one round at the fugitives, and then hold their hand to avoid hitting the 'Tigers' and the 12th men, who have scrambled up the counterscarp of the ditch and are now scattered in pursuit of the flying foes. There is no time to reload, and the bayonet does its deadly work. The swifter-footed of the fugitives gain the shelter of the bush, and then the bugles sounding the 'Recall' check the pursuit. The repulse is complete.

"The dead and wounded are collected. There are between forty and fifty natives left on the field, and most of the wounds are mortal.

"Amongst the wounded was one youth of striking aspect. His long black hair and regular features would have made him appear effeminate but for the length of limb and splendid muscular development which caught the eye even as he lay on the ground, looking like a dusky Antinous. A good-natured soldier, one of the 'Tigers,' hearing him moaning something which sounded like '*wai*' (water), was trying to make him drink from his canteen, saying, 'Here, Jack, here's *wai* for you.' The soldiers always addressed the Maoris as 'Jack,' and the Maoris the soldiers as 'Tiaki' also. My knowledge of the language enabled me to recognize that the wounded man was moaning '*Kia maranga*,' meaning that he desired to be raised up. I noticed the small red mark in his chest which showed that a bullet had probably penetrated a lung, the bleeding from which was choking him. So kneeling down and putting my arms round him I raised him gently and supported him in a sitting position. He smiled and whispered, 'It is well'; but the blood gushed from his mouth, and he fell heavily back in my arms as I knelt behind him. After a little he rallied, and I heard him panting as in whispers he endeavoured to repeat the Maori rendering of the Lord's Prayer, '*Murua o matou hara*' ('Forgive us our trespasses'). So far he got in an agonized and almost inaudible whisper, and then the blood poured from his mouth again; there was a short struggle, and the weight I was supporting became very heavy. Slowly I laid him down, and I am not ashamed to say that my eyes grew dim as I thought how desolate some heart in the far Waikato land would be when the morning's work was known.

"As I turned away I saw sitting near me, propped up with a bundle of rugs and mats, an elderly grey-haired Maori, whose name I afterwards heard was Marakai, or Malachi. (This was a man of Ngati-Mahuta.) He was gravely smoking, and had been watching the poor youth's end. From him I learned the lad's name, and that he was one of the Ngati-Maniapoto Tribe. The name I treasured in my memory, and some two years later, when I had been sent on a political mission to the warlike and resentful Ngati-Maniapoto, I found myself one night at the village from which the dead warrior came, and was able to relate to his mother the particulars of her son's death. Several of my then hearers confessed that they had been of the attacking-party on that 23rd January, and proudly exhibited the scars of bullet-wounds on their bodies. They told me that their original design had been to make a simultaneous attack on all three redoubts..

"Knowing that Marakai was wounded, I inquired if he was in much pain. With a courtly, half-sarcastic smile he inclined his head so as to direct my attention to his knee, which had been frightfully damaged by the explosion of a shell or hand-grenade, quietly remarking, 'With a wound such as that one must suffer somewhat.' Poor old fellow! What a noble man he was! A nobleman in fallen circumstances if you like, but always a nobleman. I heard that he afterwards bore the amputation of his leg in the most plucky manner, but sank a day or two after the operation.

"Leaving the ghastly line of dead or dying Maoris I passed into the redoubt, where in a tent were lying our dead and wounded men. In his own tent was lying poor old Lieutenant Jackson, of the 40th, who had received a bullet through his forehead while leaning over the parapet at the beginning of the attack and firing his revolver at the natives."

The British losses in the No. 3 Redoubt fight were five killed and eleven wounded. The Maoris lost quite fifty killed outright or mortally wounded. Among the dead were the chiefs Te Retimana and Paora te Uata (Ngati-Raukawa), and Ratima te Paewaka, of Waikato. Thirty-seven double-barrel and single-barrel guns and flint-lock muskets were found on the field, besides some stone *meres* and many tomahawks.

CHAPTER XXIV.

PRATT'S LONG SAP.

In the beautiful midsummer weather the advance upon Te Arei was carried on under conditions which made soldiering life a pleasure in spite of the harassing tactics of the Maori snipers and the toil of redoubt-building. The tardy progress towards Hapurona's fortress was enlivened by numerous skirmishes, and there were casualties nearly every day. The flanks of the British advance were as animated as beehives with the native musketeers, whose guerilla activities kept the Regulars' covering-parties busy. No Volunteers or Militia were employed on these operations—their attention was concentrated on the patrolling of New Plymouth and its outskirts; but they could have been of assistance to the General in scouring the bush and working round to the rear of Te Arei. Pratt, however, made no attempt to engage his antagonists otherwise than by a frontal advance. Like his successor, General Cameron, he had a horror of bush warfare, in which the mobile Maori had so great an advantage over the soldier of the line. Yet there were not only settler-soldiers but many of the veterans of the 65th who could have been formed into an excellent forest-ranging corps, competent to follow the Maori into the roughest country if given a free hand and unhampered by the rigid Imperial methods. But it was not until 1863 that the value of such bush-fighting companies was recognized.

The advance was along a plateau of inconsiderable width with a very gentle upward slant inland to Te Arei, bordered on either flank by deep lateral valleys and ravines filled with *karaka* and *rata* trees and other timber. On the left these gullies fell steeply to the Waitara River; on the right they were enclosed by rolling hills, all densely wooded. In the rear was a forest country practically untrodden by Europeans; it was known, however, that in there were large plantations at Mataitawa and other well-sheltered retreats of the Atiawa. Day after day the Maoris in their fern-masked firing-pits on the edges of the plateau made practice with their *tupara* at the working-parties and the covering-details. Nightly the soldiers, withdrawn into their field fortifications, heard the distant doleful sound of the *putatara* and the *tetere*, the warriors' war-horns, and the high, long-drawn chants of the *whaka-araara-pa*, or sentinel songs. As the summer weeks went on, the troops became impatient for the order to advance at a pace somewhat quicker than Pratt's mile a month. "When are we going to rush the *pa?*" many a Regular asked, with his eyes lifted to the entrenched positions of his foe. "Look ye here, towney," a big 65th man was heard to say to his comrade, " two glasses of rum and a shout, and we'd be into them rifle-pits and picking the Maoris out with our bay'nits."

The work on the long series of saps carried towards Huirangi and Te Arei was begun on the afternoon of the 22nd January, the day before the attack on No. 3 Redoubt. A double sap, termed also a "gabionnade" in the Royal Engineers' technical

From a drawing by Lieutenant H. S. Bates (65th Regt.).]

THE BRITISH POSITIONS AT HUIRANGI, 1861,

Showing Maoris sniping from the edge of the bush.

phraseology, directed towards the centre of the Maori position, was commenced from the front of No. 3 Redoubt, and nearly 200 feet were excavated by dark. The working-party consisted of fifty men with five Royal Engineers. During the following eleven days the sap was steadily pushed forward, often under fire. The total length of this double sap dug was 768 yards, crossing the Maori rifle-pits when they abandoned the Huirangi position. The *manuka* gabions used were generally made at the Waitara camp by men of the Naval Brigade, assisted by soldiers, under the direction of Royal Engineers non-commissioned officers.

Another redoubt, called No. 4, was constructed on the 27th and 28th January, 310 yards ahead of the place where the sap was commenced. This was a small square work, measuring 13½ yards each side inside the parapet; it was garrisoned by fifty men.

A fifth redoubt, 24 yards square, was built 200 yards farther on, and 260 yards from the nearest of the Maori rifle-pits. It was garrisoned by a hundred men, with a 24-pounder howitzer.

On the afternoon of the 1st February the Maoris were discovered to have abandoned their position at Huirangi, falling back on the main fortress on the height at Te Arei, the north-west front of the famous old *pa* of Puke-rangiora, several hundreds of feet above the Waitara River. No. 6 Redoubt was built at Huirangi, its front slightly in advance of the abandoned Maori rifle-pits, in the middle of a field of high Scotch thistles; its left-front angle was close to a patch of dense bush extending to the left and front. A portion of this bush was cleared by axemen.

From the end of the double sap at Huirangi a short single sap, 90 yards, was carried on in the direction of Te Arei. Fifty men were employed in filling in the native rifle-pits to the right of No. 6 Redoubt; they extended for half a mile. No. 6 was garrisoned by the headquarters of the 65th Regiment, and a platform was laid for an 8-inch gun.

No. 7 Redoubt was now constructed (10th to 12th February), about 1,300 yards ahead of No. 6, and about 800 yards from the front of Te Arei *pa*. Its building was carried on on the first day under a sharp fire from a line of Maori rifle-pits in commanding positions, and from the *pa* itself. This fire was replied to by a line of British skirmishers, supported by four guns and howitzers. Captain Strange (65th Regiment) was mortally wounded. The redoubt was garrisoned by four hundred men, including the headquarters of the 40th Regiment. The front face and part of the left face were surmounted with gabions filled with earth, with sandbag loopholes at intervals to protect the interior from the natives' plunging fire. A man had been killed and an officer and a man wounded within the redoubt. A screen for an 8-inch gun was erected on the left flank of the redoubt; it was 12 yards in length, and was formed of two rows of gabions surmounted by a third row, all filled and backed up with earth from a ditch in the front. A parapet was also thrown up on the right of the redoubt outside as a cover for field-guns.

On the 16th February the sappers were again set to work. A single sap was commenced from the right-front angle of No. 7 Redoubt, being directed to clear the Maoris' rifle-pits close to the precipitous banks of the Waitara. This sap was continued, often under heavy fire, until the 25th; 452 yards had been excavated 5 feet 6 inches wide. The first 62 yards of the sap were without traverses; thenceforward the work was protected with traverses at intervals at from 10 to 12 yards. Meanwhile No. 7 Redoubt was considerably strengthened. The parapets were raised, and the ditch was widened to 9 feet, the earth being laid to form a glacis outside. The sap was now abreast of a hill called by the troops " Burnt Hill," about 500 yards distant. The Maoris dug rifle-pits on the slope of this hill, and their fire considerably annoyed the working-parties.

On the morning of the 25th February the direction of the sap was changed towards the left of Te Arei *pa*, and it was carried on as a double sap. A demi-parallel was commenced on the left, about 40 yards from where the double sap commenced.

The slow but sure approach of the sappers was now seriously disturbing the Maoris, who decided that it was time to interfere more actively than by sniping from distant cover. Accordingly, on the night of the 27th February, when the troops had withdrawn to the redoubts, a large body of natives crept silently out of the *pa* and vigorously set to work to fill in the trenches. They destroyed the whole of the double sap, the portion of demi-parallel, and more or less filled in nearly 150 yards of the single sap. They carried some of the gabions into the *pa*, and burned others, and removed also the sap-rollers.

Next day, to guard the progress of the sap, another redoubt (No. 8) was constructed; its front face was 34 yards from the end of the single sap. This field-work, the last of the elaborate series, was square, with a side of 16 yards within the parapet. It was occupied nightly by a guard of fifty men.

On the morning of the 1st March the whole of the old double sap was filled in, and the single sap was connected with the ditch of the rear face of No. 8 Redoubt. A new double sap was then commenced from the centre of the front ditch of the redoubt. It was directed to the right (the British left) of the entrance to Te Arei fortress. The traverses were at intervals of 10 yards. This day it was seen that the Maoris had put the stolen gabions to use by setting them up as a screen in front of the entrance to the *pa*.

By the 3rd March the workers in the sap came under a heavy plunging fire from the front of the *pa*. A demi-parallel was now thrown out to the left, about 50 yards in front of No. 8 Redoubt, and was continued to the edge of the cliff above the Waitara River. This work was 43 yards in length; the last 20 yards were converted from a line of Maori rifle-pits.

Under many interruptions the sap was pushed forward. The ground being commanded from the *pa* and the rifle-pits, the sap was deepened to 4 feet 6 inches; the traverses were placed from 8 feet to 10 feet apart, and made two gabions in height. The demi-parallel to the river-cliff was connected by an approach with the left-front angle of the redoubt, and about 10 yards of the demi-parallel was made into a battery for howitzers and a mortar. On the afternoon of the 5th March a party of warriors from the *pa* crept through the bushes on the edge of the precipice to the left and fired a volley into the sap, killing one man and wounding four others. To draw attention from this point of attack the native garrison had commenced a brisk fire from the bush on the right rear of No. 7 Redoubt, and continued it along the whole line of their entrenchments.

As the ground rose towards the *pa* the traverses were placed 14 yards apart and made one gabion in height, and the trench was excavated to the depth of 3 feet only. Heavy rain for two days interrupted progress, then the work was pushed on again steadily. Slight changes in the contour of the ground involved alterations from time to time in the intervals between the

From a drawing by Lieutenant H. S. Bates (65th Regt.).]

THE ATTACK ON TE AREI,

Showing the advanced British positions, 1861.

traverses. On the 11th March the sappers were making the traverses 12 yards apart and one gabion in height.

For three days (12th, 13th, and 14th March) hostilities and engineering-work were suspended at the request of Wiremu Tamehana, who had just arrived from the Waikato to negotiate for peace. His efforts were not successful at the time, but peace was near.

On the 15th March, the truce having expired, the works were recommenced, and a demi-parallel was begun at the left of the sap at 236 yards from No. 8 Redoubt. The object was to drive the natives from their rifle-pits along the precipice to the British left front. This trench was dug about 50 yards in two days, and carried to the verge of the cliff into the rifle-pits, which were evacuated.

Two days were spent by strong working-parties enlarging No. 7 Redoubt and constructing platforms and cover for heavy artillery, which presently opened on the *pa*. The Maoris on the afternoon of the 15th March carried on a very heavy musketry fire all along their front. That night they made an attempt to carry off the sap-roller at the end of the demi-parallel, but their scheme was violently frustrated by the explosion of an 8-inch shell which had been placed behind it, and connected with it and a friction-tube by a lanyard. (The sap-roller was a large cylindrical bundle of manuka-branches and fern, bound round gabions filled with earth, and 6 or 7 feet thick. It was rolled along in front of the advanced sappers for head-cover.)

Two important additions to the Imperial field force arrived in January, 1861—the 14th and 57th Regiments. The 14th came to Auckland from Cork in the auxiliary-screw ship "Robert Lowe" and the ships "Boanerges" and "Savilla." Their Commander was Colonel (afterwards Major-General) Sir James E. Alexander, an officer of great experience in many climes. The 57th (First Middlesex), the famous "Die-Hards" of Albuera glory, under Major Logan—who was followed by Colonel (afterwards General) Sir H. J. Warre—arrived from Bombay in the ships "Star Queen" and "Castilian." The "Die-Hards" proved highly competent in frontier warfare, and in after-years they were called upon for a great deal of hard fighting under General Chute. They shared, in fact, with the veteran 65th the toil and the honours of the most arduous service in the campaign undertaken by the Imperial regiments.

Between the Maoris and some of the troops fighting at Te Arei the war was conducted quite in the spirit of a chivalrous tournament. The 65th, who had had very friendly relations with the Taranaki natives in the intervals of peace, were singled out for good-humoured banter and frequent injunctions from the rifle-pits to "Lie down, Hiketi Piwheté, we're going to shoot." Sometimes, as the sap drew near the *pa*, there would come a loud request, "*Homai te tupeka*," and when in response a packet of tobacco was thrown over into the Maori trenches, back would come a basket of peaches or a kit of potatoes. These amenities did not extend to the other regiments; the 57th were bidden "go back to India." For all the amusing interchange of courtesies between the opposing lines there was a great deal of hot firing, though with little result. Sergeant-Major E. Bezar (ex 57th), of Wellington, recalls that one morning before breakfast every man in his part of the advanced trenches had expended all the ammunition he had brought—120 rounds. Bezar himself one morning fired 160 rounds. It must be remembered that the Enfields which the troops used were muzzleloaders, with necessarily a rather long interval between each shot, so that the barrel did not heat so greatly as that of a modern magazine rifle.

There was now a heavy siege-train battering away at the Maori defences. The storm of shot and shell compelled the garrison to take to their underground quarters, but even there they were not always safe when the Armstrongs began to play on them. There were in front of Te Arei two 8-inch naval guns, two 8-inch and

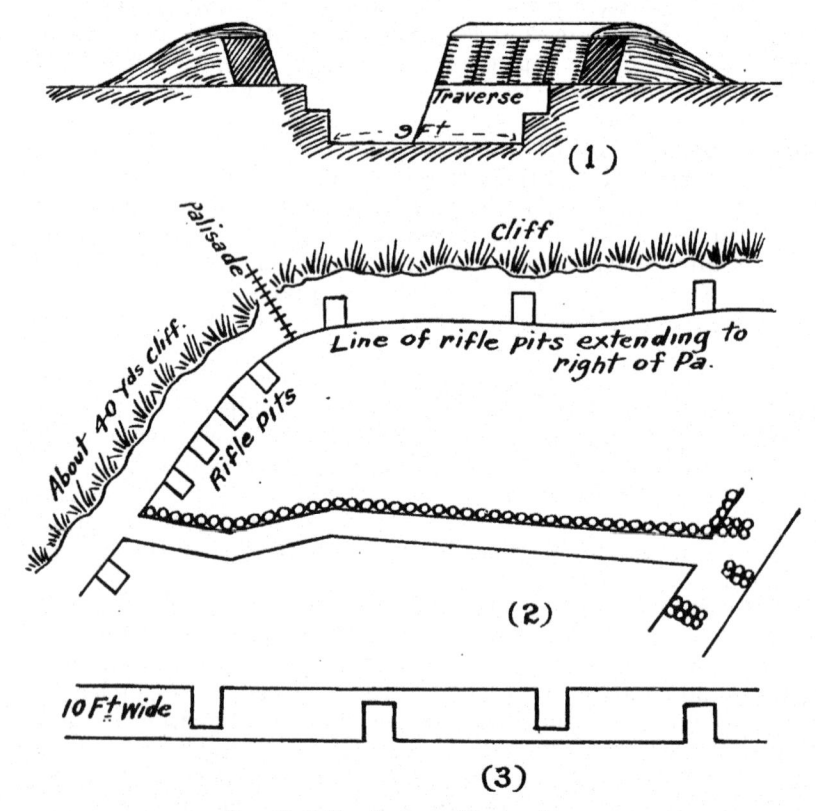

THE BRITISH SAP AT TE AREI.

(1.) Cross-section of sap, with traverse and gabions.
(2.) Head of the sap, close to Maori works, Te Arei, in March, 1861.
(3.) Remains of sap near north face of Te Arei *pa*, as existing at the present time.

two 10-inch mortars, four Coehorn mortars, two 24-pounder howitzers, three 12-pounder and one 9-pounder field-guns. The large-calibre mortars and the Armstrong field-pieces had been brought in the ship " Norwood " to Auckland (arriving 4th March,

1861) by the Royal Artillery, under Captain Mercer (killed at Rangiriri, 1863). The mortars and half the field-guns were landed at the Waitara River in surf-boats on the 13th March, and commenced firing on the *pa* from No. 7 Redoubt on the 15th March. The precision of the gunnery and the destruction caused by the bursting shells, added to the harassing effect of the night firing of the artillery, convinced Hapurona and his allies that their stronghold was no longer tenable.

On the 17th March the demi-parallel reached a point at a bend in the rifle-pits where a palisade on the cliff-edge barred further passage. Near here Lieutenant MacNaghten, R.A., was shot dead. It was he who had fired the first shot in the Waitara war, exactly a year before his death. Next day the sap, which had been suspended since the 11th, was recommenced, and 27 yards were formed during the day. The last two shells thrown into Te Arei were fired from the big mortars mounted at No. 7 Redoubt at 4 a.m. on the 19th March, 1861. The Maori white flag went up about 6 o'clock. The working and covering parties were then withdrawn and hostilities ceased.

The total length of the sap executed in this advance on Te Arei was 1,626 yards, exclusive of the 45 yards double sap filled in after having been destroyed by the Maoris, and of the final demi-parallel, 67 yards. This length is made up as follows: Double sap from No. 3 Redoubt to Huirangi, 768 yards; single sap (stopped), 90 yards; sap from No. 7 Redoubt towards Te Arei (single sap), 452 yards; from No. 8 Redoubt (new double sap) 316 yards: total, 1,626 yards.

The war was terminated by an agreement between Hapurona and the Government, Wiremu Kingi having gone to Kihikihi, Upper Waikato, to live with his friends the Ngati-Maniapoto. Mr. Donald McLean (afterwards Sir Donald), Native Secretary, and the Rev. J. A. Wilson, of the Church Missionary Society, were the chief agents of the Government, and after some days' discussion they persuaded Hapurona to accept the conditions laid down by the Governor in Council, the Waikato tribes agreeing at the same time to return to their homes. The terms agreed upon included the investigation of the title to the Waitara Block and the completion of the survey, restoration of plunder taken from the settlers, and the submission of the Atiawa to the Queen's authority. Hapurona and Wiremu Ngawaka Patu-Kakariki signed the peace treaty on behalf of the Maoris. Ngati-Ruanui declined to sign, pending a meeting of the Waikato tribes to discuss the war.

The net result of the war was the enormous destruction of settlers' property at comparatively small cost to the Taranaki Maoris. More than three-fourths of the farmhouses at Omata, Bell Block, Tataraimaka, and settlements nearer the town had been burned or sacked. The premises of 187 farming families were destroyed, many of them in daylight, and some within rifle-range of the stockades. The total value of homes and stock lost was estimated at £200,000. The blunder of the Waitara purchase had set the province back well-nigh twenty years. The Government made some compensation, but the parliamentary vote for the purpose (£25,000) went only a very small way to satisfy the ruined settlers' claims. Further financial assistance, however, was granted later on.

Notes.

A considerable portion of the sap towards Te Arei *pa*, Puke-rangiora, is still to be seen. The traveller turning up from the New Plymouth – Waitara Road from near Kairau drives along a plain studded with the ruins of British redoubts and Maori entrenchments, and when within about half a mile of Te Arei may observe on the left-hand side, in the paddocks between the road and the Waitara River, the depression in the turf which marks the line of the sap. At the end of the plain before the ascent to Te Arei begins the earthworks of No. 7 Redoubt are seen in the middle of a field on the left of the road as one goes from Kairau. Tall pine-trees grow on the grassy parapets and cast their shade over the many-angled redoubt, a camping-ground sixty years ago for four hundred Imperial troops. A little beyond this, parallel with the road, the shallow dip in the grass indicates the olden sap, and when the Government fenced scenic reserve is reached on the slant upwards to Te Arei the long trench is more clearly defined. About 200 yards of the sap, ending within 100 yards of the Maori position, are in almost perfect order. The trench here is 10 to 12 feet wide and 6 feet deep, with a low parapet on either side formed by the earth thrown up. The traverses (mounds of earth left alternately right and left in the trenches to guard against a raking fire) are still intact, as shown in sketch-plan; they are about 12 paces apart. A little above the end of the sap there are partly filled-in Maori rifle-pits and a small redoubt on the brink of the Waitara River cliff, with thick bush below, affording perfect cover for the defenders, pickets of the *pa* garrison. Above are the high fern-grown parapets of Te Arei.

Sergeant-Major E. Bezar (late 57th Regiment) supplied the following note, under date 13th January, 1921, regarding the death of Lieutenant MacNaghten, R.A., at Te Arei on the 17th March, 1861: "I have seen different accounts of the way this gallant and popular officer met his death, but they all differ. Possibly I am the only man now living who witnessed the event, and I can positively say I was the last man to speak to him before he went to his death. We were at the head of the sap. It was afternoon, and the enemy were very busy and excited, and we deemed it necessary to be prepared for a sudden rush over our way, and we fixed bayonets. Lieutenant MacNaghten expressed a desire to go to the top of the rise we were cutting through, and I remarked that it was very risky, seeing how the bullets were coming over. He climbed out of the trench and crawled through the fern to the top of the rise. I fancy they must have noticed the moving fern. He was lying flat and looking through his glasses when he received the fatal shot. A year ago that day he fired the first howitzer shot at the enemy. He was not laying a gun on this occasion, as I have seen stated, for there was not a gun nearer than No. 7 Redoubt, several hundred yards to the rear. I have a very vivid recollection of this sad event, and I never took my eyes from the officer, for the bullets were pinging over that rise by the dozen."

CHAPTER XXV.

THE SECOND TARANAKI CAMPAIGN.

Before the winter of 1861 most of the troops in Taranaki were withdrawn to Auckland, Colonel Warre remaining in New Plymouth with his regiment, the 57th. Major-General Pratt left for Melbourne after the arrival of a new Commander-in-Chief, Lieut.-General Sir Duncan Cameron, who had led the 40th Regiment at the Battle of the Alma, and the Highland Brigade at Balaclava and the siege of Sebastopol. Many of the troops sent to Auckland were employed on the Great South Road, which was being cut through the forest from Drury to the Waikato River. In Taranaki the Atiawa were amicable, but the Ngati-Ruanui and their kin remained unfriendly.

An incident of 1862 (1st September) was the wreck at Te Namu, near Cape Egmont, of the steamer "Lord Worsley," 600 tons, carrying passengers, mails, and gold from Nelson to New Plymouth and Auckland. Wiremu Kingi te Matakaatea and Eruera te Whiti (afterwards the celebrated prophet of Parihaka) befriended the shipwrecked people, numbering sixty, who were permitted to go overland to New Plymouth with their baggage, after this had been examined by the Kingite customs officers; each person had to pay 5s. on passing the Maori toll-gate established as the result of a large Maori conference at Kapoaiaia. Mr. Robert Graham, Auckland, who was a passenger, pluckily saved the gold that was on board, and twice traversed the hostile territory, carrying his loads safely into New Plymouth. A young half-caste named Hori Teira (George Taylor), who was one of the keepers of the toll-gate, obtained a horse for Mr. Graham and otherwise assisted him, and this act of friendship brought its unexpected reward in the following year, when Hori lay in prison in Auckland.

Soon after Sir George Grey had succeeded Colonel Gore Browne as Governor of New Zealand, arriving at Auckland on the 26th September, 1862, in H.M.S. "Cossack," from Cape Town, a new native policy was promulgated. A Commission had investigated the proprietary interests in the Waitara lands, and as the outcome of its inquiries the Governor issued, on the 11th

May, 1863, a Proclamation announcing the abandonment of the purchase of Teira's block and the renunciation by the Government of all claims to that area of land. This tardy vindication of Wiremu Kingi's cause had unfortunately been preceded by the armed occupation of the Tataraimaka Block, which had temporarily been abandoned in 1860, and which the Maoris now claimed by right of conquest. Three hundred officers and men of the 57th, under Colonel Warre, marched out along the south road, and on the 4th April encamped on Tataraimaka, and built a redoubt on Bayley's Farm, near the Katikara River. The Taranaki Tribe had previously informed the Governor and General Cameron that Tataraimaka would not be given up unless the British first gave up the Waitara. The march upon Tataraimaka was naturally accepted as an act of war, and Taranaki promptly sent out appeals for assistance to Ngati-Ruanui and Nga-Rauru, and to Ngati-Maniapoto and Waikato; a letter was sent to Wiremu Kingi at Kihikihi. Five weeks elapsed before the Government made amends for the error of Gore Browne and his advisers, and in the meantime hostilities had commenced.

The Ambush at Wairau.

The first shot in the second Taranaki campaign was fired on the 4th May, 1863. The Taranaki and Ngati-Ruanui planned ambuscades to cut off communications between Tataraimaka and New Plymouth, and warnings of these intended ambush tactics had been sent to the authorities in New Plymouth by friendly natives, but were lightly regarded. Sir George Grey was in the habit of riding out to the military post at Tataraimaka (fifteen miles from New Plymouth), and on the morning of the 4th May a party of thirty or forty young warriors lay in ambush waiting for the Governor and his party, who were expected to pass along the beach road that day. Among the ambush-party was the young half-caste Hori Teira, already mentioned as one of the keepers of the Maori toll-gate. His father was a ship's carpenter, and his birthplace Kororareka, Bay of Islands. Hori was a lad of eighteen. He had been educated at the mission school, and had been brought down to Taranaki by his mother's people just before the war began.

The ambuscade was laid on the coast just beyond the Oakura, at a place where two small streams, the Waimouku and the Wairau, flow down to the shingly beach. (The spot is on the farm of Captain Frank Mace.) Low but thick bush and brushwood grew close to the beach here, and in its cover between the mouths of the two streams, which are not more than 100 yards apart, the Maoris awaited their unsuspecting enemy. The Governor did not pass that day, but a small military party did. This was an escort of the 57th taking a prisoner of the regiment into New Plymouth from Tataraimaka. There were six soldiers, under Colour-Sergeant Ellers and Sergeant S. Hill. With them also were travelling two officers, Lieutenant Tragett and Assistant-Surgeon Hope, who were mounted. The officers were riding along the beach a little ahead of the soldiers. Young Hori and his companions lying in ambush let the mounted men pass by, and then fired a volley into the detachment of soldiers at a range of a few yards. Hori, relating the story, said that to his astonishment the British officers, instead of making their escape as they could easily have done, turned their horses and joined the soldiers, and so they, too, were shot down. Nine were killed, and the only man who escaped was Private Florence Kelly. A Maori named Tukino fired at one of the officers, Dr. Hope, and shot him in the face. Tukino immediately raised a yell of "*Maté rawa!*" ("He is killed!") but the officer rose and confronted his enemies again. Thereupon Hori Teira and some of his comrades fired and shot him dead. The young half-caste rushed out to plunder the dead officer—his first blood, or *mataika*. It was the first man he had helped to slay. He took a watch and chain and a ring from Dr. Hope's body, and two rifles from the dead soldiers.

It was a war custom among the Taranaki Maoris that any plunder or trophies taken from a foe whom a warrior had killed in his first battle—the "first fish"—should not be retained by the slayer, but should be given away to some other person in order to avert ill luck. It was inviting an *aitua* (a serious misfortune, even death) to keep the first spoils of war. So, on returning to the Maori headquarters, Hori was advised by the chiefs and elders to give away his war-trophies, and so placate the war-god. Hori insisted on wearing the watch and ring, declaring that they were too valuable and fine to be given away because of an old-fashioned superstition.

The ill-gotten ring brought its *aitua*. Three weeks after the ambuscade at the Wairau a small party of young warriors, of whom Hori Teira was one, laid another ambuscade near the Poutoko Redoubt, about eight miles from New Plymouth. They attacked a mounted officer, Lieutenant Waller, of the 57th. His horse was hit, and both fell. Hori, imagining that the officer was mortally wounded, and yelling "*Ki au te tupapaku!*" ("Mine is the dead man!") rushed out, dropping his rifle, and snatched out his short-handled tomahawk to deliver the finishing blow. But the officer was by no means a dead man. Jumping to his feet, he drew his revolver and fired several shots at Hori. One struck the young half-caste in the side. He was not seriously wounded, but he could not retreat, as his comrades did when a force sallied out from the redoubt. Hori was captured and identified as one of the Maoris who had ambushed Dr. Hope and his party. The fatal ring was on his finger, the watch was in his pocket, and one of the rifles was identified as Dr. Hope's. He was charged with murder—although in Maori eyes this ambush was thoroughly in accordance with the rules of war—was tried and found guilty, and sentenced to be hanged. He was taken to Auckland for execution, but his sentence was commuted to imprisonment for life. In prison a white man came to see him. This was Mr. Robert Graham, Superintendent of the Province of Auckland, the "Lord Worsley" passenger whom Hori had befriended on the Taranaki coast the previous year. Hori had cast his bread upon the waters. Mr. Graham rejoiced in the opportunity of repaying the kindness. He persuaded the Governor to reduce the sentence. Hori was released after serving four years, and he went no more upon the war-path.*

The war renewed, troops were again moved to Taranaki. The Militia and the Volunteers were once more required for guard and patrol duty around New Plymouth.

At the beginning of June more effective methods of frontier warfare were introduced by the formation of settler and Volunteer corps for the special purpose of following the Maoris into the bush and clearing the country surrounding the town of hostile bands. The soul of these free-roving tactics was Captain Harry Atkinson. His party of fifty men of No. 2 Company, Taranaki Rifles, was the first corps of forest rangers to take the field in New Zealand. The force, as the war went on, was increased to two companies, and was styled the Taranaki Bush Rangers. Day after day Atkinson

---

* Hori Teira, who is now a farmer near Parihaka, Taranaki, narrated this adventure of his youth to the writer.

Sergeant-Major Bezar, who, with a party of men, captured Hori Teira, says,—

"Hori Teira was the first prisoner taken in the war of 1863. We were in St. Patrick's Redoubt at Poutoko, and I was looking out over the parapet when I saw a man hurrying up the hill towards us on foot, and as he came closer I saw he was an officer. Seeing an officer dismounted, I immediately concluded something was wrong, and I called to some of the men, 'Get your rifles, men, quick, quick!' so that by the time the officer, Lieutenant Waller, came up we were ready. He told me what had happened, and I took my party over a short-cut to the place where he had been fired at. It was only 500 yards below our redoubt, and about four miles from where the ambush had occurred three weeks previously. We skirmished up quickly to the belt of bush where Waller had been fired at, and did it so quickly that I think we were there scarcely more than five minutes after he reached the redoubt and told me what had happened. All the Maoris but one had bolted into the bush. This one was Hori Teira. I found him crouching in the scrub. A soldier made for him with his bayonet, but I stopped him from killing him, saying that I wanted to get the young fellow to tell us where they had buried Ryan, one of the nine men killed in the previous ambuscade, whose body was still missing. This Teira did, and we found the body. I marched him to the redoubt and handed him over. Teira told me also that the Maoris had intended the ambush for Sir George Grey and General Cameron, whom they had planned to kill."

led out his war-party of practised bushmen-settlers and scoured the forest and the native tracks, and soon had the country free from hostiles for a radius of many a mile from New Plymouth. The Bush Rangers were armed with Terry breech-loading carbines and revolvers. Atkinson's principal fellow-officers in this highly useful commission were Captain F. Webster and Lieutenants Brown, Jones, McKellar, and Messenger.

THE STORMING OF KATIKARA.

Early in June General Cameron moved out against the southern tribes who were resisting the Government's title to the Tatarai-

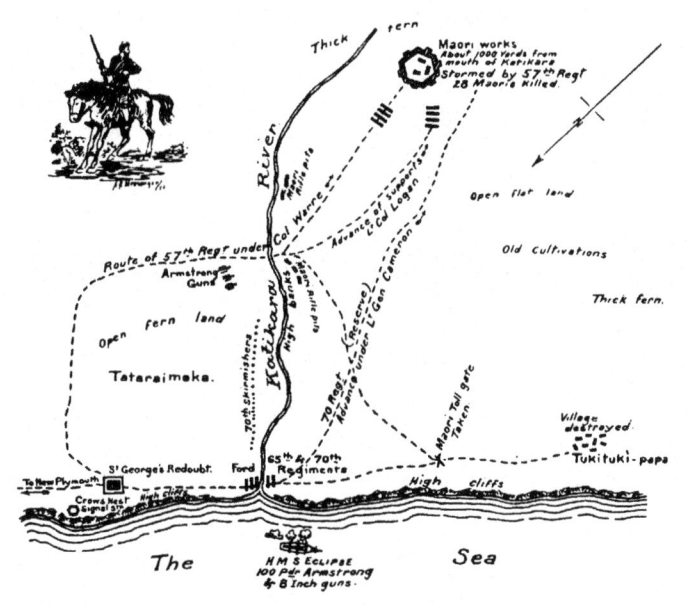

THE BATTLEFIELD OF KATIKARA (1863).

maka Block. At St. George's Redoubt, the post which he had established at Tataraimaka, he concentrated a considerable force, having previously arranged that H.M.S. "Eclipse" should co-operate by shelling the Maoris. The Taranaki, Ngati-Ruanui, Nga-Rauru, and Whanganui men had entrenched themselves in a position above a mile beyond St. George's Redoubt and near the mouth of the Katikara River. Falling in at daybreak on the 4th June the 57th (under Colonel Warre) and the 70th crossed the Katikara River and advanced upon the native entrenchments, while a preparatory bombardment was carried out by the "Eclipse"—which had anchored off the mouth of the river more than a mile from the *pa*—and by an Armstrong battery posted on the edge of the cliff above the river near the redoubt. After the shelling the 57th carried the position at the point of the bayonet, cleared the rifle-pits and trenches, and pursued the beaten foe inland. Sergeant-Major E. Bezar, one of the few surviving veterans of the 57th, took part in the charge; he thus described to the writer the storming of the trenches:—

"The Taranaki natives' position had not been completed when we attacked it. The place was about fifteen miles from New Plymouth, on the southern side of Tataraimaka and more inland. St. George's Redoubt at Tataraimaka was about a mile away. After leaving the redoubt our force had to cross a river and then advance in single file up a rough ferny ridge; at the top we halted so as to give the men time to come up, and it was a considerable time before we had enough men there to enable us to rush the *pa*. The distance we had to charge across the open was about 150 yards. In the meantime Ensign Duncan with fifty men of our regiment had been sent on to cut off the Maoris' retreat in the rear. Duncan marched up from the redoubt to within a short distance of the *pa*, but instead of taking post in the rear, as he should have done, he simply came up along the right flank of the Maoris and rushed in at the front of it as we did. Had he done his duty properly the Maoris would have been surrounded, and probably the war would have ended there.

"The place, properly speaking, was not a *pa*, as there was no parapet or palisade. It consisted simply of trench-work and rifle-pits. The main trenches, about 4 feet wide or so, roughly formed three sides of a parallelogram, with the longer side on the front which we rushed. Inside the trenches was a series of rifle-pits—three or four of them—and within again were two or three large *wharepunis*, sunk in the ground after the usual native fashion, with low roofs; they were thatched with *raupo*.

"We charged in across the trench with the bayonet, and the Maoris were soon bolting out at the rear. The glacis across which we rushed was a potato cultivation; on the south there was a maize-field. I saw one man running down across this field, and I took a shot at him and dropped him. By the time I had loaded again and caught up to my men we were in the *pa*. The *whares* were set fire to, or caught fire from the shooting close to the thatch, and as they burned the *raupo* fell in. There were several men's bodies under the burning debris when the fight was over.

"When the action was over we collected the dead and wounded. Three of our men were killed. The Maoris lost about forty killed. We carried twenty-eight bodies out across the trenches and laid them in a long row in front of the works they had defended. Then General Cameron came up with Sir George Grey, and complimented our captain, Russell, on the day's work. The dead Maoris were loaded into carts and taken down to the Tataraimaka, and all were buried in one large square pit close to our redoubt.

"A picture in the *Illustrated London News*, 1864, is a very inaccurate drawing of the fight. There was no large earthwork as shown in the sketch—only trenches and rifle-pits.

"Ensign Duncan, so far as I know, was never taken to task for his blunder; but there is no doubt that his fifty men could have disposed of the Maoris had they been in their proper position in the rear.

"The surviving Maoris, we heard afterwards, held a meeting at night in the bush, and they all decided to wage war to the uttermost in revenge for their losses that day."

A number of Upper Wanganui natives were killed in this attack, and these losses accounted in part for the readiness with which the river tribes embraced the Hauhau fanaticism in 1864.

The principal trophy captured on this successful expedition was the large board on which the list of Maori tolls was painted, set up originally by the Kingites near Te Ika-roa-a-Maui, the large assembly-house at Kapoaiaia, near Warea, and afterwards brought to Puke-tehe, in the vicinity of Tataraimaka. The tolls demanded ranged from £500 for a *pakeha* policeman to 6d. for a Maori pig carried in a cart. The board was put on board H.M.S. "Eclipse" for Auckland.

As the Waikato War had now begun, the Ngati-Maniapoto and other northern fighters who had gone to Taranaki in response to the appeal from the *runanga* at Mataitawa, when the troops occupied Tataraimaka, returned to defend their own territory, and left the west-coast tribes to continue the hostilities. There was intermittent skirmishing for some months; in these events the Taranaki Rifles Volunteers and the Militia played a conspicuous part. The principal engagement during the latter part of 1863 was an encounter on the 2nd October at Allen's Hill, or Hurford Road, five miles and a half from New Plymouth along the south road. Colonel Warre took out a strong force of the 57th and the settler-soldiers, and there was some brisk fighting on the hill and in the fields around the homestead to the west of it. Captains Atkinson, Webster, and W. B. Messenger were in charge of the Volunteers and Militia, numbering between ninety and a hundred. Captain Frank Mace and some of his mounted men were also engaged. Two V.C.s were won at Allan's Hill, by Ensign J. T. Down and Drummer D. Stagpoole, of the 57th, who went to the rescue of a mortally wounded comrade under fire near the bush.

Now and again the Regular troops, in emulation of Atkinson's active Bush Rangers, essayed to lay ambuscades for the Maoris. An incident of this kind was the ambushing of a small party of natives at the foot of the Patua Range, on which the Kaitake *pa* was built, by a detachment of the 57th, under Captain H. R.

Russell, from the Poutoko Redoubt. Seven natives were killed in this morning surprise.

The Tataraimaka Block was once more temporarily abandoned to the Maoris, and the available forces were concentrated on the defences of New Plymouth and its outposts as far as Omata and Poutoko on one hand and the Bell Block on the other. The bush-scouring parties of the Volunteers were now most useful in patrolling the broken forest country in rear of the town, and in blocking communication between the southern tribes and the Atiawa.

An example of the numerous bush skirmishes in which the settlers' corps were engaged in 1863-64 is described by Captain J. R. Rushton, now living at Kutarere, Ohiwa Harbour. Captain Rushton says,—

"Upon my arrival in New Plymouth, a few days after the ambuscade of Lieutenant Tragett and Dr. Hope at the Wairau, I joined the Bush Rangers, a scouting corps, under Captains Atkinson and Webster. Our duties were to patrol on the outskirts of the town, which was now isolated from other parts of the colony, the Maoris having burned down many houses and murdered some settlers. This is how we foiled a Maori ambuscade, through the smoke from the pipes: We had been out all night some distance past the Bell Block, and, not meeting with the enemy, started to return by the edge of the bush, through Street's Clearing, swinging along at ease in single file on the bullock-cart road. I was near the front with Bill Smart and others. The fern was high, but looking over we saw distinctly, at about 250 yards, at the edge of the bush, a small curl of smoke ahead, and upon looking again saw a group of Maoris in their mats leaning upon their guns. Captain Atkinson now got up to us and saw the Maoris, and about fifteen or eighteen of us actually formed up in line, and at the word 'Fire,' gave them a volley. We expected to get their killed and wounded, but before we got across the swamp they had dragged those hit or killed into the bush. So we did not venture in after them, being not far from Mataitawa *pa*. We got many mats with holes through them, and, I think, some guns. We now continued our way in the direction of Bell Block, and at a small rise we got a volley from behind logs. Following up the Maori party, we killed two. We now started again for home, in the direction of the Bell Block, and had not gone far when we saw coming towards us two bullock-carts. There was a strong wind blowing from them, and they told us that they never heard the firing. It was a most wonderful escape. The two ambuscades were ready for the firewood-carts from Bell Block, and it was evident that the second ambuscade never heard our first volley. We now started for town, having done a good morning's work.

"Just a word for my old comrades, the Taranaki boys. The Maoris had no chance with them, man for man, in the bush.

Skirmishing with them under Captain (afterwards Major) Sir Harry Atkinson taught me much about taking cover in bush fighting that served me well in other campaigns during nearly eight years active service in the Maori wars. It is always pleasing to an old soldier to be able to remember with affection his old officer. When spoken to by Sir Harry Atkinson one knew that he was a kind friend as well as a commanding officer."

KAITAKE PA.

South of New Plymouth towards the end of 1863 the chief activity of the Taranaki was the construction of a strongly entrenched position at Kaitake, on a north-western spur of the

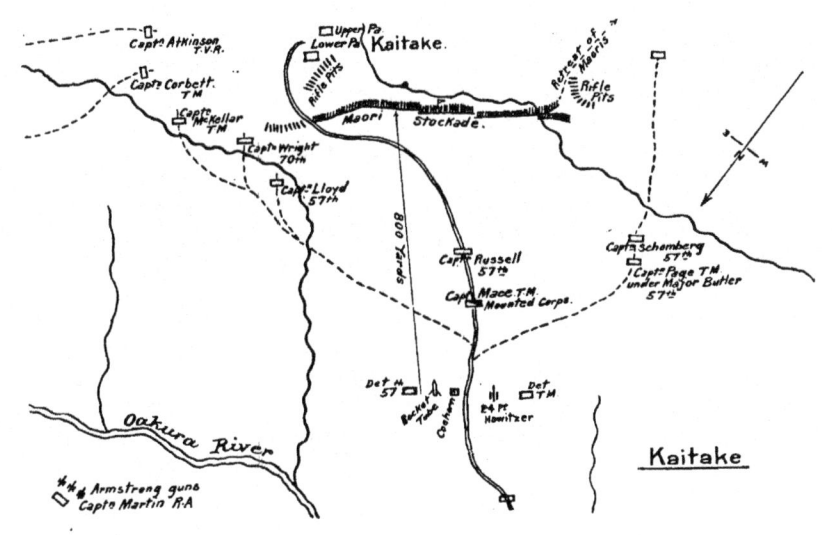

PLAN OF THE ATTACK ON KAITAKE (1864).

Patua Range; the *pa* was on the bold skyline of this ridge as seen from the main road at Oakura. The distance from the Oakura River mouth to the *pa* was about three miles. The local chief and engineer of this fortification was Patara Raukatauri, of the Taranaki Tribe; he afterwards gained celebrity as one of the emissaries or prophets sent out by Te Ua to preach the fanatic gospel of the Pai-marire among the East Coast tribes. (Patara, however, was a man of far milder character than his fellow-prophets, and did not enter into the deeds of savagery of which Kereopa was guilty.) Kaitake was a well-planned stronghold, situated in an excellent position for defence, on a steep, high ridge, with a frontal stockade covering the terminal of the spur, and two parapeted redoubts, one in rear of the other, on the heights.

There were also skilfully arranged rifle-pits flanking the direct approach to the *pas*. In December, 1863, Colonel Warre shelled the place with the Armstrong field-guns, but the final operations were deferred until the following year. The Government was now bringing in military settlers, many of them from Victoria, and the force in the province amounted to about two thousand men, including a thousand Regular troops.

Kaitake was stormed and captured by the troops on the 25th March, 1864. A force of 420 of the 57th, 70th, and Volunteers and Militia, with four guns, under Colonel Warre, moved out from New Plymouth to the base of the range. The guns were placed in position about 1,500 yards from the right of the Maori rifle-pits, and made such accurate practice that most of the defenders were driven out of those portions of the works. In the meantime a party of eighty Military Settlers, under Captain Corbett, who had left their redoubt at Oakura about 1 a.m., with great labour worked their way to the base of the spur on which the rifle-pits had been made, and took the positions in reverse. They were nine hours advancing two miles and a half through the bush. At 10.30 a.m. the guns ceased firing. The main body of the troops advanced to within 800 yards of the works, while the Volunteers and Military Settlers ascended the spur and carried in succession the rifle-pits and the *pas*, pouring a reverse fire into the trenches behind the line of palisading. The Maoris held these trenches until a portion of the main body had ascended a ridge on their extreme left. Both flanks having been turned, the Maoris retired through the bush in their rear. A redoubt for a hundred men was immediately constructed on the site of the uppermost *pa*. The enemy's works were gradually destroyed, the bush in the vicinity was cut down, and a practicable road was made to the position. A party of rejoicing settlers, including a lady, drank champagne in the captured stronghold the day after its capture. However, four days after the storming of the position the Maoris laid an ambuscade within 150 yards of the redoubt, and killed one soldier and wounded another.

It is now necessary to break the narrative of events in Taranaki, where the fighting assumed a new phase with the rise of the Pai-marire religion, and turn to the outbreak and progress of the Waikato War, 1863–64.

CHAPTER XXVI.

THE WAIKATO WAR AND ITS CAUSES.

Ka ngapu te whenua;
Ka haere nga tangata ki whea?
E Ruaimoko
Purutia!
Tawhia!
Kia ita!
A—a—a ita!
Kia mau, kia mau!

The earthquake shakes the land;
Where shall man find an abiding-place?
O Ruaimoko
(God of the lower depths),
Hold fast our land!
Bind, tightly bind!
Be firm, be firm!
Nor let it from our grasp be torn!

—*Kingite War-song.*

This chant, often heard even at the present day, embodied the passionate sentiment of nationalism and home rule for the Maoris which developed into a war-fever in Waikato. From first to last the wise and patriotic Wiremu Tamehana was a restraining force, and with him a few of the more temperate-minded of the Waikato chiefs, such as Patara te Tuhi, nephew of the old King Potatau te Wherowhero. Potatau was a firm friend of the *pakeha*, and, had he been a younger man, his undoubtedly great influence, born of his warrior reputation and his aristocratic position, probably would have prevented the Waikato throwing themselves into a test of arms with the Government. In the beginning of the King movement, as has already been explained, there was no desire to force a war. The great meetings at which the selection of Potatau as King was confirmed were attended by numerous Europeans. Government officials, missionaries, and traders were alike welcome guests at Ngaruawahia, Rangiaowhia, and the other centres of the home-rulers. The more intelligent of the Maoris saw clearly that there was nothing to be gained by a rupture of relations with the *pakeha*. But the irritation caused by the inevitable friction over

European encroachment, the treatment of the natives by the lower class of whites, the reluctance of the authorities to grant the tribes a reasonable measure of self-government, and, lastly, the sympathy with Taranaki and the bitterness engendered by the loss of so many men in the Waitara campaign, all went to mould the Waikato and their kinsmen into a powerful foe of the Colonial Government.

In the beginning the natural desire of the natives for a better system of government could have been turned to beneficial account by a prescient Administration. At a large meeting at Paetai, near Rangiriri, on the 23rd April, 1857, Potatau, Te Wharepu, and other chiefs asked the Governor, Colonel Gore Browne, for a Magistrate and laws, and *runanga* or tribal councils. To this request the Government responded by the experimental establishment of civil institutions in the Waikato, under Mr. F. D. Fenton, afterwards Judge of the Native Land Court. The new machinery, however, was not given time to develop into a useful and workable system before Mr. Fenton was recalled, and the field was left free for the exponents of Maori independence to develop their own schemes of government.

An account has been given in a previous chapter of the first meetings in connection with the establishment of the Maori kingdom. The Paetai meeting of 1857 was a highly picturesque gathering. The Lower Waikato people were assembled to meet their guests from up-river, the Ngati-Haua and Ngati-Maniapoto and some of the Waikato *hapus*, who came sweeping down the river in a grand flotilla of nearly fifty canoes. Wiremu Tamehana and his Ngati-Haua set up on the *marae* or village campus the flag of the newly selected King; this ensign was white, with a red border and two red crosses, symbolic of Christianity; it bore the words "Potatau Kingi o Niu Tireni." The speeches breathed intense patriotism. "I love New Zealand," cried one old blanketed chief. "Let us have order, so that we may increase like the white man. Why should we disappear from the land? Let us have a king, for with a king there will be peace among us. New Zealand is ours—I love it." Another, Hoani Papita, of the Rangiaowhia people, Ngati-Hinetu and Ngati-Apakura, made an eloquent plea for independence and nationalism. "Fresh water is lost when it mingles with the salt," he said. "Let us retain our lands and be independent of the *pakeha*." And he began the chant which heads this chapter, "*Ka ngapu te whenua.*" The whole two thousand natives gathered around took up the song and chanted it in a tremendous chorus. That old heart-cry of nationalism still holds power to electrify the Maori.

The formal investiture of Potatau with the dignity of King of the Maori Kotahitanga, or confederation of tribes, took place in 1858 at Ngaruawahia, and was followed by a large gathering at

Rangiaowhia, the great granary and orchard of the Upper Waikato, not far from Te Awamutu, where presently Mr. Gorst (afterwards Sir John Gorst) was placed by Sir George Grey as one of the "spades" wherewith to accomplish the downfall of the Maori national flag. The aged King Potatau died in the winter of 1860, and his son Tawhiao, grotesquely baptised Matutaera (Methusaleh), became the figurehead of the kingdom in his place.

Governor Browne and his Ministers consistently declined to recognize the Maori King or Maori nationality, but when Sir George Grey became Governor, and a peace Ministry was formed under Mr. Fox (afterwards Sir William Fox), efforts were made to conciliate Waikato. In 1861 the Governor sent John Gorst into the Waikato as Magistrate and Commissioner to watch the native political feeling and to establish European institutions in the heart of the Maori country. Grey and his Ministers introduced also a system of local government; under this plan the Maori country was to be divided into districts and "hundreds," over each of which a Civil Commissioner was to be placed to grapple with the task of governing the natives in his zone of influence, with the assistance of salaried Maori Magistrates, assessors, and policemen. The new institutions were first introduced in the Ngapuhi country and on the Lower Waikato, where the salaries and privileges were received with enthusiasm, but it was too late to entice the Kingites into the Government fold with such devices. The King's *runanga* of chiefs at Ngaruawahia told Mr. Gorst that if some plan of the kind had been carried out five or six years previously there would never have been a Maori King. Still they were willing, if the Governor was willing to let their King and flag stand, to adopt his plans and work with him for the good of all. But the Kingitanga was the stumbling-block. Grey, for all his kindly feeling towards his native friends, would have nothing to do with an alien flag, and he declared at last, at a Waikato meeting, that although he would not fight against the Maori kingdom with the sword, he would "dig around it" until it fell. This ominous figure of speech, combined with the always suspicious presence of a Government agent in the heart of the King's country, and, finally, the commencement of the military road from Drury through the forest to the Waikato River, fostered the Maori disbelief in the friendly intentions of the *pakeha*.

The Kingites' suspicions of the Governor and his Ministers were aggravated by the attempt to establish a Government constabulary station at Te Kohekohe. Grey's plan was to police the Lower Waikato district by this post, which was close to Te Wheoro's settlement on the west bank of the Waikato River, a few miles above the mouth of the Manga-tawhiri, but on the opposite side. The station or barracks was planned so as to be converted readily into a defensible place in the event of war. Te Wheoro, who

SIR GEORGE GREY.
(Period about 1860.)

afterwards became a major of Militia in charge of the contingent of Ngati-Naho friendly natives, espoused the Government's side. The Lower Waikato people were sharply divided in politics. Most of the Ngati-Tipa also favoured the Government, and their chief, Waata Kukutai, became an assessor like Te Wheoro. Ngati-Tamaoho and Ngati-Pou, on the other hand, were staunch Kingites; these were the people who inhabited Tuakau, Pokeno, and other parts close to the great westward bend of the Waikato. Two songs, current to this day among the Waikato, voice the opinions of the two factions. In one " Te Kohi," as the natives called Mr. Gorst, was urged to make the Manga-tawhiri River a close frontier against the Kingites :—

> Koia e Te Kohi,
> Purua i Manga-tawhiri,
> Kia puta ai ona pokohiwi,
> Kia whato tou
> E hi na wa!

In other words, the Civil Commissioner of Waikato was requested to " plug up " the boundary river between *pakeha* and Maori lands, and prevent the King's followers passing below its mouth to trade in Auckland, so that presently they would be reduced to a ragged condition for want of European clothing. To this piece of political persiflage the Kingites retorted with a *waiata* prompted by the Government proposal to establish a police-station at Te Wheoro's village :—

> Kuini i Te Kohekohe,
> Whakaronga mai ra nge,
> Ka pohutu atu nga papa,
> Kei Te Ia.
> Mau na wa!

> O Queen at Te Kohekohe,
> Listen to me!
> Presently we'll send your timbers splashing,
> To float down to Te Ia.

This threat was soon fulfilled, for a party of King supporters came down the river, took possession of the sawn timber that had been stacked at Kohekohe for the construction of the Government station, threw it into the river, and rafted it down to Te Ia-roa ("The Long Current"), called by the Europeans " Havelock." There they landed it in front of a trading-store kept by a young Scotsman, Mr. Andrew Kay.

The eviction of Mr. Gorst from the Waikato was the next step in the Kingites' clearance of all forms of European authority from their land. Mr. Gorst (who had at first thought of entering the Melanesian mission work under Bishop Selwyn) came under the magic spell of Sir George Grey's personality soon after his arrival in New Zealand and he became an enthusiastic instrument of the

Government in the task of civilizing and educating the Maori youth. The Church Missionary Society lent its 200 acres of land at Te Awamutu, with school-buildings, to Sir George Grey as a technical-education establishment, and there Mr. Gorst for some time carried on a useful work, schooling Maori boys in the arts of civilized life and at the same time occasionally exercising his magisterial office.

From a portrait by G. Lindauer, in the Auckland Municipal Gallery.]

TAWHIAO, THE WAIKATO KING.

(Died 1894.)

The story of Gorst's little newspaper, *Te Pihoihoi Mokemoke i te Tuanui*, or "The Lonely Lark on the House-top" (there being no sparrows in Maoriland), established by way of a counterblast to the Kingite print *Te Hokioi* ("The War-bird"), is a pivotal incident in the history of the Waikato. The pungent tone of the

Pihoihoi particularly incensed Rewi and his fellow-chiefs, and the *runanga* at Kihikihi determined to suppress Gorst and his paper. On the 25th March, 1863, when Mr. Gorst was absent at Te Kopua, on the Waipa, Rewi and a war-party of Ngati-Maniapoto, numbering eighty, invaded Te Awamutu. Wiremu Kingi te Rangitaake, of Waitara fame, accompanied Rewi. A minor chief, Aporo Taratutu, was the active agent in the raiding of the station. The Government printing-press, type, and paper, and printed copies of the fifth number of the *Pihoihoi*, were seized. Mr. Gorst was now ordered to leave Te Awamutu. When he refused, Rewi wrote to Governor Grey (then in Taranaki) requesting him to withdraw his

THE RIGHT HON. SIR JOHN E. GORST.

(Died 1916.)

Sir John Gorst came to New Zealand in 1860, in the ship "Red Jacket," from Liverpool. He was Civil Commissioner in the Upper Waikato, 1861-63. His life in the Maori country and his association with the Waikato chiefs are described in his books "The Maori King" and "New Zealand Revisited."

official. Wiremu Tamehana sadly begged Gorst to leave. "If you stay," he said, "some of the young men may grow desperate, and I shall not be able to save you." Grey recalled Gorst, who left Te Awamutu on the 18th April, 1863. He took a last look at it from the heights above the Mangapiko as he rode away; and it was more than forty-three years before he saw it again, when he revisited Waikato (December, 1906), and was warmly greeted by some of the very people who had turned him away.*

So abruptly ended the Governor's effort to wean Waikato from the charms of kingism. Rewi was condemned by Wiremu Tamehana, Patara te Tuhi, and others of the moderate party, but the great majority were delighted with Ngati-Maniapoto's *coup*, and

---

* Curious histories attach to the printing plants of the *Pihoihoi Mokemoke i te Tuanui* and the *Hokioi*. The *Pihoihoi* press and the type, after being seized by the Ngati-Maniapoto at Gorst's station, Te Awamutu, in 1863, were carted up to Kihikihi, the headquarters of the tribe. Several of the young men helped themselves to a little of the type from the cases as curiosities; otherwise there was no interference with the plant. A few days later the press and type were carted to the head of navigation and taken in a canoe down the Waipa and Waikato Rivers to Te Ia-roa (Havelock), at the mouth of the Manga-tawhiri, where they were handed over to Mr. Andrew Kay (later of Orakau), who was then a trader on the river. The property was stored in the trading-house, and Mr. Kay reported to the Government, whereupon it was sent for and carted off to Auckland. It was afterwards used in printing the *Gazette* and other Government work. A legend gained currency that the type of the *Pihoihoi* was melted down by the Kingites and moulded into bullets to fire at the British soldiers. Mr. Kay's statement and the testimony of the Maoris make it clear that the press was returned almost intact to the Government. The small quantity of type taken by Rewi's young men at Kihikihi would not have made many bullets.

The story of the *Hokioi* press is even more interesting. It goes back to the year 1859, when the Austrian frigate " Novara " was in Auckland Harbour on a cruise round the world. Dr. Hochstetter, the geologist of the expedition, was treated with much kindness by the people of Waikato when he made his tour through the interior; and when the " Novara " sailed two chiefs of the King's party, Hemara te Rerehau (Ngati-Maniapoto) and Wiremu Toetoe (Waikato, of Rangiaowhia), were taken round the world in her as guests of the Austrian Government. In Vienna they were introduced to the Emperor Franz Josef, and the Archduke Maximilian entertained them, and on parting asked the Maoris what they would like him to give them as a present. They answered, " A printing-press and type.' These were given them and brought out to New Zealand. The printing-apparatus was taken to Mangere, where King Potatau sometimes lived. One of Mr. C. O. Davis's nephews, who had learned the art of composing type at the *New-Zealander* printing-office, instructed some of the young Maoris. The plant was taken to Ngaruawahia, and was used there for the printing of the Kingite proclamations and the *Hokioi e Rere Atu na*, a name which bore reference to a mythological bird of omen, a kind of war-eagle. Patara te Tuhi (Tawhiao's cousin) was in charge of the *Hokioi* and wrote the Kingite articles, and his brother, Honana Maioha—who, like Patara, had taken a prominent part in the setting-up of the Maori King—was one of the compositors. When the troops advanced up the Waikato at the end of 1863 the *Hokioi* press and type were taken for safe keeping to Te Kopua, on the Waipa, and there they have remained to the present day. The rusted remains of the press lie on the river-bank; and a settler ploughing his land at Te Kopua has turned up some of the scattered type. The local Maoris turned the old hand-press to account in another way—to press their cakes of *torori* or home-grown tobacco.

The *Hokioi* is the rarest of all New Zealand prints; there are very few copies in existence. One in the writer's possession bears the date Hanueri (January) 13, 1863. It is a four-page paper, single-column, 11 inches by 9 inches.

Waikato was soon afire with the war-passion. The first shots were fired in less than four months after the raid on Te Awamutu.

The Kingite plan of operations was detailed by Mr. James Fulloon, native interpreter, in reports to the Government in June, 1863. (Mr. Fulloon, who was a half-caste, a surveyor by profession, was killed by the Hauhaus at Whakatane in 1865.) The original scheme of war against the *pakeha*, according to accounts given by the Maoris, was arranged in 1861, after Governor Gore Browne's threatening Proclamation. The Waikato were to come down in a body to take up a position at Paparata, in the Tirikohua district, making that their headquarters. Thence parties were to

From a photo by Mr. Hugh Boscawen, at Mangere, 1901.]

PATARA TE TUHI.

This chief of Ngati-Mahuta, Waikato, was one of the leaders in the Maori King movement, and was the editor of the Kingite paper *Te Hokioi*, printed at Ngaruawahia. He visited England in 1884 with Tawhiao and other chiefs. His attitude before the war was moderate and conciliatory, and, like Wiremu Tamehana, he endeavoured to avert hostilities.

occupy Maketu, an old *pa* east of Drury—there was an ancient track to that spot from Paparata—and Tuhimata, the Pukewhau Hill (now Bombay), overlooking Baird's Farm; also the Razor-back Range (Kakaramea). The Maketu position would menace Drury and Papakura, and from the Pukewhau and Kakaramea Hills the military traffic along the Great South Road could be attacked and the bridges destroyed. On the other side of the road (the west) the Ngati-Pou and other tribes were to attack Mauku and other settlements.

There was an alternative plan, which was favoured by most of the Kingites, and in the end was adopted; it was far more ambitious and daring than the first. The proposal was to execute a grand *coup* by attacking Auckland by night-time or early in the morning. The Hunua bush was to be the rendezvous of the main body, and a portion of the Kingite army was to cross the Manukau in canoes and approach Auckland by way of the Whau, on the west, while the Ngati-Paoa and other Hauraki coast tribes were to gather at Taupo, on the shore east of the Wairoa. The date fixed for the attack was the 1st September, 1861, when the Town of Auckland was to be set on fire in various places by natives living there for that purpose; in the confusion the war-parties lying in wait were to rush into the capital by land and sea. Certain houses and persons were to be saved; the dwellings would be recognized by a white cross marked on the doors on the night for which the attack was fixed. With the exception of those selected in this latter-day passover, the citizens of Auckland were to be slaughtered.

This was only a part of a general sudden blow against the *pakeha* race; similar attacks were urged upon the natives in the Wellington District. It was an exceedingly bold and hazardous scheme; nevertheless it would have been attempted had Governor Gore Browne remained in New Zealand. It was only the news that Sir George Grey was returning to the colony as its Governor that averted the general rising. The Maoris looked forward to his coming as the beginning of a different policy and a more friendly attitude towards their political aspirations. Then, when after all it was seen that war was inevitable, and when Governor Grey and his Ministers began an aggressive movement towards Waikato, the original plan of campaign discussed in 1861 was taken up— the raiding of the frontier settlements, with Paparata as a base of operations and camps in the Hunua forest.

In 1860 Mr. C. O. Davis informed the Government that gunpowder was being made at Tautoro (near Kaikohe, in the Ngapuhi country), and in the Waikato territory. It was believed that a Maori who had been in Sydney had learned the manufacture of powder there, and that Europeans assisted in the work. It is known that later on in the wars a European (Moffat) made a coarse gunpowder at a settlement near Taumarunui, on the Upper Wanganui. But it is improbable that the Maoris relied on locally made gunpowder to any great extent; they had sources of supply from traders, and for several years before the Waikato War had been laying in stocks of powder, lead, and percussion caps. Large quantities of ammunition were traded to the natives at Tauranga up to the beginning of the war. Tauranga was, in fact, one of the avenues of supply for Ngati-Haua as well as the Ngai-te-Rangi and other coast tribes. A common trick to evade the authorities when the restrictions on the sale of munitions were in force was for a coasting-vessel to clear outward at the Auckland Customs for Tauranga or other ports with a cargo ostensibly of empty casks (for pork) and bags of salt; each cask as often as not contained several kegs of gunpowder, and the bags were filled with lead and boxes of percussion caps. American whalers calling in at East Coast ports were believed to have bartered ammunition to the natives in return for provisions, and Sydney trading-vessels surreptitiously supplied munitions, but most of the guns and powder reached the Maoris from Auckland trading-houses.

The war now waged was very different from Hone Heke's chivalrous tournament of 1845. It was a racial war; the Maori aim was to sweep the *pakeha* to the sea, as the *pakeha* Government's object was to teach the Maori his subjection to British authority. The Europeans were not without warning that the sharp and barbarous old Maori methods of warfare were to be revived. Wiremu Tamehana himself, deeply as he sorrowed over the inevitable conflict, was compelled to place himself in line with his countrymen. He warned Archdeacon Brown, at Tauranga, that he —meaning his race—would spare neither unarmed persons (*tangata ringa-kore*) nor property. In August, 1863, he wrote to the Governor cautioning him to bring "to the towns the defenceless, lest they be killed in their farms in the bush." "But," he concluded, "you are well acquainted with the customs of the Maori race." The frontier settlers who remained on their sections did so at their own risk. No chief, not even the King or the kingmaker, could restrain a party of young bloods on the war-path seeking to flesh their tomahawks. They would quote the ancient war-proverb, "*He maroro kokoti ihu waka*" ("A flying-fish crossing the bow of the canoe") in allusion to any luckless persons whom a fighting *taua* might find in its path, and in the stern logic of the Maori there could be no reasonable protest against the practical application of the aphorism by cutting short the career of the "flying-fish."

NOTE.

During the Taranaki and Waikato Kingite wars some of the leading natives conducted correspondence on war subjects by means of a cipher code. The following is the key to the cipher, which came into possession of the Governor, Sir George Grey, about 1863:—

Letters.	Ciphers.	Letters.	Ciphers.	Letters.	Ciphers.
A	1	K	7	P	9
E	2	M	6	R	7
H	8	N	0	T	=
I	3	O	4	U	5
W		A mark resembling the symbol for "per."			
NG		O followed by an S crossed like the American dollar symbol, but with one line only.			

The figure 7 stood for both K and R, but no doubt there was some distinguishing mark or variation for one of the letters.

CHAPTER XXVII.

MILITARY FORCES AND FRONTIER DEFENCES.

In three months after the firing of the first shot in the Waikato War the whole of the able-bodied male population of Auckland between the ages of sixteen and fifty-five was on active service, bearing arms and doing duty as regular soldiers. The same conditions prevailed in Taranaki. The military expenditure of the Government was about £12,000 per month, and was on an increasing scale as the campaign developed. In addition to the equipment and pay of the Volunteers and Militia, a flotilla of armoured river-steamers and small gunboats was provided, and a field battery of six 12-pounder Armstrong guns. All this expense devolved upon the Colonial Government, besides a liability of £40 per head per annum to the Imperial Government on account of the Regular troops employed in the war. These British troops ultimately numbered about ten thousand. In a memorandum by the Defence Minister, Mr. Thomas Russell, the Volunteers and Militia on duty in the Auckland District were stated to total 3,176. The Cavalry Volunteers numbered 188, and the Rifle Volunteers 150. The local corps organized and armed were: Waiuku, 70; Mauku, 70; Pukekohe, 40; Wairoa, 60; Papakura Valley, 20; Henderson's Mill, 40; North Shore, 125; other places, 422: making a total of 847.

In addition to these Volunteers and Militia there were colonial permanent forces enrolled for the war, consisting chiefly of regiments of military settlers recruited in Australia in 1863 by Mr. Dillon Bell (Native Minister), Mr. Gorst, and Colonel Pitt. The 1st, 2nd, 3rd, and 4th Regiments of Waikato Militia raised in this way gradually relieved the Auckland Volunteers and Militia of the duties at the various posts on the Great South Road. Each regiment consisted of ten companies of 100 men. Out of the land confiscated from the Maoris each officer and man was entitled to a farm section, ranging from 400 acres for a field officer to 50 acres for a private. By October, 1863, there were about two thousand five hundred of these military settlers from Victoria, New South Wales, and Otago on permanent service in the field.

A highly useful arm of the colonial service was the Colonial Defence Force Cavalry, armed with sword, carbine, and revolver. There were two troops of Nixon's Cavalry, as this corps was locally called, in the Auckland District. There were also troops in Hawke's Bay, at Wellington, and at Wanganui; the total strength of the regiment was 375. In the Imperial Transport Service, receiving colonial pay, there were, when the war was at its height, 1,526 officers and men, with 2,244 draught animals. Captain Jackson's corps of Forest Rangers, numbering sixty, was soon augmented by a second company. Major-General Galloway was appointed to the command of the colonial forces, and gave his services to the colony gratuitously.

The Auckland Militia of the first class, unmarried men of between the ages of sixteen and forty, were first called out for active service on the 23rd June, 1863. There were no conscientious objectors in those days (or if there were they did not raise their voices), and any shirkers were dealt with severely. The first draft was 400 men, some of whom were despatched to the main camp at Otahuhu, and thence in companies to the various outposts as far as Drury. Others were retained for city patrol duty; as the war went on the older and married men relieved them of the town guard work and left the first class available for field service. The citizen recruits, drawn from all classes and occupations, were drilled in the Albert Barracks ground by the Regular Army instructors; morning after morning the drill was continued until the raw material was considered sufficiently advanced in the elements of infantry work to be despatched to Otahuhu. The duties of soldiering fell very severely upon many of the townspeople called upon to make heavy marches and live under rough camp conditions in the depth of winter, and to toil at redoubt-building and trench-digging. The large camp at Otahuhu was rather badly organized in the first hurry of war preparations, and the inferior hutting and feeding of the troops caused much sickness. The pay was half a crown a day with rations; this was increased by a shilling a day at the front.

The citadel of Auckland, Fort Britomart, stood on a commanding promontory, faced with pohutukawa-fringed cliffs 40 feet high. Major Bunbury and other commanders in Auckland had partly fortified the position, which was considerably strengthened by Major-General G. Dean-Pitt, a Peninsular War veteran, who commanded the forces in the colony from 1848 to 1851. The parapet was revetted with sods reinforced with layers of fern— an idea borrowed from the Maori *pa*-builder—and pierced with embrasures on the sea faces. On the land face there was a deep ditch in front of the parapet, with a stockade close to the counterscarp — another fashion in native fortification. Twelve fortress guns were mounted—long 24-pounders and 32-pounders, on iron garrison carriages; and there were also six 24-pounder howitzers and six 6-pounder field-guns. Within the fort were barracks for a hundred Royal Artillery and Royal Engineers men, officers' mess-room and brigade offices, military storehouses and magazines, and a main-guard house inside the gate at the trench bridge. Inland of the fort, and crowning the beautiful hill which the Maoris called Rangipuke (a large part of which is now the Albert Park), the Albert Barracks were constructed under Governor Grey's orders shortly after the conclusion of Heke's War. The barracks (accommodating a thousand men) were surrounded by a massive stone wall 12 feet high, broken into flanking bastions and loop-holed for rifle-fire, with a firing-step or banquette running along the inside of the parapet. The wall was of hard blue volcanic

From a drawing in the Old Colonists' Museum, Auckland.]

FORT BRITOMART, AUCKLAND, 1869.

stone; the construction was carried out by Maori labour under the Royal Engineers. The two gates, opening into Princes Street and Symonds Street, were protected by two flanking bastions. The area covered was sufficient to accommodate a strong garrison, and also give shelter to all the women and children in the town in case of a raid. A small section of the stone wall, ivy-grown and venerable, is still standing as portion of a boundary-wall near Government House grounds in Princes Street.

These defences were not alone intended for defence against Maori attack. There were even in that day fears of a foreign war which would involve the British colonies; the aggressive actions of the French in the Pacific, especially the annexation of

New Caledonia, had given rise to the fear that an invasion of Auckland was not unlikely.

The protection of the South Auckland outlying settlements and of the military road through the forest to the nearest point of the Waikato River necessitated the construction of many fortified posts, most of which were earthwork redoubts, others timber stockades. At Otahuhu, the principal field headquarters, there was a large fortified camp. At Howick, which was considered a vulnerable position owing to its proximity to the Wairoa Ranges, and open as it was to attack by war-canoe crews from the shores of the Thames Gulf, a field-work was erected. A large earthwork redoubt, called " St. John's Redoubt," after an officer placed in charge of it, was built between Papatoetoe and Papakura. The Village of Papakura was protected by the erection on the Auckland side of the settlement of a small redoubt, which

From a drawing by Lieut.-Colonel A. Morrow, Auckland.]

ST. JOHN'S REDOUBT, PAPATOETOE, 1863.

stood near the junction of the Great South Road and the Wairoa Road, and by the fortification of the Presbyterian church at the other side of the village. The redoubt was the camp of the local Volunteers and the Militia and a party of the 65th Regiment. The church was made bullet-proof by packing sand between the outer wall and the lining, a method used in most of the blockhouses built in the Maori campaigns. The walls were loopholed for rifle-fire. A correspondent, describing the remarkable sight of the country churches being stockaded and pierced for rifle-fire, remarked of the Papakura church, loopholed and bastioned, that it was a " visible transubstantiation of a bulwark of faith into a bulwark of earthly strength."

At Kirikiri, on the Papakura–Wairoa Road, a redoubt was thrown up on a commanding site two miles from Papakura; this came to be known as " Ring's Redoubt," after the captain of the 18th Royal Irish Regiment, who garrisoned it with his company in the early part of the war. A short distance farther along the Wairoa Road the "Travellers' Rest," an inn, store, and farmhouse combined, kept by Mr. W. B. Smith—a sturdy veteran of the Californian diggings and an old sailor—was put into a state of defence, and the owner and his family occupied it all through the war. The building was reinforced with heavy timbers, and rifle-slits were cut in the walls. The inn was the headquarters of Jackson's Forest Rangers during the early part of the war, and some of the Colonial Defence Force Cavalry were stationed there.

The Wairoa South Settlement (now Clevedon), eight miles from the mouth of the Wairoa River, was defended by the building of a redoubt on the left bank (west side) of the river and a stockade on the opposite side. The redoubt, a square work with flanking bastions, was built on Mr. Thorpe's farm. It was held by Major (afterwards Colonel) William C. Lyon and two hundred men, mostly Militia from Auckland. The stockade on the east bank was a formidable-looking post, a structure of heavy palisade timbers. It was 60 feet square, with very thick walls, bullet-proof and loopholed. Inside the stockade a corrugated-iron house, 40 feet by 16 feet, was built. This place, designed for from fifty to sixty men, was built by Mr. Snodgrass for the Auckland Provincial Government, and was occupied by the armed settlers of the district, the Wairoa Rifle Volunteers. Later, a redoubt was built lower down the river, on Mr. Salmon's property near the mouth of the Wairoa.

At Drury (the Tauranga of the Maoris), the head of navigation for cutters from Onehunga, there was a large military establishment, and a redoubt was built on the highest part of the settlement. At Pukekohe East (the present site of Pukekohe Town was then dense bush) the little Presbyterian church was enclosed by a trench and a stockade of logs laid horizontally. At Mauku the English church was stockaded and loopholed. Major Speedy's house, "The Grange," at Mauku, was loopholed and garrisoned by the settlers for defence; later, a stockade was built at the landing-place. A similar place of defence was provided at the Waiuku Settlement.

In many instances the settlers in the bush districts refused to leave their homes, and remained to brave the dangers of life on a troubled frontier.

From Drury the Great South Road through the forest to Pokeno was safeguarded by redoubts at short intervals. The principal posts were at Sheppard's Bush (Ramarama); Martin's Farm, on the plain a short distance north of Pukewhau Hill (now Bombay); Baird's Hill stockade, at the north end of Williamson's Clearing (the present site of Bombay Township); the Razorback Redoubt, on Kakaramea Hill, Pokeno Ranges; and then the field headquarters at Queen's Redoubt, on Pokeno Flat. At "The Bluff," on the right bank of the Waikato River just below Te Ia-roa, at the mouth of the Manga-tawhiri Stream, a strong timber stockade, 50 feet by 46 feet, enclosing a blockhouse, was erected ; two guns were mounted here. At Tuakau the 65th Regiment, soon after the beginning of the war, constructed a large redoubt in an excellent strategic position on the level top of a high bluff above the river : this post was named the Alexandra Redoubt.

At the few settlements on the Coromandel Peninsula there was some danger of attack from the Ngati-Paoa and other Kingite natives. A veteran Forest Ranger, Mr. William Johns, of Auck-

From a drawing by Lieutenant H. S. Bates (65th Regt.).]

THE QUEEN'S REDOUBT, AND ENCAMPMENT, POKENO.

land, recalls the fact that temporary defences were provided at Cabbage Bay, under the western side of the Moehau Range, where there was a large sawmill owned by an Auckland firm. Johns, who had been a sailor and served in the Royal Navy, was early in 1863 in charge of a cutter, the "Miranda," trading between Auckland and the Cabbage Bay mill. The natives in the district came under suspicion, as it was believed they would join the Kingites, and so one day the master of the cutter found twenty stand of arms ("Brown Besses" and a few rifles) delivered on the cutter by order of Colonel Balneavis, then Adjutant-General, for the defence of the mill workers and the other residents of Cabbage

Bay. The guns were landed at the bay, but it was not many days before they were all stolen by the Maoris, who went on the war-path rejoicing. The mill hands built a stockade for the defence of the place, encircling the sawmill with a palisade of 3-inch planks 12 or 14 feet high. However, the men were soon withdrawn.

At Raglan, on the Whaingaroa Harbour, west coast, there was fear that the small European settlement would be attacked by the Kingites from Kawhia or inland. Many of the settlers sent their families to Onehunga by the trading-vessels, but some of the women and children remained. A place of defence was considered necessary, and Mr. Richard Todd, a Government surveyor (who was shot on Pirongia Mountain by the Kingites in 1870), took charge of the work of fortification, and employed a number of friendly natives in digging a trench around the Courthouse and gaol, and in making rifle-pits to protect the principal houses. The entrenchment defending the Government buildings took in about an acre of ground. The main building was strengthened with thick timbers, and was loopholed. Early in 1864 a redoubt was built at the head of Raglan Harbour by Colonel Waddy's expeditionary force (50th Regiment and three hundred Waikato Militia).

The military road through the forest and over the range from Drury to the Mangatawhiri River was constructed in 1862 by a body of Imperial troops, the 12th and the 14th Regiments at the Pokeno end, and the 65th and 70th at the Drury end, with some Royal Engineers to direct the details of the work. Lieut.-General Cameron, in execution of Grey's plan for the employment of the troops in this work, fixed his headquarters at Drury Camp. Colonel Sir James Alexander (14th) was in command at Pokeno, where the Queen's Redoubt was built. The troops in December, 1861, marched along the Maori track over the range called the Razorback, and camps were established at points along the route, at which redoubts were afterwards built. Colonel Wyatt commanded the 65th at Drury, Colonel (afterwards General) Chute the 70th at Kerr's Farm. Brigadier-General

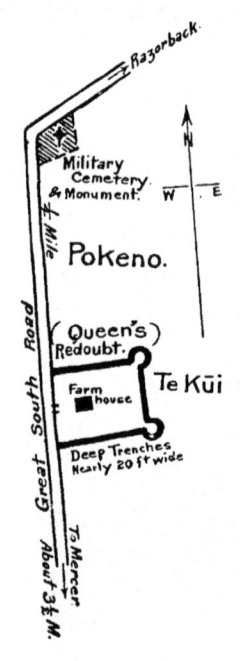

QUEEN'S REDOUBT, POKENO, AS IT IS TO-DAY.*

---

* The middle of the entrenchment is occupied by a farmhouse. The work is 100 yards square; there were originally four small angle bastions.

MILITARY FORCES AND FRONTIER DEFENCES. 243

Galloway and Lieut.-Colonel Leslie (40th) established a camp at Baird's Farm, and Lieut.-Colonel Nelson, with a detachment of the 40th, was at Rhodes's Clearing, on the southern end of the range, overlooking the Pokeno plateau. Of the twelve miles of good road cleared a chain wide, formed, and metalled (18 feet 9 inches wide) by the troops, seven miles penetrated the heavy forest.

From a drawing by Lieutenant H. S. Bates (65th Regt.), 1863.]

THE BLUFF STOCKADE, HAVELOCK, LOWER WAIKATO.

CHAPTER XXVIII.

THE FIRST ENGAGEMENTS.

On the 9th July, 1863, the Government issued an order requiring all natives living in the Manukau district and on the Waikato frontier north of the Manga-tawhiri to take the oath of allegiance to the Queen and to give up their arms, and warning the Maoris that those refusing to range themselves on the side of the British must retire to the Waikato. Those not complying with this instruction were to be ejected from their settlements. This ultimatum was followed by the following Proclamation sent to the Kingites summarizing the reasons which prompted the military measures adopted by the Government:—

CHIEFS OF WAIKATO,—
    Europeans living quietly on their own lands in Waikato have been driven away; their property has been plundered; their wives and children have been taken from them. By the instigation of some of you, officers and soldiers were murdered at Taranaki. Others of you have since expressed approval of these murders. Crimes have been committed in other parts of the Island, and the criminals have been rescued or sheltered under the colour of your authority.

    You are now assembling in armed bands; you are constantly threatening to come down the river to ravage the Settlement of Auckland and to murder peaceable settlers. Some of you offered a safe passage through your territories to armed parties contemplating such outrages. The well-disposed among you are either unable or unwilling to prevent these evil acts. I am therefore compelled, for the protection of all, to establish posts at several points on the Waikato River, and to take necessary measures for the future security of persons inhabiting that district. The lives and property of all well-disposed people living on the river will be protected, and armed and evil-disposed people will be stopped from passing down the river to rob and murder Europeans.

    I now call on all well-disposed natives to aid the Lieutenant-General to establish and maintain these posts, and to preserve peace and order.

    Those who remain peaceably at their own villages in Waikato, or move into such districts as may be pointed out by the Government, will be protected in their persons, property, and land.

    Those who wage war against Her Majesty, or remain in arms, threatening the lives of Her peaceable subjects, must take the consequences of their acts, and they must understand that they will forfeit the right to the possession of their lands guaranteed to them by the Treaty of Waitangi, which lands will be occupied by a population capable of protecting for the future the quiet and unoffending from the violence with which they are now so constantly threatened.

G. GREY,
Auckland, 11th July, 1863.   Governor.

On the 12th July General Cameron detailed a force from his army encamped at the Queen's Redoubt at Pokeno to make the first advance into the Waikato. The second battalion of the 14th Regiment, under Lieut.-Colonel Austen, crossed the swamp-fringed Manga-tawhiri Stream at the termination of the military road, and took up a position to the left, on the site of an old *pa* on a hill above the river, a spur of the Koheroa Range. A few days later this body was reinforced by detachments of the 12th and 70th Regiments, and was now five hundred strong. Three field-works were thrown up on the hill.

The process of ejection of those natives who could not bring themselves to abandon their fellow-countrymen was now carried out at the Manukau, Papakura, Patumahoe, Tuakau, and other districts between Auckland and the frontier waters. The principal tribe evicted was Ngati-Pou, who had a settlement on the right (north) bank of the Waikato at Tuakau, with large cultivations of food crops and fruit-groves. In the middle of July Mr. Dillon Bell, Native Minister, and Mr. Gorst carried out a rather perilous mission in the forested ranges above Papakura, at a small settlement called Te Aparangi, on the Kirikiri Stream, about two miles east of Papakura. Here a considerable number of Maoris had congregated, and, as most of these were known to be Kingites in politics, it was considered necessary to remove them south of the border-line. Te Aparangi was the village of the old chief Ihaka Takaanini and his people of Te Akitai and Te Uri-a-Tapa, *hapus* of the Ngati-Tamaoho; another *rangatira* of Te Akitai was Mohi te Ahi-a-te-ngu. The permanent population of the settlement was small, but some scores of young men from the Auckland side who had decided to join the Kingites had made it their rendezvous, and were believed to be fortifying themselves in the bush. Just above Te Aparangi on the foothills of the ranges is a level-topped hill known as Puke-kiwi-riki, formerly a strongly trenched fort belonging to the Ngati-Tamaoho Tribe. The ancient *pa* presented a tempting site for a freebooting stronghold. Mr. Bell gave the Akitai and their kin the choice of making a declaration of allegiance to the Queen or of going unmolested to the Waikato. He urged the former course, saying that the Government had no wish to drive them from their land. Mohi spoke in appreciation of Mr. Bell's generosity in going unarmed among the Maoris at such a time to carry a message of peace and good will, and declared that if the Minister had arrived a few days earlier with such an offer he and most of his people would have remained peacefully in their homes. But the Governor had crossed the Manga-tawhiri and invaded Waikato, and the Ngati-Tamaoho *hapus*, who previously had opposed Rewi and his war-party, now felt it their duty to join Waikato.

When the Minister and Mr. Gorst rode back to Drury that afternoon they heard the news of the first blow of the war. A settler named Michael Meredith and his young son had been found tomahawked on their bush farm near Ramarama, about four miles from Drury; they were out fencing when the marauders caught them. Some blamed Ihaka's people, but wrongly; the killing was the deed of a party of young men who sought to distinguish themselves by drawing first blood. A force of Nixon's Cavalry (Otahuhu troop, numbering thirty) and the 65th Regiment (three hundred) invaded Te Aparangi and took prisoner Ihaka and a number of others, chiefly old men and women and children, but the young armed men escaped and joined their relatives at Waikato.

Canoe-paddles dipped and flashed all along the broad Waikato as the Upper Waikato tribes and Ngati-Maniapoto, Ngati-Haua, and Ngati-Raukawa came hurrying down the river, eager to measure their strength with the *pakeha*. There were men even from Taranaki and the Upper Whanganui among the war-parties. Before the main body of the Kingites had had time to concentrate on the south side of the Manga-tawhiri the first encounter of the war was precipitated by an advance force of Waikato, numbering between two and three hundred, under Te Huirama, a near relative of King Tawhiao. Te Huirama had a fortified position at Te Teoteo, an old Maori *pa* on a bluff immediately overlooking the Whanga-marino Stream, which joins the Waikato a short distance above the present Township of Mercer. From this point the range of the hills on which Te Teoteo stands trends in a crescent, the northern horn curving in again towards the Waikato at the point where the Manga-tawhiri comes down into the swamps near the main river. Near the tip of the northern horn of the hills was the British advanced camp, under Lieut.-Colonel Austen. Te Huirama and his men hastened to provoke an attack from the British troops, and dug a succession of trenches across the narrow ridge.

The movements of Waikato were observed from the 14th Regiment's camp on the south side of the Manga-tawhiri on the forenoon of the 17th July. Lieut.-Colonel Austen immediately ordered his battalion under arms, and moved out to meet the Maoris, followed by a detachment of the 12th and 70th Regiments. General Cameron, from the Queen's Redoubt, overtook the column on its march to the ranges, over low hills covered with fern and manuka.

The force had advanced in skirmishing order for about two miles when the Maori outposts opened fire. They fell back, taking advantage of the broken ground to continue their firing. From their rifle-pits they opened a heavy fire when the leading troops were well within gunshot, and the young soldiers of the 14th hesitated momentarily after some men had fallen. The gallant General Cameron rushed forward waving his cap, and shouted to the 14th to come on. Cheering, the young battalion

THE FIRST ENGAGEMENTS. 247

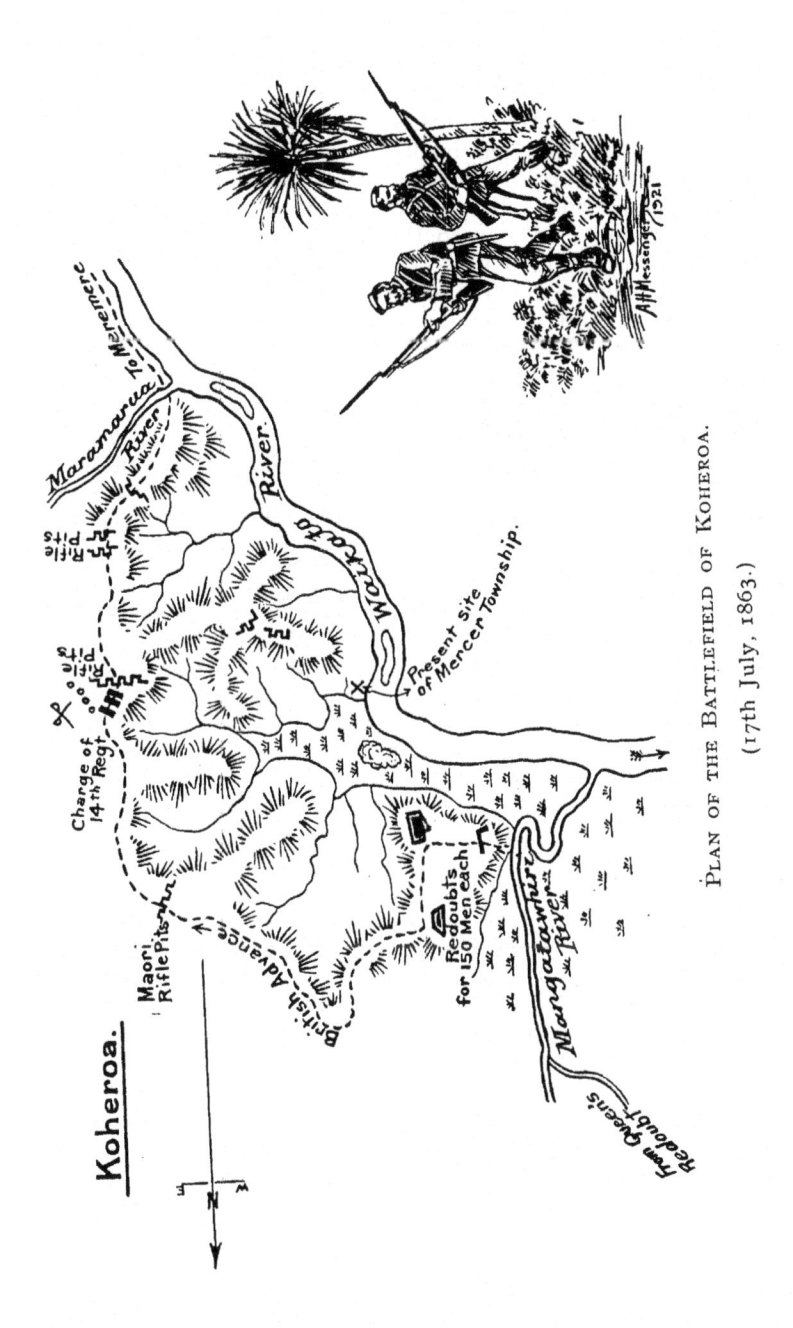

PLAN OF THE BATTLEFIELD OF KOHEROA.
(17th July, 1863.)

now swept forward at the charge, their officers—Captains Strange and Phelps, and Lieutenants Glancy and Armstrong — leading them sword in hand; and the lines of entrenchments were taken at the point of the bayonet. The Maoris, leaving many dead in and around the trenches, retreated south along the fern-hills, fighting as they fell back from one line of defence to the next, until they were driven to the heights above the Maramarua and Whanga-marino. Some escaped down a gully on the east, but lost a number of men to the heavy converging fire from the high ground on either flank. The majority of the survivors made for the south side of the Whanga-marino and thence to Meremere; others took to their canoes in the creek and paddled out into the Waikato River. The creek and the great swamp beyond stayed the further progress of the troops. The British loss was one killed; twelve were wounded, including Colonel Austen. (This officer afterwards was fatally wounded at Rangiriri.) Of the Maoris, the leader, Te Huirama (Ngati-Mahuta), and about thirty others were killed, many of them with the bayonet; a number of wounded were taken away in canoes. Many spades and some double-barrel guns, antiquated flint-lock pieces, and tomahawks were found on the battlefield.

After this sharp bayonet-work a British detachment was sent to hold a position on the south side of the heights commanding the Whanga-marino Stream. The spot selected was the summit of a bluff close to the old Maori *pa* Te-Teoteo, and a short distance east of the junction of the Whanga-marino with the Waikato. (The redoubt-site is almost immediately above the spot where the Great South Road crosses the Whanga-marino about half a mile south of Mercer.) This post was armed with two field-guns, under Lieutenant Pickard, R.A.

The Waikato Maoris, in referring to the engagement on the Koheroa Hills, speak of it as the fight at Te Teoteo.

The second skirmish of the campaign was the first of a series of surprise attacks upon British convoys and pickets along the Great South Road. The fight occurred on the 17th July, the same day as the engagement at Koheroa. A war-party of Ngati-Paoa, under Hori Ngakapa and some other chiefs, laid an ambuscade on the forest road at the northern base of the Pukewhau Hill (now Bombay). Here a settler named Martin had his farm, a small clearing cut out of the dense *puriri* forest. Much of the beautiful woodland still exists close to the road. A mile and a half to the north was the Sheppard's Bush Redoubt (Ramarama); the nearest redoubt on the south side was the post at Baird's Hill, on the northern slope of Williamson's Clearing (the site is that of the present Bombay Presbyterian Church and burying-ground). A convoy of six carts, escorted by fifty men of the 18th Royal Irish Regiment, under command of Major Turner and Captain Ring, was passing

THE FIRST ENGAGEMENTS. 249

along the road over the Pokeno Ranges from the Queen's Redoubt to Drury. On the left (west) side of the road there was a small stream ; on its banks, thickly clothed with a jungly undergrowth, part of the Kingite ambush-party crouched ; others occupied the cover near-by on the opposite side, within a few yards of the metalled road. The escort was marching at ease, unsuspicious of danger, when heavy fire was opened from both sides of the road. The first volley killed and wounded several soldiers, and

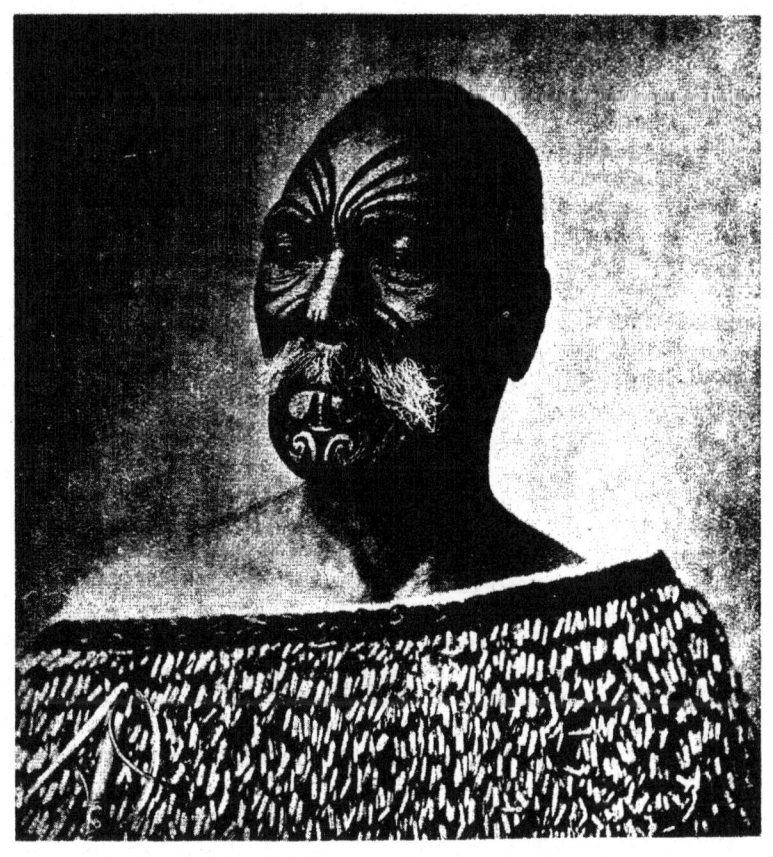

Photo by Iles, at the Thames.]

HORI NGAKAPA TE WHANAUNGA.

This warrior chief was one of the leaders in the attack on the British escort at Martin's Farm, Great South Road, 17th July, 1863. He was the head of the Ngati-Whanaunga, a subtribe of Ngati-Paoa, of the Hauraki Gulf coast. In 1851 he was a leader of the war-canoe expedition of Ngati-Paoa to the Town of Auckland (see note in Appendices). Hori fought at Rangiriri, and escaped by swimming across a lagoon. His brave wife, Hera Puna, accompanied him on the war-path in 1863.

some of the cart-horses were hit. The natives attempted to cut off the rearguard of about a dozen men from the main body, but the party, some of whom had been wounded, charged with the bayonet and fought their way through. The convoy was set under way again, and the soldiers resumed their march for Ramarama, doing their best to keep the Maoris off until reinforcements arrived. The Ngati-Paoa skirmished from tree to tree along both sides of the road, keeping up a hot fire. A detachment of the 18th came doubling up in the rear from Baird's Hill; other reinforcements presently arrived from the direction of Drury, and the attackers retreated. The British casualties were five killed and eleven wounded. The Maori loss was slight; they carried off their disabled men.*

The next engagement—Kirikiri (22nd July)—was fought still nearer Auckland. A number of settlers whose farmhouses stood on the fringes of the Hunua forest, from Papakura to Drury, had remained on their holdings, believing that they were unlikely to be attacked by the Kingites. In several instances here, as elsewhere, two or three families from the out-districts had taken up their quarters with friends in the larger houses for mutual protection. One of the pioneer settlers was Mr. Hay, whose home stood close to the Great South Road between Papakura and Drury; the site is very nearly that of the present Opaheke Railway-station. Captain Clare, an Indian Army veteran, had come into Mr. Hay's with his family from the Hunua bush; a member of the family was Mr. J. M. Roberts (now Colonel Roberts, N.Z.C.) On the morning of the 22nd July the alarm was given at Hay's that the Maoris had shot a man named James Hunt, cutting timber with his employer, Mr. Greenacre, and two others. A band of forty or fifty natives had surprised them in the bush, and, after giving them a volley, pursued them. Hunt fell with a fatal wound; the others escaped to Hay's. Mr. Roberts rushed to load all the rifles in the house. His responsibilities were heavy in the event of an attack, for there were four women dependent on his protection; one was his mother. He got up on the roof of the kitchen and kept a lookout for the Maoris. The raiders, however, were diverted

---

* The Martin's Farm ambush was the 18th (Royal Irish) Regiment's first taste of Maori warfare. This fine corps served in most of the actions of the Waikato War, and later was transferred to the west coast. The Royal Irish (2nd Battalion) came out from Portsmouth in the ships " Elizabeth Ann Bright" and " Norwood"; it was a new battalion recruited at Inneskillen in the late " fifties." The " Elizabeth Ann Bright" arrived at Auckland on the 2nd July, 1863, and the " Norwood" on the 2nd August; the strength landed was seven hundred officers and men. The Royal Irish Regiment was the last Imperial corps to leave New Zealand; the main body sailed from Auckland on the 28th February, 1870, leaving between three hundred and four hundred men who had taken their discharges to settle in the country.

by the arrival at the double of a small detachment of Militia from Papakura, under Captain Clare ; these men were soon joined by a hundred of the 18th Regiment, under Captain Ring, from the newly built redoubt at Kirikiri.

The Imperial soldiers found the Militia already in action on the edge of the bush. The united force skirmished with the Kingites in the bush in the direction of the hill Puke-kiwi-riki, above the deserted settlement of Ihaka Takaanini at Te Aparangi. The natives were gradually driven up into the hills, and occupied Captain Ring's first entrenchment on a knoll in a small clearing. From this place they were forced back by the Militia and the 18th,

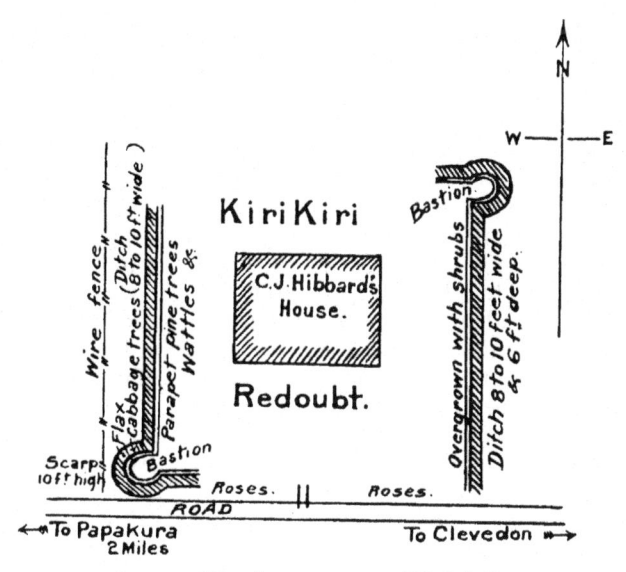

REMAINS OF RING'S REDOUBT, KIRIKIRI, 1921

The redoubt at Kirikiri (now locally misspelled Kerikeri) came to be known as Ring's Redoubt, after the captain in command. Like the Queen's Redoubt at Pokeno, its walls and trench, partly demolished, now enclose a farmhouse. The old fort stands alongside the main road two miles from Papakura on the way to Clevedon, Wairoa South. It is on part Section 29, Hunua Parish, and is the homestead of Mr. C. J. Hibbard.

but they presently threatened the flanks of the British force, which was almost surrounded. One of Ring's men had been killed at close quarters, and his rifle and bayonet seized by the Maoris. Under cover of the earthworks and logs the troops kept the Maoris back by heavy and accurate firing, and awaited reinforcements. Their position was now one of some anxiety. It was near sunset when Colonel Wyatt, with a force of the 65th and some of Lieutenant Rait's Mounted Artillery troopers, armed with swords and revolvers, came to the rescue and vigorously engaged the Maoris, whose numbers seemed also to have been reinforced. The troopers dismounted to enter the bush with the 65th, and this diversion compelled the Maoris to draw off from Ring's force. The united column, after recovering the body of the soldier killed, withdrew from the forest, and Ring returned to his redoubt above Kirikiri. This was the first occasion on which the Militia had been engaged with the Maoris, and Clare's few men behaved with skill and courage in the forest skirmish.

On the 10th August a scouting-party of thirty-five men of the Wairoa Rifle Volunteers and No. 4 Company, Auckland Militia, under Lieutenant Steele, discovered the great secret encampment of the Kingites in the Hunua Ranges, which it was believed had been prepared for a war-party essaying an attack upon Auckland from the east. This party, marching from the Wairoa stockade, explored the bush through to Drury. Passing Buckland's Clearing, a tract of open fern land in the bush, the scouts came to another fern opening, and advanced in skirmishing order upon a large encampment intended as the headquarters of a Maori army. This *nikau*-thatched township consisted of thirty-one *whares* from 20 feet to over 100 feet long, and capable, in Steele's opinion, of containing about fifteen hundred people. This camp was in the open, where the bush road from Drury emerged from the forest. On the road, and about a mile nearer Drury,-they found a few small *whares*, and again some huts three-quarters of a mile farther on, which appeared to have been used as advance posts.

The Kingite Maoris who gathered in the Hunua and Wairoa Ranges and thence made their forays were chiefly members of the Ngati-Paoa Tribe, from the Hauraki coast villages, under Hori Ngakapa and other chiefs; the Koheriki, a *hapu* of that tribe, headed by Wi Koka, from the country around the mouth of the Wairoa River; some of the Ngati-Haua, from the Upper Waikato and the Upper Thames Valley; and a number of the Ngai-te-Rangi and Piri-Rakau Tribes, from Tauranga, led by Hori Ngatai and Titipa. The Koheriki party did not number more than thirty to thirty-five fighting-men, but they were all active and ruthless fellows: they fought right through the war, and the survivors shared in the defence of the Gate *Pa* at Tauranga in 1864. With them were some women; one of these was a remarkably gifted and courageous young half-caste woman, Heni te Kiri-karamu— later otherwise known as Heni Poré (Foley)—who followed her brother Neri into the war; she was armed with a gun and used it. She took her young children with her, and her mother and sister accompanied her on the bush trail.

Most of the outlying farmers had abandoned their homes and were serving in the district Militia or Volunteers, but the smoke rising from the chimneys in some of the forest-clearings showed that a few stout-hearted settlers had determined to remain on their sections. One was Captain Calvert, whose home was on the Papakura–Wairoa Road, three miles from Papakura and a mile beyond Captain Ring's redoubt at Kirikiri. Early on the 24th July the alarm was raised at Calvert's that a party of armed Maoris was surrounding the house. The captain jumped out of bed, and just as he had snatched up his revolver some of the natives rushed into the kitchen, and one of them fired at the inmates. Calvert and his son Sylvester, a boy of sixteen, fired in return. The lad was mortally wounded. The captain, having emptied his revolver, rushed furiously at the enemy with his sword. They retreated before the brave old soldier, and fired heavily on the house from a hillock. The firing was heard at the Kirikiri Redoubt, and a party of soldiers drove the Maoris into the forest. Young Calvert was carried to the redoubt, where he died. On the same day Mr. George Cooper, a settler in the Wairoa Ranges, was shot down and killed when he went out to drive his cows up for milking. These attacks on bush-country settlers gave impetus to the formation by the Government of a special corps of guides or bush fighters, and the first company of the Forest Rangers, under Lieutenant Jackson, was soon enlisted.

After the attack on the Imperial convoy at Martin's Farm on the 17th July measures were taken to destroy the cover for the Maori parties in the most dangerous parts of the Great South Road, and the felling of the forest, making clearings a quarter of a mile wide, was begun on both sides of the road in Sheppard's Bush, at Martin's Farm, and along the west slope of Pukewhau Hill and part of the Razorback Range. This work was done chiefly by contract, under the superintendence of Mr. Martin. General Cameron ordered that the bushfellers should in every case be protected by a covering-party. The neglect of this precaution in one instance involved a party in a one-sided skirmish which provided the Maori raiders with a welcome supply of arms. This attack occurred on the west face of the Pukewhau Hill; the site, then known as Williamson's Clearing, is the present settlement of Bombay. On the 25th August twenty-five men of the 40th, under a non-commissioned officer, besides some bushmen, were engaged felling timber, leaving their rifles piled on the edge of the road in charge of a sentry. Suddenly a volley was fired from the bush, and two of the 40th fell. A party of Maoris rushed out from their ambush and easily captured the stacked rifles, twenty-three in number, and the pouches of ammunition. The bushfellers were rescued by the advance-guard of a convoy escort from Drury, under Captain A. Cook, of the 40th, and retired after fighting a skirmish with further reinforcements. Three of the natives were shot in the skirmish, and one of the 18th was wounded, besides the two shot dead in the first attack.

On the morning of the 2nd September, 1863, Ensign C. Dawson (2nd Battalion, 18th Royal Irish), subaltern in charge of the

Pokeno picket, had a lively skirmish with a large body of Maoris within a short distance of the Queen's Redoubt. The picket, consisting of two sergeants and sixty men of the 18th, left the redoubt at 7 a.m., and marched towards the Pokeno native village (which had been deserted by its owners, the Ngati-Tamaoho, on the outbreak of the war). Near the village the force was fired upon from the rear by a large body of Maoris. Dawson faced his men about and charged with the bayonet. He drove them down a gully towards the swamp and into the bush on the east side of Pokeno. After following the Kingites for about half a mile on the track inland towards Paparoa, he heard yells in the direction of the village in his rear, and returned with his force. He was saluted with a volley from Maori musketeers extended across the clearing, encumbered with logs and felled trees, between him and the settlement, and also was fired upon by some men in the bush on his right, near the hills. The soldiers, taking cover, in skirmishing order, kept up a steady fire and inflicted some casualties; the Maoris were seen carrying off their wounded. At this stage Captain Trench, of the 40th, came up with supports from the redoubt, and the reinforced skirmishers advanced and drove the Maoris out of the *kainga* and the log clearing into the bush.

A few days later (8th September) some of the Maoris attacked the British redoubt which had been erected on the top of Kakaramea, the northern spur of the Pokeno Ranges, over which the Great South Road was cut, between Williamson's Clearing and Rhodes's Clearing, overlooking Pokeno. This field-work was perched on the narrowest and most commanding part of the ridge which carried the road, but there was a higher hill a short distance to the east. The present road cuts through the western angle of the old fortification. A sentry outside, about 60 yards from the redoubt, at 10 a.m. saw a Maori stealing up on him through the bush. He fired at him, and the fire was returned by a war-party from the partly cleared hill about 100 yards on the east side of the road. The garrison (one hundred of the 65th Regiment, under Lieutenant Talbot) turned out and kept up a steady fire on the natives, who had the cover of felled timber and stumps. Ensign Ducrow, of the 40th, came up with forty men from Rhodes's Clearing, the next post on the south, and Talbot took half the detachment at the post and skirmished out, driving the attackers into the bush. Further reinforcements arrived from Williamson's Clearing, but they were not needed. The dead body of a Maori was afterwards found; there were no British casualties.

On the north bank of the Lower Waikato, between the Tuakau Redoubt and the Heads, an army depot had been established as a half-way station for stores shipped up the river to the British field headquarters. This station, named Camerontown, after the General, was in charge of two Europeans, and was

THE FIRST ENGAGEMENTS.

guarded also by friendly natives, chiefly Ngati-Whauroa, who had a small *pa* on a hill, weakly stockaded. Mr. James Armitage, the Resident Magistrate on the Lower Waikato, was engaged in superintending the work of taking the stores up the river; this was done by Maoris, under Wiremu te Wheoro, of Kohekohe, and Waata Kukutai, of Kohanga. The tribes engaged in this canoe transport were chiefly Ngati-Naho and Ngati-Tipa. The barque " City of Melbourne," laden with stores, was lying at anchor inside the Waikato Heads early in September, and Mr. Armitage was busily loading his flotilla of large canoes and despatching them up to the Manga-tawhiri. On the 7th September he had returned to the depot from the Bluff stockade at Te Ia-roa, when he was shot down in his canoe by a party of Maoris and killed, together with the two men of the Camerontown station (William Strand, a carpenter, and Heughan, a blacksmith), a half-caste named Wade, and a friendly Maori, one of the canoe-crew. Ngati-Whauroa did not attempt to defend the Europeans from their assailants, mostly Ngati-Maniapoto; but Te Wheoro and his tribe, who arrived from Te Ia-roa in several canoes shortly after the ambuscades, engaged the enemy at Camerontown, and fought a skirmish in which a great deal of ammunition was fired away for little result. The hostile force was estimated at about a hundred. The Kingites sacked the stockade of the friendly Maoris above the depot, and destroyed a large quantity of commissariat stores. The Kingites' antipathy to Mr. Armitage (" Te Amatiti " of the Maoris) arose not so much from the fact that he was a Magistrate—in that capacity he had been greatly esteemed along the Lower Waikato—as from his participation in the work of military transport. His companion, Mr. Strand, formerly of Kohanga, had assisted in the piloting of the war-steamer " Avon " up the river.

The heavy firing in the skirmish between the friendly natives and the Kingites at Camerontown was heard at the Alexandra Redoubt, Tuakau, and a party of Maoris came paddling up in great haste to report the death of Mr. Armitage and the burning of the stores. Captain Swift, of the 65th, who was in charge of the detachment at the redoubt, marched at once for Camerontown, with Lieutenant Butler and fifty men, in an attempt to intercept the attacking-party. The senior non-commissioned officer of the detachment was Colour-Sergeant E. McKenna. An engagement which took place that afternoon in the bush near Camerontown resulted in the death of Captain Swift and three men, and the disabling of Lieutenant Butler. Swift, as he lay dying, ordered McKenna to lead on the men, and the non-commissioned officer conducted the bush skirmishing with great skill and judgment. His little party sustained a heavy fire from the natives, and had to spend the night in the forest, struggling out to Tuakau in the morning. The colour-sergeant estimated the Maori loss at between twenty and thirty killed and wounded. He saw seven shot dead; their bodies were dragged into the bush by their comrades. Lieutenant Butler recovered from his severe wound. McKenna was awarded the Victoria Cross for his valour, and was also given a commission as ensign in his regiment. He settled in New Zealand, and was for many years a stationmaster in the Government railway service. Lance-Corporal Ryan was also awarded the V.C., but before he received it he was drowned in the Waikato in an attempt to save a comrade. Four of the privates engaged—Bulford, Talbot, Cole, and Thomas—were each decorated with the medal for distinguished conduct in the field.

After the tragedy at Camerontown the Ngati-Whauroa, with their chief Hona, who up to this time had nominally been friendly to the Government, turned to the Kingite side and joined their kinsmen in the war.

From a sketch (1863) in the "Illustrated London News."]

THE ALEXANDRA REDOUBT, TUAKAU.

This large redoubt, on the right bank of the Lower Waikato, was built in July, 1863, by a detachment of the 65th Regiment. The position, on a bold bluff about 300 feet above the river, was commanding and of great strategic importance. The redoubt is the best preserved of all the military posts built in 1863-64. The present entrance is from the roadway in the rear into the north-west flanking angle, where a monument erected by the Government bears the names of British soldiers who fell in the district. The redoubt covers an area of about three-quarters of an acre, and is a parallelogram, with the usual two flanking angles at diagonally opposite corners of the work. The surrounding trench is still in most places 4 feet or 5 feet in depth, and from the bottom of the ditch to the top of the fern-grown parapets the height varies from 10 feet to nearly 20 feet.

CHAPTER XXIX.

THE FOREST RANGERS.

*The cautious camp, the smother'd light,
The silent sentinel at night.*

—JOAQUIN MILLER (" The Ship in the Desert ").

The crossing of the Manga-tawhiri River by Cameron's troops was immediately followed by Maori attacks upon some of the venturesome settlers who remained upon their farms on the frontier, and even after the army had advanced up the Waikato its rear was threatened by roving bands of Kingites. The broken forest country of the Hunua and Wairoa Ranges, bordering the left flank of the British advance, was the camping-place and war-ground of these natives, who from the cover of the bush could raid farmhouses and ambush military convoys with little loss to themselves. Neither the Regular soldiers nor the newly enrolled city Militia were competent at the time to pursue the Maoris in their forests, and it soon became clear to the military heads that a special force was necessary to meet the natives on their own ground and levy guerilla war with the object of clearing the bush on the flanks and safeguarding the army's communications and the out-settlements. Taranaki had set an example in the formation of a corps of Bush Rangers, composed largely of country settlers and their sons. There was equally good material in the Auckland settlements, and there was also at hand a body of gold-diggers at Coromandel ready to turn to new adventures now that the excitement and the profits in the primitive mining of that period were dwindling. The Government, urged by the Press and the public, resolved to form a small corps of picked men, used to the bush and to rough travelling and camp life, to scout the forests and hunt out the parties of marauders.

In the first week of August, 1863, the following attractive invitation to arms appeared for several days in the *Southern Cross* newspaper, Auckland :—

NOTICE.

TO MILITIAMEN AND OTHERS.

ACTIVE YOUNG MEN, having some experience of New Zealand Forests, may now confer a benefit upon the Colony, and also ensure a comparatively free and exciting life for themselves, by JOINING a CORPS of FOREST VOLUNTEERS, now being enrolled in this province to act as the Taranaki Volunteers have acted in striking terror into the marauding natives, by operations not in the power of ordinary troops.

By joining the Corps the routine of Militia life may be got rid of and a body of active and pleasant comrades ensured.

Only men of good character wanted.

For further information apply to the office of the *Daily Southern Cross*, O'Connell Street, Auckland.

31st July, 1863.

This appeal soon filled the ranks of a company of Forest Rangers, sixty strong, under the command of Lieutenant William Jackson, a young settler of the Papakura district (afterwards Major Jackson and M.H.R. for Waipa). Towards the end of the year a second company was formed under the command of Captain Von Tempsky. The pay at first was 10s. a day, but it was later reduced to 4s. 6d. a day and rations, and a double ration of rum on account of the rough character of the work.

The Rangers' arms were a breech-loading Calisher and Terry carbine, a five-shot revolver, and, in Von Tempsky's company, a bowie-knife with a blade 10 inches or 12 inches long. Von Tempsky took intense interest in teaching the men the use of the bowie-knife, gripped in the left hand (the right was for the revolver), with the blade along the arm. There was a drill for it—a perfect method of guard and attack in hand-to-hand action. As King Agis answered the Athenians who laughed at the short swords of the Spartans, " We find them long enough to reach our enemies with," so the Rangers could have said of their bush-knives that they were quite long enough for close quarters. They were more useful than bayonets or cutlasses in the tangled forest. Von Tempsky was a master of the weapon, the use of which he had learned in Spanish America in guerilla warfare. In instructing his men he challenged them to stab him, and demonstrated his perfect ability to defend himself. The knife could also be thrown with deadly effect, being so heavy. When slashing a way through the supplejacks and other undergrowth in the trackless bush it was a first-class tool. Captain Jackson affected to despise the knife as a war-weapon, but one or two of his men adopted it.

Colonel J. M. Roberts, N.Z.C., who began his military career in the Forest Rangers, and was a subaltern in No. 2 Company, 1863–64, was one of the young bushmen-soldiers who appreciated the bowie-knife. "It was rather awkward in the bush sometimes," he says, "for it was nearly as long as a bayonet, but it certainly was very handy for cutting tracks. We were taught to hold the knife with the blade pointing inward and upward, laid along the inner arm. With the arm held out, knife-defended

MAJOR WILLIAM JACKSON.

In 1863–64 Major Jackson commanded No. 1 Company of Forest Rangers. In the "seventies" he was in command of Te Awamutu troop, Waikato Cavalry Volunteers, formed for the protection of the Upper Waikato frontier.

thus, a blow could be warded off, and then out would flash the blade in a stab. When we were in camp at Paterangi in 1864 my fellow-subaltern Westrupp and I frequently went out in the *manuka* together and practised the fighting drill. At Orakau we found the knife very useful—not for fighting, but for digging in. Our position was on the east side of the *pa*, a cultivation-ground bordered with low fern—a place very much exposed to the Maoris' fire. We lay down on the edge of this cultivation and went to work as hard as we could with our long knives, each man digging a shallow shelter for himself and throwing up the earth in front; the bullets were coming over thick that day."

The men who were provided with these arms were as efficient as the weapons they carried. They were a varied set of adventurers. The bush-trained settlers of Papakura, Hunua, and the Wairoa were the dependable nucleus of the corps, and to their ranks were added sailors, gold-diggers, and others who had seen much of the rough end of life. Von Tempsky, describing (in an unpublished manuscript journal) his company of fifty men at the end of 1863, wrote: " Like Jackson, I had two black men, former men-o'-war's-men; one had also been a prize-fighter. I had men of splendid education, and men as ignorant as the soil on which they trod." All nationalities were in the ranks—English, Welsh, Scotch, Irish, Germans, and Italians. Some of Von Tempsky's best volunteers had been members of the 1st Waikato Regiment of Militia.

The Rangers' field equipment was simple. On the war-path in the Wairoa and Hunua bush their bed was a bundle of fern, and the forest was their tent. " In our campaigning in the Waikato," says a survivor of the corps, " we used blue-blanket tents. These were army blankets, with fastenings for use as bivouac shelters; there were two blankets to every four men. Two of the four would carry the blankets when on the march, and the other two would pick up and carry along sticks for tent-poles (unless, of course, they were in the bush). The two blankets joined over a ridge-pole sheltered the four men; at any rate, they kept off the dew."

An important item of Ranger equipment was the rum-bottle, cased in leather to prevent breakage. Two good tots a day was the allowance. " It was the rum that kept us alive," says one of Jackson's veterans, ex-Corporal William Johns; " we had so much wet, hard work, swimming and fording rivers and creeks, and camping out without fires. When we camped in the bush on the enemy's trail it was often unsafe to light a fire for cooking and warmth, because we never knew when we might have a volley poured into us. So we just lay down as we were, wet and cold, and we'd have been dead but for the rum."

In the early expeditions the work of the Rangers was carried out in the forest hills of Wairoa, above Papakura and Hunua, and the ranges trending to the Thames Gulf and the Manga-tawhiri headwaters. The Wairoa frequently had to be crossed, and when in flood it was a dangerous river. Most of the Rangers could swim, but there were always several men who had to be helped over by their comrades, in this fashion: Large bundles of dry fern were cut and placed under the non-swimmer's chin and breast as he took the water, and he was hauled across with hastily made flax ropes by his mates, the fern making a temporary float. Always in crossing a river in the enemy country the best swimmers went over first, holding their carbines over their heads. These men would be ready at once to act as advance guard on the farther bank and cover their comrades' crossings. The marching was very severe—far more so than that of any other corps—as the men were at work continuously covering large areas of rugged country, and it was necessary to take special care of the feet. Many a man knocked up, and comparatively few went through the campaign from beginning to end in the Rangers.

MAJOR VON TEMPSKY.

In 1863-64 Von Tempsky was Captain of No. 2 Company of Forest Rangers. He afterwards served in the West Coast campaigns, and was killed at Te Ngutu-o-te-manu in 1868.

Of the Rangers' two commanders, Gustavus Von Tempsky, Captain of No. 2 Company, was by far the more experienced bush fighter. Of aristocratic Polish blood, he began his military life in the Prussian Army in the early "forties," but quickly sought a career more to his taste. In Central America he commanded at one time an irregular force of Mosquito Coast Indians against the Spanish, and he guided British naval parties against

Spanish stockades in one of the little wars in those parts. Later, we find him trying his fortune in California in " the days of Foity-nine," and travelling adventurously through Mexico. The news of the gold find at Coromandel brought him to New Zealand from Australia, and when the Waikato War began he was working No. 8 claim on the diggings. The first shots of the Waikato War excited the old war-fever, and after trying unsuccessfully to form a diggers' corps at Coromandel captained by himself—there was some prejudice against him on the score of his nationality—he joined the *Southern Cross* newspaper in Auckland as a temporary war correspondent, hoping presently to have an opportunity of getting into action. Lieutenant Jackson he frequently met at the first Forest Rangers' headquarters, the " Travellers' Rest " inn, on the Papakura–Wairoa Road. He accompanied Jackson as correspondent on one of the early expeditions into the Wairoa Ranges ; and it was on this excursion, lasting three days, that the young Rangers' officer discovered that the lean, swarthy ex-digger with the very pronounced foreign accent was far better fitted than himself to command a fighting corps. So Von Tempsky soon found himself invited to join the Rangers as subaltern and military adviser, and the Government gave him a commission as ensign. The early prejudice against the roving soldier soon disappeared when his comrades realized his soldierly talent, and when he was commissioned to enlist a company of his own he was able to pick a little body of first-class men from the many recruits offering. The first body of Rangers was disbanded after three months' service, and toward the end of the year 1863 two companies were formed, each of fifty men.

Paparata and a Scouting Adventure.

From the hills near the Queen's Redoubt the fortified position of Paparata, on the open country to the east, was plainly visible, a long line of freshly turned yellow clay showing against a prominent fern ridge. This was a Kingite half-way post between the Waikato River and the shores of the Hauraki ; from its shelter war-parties could raid in either direction, or could enter the Wairoa Ranges at will. Below was a valley covered with fields of wheat, potatoes, and maize, and with many groves of peach-trees ; the Manga-tawhiri, here a clear gravelly stream, flowed through the cultivations. Here and there along the rim of the valley were patches of native forest. The distance from the Queen's Redoubt was about ten miles, but the most convenient approach was from the Koheroa ridge, on the south of the Manga-tawhiri.

General Cameron was anxious, after a futile reconnaissance towards Paparata, 1st–2nd August, to obtain accurate information regarding the route and the character of the fortifications, and Von Tempsky and Thomas McDonnell volunteered to scout the position. McDonnell (afterwards colonel in command of the Armed Constabulary Field Force) was, like Von Tempsky, well qualified for the enterprise. He was a young officer in Nixon's Colonial Defence Force Cavalry, was eager for any dashing and perilous mission, and had a perfect knowledge of the Maori tongue. The two scouts set out from the Whanga-marino Redoubt at night, after reconnoitring their route with field-glasses from the Koheroa hills. The track lay in a general north-east direction from the ridge, along an open belt of fern land with swamps on each side. Each scout was armed with two revolvers, and McDonnell carried a tomahawk and Von Tempsky his bowie-knife.

The two scouts crossed the open ground in the darkness, and just before daylight found themselves almost within the first line of the Maori entrenchments. They had intended to take cover in a neighbouring belt of bush, but it was fortunate for them that they were unable to do so, for soon after daylight the bush was swarming with Maoris pigeon-shooting. Hidden in high flax-bushes on the edge of the swamp and alongside the track from Paparata to Meremere, they watched their enemies all day through the loopholes of leaves. Once they were all but discovered by a pig-hunting dog. When it began to rain in the afternoon and the Maoris retired to their *whares* the scouts felt themselves secure; they knew also that the rain would obliterate their footmarks near the hiding-place. It was dark before they ventured to leave their flax-clump, after light-heartedly laying a train of broken biscuits from their nest in the flax to the track, by way of puzzling the Maoris next morning. They returned safely from their perilous mission, and for the information they were able to give the General they were highly complimented. Both soon afterwards received commissions as captain. Von Tempsky fell at Te Ngutu-o-te-manu in 1868. McDonnell lived to receive the decoration of the New Zealand Cross for his scouting-work at Paparata.

The remains of biscuit and some empty meat-tins which the officers left at their hiding-place had a curiously important effect upon the Maoris and the campaign. It came to be known some time afterwards that the natives were so disturbed by this evidence of *pakeha* scouts in their midst that they concluded their stronghold would soon be untenable, and it was not long before they evacuated it. In December, after the troops under Lieut.-Colonel Carey had built a chain of redoubts across the ridges from the Miranda, Von Tempsky, with his subaltern, Mr. Roberts, and a dozen men, made a reconnaissance of the scene of his scouting exploit. The Surrey Redoubt had been built on the south-eastern rim of the Paparata Valley, and the Ranger officers, accompanied from the redoubt by McDonnell, explored the works before which they had crouched in the flax-clump. "From what we saw," wrote Von Tempsky in his journal, "it appears that we had been encircled within two hundred yards of a zigzagging line of rifle-pits traversing nearly the whole valley. A sharp elbow of the river (the Manga-tawhiri), with its convex angle towards Koheroa, had been taken advantage of in the following way: The inner side of the bank had been dug out in proper traversed shape in their usual fashion of rifle-pits, but the earth had been thrown into the river, so that an enemy could never have expected the existence of these rifle-pits till within a dangerous distance of a volley from pieces resting on the very ground on which you trod. Moreover, a few withered bushes had been allowed to remain immediately in front to mask still more the formidable line. *Whares* with bullet-proof flax mats for roofs were built all along inside the rifle-pits." On the ridge above was the stockaded and rifle-pitted *pa*. The *whares* in the various entrenchments were capable of accommodating nearly a thousand men.

CHAPTER XXX.

THE DEFENCE OF PUKEKOHE EAST CHURCH STOCKADE.

Looking due east from the higher part of Pukekohe Town one will see on the skyline, a mile and a half air-line distant, an isolated dot of white. In the late afternoon the speck of a building becomes a heliograph when the westering sun strikes flashes from its windows across the valley. This is the little Presbyterian church of Pukekohe East, a monument to-day to the pluckiest defence in the South Auckland War of 1863. Stockaded and occupied as a garrison-house by the settlers of the place, it was the scene of an attack by a strong war-party of Kingite Maoris, against whom it was held successfully by only seventeen men until reinforcements arrived.

The Pukekohe East church, two miles from Pukekohe Railway-station by the road, stands in a commanding position on the eastern and highest rim of a saucer-shaped valley, the crater basin of an ancient volcano, about half a mile across at its greatest axis, east and west. The lower lip, facing Pukekohe Town, has been eroded through to the level of the old crater-floor, and a small stream, rising in the bushy slopes below the church and flowing through a swampy valley, issues from this break. The trench, 6 feet wide and 3 or 4 feet deep, which surrounded the church is still plainly to be traced; a regular grassy depression about 1 foot deep remains, and the small flanking bastions are well marked. Splintered bullet-holes can be seen in the building and in a gravestone on the edge of the hill. The church is a plain little building with tiny porch and belfry; it was built in 1862 of *totara* and *rimu*. In dimensions it is only 30 feet by 15 feet. Unlike the Mauku Church of St. Bride's, the building itself was not loopholed, but was defended by a surrounding stockade in which openings were cut for rifle-fire.

Pukekohe East was first settled in 1859 by people from Scotland and Cornwall—the families of McDonald, Comrie, Scott,

Roose, Robinson, Hawke, Easton, and others. The Comries came from Perthshire. The Roose family, from Cornwall, arrived at Auckland by the ship "Excelsior" in 1859. Adjoining their holding and between the church and the site of the present Town of Pukekohe was the section of the Scotts. When the war began the able-bodied men—in fact, every man and youth who could handle a rifle—were formed into a company of the Forest Rifle Volunteers to defend their district, and their families were sent to Drury or Auckland. Sergeant Perry, the only drilled man in the district, was placed in charge of the stockade now commenced. Lieutenant D. H. Lusk, in command of the defences from Waiuku to

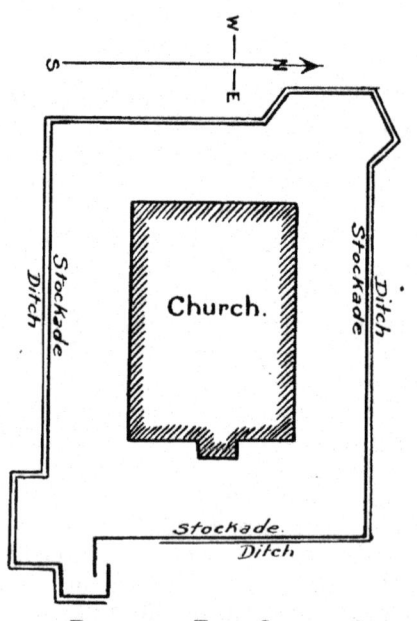

GROUND-PLAN OF PUKEKOHE EAST CHURCH STOCKADE, 1863.

The south-east angle (front), facing the road and covering the right flank and the entrance, was defended by Joseph Scott and James Easton.

Pukekohe East, hurried the settlers in their entrenchment-work, but in spite of his warnings they had not completed it in time.

The stockade was built at a distance of 10 feet from the church all round; outside it was the trench, the earth from which was thrown up against the timbers. The stockade consisted of tree-trunks, small logs from the bush, averaging about 6 inches in diameter, and not set upright, as was the usual way, but laid horizontally on one another and spiked to posts. This wall was to have been 7 feet high all round, but it had not been completed when the place was attacked, and was not more than 5 feet high in most places, and gave poor head-cover. The stockade was to have been reinforced with a front of thick slabs set upright outside and spiked to the logs, but this work had only partly been carried out when the Maoris delivered their assault. The timbers for the walls were hauled from the bush across the road in front of the church on the east and south sides, and some of the material (slabs) was brought from Mr. Comrie's homestead, where it had been cut for a new house. Rifle loopholes were cut in the upper and lower logs, about 10 inches in length, vertical, by 3 or 4 inches in width. In places the logs did not fit very closely, and Maori bullets came through the interstices. The taller men had to stoop to avoid the enemy's fire; the top logs of the stockade had not been spiked on when the attack came. The defence work, as measured by the trench depression in the ground to-day, was 21 paces long by 13 paces wide at the flanking bastions.

On the 31st August Lieutenant Lusk found the stockade in an incomplete state, and made the Volunteers strengthen the foot of the log wall by piling up the earth from the trench. The garrison neglected, however, to clear the bush to a safe distance from the stockade.

Four young men, members of the stockade garrison, Privates Joseph Scott (afterwards Captain Scott, of Epsom, Auckland), Elijah Roose, and Hodge, and a special constable sent up from Drury, had a perilous adventure the day before the attack. A fortnight previously Mr. Scott, sen., had been mortally wounded on his farm by a party of Maoris; and the four Volunteers, too, fell in with a war-band when they visited the farm to see to the stock. Taking cover behind some *rimu* logs, they opened fire on the raiders, but found that another small party of natives was in their rear. The four men separated, Scott and Roose keeping together as they ran for the shelter of the bush, and the other two making for the stockade. Hodge and his companion were not pursued far, and they safely reached the post. Scott and Roose raced for the bush in the valley on the west; the Maoris were between them and the stockade. As they were crossing a fence they received a volley at less than 40 yards. Scott happened to turn his head to look behind him, and a bullet grazed his right eyebrow. The Maoris usually fired too high at close range; seven bullet-holes were afterwards found in a tree at that spot, at about 12 feet above the ground. The fugitives ran through one small patch of bush and then took shelter in the main tract of forest, about 60 acres in extent, in the bottom of the valley. The Maoris surrounded this bush and parties of them searched it for the settlers, who kept moving about as they heard the voices of the enemy, creeping up after them so that they could keep within hearing and retreating when they heard their pursuers returning.

As night came on the Maoris lit large fires in the fern around the bush, illuminating the whole place and making it impossible for the two men in hiding to emerge without being seen. At last, however, a storm of wind and rain extinguished the fires, and after midnight the two fugitives scouted cautiously out of their refuge, and reached the stockade in the early morning in time to take part in the defence.

Between 9 and 10 o'clock on Monday morning, the 14th September, while some of the men were cleaning their rifles and others engaged in the cooking-shed a few yards in front of the stockade gateway, a single shot was fired from the bush on the right front. The *puriri* forest almost surrounded the stockade; on

THE PUKEKOHE EAST PRESBYTERIAN CHURCH.

This historic little church still bears marks of the Maori attack in 1863. There are two bullet-holes in the front of the porch (one of these, however, appears too small and clean cut for the large-calibre bullets of the "sixties"), and there is one inside in the rear wall, above the pulpit, besides several splintered bullet-holes in the ceiling. The shingled roof has been replaced by iron, but the original ceiling lining remains. Outside in the rear wall, high up, there is another bullet-hole. This was drilled by a shot fired from a *rimu* tree which stood on the steep side of the gully below the church. A Maori was shot down from the upper branches of this tree during the fight. In the burying-ground the oldest memorial is one which made a target for a bullet fired from the *rimu* tree. This gravestone bears an inscription to the memory of "Betsy, the beloved wife of William Hodge, who died July 3rd, 1862, aged 24 years." In the back of the tombstone there is a large splintered bullet-hole. The stone is just outside the south-west corner of the stockade line.

the side first attacked it was within 40 or 50 yards of the defences; some isolated trees were nearer, and at most parts the bush was not 100 yards away, and logs and stumps gave cover for attackers. The first shot was followed by a charge. In an instant scores of figures leapt out from the trees, fired heavily on the stockade and on the riflemen running for shelter, and rushed down on the log fence, darting from stump to stump, some firing the remaining barrel and reloading, others reserving their fire for close quarters. With the warriors was a woman, armed with a single-barrel gun, a cartridge-belt buckled about her waist. The little clearing, so quiet a few moments before, was filled with the bellowing of heavily loaded *tupara* and the sharp crack of rifles. High above the other sounds rose the screaming voice of the Maori amazon as she exhorted her warrior comrades, "*Riria! Riria!*" ("Fight away! Fight away!")

The defenders of the stockade numbered seventeen. They were Sergeant Perry, Privates Joseph Scott, Elijah Roose, William Hodge, George Easton, James Easton, and three generations of the McDonald family (Alexander McDonald, his son James McDonald, and grandson James), besides nine volunteers enrolled as special constables. The young boy, James McDonald, pluckily helped by carrying out ammunition from the church to the riflemen. There were three other members of the garrison, J. Comrie, J. B. Roose, and T. Hawke, but they were absent when the attack was made. Comrie and Roose, who had been on leave to see their families, were returning on horseback from Drury when they saw the church was attacked, and they galloped back to Drury for reinforcements.

Sergeant Perry's first order to his little force was "Fix bayonets!" He ordered them on no account to fire a volley. The reason was that while the defenders were reloading their muzzle-loading Enfields the Maoris might charge in. Each man ran to a loophole, and in a moment the outer wall was bristling with bayonets projecting through the rifle-slits. Independent firing began, and for the next six hours the settlers and their comrades the special constables fought a battle against many times their number of brown skirmishers, who kept up an extraordinarily heavy fire from behind trees, logs, and stumps, and from the tree-tops, and others from the shelter of a house (Easton's), about 100 yards away, above the gully on the defenders' right flank. Every tree along the ragged edge of the bush on the front and the flanks covered its musketeer. Most of the Maoris, after the first rush, took cover on the right front, where some of the ancient *puriri* survive to-day.

The war-party was estimated by some of the garrison at three to four hundred men, but according to a Maori survivor, the old warrior Te Huia Raureti, of Ngati-Maniapoto, it did not exceed

270   NEW ZEALAND WARS.

THE ATTACK ON THE PUKEKOHE EAST CHURCH STOCKADE. (14th September, 1863.)
From a drawing by A. H. Messenger.

two hundred men. Te Huia (at Te Rewatu, on the Puniu River, 14th November, 1920) said:—

"Our *ope* which attacked the Europeans at Pukekohe East barracks [*i.e.*, the stockade] consisted of a part of my tribe, Ngati-Maniapoto, some other Upper Waikato people, and the Ngati-Pou, of Lower Waikato. In all we numbered between a hundred and seventy and two hundred. With us was a fighting-woman named Rangi-rumaki; she was an elderly woman, of determined countenance, and perfectly fearless. We came down the Waikato River from Meremere in three war-canoes, and were joined by Ngati-Pou. We landed near Tuakau, and were guided through the bush to Pukekohe by Ngati-Pou, whose land it had been. At Tuakau we had a preliminary skirmish; we gathered in the bush on the ridge near the British *pa* [the Alexandra Redoubt] and fired heavily on the British soldiers, who replied as heavily. We had plenty of ammunition, and we fired much of it away there. Then we marched inland and north, keeping to the level forest land on the west of the Pokeno and Pukewhau Ranges. We slept one night in the bush on the way; it was a Sunday. At our bivouac that night the chiefs Raureti Paiaka (my father) and Hopa te Rangianini spoke in council, saying, 'In the battle to come let us confine ourselves strictly to fighting; let no one touch anything in the settlers' houses, or their stock, or otherwise interfere with their property.' To this all the warriors agreed. At daylight in the morning the march was resumed. Wahanui Huatare with a number of his Ngati-Maniapoto men went on ahead, keeping under the shelter of the bush. We saw them enter a settler's house and loot it, removing the goods it contained. This breach of our agreement made us angry; it was a bad omen for us in the fight that presently began. It was not right that Wahanui and his comrades should thus trample on our accepted rules of fighting. Then the leading sections made a dash for the stockade, which stood in a small clearing. The rest of us, under Raureti and Hopa, also charged along the level ground. Raureti and Maaka, with whom was the woman Rangi-rumaki, saw a sentry on a stump outside the defences and fired at him; he ran inside the stockade, which enclosed a building [the church]. Rangi-rumaki was exceedingly active and courageous. She charged daringly close up to the stockade, armed with a single-barrel gun; round her waist was buckled a cartridge-belt. An old Waikato fighting-man, Rapurahi, was the leader of the charge, and the woman was close up to the front; Renata and Ara_ma followed. When we reached the front of the stockade we saw the muzzles of the guns with fixed bayonets pointing at us, and we seized some of the guns by the end of the barrel and tried to pull them out through the loopholes, but the rifle-slits were not large enough to let the stocks come through."

Soon after the first dash of the Maoris had been stayed, the attackers, as they fell back to take cover, seized the defenders' dinner of meat and potatoes, which was cooking in iron pots in the shed in front of the stockade. It was a perilous enterprise, within a few yards of the log wall, and several warriors fell dead or wounded, but the natives succeeded in carrying off the pots, and feasted on their contents in the gully below the right front of the church.

Hour after hour the firing continued in the smoke-filled clearing. The powder-grimed garrison, with smarting eyes and parched throats, stuck manfully to their posts, firing with care, for their

CAPTAIN JOSEPH S. SCOTT.

Captain Scott (No. 3 Company, Pukekohe Rifles, 1872), of Epsom, Auckland, is one of the three survivors of the Pukekohe East Church Stockade defence. At the time of the attack he was a private in the newly formed Forest Rifle Volunteers, Pukekohe Company, numbering twenty-three all told.

ammunition was running short. It was only the sight of the bayonets projecting from the loopholes that prevented the Maoris from charging over the unfinished stockade. The angle holding the narrow gateway on the right front of the stockade was defended by two men, Joseph Scott and James Easton. They had the hottest work of all, for most of the attackers were concentrated on that section of the front. Both were good shots and did not waste cartridges.

Many Maoris fell; the dead and wounded were swiftly removed by means of supplejacks fastened round the ankles by men who crawled up on their hands and knees; the fallen ones would be seen disappearing over the face of the hill into the valley, or hauled by unseen hands into the cover of the bush.

On the south-east face, just on the road-boundary of the church-grounds, not more than 20 yards from the stockade, stood a large *puriri* tree. Some of the Maoris climbed the tree, and from the cover of the thick flax-like growth of *wharawhara*, or astelia, in the forks of the main branches, fired over the log wall. One at least of these snipers was shot. Another of the attackers, firing at the garrison from the roof of Easton's house under cover of the wide slab chimney, received a bullet as he incautiously exposed his head and shoulders for a moment, and came tumbling to the ground.

Some of the Maoris came up so close that they threw sticks over the wall and challenged the defenders to come out in the open. One warrior took cover behind a *puriri* stump just outside the stockade, so close up that he was unable to move to load his gun and had to crouch down low under the loopholes. The woman Rangi-rumaki gave inspiration to the attack with her loud cries of encouragement—" *Riria, riria, riria!* "—but even her exmple and her war-shouts could not prevail upon her men to hurl themselves upon the sharp steel that glinted in the rifle-flash from each fire-aperture.

The first reinforcements were joyfully greeted by the out-numbered little garrison about 1 o'clock in the afternoon, when Lieutenant Grierson and thirty-two men of the 70th Regiment arrived from the Ramarama post. Grierson had heard the firing at 10.30 a.m. Skirmishing with the besiegers at the edge of the bush, they advanced at the double across the clearing and joined the defenders in the stockade. It was the salvation of the garrison, whose ammunition-supply was very low; some men had only a round apiece remaining. The strengthened force now was able to keep the Maoris close to their cover.

A detachment of the 1st Waikato Militia, under Captain Moir, with three carts containing ammunition, reached the stockade from Drury in the afternoon, and there was a sharp encounter with the Maoris in the clearing. One of the Militia was shot in the knee and wounded by a tomahawk-cut in the head. About 4 o'clock in the afternoon the sound of British bugles was heard in the bush, and 150 soldiers of the 18th Royal Irish and the 65th charged across the clearing and engaged the Maoris, who were then within 40 yards of the stockade. The troops were led by Captain Inman and Captain Saltmarshe; the latter received a severe wound in the mouth. The fighting that followed, lasting for about an hour, was chiefly on the right front and flank of the church. Many of the Maoris held the cover in the hollow immediately below the church-ground on the south side, and stood their ground there until several had been killed. Five natives were buried here, on Easton's land; the spot is in a field sloping steeply to the gully, just outside the churchyard fence on the south, a few yards from the road. The British loss was three killed or mortally wounded, and eight wounded. Not a man of the stockade-defenders was struck by a bullet; the one casualty was a slight wound inflicted by a flying splinter of wood. The garrison's only loss was a good dinner, which had gone into the Kingites' stomachs. The little church showed many a scar and splinter of battle: the upper parts were well riddled with bullets, and many of the window-panes were either perforated or broken.

A curious incident of this combat was narrated by some of the defenders. A native pigeon, dazed by the firing and the smoke of battle, and frightened out of the bush by the yells and shooting of the Maoris, flew on to the high-pitched roof of the church and remained there for some time, unhurt by the bullets that whistled about it. The beautiful *kereru* perched in such a precarious sanctuary seemed a harbinger of hope and an omen of success to the hard-pressed settlers. The story is one of those legends of the past of which it is difficult now to obtain confirmation. Captain Joseph Scott says that he did not himself see the pigeon; it would be difficult for most of the defenders to see anything on the ridging from within the stockade, owing to the narrow space between the log wall and the church. However, he considers the incident is probably authentic. The Hon. Major B. Harris, M.L.C., who was on active service in the district at the time, though not a member of the Pukekohe church garrison, says, "I believe it is true that a bush-pigeon settled on the roof of the church during the firing, and was regarded by the defenders as a mascot, or a bird of good omen."

"In this encounter," says Te Huia Raureti, "we lost, I think, more than forty men killed. Ngati-Pou suffered most; they had about thirty men killed. Most of the dead were carried off the field, but we had to leave them on the way, and some of the bodies were concealed in the hollows and the branch forks of large trees, among the *wharawhara* leaves, so that our enemies should not find them. We had no time to bury them. Of our party from up the river the killed included Te Warena, Wetere Whatahi, Moibi Whiowhio (of the Ngati-Matakore Tribe), and Matiu Tohitaka (Ngati-Rereahu). Te Raore Wai-haere, brother of Rewi Maniapoto, was wounded. My father, Raureti Paiaka, was wounded in the right arm."

On the day following the engagement a detachment of Militia, from Drury, arrived to garrison the church and relieve the volunteers and special constables. Sergeant Perry, in recognition of his capable leadership in the defence, was given a commission as ensign in the 2nd Regiment, Waikato Militia.

THE ATTACK ON BURTT'S FARM, PAERATA.

On a partly wooded upswell of land at Paerata, midway between Pukekohe and Drury by a branch road, stands an old farmhouse of the substantial kind built by the frontier pioneers. "Glenconnel" is painted on the road-gate, but its name in 1863 was Burtt's Farm, a name associated with one of the incidents which proved the spirit of the settlers who remained on their farms after the outbreak of war. The homestead was attacked by a party of Maoris on the 14th September, 1863, the same day as the Battle of Pukekohe East Church Stockade, a few miles

PAERATA BLUFF AND BURTT'S FARM.

A fortified *pa* of the Ngati-Tamaoho Tribe, named Te Maunu-a-Tu ("The War-god's Lure"), stood on the western end of the Paerata ridge in ancient days.

away. Burtt's Farm is three miles from Pukekohe by the road which diverges to the eastward of the railway-line at Paerata, then crosses a stream flowing from the Tuhimata hills, and winds up a steep hill, terminating on the westward in a bold bluff like a battleship's ram bow. The southern and southwestern sides of the hill are wooded, and many great oak-like *puriri* shade the approach to the homestead. Sweet-peas and roses climb the front of the dwelling, a comfortable old place, with the high-pitched roof and wide veranda that distinguished the homes of the early days. James Burtt, an Auckland merchant, built this place about 1859, when heart of *kauri* and *totara* and the best *rimu* were used. There are two bullet-holes, made by large-calibre balls, in the front weatherboards near a window on the veranda, and another hole drilled in 1863 is to be seen in the front of a square, strongly built workshop of pit-sawn timber in rear of the farmhouse; the building is almost hidden in ivy.

On the morning of the 14th September a war-party of about twenty Maoris from the Lower Waikato, chiefly Ngati-Pou, came up through the *puriri* and *rata* forest on the south side of the Paerata ridge and surrounded the homestead. The occupants of the place were Mr. Watson, manager for Mr. Burtt, and his family, three sons and two daughters, and two farm workers named Knight and Hugh McLean. The men had rifles, and they

Photo, J. C., 1920.]

BURTT'S FARMHOUSE, PAERATA HILL.

were accustomed to take their arms with them when they went to their work about the farm. That morning Watson and one of his sons (Robert) were engaged in putting up a fence some distance from the house, and McLean and the eldest son, John Watson, were ploughing near the bluff on the west, a third of a mile from the house. Mrs. Watson was lying ill in bed in the house. The attack began about 10 o'clock, when shots were fired at Watson and his son, and the boy Robert, a lad of fourteen, was mortally wounded. Watson and Knight took cover, and replied to the Maori fire with their rifles until they had exhausted

THE ATTACK ON BURTT'S FARM, PAERATA.

their ammunition. They were cut off from the house by the Maoris, about a dozen of whom had commenced firing into it. In the other direction the ploughman McLean and young John Watson, a lad of eighteen, were at work when they heard shots, and running towards the house they found it surrounded by natives. Ten Maoris engaged McLean, who used his rifle bravely against them, while Watson got the ammunition ready. The cartridges were soon expended, and McLean ran down the hill eastward, chased by several Maoris. John Watson, taking off his boots, ran for his life to summon help. He caught up with

From a water-colour drawing by Major Von Tempsky, 1863.]

THE MAORI ATTACK ON BURTT'S FARMHOUSE.

The three figures on the right in the picture are Mr. Hamilton, Miss Watson, and Alex. Goulan.

one of his brothers, William, who had been sent off by his father for assistance. They gave the alarm at Drury, and an armed force was soon on the way to raise the siege.

In the meantime ten or a dozen Maoris were firing into the doors and windows of the house. Mrs. Watson, in her terror, got under the bed for safety, while one of the daughters ran through the thickly planted garden at the side unobserved by the Maoris, and under cover of the bush raced down across the slopes and up the opposite hill to the home of the nearest neighbour, Mr. James Hamilton, half a mile away to the east, near Tuhimata. Mr. Hamilton and his employee, Alexander Goulan, had already heard the firing, and had armed themselves with Enfield rifles and bayonets (they were Militiamen), and were coming to the rescue. Taking advantage of the bush cover, they opened fire on the Maoris, who were peppering the house briskly with their guns. Keeping well concealed and firing rapidly, they drove the Kingites off from the house into the *puriri* bush. Imagining that they were attacked by a considerable number of *pakehas*, the Maoris retreated, and the relieving-party met Mr. Watson and his man, who had been cut off from the home, and entered the house to find the invalid woman very frightened but unhurt.

A party of troopers (Mounted Artillery), under Lieutenant Rait, presently galloped up from Drury, followed by forty infantrymen; but the Maoris by this time had retreated into the forest. The courage and prompt action of Hamilton and Goulan deserved all the praise bestowed by the military, for they had not hesitated a moment to come to the rescue, against great odds, and by their skill in using the cover around the house they succeeded in concealing the weakness of their party.

Burtt's Farm people were escorted into Drury, Mr. Watson carrying his mortally wounded son. The boy died in the military hospital. After their departure the Maoris returned and sacked the house. A few days later the body of Hugh McLean was found in the swamp, shot through the heart; his rifle had been carried off.

Burtt's Farm now was made the headquarters for a time of a Flying Column (or Movable Column) formed, under the command of Colonel Nixon, for the purpose of scouring the tracks in the bush between the Great South Road and the Waikato River. It was also used by Jackson's Forest Rangers as a convenient field base in scouting-work around the district.

NOTE.

John Watson's Narrative.

The following account of the attack on Burtt's Farm is contained in a letter (7th May, 1922) from Mr. John Watson, of Riversdale Road, Avondale, Auckland; he was one of the two boys who escaped from the Maoris and ran for help to Drury. Mr Watson is the last survivor of the family. After confirming the narrative given in this chapter, he wrote:—

" The Paerata farm, belonging to Mr. James Burtt, consisted of 900 acres. The road going over the Paerata Hill cut the farm in two sections, the homestead on one side and the bluff on the other. There was a very high *rata* tree growing on the bluff side of the road, towering above the rest of the trees in the clump of bush there; it could be seen for miles around. My father was on Paerata farm in 1859; the rest of us went out in 1861. At that time there was no one living within three miles except Mr. Hamilton and Mr. Samuel Luke. The latter lived down in the valley behind the Paerata farm; he was very fortunate, for he and his wife left for Drury two or three days before the raid in September, 1863. The Maoris camped in his house the night before they attacked us, or the night after.

"As you correctly state, Hugh McLean and I were ploughing on the bluff when the attack was made. The morning was beautifully fine and calm. About 10 o'clock we heard firing in the direction of Pukekohe East Church Stockade. It was not five minutes later when firing commenced at our house. We at once unharnessed our horses and turned them adrift. Then we made for the house as fast as we could run. Instead of keeping the direct road which led through thick scrub and tea-tree we made a half-circle round the bush and came out in the open in front of the house. It was well we did so, for otherwise we would have been tomahawked, as four or five of the Maoris came from the road we always used except this time. When we were about 400 yards from the house we saw five or six natives come up the rise from where we afterwards were told they attacked my father and brother and the man Knight. McLean opened fire on them. He had a rifle. I had nothing unfortunately; I left mine at home that morning. The firing brought out of the scrub the Maoris who were lying in wait for McLean and me, and we had five more on the other side closing in on us like the letter V. Their fire became too hot for us, and we had to retreat. There was no cover for us to take shelter in. I took the road to Drury, and McLean turned to the right, in an easterly direction. There was a redoubt with troops about two miles from Drury that could be seen from our side; it would be between two and three miles across country, more than two miles nearer than Drury, but it was through fern hills and swamps. Undoubtedly it was for this redoubt McLean was making. I preferred to keep the road to Drury; I was afraid of the swamps after winter rains. As we took different directions one half the Maoris followed McLean, the others followed me and kept up a running fire. I had some narrow escapes, but I got out of their range when I was half-way to Drury. McLean, after getting about half-way to the redoubt on the south road, got stuck in a swamp, where he was evidently shot at close quarters.

"Our retreat drew at least ten of the Maoris from the attack on the house, and enabled my father and Knight to join Mr. Hamilton and Alex. Goulan, who stuck to their posts until a detachment of Mounted Artillery arrived. As soon as I arrived at the camp at Drury and reported they were in their saddles and off, but when they got to the farm the Maoris disappeared.

"When my brother—the one who was with my father and the man Knight—was shot by the Maoris he took cover in a thicket of scrub. He was able to tell us before he died that he heard the natives passing quite near him, but they did not find him. That was how he escaped being tomahawked."

Regarding his sister's share in the events of that perilous morning, Mr. Watson said:—

"There were two girls in the house, my sisters. When the firing commenced, Mary Ann—she was the one that had the most pluck to do anything—rushed out of the house to let a watch-dog off the chain, but the dog was so furious about the firing she could not undo the strap. She had to return to the house for a knife to cut the strap. While she was doing so she was fired on, but escaped. The dog then rushed into the bush. He was a savage one to strangers: it took the Maoris some time before they got him killed. In the meantime Mary Ann made off as fast as she could run for Mr. Hamilton's. When about half-way she met Hamilton and his man, who had hurried off when they heard the firing. As to Mr. Hamilton arming my sister with a rifle [as shown in Von Tempsky's sketch], I do not remember hearing about that, nor do I think it was possible for him to do so, because it is not likely he and Goulan would take more arms than they could use. If Von Tempsky sketched her carrying a rifle he could have done it when he was billeted in the house. He with Captain Jackson and Captain Heaphy—afterwards Major Heaphy, V.C.— put up in the house at night for three weeks. The Forest Rangers had no tents. Colonel Nixon and the Flying Column were camped on the road on the top of the hill. It is quite likely that Von Tempsky sketched her for amusement. Every one connected with the attack is dead but myself—my sisters and all. Before Von Tempsky came to New Zealand he was in the California gold rush, and at night I have heard him telling the other officers of the wonderful adventures he had."

CHAPTER XXXI.

OPERATIONS AT THE WAIROA.

In September of 1863 the Koheriki and other parties of Kingites who roamed the ranges of Wairoa South and the Hunua turned their attention to the scattered settlements on the lower part of

Drawn by Lieut.-Colonel A. Morrow.]

CAMP OF A MOVABLE COLUMN, NEAR PAPATOETOE (1863).

This column, consisting of detachments of the 70th Regiment, Pitt's Militia, and the Auckland Rifle Volunteers, was encamped for a time between St. John's Redoubt, Papatoetoe, and the hills on the west side of the Wairoa.

the river. They pillaged the houses of outlying farmers who had gone into the stockade opposite the Galloway Redoubt or into Papakura, and scouted the edge of the bush awaiting an opportunity to cut off settlers returning to their sections. Major Lyon, a Crimean veteran, was in command of the Militia district, with his quarters in the Galloway Redoubt. To relieve the Militia garrison doing duty in the redoubt, detachments of the Auckland Rifle Volunteers were sent down to the Wairoa in the

Government armed steamer "Sandfly." It was on this service that the city Volunteers first engaged the Maoris; their previous duty had chiefly been in garrison in Auckland, varied by service at Otahuhu and Drury, and an expedition as part of a "Flying Column" with the 70th Regiment, encamped near St John's Redoubt, Papatoetoe.

On the 15th September some of the garrison when playing cricket, and a fatigue-party getting slabs, near the stockade, were fired on at a distance of about 150 yards, and heavy firing followed. Two days later a detachment of fifty-five men led by Major Lyon marched up the valley towards Otau in pursuit of a large raiding-party which had been plundering settlers' houses on the outskirts of

From a drawing by Lieut.-Colonel A. Morrow.]
THE GALLOWAY REDOUBT, WAIROA SOUTH (1863).

the village. In the skirmish which followed the Volunteers behaved with steadiness and judgment, and inflicted some casualties on the Kingites. Lyon extended his small force across the face of the hill surrounding the native village and kept up a heavy fire, to which the Maoris replied by independent firing as well as by volleys from numbers of men formed into large squares. Each square, having delivered a volley, fell back behind the *whares* to reload.

Before daylight on the morning following this engagement Major Lyon marched from the Galloway Redoubt with a force composed of fifty men from the Auckland Rifle Volunteers and twenty Wairoa Rifles from the stockade, under Lieutenant Steele, to deliver an attack upon the natives at Otau. The troops silently took up a position on the bank of the flooded river opposite the *whares*, and in the gray dawn opened a heavy fire on the sleeping camp. It was a complete surprise, for the Maoris had not expected a renewal of the attack so soon. There were between one hundred and fifty and two hundred natives in the settlement. The rudely aroused men, women, and children rushed out in great confusion and took shelter in the bush. A number of them replied to the Volunteers' fire, but the whole body soon retreated into the ranges.

Among the Maoris was the young half-caste woman Heni te Kiri-karamu, who had gone on the war-path to share the fortunes of her brother Neri (Hone te Waha-huka), of the Koheriki. Describing the surprise attack Heni said, " We had intended to march down and attack the *pa* of the soldiers on the Wairoa, but they forestalled our plan. We camped in some deserted *whares* near the river-bank, and did not expect an early-morning visit, so there was a panic when we were awakened at daybreak by a terrific volley fired into our huts. The troops had lined up on the opposite side of the Wairoa, and at short range volleyed at us; it was a wonder that any of us escaped. Instead of making a stand we retreated rapidly into the forest. I carried my baby on my back. Most of us were assembled in a large *whare*, and in running out of it the chief Titipa, from Tauranga, was shot dead just in front of me. Another man from Tauranga named Tipene was killed, and many were wounded. The Tamehana boys, of Ngati-Haua, were both there."

As the river was still flooded, the European force could not cross to follow up the Maoris, so Major Lyon marched his men back to the redoubt. Later on in the day twenty men of the 18th Regiment, under Lieutenant Russell, were despatched to occupy the position in front of the Maori camp which had been held in the morning, while the commanding officer, with seventy-five of all ranks, marched by a track on the other side of the river to take the settlement in the rear. The troops found, however, that the natives had evacuated the place.

In these skirmishes the Maoris lost eight men killed.

On the 13th October a party of the Koheriki retaliated with an attack on unarmed Europeans within a short distance of the Galloway Redoubt. An elderly man named Job Hamlin was killed, and his companion, a boy named Joseph Wallis, about thirteen years of age, was terribly tomahawked, but by a miracle survived his wounds. Joseph Wallis's people were shifting their property to town from their farmhouse near the Wairoa Road, for fear of the Maoris, and Job Hamlin was employed in carting the goods; which were loaded into a bullock-dray. The boy was riding on horseback, and Hamlin was driving the team. Suddenly some Maoris ran out from the bush and fired on them. The boy's horse refused to go on, and when he got off it to lead it, or to run the Maoris chased him. One of them caught him and delivered two tomahawk-cuts crosswise on the side of his head and face, inflicting an X-shaped wound. The top of his head was also smashed in with the butt of a gun. The soldiers at the redoubt ran up on hearing the firing, and found him lying there apparently dead; he was taken to the camp hospital at Papakura. Job Hamlin was found dead, tomahawked. The Maoris had left Wallis for dead. He recovered, and he is to-day farming in the Waikato, but he has suffered all his life from the gun-butt blow. He is the younger brother of Mrs. Harris, wife of the Hon. Major B. Harris, M.L.C.

On the 15th October an old soldier named Fahey and his wife, who were settled on a small bush farm near Ramarama, were out milking their cows when they were surprised by some of the Koheriki and shot and tomahawked. Mrs. Fahey was dead when found, and her husband died soon afterwards.

A party of twenty Koheriki natives on the 26th October raided Kennedy's Farm at Mangemangeroa, a few miles beyond Howick in the direction of Maraetai. Mr. Trust, who was in charge of the farm, was away in Auckland at the time, but there were three of his sons in occupation, besides two men, Courtenay and Lord. Ambrose Trust was the eldest son; the others, Richard and Nicholas Trust, were nine and twelve years of age. Lord, who was a workman on the place, was leaving the farmhouse at about 7 o'clock to go to his house when he saw a number of armed Maoris crouching in a ditch near the house. Lord and Courtenay escaped, but the latter was wounded. The Maoris fired through the front window. Ambrose Trust, taking his little brothers by the hand, ran out at the back and hurried in the direction of the nearest neighbours. The Maoris gave chase and shot down the two small boys. Ambrose, wounded in the shoulder, with difficulty escaped. The boys were tomahawked.

Major Peacocke, in command of the redoubt at Howick, started in pursuit of the Koheriki with some Militia, and a detachment of the Defence Force Cavalry and Otahuhu Volunteers, numbering fifty, took up quarters at Kennedy's Farm. Peacocke followed the track of the Maoris for some miles, but they had made off in the direction of the Hunua Ranges. H.M.S. "Miranda" steamed down the gulf in the afternoon with a force of a hundred Auckland Naval Volunteers and the same number of Rifle Volunteers, under Major de Quincey, and anchored off Mangemangeroa, but the raiders by that time had crossed the line of posts between Wairoa and Papakura, and there was therefore no chance of cutting them off.

Some weeks after these events at the Wairoa the Forest Rangers made a successful surprise attack on a camp of the Koheriki *hapu* in the heart of the ranges. By this time (14th

December) the Rangers had been reorganized, and two companies were formed, one under Jackson and the other under Von Tempsky. Jackson's No. 1 Company had the skirmish all to themselves; Von Tempsky, to his great disappointment, missed the opportunity, although he had observed the native tracks, by following a trail which led him towards Paparata. Jackson, setting out from the Papakura Camp with Lieutenant Westrupp and twenty-five men, marched to Buckland's Clearing in the Hunua Ranges, and descended into the densely wooded upper valley of the Wairoa River. Maori tracks were found leading toward the source of the Wairoa, and a lately deserted camp was passed. The trail led across the head of the Wairoa and for several miles beyond into the *terra incognita* towards the river-sources near the higher parts of the Kohukohunui Range. The

MAORI WAR FLAG CAPTURED BY THE FOREST RANGERS.

(14th December, 1863.)

trail at last was lost, but smoke was seen rising from a distant gorge in the forest, and as the Rangers scouted in that direction they heard a cow-bell ringing irregularly, as if a child were playing with it. The sound guided them toward a secluded camp by the side of a creek. Ensign Westrupp with six or eight men cautiously advanced down the rocky stream. A coloured man, George Ward, who was the first to emerge from the bush, found a Maori bathing; the astonished Maori, thinking Ward possibly a friend, beckoned to him to approach, but the Ranger shot him dead. Westrupp dashed into the camp, followed by the rest of the party. The Maoris were taken completely by surprise. It was a Sunday; they had had a religious service, and some of the party were cleaning their guns, while others were bathing.

A few of them made desperate resistance, and there were one or two hand-to-hand combats, but it was very soon over. Several fired, but had no time to reload before the Rangers' carbines and revolvers laid them low. A woman was shot accidentally while assisting a wounded warrior who was endeavouring to give the *pakehas* a final shot. A tin box containing three flags was captured by Corporal W. Johns. One of these was a red-silk flag, bearing a white cross and star and the name "Aotearoa"; it had been made by Heni te Kiri-karamu for her chief Wi Koka. It is now in the Auckland Old Colonists' Museum. Four dead Maoris were left on the ground, and three dead were seen carried off; several were wounded. The Rangers sustained no casualties.

"Shortly before this," narrated Heni te Kiri-karamu, "it had been decided that we should make for the Waikato, and we were to travel south through the bush by way of Paparata. In our party was an old *tohunga*, a man named Timoti te Amopo; he was gifted with the power of *matakite*, or second sight. As the result of some vision or foreboding—a warning from his personal god, Tu-Panapana—Timoti advised us not to follow the track which ran straight toward Paparata, but to disperse into small parties and make our way through the bush to the common meeting-place, so as to throw the troops off our trail. A number of our people, however, did not accept the seer's advice, and continued on the well-marked track, while the rest of us, with Timoti, split up into small sections and struck into the trackless parts of the forest for a rendezvous to the southward. The consequence was that we escaped, while those who disregarded the old seer's counsel fell in with the Forest Rangers and had several men killed and wounded, It was on a Saturday that we parted company; the fight took place next day. The survivors of this skirmish joined us in the forest near the headwaters of the Manga-tawhiri River."

This surprise attack in the forest took place deep in the ranges near the sources of the Wairoa and the Manga-tawhiri. It is sometimes described as having occurred at Paparata, but this is an error; the spot was nearer Ararimu, in the Upper Wairoa district.

"One of the Maoris in the camp," said Heni, "was a man named Te Pae-tui. He was terribly wounded, shot through both hips. His elder brother, Te Tapuke, seeing him fall, ran back to his assistance, and stood by him reloading his double-barrel gun, determined to defend his brother to the death. Te Tapuke a few moments later received a bullet through the forehead and fell dead by his wounded brother. After the fight the Forest Rangers attended as well as they could to Te Pae-tui's injuries, laid him on blankets found in the camp, and gave him drink and food. His wife came out from the bush, weeping over her husband, and they treated her kindly, but they could do nothing more for her husband, and they left her there. She remained tending the mortally wounded man until he died several days later. She was all alone then. She could not shift him, so she dug a grave herself and buried him there in the forest."

NOTE.

The following is the roll of Jackson's Forest Rangers engaged in the fight in the Wairoa Ranges, 14th December, 1863: William Jackson (Captain Commanding), Charles Westrupp (Lieutenant), A. J. Bertram (Sergeant-Major), Thomas Holden, William Johns, John Smith, Robert Alexander, Robert Bruce, William Bruce, Lawrence Burns, George Cole, Robert Gibb, Joseph Grigg, William Thomson, Henry Hendry, Richard Fitzgerald, Harry Jackson, Patrick Madigan, Stephen Mahoney, John Roden, Henry Rowland, Charles Temple, James Peters, Matthew Vaughan, James Watters, George Ward, and William Wells.

THE SETTLERS' STOCKADE AT WAIROA SOUTH.

This stockade (see pages 240 and 282) was held by the Wairoa Rifle Volunteers. It was the scene of an attack on the 15th September, 1863. The drawing is after a sketch by Lieut.-Colonel A. Morrow, of Auckland, who served in the operations at Wairoa South as an ensign in the Auckland Rifle Volunteers.

CHAPTER XXXII.

MAUKU AND PATUMAHOE.

The Mauku and Patumahoe districts, contiguous to Pukekohe and extending to the southern tidal waters of the Manukau Harbour, are attractive to-day with the twin charms of natural landscape beauty and the improvements made by the farmers' hands during more than sixty years of settlement. Even before the Waikato War the Mauku, first settled in 1856, was a fairly-well-peopled locality, when the site of the present Town of Pukekohe was still a forest of *puriri* and *rimu*. The branch railway-line from Pukekohe to Waiuku passes within a short distance of the pretty, antique-featured building upon which the war-history of Mauku is centred. The Church of St. Bride's is of an eye-pleasing design that belongs to many of the churches planted by the pioneers, whose first care, after establishing their homes, was to set up a place of worship in their midst. Built of *totara*, its shingled roof dark with age, its spire lifting above the tree-tops, it stands picture-like on a green knoll in the midst of its little churchyard. Walk round its walls and count the rifle loopholes in its sides—narrow slits that remind one that the place was once a fort as well as a church. There are fifty-four of those rifle-slits, now neatly plugged with timber or covered with tin and painted over. The cruciform design of the building exactly lent itself to fortification, and gave the defenders the necessary flanking bastions. When the Mauku men erected their stockade of split logs, small whole tree-trunks and heavy slabs, 10 feet high, they planted the timbers alongside one another close up against the walls of the building. The openings for rifle-fire were cut through walls and stockade; the garrison therefore could point their long Enfields through the double defence. These loopholes, at regular intervals all round the church, at about 5 feet from the floor, are 9 inches in length vertically by about 3 inches in width; the cuts in the palisade were necessarily a little wider to give the rifles play.

At the tidal river-landing, about a mile distant to the west, stood the Mauku stockade, a small iron-roofed structure defended by a wall of upright logs. This stood at the spot where cutters from Onehunga landed stores for the local forces.

The first alarm of a racial war occurred in October, 1860, when a Maori of the Ngati-Tamaoho Tribe named Eriata was found shot dead in the bush at Patumahoe. The natives imagined he had been murdered by a European, and a war-party of Waikato and Ngati-Haua came down in canoes to Te Purapura to investigate the matter. Wiremu Tamehana accompanied them to exercise a restraining influence, for the chiefs of the war-party had declared that if it were true that a *pakeha* had killed the Maori they would begin a war. Possibly war would have been precipitated but for the intervention of Bishop Selwyn and Archdeacon Maunsell, who met Tamehana and the *taua* and persuaded the force to return. Mr. Donald McLean and Mr. Rogan, of the Native Department, also went to investigate the matter and met the Patumahoe people. The conclusion arrived at was that the Maori had accidentally shot himself.

It was Mr. Daniel H. Lusk (afterwards Major Lusk), a surveyor by profession—he had helped to lay out the City of Christchurch in 1851—and owner of a bush farm in the district, who was chiefly instrumental in forming the Forest Rifle Volunteers. Mr. Lusk had been in New Zealand since 1849; he was a frontiersman of the best kind, energetic and observant, used to the bush, and endowed with a natural gift of leadership. To him more than to any other settler-soldier the credit was due of placing the district west of the Great South Road in a state of defence. He had organized local Volunteer corps during the first Taranaki War. When that campaign ended in 1861 many settlers imagined that fighting had definitely ceased in New Zealand, and most of the rifles at the Mauku were returned to store. However, Mr. Lusk was firmly of opinion that there would be war in the Auckland District, and early in 1863 he was the principal means of forming three companies of Forest Rifles—one at Mauku, one at Waiuku, and one at Pukekohe East.

The first skirmish in which the Forest Rifles were engaged was fought on the 8th September — the morning after the encounter near Camerontown in which Captain Swift, of the 65th, was killed. Early that morning a small body of colonial troops, consisting of about thirty-five of the Forest Rangers, under Lieutenant Jackson and Ensigns Von Tempsky and J. C. Hay, and fifteen of the Mauku Company of Forest Rifles, under Lieutenant Lusk, started out from the Mauku stockade on a bush-scouting expedition in search of Maoris. They began by reconnoitring the forest and the bush-clearings in the direction of Patumahoe and Pukekohe. They reached the farms of Lusk and H. Hill, between Patumahoe and Pukekohe

[After a sketch by G. Norbury, 1863.]

Hill, and found that the Maori marauders had been there. Lusk's house had been pillaged. On the edge of what was known as the "Big Clearing," belonging to Mr. Hill, they found traces of the raiders. The Maoris shot a bullock in this clearing, which was nearly half a mile square, covered with burnt stumps and logs. The force, hearing the shots, divided, and twenty, under Jackson, Lusk, and Von Tempsky, scouted about the fringes of the paddock, keeping under cover of the bush. They received a sudden volley at a range of a few yards, and replied briskly. The natives were sheltered behind masses of fallen trees and undergrowth interlaced with supplejack. The other party of Rangers skirmished up on Jackson's left and joined their comrades. At last the Maori fire grew slacker, and the Rangers and Mauku Rifles charged into the bush, but their

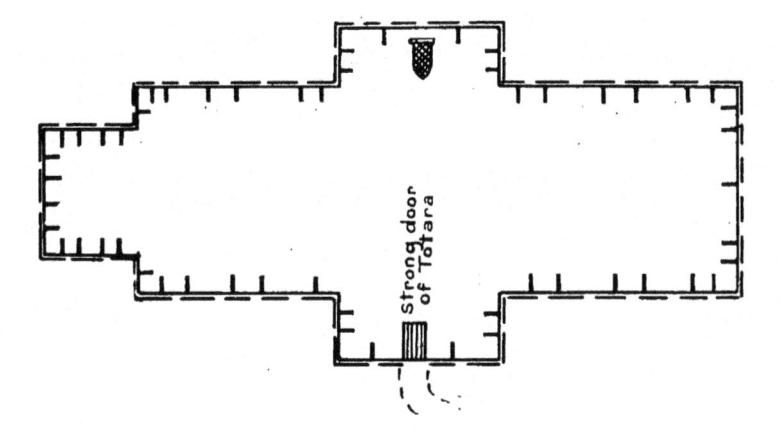

Sketch-plan, J. C., 1920.]

PLAN OF MAUKU CHURCH,

Showing positions of loopholes in the walls.

opponents had disappeared. An encampment was found with about a dozen rough huts. Only fleeting glimpses of the Maoris had been obtained during the skirmishing, and any killed or wounded were carried off the field. It was reported afterwards that five had been killed. The war-party was composed chiefly of Patumahoe natives, the Ngati-Tamaoho and other *hapus*, who, after deserting their settlements, were prowling about the bush, plundering the outlying homesteads. The European force suffered no casualties, although several of the men had received bullets through cap or clothes.

It was the maiden fight of the Rangers and Mauku Rifles. The guerilla veteran Von Tempsky in his journal gave high praise to some of the settler-soldiers. Lusk he described as "a man of consummate judgment about Maori warfare." In the height of the skirmish he found time to admire the *sang froid* of the Mauku men: "There are some cool hands amongst those Mauku Rifles. There are big Wheeler and little Wheeler, and Kelahan, watching the Maoris like cats; they have holes through their coats, but none through their skins as yet. Lusk is cool and collected, keeping the men together." The best marksmen were Jackson and Hay, both crack shots.

This was one of the first fights in the war conducted after the traditional manner of North American Indian warfare, skirmishing from tree to tree. For some time after this skirmish the Forest Rangers remained at Mauku, making the fortified church their headquarters and scouring the bush.*

THE ENGAGEMENT AT TITI HILL, MAUKU.

Less than a mile south of the Mauku church and village is a gently rounded hill of red volcanic tufa, crowned by a farm-homestead and crossed by a road. In 1863 this hill, known as the Titi, was a partly cleared farm belonging to Mr. Wheeler. Beyond, on the southern side, the land slopes deeply to a valley, on the farther side of which, nearly a mile distant, are the heights known as the Bald Hills. The distance of the Titi from the nearest part of the Waikato River is about six miles; the intervening country in the war-days was mostly dense forest, threaded by one or two narrow tracks—old Maori fighting trails.

Early on the morning of the 23rd October, 1863, the sound of heavy firing in the direction of the Bald Hills was heard by the little garrison of Forest Rifles and Militia at the Mauku church stockade and the lower stockade near the landing. Lieutenant Lusk, commanding the Forest Rifles, was at the lower stockade at the time, and, thinking that possibly the church was being attacked, he advanced quickly with twenty-five men to St. Bride's to reinforce the force there. Then it was thought

---

*The skirmish in Hill's Clearing, near Patumahoe, west of Pukekohe, was fought on a level tract of country traversed by the present road from Pukekohe. The scene of the principal fighting, as nearly as can be located now, is on the right-hand side (north) of the main road from Pukekohe to Mauku and Waiuku, after passing the turn-off to Patumahoe at Union Corner, three miles from Pukekohe and the same distance from Mauku. Soon after passing Union Corner (Steinson's) the traveller will notice on the right a very large *puriri* stump, forming part of the post-and-rail fence dividing the road from the fields: this stump indicates the scene of some of the skirmishing in the edge of the bush. There are still remnants of the olden *puriri* forest on both sides of the road.

Major Von Tempsky's MS. narrative of this skirmish is given in the Appendices.

that the volleys in the distance might be the Waiuku Volunteers out practising, and Mr. John Wheeler and a comrade scouted up through the bush and the clearing to reconnoitre. They discovered Maoris shooting cattle on Wheeler's Farm, between the Titi summit and the Bald Hills. When Lieutenant Lusk received this report he despatched a man to the lower stockade, instructing Lieutenant J. S. Perceval, who had been left in charge of the Militia (1st Waikato Regiment), to join him at once at the church with half his force. At the same time one of the settler Volunteers, Mr. Heywood Crispe, was sent off to Drury for reinforcements. Lieutenant Perceval set out as ordered, at the head of twelve men, but instead of following instructions to join the others at the church he struck off to the right for the crown

THE MAUKU CHURCH, PRESENT DAY.

of the Titi Hill, with the object of taking the Maoris in the rear. These rash tactics quickly involved Perceval and his small party in a perilous position from which it was necessary for Lusk to extricate them. Perceval entered the bush, but the natives, having ended their cattle-shooting, came skirmishing over the hill and almost surrounded the Militia. The fight was now visible from the church stockade, where Lusk had been waiting for Perceval to join him, and in a few moments the Forest Rifles were dashing up the rise towards Wheeler's Clearing. Perceval when joined by the church-stockade party was retiring in good order, hotly pressed, but without casualties so far. At this time Lieutenant Norman, a Militia officer who was in charge of the church garrison, and who had ridden into Drury for the men's pay, returned and, armed with a rifle, caught up to the fighters on the hill.

Lieutenant Lusk, considering his force of about fifty was strong enough to drive back the Maoris and enable him to return, now boldly attacked, and before the steady advance with fixed bayonets the raiders fell back through a strip of Wheeler's felled but unburned bush to the open ground. The Maoris, however, skirmished rapidly through the standing *puriri* and *rata* forest on Lusk's left flank, and as they greatly outnumbered the riflemen it was necessary to retire in order to avoid being outflanked and surrounded. The Kingites were endeavouring to cut the little force off from the church stockade, and Lusk had need of all his bush-fighting skill to counter their tactics. When recrossing this ragged strip of felled timber, taking advantage of every bit of cover and fighting from behind logs and stumps as they fell back, the Volunteers and Militiamen were charged fiercely by the warriors in their full strength, about a hundred and fifty.

Now came a desperate close-quarters battle, lasting ten minutes or a quarter of an hour. At very short range—Lieutenant Lusk afterwards stated it at 20 yards—the opposing forces poured bullets into each other as fast as they could load and fire. Every log and every stump and pile of branches was contested. In the centre, facing the Maoris' front, the gallant Perceval recklessly exposed himself, and it was with difficulty that the Mellsop brothers, three young settlers, prevented him from charging at the enemy. Twice they saved his life by pulling him under cover. At last, after shooting several of his nearest opponents, he was shot himself, and fell dead in front of his men. Lieutenant Norman also was shot dead, and several other men fell. Some of the Maoris, throwing down their guns, charged upon the bayonets with their long-handled tomahawks. Lusk, finding himself outflanked on both sides, ordered his men to take cover in the bush on the right. In this movement the troops had to run the gauntlet of a heavy cross-fire, and man after man was hit. One of the Forest Rifles, Private Worthington, was tomahawked as he was reloading his rifle; another man was killed with the tomahawk while he was in the act of recovering his bayonet which he had driven through a Maori's body. One of the wounded, Johnstone, was assisted by two comrades into the bush, and as he could not walk he was concealed in a hollow *rata* tree, where he huddled until the relief force rescued him on the following day.

Under cover of the bush Lusk's force had a short breathing-space, and their accurate shooting soon cleared the smoky clearing of the Maoris, but it was impossible to venture into the open space to carry off the eight dead who lay there. The officer in command re-formed his men and retired in good order upon the church stockade, keeping carefully to the timber cover most of the way. This rearguard action, firing by sections as the retirement was made, was carried out with excellent judgment, and the little force behaved with the steadiness and coolness of veterans. The headquarters at the stockade and the post at the church were reached without further casualty. The force

MAJOR D. H. LUSK.
(Died 1921.)

After his active service in command of the Forest Rifles, Major Lusk joined General Cameron's army in the Upper Waikato as an officer attached to the Transport Corps. When the steamer "Avon" sank in the Waipa River with her cargo of supplies (February, 1864) he succeeded in getting commissariat through to the troops at Te Rore with a Militia force, by rapidly cutting a pack-track from Raglan Harbour over the ranges to the Waipa, and kept the army supplied in this way till the "Avon" was replaced.

lost two officers and six men killed; but grief at the fall of good comrades and at the necessity of leaving their bodies to the tomahawk was tempered with the satisfaction of having killed or wounded several times that number of the enemy.

Lusk and his comrades during the fight had cast many an anxious glance towards the village in the direction of the church stockade, hoping for the reinforcements from Drury. But when the long-awaited troops at last arrived all was over, and the battle-grimed Volunteers and Militia were back in their quarters. Heywood Crispe, who had galloped the twelve miles to Drury in three-quarters of an hour, had an exasperating interview with the Imperial officers at the camp. "Colonel Chapman was in charge there," narrated Mr. Crispe, "and with him was young Colonel Havelock (Sir Henry Havelock, son of the Indian Mutiny hero), who was on General Cameron's staff. I told them that I had seen the Maoris shooting cattle, and they almost laughed me to scorn, and said it was impossible for natives to be there. I most earnestly solicited them to send for Major Rutherford's 'Flying Column,' which I knew was in camp at the Bluff near Pokeno, and get the force to go through Tuakau and on to Purapura, on the Waikato, where they would be sure to intercept the Maoris returning from Mauku, as it was their only way of retreat to cross the Waikato." Crispe also begged for mounted men, some of the Defence Force Cavalry, to be hurried off to the Mauku, but all that was done was to send two companies of infantry—the Waikato Militia—who arrived there in the evening, too late to be of any use.

Early next morning firing was heard in the direction of the Bald Hills, and some natives were seen there, but when a force of about two hundred men advanced to the Titi Farm the Kingites had disappeared. It was learned afterwards that these Maoris were some who had met the returning war-party on the Waikato River, and, on hearing that they had not fired a volley over the battle-ground after the battle by way of claiming the victory, had marched in themselves and fired off their guns near the spot. The troops found the bodies of the slain men, all tomahawked and stripped of arms and equipment and part of their clothes, laid out side by side on the grass in the clearing. A pole on which a white haversack had been tied indicated the place. The bodies, with the exception of Worthington's, which was buried at Mauku, were sent in to Drury for burial. A force was sent through the bush to Purapura, following the trail of the Maoris, and numbers of *kauhoa* or rough bush-stretchers for carrying the dead and wounded were found. It was estimated that the natives had lost between twenty and thirty killed, besides many wounded. The "Flying Column" had in the meantime marched across country via Tuakau to intercept some of the raiders, but they only reached Rangipokia, near Purapura, in time to open fire on the last of the canoes crossing the river. The Maoris returned to Pukekawa, the field headquarters of Ngati-Maniapoto.

NOTES.

This curious story with reference to Lieutenant Norman was related to me by Major D. H. Lusk:—

Lieutenant Norman, who had just returned from Drury with the pay for the Mauku Forest Rifles and Militia garrison, had about £200 in his possession, mostly in bank-notes. He was shot through the chest and killed; the fatal shot was fired at such close range that his clothes were forced into the wound. When the body was searched next day the money could not be found. Its disappearance remained a mystery to Lusk for nearly fifty years. Then a half-caste member of the Ngati-Maniapoto Tribe told him that some years after the war a Maori brought him one day a bundle which proved to be a large roll of bank-notes stuck together with earth and blood. With much care the notes were separated and dried, and in the end the Maoris succeeded in passing them at the banks. This bundle, the natives said, formed part of the loot brought by Ngati-Maniapoto from the Titi fight in 1863. Without a doubt it was the missing pay for the Mauku men, and the blood which caked the notes together was Norman's life-blood.

The Maoris took a prisoner, a Portuguese named Antonio Arouge, in the employ of the Crispe family. He was captured by the cattle-shooting party and tied to a tree. After the fight he was taken into the Waikato, and remained a prisoner for some months, when he was allowed to return to the Europeans. It was, no doubt, his swarthy skin that saved him.

Many stories were told of the brave conduct and accurate shooting of the Volunteers and Militia. There were also a few good shots among the natives. Just before Lusk advanced from the church stockade to Perceval's relief he saw, through his field-glasses, a Maori marksman in a conspicuous dress taking deliberate sniping shots from the cover of a log. Although the sniper was quite 1,000 yards away he put a bullet through the soft-felt hat of Tom Harden, a Volunteer a few feet away from Lusk, and sent two or three other bullets remarkably close to him. The Maori was evidently using a captured British rifle. Lusk was a good rifle-shot, and, sighting for 1,000 yards, his first shot made the Maori sniper leap back hurriedly for cover. In the skirmish which followed as the force advanced Tom Harden had the satisfaction of taking compensation for his damaged hat by killing the native marksman.

Lusk in his report gave praise to Sergeant Harry W. Hill and Private John Wheeler, of the Forest Rifles, who distinguished themselves by their determined gallantry. Another settler who behaved with special courage was Felix McGuire, afterwards a member of the House of Representatives.

Major Lusk narrated this incident which immediately preceded the outbreak of the war :—

The Ngati-Pou and Ngati-Tamaoho Tribes, of Waikato and Patumahoe, had, it is believed, fixed a day for a general attack on the settlers. By a curious coincidence it happened to be the date on which the *pakeha* residents were loyally celebrating the marriage of the Prince of Wales (afterwards King Edward VII) and the Princess Alexandra of Denmark. The frontier settlers kindled bonfires at dark that night on prominent hills, and those of the Mauku, including Lusk and some neighbours, lit theirs on the Bald Hill, where it was visible for many miles around and as far as the Waikato River. The Maoris, it was said, were about to start out on their raid, anticipating the British declaration of war, but the unexpected glare of the bonfires alarmed them into the belief that their plans had been discovered, and that the fire was a signal for a general attack on the Kingites. Lusk and several fellow-settlers were returning from the bonfire hill late at night, when they met a party of about fifteen Maoris, some of them armed, who had evidently been to Lusk's house. He demanded their business there. They replied that they had been alarmed by the bonfires and inquired if they were a signal for an attack upon the natives. Shortly after this incident Major Speedy (a retired Imperial officer), who was Resident Magistrate and Native Agent for the Mauku, Waiuku, and Pukekohe districts, was directed to read the Governor's Proclamation to the natives requiring them either to take the oath of allegiance to the Queen and to deliver up their arms or to retire into the Kingite country, so that the Government might be able to discover who were their friends. As it was evident that the Maoris would not willingly give up their arms and leave their land, Major Speedy instructed Lieutenant Lusk to organize all the able-bodied settlers of the districts into three rifle volunteer companies, which came to be known as the Forest Rifles.

Mrs. Jerram (Remuera. Auckland), a daughter of the late Major Speedy, of Mauku, says that the family's home at " The Grange," near the Mauku landing, was loopholed and garrisoned by the settlers for defence against the natives in 1863. This was before the stockade was built at the landing-place. Mrs. Jerram and Mrs. B. A. Crispe describe the scene in " The Grange " in the time of alarms, when for three nights the women and children of the settlement took shelter there, waiting for the cutter which was to take them to Onehunga. The armed settlers kept guard in twos; those off guard lay down on the floor in their blankets, their loaded rifles on the table. There were numerous false alarms, especially just before the dawn, the Maoris' favourite time of attack. " The Grange " was not the best of places as a defensive shelter, for there was a thick growth of trees and creepers close up to the house, affording perfect cover for an enemy.

Tohikuri, of the Ngati-Tamaoho Tribe, Pukekohe, gives the following explanation of the place-name Patumahoe, that of the gently rounded hill near the battlefield of Hill's Clearing :—

The chief Huritini, of the Ngaiwi or Waiohua Tribe, of the Tamaki district, came to these parts to make war upon Hiku-rere-roa and Te Ranga-rua, the leaders of the Ngati-Tamaoho Tribe, six generations ago. The *pa* of Ngati-Tamaoho was on the Titi Hill. The battle began on the western side of the present Mauku Railway-station, near the church. Huritini was killed with a blow delivered with a *mahoe* stake or part of a sapling snatched up hurriedly from the ground by a Ngati-Tamaoho chief who had dropped his weapon; and the Ngaiwi men were defeated and driven from the district. Hence the name: *Patu*, to strike or kill; *mahoe*, the whitewood tree *(Melicytus ramiflorus)*.

Tohikuri is a direct descendant of Ranga-rua.

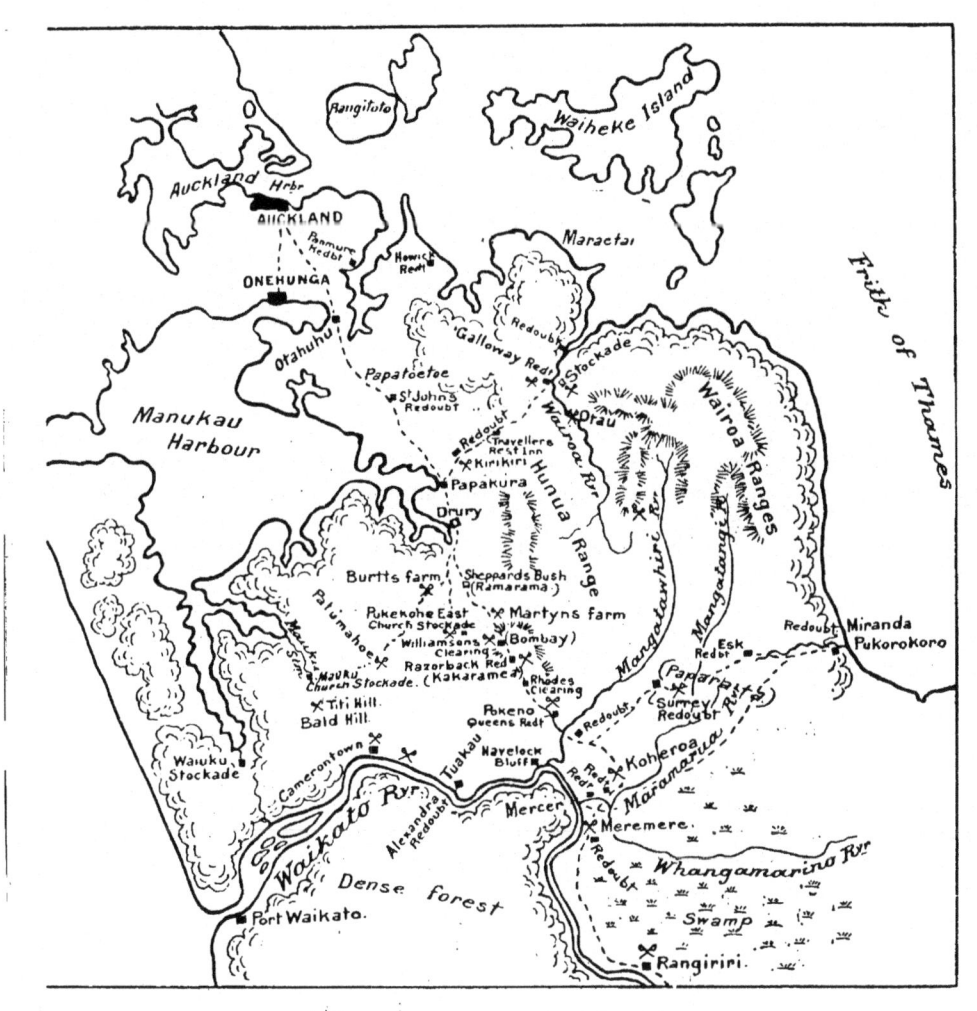

THE SOUTH AUCKLAND DISTRICT,

Showing military posts and scenes of engagements, 1863.

CHAPTER XXXIII.

THE RIVER WAR FLEET.

It was necessary to organize a small fleet of protected vessels for the Waikato River in order to carry the war into the Kingite territory. The first craft procured was the little paddle-steamer "Avon," of 40 tons, 60 feet in length, and drawing 3 feet of water. She had been trading out of Lyttelton before the purchase by the Government. She was brought up to the Manukau, and at Onehunga was armoured for the river campaign. She was armed with a 12-pounder Armstrong in the bows. The work of making the hull bullet-proof was carried out by the engineer, Mr. George Ellis (now of Auckland), who states that the "Avon" was converted into an armoured steamer by having iron plates bolted inside her bulwarks. These plates were $\frac{1}{4}$ inch thick and measured 6 feet by 3 feet. The wheel was enclosed by an iron house of similar-sized plates, with loop-holes. "I put the same thickness of iron protection on some smaller craft," said Mr. Ellis. "These were armed barges for towing troops. The gunboat-barges were each 30 feet to 35 feet in length; they had been open fore-decked cutters in Auckland Harbour, and were taken over on trucks to Onehunga. I armoured them with lengths of bar iron, $\frac{1}{4}$ inch thick and 3 or 4 inches in width, along the outside of the hull from the gunwale to the water-line. In the bows of each boat was a gun-platform for a 12-pounder. The troops were put into these barges, which were towed up by the steamers. The bulwarks protected the soldiers quite well, but the barges were never attacked. There was another vessel, the 'Gymnotus,' but she was not armoured. She was a curious-looking craft like a long narrow canoe, and had been built for ferry service on Auckland Harbour. She was the first screw steamer on the Waikato, and was employed in carrying stores up the river."

The paddle-wheeler "Avon" was the first steam-vessel to float on the waters of the Waikato. She was towed to Waikato Heads on the 25th July, 1863, by H.M.S. "Eclipse," and Captain Mayne, the commander of that ship, took her inside the Heads and anchored that night eight miles below Tuakau. Next day, watched with intense excitement by the Maoris, friendlies, and hostiles alike, she reached the Bluff, otherwise known as Havelock—Te Ia-roa of the Maoris—just below the junction of the Manga-tawhiri with the Waikato. She was not fired upon, contrary to the expectations of her crew, who expected a volley from the southern bank of the river at the narrower parts. Mr. Strand, of Kohanga, assisted to pilot the "Avon" up the river.

On the 7th August Captain Sullivan (H.M.S. "Harrier"), senior naval officer in New Zealand, took the vessel on a reconnaissance up the river, and near Meremere she became a target for Maori bullets for the first time. A volley from some Maoris under cover on the river-bank was replied to with the 12-pounder Armstrong. On several occasions later in the campaign the "Avon" was under fire. This little pioneer of steam traffic on the Waikato proved an exceedingly useful vessel. When the army reached the Waipa Plains she carried stores up as far as Te Rore, on the Waipa; it was near there that Lieutenant Mitchell, R.N., of H.M.S. "Esk," was killed on board her (February, 1864) by a volley from the east bank of the river. Lieutenant F. J. Easther, R.N., was in command of the "Avon."*

The second steam-vessel of war placed on the Waikato was the "Pioneer"—a name that more properly might have been bestowed on the "Avon." The "Pioneer" was specially designed for navigation in shallow waters, and was a well-equipped river

---

* Mr. George Ellis, of Auckland, who was engineer of the "Avon," says:—

"Lieutenant Mitchell's death occurred in this way: We carried out rather dangerous work in the later stages of the war when running up and down the Waipa River. Sometimes we took shots at anything that offered on the banks, and even landed to go pig-hunting. One very warm summer day, when steaming up the Waipa near Whatawhata, Mr. Mitchell remarked that it was too hot to remain in the iron wheel-house and that he would go outside; he declared that he would not be shot that day. He walked out on to the open part of the bridge-deck, and Lieutenant Easther (in command) and Midshipman Foljambe (father of the present Lord Liverpool) followed him. They had not been long there before a sudden volley was fired from the scrub-covered bank of the river—the east or proper right bank. The three officers were close together, with Mr. Mitchell in the middle, and, curiously, it was only the man in the middle who was hit. The volley was fired at an oblique angle. Mr. Mitchell was shot right through the breast, and died next day. We never saw a Maori, so thick was the cover on the bank."

The "Avon," besides plying on the Waipa, made a number of trips from Ngaruawahia to General Cameron's advanced camp at Pukerimu. This perilous passage through the hostile country was generally made at night. The "Avon" was never fired at on this part of the Waikato—usually called the Horotiu above Ngaruawahia—but there were anxious moments when she was passing through the narrows, where the high banks closely approach each other, above the present town of Hamilton.

gunboat. She was built for the New Zealand Government by the Australian Steam Navigation Company at Sydney, and was an iron flat-bottomed stern-wheel paddle-steamer of nearly 300 tons, with a length of 140 feet and beam of 20 feet, drawing only 3 feet of water when fully loaded. The engine-room and other vital parts of the vessel were all well protected. Her most conspicuous deck feature was the pair of iron turrets or cupolas, 12 feet in diameter and 8 feet in height. Each tower was pierced for a 12-pounder gun and for rifle-fire. (One of these cupolas afterwards stood on the river-bank at Mercer for many years; it was at one time used by the police as a lock-up. It now forms the lower part of Mercer's memorial to the local soldiers in the Great War.)

The "Pioneer," rigged for the voyage as a three-masted fore-and-aft schooner, left Sydney for the Manukau on the

THE RIVER GUNBOAT "PIONEER."

This drawing, from a sketch in 1863, shows the "Pioneer" in seagoing rig. The mainmast was removed before she entered operations on the Waikato River.

22nd September, 1863, in tow of H.M.S. "Eclipse," and, after a stormy voyage, reached Onehunga on the 3rd October. She was taken into the Waikato later in the month, after undergoing a few alterations, and until the end of the war was actively engaged in reconnaissances and conveyance of troops and supplies.

The four small armoured barges, or gunboats, mentioned by Mr. Ellis were taken into the Waikato about the same time, and each of them was placed under the command of a junior naval officer. Midshipman Foljambe (father of Lord Liverpool, recently Governor of New Zealand) was in charge of one of these boats, which he called the "Midge"; it was manned by seven sailors, and was armed with a 12-pounder and a $4\frac{2}{5}$-inch brass Coehorn mortar.

Later in the war two stern-wheel iron gunboats, called the "Koheroa" and the "Rangiriri," were procured in Sydney, and were brought over in sections and put together at the Government's dockyard and stores depot at Putataka, Port Waikato. The high bulwarks of each steamer were pierced for rifle-fire, and there was a gun-position on the lower deck amidships. The "Koheroa" on one occasion towards the close of the campaign went up the Waikato River as far as a point near the present town of Cambridge.

Without this river flotilla General Cameron could not have carried on the Waikato campaign. The gunboats and the troops they carried enabled him to outflank the Maori positions at Meremere and Rangiriri, to capture Ngaruawahia unopposed, and to keep his army fed and equipped on the Waipa Plain. It was the great water-road into the heart of the country, Waikato's noble canoe highway, that gave the British troops command of the Kingite territory and prepared the way for the permanent European occupation.

THE RIVER GUNBOAT "RANGIRIRI."

(Sister ship, "Koheroa.")

The New Zealand Government's iron gunboats "Koheroa" and "Rangiriri" were constructed at Sydney by P. N. Russell and Co. from designs by Mr. James Stewart, C.E., of Auckland, who was sent to Sydney to superintend the work. A correspondent gave the following description of the "Rangiriri" in 1864: "This boat, which can turn easily in the space of a little more than her own length, may follow the bendings of such a river as the Waikato in its narrowest part, and may either be used as a steam-tug, towing flats for the conveyance of troops, or may be armed with guns at each of the singular-looking portholes [embrasures] which are closed with folding-doors in the middle of the lower deck; while the bulwarks on each side are pierced with twenty or thirty loopholes for rifle shooting, and the covered platform or tower amidships will afford cover to a number of men whose fire commands the river and its banks. The paddle-wheel is placed astern of the vessel so as to take up less room. The first of these gunboats, the 'Koheroa,' was built in less than six weeks after Messrs. Russell got the contract.' Both vessels were sent in sections to New Zealand and put together at Port Waikato.

Some small vessels were necessary for despatch and patrol work on the coast. The Colonial Government bought the s.s. "Tasmanian Maid," 90 tons, renamed her the "Sandfly," and armed her. Under the command of Captain Hannibal Marks, the "Sandfly" carried out useful work as a gunboat and despatch-vessel on the east coast, particularly in the Hauraki Gulf and in the coast operations near Maketu (1864). The "Sandfly" was protected against a sudden attack by canoe-crews by an arrangement of galvanized wire stretched between stanchions fitted on the bulwarks, thus forming a strong boarding netting. As a further defence, canvas mattress-cases stuffed with flax were provided, to be placed against the wire netting as a bullet-proof barrier. Another patrol-vessel was a fore-and-aft schooner,

After a sketch by Mr. S. Percy Smith.]

PUTATAKA, PORT WAIKATO, 1864.

Extract from Mr. S. Percy Smith's diary: "10th October, 1864.—Pulled from survey camp at Maioro down to Putataka to take some angles and spend a couple of hours in looking about the place. There were the steamer 'Koheroa' undergoing repairs, the 'Avon' being dismantled, having done her work on the Waipa nobly, and the 'White Slave,' a new steamer, being built, besides the building of barges and boats. There are several large and good stores for commissariat purposes, both Imperial and colonial, barracks, and officers' quarters on a hill overlooking the dockyard; a few men of the 14th Regiment are in garrison.'

the "Caroline," armed with a gun; she was used for a time in Auckland waters, and on one occasion took a party of Naval Volunteers on a cruise in search of a schooner trading in contraband of war.

THE BRITISH SCREW CORVETTES "MIRANDA" AND "FAWN."

Before coming to New Zealand the "Miranda," a fifteen-gun corvette, had been engaged in the blockade of Archangel during the war with Russia, 1853-54. She was employed in the Hauraki Gulf in the Maori War of 1863, and in 1864 was sent to Tauranga, where the Captain (Jenkins) and a detachment shared in the disastrous attempt to storm the Gate *Pa*. The "Fawn," which was at Auckland in 1862, was a seventeen-gun corvette.

From a painting by W. Forster.]

THE GUN-SCHOONER "CAROLINE," 1863.

The small schooner "Caroline" (afterwards the "Ruby") was used by the Government in 1860–63 as a despatch and patrol vessel on the west coast and in the Hauraki Gulf. She was armed with a gun. At one time she was commanded by Lieutenant S. Medley, R.N.

Other vessels used on the Hauraki Gulf patrol were the s.s. "Auckland," which carried two 12-pounder guns, and the cutter "Midnight," 33 tons, armed with a 4-pounder gun and manned by a crew of fifteen Auckland Naval Volunteers.

The Naval Brigade, made up from the crews of the several naval ships in New Zealand waters, was a highly useful reinforcement to the land army. In October of 1863 there were five ships of the Australasian Squadron, all with steam-power, lying in the Auckland and Manukau Harbours. The flagship was the steam-frigate "Curaçoa" (Commodore William S. Wiseman), mounting twenty-three guns—sixteen plain-bored 8-inch guns on her main deck, six 40-pounder Armstrong guns on her quarter-deck, and one 110-pounder Armstrong pivot gun on her forecastle. Her tonnage was 1,571 tons, and her engines were 350 horse-power.

H.M.S. "ECLIPSE."

The "Eclipse," first under Commander H. G. Mayne and afterwards under Captain (now Admiral) Sir E. R. Fremantle, carried out much useful service on the New Zealand coast, 1863–65. She was the first vessel of the British Navy to enter Waikato Heads. The "Eclipse" was a barque-rigged steamer of 750 tons, capable of steaming 11 knots per hour. She had a crew of ninety men, and was armed with a 110-pounder Armstrong gun and a 68-pounder, both pivot guns, besides two 32-pounders. The "Eclipse" served on the Taranaki coast and in the Manukau, and later (1865) was engaged in operations against the Hauhaus in the Bay of Plenty and about the East Cape.

The "Miranda," Captain Robert Jenkins, was one of the screw corvettes of the "Niger" order; she measured 1,039 tons, carried fifteen guns, and had engines of 250 horse-power. The "Esk" was the latest addition to the squadron. She was one of a numerous family of twenty-one-gun corvettes, of 1,169 tons, with engines of 250 horse-power. Her armament was powerful for those days, consisting of sixteen plain-bored 8-inch guns, four 40-pounder and one 110-pounder Armstrong field-guns. The "Esk" was under the command of Captain John Hamilton; he fell in the assault of the Gate *Pa* in 1864.

The two remaining ships, "Harrier" (700 tons) and "Eclipse" (750 tons), were the guardians of the Manukau waters.

THE BRITISH TROOPSHIP "HIMALAYA."

The ship-rigged steamer "Himalaya," 3,570 tons, was a celebrated British transport in the days of the Crimean War and the Indian Mutiny, and carried many thousands of troops to the East. She was built in 1853 for the P. and O. Company. On the 14th November, 1863, she arrived at Auckland from Colombo, bringing the 50th Regiment, numbering 819 officers and men, under Colonel Waddy, C.B. Captain Lacy commanded the "Himalaya."

CHAPTER XXXIV.

THE TRENCHES AT MEREMERE.

Maori artillery, emplaced on the long narrow ridge of Meremere, saluted the first steam-craft that came paddling up the Waikato. The roar of these Kingite-manned guns — old ship's pieces conveyed with great labour from the west coast and loaded with a strange variety of projectiles—gave a deeper note of determination to the struggle for independence. Every tribe acknowledging the authority of the Maori King sent its warriors to garrison Meremere. At one period of its occupation there were more than a thousand men there, from the tribes of Waikato, from Ngati-Maniapoto, Ngati-Haua, Ngati-Koroki, Ngati-Raukawa, Ngati-Tuwharetoa, and even from Taranaki and the Upper Wanganui. Inland again, in the direction of the Wairoa and the Hauraki, was the Paparata series of entrenchments, designed to bar the British advance on the eastern side, and to keep communication open with the Thames Gulf and the Wairoa Ranges. On the other side of the Lower Waikato, in the elbow of the river, was Pukekawa, the advanced field base of Ngati-Maniapoto ; from its domed crown they could overlook the river and the movements of the troops from Whangamarino down to Tuakau and Camerontown. Meremere held the centre; it was the key of the Waikato, and had the Kingites been armed on equal terms with the British they might, for all their inferior numbers, have swept the river clear, and maintained indefinitely the independence of the interior.

The Great South Road, which skirts the proper right bank of the Waikato south of Mercer, cuts through the site of the Meremere fortifications of 1863. The principal remains of the Maori works extend obliquely along a ridge—now a dairy farm— rising in places in irregular terraces parallel with the river, on the southern side of the Whangamarino flax swamp. A system of marshes, converted into lagoons in time of flood, bounds the long Meremere ridge, or succession of ridges, on the east, and when the Waikato ran high the Maori position was practically an island. At its greatest elevation it was about 130 feet above the river. The northern terminal of the ridges is about two miles south of the Mercer Railway-station. As the Great South Road, after crossing the swamp, ascends this end of the long hill it intersects the ruins of the first line of rifle-pits ; on the clay spur, grown with gorse and pine-trees, the remains of the Maori trenches and shelter-holes are still plainly to be traced. From this point southwards for nearly half a mile the road runs close to the lines of trenches. On the edge of the steepest part of the slope above the Waikato irregular outlines of rifle-pits and dug-in *whares* are traceable in the uneven turf of the paddock. On the opposite side of the road (east), about 150 yards from the highway and on the crest of the ridge, are the well-preserved remains of the British redoubt constructed upon the site of the Maori *tihi* or citadel. This field-work, cut in a stiff clay, retains its original proportions well; the trench shows 15 feet scarp at the highest point, with a counterscarp of about 6 feet.

The Maori artillery in the Meremere works consisted of three ship's guns, which the natives regarded with great pride; they

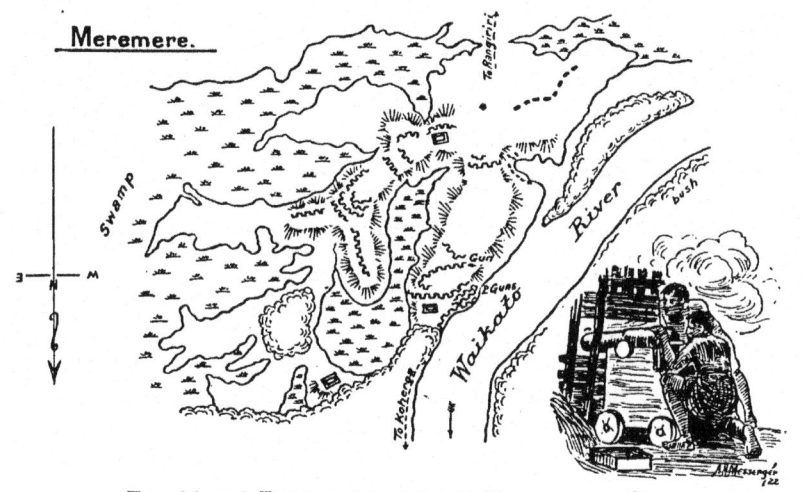

THE MAORI ENTRENCHMENTS AT MEREMERE, 1863.

expected with them to prevent any *pakeha* vessel running the blockade of the Waikato. Patara te Tuhi, who was in Meremere with his tribe, informed me that two if not all of the guns had been given to the Ngati-Tabinga Tribe, at Whaingaroa, on the west coast, many years before by the trader Captain Kent ("Te Amukete" of the Maoris). They had been transported over the ranges by man-power, and taken by canoe from the Waipa down to Meremere.* The native gunners were taught

---

* Tohikuri, of Ngati-Tamaoho, gives the following names of the largest war-canoes manned by the Waikato tribes during the river war of 1863: Maramarua, Tawhitinui, Te Marei, Te Aparangi, Te Ata-i-rehia, Te Winika, Tahere-tikitiki, Ngapuhoro, and Te Toki-a-Tapiri. The last-named was among the canoes belonging to the Ngati-te-Ata seized by the Naval Volunteers in the Manukau creeks; it is now in the Auckland Museum.

the art of loading, laying, and firing the pieces by a European who lived in the Maori country before the war. This was an old East India Company's gunner, who was detained by the Kingites until he had trained the brown artillerymen. Tohikuri, of Ngati-Tamaoho, says that the guns were under the charge of Nganiho Panapana, a relation of Major te Wheoro, of the Ngati-Naho Tribe. This gunner succeeded one day in firing a steelyard weight into the "Pioneer." His difficulty was the want of proper projectiles; for lack of shot he loaded his guns with pieces of iron chain and with *paoro weeti* (pound weights) taken from the traders' stores. Panapana afterwards was taken prisoner at Rangiriri, and was one of those who escaped from Kawau Island in 1864. Tai-whakaea te Retimana was one of the gunners; he had worked as assistant to a blacksmith. Later on he was in charge of the two guns which the Kingites emplaced in Paterangi *pa*, in the Upper Waikato.

The first line of defence began at a palisading close to a belt of bush on the Maoris' extreme right, on the edge of the Whangamarino Swamp and close to the river. In front of the landing two ship's guns were in place; one of these was a small swivel 6-pounder. There were two embrasures in a kind of chamber cut in the clay bank; these openings covered the approach up or down the river, and the gun was shifted from one embrasure to the other with rope tackle. In rear of the battery were eleven tiers of traversed pits, covering the landing. A covered way led from the first gun to the second, which was mounted on a rough carriage with wooden wheels. The next system of entrenchments consisted of lines of rifle-pits, extending for several chains along the face of the ridge. Here a 24-pounder gun was emplaced. Beyond these pits, and on the summit of the hill, was the trenched *pa*, 28 yards by 20 yards, lightly palisaded.

On the 6th August the "Avon," commanded by Captain Hunt, when steaming up the river eight miles above Te Ia-roa, was fired on from the left bank. The Maori bullets flattened harmlessly on her plates. The steamer fired six rounds from her Armstrong gun, besides three war-rockets, and inflicted some casualties. On the 12th August the "Avon," with General Cameron on board, made a reconnaissance of Meremere. Anchoring within 1,000 yards of the *pa*, she sent some shells and rockets into the Kingite rifle-pits. The Maoris had begun their fire on the steamer from the bush on the bank, and as she swung round to return down the river they fired one of their pieces of artillery at her at point-blank range—about 100 yards. The gun was loaded, in lieu of other shot, with long iron nails, which furrowed the water astern of the gunboat. One of the seamen received a slight scalp-wound.

On the 29th and 30th October the gunboat "Pioneer" made reconnaissances of the Meremere position. General Cameron and his staff were on board. The gunboat was fired on heavily by the Maoris, who used their cannon as well as small-arms, but the fire was not effective. Most of the shots fell short, but on the 30th a 7 lb. steelyard weight fired from the upper gun, a 24-pounder, penetrated the upper works of the gunboat and lodged in a cask of beef. Fragments of iron used as projectiles rattled against the plating and the cupolas, but did no damage. On the first day's reconnaissance the "Pioneer" replied to the Maoris' cannonade with her gun, and the 40-pounder Armstrongs in the Whangamarino redoubt also sent several shells into the Meremere entrenchments.

Drawn from a sketch by an officer of H.M.S. "Curacoa."]
THE GUNBOAT "PIONEER" AT MEREMERE.

On the 29th October, 1863, the "Pioneer," with Lieut.-General Cameron and staff on board, reconnoitred the Kingite entrenchments on the Meremere ridge. The gunboat anchored in the Waikato 300 yards from the shore, and remained there for more than two hours under fire. A correspondent in the "Pioneer," describing the reconnaissance, wrote:—
"A cloud of white smoke burst from the bank at the landing. The Maoris had fired their lower guns. . . . Another puff of smoke sprang up, this time from a kind of embrasure in the upper line of rifle-pits. This shot fell short, endangering the Maoris more than the people in the steamer. Again the same gun fired, and with similar effect, the langridge splashing up the water, but nearer to the rifle-pits than to the steamer. The gun at the landing belched out again, and a jet of water spouted up alongside the gunboat; she was hit at last. A broken rocket-tube fell on board, but without any injury resulting. The natives had evidently dug up this projectile and used it as a charge of langridge. The side of the steamer was in a moment enveloped in white smoke, and the fragments of a shell tore up the ground about the rifle-pits at the landing. Another followed, and another, while not a movement was made

in the native position. Now a sharp crack was heard in another direction, followed by a sustained hissing sound—the 40-pounder Armstrong gun had sent its shell from Whangamarino, and this burst over the long line of rifle-pits on the hilltop. The steamer again fired, and alternately the 40-pounder fired, the missiles bursting over every part of the position. The time-fuse appeared rather short for the 40-pounder range, and the shells burst in the air, but the percussion fuse exploded the other shells as they struck the ground, and each sent a shower of earth into the air. The natives made no reply for a time, but at length, from a point near the water, where a palisade had been erected to arrest the march of any troops that might attack the place from the Whangamarino side, a sharp volley of musketry rattled out, succeeded by another, and then came a dropping fire from the whole extent of rifle-pits. The balls pinged on the steamer and pattered on the iron plating, occasionally going through an opening or glancing sharply off the cupolas. No one was struck, save perhaps some man in his coat-skirt or the brim of his hat. For half an hour now the steamer lay without firing a shot. General Cameron and his staff had now made themselves acquainted with the nature of the position; at each loophole a sketch was being made, while the natives expended their ammunition in vain."

The "Pioneer" again reconnoitred the Meremere entrenchments on the 30th October and was fired on heavily.

After the reconnaissance in the "Pioneer" on the 30th October General Cameron returned to the Queen's Redoubt, and orders were given for the embarkation of a column of six hundred men, consisting of detachments of the 40th and 65th Regiments, and two gun detachments of the Royal Artillery. These marched to the naval camp on the Manga-tawhiri, and were taken off to the "Pioneer" as she lay at her moorings in the Waikato near the Bluff. The expedition before daybreak on the 31st October had passed the enemy's position at Meremere, fired upon by the upper and lower battery and rifle-pits as she steamed up the flooded river. Without returning the fire, the "Pioneer," accompanied by the "Avon," and having in tow several of the small gunboats, steamed for about eight miles above Meremere, and the force was landed. An entrenchment was thrown up on the high ground on the right bank and on the track from the landing to Rangiriri and Meremere. Three guns were got into position early in the day. One of the small gunboats was left in the river to cut off the Maoris' communication from the interior by water, and the "Pioneer" and "Avon" returned, towing the remaining gunboats.

The Maoris realized the importance of this move, and attempted to dislodge the British force by an attack on the field-work early next morning, but they were repulsed. A force of about six hundred men was to have embarked on the 1st November to form a junction with the advance force and march back to Meremere, attacking it about dawn on the left flank and rear. The Maoris forestalled this movement by a retreat. The flooded state of the country favoured their escape from the rear; and about 2 o'clock a despatch from Captain Phelps, of the 14th Regiment, in command at Whangamarino, gave the first news that the natives were crossing the lagoon in canoes from Meremere towards Paparata and the Thames. General Cameron, accompanied by his staff, immediately left the Queen's Redoubt, and in passing the Koheroa redoubts gave orders for 250 men of the 12th and 14th Regiments to embark in the "Pioneer." The General went ahead in the "Avon" to reconnoitre, and on being joined by the "Pioneer" the expeditionary force landed. Meremere was found deserted; two of the heavy guns, one musket, and three canoes were all that were captured. The troops occupied the position, and built a redoubt on the highest point.

THE MIRANDA EXPEDITION.

On the 16th November a force of about nine hundred men, under Lieut.-Colonel Carey, embarked at Auckland for the Thames Gulf. The object of the expedition was to occupy the principal Maori settlements on the western shore of the gulf, whence men and supplies had been sent to the Waikato, and to establish a line of forts across country from the sea to the Queen's Redoubt. The Kingite position at Paparata still threatened the rear of Cameron's army, and raiding-parties were able to cross the frontier at will and rove the Wairoa Ranges. Carey's expeditionary force consisted of two companies of the Auckland Coastguards (Naval Volunteers) (Captain William C. Daldy), sixty of the Colonial Defence Force Cavalry (Captain Walmsley), detachments of the 12th and 70th Regiments, and the 1st Regiment of Waikato Militia. The warships "Miranda" and "Esk" headed the fleet of transports, which included the Government gunboat "Sandfly,' the steamers "Corio" and "Alexandra," the brigantine "Jessie," and seven or eight cutters. The cavalrymen and their horses were taken down in the "Corio" and "Alexandra."

For eight days the vessels lay at anchor in Waiheke Passage, weather-bound. At last the fleet brought up off Wakatiwai, north of the Pukorokoro, a small stream which flows out into the mangrove-fringed gulf near the spot now known as Miranda. The Coastguards were boated ashore at Wakatiwai, and, cutting their way through bush and scrub, they reached the main ridge and marched along it towards the Pukorokoro, about six miles. In the meantime the gunboat steamed southward. From Wakatiwai a beautiful shelly beach extended nearly to Pukorokoro. This stretch of beach and the rising ground behind were thick with enemy rifle-pits, in two lines, extending over about a mile north and south. The Maoris had also blocked the mouth of the Pukorokoro with large limbs of *pohulukawa* trees. (The "Miranda" and "Sandfly" had reconnoitred Pukorokoro a fortnight previously, when three of the native villages were shelled.) The Coastguards, hurrying along the ridge, were just in time to see the Kingites retreating quickly across the creek in the direction of Waitakaruru and the Piako Swamp. The officer commanding the Coastguards (who had by this time been joined by the rest of the military force) obtained permission to lead the attack on the native village at Pukorokoro, which stood a short distance south of the stream. Doubling up past the Regulars and Militia, the bluejackets took the lead and crossed the creek. The Maoris made no stand, but quickly retreated along the narrow level

THE ESK REDOUBT.

This redoubt, for 150 men, named after H.M.S. "Esk," was constructed at the end of November, 1863, by the force under Colonel Carey. It was situated on a commanding ridge between the Miranda post (Pukorokoro) and the Surrey Redoubt, south of Paparata, and formed one of the chain of redoubts from the Thames Gulf to the Waikato River.

belt between the mangroves and the hills for about two miles towards the Piako Swamp.

On the bluff above the creek-mouth the troops built a redoubt for 120 men. It was named the Miranda, after the warship. Working detachments were sent out later along a route westward selected for a line of posts to the Waikato, and two redoubts, named the Esk and the Surrey, were constructed along the Miranda–Manga-tawhiri line, linking up with the Queen's Redoubt.

Operations of the Naval Volunteers.

The Auckland Coastguards—later known as the Auckland Naval Artillery—who took a prominent part in the Miranda expedition, performed very useful service during the year in scouring the shores of Manukau Harbour and the Hauraki, and (in conjunction with the Onehunga Naval Volunteers) in seizing the flotilla of Maori war-canoes in the South Manukau creeks.

Lieut.-Colonel Henry Parker, of Devonport, who served for nine months as a seaman in the Auckland Coastguards, narrating the services of the corps (1918), stated that the first call to war came on the 18th July, 1863. The corps had a flagstaff near Government House, overlooking the town and harbour, and a gun was mounted there. The signal went up to muster, and at 2 p.m. the company fell in at Princes Street fully armed and accoutred, under Lieutenants Guilding and Stevenson. On reaching the rendezvous the Navals found that sixty armed friendly Maoris were to accompany them to the Manukau. They objected to march with the natives unless the latter were disarmed, as they did not trust them. The Defence Minister, after a conference with his officers, had the rifles and ammunition taken from the Maoris. The Volunteers marched out to Onehunga, and on reaching the Manukau were embarked in cutters. With the flood tide the flotilla stood up the south bay, and at 2 o'clock next morning the force landed at a point on the left-hand side of the tidal river, sailing up. Here there was a settlement of Kingite Maoris (Ngati-te-Ata) who were in possession of many large canoes; these canoes, it was believed, were to be used to transport war-parties of Kingites across the Manukau to Blockhouse Bay for an attack upon Auckland. Immediately the Maoris in the fenced village of *raupo* huts observed the presence of an enemy in the channel they opened fire on the troops. In the meantime a considerable number of the men had landed and gained the shelter of the cliff. The company advanced, and when the natives discovered the landing-party they retreated. The Volunteers suffered only one casualty—Seaman Thomas Barron (afterwards a well-known Auckland oarsman), who was hit in the ankle by a slug from a Maori gun. The force on returning to the village threw the Maori drays, ploughs, and other movable property into the harbour. After enjoying the *kumara* and other stores, the men endeavoured to set fire to the timber palisading around the *pa*, but it would not burn. The Navals explored the Papakura Creek, where H.M.S. "Harrier" was lying, and searched all the native villages. One of the main objects of the expedition, the capture of the enemy's means of transport across the Manukau, was successfully accomplished. Twenty-one large canoes were secured; these *wakas* were capable of carrying from thirty to fifty men each. The force also found an historic craft, the war-canoe "Toki-a-Tapiri" ("Tapiri's Axe")—which now reposes in the Auckland Museum. The "Axe" could carry quite a hundred warriors. At Onehunga the canoes were handed over to the troops. Most of them were broken up and used for firewood or otherwise destroyed. The contingent then marched back to Auckland, after an absence of a week.

The Auckland Coastguards' next warlike mission was a minor expedition to carry despatches. Ten of the volunteer bluejackets, under Chief Petty Officer (afterwards Captain) W. C. Daldy, were ordered to carry despatches to the head chief of the native *hapu* on the Wairoa River; this was Hori te Whetuki, of the Koheriki Tribe. The detachment embarked in the gun-schooner "Caroline," Captain Hannibal Marks. Arriving off the mouth of the Wairoa in the early morning, the schooner anchored, and the boat's crew was ordered away to carry the despatches up the river. Chief Petty Officer Daldy and four men formed the crew, Daldy steering; one of the oarsmen was Seaman Parker. The bluejackets had pulled about two miles up the river when they were fired on by a party of natives in the bush on the bank. In the bottom of the boat, under the thwarts, were loaded Enfield rifles, but as the crew was so small it was deemed advisable not to return the fire. Not a Maori could be seen—only the smoke that hung about the edge of the bush. This hostile reception compelled the despatch-carriers to return to the schooner. They pulled down the river and out to the "Caroline," and a few hours later were back in Auckland.

Three days later the Coastguards received orders to go to the Wairoa again. The Government had chartered the steamer "Auckland," and Nos. 1 and 2 Companies (the second company had just been formed), totalling about two hundred men, were ordered aboard, and all preparations were made for fighting. The steamer anchored off Ponui (Chamberlin's Island), several miles off the mouth of the Wairoa, and all the boats were put into the water. The force rowed ashore, but not a Maori was found; all the coast settlements were deserted. The expedition, finding no foe whereupon to play Enfield and cutlass, returned to town.

A week later the Coastguards were ordered out to the military camp at Drury. For several weeks the Volunteers were employed on convoy duty in the district between Drury, Mauku, and the Queen's Redoubt. On one occasion, the day after the fight at the Titi Farm, Mauku, a convoy of the Coastguards was ordered to take stores of food up to the soldiers at the Mauku stockades. The convoy had covered about half the distance, over a very bad road cut through the dense forest, when the bullock-drays became bogged. Some Maoris had taken post in a wooded gully flanking the road. By this time it was dark, and the Maori fires could be seen twinkling through the screen of foliage. The enemy opened fire on the convoy. The fire was effectively returned, the natives were driven off, and the convoy delivered the stores at Mauku and returned to Drury without further molestation.

This convoy duty and working cargo on the Drury tidal landing from the small craft that plied from Onehunga were arduous, but were cheerfully undertaken by the Coastguards. They openly rebelled, however, against an order to build a redoubt. Captain Daldy paraded the corps one day, and informed them that orders had been given by the Imperial officers to turn to and build an earthwork for the troops. This order met with very strenuous objections from the men, who protested that they had come to fight and not to build redoubts for the Regulars. They considered that as there were then some thousands of soldiers at Drury the troops could set to at their own fortifications. The protest held good. The officer in command rescinded his order, and the Coastguards presently received orders to return to Auckland.

In the town the Coastguards were continuously engaged in garrison duty; the pay was two guineas per week.

Later in the year (November) an expedition of Onehunga Navals and Rifle Volunteers, under Captain Purnell, scoured the southern and western shores of the Manukau in the s.s. "Lady Barkly," and brought in canoes overlooked by the first expedition. The "Toki-a-Tapiri," which had not been removed by the force in July—only the stern portion of the hull had been taken—was brought up to Onehunga. At Waiuku it was learned that a party of Maoris had cut down the signal-mast at the South Manukau Head, and had taken away two boats. The shore was searched, but the raiders had disappeared. A few days later there was another expedition in the steamer, this time to Awhitu, where it was reported that Kingite Maoris had appeared in force. The Navals landed, and in skirmishing order rushed the *kainga*, but the Maoris took to the bush, where it was not practicable to follow them.

CHAPTER XXXV.

THE BATTLE OF RANGIRIRI.

Fifty-six miles south of Auckland the Main Trunk trains pass the station of Rangiriri. Nothing is to be seen there of the battle-ground of the 20th November, 1863—the view is of swamps and lagoons and a forest of weeping-willows bordering the Waikato River—but from the line a little distance north of the station one may see, a mile away, the hill where the engagement was fought. Westward of the railway is the still, sedge-bordered Lake Kopuwera, now a bird-sanctuary, alive with wild duck and swans and wading-birds. This lagoon extends to the eastern base of a ridge marked by a dark plantation of pines: that is the spot where the Maoris of Waikato built their redoubt and dug out their rifle-pits and trenches to resist General Cameron. On the west side sweeps the Waikato River, here a full third of a mile wide. The Great South Road, running west of the railway, traverses the battlefield. Half a mile before reaching Rangiriri Township going south from Auckland the traveller motors or rides over the actual site of the entrenchments. The central redoubt of Rangiriri was just on the western side of the present road. The trenches and rifle-pits extended down the slopes on either side to the Waikato on the west and to the small lake on the east. The long double trench and parapet on the north (or front) face of the position can still be traced from the hilltop; it is about three-quarters of a mile in length, stretching from water to water. The redoubt in the centre of the works, the apex of the ridge, is indicated by a ditch still about 6 feet deep, with a parapet extending westward over the crown of the hill.

In rear of the left centre of the main line and at right angles to it there was a line of trenches and rifle-pits parallel to the Waikato River, designed to resist troops landing from the war-steamers. In rear again and some distance from the *pa* there was a separate earthwork on the spur, the southern terminal of the ridge. This work General Cameron had observed on a reconnaissance, and arranged to attack it by landing a force from the steamers simultaneously with the land attack on the front of the main position. The distance between the central redoubt on the ridge and this entrenchment in rear immediately overlooking the swamps and lakes was about 500 yards. The whole of the Kingite defences consisted of earthworks; no palisading was used.

General Cameron, after reconnoitring Rangiriri on the 18th November in the "Pioneer," moved against the Kingite stronghold on the 20th. The whole of the river fleet was engaged in taking up sailors and soldiers from the Manga-tawhiri, while the troops encamped at Meremere and Takapau marched up along the right bank of the river. The "Pioneer" and "Avon" brought up the headquarters of the 40th Regiment, about 320 strong. In tow of the steamers were the four armoured gunboats filled with men. Commodore Sir William Wiseman commanded the flotilla. A Naval Brigade of a hundred men, under Lieutenant Alexander, of H.M.S. "Curaçoa," marched up the bank with the infantry column. The force which assembled on the north front of the Rangiriri ridge at 3 o'clock in the afternoon after a hot march totalled about 850, made up as follows: Royal Navy, 100 officers and men, with a 6-pounder Armstrong; Royal Engineers, 15; Royal Artillery, 54, with two Armstrong guns; 12th Regiment, 112; 14th Regiment, 186; 65th Regiment, 386. On the river side of the operations much delay was caused, as the "Pioneer" became unmanageable and was not able to anchor at the point arranged, owing to the powerful current of the flooded Waikato and the strong wind blowing.

The attack began with an artillery bombardment at a range of about 700 yards. The three Armstrong guns shelled the Maori works for nearly two hours; a fire was also directed on the *pa* from the gunboats. The solid earthworks suffered very little from the shelling, but many casualties were inflicted on the Maoris crowded in their trenches and pits. The heaviest gun employed was a 12-pounder Armstrong. Then General Cameron, concluding that this artillery preparation was sufficient, ordered an assault of the Kingite trenches. For this task the 65th Regiment was detailed. The leading company, under Lieutenant Toker, carried scaling-ladders and planks; with the stormers was a small detachment of the Royal Engineers, under Captain Brooke. Three companies of the 65th followed, with the 14th in support. The storming-party, with fixed bayonets at the charge, swept gallantly up the manuka-grown slope of the hill, and quickly forced the defenders out of the first line of entrenchments, but lost several men. A bullet smashed Captain Gresson's right arm.

The Kingite warriors fell back to defend the second line of rifle-pits, and for a few minutes held the position with great determination, but this system of defences also was captured at the point of the bayonet.

320 NEW ZEALAND WARS.

THE MAORI ENTRENCHMENTS AT RANGIRIRI.

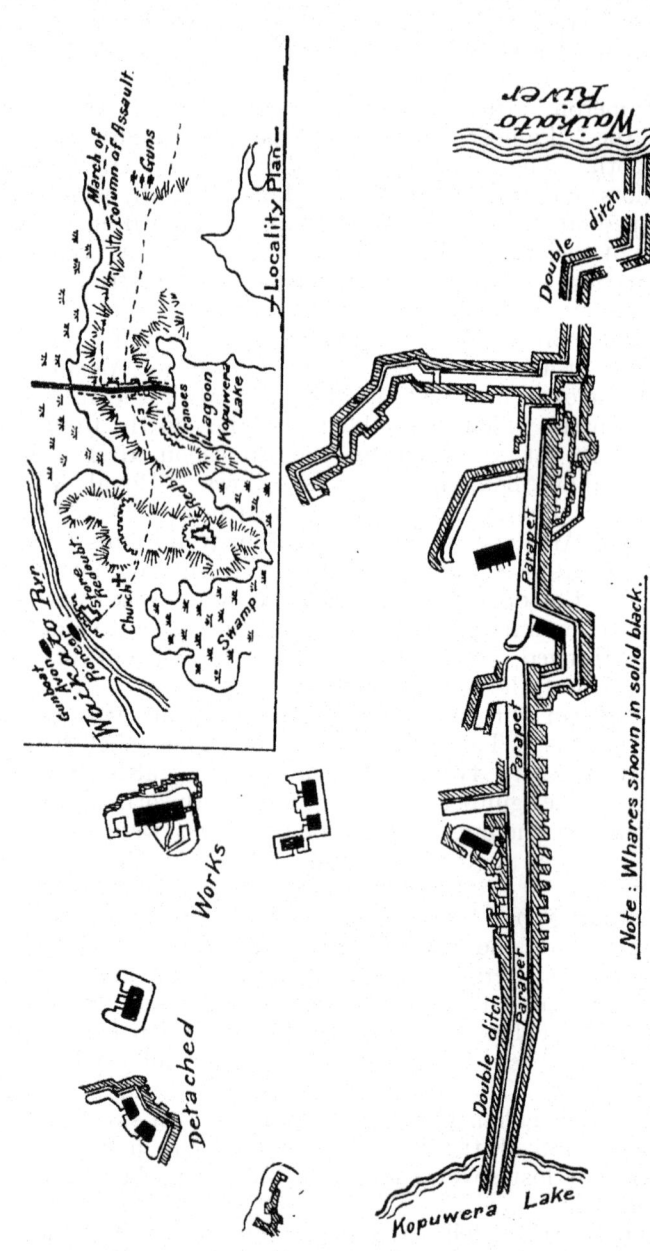

From plans by Captain E. Brooke, R.E., 1863.

THE BATTLE OF RANGIRIRI.

The long lines of outer works were now in the British hands, and the greater number of the defenders crowded into the central redoubt, a rectangular citadel of high and broad parapet surrounded by an unusually wide ditch. The scarp of the earthworks was 17 or 18 feet in height from the bottom of the trench. From the rough banquette inside the rampart the defenders, resting their guns on the top, fired heavily on the troops. Many of the Maoris, however, were unable to reach this redoubt on the hilltop. When the outer trenches were stormed the musketeers on the Maori right flank ran for the lagoon and the swamps in the rear, but were fired on hotly by detachments of the 65th, which pursued them. Some of these were hit and wounded in swimming away, and most of the other fugitives lost their guns.

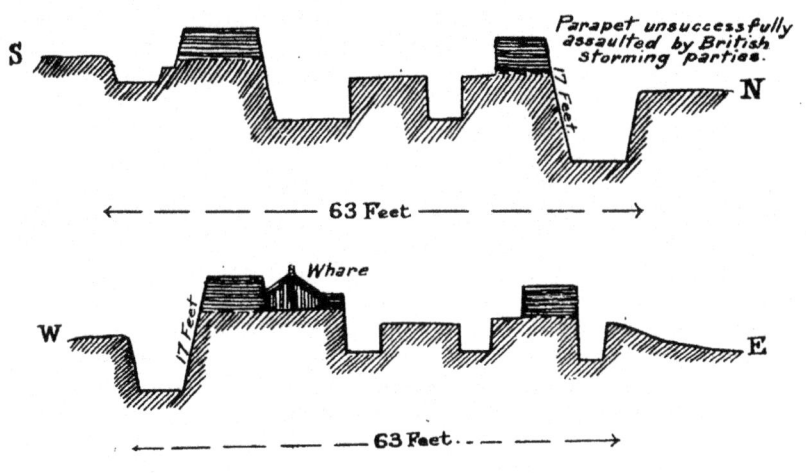

CROSS-SECTIONS OF THE CENTRAL REDOUBT, RANGIRIRI.

The 40th Regiment, late in the afternoon, succeeded in landing from the steamers where the present township of Rangiriri stands, in rear of the *pa*, and attacked and captured a series of entrenchments on a spur above. The defenders of this outwork fled across the swamps and made for Lake Waikare, which they crossed in canoes. A portion of the 65th Regiment now worked round to the Maoris' left rear, crossing the deserted double trench and parapet which extended from the crown of the ridge to the Waikato River. By this time an attempt by the main body of the 65th and the 14th to storm the central redoubt failed, because the ladders brought were too short to reach to the top of the parapets; and although a few did mount the high rampart they were hurled back or shot down.

The Maoris in the main work were now fighting with desperate determination, firing at close range as quickly as they could

11—N.Z. Wars.

load their guns. There were women among them: after the battle a beautiful girl was found lying dead on the hilltop, killed by a fragment of shell.

Late in the afternoon General Cameron issued the most extraordinary order of the day. A detachment of the Royal Artillery, armed with revolvers and swords, was to storm the redoubt. Captain Mercer led thirty-six of his men to the assault. Leaping into the wide trenches, they attempted to gain the top of the parapet, but only one or two succeeded in planting foot upon it. Sergeant-Major Hamilton reached the top and fired his revolver into the Maoris, but was forced back with a severe gunshot wound in the right arm. Captain Mercer fell, mortally wounded, outside the trench; he was shot through the mouth.

This repulse only strengthened Cameron's stubborn resolution to take the redoubt, and another assault was ordered. This time the Royal Navy men were selected for the forlorn hope. Captain Mayne, of H.M.S. "Eclipse," was directed to make a frontal attack with ninety sailors of the Naval Brigade, consisting of portions of the crews of the "Eclipse," "Curaçoa," and "Miranda." The bluejackets, with rifle and cutlass, dashed at the works and endeavoured to swarm up the straight-scarped parapet, but once more the stormers were thrown back, and dead and dying men strewed the ditch and the ground in front of it. A few reached the top of the parapet. Midshipman Watkins was one of them; he fell back into the trench with a bullet through his head. Commander Mayne was severely wounded in the left hip; Lieutenant Downes, of H.M.S. "Miranda," was shot through the left shoulder; and two officers of the "Curaçoa" suffered bad wounds, Lieutenant Alexander in the right shoulder and Lieutenant C. F. Hotham (afterwards Admiral) in the right leg.

When this attack failed a party of seamen, under Commander Phillimore, of the "Curaçoa," charged up to the ditch and threw hand-grenades over into the redoubt, but this attempt did not alter the position. In the Naval Brigade was Midshipman C. G. Foljambe ("Curaçoa"), afterwards Earl of Liverpool and father of a recent Governor of New Zealand. He and his comrades made several attempts to scale the parapet, but the task was hopeless.

It was now almost night, and the General was compelled by the darkness to cease the waste of brave men's lives. The *pa* was surrounded by the troops in readiness to renew the combat in the morning, and sailors and soldiers lay in the main ditch all night listening to the shouts and war-songs of the maddened Maoris, and occasionally returning the fire directed at them from the parapet. Many of the Maoris contrived to escape during

THE BATTLE OF RANGIRIRI.

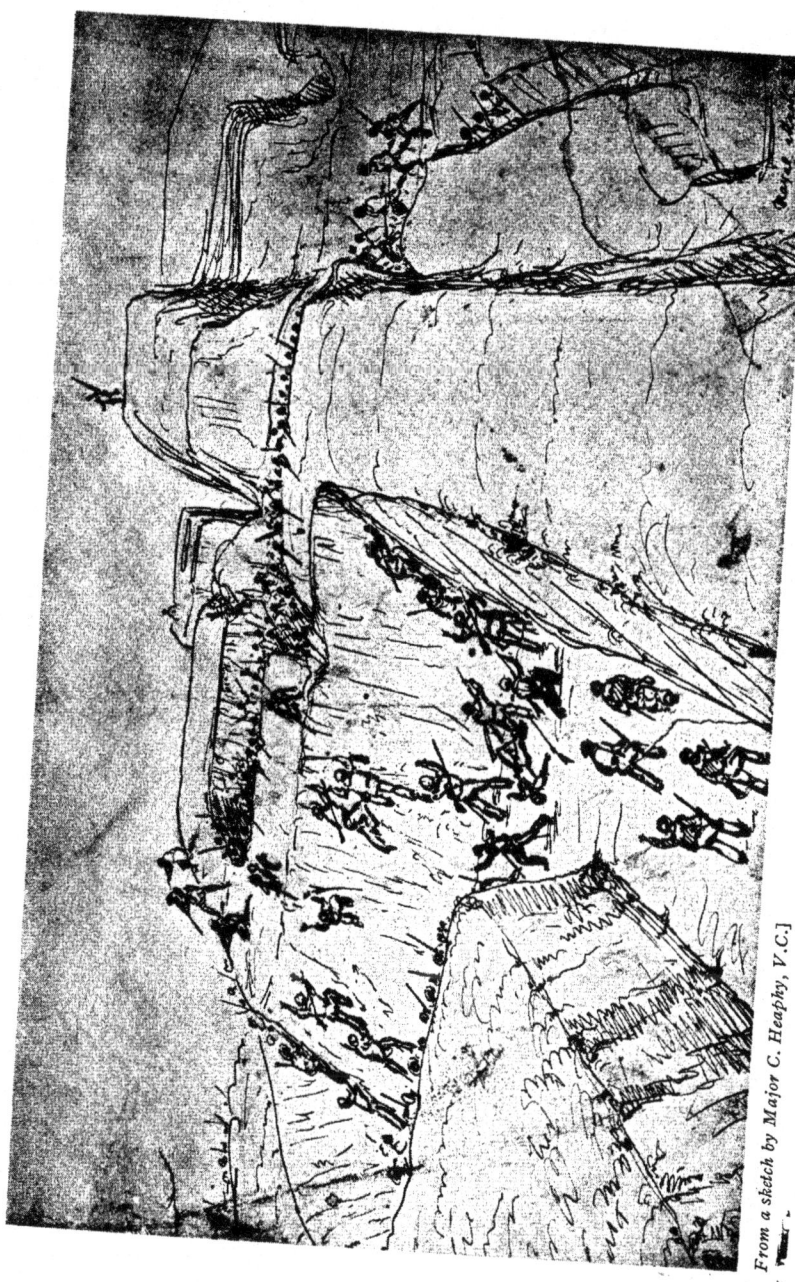

THE REPULSE OF THE ROYAL NAVY STORMING-PARTY, RANGIRIRI PA. (20th November, 1863.)
[From a sketch by Major C. Heaphy, V.C.]

the night ; among them was Te Wharepu, a leading warrior, who was severely wounded. Hand-grenades were thrown into the redoubt in the darkness and caused a number of casualties.

The British casualties in this second Ohaeawai totalled 128. Of this number two officers were killed outright (Mr. Watkins, R.N., and Lieutenant Murphy, 14th Regiment), four died from their wounds (Lieut.-Colonel Austen, 14th, Captain Mercer, R.A., Captain Phelps, 14th, and Ensign Ducrow, 40th), and nine others were wounded. Forty-one men were killed or died of wounds, and seventy-two were wounded. The Maori losses were greater ; thirty-six dead were buried after the capture of the *pa* on the following day, and many were shot or wounded in escaping across the flooded lagoons.

Before daybreak next morning (21st November) the men of the Royal Engineers, under Colonel Mould and Captain Brooke, made an attempt to mine the main *pa*, and a gallery was run in under an angle of the parapet for the purpose of blowing it up and making a breach. It was found, however, that the fuses had been mislaid on board the " Pioneer." Picks and shovels were afterwards used to bring the parapet down, but shortly after daybreak the Maoris ceased firing and hoisted a white flag in token of surrender.

One of the staff interpreters, Mr. Gundry, was sent forward, and after some discussion the principal chiefs, headed by Tioriori, of the Ngati-Koroki (a section of Ngati-Haua), agreed to submit unconditionally. The gallant Tioriori had sustained three wounds when chivalrously attempting to remove a wounded officer out of the line of fire. The defenders surrendered to the number of 183, and gave up 175 stand of arms of varied makes, chiefly double-barrel shot-guns. The troops entered the redoubt —a pitiful scene after the battle—and the prisoners of war were escorted to the native church near the river ; they were afterwards taken down the Waikato in the " Pioneer," and marched from the Manga-tawhiri to Auckland.

Soon after the surrender of the *pa* a large force of Maoris was seen near Paetai, on the south side of the Rangiriri Stream. An interpreter found that they were a body of reinforcements, under Wiremu Tamehana. The leader was desirous of surrendering, and sent his greenstone *mere* to the General as a token of peace. His men, however, were strongly opposed to giving up themselves or their arms, and Tamehana accordingly retired with them to Ngaruawahia.

Many prominent Kingite chiefs were captured when Rangiriri surrendered, besides Tioriori. The Maori of highest rank was Ta Kerei (" Sir Grey ") te Rau-angaanga, a near relative of the Maori King. Others who surrendered were Wiremu Kumete (Whitiora), Tarahawaiki, Te Kihirini, Te Aho, Tapihana (of Kawhia), Wini Kerei, and Maihi Katipa. Te Wharepu, the

THE BATTLE OF RANGIRIRI.

principal engineer in the construction of the *pa*, escaped badly wounded. Among the men of importance killed were Te Tutere, of Ngati-Haua, and Amukete Ta Kerei, son of Ta Kerei te Rau-angaanga. The total Maori loss in killed was between forty and fifty.

A veteran of the Ngati-Tamaoho Tribe says that the principal reason for the surrender of Rangiriri on the second day was the fact that all the ammunition was expended. "The highest chief who remained in the *pa*, Ta Kerei te Rau-angaanga, spoke to the

THE ENTRENCHMENTS AT RANGIRIRI, PRESENT DAY.

This photograph, taken from the site of the central redoubt of Rangiriri *pa* (intersected by the Great South Road), shows the long parapet and double ditch extending westward from the hilltop to the Waikato River.

interpreter sent forward by the General and said, '*Kaore e mau te rongo*' ('Peace shall not be made'). In response to the summons to surrender he declared, 'We will fight on.' Then he made the request, '*Ho mai he paura*' ('Give us some gunpowder'). He thought it would be fair play if the soldiers gave the Maoris some powder to continue the fight. But the interpreter said, 'No.' Ta Kerei and his people therefore decided to surrender."

The same authority says, "Wiremu Kingi te Rangitaake, of Taranaki, was in Rangiriri at the beginning, but retreated when he saw the war-steamers coming up the river."

NOTE.

The Escape from Kawau Island.

On the night of the 11th September, 1864, the Waikato prisoners of war taken at Rangiriri escaped from Kawau Island to the mainland. The escape was planned chiefly by Tapihana, of Kawhia; other leading men in the party were Wi Karamoa (the Waikato lay reader, who was the only man to surrender at Orakau) and Wiremu Kumete te Whitiora, of Ngati-Mahuta. Tioriori and Ta Kerei had been released. The prisoners, after a confinement of many months in the hulk " Marion " in Auckland Harbour, under a guard of fifty Militia (Captain Krippner), had been removed to the Kawau, but no charge was laid against them, nor were they tried by any tribunal. This uncertainty and their home-sickness were quickened by wild reports that they were to be taken out to sea in a vessel and sunk by gun-fire—a story which had gained currency owing to a warship having carried out target practice off the island. Their quarters were near the old sulphur-workings on the Kawau. They were allowed the use of boats for fishing, but the oars and rowlocks were locked up at night. To the number of nearly two hundred they crowded into the boats, taking all the craft on the island, and worked their way across to the nearest point of the mainland with their spades and shovels and pieces of board which they had shaped into paddles. The fugitives landed at Waikauri, and ascended the mountain Otamahua, overlooking Omaha and Matakana. There they entrenched themselves on a narrow ridge commanding a view over the surrounding country for many miles. Their *nikau*-hut camp, partly fenced and ditched around, was about 150 yards in length by 15 to 20 yards in width; on either side were precipices, and the only approach was up a steep spur. Here they watched for pursuers, and were visited by many of the neighbouring Ngapuhi people, who supplied them with food. They were visited also by Government agents and their late keeper, who tried to coax them back to their prison island; but Wiremu Kumete asked sardonically, " How many birds, having escaped from the snare, return to it ? " The Government wisely left them alone, and they presently made their way across to the Kaipara, and thence to West Waikato.

There had been some discussion between the Governor and his Ministers with regard to the treatment of the prisoners from Rangiriri, and some ill-natured critics even professed to believe that Sir George Grey had connived at their escape from his island home, the Kawau. Upon this the entertainer Richard Thatcher, whose topical songs were highly popular among the Auckland audiences of the " sixties," wrote and delivered a song (to the old-fashioned tune of " Nellie Gray "), one verse of which ran—

> Oh, *ka kino!* Hori Grey,
> For you let us get away,
> And you'll never see your Maoris any more;
> Much obliged to you we are,
> And you'll find us in a *pa*
> Rifle-pitted on the Taranaki shore.

CHAPTER XXXVI.

THE ADVANCE ON THE WAIPA.

The trumpet-call of "Boot and saddle" in the cavalry and mounted artillery camps, and the infantry "Assembly" bugle, set all hearts bounding when the news came that Cameron's march for the Upper Waikato had begun. Already large infantry detachments had gone forward from the advanced camp at Rangiriri to Ngaruawahia, where the British flag was hoisted on the 8th December, and the main army was now to be transported into the heart of the Maori country. Horse, foot, and guns streamed southward in the beautiful midsummer weather; in their train came an endless procession of munitions and stores in transport-carts. The river was alive with the steam flotilla and the boats and canoes of the transport service. Bend after bend of the broad Waikato was invaded by the steadily churning gunboat-paddles and the flashing oars of the heavy boats manned by the newly organized Water Transport Corps. The time-songs of Te Wheoro's and Kukutai's friendlies rang like war-cries along the Waikato as they came sweeping up in their long canoes, carrying thirty or forty men apiece, and loaded, like the boats, with commissariat stores. Then, too, one would hear English sea-songs strangely far inland, for most of the *pakeha* Water Transport Corps were sailors, and they chantied as they stretched out on their oars that they would "go no more a-roving," and at their camp-fires they raised the old choruses of "Good-bye, fare you well," and "Rio Grande." And many a man of Jackson's and Von Tempsky's Forest Rangers — now two independent companies — swinging lightheartedly along the bank, joined in the chanties, for a large proportion of the blue-shirted carbineers had at one time or another followed the sea.

Crying their farewells to their old homes and chanting the ancient *tangi* laments over sacred Taupiri, their mountain necropolis, the Kingites abandoned their hold on mid-Waikato and drew off to the open delta that lay between the Horotiu and the Waipa. They realized now that the *pakeha* would not be satisfied until the garden of the Upper Waikato was occupied,

328   NEW ZEALAND WARS.

and that Cameron intended to break the Maoris by cutting them off from their main source of food-supply, the cultivations at Rangiaowhia and the surrounding districts. So, after evacuating Ngaruawahia, they set desperately to work fortifying the principal avenues of approach to the central granary of the Kingitanga. Two main tracks led to Rangiaowhia from the river highways. The usual route was from the Waipa at Te Rore in an easterly direction across the hills of Paterangi and Te Rahu; this was a Maori cart-road used for the transport of wheat and flour to the Auckland market. The other was from Kirikiri-roa (now Hamilton), on the Horotiu—the name for the upper part of the Waikato River, where the current is swift

THE MAORI KING'S CAPITAL, NGARUAWAHIA.

This drawing was made by Lieutenant (afterwards Colonel) H. S. Bates, of the 65th Regiment, staff interpreter, in the early part of 1863, before the war. The sketch shows the junction of the Waikato and Waipa Rivers, and the Kingite village, the site of the present town and railway-station of Ngaruawahia.

and the banks high, from the water-junction at Ngaruawahia to the rapids near the base of the Pukekura Range. There was also a track from Ngaruawahia parallel with the Waipa, passing Tuhikaramea, Whatawhata, and Pikopiko. At Pikopiko (Puketoki) and Paterangi the Maoris now constructed the most formidable systems of redoubts and entrenchments built in this campaign; and in rear again they threw up fortifications almost as strong, at Rangiatea and Manga-pukatea, completely barring the way to Rangiaowhia. Wiremu Tamehana's people, the Ngati-Haua, presently occupied a stronghold of their own at Te Tiki o te Ihingarangi, on the west bank of the Waikato, a short distance above the present Town of Cambridge. Paterangi was the headquarters; here at one time in the early part of 1864 nearly two thousand Maoris were in garrison, the largest Kingite force ever assembled in the war.

The Maoris had made some preparation for the defence of Ngaruawahia. When, on the 8th December, General Cameron's advanced force occupied the abandoned Kingite capital and hoisted the British colours on Tawhiao's flagstaff it was found that some trenches and rifle-pits had been dug on the point of land at the junction of the Horotiu and the Waipa, and a partly constructed earthwork *pa*, 30 yards square, overlooked the mouth of the Waipa, about 200 yards up the bank of that river. A suggestion had also been made to bar the progress of the troops at Taupiri, where the opposing lofty ranges made a grand natural gateway, forested Taupiri on the east side and a spur of the Hakarimata Mountain on the west. But without artillery the defence of these points was hopeless against Cameron's armoured gunboats.

The small steam fleet on the Waikato was now busy transporting troops from a point near Rangiriri to Ngaruawahia, and by the end of 1863 there were nearly three thousand soldiers, Imperial and colonial, assembled at the apex of the Waikato-Waipa delta for the conquest of the territory to the southward. General Cameron moved his field headquarters forward to Tuhikaramea, with the Waipa River on his right flank. By this water highway great quantities of army supplies were hurried to the front. Later, supplies were also brought across by packhorse from Raglan, when the "Avon" was temporarily out of service through striking a snag and sinking in the Waipa. At the end of January Cameron moved the army headquarters forward to Te Rore, three miles from Paterangi, and Colonel Waddy, with six hundred men, took up an advanced position three-quarters of a mile from the *pa*.*

---

* Describing the advance on the Kingites' new positions, Von Tempsky wrote in his journal :—

"On the 27th of January, 1864, the two columns from Tuhikaramea and Whatawhata started on the main road for Pikopiko. For miles and miles now there was an unbroken stream of soldiers, bullock-drays, artillery, packhorses, and orderlies meandering over the plains and fern ridges of the sacred Maori delta. Yellow clouds of dust hovered along our road, to the great disparagement of our faces, sight, and clear speech. We had the special honour to escort on the first day some Armstrong guns dragged by bullocks. On a low backed ridge of considerable width, near a deserted village, the army encamped under their blanket tents. I saw Jackson's blue-blanket tents in the Tuhikaramea column. We had discarded even that trouble and slept in the fern, in line of battle, at the most exposed flank, opposite the bush.

"On the following morning we sighted Pikopiko, and one's heart began to beat as soon as the General began to mass his troops in columns before the Maori stronghold. There it lay, no despicable object even in the eyes of the greatest ignoramus of works of defence. There were the Maoris—at least, their black heads visible on the parapet; here and there sentries walking on the parapet, and again, some fellows dancing on it and waving to us and shouting 'Come on!'

"For more than an hour we were kept in suspense regarding the intentions of the General. (The loyal chief Wiremu Neera, of Raglan, now made his appearance with a party on horseback.) Our suspense was broken at last by the columns filing away to the west, past Pikopiko, towards the Waipa, and this night we camped unmolested near Te Rore. Our encampment extended nearly a mile from the banks of the Waipa to the hills opposite Paterangi. The headquarters were pitched in a grove of fruit-trees on an eminence isolated by gullies on three sides, and at the foot of it the two companies of Forest Rangers were ordered to pitch their camp. We had also charge of a picket guarding the entrance to a valley on the Waipa where all the commissariat stores and munitions of war were kept. We were, moreover, to be ever ready to move to any one point, be it night or be it day; and we felt proud of this kind of honour, and to the last man in the two companies our alertness was never found deficient.

"From our most advanced post, under Colonel Waddy, of the 50th Regiment, you could see the daily life going on at Paterangi. A little battery of Armstrongs kept the alertness of the Maoris somewhat in practice, and from a still more advanced hill a picket amused itself daily by long shots at the Maoris.

"I had a great desire to make a sketch of Paterangi," Von Tempsky continued, "so, getting leave of the General, I took five men with me and started. I had chosen five of my best shots, to keep heads below the parapet while I made my sketch, and I also had chosen them from amongst the new men to see what effect the whistle of a bullet would have upon them. I passed the picket hill, and, leaving my men with Roberts in some fern, I advanced to see how far the Maori sharpshooters would allow me to come. An Enfield bullet striking the ground at my feet soon convinced me that I was far enough. On returning to my men I told them to commence whenever they saw a shot. I also began my sketch. It was not long, however, before another Enfield bullet struck within a foot at my right. I shifted to the left. Another one checked as closely as before my shifting in that direction. However, I persevered with my work, and my men blazed away as happy as larks—till again that same rifle cracked and a bullet struck the ground in front of me. I shifted once more, but got two more close shaves from the same rifle (evidently out of a casemate hole), and having finished my sketch I waved a complimentary adieu to my friend with the Enfield rifle and departed, highly contented with the behaviour of my men and with the acquisition of the sketch, which I had intended for the General."

"It was little wonder," says a veteran of Nixon's Cavalry, "that General Cameron declined to assault Paterangi *pa*. The place was immensely strong. We felt very dubious about it as we watched it week after week and waited for the General's decision. An attempt to storm it would have cost even more lives than Rangiriri." And an Imperial officer who had fought in the Crimea declared, when he inspected the fortifications later

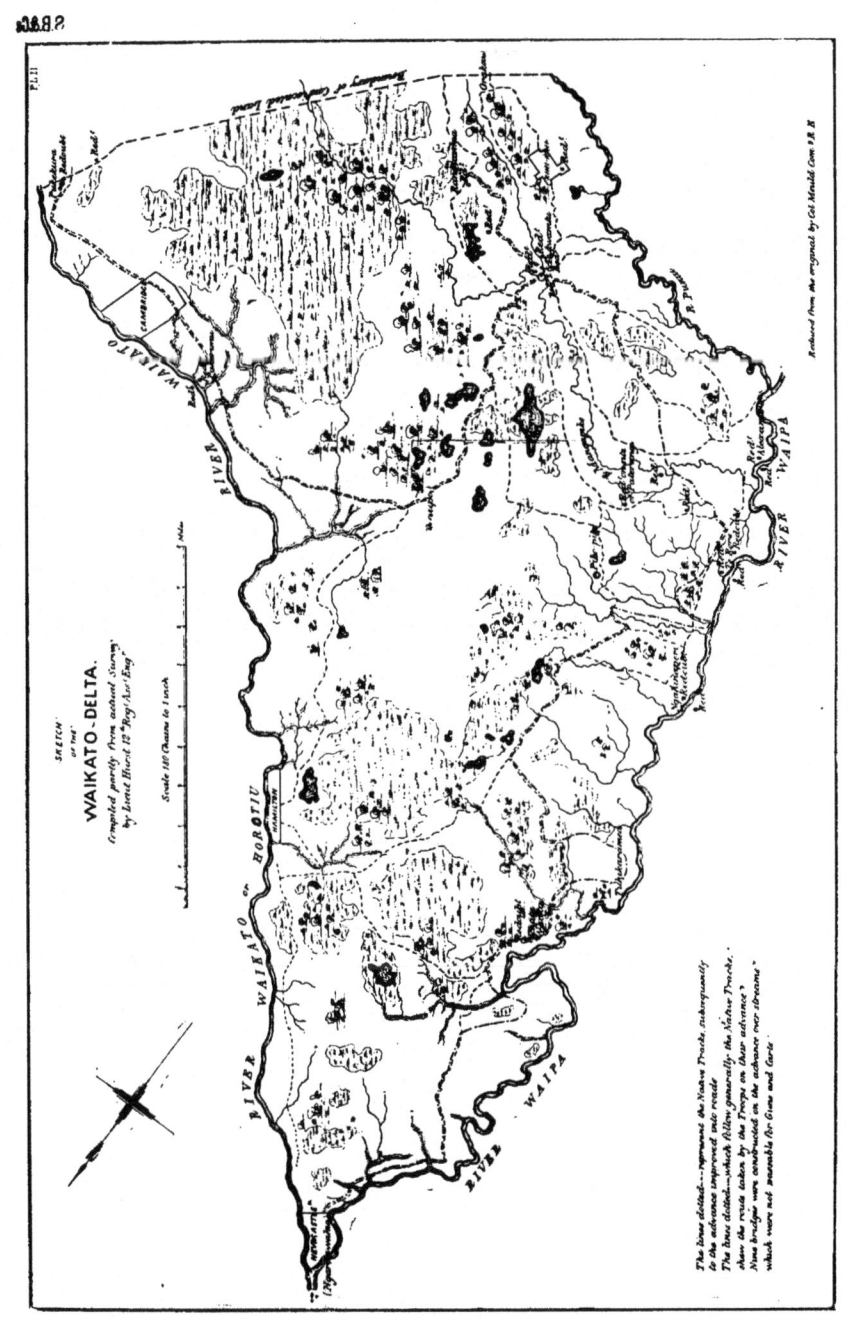

MAP OF THE WAIKATO-WAIPA COUNTRY,

Showing military routes and positions of redoubts, 1864.

From military surveys, 1864.]

in the year, that the Paterangi works were stronger and more skilfully designed than even the Redan. Some of Cameron's staff, like Despard at Ohaeawai, declined to believe that the Maoris were capable of planning such ingenious defences, and imagined that some European must have assisted them. It was difficult to convince some of the Regulars that, like Kawiti and Pene Taui in 1845, the men who drew the lines of the Paterangi redoubts and intricate trench-system, though none of them held a Royal Engineers commission or had gone through a staff college course, were military engineers of a high order.

The Paterangi works occupied a bold and commanding site, formidable of front, with a comparatively open rear. The highest central part only was stockaded; the rest of the works consisted of a network of trenches and parapets. The frontal earthworks were unusually solid and broad; and it was on these parapets that the natives, as they saluted the coming of the troops with a great war-dance, gave many of the troops their first view of the Maori forces in large numbers. The hill-crest which formed the front is the western terminal of a long ridge trending east and west, with low and swampy country on three sides of it. It overlooked the whole valley of the upper Waipa, from the mountain-range of Pirongia on the west to Maunga-tautari on the east. The position can readily be identified to-day, and an exploration of the hill and the sloping ground on the south reveals many traces of the works of 1863-64. As in so many battlefields of the Waikato, a road passes through the middle of the works. This is the road connecting Pirongia and Te Rore, on the Waipa, with the Ohaupo–Te Awamutu main road on the east. Paterangi village and churches are one mile east of the *pa* site, and the Township of Pirongia is three miles to the south-west.

Our plan of Paterangi, from a survey made by Captain Brooke, R.E., in 1864, shows how cleverly the Maori engineers entrenched the whole western and south-western faces of the ridge with works completely blocking an advance over the ground between the flanking swamps. The central works, on the hilltop, consisted of three strong redoubts; the two on the east—separated from the other by the present line of road—were connected with the western hill-crest *pa* by a line of covered way, about 100 yards in length, a deep ditch with a frontal parapet and a roofing of timber and earth. Close to this trench was a deep well. From the south side another trench with a high rampart curved down the hillside and across the road to a hollow under the slopes. In this depression was a spring of water; the trench and the wall, about 10 feet high, protected the water-carriers from observation. Thence the line of ditch and bank extended in a south-easterly direction to the lower hill

THE ADVANCE ON THE WAIPA. 333

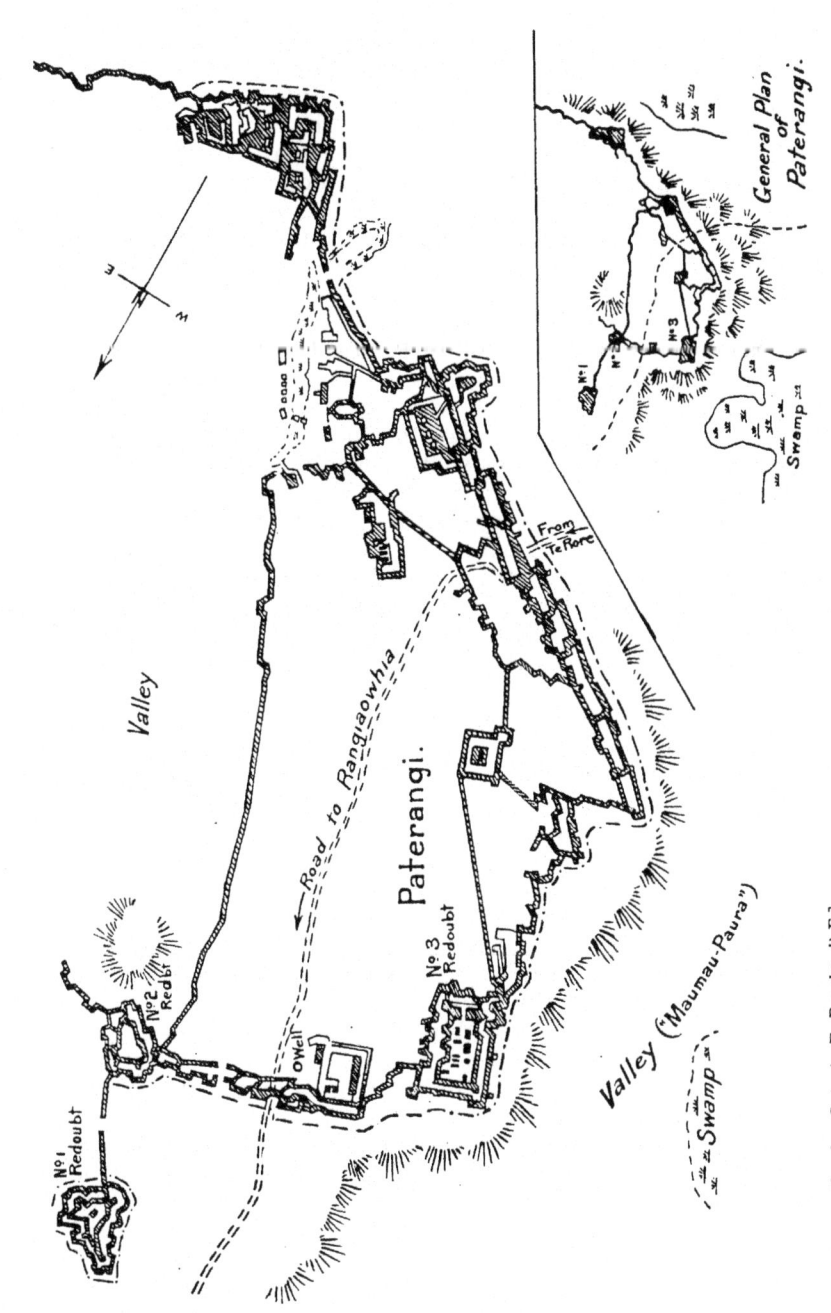

THE MAORI ENTRENCHMENTS AT PATERANGI, 1864.
From a plan by Captain E. Brooke, R.E.

of the ridge, and effectually barred any attempt to mount the ridge on that side. The native cart-road which ran from the Waipa landing at Te Rore through Paterangi to Te Rahu and Rangiaowhia, across which the entrenchments were made, is followed almost exactly by the modern road. A portion of the parapet, about 6 feet high, defending the way to the water-spring, is still standing, on Mr. H. Rhodes's property, "Parekura," on the south-west slope of the hill.

The general outline of the main redoubt and trenches on the level crest are indicated by slight depressions extending over an area of about 2 acres, and on the eastern side of the road the traces of a *pa* converted into a British redoubt after the occapation are equally plain in the turf. Te Huia Raureti, when pointing out the sites of the redoubts, showed a depression in the ground which marked the place where a large shell-proof *whare* was constructed by Ngati-Maniapoto and occupied by Rewi, Raureti, and their party. This slight hollow, retaining the shape of a house-excavation, is near the southern end of the main works on the hilltop west of the road. About it are the traces of other excavations and of parapets. The roofs of some of the shell-proof *ruas* (or dug-in shelters) and *whares* in the *pa* were so strong, covered with heavy timber and with earth, that drays were driven over them. These drays were used by the Maoris in carting in provisions to the *pa* from Rangiaowhia, ten miles in the rear.

On the western side the hill of Paterangi falls steeply to a narrow swamp of *raupo* and *manuka*, on the opposite side of which the land rises into undulating country about 200 feet below the level of the *pa* on the crest. The scrub- and fern-covered slopes here and the swampy valley were the favourite lurking-grounds of the Maoris, who were accustomed to skirmish daily with the troops, without much damage to either side. From the large expenditure of ammunition there the natives gave the place the name of "*Maumau-paura*," or "Waste of gunpowder." The advanced British camp, under Colonel Waddy, was on the slightly rising ground to the south of Maumau-paura and about south-west of the *pa*; the road now passes through the spot, half a mile from the site of the fortification. The Armstrong guns were posted there, and frequently threw shells into Paterangi without inflicting much damage.

Te Huia Raureti states that Rangiatea was the first fortification built for the defence of the Rangiaowhia country. The second *pa* constructed was Manga-pukatea, intended to block the road from Kirikiri-roa via Ohaupo; it was built by Ngati-te-Kohera, from West Taupo. When these forts were completed the united force of the Kingites threw up the large defences of Paterangi. The entrenchments at Pikopiko — usually called

Puketoki (Axe Hill) by the Maoris—were made by Ngati-Apakura and other Waikato tribes; the place is two to three miles north of Paterangi.

As in Meremere, the Kingites in Paterangi derived some moral support from the possession of artillery of a kind. They had two cannon—old ship's guns, originally from Kawhia Harbour. A Ngati-Maniapoto veteran, Pou-patate Huihi, of Te Kopua, who was with Raureti in the Paterangi trenches, says that these guns had been carried overland to Te Kopua long before the war, and stood near the mission station there. They were borne over the Rau-a-moa spur of Pirongia Mountain from Oparau, via Hikurangi, slung on strong poles, which were shouldered by parties of men in frequent reliefs. The guns lay on the bank of the Waipa at Te Kopua for many years. When Paterangi was fortified they were taken down in canoes to Te Rore and carted

From a sketch by Captain E. Brooke, R.E.]

NO. 1 REDOUBT, PATERANGI PA, 1864.

This Maori redoubt was one of a series of strong field-works on Paterangi Hill, connected by lines of trench and parapet. The site is very close to the present homestead of Mr. H. Rhodes. The view is south-west, looking towards No. 3 Redoubt, on the crest of the hill; Mount Pirongia in the distance.

to the fort, where they were mounted behind the parapets (in which there were embrasures) on the south-west front, in a position that would sweep the only road by which the troops could advance. The gunner who had charge of them was Te Retimana, who had had experience with the artillery at Meremere. He was a man of very short stature, belonging to Ngati-Wairangi, a *hapu* of Ngati-Raukawa. Retimana had been in a blacksmith's employ before the war, and spoke English. The cannon were loaded with heavy charges of powder and crammed with pieces of bullock-chain (*tini-kau*), steelyard-weights, and scraps of iron. The little gunner had a small fire burning close by, and in this he had an iron heating, ready to fire the guns. He slept by his artillery; he was ever on the alert for the advance of the soldiers. But the troops did not come within range, to Retimana's great disappointment, and so the guns were never fired. They were reserved for the always-expected rush. The two pieces were

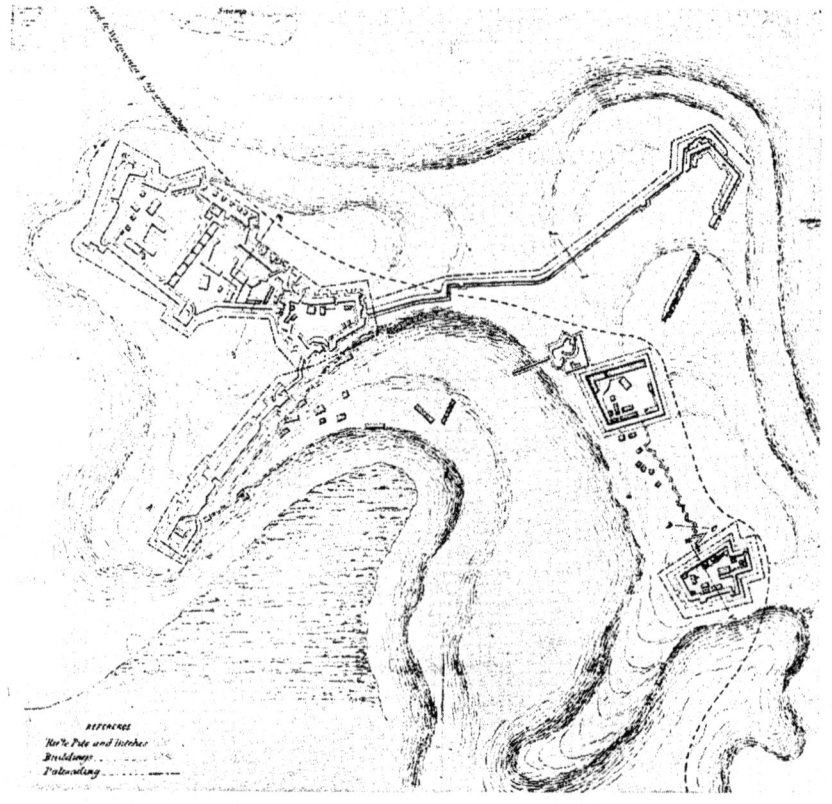

From a plan by Captain E. Brooke, R.E.]

THE MAORI ENTRENCHMENTS AT PIKOPIKO (PUKETOKI).

within a few yards of each other, one on either side of the road. Stout sections of tree-trunks were sunk in the ground, and each gun was made fast to these posts with *aka* vines, in lieu of rope breeching, to prevent capsize from the recoil. One of the guns now lies in the disused well on the eastern side of the road.

Rangiatea *pa*, a strong fortification, was built in rear (eastward) of Paterangi in order to cover more effectually the sources of food-supply at Rangiaowhia. The *pa* was on the crown of a narrow ridge of land, and the trenches ran down to a deep swamp on one hand and the swampy border of the Ngaroto lakes —now partly drained—on the other. It was along this ridge, the prolongation of the Paterangi high ground, that the Maori cart-road passed from Rangiaowhia to Paterangi and to the canoe-landing at Te Rore. The present road from Pirongia and Paterangi eastward to the Ohaupo – Te Awamutu main road and Te Rahu passes through the Rangiatea works, long since obliterated by the road and by filling-in and ploughing. The spot is on Mr. W. Taylor's farm, a quarter of a mile west of the junction of the Paterangi, Te Awamutu, and Ohaupo Roads. On Mr. George Finch's farm, along the same road, near the Lake Road Station, are the tree-covered remains of a fort named Tauranga-mirimiri, occupied for a time during the war period 1863-64. The position is on a commanding hill, with the Ngaroto lakes below on the northern side. Near the eminence known as "Green Hill," overlooking Te Awamutu, there was a Maori settlement named Te Rua-kotare, but this was not occupied as a fortification.

The Engagement at Waiari.

As the expected assault on Paterangi was never delivered, the fighting was mostly long-range sniping, varied by occasional shelling from the British guns; but the period of waiting for action was relieved on the 11th February, 1864, by a sharp skirmish at Waiari, on the Mangapiko River, a mile south of the fortifications. In this encounter five soldiers and forty-one Maoris were killed. The central scene of the engagement is an ancient earthwork fortification of the Ngati-Apakura Tribe, built in a loop of the Mangapiko. The river doubles back on itself here, and across the narrow neck of land on the left bank of the stream are three lines of very high and broad parapet and deep ditches. Covered with thick *manuka* and fern in 1864, the place is in very much the same jungly condition to-day. Just above the *pa* the river is very narrow, at one place not more than 15 feet in width, and across this deep run at the time of the fight there lay a precarious Maori bridge, a single tree-trunk, smoothed on the upper surface. A short distance from the old fortress was a large pool which the soldiers in Colonel Waddy's advanced camp used as a bathing-place.

Colonel Waddy's camp, the most advanced British post, was situated on a hill with an abrupt front towards Paterangi, and a gentle slope at the back where the tents of the 40th and 50th were pitched, sheltered from Maori bullets. The native scouts reported that if they worked round to the rear of the hill they would be able to surprise the camp by night from that side.

The Paterangi leaders therefore planned an attack to be delivered by about a hundred warriors, who could conceal themselves during the day at the Mangapiko Creek, below the camp. After their first volleys on the camp in the night they were to be supported by large bodies from Paterangi. However, Colonel Waddy had sent that day a large bathing-party of the 40th Regiment to the creek. The Maoris were hidden in the bushes on the south side, close to the water and a short distance from Waiari *pa*. They could not resist firing on the bathing-party and the small covering detachment of soldiers. The soldiers were

From a water-colour drawing by Major Von Tempsky, 1864.]

THE FOREST RANGERS AT WAIARI.

(11th February, 1864.)

soon reinforced by two hundred men of the 40th and 50th from the advanced camp, under Lieut.-Colonel Havelock. With the reinforcements came Captain William Jackson, of No. 1 Company Forest Rangers, and Captain C. Heaphy, of the Auckland Rifle Volunteers. In the skirmishing that followed Jackson shot a Maori in the river, and secured his double-barrel gun.

Some of the troops crossed the stream and closely engaged the Maoris in the *manuka* and fern; others fired across the narrow gully of the river. The natives were driven down-stream and took cover in the overgrown ditches of Waiari.

Reinforcements were hurrying down from Paterangi and threatening the British rear and flanks. Von Tempsky and half of the Forest Rangers were in their camp at Te Rore, two miles away, when the firing began, but with their usual eagerness they rushed off at their utmost speed when the news of the fight reached them. Colonel Havelock, carbine in hand, was directing the attack when Von Tempsky and his panting Rangers reached the southern side of the Mangapiko. He requested Von Tempsky

Photo by J. Cowan, 1920.]
THE MANGAPIKO RIVER AND WAIARI.
(From the north bank.)

to clear out some Maoris who had taken cover in the thicket that filled an olden trench in the rear of the British party, and away the Rangers went. "A ditch of the breastwork of an ancient *pa* sloped down into the river," Von Tempsky wrote. "It was densely covered with scrub, as well as the banks of the river. My men bounded down into it like tigers. On our hands and knees we had to creep, revolver in hand, looking for our invisible foes. The thumping of double-barrel guns around us announced soon that we were in the midst of the nest. I had in all about thirty men. Some were stationed on the top of the bank, others in the very river, and the rest crawling through the scrub. There were some strange meetings in that scrub. Muzzle to muzzle, the shot of despair, the repeating cracks of revolvers and carbine thuds, and the brown bodies of Maoris made their appearance gradually, either rolling down the hill or being dragged out of the scrub."

It was nearly dark by the time the old *pa* was finally cleared of the Maoris, and the troops returned to camp, skirmishing with large bodies of Maoris under cover of low bush and *manuka* on the right flank of the route. The Rangers covered the return of the force and remained in action until darkness fell.

Soon after the battle opened at Waiari Captain Charles Heaphy, of the Auckland Rifle Volunteers, performed a deed for which he was promoted to Major, and received the only Victoria Cross awarded to a colonial soldier in the Maori wars. Heaphy was attached to the force as staff surveyor. He had arrived in the colony in 1839 as one of the New Zealand Company's survey staff, and had distinguished himself as an explorer in the South Island. While trying to rescue a wounded soldier he raised the man's head in his arms, and in doing so received a volley from thick cover, at close range, five bullets grazing and contusing him. A soldier of the 40th came to his assistance, and Heaphy directed others to where the natives were; five of the Maoris were shot.

The Maoris who fell in this skirmish numbered forty-one. Twenty-eight bodies were counted; others fell in the river. Two wounded prisoners were taken. Many of those engaged were Kawhia men who had only recently arrived at Paterangi. One of their principal chiefs killed was Te Munu Waitai, of Ngati-Hikairo; others were Taati, Te Kerei, Taare, Te Kariri, and Hone Ropiha (Ngati-Maniapoto). Some of the dead were buried on the north side of the river, and close to their graves the troops, soon after this fight, built a redoubt to guard the crossing at Waiari. The parapets and trench of this redoubt (on Mr. H. Rhodes's farm) are still well preserved, and are marked by a grove of acacia.

CHAPTER XXXVII.

THE INVASION OF RANGIAOWHIA.

The summer of 1864 was well advanced before General Cameron found himself able to execute the final strategic movement of the campaign, the outflanking of the Kingites' heavy defences at Paterangi and Rangiatea. Two half-caste guides attached to headquarters, James Edwards and John Gage, who had lived in Rangiaowhia and Kihikihi before the war, furnished the staff with detailed information about the country, and a surprise expedition was planned to advance on the Maoris' chief sources of food-supply by way of the mission settlement at Te Awamutu. The forward move was made under cover of darkness on the 20th February. At half-past 10 o'clock at night a force of nearly a thousand men (about half the troops at head quarters) fell in at Te Rore; the others were to follow in the daytime with the baggage and supplies, leaving a sufficient garrison in front of Paterangi. The utmost silence was preserved. No bugle sounded; the swords and bridle-chains of the cavalry were muffled with cloth. The advance-guard, commanded by Captain Von Tempsky, consisted of No. 2 Company of the Forest Rangers, with one hundred men of the 65th Regiment, under Lieutenant Tabuteau; Colonel Nixon's Colonial Defence Force Cavalry corps and Rait's Mounted Artillery, doing duty as cavalry, followed. The main infantry body was composed of detachments of the 50th, 65th, and 70th Regiments, with No. 1 Company of the Forest Rangers as rearguard. The guide was Mr. Edwards ("Himi Manuao" of the Maoris). The route was via Waiari, where the Mangapiko was crossed, thence well across the fern ridges to Te Awamutu, passing near the old *pa* Otawhao (in the neighbourhood of the present railway station at Te Awamutu). Bishop Selwyn rode with General Cameron. The spire of the Rev. John Morgan's mission church was in sight at daylight. The troops made no halt at Te Awamutu, but pushed on to Rangiaowhia, three miles distant, along a hilly road above the deep swamps and *kahikatea* forest that fringed the Manga-o-Hoi Stream. The ridge of Hairini surmounted, about a mile and a half from the mission station, the large unfortified settlement of Rangiaowhia came in sight, a scene of peace and beauty. Fields of wheat, maize, and potatoes extended over long gentle slopes, and peach-groves shading clusters of thatched houses were scattered along a green hill trending north

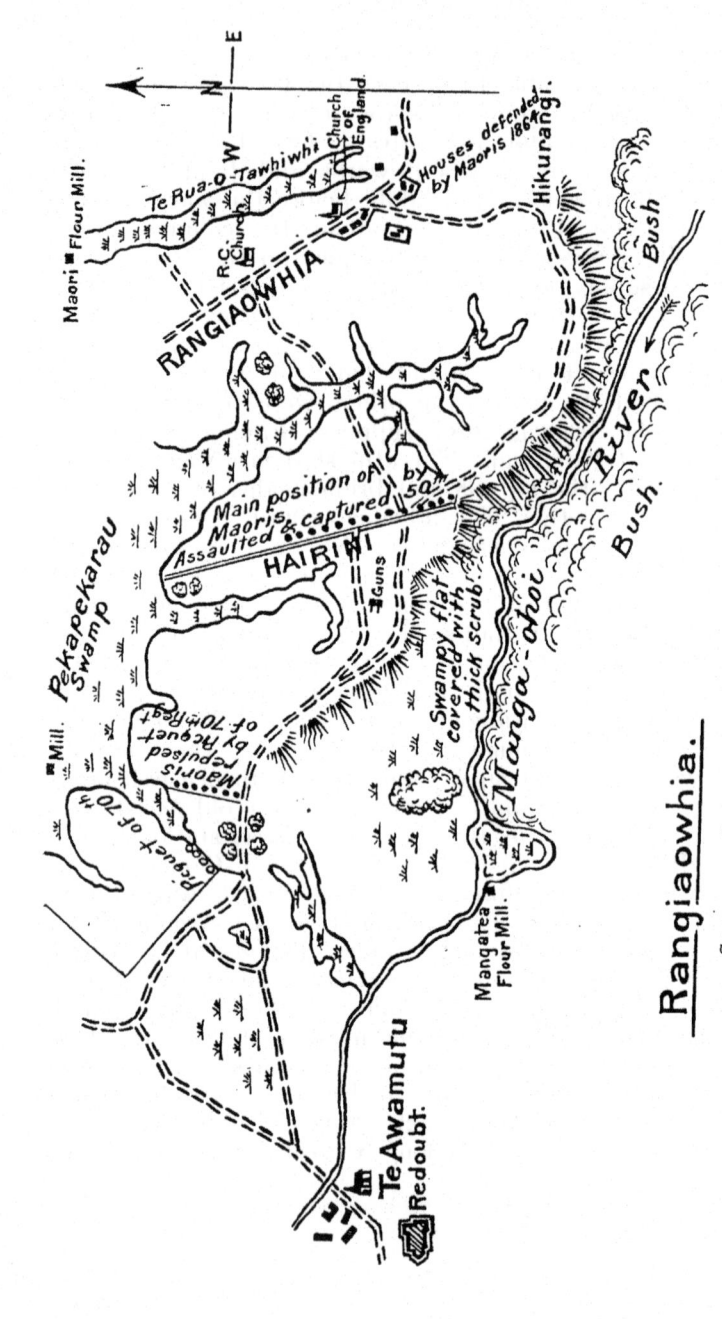

Rangiaowhia.

SCENE OF OPERATIONS AT RANGIAOWHIA AND HAIRINI,
Showing positions captured by the British on the 21st and 22nd February, 1864.

and south, the crown of the village, with the steeples of two churches rising above the trees, a quarter of a mile apart. In the swampy and part-wooded valley of Pekapeka-rau, below on the left as the invading army marched along the southern rim of the Rangiaowhia basin, the morning mists curled up from the *raupo*-bordered waters of a little lagoon, the dam which supplied the power for a flour-mill.

Nixon's cavalry galloped ahead, and the crack of carbines and popping of revolvers, replied to with double-barrel guns, broke the quiet of Rangiaowhia. The main forces of the Kingites were in Paterangi and Pikopiko; those occupying Rangiaowhia were chiefly people of the Ngati-Apakura and Ngati-Hinetu sections of Waikato, engaged in supplying food to the garrisons at the front. There were about a hundred men in the settlement, with many women and children. Alongside the road, lined with *whares* extending from the south end of the village to the hill on the north where the Roman Catholic church dominated Rangiaowhia, great quantities of food were laid out—potatoes, *kumara*, pigs, and fowls—packed ready for carting to Paterangi. The Maoris, recovering from their first astonishment at the attack, took cover in their *raupo* huts and in one or two houses of sawn timber, and opened fire on the cavalrymen. The Rangers were soon up in the centre of the village, followed by the 65th, and the skirmish spread along the street between the rows of houses. The cavalry gave their attention to some large *whares* to the south and south-east of the English church; these houses, one of which was the home of the chief Ihaia ("Isaiah"), of Ngati-Apakura, were clustered at a spot called Tau-ki-tua, about the head of a long swampy valley which extended in a northerly direction; a little to the south was Tioriori *kainga*. Lower down this valley, the Rua-o-Tawhiwhi, was a flour-mill similar to that at Pekapeka-rau. The Forest Rangers found the Roman Catholic church crowning the mound at the north end of the settlement, called Karanga-paihau, crammed with armed Maoris, who showed a white flag, and so were not pressed further. In rear of the church, surrounded by lines of *whanake* or cabbage-trees (these *whanake*, now grown to enormous trees, still adorn the old village-site), was the *kainga* Te Reinga, the headquarters of Hoani Papita ("John the Baptist") and his people of Ngati-Hinetu. Between the church and this settlement was the house of the priest of the district. The Rangers, fired at here and there from *whares*—one or two of these snipers were women—hurried down to the right, where heavy firing was now going on. The English church, too, was filled with Maoris, and some shots came from the windows, but the action centred in one of the large houses on the slope above the spring at the head of the little valley. Close by was a house which belonged to a European, a man named Thomas Power, who had a Maori wife. In both of these houses a number of Maoris had taken refuge.

344   NEW ZEALAND WARS.

Colonel Nixon's cavalrymen, dismounting, surrounded the *whares* near the swamp-head (the spot is in the angle formed by the junction of the present Kihikihi–Rangiaowhia main road and the road eastward from Te Awamutu to Puahue and Panehakua). The Colonel sent Lieutenant McDonnell and Ensign William G. Mair (interpreter—afterwards Major Mair) to summon the Maoris in the large house to surrender, assuring them of good treatment. The reply was a volley. Then began independent firing from scores of carbines, rifles, and revolvers, perforating the *raupo* walls of the house everywhere; the troops were drawn round the place on three sides. The

THE ENGLISH CHURCH AT RANGIAOWHIA.

This historic mission church was built for the Ngati-Apakura people some years before the Waikato War, and was one of many churches established under the first Bishop Selwyn. It is now used by the European residents of Rangiaowhia and Hairini. The principal scene of the fighting on the 21st February, 1864, was a short distance to the right of the picture, and many Maoris took refuge in the church.

occupants of the *whare*, however, had good cover for a time, as the interior was excavated a foot or two below the level of the ground outside, and, crouching on the floor, the Maoris could deliver their fire through holes in the bottom of the walls, as in a shallow rifle-pit. An excited cavalryman, Sergeant McHale, rushed forward eager to storm the *whare*. He reached the low doorway, and was stooping firing into it with his revolver when he was shot dead and dragged inside. A 65th soldier was also shot dead in front of the house. The Maoris secured McHale's carbine and revolver, with about twenty rounds of carbine ammunition, and, using the captured firearms and their own guns, continued their resistance. Hundreds of shots were poured into the *whare*, and Colonel Nixon himself fired into it with his revolver. He was shot through the lungs from the open doorway, and fell in front of the house. McDonnell and Mair ran to his assistance, and Mair pulled off a door from a hut and laid the mortally wounded colonel on it. Some of the neighbouring *whares* were now on fire, either ignited by the firing through the thatch or set on fire by the troopers.

From a drawing by J. A. Wilson, 1864.]

THE FIGHT AT RANGIAOWHIA.

(21st February, 1864.)

The soldier shown falling is Colonel Marmaduke Nixon, commanding the Colonial Defence Force Cavalry, who was shot from the doorway of the Maori house in the middle of the picture.

Von Tempsky came running up with his Rangers, and, followed by a dozen of his men, rushed at the doorway of the large *whare*. Sergeant Carron thrust his head into the low doorway, seeking a target in the gloom of the house, but could see nothing at which to fire. At this moment Corporal Alexander, of the Colonial Defence Force Cavalry, ran up and, crouching at the open door, was about to fire his carbine into the house when he was shot dead. The Rangers dragged the dead corporal away from the door, and Von Tempsky quickly fired the five shots of his revolver into the corner from which he had heard the last report. Then he pulled the body of the 65th soldier away and drew his men off a little distance. One of the Rangers, a young Canadian named John Ballender—a surgeon by profession, and a very brave fellow and a fine shot—fell wounded in the hip; he died from his injury some months later. Four cavalrymen, including Sergeant Hutchinson and Trooper E. Mellon, rushed forward with a stretcher and carried Colonel Nixon out of the line of fire. Then they went back for Trooper Alexander, who was lying outside the door shot through the throat. The shot had been fired at so short a range — only a few feet — that his whiskers were burned by the powder-flash.

The garrison *whare* was now on fire, like the neighbouring huts. A veteran of the cavalry says that one of the troopers had run round to the rear of the hut and set it alight; but an old Forest Ranger considers that the thatch may have been ignited by the firing. "We put the muzzles of our carbines close to the *raupo* walls," he says, "and fired through the thatch. The Maoris inside were doing the same, and naturally the inflammable walls would soon catch fire from the flash and the burning wadding."

The flames at last drove one of the occupants out. A tall old man, clothed in a white blanket, which he was holding about his head, emerged from the doorway of the burning house. His upstretched arms showed that he had no weapon. He advanced towards the crescent of troops in surrender, facing a hundred levelled rifles. "Spare him, spare him!" shouted the nearest officers. But next moment there was a thunder of shots. Staggering from the bullets, the old hero recovered his poise for an instant, stood still with an expression of calm, sad dignity, then swayed slowly and fell to the ground dead. The episode enraged the chivalrous officers who had entreated quarter for him, and young St. Hill, of the General's staff, pointed to a soldier of the 65th Regiment and shouted, "Arrest that man! I saw him fire!" But Leveson-Gower, the captain of the detachment, replied, "No, I'll not arrest him; he was not the only one who fired." The truth was that the troops clustered promiscuously about the burning houses were not under the immediate control of their officers at the moment of the Maori's surrender; and there were many who burned to avenge the fall of their beloved Colonel Nixon.

No more Maoris surrendered after that sacrifice. The house was now wrapped in flames. A man stepped out of the pit of death, stood in front of the doorway, and fired his last shots from his double-barrel gun. A volley from the soldiers, and he fell dead. Yet another appeared from the doorway and was shot dead while aiming at his foes. The burning house crashed and fell inward. When the troops were able to approach it they found in the smoking ruins the charred bodies of Sergeant McHale and seven Maoris. The brave little garrison had numbered ten, opposed to some hundreds of the invaders, and the taking of the *raupo* hut cost, besides, three whites shot dead and two mortally wounded.

None of the other *whares* was defended in this determined manner. About a dozen houses were burned down; some of their occupants had dispersed to the northward, making across the slopes for the Catholic church on the hill; others took refuge in the swamp or fled eastward into the bush. At the Catholic church some of Hoani Papita's men made a short stand. Twenty or thirty of them rushed into the church and fired through the windows, and it was thought at first that they intended standing a siege there, but they discovered that the weatherboards were not bullet-proof. The Rangers and some Regulars attacked, and the church-walls were soon perforated with bullets. At last the defenders dashed out through the door on the northern side, and fled to the swamps.*

Twelve Maoris, including the chiefs Hoani and Ihaia, were killed in the morning's encounter, and above thirty prisoners, some wounded, were taken.

The Battle of Hairini.

The news of the General's surprise expedition and the attack on Rangiaowhia brought the main body of the Waikato and their allies pouring eastward into the invaded village, and a few hours after the fight the leaders were hastily planning the fortifications for the defence of their supply headquarters. They realized now that Paterangi, Pikopiko, and Rangiatea represented so-much heavy labour lost as the result of the British turning movement, and those forts were evacuated immediately. A position was selected for an entrenchment to block the road

---

* Mr. William Johns, of Auckland, who served as a corporal in the Forest Rangers, says, regarding the firing at the Roman Catholic church, Rangiaowhia :—

" The Natives took cover in the Roman Catholic church after most of the *whares* on the lower ground had been cleared of them; the huts were nearly all set on fire by natives firing through the *raupo* walls at the troops. The church was held by them for only a brief period; they retreated quickly before the advancing Forest Rangers and troops. The Rev. Father Vinay, who resided at the church for many years after the war, cleverly effaced and closed up the bullet-holes left in the building during the skirmish, and yet these were long visible upon close inspection. The temporary stand made by the natives in the church formed the closing scene of that morning's encounter.

" A great deal of wild talk arose as to the burning of the Maori *whares* designedly, but the firing of Maori guns and of soldiers' rifles at close range into dry *raupo whares* is a sufficient explanation."

from Te Awamutu to Rangiaowhia. The place chosen was the crest of a ridge at Hairini (" Ireland "), the highest part of the approach to Rangiaowhia from the west. An old line of ditch and bank, fencing in some large cultivations, crossed the crown of the height from north to south. This line the Maoris quickly strengthened on the morning after the invasion of the village, deepening the ditch and converting the bank into a strong parapet, with a stake fence surmounting it. The road was blocked by a rifle-trench with a narrow opening. The entrenchment ran down the hill on the north side—the defenders' right flank— into a deep swamp; on the south side the ditch and bank extended along a slope to the cover of thick bush and *manuka*, which continued thence steeply down to the *kahikatea* forest in the swampy valley of the Manga-o-Hoi. The flanks of the Kingites were thus well protected. Members of many Kingite tribes shared in the work of defence. Besides numerous subtribes of Waikato, there were many Ngati-Maniapoto, one of whose chiefs was Wahanui—a gigantic figure of a man, afterwards the most celebrated orator of the King party—some men of Ngai-te-Rangi from Tauranga, and a contingent of nearly a hundred Urewera warriors, under Piripi te Heuheu, Hapurona Kohi, Te Whenuanui, and Paerau. With the Ngai-te-Rangi was a savage fellow of Ngati-Rangiwewehi from Rotorua, named Kereopa te Rau; he became notorious in the following year as Kereopa Kai-Karu (the " Eye-swallower "), the Hauhau apostle who put the missionary Volkner to death at Opotiki.

On the morning of the 22nd February, the day following the attack on Rangiaowhia, an outlying picket on the north side of the Manga-o-Hoi Stream at Te Awamutu was fired upon by a party of Ngati-Maniapoto from the cover of some *manuka* at Matariki, on the river-bank a short distance above the bridge. The troops in the camp at Te Awamutu had been reinforced by a large body from Te Rore, including the 50th Regiment (under Brevet-Colonel Weare), a detachment of Royal Artillery, and a party of Royal Navy men from the ships at Auckland, with two 6-pounder Armstrong guns and a naval 6-pounder. The soldiers were just preparing for dinner when the " Assembly " sounded. The Colonial Defence Force Cavalry, under Captain Pye, V.C., and Captain Walmsley, led the advance upon Hairini which was now ordered, and the Forest Rangers, as usual where there was fighting in prospect, were well ahead of the other infantry corps. The General, immediately on learning that the natives had taken up a position on Hairini Hill, determined to attack before they had time to strengthen their defences, and early in the afternoon nearly a thousand bayonets flashed back the sun as the column advanced in fours along the narrow road towards the ridge with high fern on either side. (The present

THE BATTLE OF HAIRINI.   349

main road follows exactly this route.) A mile from Te Awamutu the route led under the southern crest of a rather steep spur; below was a gully of scrub and bush and swamp. A Maori skirmish line under cover of a hedge was driven in, and on a hill about 500 yards in front of Hairini height the guns were placed and opened fire on the entrenchments, now manned by five or six hundred men. The infantry went on and halted in the

From a painting by G. Lindauer, in Auckland Municipal Art Gallery.]
WAHANUI HUATARE.

Wahanui, whose home was at Hangatiki, received a slight wound in the fight at Hairini. He was the most prominent chief of Ngati-Maniapoto after the war, and was the leading representative of the Maori King party in the negotiations with the Government.

ferny hollow between the two hills, awaiting the order to storm the position. Just outside the road gateway at the trenches a wild figure leaped and brandished a *taiaha*, yelling defiance at the troops, and encouraged his comrades with cries of "*Riria, riria! Patua, patua!*" ("Fight on, fight on! Strike, kill!") This was Kereopa te Rau. The field-pieces fired shells over the heads of the Forest Rangers (mustering seventy-nine) and the 50th (480 strong)—the 65th were in support, and the 70th Regiment in reserve—and the Maoris all along the line replied heavily with their double-barrel guns. "It was as pretty a bit of hot firing as I have ever seen," says a veteran of Jackson's company of Rangers. "The Armstrongs were sending their shells screeching over us, and the Maori bullets were cutting down the fern near me with as even a swathe almost as you could cut it with a slash-hook. We were lying down within 300 yards of the enemy. At last the 'Charge' was sounded, and away we went, the whole of us, we Rangers making for the Maoris' right flank, and the 50th Regiment, on our right, for the centre. With a great cheer the 50th swept splendidly up to the parapet with bayonets at the charge. We on their left stormed the Maori line on even terms with them; we had no bayonets, but used our revolvers for close-quarters work"

The Kingite warriors maintained a heavy fire, but their bullets flew too high, and as the fatal line of steel approached they broke into confusion and flight. Some raced down to the left into the shelter of the deep swamp on the north side, and struggled across it in the direction of Rangiaowhia; others fled across the hill in the rear and into the cover of the bush on the south.

Now came the opportunity for the cavalry. One detachment of the Colonial Defence, under Captain Walmsley, advanced on the right flank, taking the high ground overlooking the Manga-o-Hoi Valley; the other troop, under Captain Pye, galloped up on the left, crossing a maize-field above the swamp, with its patches of *kahikatea* bush. The trumpet sounded the "Charge," and the troopers rode into the Maoris with their sabres, cutting down a number as they went over them. Some of the warriors bravely faced the horsemen. Captain Pye's men met a volley. "Our detachment," says a veteran of this troop, "got in among a party of Maoris who attempted to resist us. I made a cut with my sword at one man, but he jumped aside and I missed him. As I passed ahead I looked round and saw another trooper, Middleton, running his sword through him. Some of the Maoris ran down on the south side of Hairini, where we could not follow them; others retreated across the swamp at Pekapeka-rau, where the Maori dam and flour-mill were." This was one of the few occasions on which cavalry charges were practicable in the Maori wars. Cavalry were used at Orakau, a few weeks after the Hairini fight; the other principal instances of charges with the sabre occurred at Nukumaru, on the west coast, in 1865, and at Kiorekino, on the Opotiki Flat, in the same year.

The Forest Rangers, under Von Tempsky, meanwhile were firing from a peach-grove on the left upon the Maoris escaping through the swamp, and they, with some of the 50th and the 70th, skirmished up towards Rangiaowhia, where the fighting ended. The village was looted, and the Rangers and many other troops returned to Te Awamutu laden with spoils in the way of food and Maori weapons.

The day's casualties numbered two soldiers killed, one of the Defence Force Cavalry mortally wounded, and fifteen others wounded, including Ensign Doveton, of the 50th. The Maoris lost about a score killed, besides many wounded, some of whom were captured and treated in the field hospital at Te Awamutu. The troops probably would have suffered more severely when doubling along the road to the assault but for the clouds of dust that obscured them.

A British redoubt was built at Rangiaowhia, near the brow of the hill Hikurangi, overlooking the Manga-o-Hoi forest and swamp (the district school now stands close to the spot). The post was garrisoned by a company of the 65th Regiment, under Captain Blewitt. In later years, when the Waikato frontier was threatened by the King Country Hauhaus, a blockhouse was built on the site and held by the armed settlers, some of whom were old Forest Rangers of Jackson's No. 1 Company.

Other Operations.

The whole of the mid-Waikato and the fertile plain of the delta between the Waipa and the Horotiu (upper Waikato River) as far south as the Mangapiko River was now under British occupation. General Cameron left detachments to garrison Te Rore, Pikopiko, and Paterangi, and at Kirikiri-roa, on the Horotiu, established a post which became the present Town of Hamilton. The gunboats "Pioneer" and "Koheroa" steamed up the Horotiu for the first time on the 2nd March, 1864, with a detachment of the 65th, and anchored below the deserted native settlement of Kirikiri-roa. Next day the "Koheroa," under command of an officer of H.M.S. "Eclipse," ascended the strong river as far as Pukerimu, and the officers and surveyors on board made a rapid reconnaissance of the country. Redoubts were built soon after this at Pukerimu and Kirikiri-roa, and were garrisoned by detachments of the 18th and 70th Regiments; later, the settlements were occupied by men of the Waikato Militia. The Ngati-Haua and their allies, including many Ngai-te-Rangi from Tauranga, had now strongly fortified themselves at Te Tiki-o-te-Ihingarangi, where the Pukekura Range, an out-spur of Maunga-tautari, terminates above the precipitous left bank of the Waikato River. Soon after the first visit to Pukerimu the General advanced with a force of several hundred men from Te Awamutu and skirmished towards the Ngati-Haua positions. After a little firing at comparatively long range the troops retired. The *pa* was occupied for several weeks, but at last was evacuated before Cameron had made up his mind to attack it. This was the only strong position in the Waikato country remaining to the Kingites in March. There were now nearly five thousand troops, Imperial and colonial, distributed in the occupied territory; the greater number was encamped at Te Awamutu, where the army spent the winter of 1864.

The headquarters of the Ngati-Maniapoto Tribe, the large village of Kihikihi, three miles south-east of Te Awamutu, was invaded on the 23rd February. It was an attractive place in those days, with its clusters of thatched houses spaced over a considerable area of hill and valley, shaded by peach-groves and surrounded by large cultivations of potatoes and maize which extended in the direction of the Puniu River to the south and to the outskirts of the forest and swamps on the east. Here was Rewi Maniapoto's home; and on the gentle southern slope of Rata-tu Hill, on which the principal settlement stood, was the carved house "Hui-te-Rangiora," in which Rewi and his *runanga* of chiefs had framed the belligerent policy which precipitated the Waikato War. No attempt was made by Ngati-Maniapoto to defend Kihikihi. They could have blocked for a time the advance of the troops from Te Awamutu by entrenching the steep northern and north-west face of the ridge on which Kihikihi stood (the present road ascends this face), and extending the wings of the defences to the swamps on either flank. But Rewi and his people abandoned Kihikihi after the fighting at Rangiaowhia, and, crossing to the south side of the Puniu River, encamped at Tokanui, on the slopes overlooking their old homes. From there they saw the flashing of the bayonets as a body of troops marched into Kihikihi, and presently watched the smoke and flames ascending from their council-house, destroyed by the soldiers. Rewi's flagstaff was also demolished, and the village was looted by the Regulars and the Forest Rangers. A redoubt was soon afterwards built on the crest of the Rata-tu Hill, a commanding site overlooking the whole of the Kihikihi and surrounding country for many miles. This post was first garrisoned by detachments of the line regiments, and afterwards by a force of the 1st Waikato Militia, under Colonel T. M. Haultain.

Numerous scouting expeditions were made from headquarters at Te Awamutu by the Forest Rangers and by the Colonial Defence Force Cavalry. It was after one of the troopers' rides to the neighbourhood of Kihikihi, where Maoris were again seen to be gathering—one was shot at long range by Lieutenant (afterwards Colonel) McDonnell—that it was decided to build the redoubt just mentioned. An expedition marched before daylight one morning, under Colonel Waddy and Colonel Havelock, with the Forest Rangers, as usual, forming the advanced guard, to pay a surprise visit to Kihikihi, but the natives again retired in time. Von Tempsky went on through some maize-fields and skirmished across a swamp with some of the Maoris, but did not get close to them. That night he took the men into the *kahikatea* bush and swamp which flanked Kihikihi, in an attempt to reach the Maoris who had retreated into some distant *whares* on a rise, and after a very rough experience,

Photo by W. Beattie, 1906.]

ST. JOHN'S CHURCH, TE AWAMUTU.

This mission church was built in the early "fifties," when Te Awamutu was the station of the Rev. John Morgan, of the C.M.S., who introduced civilization and English methods of agriculture among the tribes of the Upper Waikato. Mr. Morgan carried on mission work and industrial education here from 1841 until the beginning of the Waikato War. The soldiers who fell at Orakau and other fights in the district were buried in the churchyard.

scrambling through the swamp and jungle in the darkness, reached the *whares* at daylight and rushed them, but found them empty. Sergeant Carron reported that there were Maoris in the bush which nearly surrounded this settlement, a little distance to the eastward of Kihikihi Village. Von Tempsky withdrew his men from the *whares*, and received a harmless volley from the bush-covered hill. He took up a position within 300 yards of the huts, under cover of logs and fern, and awaited a Maori advance, but the Ngati-Maniapoto party wisely remained in their cover. The Rangers returned to Kihikihi, and from the central hill that afternoon they saw some hundreds of Maoris in the distance driving their cattle and horses into safety southward of the Puniu.

NOTES.

The site of Rewi Maniapoto's council-house " Hui-te-Rangiora," burned by the troops, is a little distance to the south-west of the present Presbyterian church in the Kihikihi Township. Near this church is the house which the Government built for Rewi shortly before the Kingites finally made peace in 1881; close to the house at a street-corner is his grave; he died in 1894 The name " Hui-te-Rangiora," celebrated in Maori-Polynesian tradition, is still honoured among Ngati-Maniapoto; it has been given to the house (a gift from the Government) on the south bank of the Puniu River in which Rewi's widow, Te Rohu, now lives.

The redoubt on Rata-tu, the highest part of the Kihikihi ridge, was a military post for about twenty years after its construction. It was occupied as a barracks by the Armed Constabulary, 1870–83, and was an important place in the chain of defences along the frontier against the often-threatened Kingite and Haubau invasions of the Upper Waikato. The lines of the redoubt can be traced just behind the present police-station in Kihikihi Township.

The head of river navigation for the wheat-growers of Kihikihi, the headquarters of Ngati-Maniapoto, was at Tokatoka, afterwards known as Anderson's Crossing, on the Puniu River, about two miles from the village. Large canoes carrying sixty or seventy men could come up the Puniu River in the old days, before it was blocked with willows, and cargoes of wheat and potatoes loaded there were taken down into the Waipa, and thence into the Waikato for Auckland. A mile north of the Tokatoka landing was the flour-mill of the Kihikihi Maoris; the water-power was supplied by a small stream which drained the Whakatau-ringaringa swamp on the west and south-west side of the Kihikihi ridge.

CHAPTER XXXVIII.

THE SIEGE OF ORAKAU.

Three miles to the east of General Cameron's advanced post at Kihikihi the village of Orakau ("the Place of Trees") lay among its fruit-groves and its cultivated fields, gently tilted to the quarter of greatest sunshine. This easy northward-looking slant of the country is a topographical feature particularly marked in these parts of the Waipa basin. The contour of Rangiaowhia, Orakau, and the neighbouring terrain of Otautahanga and Parawera is distinguished by a gradual upward slope to the south, and then a sudden break in a descent of a hundred or two hundred feet to the swamps and wooded levels. The Orakau settlement, a collection of thatched hamlets, was spread over half a square mile of the slopes and plain extending from the ridge called Karaponia, on the south, to the edge of the swamps and *kahikatea* forest through which the Manga-o-Hoi coiled in its sluggish course to join the Mangapiko at Te Awamutu on the west. These swamps and the creek separated the Orakau country from the higher land of Rangiaowhia. To the east the range of Maunga-tautari made a rugged skyline; to the south the blue mountains of Rangitoto marked the source of the Waipa River in the heart of the Ngati-Maniapoto country. The crest of the Orakau ridge broke off abruptly to a *manuka* swamp; from the northern part of this swamp watercourses drained into the Manga-o-Hoi, and from the southern side of the imperceptible watershed the eel-waters flowed toward the Puniu, a clear stream running over a gravelly bed in a westerly course two miles away.

Orakau was an idyllic home for the Maori. Like Rangiaowhia, it was a garden of fruit and root crops. On its slopes were groves of peaches, almonds, apples, quinces, and cherries; grape-vines climbed the trees and the thatched *raupo* houses. Potatoes, *kumara*, maize, melons, pumpkins, and vegetable-marrows were grown plentifully. Good crops of wheat were grown in the "fifties" and early "sixties" on the northward-sloping ground between Karaponia* Hill crest and the groves of Orakau and Te Kawakawa. The Maoris at one time were paid 12s. a bushel for the wheat from Rangiaowhia and Orakau. "Ah," said old Tu Takerei, of Parawera, who was born in Orakau, "it was indeed a beautiful and fruitful place before the war. The food we grew was good and abundant, and the people were strong and healthy—there was no disease among them; those were the days of peace, when men and women died only of extreme old age."

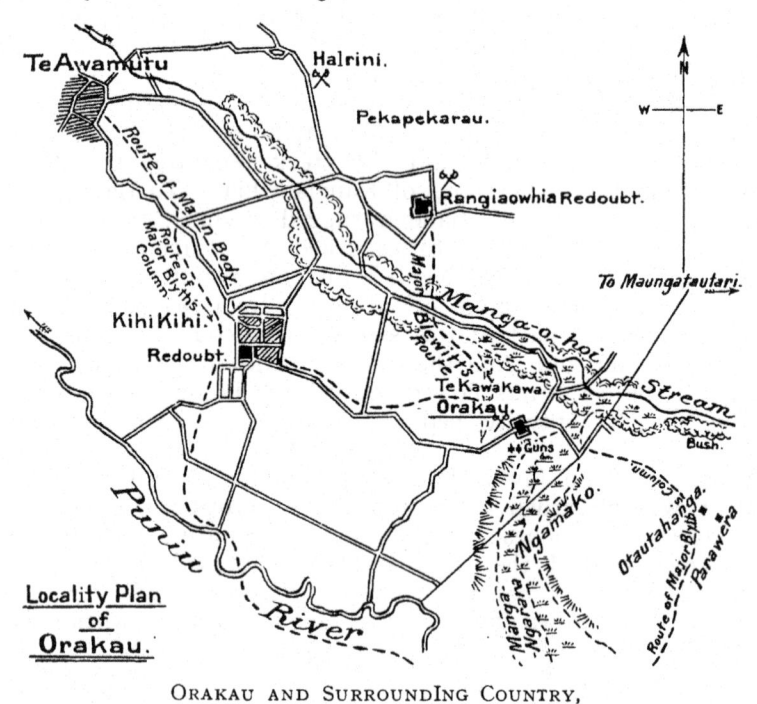

ORAKAU AND SURROUNDING COUNTRY,

Showing the routes of the British march, 1864.

* The name Karaponia ("California"), bestowed upon the hill of the wheat-fields at Orakau, has a curious history. One or two natives of the district who had gone to Auckland in the early "fifties" shipped in a New Zealand vessel bound for San Francisco, where the gold-diggings of the Sacramento had created a demand for wheat, flour, and potatoes from the South Pacific colonies. After trying their luck at the diggings they found their way back to New Zealand, and when they reached their homes narrated their travels to California (Maorified into "Karaponia"). The word appealed to the native ear as a pleasant-sounding name—"*He ingoa rekareka, ingoa ngawari,*" says the Maori. So "Karaponia" presently came to be given to the wheat-farm terminating in the ridge on which the British guns were emplaced in 1864.

THE SIEGE OF ORAKAU. 357

The people of Orakau were the Ngati-Koura *hapu* of Waikato, with a section of Ngati-Raukawa. The focus of the settlement was the Maori church, which stood on the crown of a knoll on the west side above a deep but narrow swamp, through which a small watercourse, the Tautoro, flowed toward the Manga-o-Hoi. (On this elevation Mr. W. A. Cowan, father of the present writer, built his homestead a few years after the battle.) Near the church the chief Te Ao-Katoa, of Ngati-Raukawa, lived before the war. He was a *tohunga* of the ancient Maori school; later, he became a war-priest of the Hauhau fanaticism. To the north a short

THE BATTLEFIELD OF ORAKAU, PRESENT DAY.

The eucalyptus tree in the foreground was planted by the Armed Constabulary in the "seventies" to mark the position of the British Armstrong guns on Karaponia Hill.

distance along the slopes were the *whares* and peach-groves of Te Kawakawa; beyond was Te Ngarahu, where under the acacias on the swamp-edge Dr. R. Hooper lived (1848–63); he had a half-caste wife, and received a small salary from the Government for dispensing medicines to the natives.

Such, before the war, was Orakau, soon to become a place of sadness and glory, the spot where the Kingites made their last hopeless stand for independence, holding heroically to nationalism and a broken cause.

There was a military expedition to Orakau a month before the construction of the *pa* to which the British troops laid siege. This was on the 29th February, 1864, when Colonel Waddy, of the 50th, led a column out from Te Awamutu, six miles away, with the object of dispersing some Maoris who it was reported were digging rifle-pits. The Forest Rangers were in the advance. A little more than half-way between Kihikihi and Orakau (at a spot where the present main road ascends a small hill above a narrow swamp) the Rangers encountered a newly built stake fence; a high bank rose behind it, and the crown of this bank looked suspicious to Von Tempsky. He ordered his men to throw down the fence, making a gap; they then rushed the bank. As expected, there was a line of rifle-pits there; the trenches were masked with branches of *manuka* stuck into the earth. The position was deserted, but a few shots were fired at long range by some Maoris, who fell back on Orakau. The village was abandoned, and the Rangers went through it in skirmishing order. The natives made no stand, but drew off eastward in the direction of Otautahanga, and the troops, after burning some of the *whares*, returned to Te Awamutu.

After the defeats at Rangiaowhia and Hairini, and the British occupation of Kihikihi, Ngati-Maniapoto with some of the other tribes gathered at Tokanui, below the group of terraced hills now called the " Three Sisters." Thence they travelled southward to Otewa, on the Waipa, and from there they were called to a conference at Wharepapa, a large village about three miles south of the Puniu. The gathering discussed two questions : (1) Whether or not the war should be renewed ; (2) whether a fortified position should be taken up on the northern side of the Puniu River or on the southern side. The decision to continue the war was unanimous. As to the site of the new fighting *pa*, it was resolved to confine the war, if possible, to the northern side of the Puniu. Rewi made a proposal to consult Wiremu Tamehana at the stronghold Te Tiki o te Ihingarangi, on the upper Waikato, on the question of the future conduct of the campaign. It was decided to send to the kingmaker and ask his advice, and Rewi and a small party of his men set out for Te Tiki. They marched by way of Ara-titaha, on the southern spur of Maunga-tautari. There they met an Urewera (Tuhoe) war-party, 140 strong, under the chiefs Piripi te Heuheu, Hapurona Kohi, Te Whenuanui (Ngakorau), the old warrior Paerau te Rangi-kai-tupu-ake, Te Reweti (of the Patu-heuheu), Ngahoro (of Ngati-Whare), and Hoani (Tuhoe and Patu-heuheu). Tuhoe proper numbered fifty ; the Ngati-Whare and Patu-heuheu party was also fifty strong. The prophet Penewhio sent two *tohungas*, Hakopa and Tapiki, with the contingent. In the contingent were twenty men of the Ngati-Kahungunu Tribe, from the Wairoa, Hawke's Bay, under Te Waru Tamatea. The main body of this force, numbering a hundred, led by Piripi te Heuheu, had fought in some of the engagements of the war, including Hairini, and had helped to garrison Manga-pukatea and Paterangi. The Ngati-Kahungunu party did not arrive until after Hairini had been fought. About the end of 1863 Rewi had made a recruiting journey to the Rangitaiki country and to the Ngati-Whare and Tuhoe headquarters; there were old ties of friendship between his section of Ngati-Maniapoto and the Warahoe people and some of their Urewera kinsmen. Rewi visited Tauaroa, Ahikereru, and Ruatahuna, accompanied by Te Winitana Tupotahi and Hapi te Hikonga-uira, and aroused the fighting-blood of the mountain tribes by his appeal for assistance and his chanting of two thrilling war-songs. The first was the Taranaki patriotic chant beginning "*Kohea tera maunga e tu mai ra ra?*" ("What is that mountain standing yonder?") referring to Mount Egmont. The second was the song that began "*Puhi kura, puhi kura, puhi kaka*" ("Red plumes, red plumes, plumes of the *kaka*"), his favourite battle-chant. These impassioned war-calls intensely excited the young warriors of Tuhoe, and in spite of the advice of some of the old chiefs they raised a company for the assistance of the Maori King. Two casks of gunpowder were given to Rewi's party. One of these—presented by Harehare, Te Wiremu, and Timoti, of the Ngati-Manawa, at Tauaroa—had been sent from Ohinemuri by the old cannibal warrior Taraia Ngakuti, of Ngati-Tamatera. The *tohungas* had recited charms over the cask of powder to render the contents doubly efficacious against the *pakeha;* and it had been given a name, "Hine-ia-Taraua." Takurua Koro-kai-toke joined Rewi; he was the elder brother of Harehare, the present chief of Ngati-Manawa at Murupara, on the Rangitaiki. He and his wife Rawinia (Lavinia) were both wounded at Orakau. Harehare himself, having no grievance against the Europeans, did not join, saying that he would fight the troops if they invaded the Rangitaiki country, but not otherwise. But Tuhoe and Ngati-Whare entertained no such punctilio; they were eager to make use of their weapons, and would travel far for the pure love of fighting. A small war-party of Tuhoe had already gone to the Waikato. This *taua* consisted of twenty men from Ruatahuna led by Piripi te Heuheu. These warriors assisted Ngati-Maniapoto in the Lower Waikato in the latter part of 1863, but did not share in the defence of Rangiriri, and returned to Ruatahuna. It was then in response to Rewi's appeal for reinforcements that the larger expedition was formed. It numbered a hundred men *(rau taki-tahi).* After Hairini, the Urewera remained at Arohena with Ngati-Raukawa; and the Ngati-te-Kohera section of this tribe was assembled with them at Ara-titaha when Rewi reached that village.

The Urewera chiefs, strongly supported by Ngati-Raukawa, urged that a fort should be built at or near Orakau as a challenge to the troops, and Te Whenuanui chanted a song composed by the chief *tohunga* of the Urewera, prophesying the defeat of the Europeans and the reconquest of the land by the Maoris. Rewi replied that he had no faith in such a prophecy, and proposed that the chiefs should all consult Tamehana before renewing the war. He opposed the suggestion to fortify Orakau, but the Urewera were persistent. Their *tohungas*, Hakopa and Tapiki, said, " Let us go on ; let us challenge the *pakeha* to battle. We are bearing heavy burdens [guns and ammunition] ; let us use them." Rewi angrily replied, " If you Tuhoe persist in your desire for battle I alone will be the survivor " ; and he chanted this song of warning, foretelling defeat :—

> *Tokotokona na te hau tawaho,*
> *Koi toko atu*
> *E kite ai au*
> *I Remu waho ra,*
> *I kite ai au,*
> *I Remutaka ra,*
> *I kite ai au*
> *Mate kuku ki Wai'mata ra e.*
> *Tohungia mai e te kokoreke ra*
> *Katahi nei hoki ka kite*
> *Te karoro o tua wai,*
> *Tu awaawa ra.*
> *Na te kahore anake*
> *E noho toku whenua kei tua,*
> *Tera e whiti ana,*
> *E noho ana,*
> *Ko te koko koroki ata,*
> *" Ki—ki—tau."*

In this chant, a *mata* or prophecy, Rewi in figurative language endeavoured to dissuade Tuhoe from again entering the campaign. He sang of the winds of war, of the enemy troops gathering at the seaports, in the south and on the Waitemata, to sweep over the lands of the people; and concluded with an allusion to the *koko* (tui) singing in the dawn. He was the bird of dawn; by this he meant that he would be the lone survivor of the battle. " But this," says an Urewera survivor, " did not change our purpose, although Rewi repeated his warning and again declared, ' If you persist I alone will be the survivor,' for he had a strong presentiment that we would be defeated."

Rewi, abandoning his visit to Tamehana, gloomily returned to Waikeria. He had dreamed, he told his people, that he was standing outside the church in Orakau and flying a kite, one of the large bird-shaped kites made of *raupo* and adorned with feathers. At first it soared strongly upwards to the clouds; then it broke loose and came to the ground in pieces. The shattering of the kite he interpreted as a portent of the utter defeat of the Maoris. But Rewi's recital of his *matakite*, or vision of omen, did not turn his tribe from their resolve to renew the war; they were burning to join the Urewera and strike another blow in defence of their land. Now, reluctantly and against his better judgment, he acceded to the general wish.

The war-parties united at Otautahanga, and marched to Orakau, two miles to the west, to select a site for the fort. Near Ara-titaha some of the people had begun to fortify a mound called Puke-kai-kahu, but the majority of the warriors demanded that a position be taken up nearer the British advanced post. One important reason for the selection of Orakau was that it was in a convenient position for the supply of food to the garrison.

Only a few of the Waikato people living at Orakau joined in the forlorn hope of the Kingites. The greater number of Ngati-Maniapoto had gone southward for safety, and did not return in time for Orakau, and the war-party of that tribe consisted chiefly of Rewi's immediate kinsmen, in number about fifty. The backbone of the defence was furnished by the war-loving Urewera and Ngati-te-Kohera.

The ground chosen for the fort was the gentle slope of Rangataua, in the midst of the Orakau peach-groves.* Rewi saw the folly of constructing the works in such an exposed position, and urged, now that he had consented to the building of a *pa*, that it should be placed more to the north, on the lower part of the Orakau slopes and close to the *kahikatea* forest of the Manga-o-Hoi; this bush would afford a way of retreat. Others suggested that the site should be near the church at the edge of the hill above the Tautoro swamp on the west; the land here fell rather steeply on the Kihikihi face, and could be entrenched strongly. But these counsels were overruled; and

---

* Pou-patate, of Te Kopua, who was sent as one of the messengers to assemble the people at Wharepuhunga and other places for the defence of Orakau, states that a proposal was made by some of Ngati-Maniapoto, when the refugees were gathering near the Puniu, to build a fort at Kiharoa. This is on the crown of the high ground just to the north of the three round hills at Tokanui, two miles south of the Puniu River, on the road from Kihikihi to Otorohanga. But by this time the chiefs had decided upon Orakau.

Another Maori survivor says that when the warriors gathered at Orakau to select the site of the *pa* it was seen that the crest of the hill at Karaponia was the most suitable spot, but upon consideration it was disapproved because there was no water there, and Rangataua was chosen because it was close to a water-spring and also was in the middle of the food cultivations.

PLAN OF THE BATTLEFIELD OF ORAKAU,

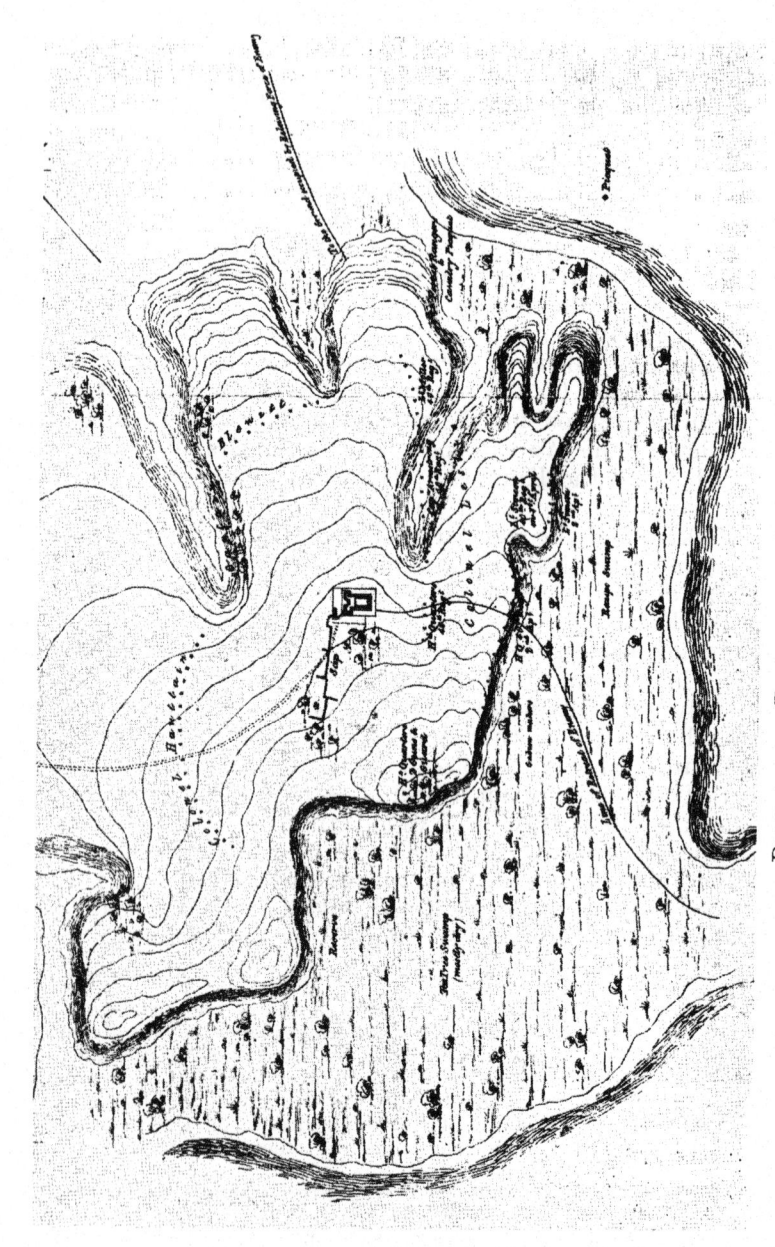

Showing disposition of the British troops, 31st March and 1st and 2nd April, 1864.

on the crown of the slightly rising ground at Rangataua, about 400 yards from the native church and 250 yards from the southern crest of the Karaponia ridge, the lines of the Orakau entrenchments were drawn.

The main work thrown up by the natives, working in relays because there were not sufficient spades, was oblong in figure, about 80 feet in length by 40 feet in width, with its greatest axis north and south. The design was an earthwork redoubt with external trench and a broad parapet, inside which was another ditch, well traversed against an enfilading fire, and converted into a series of *ruas*, or burrows, partly covered over for protection from shell-fire. The main parapet was about 6 feet thick; the height from the bottom of the ditch was 6 to 8 feet. In constructing the rampart the builders used alternate layers of earth and armfuls of newly pulled fern; the fern helped to bind the friable soil, and gave the wall an elastic quality which greatly reinforced its resistance to shot and shell. The interior scheme, divided into a number of *ruas*, also neutralized to some extent the shell-fire; a shell dropped into one of these burrow-like compartments would have a very circumscribed radius of damage. In portions of the earthwork the builders made long horizontal rifle loopholes or embrasures, with sections of board for the upper part and short pieces of timber at the sides. There was no palisading, but surrounding the redoubt was a post and three-rail fence. This fence, harmless-looking enough, was in reality a serious obstacle to any rush; it was partly masked by flax-bushes, high fern, and peach-trees. The *pa* was built in a scattered grove of peach-trees, and the defences were only a few feet above the general level of the ground. Orakau *pa*, flimsy as it was, proved an unexpectedly difficult problem for the assaulting forces.

In advance of the north-west angle of the redoubt, and connected with it by a short trench, a small outwork was built by the Ngati-te-Kohera and Ngati-Parekawa. This bastion was not completed when the attack began, and the outer trench was not more than 3 feet deep. There was a proposal to strengthen the fortifications by constructing another redoubt on the crest of the ridge at Karaponia—where the British headquarters presently were fixed and where a blockhouse was built during the Hauhau wars—and connecting the two works by a parapet and double trench. This would greatly have increased the defensible value of Orakau, but the swiftness of the British attack prevented any extension of the kind.

While the people were entrenching the position several men were sent, on the suggestion of a prophetess, to procure some *otaota* (fern, or leaves of shrubs) from the scene of the bloodshed at Rangiaowhia. The *otaota* was to be used in ceremonies to propitiate the deities and ensure the successful defence of the fort. But the scouts did not reach Rangiaowhia. One of them was shot in an encounter with some troops near the Manga-o-Hoi, and the others returned without the material for the luck-bringing rite.

The builders and defenders of the fort in the peach-groves numbered scarcely more than three hundred; among them were about twenty women and some children. The units were—Urewera, Ngati-Whare, and Ngati-Kahungunu, about 140; Ngati-Raukawa and Ngati-te-Kohera, with a few of Ngati-Tuwharetoa,

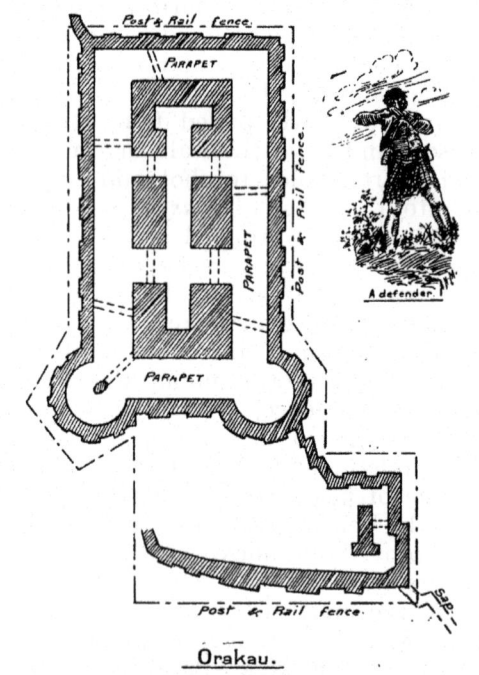

From a sketch-plan by Captain W. N. Greaves, April, 1864.]

PLAN OF ORAKAU PA.

The shaded parts indicate the trenches and the dug-outs for shelter from shell-fire. Maori survivors of Orakau state that this is a more accurate plan of the redoubt than the one which follows. The flanking bastions at the north end are here shown of a rounded form, resembling the plan usually adopted in a British field-work. The defences at the north end (foot of the plan) had not been completed by Ngati-Parekawa and other *hapus* when the troops attacked the position.

about 100; Ngati-Maniapoto, 50; Waikato, 20: approximate total, 310. A number of the wives and sisters of Urewera and other warriors shared in the toil and peril of the enterprise,

THE SIEGE OF ORAKAU. 365

and several of the Orakau families joined the garrison and carried in food-supplies. Ngati-Maniapoto held the south-east angle and the east flank; the Urewera the south-west angle

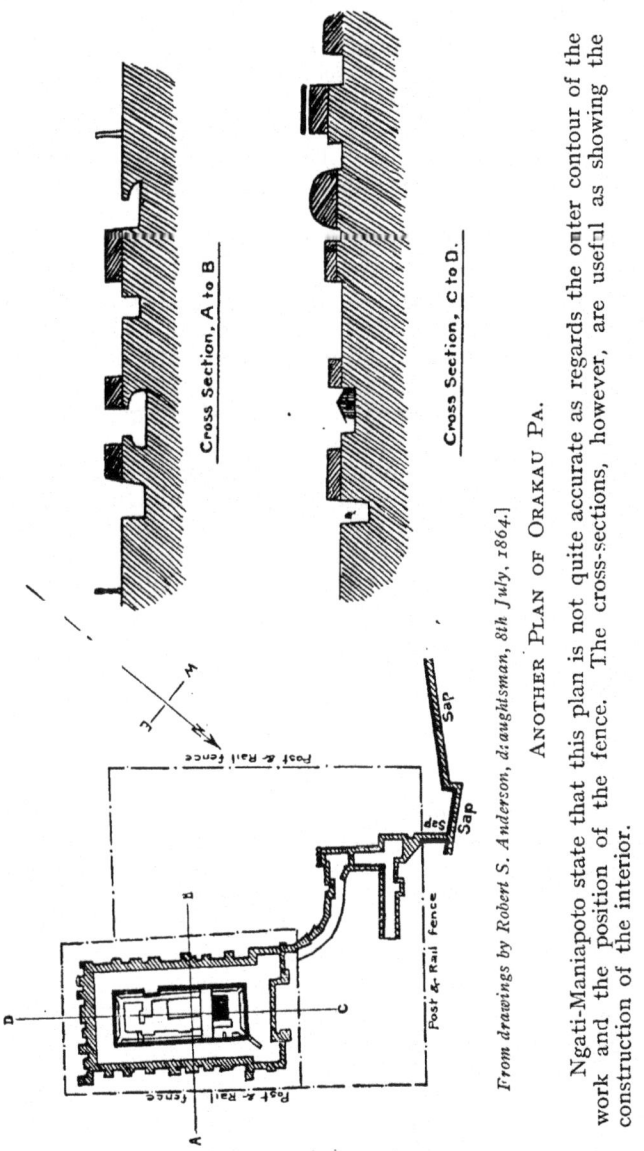

ANOTHER PLAN OF ORAKAU PA.

[From drawings by *Robert S. Anderson, draughtsman, 8th July, 1864.*]

Ngati-Maniapoto state that this plan is not quite accurate as regards the outer contour of the work and the position of the fence. The cross-sections, however, are useful as showing the construction of the interior.

and part of the west flank, facing Kihikihi; the north-west angle and the outwork were defended by Ngati-Raukawa, Ngati-te-Kohera, and some men of Ngati-Tuwharetoa.

Rewi Maniapoto was by common consent the chief in supreme control, but he consulted his fellow-chiefs on important questions. The principal men of the various tribes under Rewi's generalship were: Ngati-Maniapoto — Te Winitana Tupotahi, Raureti Paiaka, Te Kohika; Waikato — Wi te Karamoa (Tumanako), Te Paewaka, Aporo, Te Huirama; Ngati-te-Kohera, Ngati-Parekawa, and allied sections of Ngati-Raukawa — Te Paerata, his sons Hone Teri and Hitiri te Paerata, Henare te Momo, Hauraki Tonganui; Ngati-Tuwharetoa—Rawiri te Rangihirawea, Nui, Rangi-toheriri; Urewera—Te Whenuanui, Piripi te Heuheu, Paerau, Hapurona Kohi; Ngati-Kahungunu—Te Waru Tamatea, Raharuhi.

One of Rewi's lieutenants, his cousin Te Winitana Tupotahi, was a man of enterprise and some adventures. He was one of several Maoris who had voyaged to Australia, attracted by the gold rushes of the "fifties" in Victoria. Tupotahi worked on the diggings at Ballarat, and returned with a little hoard of gold, although he had suffered losses by robbery on the goldfields. At the gold-diggings he learned a good deal about shaft-sinking, tunnelling, and boarding-up, and this knowledge he turned to account in military engineering when the Waikato War began. Tupotahi was severely wounded at Orakau. Another notable man was Te Waru Tamatea, the leader of the small Ngati-Kahungunu party; his home was at Te Marumaru, Wairoa (Hawke's Bay). He was a veteran of the olden Maori wars, a figure of the pre-European era in his attire of flax-mats, with his long hair twisted up in a knob on top of his head and adorned with feathers. His son Tipene te Waru, who was taken prisoner and had an arm amputated after Orakau, became a desperate Hauhau in the war of 1868-70. At last he and his father surrendered. Another warrior of the ancient type was Te Paerata, the leader of the Ngati-te-Kohera. When his party reached Orakau, the ancestral home of his people, he declared, "*Me maie au ki konei*" ("Let me die here"), and he and his son Hone Teri insisted on the *pa* being built where he halted on Rangataua Hill. They both fell on the last day of the battle. There were lay readers or *minita* of the Church of England in the garrison—Wi Karamoa, of Waikato, was the principal *minita*—who led in the religious services, but the ancient Maori rites were not neglected. Most of the people, including Rewi himself, while adopting the faith of the missionaries, turned to the old religion in their extremity. When the ancient Celts and Norsemen began to amalgamate, the people are described as having been "Christians in time of peace, but always certain to invoke the aid of Thor when sailing on any dangerous expedition." There was as curious a mixture of Christian and pagan beliefs in the hearts of the Orakau defenders. The principal *tohunga Maori*,

THE SIEGE OF ORAKAU.

or men skilled in ceremonies and incantations and arts of divination, were Apiata and Tiniwata te Kohika; and the latter's wife, Ahuriri, was gifted with the powers of *matakite*, or "second sight," and of prophecy. There was also an old *tohunga* named Te Waro, who had fought in the Taranaki Wars. Pou-patate says that Te Waro was the priest of the god Tu-kai-te-uru, whose *aria*, or visible form, was a fiery glow on the horizon seen on certain occasions.

Not all the garrison were armed with guns. Peita Kotuku, a veteran of the first Taranaki War, says that he laboured in the building of the Orakau *pa*, but he had no firearm. Te Huia Raureti says: "Our weapons were mostly double-barrel guns, with some flint-muskets and a few rifles; some of us also carried greenstone and whalebone *mere*, *taiaha*, and tomahawks. We carried our ammunition, roughly made up in paper-cased cartridges, in wooden *hamanu*, or cartridge-holders, fastened on leather belts, which we wore either as cross-shoulder belts or buckled around the waist. These *hamanu* were made out of *kahikatea*, *pukatea*, or *tawhero* wood; they were curved in form so as to sit well to the body, and each was bored with auger-holes for eighteen or twenty cartridges. Many of us wore three *hamanu* buckled on for the battle. We were, however, short of ammunition; most of our powder and lead had been left in our deserted villages, and the troops were in occupation before we could obtain it." Before the attack a man was sent to Kihikihi to recover a bag of bullets left there, but he found a sentry walking up and down on the very place where it had been buried. Pou-patate was armed with a Minie rifle; it was one of fifteen captured rifles which had been brought from Taranaki by the victors of Puke-ta-kauere in 1860.

As for food, there was little in the *pa* when the attack began, but under cover of night and the bushes some of the young men stole out during the siege and brought in kits of maize, potatoes, pumpkins, and *kamokamo*, or vegetable marrows. The water-supply on the east side was cut off early in the battle, and all the defenders then had to quench their thirst were raw potatoes and *kamokamo*. The women, who worked under fire like the men, ground flour from wheat in small steel hand-mills (such as were in general use in the country at that period), and baked bread at the beginning of the siege. Potatoes also were cooked in the excavations on the inner side of the main parapet, but the people were unable to swallow this food when the water-supply in calabashes *(kiaka)* was exhausted.

On the morning of Wednesday, the 30th March, two surveyors, Mr. Gundry and Mr. G. T. Wilkinson, from the eastern hill of Kihikihi observed through a theodolite telescope a large number of natives at Orakau working at entrenchments. Lieutenant

From a photo by Pulman, Auckland, 1883.]

REWI MANIAPOTO (MANGA).

(Died 1894.)

Lusk, of the Mauku Forest Rifles, attached to the Transport Corps, also reported the presence of Maoris at Orakau. The news was sent to headquarters, and Brigadier-General Carey, who was then in command—General Cameron was at Pukerimu—at once organized an expedition. Three columns were despatched, with the object of surprising and surrounding the Maoris. No. 1 column, starting from Te Awamutu about midnight, was to take the natives in the rear; it consisted of about half of Von Tempsky's company of Forest Rangers as the advance guard, and detachments of the 40th and 65th Regiments, the whole numbering about three hundred men, and commanded by Major Blyth, of the 40th. This force marched to the west of Kihikihi, flanking the Whakatau-ringaringa swamp, fording the Puniu, and taking a track along the south side of the river as far as Waikeria, where the Puniu was recrossed and a route followed that brought the column well in rear of Orakau. John Gage, half-caste, who had lived in Kihikihi before the war, was the guide. No. 2 column, the main body, consisting of six hundred men of the various regiments, with two 6-pounder Armstrongs, under Brigadier-General Carey, started from Te Awamutu shortly after daylight, and marched by the cart-road to Orakau, picking up at the Kihikihi redoubt a detachment of the 65th and a company of the 1st Waikato Militia (Colonel Haultain). Lieutenant Roberts and nineteen men of the Forest Rangers marched with this body, holding the usual post of honour as advance guard. (Jackson's company was camped at Ohaupo, and did not arrive till the next day.) No. 3 column was a smaller force—detachments of the 65th and Waikato Militia from the redoubt under Captain Blewitt's command at Rangiaowhia; this force crossed the Manga-o-Hoi River and advanced through the bush and swamp, guided by Sergeant Southee, of the Forest Rangers.

Major Blyth's column, after a rough and wet march, came out on the Orakau–Aratitaha track soon after daylight, at a spot near the old *pa* Otautahanga, and close to where Mr. Andrew Kay's homestead now stands. Here Von Tempsky's leading men fired at five Maoris at the head of the swampy gully on the right (north) and killed one (Matene), hit by Sergeant Tovey. Then, quickly advancing westward again in extended order, Major Blyth moved in the direction of heavy firing which was now heard, and came in sight of the Orakau ridge, veiled in gunpowder-smoke.

The first attack on the *pa* was delivered early in the morning of the 31st March by the Forest Rangers (the advanced guard of Carey's main body) and 120 men of the 18th Royal Irish, under Captain Ring, supported by a company of the 40th Regiment. The work of the garrison in relays of diggers had gone on continuously for two days and two nights, but the parapets and post-and-rail fence on the east side and the outwork at the north-west angle were still unfinished. Most of the Maoris were outside the fort, and were holding morning prayers when the troops were first seen. "Wi Karamoa, the lay reader, was praying to Jesus Christ to guard and uphold us, and protect us against the anger of the *pakeha*," said Tupotahi, narrating his experiences in the battle, "and the people were bowed with their hands over their eyes, so. I was a little distance away, and happened to look toward the parapet, and saw a Ngati-Raukawa man beckoning to me and pointing. I looked towards Kihikihi, and there I saw in the distance the bayonets and rifles of the soldiers glinting in the morning sunshine. I waited until prayers were over, and then gave the alarm. Then, too, Aporo, who from his post on the parapet had seen the soldiers, raised the shout, *He whakaariki! He whakaariki—e!* (A war-party, a war-party!) and each man ran for his gun."

Now Rewi gave his orders for defence, as the British column came marching in fours along the track past the groves of Te Kawakawa and into the fields of Orakau. The majority of the garrison he had instructed to take post in the outer ditch, leaving about forty, including the older warriors, inside the parapet. He bade the *tupara* men hold their fire until the soldiers were close up to the post-and-rail fence, and then fire one barrel in a volley, reserving the other barrel for a second volley.

The troops could see little of the defences as they approached through the fern and the fallow cultivations. All that were visible were low parapets of freshly turned soil in a grove of peach-trees, with a post-and-rail fence. The line advanced in skirmishing order on the west and north-west sides of the position, the Forest Rangers on the left of the line. The bugle sounded the "Charge," and the Royal Irish, led by Captain Ring, and the Rangers, under Lieutenant Roberts, dashed at the apparently weak position. The Maoris held their fire until the attackers were within 50 yards. Then Rewi shouted to the defenders in the outer trench "*Puhia!*" ("Fire!") Two hundred guns thundered as a line of flashes and smoke-puffs ran along the front of the works and back again. The tops of the flax-bushes and the fern were mowed off in swathes, and but for the usual Maori fault of too heavy a charge of powder and too high a fire the British losses would have been heavy; as it was the first rush was stopped. Captain Ring fell mortally wounded near the ditch, by Lieutenant Roberts's side, and several others of his regiment were hit. The "Retire" was sounded, and the assaulting column fell back to re-form, and was reinforced by another company of the 40th. But the second bayonet charge was no more successful than the first. Reserving their fire, the garrison waited until the leading files were close to the fence; then Rewi gave the orders, "*Puhia, e waho! Puhia,*

THE SIEGE OF ORAKAU.

e roto!" ("Fire, the outer line! Fire, the inner line!") and the volleys swept the glacis. Several men of the 18th and 40th were killed, and Captain Fischer (40th) and some men were wounded. Captain Baker, of the 18th, who was Deputy Adjutant-General, galloped up on Captain Ring's fall, dismounted, and rallied the men of his regiment; but this gallant effort was also repulsed by the heavy fire from the trenches at point-blank range. Lieutenant Roberts and his Rangers advanced to within a few yards of the defenders, who had now all retired behind the parapet, and a few of the men got into the outer ditch, close enough to get a glimpse of the dense row of Maoris lining the earth-wall, with many a long-handled tomahawk gleaming for the expected combat at close quarters. The natives yelled defiance and derision as each storming-party fell back; some of them cried in English, "Come on, Jack, come on!"

A soldier had fallen just outside the fence. The old warrior-*tohunga* Te Waro, of Ngati-Paea, seeing the man lying there, pulled out his knife, and called to some of the young men to rush out of the fort and drag the body into the ditch, in order that he might cut out the heart for the rite of the *whangai-hau*. The heart of the first man killed (the *mata-ika*) must be offered in burnt sacrifice to Uenuku, the god of battle. But Rewi and his fellow-chiefs and Wi Karamoa, the lay reader, forbade this return to the savage war-rites of old. Te Waro argued that if the heart of the *mata-ika* were not offered up to Uenuku the garrison would be deserted by the Maori gods. "I care not for your *Atua Maori*," said Rewi, "we are fighting under the religion of Christ."

Finding that the *pa* was a more formidable place than it appeared at first view, the Brigadier drew off his troops, and, as Major Blyth and Captain Blewitt were now at their appointed posts, he determined to invest the place closely and play upon it with artillery. The two 6-pounder Armstrongs were brought up and emplaced on the highest part of the Karaponia ridge. At a distance of 350 yards the guns began to throw shells into the redoubt, but the shells made very little impression on the earthworks, resilient with their packing of fern.

The Brigadier now decided, upon the suggestion of Lieutenant Hurst, of the 18th, acting Engineer officer, to approach the redoubt by sap. A trench was opened on the western side of the *pa*, in a slight hollow covered by some peach-trees and flax, about 120 yards from the Maori position. The sap was first carried in a northerly direction, crossing the line of the present road, and then continued easterly towards the *pa*, with many turns and angles, and traversed every few yards. The necessary gabions for head-cover were first ordered up from Te-Awamutu, where a supply had been prepared for an impending attack upon Wiremu Tamehana's *pa* at Te Tiki o Te Ihingarangi, and a party of the 40th Regiment was sent down to the edge of the swamp on the south to cut *manuka* and make more gabions.

On the east side of the *pa* the cordon of troops was completed by Von Tempsky and his Forest Rangers, who were stationed under the fall of the ground near the swamp which trended toward the Manga-o-Hoi. Von Tempsky, observing that a large party of Maori reinforcements had appeared in the distance eastward, placed a picket of his men near a sawn-timber house (formerly occupied by a European named Perry) which stood on a hill on the east side of the swamp, commanding a view of the quarter from which the Maori relief was coming.

The Maoris in the *pa* had early observed the approach of reinforcements, and raised loud shouts in chorus and fired volleys, which brought responsive calls, although the intervening distance was more than a mile. A warrior in the *pa*, pitching his voice in the high-keyed chant that carries over long distances, called route directions to the advance skirmishers of the relief who had made their way across the swamps. Then the British riflemen and the sap-workers heard the Orakau garrison burst into the stamp and chorus of a war-dance. One of the songs chanted, as Tupotahi narrated, was the Kingite *haka* composition likening the Government and its land-hunger to a bullock devouring the leaves of the *raurekau* shrub:—

> *He kau ra,*
> *He kau ra!*
> *U—u!*
> *He kau Kawana koe*
> *Kia miti mai te raurekau*
> *A he kau ra, he kau ra!*
> *U—u—u!*
>
> [TRANSLATION.]
> Oh, a beast,
> A beast that bellows—
> Oo—oo!
> A beast art thou, O Governor,
> That lickest in the leaves of the *raurekau*—
> A beast—oh, a beast!
> Oo—oo!

The Maori reinforcements (Ngati-Haua, Ngati-Raukawa, and other tribes) who were gathered at Otihi, on the Maunga-tautari side of the Manga-o-Hoi swamp, responded to this bellowing chorus with volleys of musketry and the chanting of war-songs. The Orakau garrison saw them rush together in close column and leap in the action of a *peruperu*, or battle-dance, with their guns and long-handled tomahawks flashing in the sun as they thrust them above their heads at arm's length. The action and the rhythm told the watchers that the *peruperu* was the

THE SIEGE OF ORAKAU.

great Taupo war-song "*Uhi mai te waero.*" Skirmishers from the party of reinforcements soon appeared on the nearer edge of the bush and fired at long range at the Forest Rangers' line, but could not venture across the intervening open ground.

The Forest Rangers had a rather uncomfortable position in their hollow on the eastern flank of the *pa*, for the soldiers who covered the sap-workers with their rifle-fire dropped many of their bullets into the lines on the other side. Heavy firing continued all the afternoon, and all night long there was an intermittent fire from the Maoris and the troops. The soldiers'

Photo by J. Cowan, at Te Rewatu, 1920.]

TE HUIA RAURETI.

This veteran of Ngati-Paretekawa *hapu*, Ngati-Maniapoto Tribe, is a nephew of Rewi Maniapoto. and with his father, Raureti Paiaka, shared in the defence of Orakau *pa*, and helped to safeguard Rewi on the retreat to the Puniu. Te Huia was born about the year 1840. Much of the information embodied in these chapters was given by him.

investing detachments, lying in the sap-trenches or in shallow holes scraped with bayonet and bowie-knife, heard bullets whistling over their heads, cutting off the fern or dropping in their midst, until the early hours of the morning. All night the

Royal Artillery troopers, under Lieutenant Rait, patrolled the lines. The strength of the force investing the redoubt had now been increased to about fifteen hundred men by the arrival of two hundred more of the 18th Regiment, under Captain Inman, from Te Awamutu.

In the *pa* the sentinels, or *kai-whakaaraara-pa*, paraded the rampart, chanting their high songs and bidding the garrison be on the alert. The first of these inspiriting watchmen, Aporo, of Ngati-Koura, was shot dead before night. The second was Te Kupenga, of Ngati-Raukawa; but he made a *whati*, or break, in one of his chants, which was unlucky; and his place was taken by Raureti Paiaka, of Ngati-Paretekawa (Ngati-Maniapoto), who continued to chant sentinel songs and war-cries until the last day of the siege.

"The second morning of the battle dawned," narrates Te Huia Raureti. "A thick fog enveloped the *pa*, and completely concealed the combatants from each other. By this time Tupotahi had discovered that the greater part of our ammunition had been fired away, and that there was no reserve of powder and bullets; also that there was no water, and that the people were eating raw *kamokamo* and *kumara* to relieve their thirst. Tupotahi therefore made request of the council of chiefs that the *pa* should be abandoned, in order to save the lives of the garrison, under cover of the fog. The *runanga* considered the question, but resolved not to abandon the *pa*. This was the announcement made by Rewi Maniapoto: 'Listen to me, chiefs of the council and all the tribes! It was we who sought this battle, wherefore, then, should we retreat? This is my thought: Let us abide by the fortune of war; if we are to die, let us die in battle; if we are to live, let us survive on the field of battle.'* So we all remained to continue the fight. When the sun was high the fog lifted from the battlefield, and then again began the firing. When the sun was directly overhead we made a sally from the *pa*—a *kokiri*, or charge, against the troops on our eastern flank. Every tribe took part in this *kokiri*, which was directed against the troops who formed a cordon between us and the quarter from which we expected relief. Most of us rushed out on that flank, but on all four sides of the *pa* warriors leaped outside shooting at the soldiers. The Urewera, Ngati-Maniapoto, Waikato—all sallied out. My father, Raureti, was on top of the parapet, firing. Just before we rushed out many of us formed up on the east side of the works, and there we

---

* Rewi's words translated above were: "*Whakarongo mai te runanga, me nga iwi: Ko te whawhai tenei i whaia mai e tatou, a i oma hoki hei aha? Ki toku mahara hoki, me mate tatou mate ki te pakanga, ora tatou ora ki te marae o te pakanga.*"

leaped in the movements of the war-dance and we chanted the war-song of the Ngati-Toa and Ngati-Maniapoto :—

> "*Awhea to ure ka riri ?*
> *Awhea to ure ka tora ?*
> *A ko te tai ka wiwi,*
> *A ko te tai ka wawa*——"

[TRANSLATION.]
Oh, when will your manhood rage ?
Oh, when will your courage blaze ?
When the ocean tide murmurs,
When the ocean tide roars——

"But we were too impatient to finish the chant. When we shouted the word '*wawa*,' with one accord we all dashed out of the *pa* to meet the soldiers. Rewi Maniapoto directed the charge from the parapet, and as we rushed out to the east we heard his voice crying, '*Whakaekea, whakaekea!*' ('Dash upon them, charge upon them!') Only one man was in high command, and that was Rewi. He carried a famous hardwood *taiaha*, called 'Pakapaka-tai-oreore'; it had been taken in battle long ago in the Taupo country; in his belt glistened a whalebone club, a *patu-paraoa*. I lay down and reloaded after firing off my two barrels as the troops fell back before us, and fired again. In reloading my *tupara* I did not wait to use the ramrod, but dashed the butt of the gun on the ground to settle the bullets down; this was our way with the muzzle-loader when we were in the thick of a fight. Our charge down the slopes extended as far as from here to yonder fence [about 200 yards]. One of our chiefs, Te Huirama, was shot dead; he fell near the grove of elderberries below the *pa*, close to where a tall poplar-tree now stands on the right-hand side of the road as you descend the hill eastward. We fell back on the *pa* as quickly as we could, but some of us were cut off from the work by the lines of soldiers, and had to lie concealed in the fern and creep back under cover of night.

"We were in better spirits after our fight in the open; nevertheless we realized that our position was hopeless, short of food and water, short of lead, and surrounded by soldiers many times outnumbering our garrison, and with big guns throwing shells into our defences."

Further reinforcements arrived on the second day (1st April), including Jackson's No. 1 Company, Forest Rangers, from Ohaupo. There were now a hundred Rangers with their carbines and five-shot revolvers guarding the east flank.

The sap was pushed on vigorously, in spite of two *kokiri*, or rushes, made by the warriors, who delivered their fire as they charged into the head of the trench. The Armstrongs threw some shells at the Maori reinforcements near the Manga-o-Hoi. On the hills to the east, in the direction of Owairaka, were some

Ngati-Tuwharetoa, from West Taupo, under Te Heuheu Horonuku, but they were powerless to assist the garrison.

The day had been very hot, and the garrison, surrounded by that ring of fire and helpless to stay the steady approach of the sap, were quite without water. Wounded men were lying about the *pa* tortured with thirst. That night a young warrior, Hitiri te Paerata, crept out through the British lines to the spring in the gully on the east side and returned with a calabash of water for the wounded. Hitiri, narrating this, said, " I passed right through the line of soldiers. Perhaps they knew what I wanted the water for, because they did not fire at me." A British sentry told his comrades next day that when on duty in the night on the east side of the *pa* he saw a woman creeping down through the fern to the spring to obtain water, and he allowed her to pass, pretending he did not see her.

That evening Tupotahi proposed to Rewi that the garrison should fight their way out of the *pa* under cover of darkness. Rewi agreed, and suggested that he should speak to the other chiefs in their trenches and obtain their opinions. After dark the chiefs assembled and discussed the question. Rewi declared in favour of evacuating the *pa* that night. Hone Teri te Paerata strongly opposed this. " If we do not break out through the soldiers to-night," said Rewi, " we will all perish. If we retreat in the darkness we will be able to fight through with little loss. Do not wait for daylight, but go to-night, so that the soldiers will be confused and will not know our line of retreat." Rewi pointed out the way of flight he suggested, in the direction of the Maori force on the north-eastern side of the Manga-o-Hoi.

But the Paerata family and the Urewera chiefs were stubborn in their decision not to retreat but to continue the battle. (" *Kaore e pai kia haere, engari me whawhai tonu.*") " *E pai ana* " (" It is well—so be it "), said Rewi, submitting to the general voice of the council.

The supply of lead was now running very short, although there was some powder in reserve. Rewi instructed his people to reserve their bullets for daylight firing, and to use pieces of wood for the night fighting. The chiefs experimented with the wood of peach and apple trees and *manuka*, cut up into small pieces, about 2 inches in length. The sections of apple-branches proved the most solid and carried the farthest. That night Ngati-Maniapoto and their allies fired chiefly wooden bullets. Several of the men smashed off the legs of their iron cooking-pots for projectiles; others fired peach-stones. Some of the old smooth-bores began to give way from the heavy powder-charges and the jagged iron bullets, to the rage of their owners, who made shift heroically with their damaged guns. In spite of the poorness of the ammunition, the Maori shooting was accurate enough to make the troops keep close to cover.

CHAPTER XXXIX.

THE SIEGE OF ORAKAU—*continued*.

THE LAST DAY.

As the first faint glimmer of coming dawn spread over the battlefield, the chiefs of the beleaguered redoubt held council. Tupotahi, as shrewd a soldier as his cousin Rewi, realized that now or never was the hour to make a dash for liberty, with a fighting chance of escaping in the uncertain light. He proposed to Rewi that the *pa* should be evacuated at once. "Let us charge out before it is day," he said; "if we retreat now we may fight our way through." Rewi smiled grimly, and bade Tupotahi consult Raureti Paiaka and the other chiefs. When the question was put to Raureti he refused to abandon the *pa*. Nor would any of the other tribal leaders agree to the proposal. "We shall remain here," they declared; "we shall fight on." But many of Ngati-Maniapoto were of like mind with Tupotahi, and voiced their anger at Raureti's stubbornness. They stood by their chiefs, however, and all prepared to resist to the end.

Rewi's first order to his people, as early morning came, was to cook food. They roasted potatoes in the excavations on the inner side of the parapets, but the parched throats refused the food. There was not a drop of water in the redoubt. Rewi went from man to man of his tribe questioning him about the meal, and each one returned the same answer, "I cannot swallow the potatoes." Rewi returned to his quarters in the centre of the *pa*. "We shall have to go," he told his fellow-chiefs, "but we shall not go as Waikato did at Rangiriri [as prisoners]. We shall retreat fighting." He strapped six cartouche-boxes about him—three in front and three at the back—and took two guns. Hone Teri te Paerata suggested that all the best men should be gathered to start the rush through the British lines. But now it was too late; it was clear daylight. The morning haze swept away from the battlefield, and the smoke of heavy musketry took its place.

The morning grew warm, and the sufferings of the thirst-racked garrison increased. The sappers had been at work all night, and early in the forenoon the trench had reached the post-and-rail fence and was within a few yards of the north-west outwork. Lieut.-Colonel Sir Henry Havelock, D.A.Q.M.G., came in from Pukerimu via Ohaupo, and with him came some of the Colonial Defence Force Cavalry, leading packhorses loaded with hand-grenades. The sap was now close enough to the outwork for the grenades to be thrown over the parapet, and this service was carried out by Sergeant MacKay, R.A., under a hot fire. Two colonial officers distinguished themselves by their gallantry at the head of the sap—Captain Herford, of the Waikato Militia, and Lieutenant Harrison, of the same corps, both of whom fought at the head of the sap, keeping down the fire of the Maoris with their rifles. Captain Herford, in attempting to cut down a post of the fence later in the day, was shot in the head and lost an eye. The bullet remained in the back of his head, and caused his death some time afterwards at Otahuhu. Captain Jackson, of the Forest Rangers, who was a very good shot, also assisted with his carbine in covering the workers at the head of the sap.

In a short *kokiri* or rush out of the *pa* in the morning two old men were killed; one was Te Waro, the warrior-*tohunga* who had predicted misfortune after the chiefs prevented him from cutting out the heart of the first soldier killed.

At noon General Cameron and his staff arrived from Pukerimu with an escort of the Colonial Defence Force Cavalry. There were now eighteen hundred British and colonial troops surrounding the *pa*. One of the 6-pounder Armstrong guns was taken into the sap near the head, and opened fire on the outwork, making a breach in the defences. Under the storm of shells, hand-grenades, and rifle-bullets, the garrison now suffered many casualties. Dead and wounded were lying in every trench, but the desperately pressed men and women still held the fort. By noon some of them were quite out of ammunition, but most were reserving one or two cartridges for the last rush. Pou-patate, who was one of the few armed with rifles, was sparing of his ammunition, which could not be replaced. In the first day's fighting, he says, he expended twenty cartridges — a pouchful. On the last day he had ten cartridges left at the close of the fighting; he was reserving them in case the British pursuit was continued. One of the Urewera survivors, Paitini, says that he fired during the siege thirty-six rounds, the contents of two holders, or *hamanu*. The British, man for man, fired a far greater amount of lead than the Maoris.

The defenders hurriedly buried their dead in shallow graves scooped in the pits and trenches. One man, Matiaha, of Ngati-

Tamatea and Ngati-Ruapani (grandfather of Hurae Puketapu, of Waikaremoana), was blown to pieces by the explosion of a shell. The casualties included several of the women.

The first of the hand-grenades (*rakete,* or " rockets," the Maoris call them) thrown into the *pa* from the head of the sap had long fuses, and some daring fellows snatched out the burning fuses (*wiki,* or " wicks ") and poured the powder out for their own cartridges. Others they threw back into the sap before they had time to explode, and they burst among the men who had hurled them. One of the warriors who returned the grenades in this way was Hoani Paruparu, of Ngati-Maniapoto ; he had become familiar with the action of shells in the Taranaki War. But the Royal Artillery men shortened the fuses, and when Hoani attempted to repeat his performance he was killed by the explosion of one of the bombs.*

Early in the afternoon General Cameron, impressed by the Maoris' courage, decided to give the garrison an opportunity of making surrender. The buglers sounded the " Cease fire," and two interpreters of the staff, Mr. William G. Mair (afterwards Major Mair), then an ensign in the Colonial Defence Force Cavalry, and Mr. Mainwaring were sent into the sap with a white flag to invite the natives to capitulate. The din of musketry was stilled, and the Maoris crowded the walls as the interpreters approached the head of the sap, now within a few yards of the north-west outwork. Many of them were suspicious of the flag of truce ; the Urewera at first imagined it a piece of deceit on the part of the British. Controversy has raged over the details of this historic interview ; many a picturesque fiction has been printed, and artists have depicted Rewi Maniapoto posed in a heroic attitude on the parapets hurling defiance at the troops. The bare facts are sufficiently thrilling and inspiring without the decorations of fiction. The British and Maori versions of the " challenge scene "

---

* At Ohaeawai in 1845 many of the shells thrown into Pene Taui's *pa* by Colonel Despard's artillery proved harmless, as the fuses were defective and the shells did not explode. A good deal of powder was thereby furnished to the Maoris, who poured the powder out of the shells to make their cartridges.

An incident curiously resembling the episode of the hand-grenades at Orakau occurred in 1844 in the French-Tahitian war, when the natives of the Society Islands resisted the aggression of Admiral Du Petit Thouars and Commandant D'Aubigny, and when Queen Pomare took refuge in a mountain-camp on the island of Raiatea. In a fight in rear of the present town of Papeete the natives lost about seventy and the French twenty-five killed. Being in want of gunpowder, and discovering the secret of the explosion of the shells fired by the French artillery, the Tahiti warriors watched for the alighting of the projectiles, when they fearlessly seized them and removed the fuses on the instant before they had time to explode. From each shell or bomb they obtained powder for many musket-charges. The emptied shells they converted into drinking-cups.

differ in some details, as will be shown, but the essential facts remain. The men and women of Orakau chose death on the battlefield rather than submission. Another fact which emerges from the many narratives gathered is that Rewi Maniapoto did not personally confront the General's messenger, but remained with the council of chiefs, delegating the delivery of the ultimatum to others.

MAJOR W. G. MAIR.

Major William Gilbert Mair and his younger brother, Captain Gilbert Mair, N.Z.C., were two of the most distinguished colonial soldiers who fought in the Maori wars. William Mair, after Orakau, was Resident Magistrate and Government Native Agent in various districts. As an officer in command of Arawa and other Maori contingents he fought the Hauhaus in the Bay of Plenty and the Urewera country, 1865–69. One notable success was his capture of Te Teko *pa*, on the Rangitaiki River, by means of sap, which forced a surrender (described in Vol. II). For many years after the wars he was Judge of the Native Land Court.

An account of the interview with the garrison given to the writer in 1906 by Major Mair, the interpreter who spoke to the Maoris, is of first importance, as it preserves the actual phrases used in demanding the surrender, and the words of the Maori reply. Mair wrote the account in the form of a letter to a relative shortly after the capture of the *pa*:—

"I got up on the edge of the sap and looked through a gap in the gabions made for the field-piece. The outwork in front of me was a sort of double rifle-pit, with the *pa* or redoubt behind it. The Maoris were in rows, the nearest row only a few yards away from me. I cannot forget the dust-stained faces, bloodshot eyes, and shaggy heads. The muzzles of their guns rested on the edge of the ditch in front of them. One man aimed steadily at me all the time—his name was Wereta.

"Then I said, '*E hoa ma, whakarongo! Ko te kupu tenei a te Tienara: ka nui tona miharo ki to koutou maia, kati me mutu te riri, puta mai kia matou, kia ora o koutou tinana.*' ('Friends, listen! This is the word of the General: Great is his admiration of your bravery. Stop! Let the fighting cease; come out to us that your bodies may be saved').

"I could see the Maoris inclining their heads towards each other in consultation, and in a few minutes came the answer in a clear, firm tone:—

"'*E hoa, ka whawhai tonu ahau ki a koe, ake, ake!*' ('Friend, I shall fight against you for ever, for ever!')*

"Then I said, '*E pai ana tena mo koutou tangata, engari kahore e tika kia mate nga wahine me nga tamariki. Tukuna mai era*' ('That is well for you men, but it is not right that the women and children should die. Let them come out').

"Some one asked, '*Na te aha koe i mohio he wahine kei konei?*' ('How did you know there were women here?')

"I answered, '*I rongo ahau ki te tangi tupapaku i te po*' ('I heard the lamentations for the dead in the night').

"There was a short deliberation, and another voice made answer:—

"'*Ki te mate nga tane, me mate ano nga wahine me nga tamariki*' ('If the men die, the women and children must die also').

"I knew it was over, for there was no disposition on the part of the Maoris to parley; so I said, '*E pai ana, kua mutu te kupu*' ('It is well; the word is ended'), and dropped quickly into the sap.

"Wereta, the man who had been aiming at me, was determined to have the last say in the matter, and he fired at me. His bullet just tipped my right shoulder, cutting my revolver-strap and tearing a hole in my tunic. Wereta did not long survive his treachery, for he was killed by a hand-grenade soon after.

"The people in this outwork were Ngati-te-Kohera, of Taupo, under their chief Te Paerata, whose sons, Hone Teri and Hitiri, and his daughter, Ahumai (wife of Wereta), were with him in the trench. There were also some of the Urewera under Piripi te Heuheu. Very few of them escaped."

Mair reported the interview to General Cameron, who was greatly impressed with the stubborn devotion of the Maoris. "He certainly does not like killing them," wrote Mair. "Colonel Sir Henry Havelock said, in his jerky way, ' Rare plucked 'uns, rare plucked 'uns!'"

---

* The Maori accounts differ somewhat from Major Mair's in regard to the answers given by the chiefs. A current version of the defenders' reply to the demand to surrender gives it in these words: "*Ka whawhai tonu matou, ake, ake, ake!*" ("We shall fight on, for ever, and ever, and ever!") The actual phrase of defiance used by Rewi and repeated by the people, according to Ngati-Maniapoto; was "*Kaore e mau te rongo—ake, ake!*" ("Peace shall never be made—never, never!")'

Raureti Paiaka, the Ngati-Maniapoto survivors state, was the principal intermediary between the council of chiefs, headed by Rewi, and the General's interpreter. A Ngati-te-Kohera account, obtained at Taupo, states that Hauraki Tonganui replied to the first demand for surrender by a refusal, and added, "*Hokihoki koutou katoa ki Kihikihi, ka hoki matou ki to matou kainga, me waiho atu Orakau nei*" ("Let all of you return to Kihikihi, and we will go to our homes and abandon Orakau"). Te Huia Raureti, son of Raureti te Paiaka, agrees that such a reply was given to the first demand, but says it was uttered by his father, and that it voiced the opinion of Rewi and most of the chiefs. Rewi was at that time sitting inside the parapets, near the north end of the *pa*. The first message was taken to him by Te Paetai, a man of Ngati-Maniapoto. Rewi himself did not see the interpreter at that time. Some of the chiefs in council proposed to accept the offer of peace, but Rewi and others dissented (they had Rangiriri in their minds), and they proposed that the troops should leave the battlefield, and that the Maoris on their part should evacuate the *pa*. After discussion it was decided to refuse the General's offer and to continue the defence. Rewi cried, "*Kaore e mau te rongo—ake, ake!*" ("Peace shall never be made—never, never!") Raureti returned to the outer parapet, stood up on the firing-step a few yards from Mair, and delivered this decision, and all the people shouted with one voice, "*Kaore e mau te rongo—ake, ake, ake!*" Rewi came out to the north-west angle when the final decision had been made, and stood in the trench a few yards in rear of Raureti. "As to the reported words, '*Ka whawhai tonu matou, ake, ake, ake!*'" says Te Huia, "I did not hear them uttered."

That is the version of Ngati-Maniapoto. But a different story is given by some of the Ngati-te-Kohera and Ngati-Tuwharetoa. Moetu te Mahia (died 1921), whose home was at Kauriki, near Manunui, on the Main Trunk Railway, declared that it was Hauraki Tonganui who delivered Rewi's reply to Mr. Mair. Moetu fought at Orakau; he was then about twenty years old. He and Hauraki were both of Ngati-Tuwharetoa and Ngati-te-Kohera, and were first cousins. Rewi Maniapoto was a cousin of theirs several times removed. Hauraki was a man with a very powerful voice, and Rewi kept him with him throughout the siege to act as his spokesman. Hauraki's voice, according to Moetu, could be heard at times above the din of battle. Apparently Hauraki was used as a kind of crier or human megaphone for Rewi, and no doubt it was he who called route directions to the reinforcements in the distance during the siege. If he replied to Mair on behalf of Rewi—and this Ngati-Maniapoto, in their Highlander-like clan jealousy, will not admit—he apparently did not use his leader's exact words, but improved upon them with the phrase reported by the interpreter, "*E hoa, ka whawhai tonu ahau ki a koe, ake, ake!*"

The request to send the women and children out of the *pa* was taken to Rewi, Te Huia Raureti believes, by a Tuhoe man; this probably was Hapurona. But the women did not wait for the decision of the chiefs. Ahumai, a tall handsome young woman, daughter of the old West Taupo chief Te Paerata, stood up and made heroic reply, "If the men are to die, the women and children must die also." It was her husband, Wereta, who all the time had his gun steadily aimed at Mair.

"Wereta," says Te Huia, "was standing beside me in the trench while my father, standing on the earthwork a little above me, was speaking to the General's messenger. He was a tattooed man, of the Ngati-te-Kohera. He loaded his gun in a furious hurry and, resting it on the parapet, aimed at the *pakeha*. As the last words were spoken I saw that Wereta was on the point of firing, and I caught hold of him and tried to pull him back, but he pressed the trigger just as I caught him. His aim, however, was bad through his excitement, or else I diverted it, for the bullet only grazed the *pakeha*, though the range was so close." It was Te Huia, therefore, who saved Mair's life that day.*

---

* Neither Mair nor his comrades then knew any of the Maoris; but long after the war the Major, then Judge of the Native Land Court, met the aged Hauraki Tonganui, of Ngati-te-Kohera and Ngati-Tuwharetoa, who reminded him of the day they confronted each other at Orakau. Mair then, after inquiry, came to the conclusion that it was Hauraki who spoke to him from the parapet and delivered the Maori reply to the demand for surrender. No doubt more than one man spoke to Mair. One thing is certain, that Rewi himself did not appear on the ramparts or speak to the interpreter.

The following note is made for the guidance of artists who may essay some day to paint the historic scene at Orakau:—

Te Huia Raureti said (31st May, 1920): "My father, Raureti Paiaka, who delivered the final reply of Rewi and his fellow-chiefs to the British General's demand for their surrender, wore this costume: Shirt and waistcoat, *rapaki* (waist-garment) of white calico, and a piece of red calico worn like a shawl over the left shoulder, where it was tied, and under the right arm. He wore three *hamanu*, or cartridge-belts—two round the waist and one over the left shoulder. These were leather belts with wooden boxes each bored for about eighteen cartridges; one of these ammunition-holders came across the breast, one was in front of the waist, and one at the back. Raureti Paiaka was a partly tattooed man with a short greyish beard. He was about the same age as his cousin Rewi."

Tupotahi described Rewi Maniapoto's war-dress, an historical detail which may also be of use to our artists when the incidents of Orakau come to be painted. "Rewi wore," he said, "a short *parawai*, a mat of soft flax, about his waist; over that he had a flax *piupiu* kilt; he also wore a shirt and waistcoat. In his girdle was a whalebone *mere*, or *patu-paraoa*." Many Maoris wore *pakeha* waistcoats when fighting, for the reason that the pockets were very convenient for holding percussion caps.

Now the firing recommenced hotter than ever. The hand-grenades hurled in from the sap-head killed and wounded many. Te Huia says the casualties through the explosion of these bombs numbered scores. The artillery-fire at short range also inflicted losses, besides battering the works. Two attempts to rush the north-west outwork were made by the Waikato Militia and other men, but were repulsed with loss. It was now 4 o'clock in the afternoon. The sap was within a few feet of the outwork. The end was near.

The story of the last day in Orakau imperishably remains as an inspiration to deeds of courage and fortitude. Nowhere in history did the spirit of pure patriotism blaze up more brightly than in that little earthwork redoubt, torn by gun-fire and strewn with dead and dying. The records of our land are rich in episodes of gallant resistance to overwhelming force, but they hold no parallel to Orakau. Suffering the tortures of thirst, half-blinded with dust and powder-smoke, many bleeding from wounds which there was no time to stanch, ringed by a blaze of rifle-fire, with big-gun shells and grenades exploding among them, the grim band of heroes held their crumbling fort till this hour against six times their number of well-armed, well-fed foes. Now they must retreat, but they would go as free men.

Rewi and the chiefs sent round the word. Those who still had cartridges loaded their guns for the last time; others gripped long-handled tomahawks. The sap had been connected with the trench of the outwork, and Ngati-te-Kohera fell back into the main work. The women and children were placed in the middle of the massed warriors, and with the best men in advance to fight a way through they broke down a part of the earthwork on the south-east angle of the *pa* and rushed out. Only one unwounded man remained in the *pa*. This was the lay reader, Wi Karamoa Tumanako, of Ngati-Apakura, who stayed to surrender, holding up a stick with a white cloth.*

"Haere! Haere!" shouted Rewi when he ran out from the *pa*. It was the Maori "*Sauve qui peut.*" But the people

---

* Wi Karamoa was the only man who advocated acceptance of the General's offer. When the council of chiefs resolved to continue the defence of the *pa* he stood up and declared that he would make peace. Rewi and his fellow-chiefs told him that they would not suffer their people to be made prisoners. "Wait until we have left the *pa*," said Rewi, "then you can make your own peace."

"At 3.30 the enemy suddenly came out of their entrenchments into the open, and in a silent and compact body moved without precipitation. There was something mysterious in their appearance as they advanced towards the cordon of troops, without fear, without firing a shot, or a single cry being heard even from the women, of whom there were several among them."—(Journals of Lieut.-Colonel D. J. Gamble, D.Q.M.G., published by the War Office.)

preserved a solid formation for some distance, going at a steady trot, as a survivor narrates, and there was some firing from both flanks. By this time the soldiers in the sap-head had rushed into the *pa*, and some were firing at the retreating Maoris from the parapets. The last to leave the fort encountered the bayonet, and the troops on either side closed in towards the natives; but here the hesitation to fire for fear of hitting each other was the salvation of many of the Maoris.

The main body of the fugitives made for the dip in the lower end of the ridge, just to the east of the hill on which the Orakau blockhouse was afterwards built. Here there was a steep fall of 20 or 30 feet to the fern flat at the edge of the *manuka* swamp. Along the lower face of the ridge there was a scarped bank with a ditch, made by the Maoris to keep the wild pigs out of the cultivations. Immediately below this was a thin cordon of soldiers, men of the 40th Regiment, under Colonel Leslie; others were employed at the edge of the swamp cutting *manuka* for sap-gabions. Before the leading men had reached the edge of the dip the close body of fugitives had been broken up into groups and the pace became a run.

Yelling and shouting in pursuit came the soldiers, the various corps all mixed up, eager for a final shot at their enemies. Down over the gully-rim poured the fugitives. The surprised 40th were unable to stay the rush, although they shot or bayoneted some of the leaders. A man named Puhipi was killed in penetrating the line, and the foremost men momentarily hesitated; but Raureti Paiaka and his comrade Te Makaka dashed at the nearest soldiers and broke through, and the rest of the fugitives followed them. As the leaders leaped down over the scarped bank Raureti shot two soldiers, one with each barrel, close to the ditch. He received a slight wound in this dash for freedom. Another man who distinguished himself was the half-caste Pou-patate, a tall, athletic young man (his figure is stalwart to-day, but he is quite blind). "Pou-patate was a hero that day," says Te Huia. "He was a very quick, active man in breaking through the line of troops." Another warrior, Te Kohika, uncle to Te Huia, was armed with a gun, but his ammunition was all expended. Glancing back as he rushed through the cordon for the swamp, he saw a Maori fall, shot dead, and thinking it might be his brother he stopped and turned back. He was surrounded by a group of soldiers, who tore his gun from him and tried to bayonet him, but, leaping aside, he escaped. His knee was badly hurt by a blow with the butt of a rifle. A shot at very close quarters missed him, but so narrowly that the powder scorched his bare shoulder. He reached the swamp, where he lay concealed in the *manuka* until night, and then he hobbled along to the Puniu, suffering great

13—N.Z. Wars.

pain from his injured knee, and joined the survivors on the south side of the river. As for Rewi, his retreat through the swamp of death was safeguarded by a devoted body-guard consisting of twelve of his kinsmen, including Raureti Paiaka and his son Te Huia, Pou-patate, Matena te Paetai, Rangi-toheriri, and Tamehana.

Pou-patate, describing the flight, gave a dramatic narrative of his retreat with Rewi to the gully and through the swamp from which the Manga-ngarara Stream flows to the Puniu. "The

HITIRI TE PAERATA.

(Ngati-Raukawa and Ngati-te-Kohera, West Taupo.)

Hitiri and his sister Ahumai were the only survivors of their family at Orakau. Their father, the old chief Te Paerata, was killed in the retreat on the 2nd April, 1864.

bullets," he said, "were flying all around us; they whistled *whi-u! whi-u!* about my ears. When we were in the *manuka* the tops of the bushes were cut off by the bullets, swishing like a storm through the swamp. Yet not one touched me. I saw Hepi Kahotea shot dead there. The soldiers were massed all along the Karaponia ridge, firing down into the *manuka* and *raupo*. There were hundreds of rifles blazing into us. Then, on the other side of the swamp were more foot soldiers and some mounted men hurrying round to cut us off."

Rewi escaped unwounded. He and his tribe suffered less than the Urewera and the Ngati-te-Kohera, whom he had vainly tried to dissuade from the building of the challenge fort at Orakau. Many years after the war, standing on the sacred soil of Orakau *pa*, he gave a narrative of the siege. His story of the last day and the flight to the Puniu reveals the curious mingling of ancient and modern religious beliefs in the Maori mind, and the reversion to the ancient faith in hours of peril when the soul of man is laid bare.

"When we rushed out of the *pa*," said Rewi, "I prayed to God. The words of my prayer were, '*E Ihowa, tohungia ahau, kaua e whakaekea tenei hara ki runga i a au*' ('O Lord, save me, and visit not this sin upon me'). Just then I stumbled and fell down, which made me very dark in my heart, for it was an evil omen. I rose and started on again, but had only gone a short distance when I stumbled and fell once more. When I rose the second time I recited this prayer:—

"*Wetea mai te whiwhi,*
Wetea mai te hara,
Wetea mai te tawhito,
Wetea kia mataratara,
Tawhito te rangi, ta taea."

[In this *karakia* Rewi besought his Maori gods to remove from him all sins or transgressions of which he or his male relatives might have been guilty.]

"Then I slapped my thighs, and I cried out—

"*Tupe runga, tupe raro, tupe haha,*
Kei kona koe tu mai ai,
Ki konei au rere ake ai,
Rere huruhuru, rere a newa a te rangi."

[This *karakia* was used by the Maoris when after a battle the defeated warriors were being pursued by the victors. A chief singled out one of the enemy for pursuit, and this charm had the effect of causing the pursued one to fall or stop to be captured. Rewi used it here with the object of stopping the pursuit by the soldiers. The translation of the expression beginning "*Kei kona koe tu mai ai*" is "Remain there where you are. I will flee on from here, fly like a bird, rising high toward the heavens."]

"I went on across the fern slope towards the swamp," continued Rewi. "I was not yet clear of the soldiers. There were three parties of them. My only weapon was a short-handled tomahawk. I had dropped my two guns when I fell down; my younger brother took them. I called out to some of my people who were a little ahead of me and who had guns, 'Come here; one of you fire there'; to another, 'Fire over there'; to one who was standing close to me I said, 'You fire right in here.' We descended the hill and jumped down over the bank. We were fired upon here, but although the soldiers were close they did not hit us, as we were over them and they had to fire upwards. At my call one of my companions shot a soldier who had fired at me. The soldiers gave way before us, and we rushed down into the swamp. My comrades kept firing as we went on. The troops were on either side of us, on the high ground, firing across at us as we fled through the *manuka*. Now I prayed again. I uttered the words, '*Matiti, matata!*' That was all my prayer.*

"Continuing our retreat through the swamp we overtook an elderly relative of mine named Mau-pakanga. He had two guns. I took one of them. Mau-pakanga soon was shot by some of the soldiers who were firing at us from the hills. Next we overtook Hone Teri. I said to him, 'Don't run; go easily.' A short distance farther on a soldier took aim at Hone Teri and shot him dead. I went up to him to take his gun (he was shot in the head, and his gun was lying under him), and cried a farewell to him and his parents. Then we continued our flight to the Puniu River, some of us returning the fire of our pursuers. Raureti and his companions shot two troopers out of their saddles. A soldier on the Ngamako spurs rode in chase of a native named Ngata. I called to Te Whakatapu, who was reloading as he ran, to stand. The cavalryman jumped off and got behind his horse to avoid being shot by Te Whakatapu; but Ngata had by this time taken cover in the swamp, and having a good view of the soldier he shot him. Hurrying on, we forded the Puniu, and on the south side rested ourselves and collected the survivors; there were sixty of us there. Others came in later."

The Forest Rangers and the Colonial Defence Force Cavalry with some of Rait's Royal Artillery troopers had pushed on along the line of steep-faced hills on the south-eastern side of the long

---

* " Split up! Open up!" is the meaning of this magic formula, which is used only in the last extremity. In Maori mythology it was the charm uttered by the Arawa hero Hatupatu when making his escape from the clutches of the witch-goddess Kura-ngaituku—" Kura-of-the-claws." The ogress was about to seize him when he came to a great rock—it is identified to-day with a curious volcanic rock by the roadside at Ngatuku Hill, near Atiamuri—and exclaiming, " *Matiti, matata!*" the rock opened to receive him, and closed after him. To the Maori the expression carries the significance of the Christian hymn " Rock of Ages, cleft for me." Fortunately for Rewi, this " open sesame" proved as successful as in Hatupatu's case; at any rate, he escaped unscathed when his comrades were falling all round him.

THE SIEGE OF ORAKAU.

swamp in order to cut off the retreat. Von Tempsky was at his post in the valley on the eastern side of the *pa* when the loud cheering from the hill and the intensified volume of rifle-fire told him that at last the Maoris had broken cover. The *pa* ridge was thickly veiled in gunpowder-smoke, and the heavy rattle of musketry was uninterrupted. The Rangers, led by Von Tempsky and Lieutenant Roberts, dashed off southward along the Ngamako ridge, crossing small gullies and swamps, and came within shot of the fugitives as their foremost men ascended a sharp spur of fern land called Ti-kiore. The Armstrong gun on the Karaponia ridge threw some shells into the body of fugitives. The cavalry headed the Maori leaders off into the swamps again by a rough cross-country gallop, but as the first of the troopers, Rait's men, to come up with the natives had only revolvers besides their swords, they were compelled to stand off when the fugitives turned on them with their double-barrel guns, killing one or two horses and wounding some men. The Rangers by this time, having taken a short-cut across the broken ground, began to drop Maori after Maori with their accurate carbine-fire. Many warriors were shot down after delivering their last barrel. The troopers were outdistanced by the strong runners of Von Tempsky's and Jackson's corps. "There was Roberts ahead of us all," wrote Von Tempsky in his journal, "with Thorpe, of Jackson's company, and two or three others, the fleetest of the corps. That day I christened Roberts 'Deerfoot' as I panted behind him, bellowing my lungs out in shouting to the men and directing the pursuit." The Rangers followed their game for several miles; some of them crossed to the south side of the Puniu in the eagerness of the chase. About a hundred men of various regiments who had followed the escaping garrison through the swamp, using their Enfields, joined in the pursuit along the ridges to the Puniu, but they could not keep up with the Rangers, who could load their breech-loading carbines as they ran. It was dusk when the pursuit ended, at the sound of the distant bugles, and the Rangers, on recrossing the Puniu, met Colonel Havelock collecting the troops for the return to camp.

As the straggling pursuers marched back across the broken country they found several of their victims. One mortally wounded Maori, raving with thirst and fear, they tended and carried along till he died. Another was borne campward till he, too, expired from his terrible wounds. Some of the 3rd Waikato Militia were also succouring the wounded, and they and the Rangers carried into Orakau a warrior with a broken thigh.

At the camp-fires were told some of the episodes in the first rushing of the *pa*. Dead and wounded lay about the *pa*. Among the wounded were several women, and even these did not escape the bayonets of the maddened Imperials. The colonial troops behaved

390   NEW ZEALAND WARS.

better. In the flight to the Puniu a half-caste girl, shot through the arm, was on the point of being bayoneted by a soldier when a Forest Ranger saved her; and Von Tempsky's favourite scout, Sergeant Southee, protected another. In the *pa*, however, there was a pitiful tragedy. Mr. Mair, rushing in with the stormers, found some Regulars about to bayonet a wounded woman who had scraped away the light layer of earth covering the body of her slain husband for a last look at him, weeping as she brushed the soil from his face. Mair tried to beat the men back with his carbine, and knocked one of them into the ditch; then he turned to attend

WINITANA TUPOTAHI.

Tupotahi, who was cousin to Rewi Maniapoto, was one of the leading men in the defence of Orakau, and was severely wounded in the retreat. His narrative is given in these chapters.

to the poor woman. She was Hine-i-turama, a high chieftainess of the Arawa people, ninth in direct descent from Hinemoa, and celebrated as a composer of songs; she had been the wife of Hans Tapsell, the trader of Maketu, and on coming to Orakau to visit her daughter, the wife of Dr. Hooper, had been detained by the Kingites, and married another man, Ropata, who fell in the siege. Mr. Mair carried her to an angle, and then went to attend to another wounded woman; but when he returned Hine-i-turama had been bayoneted to death by some brutal soldiers in avengement of fallen comrades.*

The splendid devotion and fearlessness displayed by the Maori heroes of that retreat aroused the admiration of their enemies. Colonel Roberts, N.Z.C. — the "Deerfoot" of Von Tempsky's journal—narrates one poignant episode of the Forest Rangers' chase. "Most of the troops," he says, "abandoned the pursuit at the Puniu River, but several of us Forest Rangers and two or three men of Rait's Artillery crossed the river and went on in chase for a little distance. We caught up on one Maori, who repeatedly turned and deliberately knelt and levelled his single-barrel shot-gun (he was endeavouring to cover the retreat of some of the wounded). I and the Ranger who was near to me took cover among the *wiwi* rushes and scrub, fired, and were reloading as we lay there. The Maori retreated a few yards, then turned and presented his gun at us as before. Several shots were fired at him, but he did not reply. At last one of us shot him dead. We went up to the plucky fellow as he lay there in the rushes, and we found that his gun was empty; he had not a single cartridge left. On the middle fingers of the left hand he wore a little bag which held a few percussion caps. I was terribly grieved—we all were—to think that we had killed so brave a man. Of course we did not know he was pointing an unloaded gun at us; we had to save ourselves from being potted, as we thought. Had he dropped his useless gun, and stood up and shown that he was unarmed and helpless, we would have been only too glad to have spared him. But at that time none of us knew enough Maori to call upon him to surrender."†

---

* Major Mair said, "There was great indignation in camp at Te Awamutu over the bayoneting of the woman Hine-i-turama, and I went with Lieutenant Albert Jackson, of the 18th Regiment, through the tents of one regiment hoping to detect the men, but I could not identify them."

† Captain Gilbert Mair, N.Z.C., narrates another incident of heroism in this retreat from Orakau. In the year 1888 he was interpreting an account given by Hitiri te Paerata in Parliament House, Wellington, describing the Battle of Orakau. Major Jackson, M.H.R. for Waipa, who at Orakau commanded No. 1 Company of the Forest Rangers, asked, "Who was the Maori in the white shirt whom I was chasing?" It was stated that this Maori was assisting a young woman who was wounded to escape. Hitiri remembered the incident. The young Maori warrior described succeeded in helping this girl, who was wounded in the thigh, through the cordon of soldiers, and through the swamp and scrub to the Puniu. He kept his pursuers in check by repeatedly turning, kneeling down, and aiming his gun at them, while the girl hobbled on towards the river and safety. At last the pair crossed the Puniu, and in the Maori country they came to a sheltered place where there was a grove of peach-trees. There they remained, resting, and living on the peaches, until the girl was able to travel to her people.

"Well, what happened?" Hitiri was asked.

"Oh, nothing happened; but what I was going to tell you was that the Maori's gun was unloaded all the time. He had not a charge left when he knelt down and kept the troops off with his levelled *tupara*."

The British casualties in the three-days battle were seventeen killed or died from wounds and fifty-two wounded. The dead were buried in the English Mission Churchyard at Te Awamutu.

More than half the gallant Maoris lay dead when the sun went down that night of the 2nd April. Out of a very few more than three hundred, quite one hundred and sixty were killed, and of the survivors at least half were wounded. Of the twenty-six prisoners taken nearly all were wounded, and several died in the field hospital at Te Awamutu. Brigadier-General Carey reported 101 killed, besides eighteen to twenty stated by the Maoris to have been buried in the *pa*. The total killed was, however, heavier than this estimate. Forty were buried by the soldiers in the trenches on the northern side of the *pa* (the spot is just within the farm-fence on the north line of the present main road). As many more were buried on the edge of the swamp near the place where the fugitives broke through the lines of the 40th Regiment, and many were laid to rest on the spur on the opposite side of the swamp, near Ngamako, and further along the line of retreat to the Puniu. The dead at the *pa* were buried in their own trenches on a beautiful sunny morning, and so near to the surfaec that one clenched hand rose above the surface, and a soldier trampled on it to press it under

Ngati-te-Kohera and the Urewera suffered the heaviest casualties. Hitiri te Paerata and his sister Ahumai were the only survivors of a family. Their father, the old warrior Te Paerata, his son Hone Teri, and several others of the house fell in the retreat. Ahumai—she who declared that the women would remain in the *pa* and share the fate of the men—was wounded in four places. She was shot through the body, the bullet going in on her right side and coming out on the left, through the shoulder, and through the wrist, hand, and arm. Yet she survived that terrible flight and recovered from her wounds; she died at Mokai, near Taupo, in 1908. The Urewera lost thirty killed, and a great many were wounded; they sustained probably over 50 per cent. of casualties. Paitini te Whatu, who was badly wounded, and whose father was killed, gives the following list of the principal people of the contingent of Urewera and their kin who fell at Orakau; the killed, he states, included three out of the six women who were with the company: Piripi te Heuheu and his wife Mere, Te Kaho, Rakuraku, Te Parahi, Wiremu Tapeka (Paitini's father), Paiheke, Te Teira, Penehio, Kaperiere, Hoera, Reweti te Whakahuru and his wife Marata Kopakopa; also Matiaha, of Ngati-Tamatea, and Raharuhi Tamatea, of Ngati-Kahungunu.

Paitini, describing his experience in the retreat, said: " I fired a shot and brought down a soldier as we descended the steep bank above the *manuka* swamp. In fact, I dropped down the bank on to the man I shot, and I could not recover my double-barrel gun. A soldier shot me in the left thigh, causing a very bad wound. I managed to reach the cover of the *manuka* and went slowly along toward the Puniu, bleeding very much and in great pain. Many of our wounded lay out in the swamp all that night and next day. My father was killed in the retreat, outside the *pa*. He was behind me; I did not see him fall. Our chief Piripi te Heuheu was killed in the *pa*.

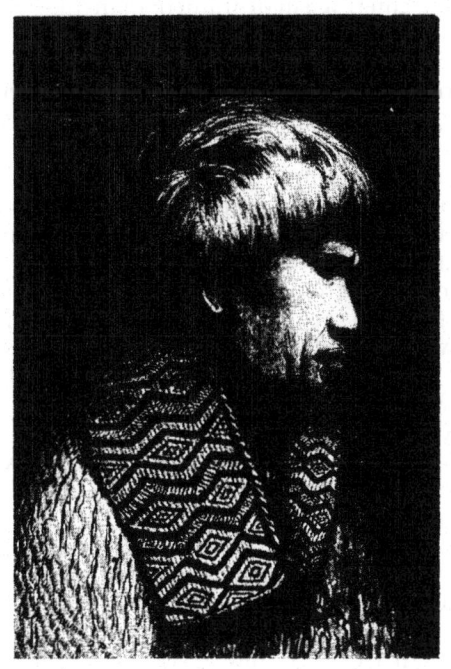

From a drawing, at Taupo, by Captain T. Ryan.

AHUMAI TE PAERATA.

Ahumai was the woman who made the heroic reply at Orakau that the women would die with the men. She was very severely wounded in the retreat. In the following year she saved the life of Lieutenant Meade, R.N., who was in danger of death at the hands of the Ngati-Raukawa Hauhaus, near Taupo.

Paraki Wereta, now living at Te Umuroa, escaped from Orakau unwounded."*

Peita Kotuku, who is part Ngati-Maniapoto and part Patu-heuheu, was a member of the Urewera contingent. He narrates

---

*Statement by Paitini te Whatu, to the writer, at Omakoi, Urewera country, 23rd January, 1921.

that a *pora*, a thick shaggy shoulder-cape of flax, which he was wearing deflected one or two bullets that struck him. Four of his mother's people, the Patu-heuheu, were killed in the battle; one was his uncle Peita, whose name he took in memory. The old chief Paerau, of Tuhoe, escaped, and, like Peita, became a strong Hauhau partisan.

Ngati-Maniapoto did not suffer so severely as the other clans—at any rate, none of their leading chiefs was killed. Tupotahi had his collar-bone broken by a bullet when he was leaving the *pa*. The wiry old chief, a small-framed man like Rewi, narrated that the bullet went out at the back of his right shoulder, and the arm hung helpless. He picked up his gun in his left hand, and ran on after his comrades, supporting his right arm by clenching the fingers between the teeth. At last he had to drop his gun and support his right hand and arm with his left, and so hurried on to the swamp. Men fell all around him, but he was not hit again. Half-dead with pain and loss of blood and tortured with thirst, he lay in the *manuka* for some time unable to move. At last, when it was dark, he rose and struggled on through the scrub to the Puniu. With many of the other wounded he was taken to the Otewa Village, on the Waipa, where his hurt was tended. Some of the survivors gathered at Korakonui and Wharepapa, a few miles south of the Puniu; others of Ngati-Maniapoto returned to Hangatiki.

The Urewera survivors collected at Ara-titaha and Waotu, and made their way home to their mountains, travelling slowly because of their many wounded. Harehare, of Ngati-Manawa, says: "We who had remained at home at Tauaroa (on the Rangitaiki) waited anxiously for news of our relatives and friends. One of our old men had a premonition of disaster. He beheld a *wairua* — an apparition — which he interpreted as a message from the dead, and he told us that misfortune had befallen our people in the Waikato. A few days later the *morehu* — the survivors—began to arrive, among them my brother Takurua and his wife, both wounded, and then we found that the Battle of Orakau had been fought just about the time the vision appeared to our old seer."

Notes.

The present main road from Kihikihi eastward toward Maunga-tautari passes through the site of Orakau *pa*. A stone monument on the roadside now marks the spot. The only trace on the roadway of the olden entrenchment is part of a ditch on the southern side of the road-cutting. Just inside the fence of the field on the northern side, where the north-east angle of the *pa* stood, there is a large mound surrounded by uneven lines of depression, indicating trenches. This is where forty Maoris were buried in the outer trench by the troops. This sacred spot was fenced in over

THE SIEGE OF ORAKAU. 395

From a photo by G. Bourne.]

Te Wairoa Phripi. Hekiera te Rangai. Pou-Patate Huibi. Te Huia Raureti. Matiu te Manu. Te Wharerangi Parekawa.

AFTER FIFTY YEARS.

Ngati-Maniapoto survivors of the war, at the jubilee gathering on the battlefield of Orakau, 1st April, 1914. All but Hekiera shared in the defence of Orakau *pa*, and fought through to the Puniu River in the retreat.

fifty years ago by the then owner of Orakau, Mr. W. A. Cowan, and was planted with blue-gums; but the little cemetery is now part of a paddock, and the fence and the memorial trees have disappeared. Great poplar-trees, planted about the same time, line the southern side of the road. For many years after the war the bullet-riddled peach-trees stood dotted about the battlefield. The outlines of the British sap of 1864 are now indistinguishable except for a few yards in the field on the north side of the road where a slight depression in the turf indicates the olden trench towards the position on the round of the hill. Te Huia Raureti, when pointing out the line of the sap, said it was started in a peach-grove in the western side of the gentle rise about 150 yards from the *pa*. The first trench ran northward, parallel to the west flank, for a few yards and crossed the line of the present road; then the sap was directed toward the northwest angle of the fort and zigzagged (*haere kopikopiko ana*) easterly, parallel with the road. The sap was traversed every few yards, and was cut with many turns. There were also demi-parallels, occupied by the covering-parties of riflemen. The sap was not very deep, said the old warrior, but the soldiers digging it were sheltered by means of *peke oneone* (gabions, large wicker baskets made of *manuka* and filled with earth from the trench) placed along the edge of the ditch for head-cover. At the head of the sap as it went on they rolled along a *peke rakau*—a sap-roller—made of green *manuka* tightly bound together, 4 or 5 feet in thickness, for protection from the Maoris' fire. There was a good deal of cover on the ground traversed by the sap—peach-trees and flax and fern.

Among the wounded prisoners taken at Orakau (2nd April, 1864) was a young warrior named Tipene te Waru, whose after-career was rather remarkable. He was taken to the military hospital at Te Awamutu, where his left arm was amputated by Dr. Spenser, and on recovering was sent home to his people at Wairoa, Hawke's Bay. His father, Te Waru Tamatea, of Marumaru, was the leader of the small Ngati-Kahungunu contingent which had joined the Urewera war-party. Tipene took revenge for the loss of his arm by joining the Hauhaus when the Pai-marire warfaith reached the Wairoa in 1865. His history is related by Captain G. A. Preece, N.Z.C., in the following note (15th July, 1922) :—

"This man, Tipene te Waru, who had lost his left arm from a wound at Orakau, fought against us at Manga-aruhe or Omaru-hakeke on Christmas Day, 1865, and at Te Kopane, near Lake Waikare-moana, on the 18th January, 1866. The elder Te Waru and all his tribe surrendered to us about February, 1866, and after the lands were confiscated they and the Waiau natives were allowed to go back to their settlements at Whataroa and the Waiau Valley (south of the lake), where they remained quietly until after Te Kooti landed on his escape from the Chatham Islands in 1868. Indeed, after the fight at Ruakituri (inland of Gisborne) Te Waru pretended to be loyal, and came to Wairoa and got twenty stand of rifles to protect himself against Te Kooti, and professed to give information as to his (Te Kooti's) movements. This continued up to the time he murdered Karaitiana Roto-a-Tara and his three fellow-scouts at Whataroa in October, 1868. Te Waru (the elder) himself was not present when the scouts were treacherously killed in the *whare* given them, but it was prearranged. His brother Reihana or Horotiu [afterwards notorious as Te Kooti's ' butcher,' or executioner of prisoners] actually committed the murders, but they were all implicated. Te Waru, Tipene te Waru, Reihana or Horotiu, Hemi Raho, another brother, and the whole of the *hapu* then living (about forty people in all) came out of the Urewera country at Horomanga and surrendered to me at Fort Galatea, on the Rangitaiki, on the 9th December, 1870. When I was Resident Magistrate at Opotiki in 1877 Te Waru and the little tribe were living at Waiotahi, where they had been given some land. In that year Tipene te Waru, while out pig-hunting, ran a *manuka* stake through his right foot, and got in such a bad way that he was sent to the Auckland Hospital. However, he got *mokemoke* (lonely, home-sick) there, and returned to Opotiki, and at last the leg had to be amputated. Dr. Reed, assisted by Captain Northcroft, N.Z.C., took it off. We got a wooden leg for him from Sydney, and the one-armed and one-legged warrior used to ride all over the country. I think Hemi Raho was allowed to return to Wairoa, but none of the other members of the rebel tribe went back to their old homes, and I paid them a sum of £400 or £500 for all their interests in the Wairoa lands."

Another wounded prisoner taken at Orakau proved less amenable to the surgeon's skill. This was an old man named Te Wiremu, who had his thigh broken by a bullet from Mr. Mair's carbine. Mair took a friendly interest in Te Wiremu in the hospital at Te Awamutu, but the old warrior was determined to die. "He defied the doctors and hospital attendants to the end," Mair wrote. "Nor could the chaplains make anything of him. One day he would call himself a 'missionary,' and the next he was a 'Catholic'; indeed, he succeeded in establishing something like a coolness between the worthy representatives of the two denominations. He was buried in Te Awamutu churchyard with the other prisoners who died of wounds. The men of the 65th Regiment, who held the Maori people in great esteem, erected a head-board over the grave, bearing an inscription written by Bishop Selwyn."

CHAPTER XL.

THE END OF THE WAIKATO WAR.

Although the Battle of Orakau was the final and decisive blow delivered in General Cameron's Waikato campaign, it did not end the Maoris' preparations for resistance. Ngati-Maniapoto fully expected that the British would follow up their victory, and would invade the country south of the Puniu River. The scattered *hapus* were collected, and the defence of the territory in the southern part of the Waipa basin was decided upon. The first fortification built was designed to block the advance of troops towards Hangatiki, the home of Wahanui Huatare and a large section of Ngati-Maniapoto. It consisted of entrenchments thrown up at Haurua, across a ridge on the main track between Otorohanga and Hangatiki, with swamps on the flanks. The ditches and parapets of this work are intersected by a riding-track on the west side of the railway-line a short distance south of Otorohanga. In rear of this advance work was a stronger position, Te Roto-Marama, an entrenched hill near the present Village of Hangatiki. The third *pa* built was Paratui, a hill-fort between the Mangaokewa and Mangapu Streams, a short distance south of Hangatiki; the site is to the west of the Main Trunk Railway. The whole strength of Ngati-Maniapoto was concentrated on the construction of these fortifications, under Rewi, Raureti, Wetini, Paku-kohatu, Te Rangi-ka-haruru (" The Thundering Heavens "), and Hauauru and his brother Patena, the chiefs of the Ngati-Matakore subtribe, both warriors of the old days of intertribal strife. Topine te Mamaku, from the Upper Wanganui, was also there. Haurua was for some time the headquarters of these Kingites, resolved to bar the southward march of the troops. But Cameron's advance had ended, and Kihikihi remained the most southern outpost of the troops.

It was at Ara-titaha, a Ngati-Raukawa settlement on the southern spur of Maunga-tautari, that the last shots of the Waikato War were fired, in a slight skirmish. This was a reconnaissance affair, about three months after Orakau. A Roman Catholic priest, the Rev. Father Garavel, arrived at Te

Awamutu one day from Taupo via Orakau, and mentioned that he had seen an armed party of Maoris at Ara-titaha, where the track ascended from the plain near Waotu. Lieutenant Rait, commanding the mounted artillery, on patrol around the advanced posts, organized a secret expedition, which was joined by detachments of the 65th and other corps from Kihikihi and Rangiaowhia, under Captain Blewitt and other officers. The mounted men were engaged at long range by some Maori skirmishers near the Village of Ara-titaha, but the artillery troopers, having only revolvers, could not reply to the fire, and the infantry were some distance in the rear. Ensign Mair, the interpreter, however, was armed with a carbine, and he returned the Maoris' fire, and fired the last shot in the campaign. The force withdrew to the camps without carrying hostilities further.

Soon after the capture of Orakau the Ngati-Haua and their allies from Tauranga, who had entrenched themselves at Te Tiki o te Ihingarangi, evacuated their stronghold. The fortification, a *pa* of ancient days, had been strengthened by deepening the trenches, digging covered ways, and erecting palisades. The main *pa* stood on the edge of a high cliff overlooking the rapid Waikato, at the foot of the Pukekura Range; in rear was a higher *pa* of small area. General Cameron had made preparations to shell the place, and had gathered a strong battery at Pukerimu. Tamehana and his people did not wait for the bombardment. They abandoned the place under cover of night, crossing the river in canoes — a dangerous feat, for the current was very swift, and there were rapids just below the crossing-place. Men, women, and children all safely reached the eastern side and marched across the plain to Peria, near Matamata. For some time after the British occupation of Te Tiki o te Ihingarangi a force of Militia garrisoned a redoubt on the site of the upper *pa*. Wiremu Tamehana made his peace with the British, after his long and hopeless struggle, by meeting Brigadier-General Carey at Tamahere on the 27th May, 1865, and signing a document acknowledging submission to the law of the Queen. His tribe lost some land by confiscation, but Waikato were the heaviest sufferers; they were dispossessed of all their territory east of the Waikato River, and remained on the lands of their friends the Ngati-Maniapoto for nearly a generation after the war.

Te Awamutu was the winter quarters for the Waikato army of occupation. When the Government fixed the confiscation-lines the Puniu River was made the frontier, and no attempt was made to drive the defeated Kingites farther south. Four thousand regular troops remained at Te Awamutu and the outposts until the end of 1864, and as they were withdrawn the military settlers embodied in the regiments of Waikato Militia took their places and established frontier villages, each defended by

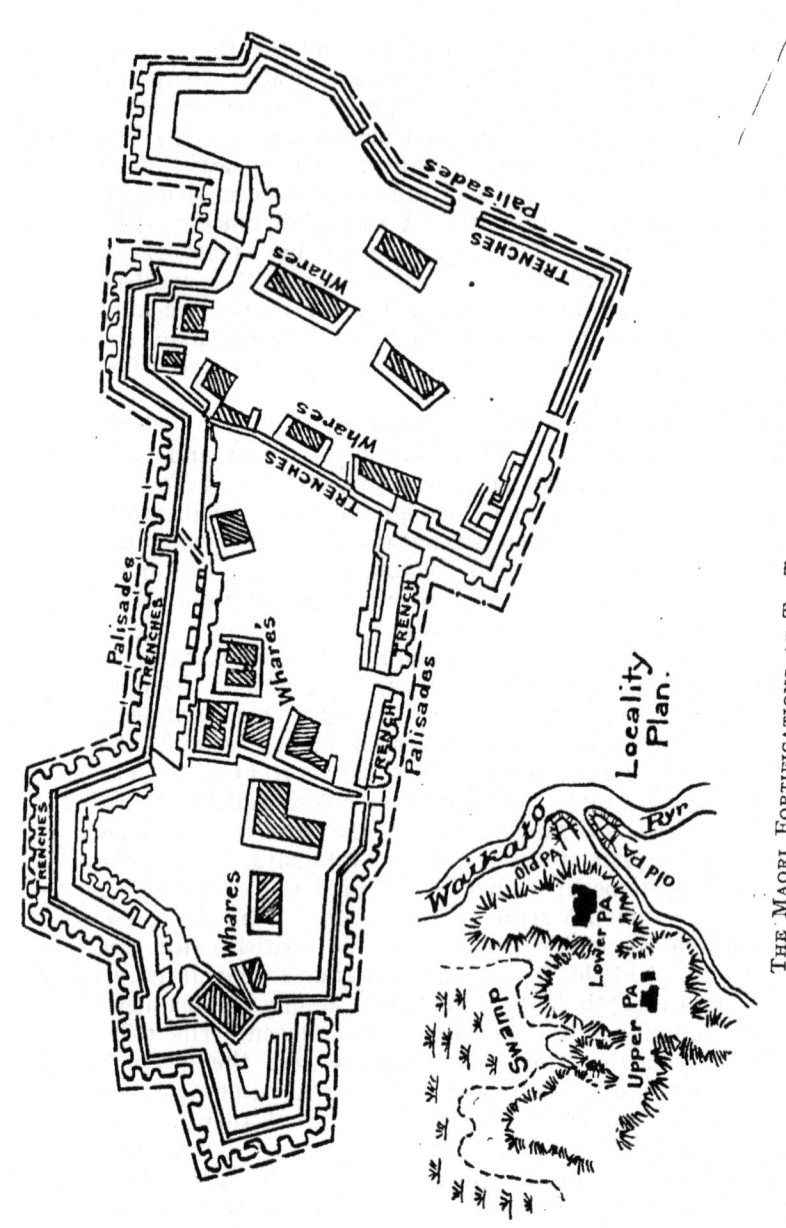

THE MAORI FORTIFICATIONS AT TE TIKI O TE IHINGARANGI.

The large plan is that of the main or lower *pa*, Ngati-Haua's headquarters early in 1864, on the west bank of the Waikato River, opposite and above the present Town of Cambridge. The drawings are from plans made in April, 1864, by Brevet-Majors F. Mould and E. Brooke, of the Royal Engineers.

THE END OF THE WAIKATO WAR. 401

a redoubt, which developed into towns as the settlement of the surrounding confiscated lands gradually increased. The 1st Regiment of Waikato Militia were given their sections of land at Tauranga; the other three regiments garrisoned and settled the southern Waikato—the 2nd at Alexandra (now Pirongia, at the head of steamboat navigation on the Waipa River) and Kihikihi; the 3rd Regiment at Cambridge, at the head of the

Rewi Maniapoto (Manga).   Tawhana.   Taonui.   Hone Wetere te Rerenga.

Te Rangituataka.   Te Naunau.

THE CHIEFS OF NGATI-MANIAPOTO.

This photograph, taken at a settlement in the King Country about 1884, shows most of the leading chiefs of the Ngati-Maniapoto Tribe from the Puniu to the Mokau. Wetere te Rerenga was the leader of the small war-party of Mokau men who killed the Gascoignes and the Rev. John Whiteley at Pukearuhe Redoubt, White Cliffs, in 1869.

Horotiu navigable waters; and the 4th at Hamilton, formerly Kirikiriroa. The river-steamer "Rangiriri," from Mercer, landed the first of the military settlers at the site of the present Town of Hamilton on the 24th August, 1864; they numbered about one hundred and twenty men, under Captain W. Steele. Each

Waikato military settler received a grant of one town acre and a section of from fifty acres upward, according to rank. Jackson's and Von Tempsky's Forest Rangers were given land at Rangiaowhia, Te Rahu, Kihikihi, and Harapepe. South of the frontier most of the Kingites remained in isolation, planning the reconquest of the Waikato, but deterred from a renewal of the war by their lack of good arms and by the presence of strong and well-trained bodies of soldier farmers on the fringes of the conquered territory. It was not until 1881, when Tawhiao laid down his guns at Major Mair's feet at Alexandra, that Waikato and Ngati-Maniapoto definitely and finally made their peace with the Government of the colony.

NOTES.

The New Zealand Settlements Act of 1863, under which the confiscation of native lands was carried out, set forth in the preamble that it was necessary "that some adequate provisions should be made for the permanent protection and security of the well-disposed inhabitants of both races, for the prevention of future insurrection or rebellion, and for the establishment and maintenance of Her Majesty's authority, and of law and order throughout the colony." The best and most effectual means of attaining those ends would be by the introduction of a sufficient number of settlers, able to protect themselves and to preserve the peace of the country. As there were large tracts of land lying unoccupied, useless, and unproductive, which might be made available for the introduction and location of such settlers "with benefit to themselves, and with manifest advantage to the colony," it was enacted that the Governor in Council might take native land where desirable in order to set apart sites for settlements. The money derived from the sale of land was to be devoted to recouping the expenses of the war, in the construction of public works, the establishment of schools and other institutions, and in promoting immigration for the colonization of the confiscated territory.

An enormous area of the Waikato and neighbouring country was confiscated under this Act. It embraced the whole of the country on the east side of the Waikato-Waipa basin, from the Manga-tawhiri south to the summit of Mount Pirongia, thence along the Puniu River to the Waikeria, and from there across to Pukekura, on the foothills of the Maunga-tautari, thence northward to the Thames Gulf. Portions of this area were afterwards returned to *hapus* who had not shared in the war, but by far the greater portion was parcelled out for white settlement.

In 1866 Dr. Edward Waddington, who was for many years the Government military surgeon in the Waikato, in a report on the district gave the following statement of the strength of the principal military settlements (number exclusive of officers):—Alexandra (now Pirongia): 2nd Waikato Regiment—675 men, 102 women, 183 children. Cambridge: 3rd Waikato Regiment—843 men, 87 women, 198 children. Hamilton: 4th Waikato Regiment—432 men, 282 women, 751 children.

In addition to these chief settlements there were the Militia township at Kihikihi and the Forest Rangers' allotments already mentioned. In all, the Government introduced about three thousand military settlers into the Upper Waikato country.

THE END OF THE WAIKATO WAR. 403

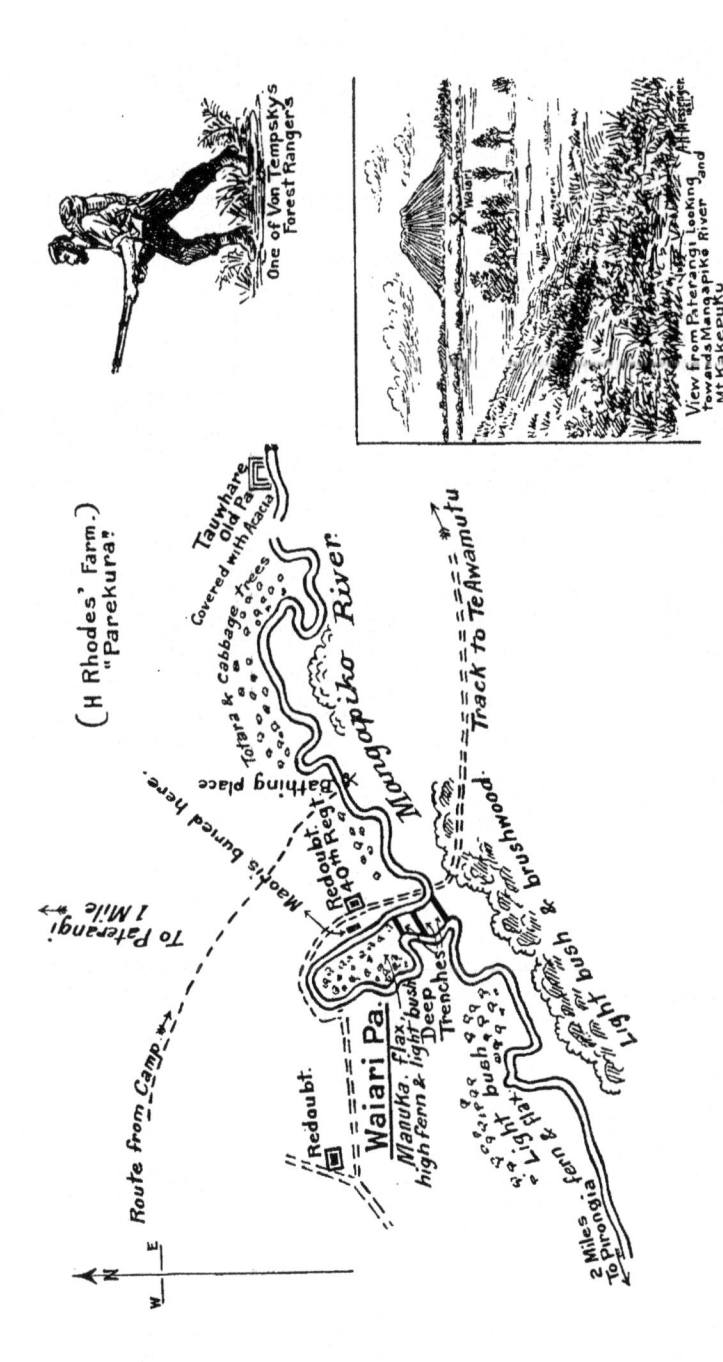

PLAN OF WAIARI, ON THE MANGAPIKO RIVER.
Scene of the engagement of 11th February, 1864. (See pages 337–340.)

CHAPTER XLI.

THE ARAWA DEFEAT OF THE EAST COAST TRIBES.

The Maori King movement had gained strong support among many of the tribes of the East Coast, along the shore of the Bay of Plenty from Matata to Opotiki, and thence round the East Cape as far as Turanganui (Gisborne) and the Wairoa. By the end of 1863 a formidable crusade in aid of hard-pressed Waikato and their kin was set on foot on the coast, and half a score of tribes joined in a strong contingent of reinforcements. The design was to gather at a point in the Bay of Plenty, and thence march through the Arawa country to the Upper Waikato plains, passing Rotorua on the way. By January of 1864 the plan of campaign was matured, and a war-party which swelled to the proportions of a small army was soon assembled at Matata, the headquarters of the Ngai-te-Rangihouhiri, for the advance upon Waikato, where General Cameron was temporarily blocked by the heavy entrenchments on the Paterangi ridge. It was now that the Arawa people definitely ranged themselves on the side of the Queen as defenders of their territory against the Kingites.

From 1856 to 1863 the majority of the Arawa Tribe were scattered over the North Auckland country digging kauri-gum. By their industry they had acquired a fleet of small cutters and schooners, which were engaged largely in the carrying trade between Auckland and the East Coast ports. In 1863 they had spread up north beyond the Bay of Islands. Then rumours began to reach them of the intention of the East Coast tribes to send a large force through to support the Waikato Kingites. These reports became so alarming and urgent that the Arawa exhumed the bones of their numerous dead in various parts of the gumfields of the north, and setting sail in their small craft early in January, 1864, they arrived at Maketu to defend their ancestral soil. In their eagerness to get into action some of them drove their vessels ashore; others dropped anchor out in the stream at Maketu and hastened ashore without taking time to stow their sails. During the six or seven years' fighting that followed, all the vessels sank at their anchors or rotted on the beach. Another result was that sandbanks formed round the sunken vessels and quite ruined the little harbour of Maketu.

Now it became known that about seven or eight hundred hostile natives of the Bay of Plenty and the East Cape were on the way to the Rotorua district. By this time the contingent of Ngati-Porou and other Tai-Rawhiti tribes had been swelled by the addition of the Whanau-a-Te Ehutu, Ngai-Tawarere, Te Whanau-a-Apanui, the Whakatohea, Ngati-Awa, Ngati-Pukeko, and other clans, and finally the Ngai-te-Rangihouhiri at Matata. Te Puehu visited the Arawa country as a herald, asking the lakes tribes to permit them to pass through to help Waikato against the whites, but permission was peremptorily refused. Had the Tai-Rawhiti tribes been allowed to pass through to join the King party the addition of several hundreds of well-equipped warriors would obviously have exercised a powerful influence on the fortunes of the campaign, and would at least have prolonged the war. The Arawa found themselves in this position: that, never having expected any war, they had neglected to provide themselves with arms and ammunition and the necessary equipment for a campaign. They had not followed the example of the other tribes, who all eagerly set to work purchasing guns and ammunition on the relaxation of the arms restrictions by Gore Browne in 1857.

When the plight of the Arawa was realized, with the invaders only a few days' march away, several delegates of the tribe were despatched from Rotorua to Maketu, where they interviewed the Civil Commissioner and asked him to supply them with arms to defend their land against the Queen's enemies. The request was declined. Fortunately, Mr. William Mair (the interpreter at Orakau), who had lately been appointed Magistrate at Taupo, arrived at Maketu at this juncture, and, seeing how necessary it was that these people should receive help, he returned to Tauranga and begged the Imperial military officers there to give him the whole of their sporting ammunition for the loyal Maoris. He succeeded in obtaining about three hundredweight of powder, several hundredweight of shot, and a large quantity of percussion caps. He went to the local storekeepers, and they even emptied their chests of tea and gave Mair the lead. At Maketu the timely munitions-supply was given to the Arawa, who took their warlike stores inland to Mourea, the village on the Ohau Stream, which connects Lakes Rotorua and Rotoiti; there all set to work making cartridges.

Meanwhile some Taupo men had arrived under Rawiri Kahia and Hohepa Tamamutu, and this contingent joined Ngati-Whakaue at Ohinemutu. The allied force crossed the lake in a flotilla of large canoes—" Te Arawa," the largest, could carry nearly a hundred men—and combining with the others at Mourea.

the whole force, some four hundred strong, swept down Lake Rotoiti in true ancient warlike state to meet the advancing Tai-Rawhiti army, who were marching up from Otamarakau by way of Rotoehu and Hongi's Track through the bush to the east end of Rotoiti.

The fighting which followed occurred on the 7th, 8th, and 9th April, 1864. The great war-party of the East Coast tribes

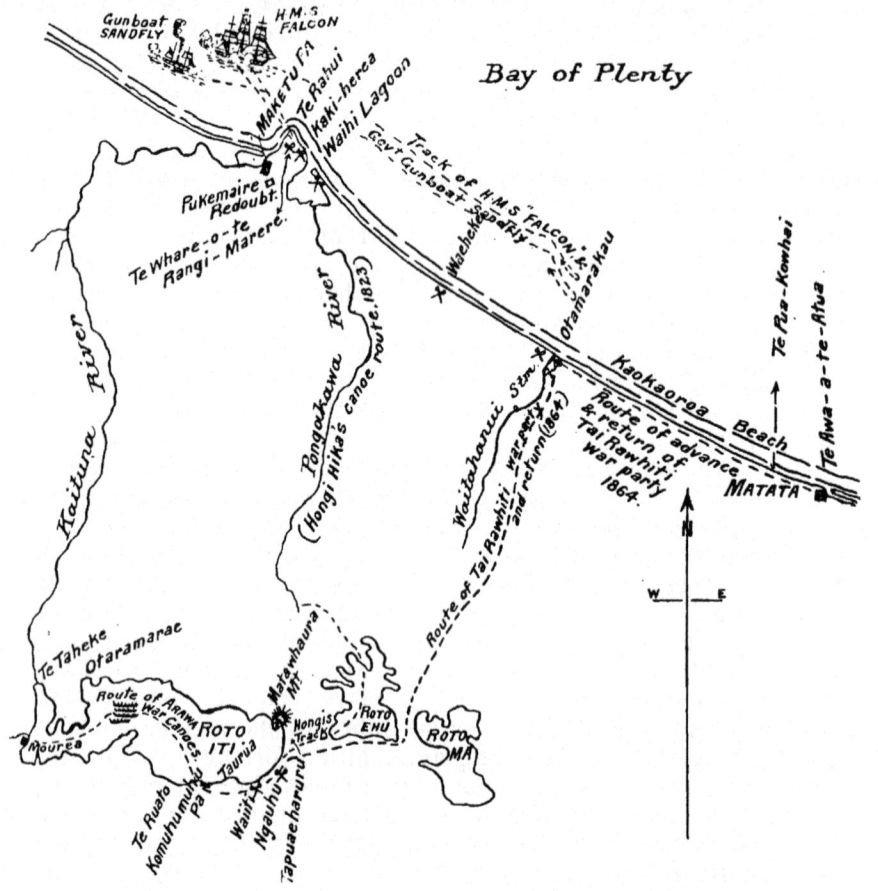

THE BATTLEFIELDS AT LAKE ROTOITI, MAKETU, AND KAOKAOROA.

emerged from the forest and encamped at Tapuae-haruru ("The Beach of the Resounding Footsteps"), with the forest in their rear and the beautiful wooded range of Matawhaura lifting above them like a wall on their right. The Arawa made the Komuhumuhu *pa*, a palisaded village on the south side of the lake, their headquarters, and from there advanced along the shore now traversed by the main road from Rotorua to the eastern lakes and Whakatane. The three days' skirmishing ended in the complete repulse of the invaders. The fighting began at Ngauhu, near Wai-iti. On the second day a hot battle was fought on the Taurua ridge and the lake-edge between Komuhumuhu and Wai-iti. About twenty of the invaders were killed, including the chief Apanui, who fell at Te Tu-arai, the wooded headland near Emery's house at Taurua. The Arawa lost three of their men. The enemy retreated to the sea-coast, announcing that they would next invade Maketu; to which the Arawa chief Te Mapu te Amotu replied, "That is well; we shall finish our battle there."

NOTE.

THE FIGHTING AT LAKE ROTOITI (1864).

At Otaramarae, Lake Rotoiti (6th January, 1919), Hohapeta te Whanarere, a veteran of the Ngati-Pikiao Tribe, gave Captain Gilbert Mair and myself a narrative of the encounter at Taurua with the Kingite reinforcements from the East Coast. After describing the gathering of the Arawa force and the canoe expedition to the eastern end of Rotoiti to stay the advance of the East Coast army, the old warrior said :—

"Our first skirmish with the Tai-Rawhiti men was at Ngauhu, just beyond Wai-iti, and close to the lake-beach at Tapuae-haruru, where the track from the coast by way of Rotoma and Rotoehu comes out of the bush. We held the East Coast men there, and at last they retired to Tapuae-haruru, and on the evening of the second day we returned to our palisaded *pa* on the lake-side at Komuhumuhu. In the skirmishing we cut bunches of fern and stuck them in the ground for cover and fired from behind them. We chiefly had flint-lock guns (*ngutu-parera*) and not much ammunition.

"Next morning the East Coast tribes came up along the lake-side to attack us at Komuhumuhu. We sallied out and met them at Taurua and fought a battle there. The skirmishers spread out all over the ridge of Taurua above the point where the half-caste Emery's house now stands. We scooped out little hollows—they could hardly be called rifle-pits—for cover on the bare hill; we dug them hurriedly with our tomahawks and hands. In this fighting we lost Mohi and Maaka shot dead, Topia (Mita Taupopoki's elder brother) mortally wounded; others wounded were Piwai te Wharekohatu (hand smashed), Matua-iti (jaw shot away), and Wi Pori. Several of us held a little parapet on the hill—I and my brothers Te Harete and Te Pere, Mohi, my cousin Te Pokiha and his brother Waata Taranui. Mohi had been standing up and firing at the enemy, and they fired a volley in return. A bullet pierced his brain, and he fell back dead on top of us. Down below us at the edge of the lake (near the present native store at the little jetty) the enemy were held in check by the *hapus* Ngati-Uenuku-kopako and Ngati-Kereru.

"A section of the rebels nearly succeeded in cutting us off from our *pa* by working up inland into the bush, and we were compelled to retire along the beach and fall back on Komuhumuhu. Two of our old chiefs, Te Mapu te Amotu and Te Puehu, would not retire although hard pressed, and it was then that the rebels took us in flank. One of our men, Kakahi, was shot through the chest. We only saved ourselves by a rapid retreat to the *pa*. Some of the Arawa were panic-stricken by the persistence and numbers of the enemy, and ran to the war-canoes at the beach to escape. Then, after some sharp fighting, the foe hoisted a white flag:

they had had enough of it. Hakaraia, a chief of Waitaha, came towards us with a flag of truce. The enemy retreated, and we followed them up to the end of the lake at Tapuae-haruru. Te Mapu and Te Porarere (son of Te Puehu) went out and ordered them to leave the Arawa country. Te Mapu told them that they need not rejoice over the fact that they had temporarily driven the Arawa back on Komuhumuhu *pa;* they must retire to the sea-coast lest worse befall them. '*E waru nga pu-manawa o te Arawa*' ('The Arawa have eight breaths, or eight talents'), he concluded. (This proverbial saying, famous among the Arawa, is an expression to denote courage, resolution, and resourcefulness.) The rebels' leader replied, 'I shall go and shall not return here, but I shall kindle my fires of occupation at Maketu' ('*Ka ka taku ahi ki runga o Maketu*'). To this Te Mapu returned, "That is well; we shall finish our piece of battle (*pito whawhai*) at Maketu.'

"This understanding was honourably kept," said Hohapeta. "The foe retired to the coast at Matata, and there awaited reinforcements for the march on Maketu. As for us, we returned to Mourea, where for the first time the Arawa all assembled and prepared for a campaign, and then we marched on to Maketu to meet the invaders.

"In the Rotoiti fighting we killed about twenty of the invaders. Among them was Apanui, a high chief from the East Coast. He fell at Te Tu-arai, the wooded headland just to the eastward of Emery's house, above the present road and overlooking the lake."

MAKETU AND KAOKAOROA.

The Tai-Rawhiti expedition was reinforced at Otamarakau, the ancient *pa* of Waitaha, on the sea-coast, by a company of sixty Tuhoe and Ngai-Tama, also by a section of Ngati-Makino and some Ngati-Porou. The large flotilla of war-canoes was drawn up on the beach at the mouth of the Waitahanui Stream, below the massive earthworks of Otamarakau. Towards the end of April they marched on Maketu, and their advance-guard surprised two officers, Major Colvile (43rd Regiment) and Ensign Way (3rd Waikato Militia), who were out duck-shooting in a canoe on the Waihi Lagoon, two miles east of Maketu. The officers had a narrow escape. By this time there was a small body of troops, under Major Colvile, in occupation of Maketu, and Pukemaire, an ancient *pa* on the hill above Maketu, was converted into a redoubt, in which two field-guns were mounted. Major Drummond Hay and Captain T. McDonnell had also arrived with a few men of the Forest Rangers and the Colonial Defence Force to organize the Arawa defence. Skirmishing followed for two or three days at Kakiherea and Te Rahui, on the high land overlooking the Waihi estuary and the sea, and the invaders dug themselves in on the tableland called Te Whare-o-te-Rangi-marere, about a mile east of the Maketu Village. There the line of rifle-pits is still to be seen. Then two warships appeared, H.M.S. "Falcon" and the colonial gunboat "Sandfly," and these vessels, and also the guns on Pukemaire, opened fire on the Tai-Rawhiti, and soon drove them out of their entrenchments. They recrossed the Waihi Lagoon and occupied the sandhills on the opposite side, but their position was gallantly stormed by McDonnell and his Rangers and Te Pokiha Taranui (afterwards known as Major Fox) and his Ngati-Pikiao under a very heavy fire.

By this time the main body of the Arawa had arrived from the lakes, and some three hundred of their best men pursued the Tai-Rawhiti along the beach toward Matata, while the "Falcon" and the "Sandfly," steaming along close to the coast, shelled the retreating force. A heavy shell from the "Falcon" killed several men of the Whakatohea in a group at the mouth of the Waeheke Stream, near Pukehina. At this place the Arawa skirmished with their foes, and drove them toward Otamarakau. Next day the invaders attempted to launch their fleet of about twenty war-canoes lying at the mouth of the Waitahanui. While so engaged the Arawa came upon them, drove them off, and seized the canoes; some of the long *waka-taua* had broached to in the surf and were smashed.

Next day (28th April) the pursuit was continued along the wide sandy beach called the Kaokaoroa ("Long Rib"), extending from Otamarakau to the mouth of the Awa-a-te-Atua River at Matata. The fight, lasting all day, raged over the sandhills and the *kumara* and *taro* plantations between the sea and the high sandstone cliffs. The principal Arawa chiefs engaged, beside the energetic Pokiha Taranui, were the old warrior Tohi te Ururangi (also called Winiata Pekama, or "Wynyard Beckham"), Matene te Auheke, Te Waata Taranui, Te Mapu, Rota Rangihoro, Henare te Pukuatua, Te Araki te Pohu, Te Kohai Tarahina, Paora Pahupahu, and Kepa te Rangipuawhe: these men represented all sections of the Arawa people. The arms used were chiefly old Tower muskets, flint-locks, and double- and single-barrel shot-guns. The *porera* bullets—twelve to the pound—fired from the Tower muskets inflicted smashing wounds. The Arawa had not at this time received Enfield rifles.

The spot where the Tai-Rawhiti warriors made their final stand is near Pua-kowhai Stream, about two miles west of Matata. They took cover under the bank of a small watercourse trending down through the cultivations of *kumara* and maize. About four hundred of the enemy resisted the Arawa here, with others in reserve. The Ngati-Awa and Whakatohea fired heavy volleys from their double-barrel guns, but the Arawa, advancing in quick rushes after the volleys, got up within 30 feet of them. Then a daring chief, Paora Pahupahu, armed only with a *taiaha*, dashed at the enemy's line and cut his way through, followed by the advance-party of his tribe. Meanwhile Tohi te Ururangi, standing on a low sandhill nearer the sea, was directing the movements of his warriors, shouting and pointing with his *taiaha*, when a volley laid him low. The enemy broke and fled. Most of them retreated along the beach; Hira te Popo, of Ngati-Ira, from Waioeka, Opotiki, and his detachment of the war-party escaped up a gully on the cliff-side. About fifty of the rebels were killed in this fight. The Arawa closely pursued the fugitives, and killed Te Ringa-matoru and several other chiefs of the Whakatohea on the sandhills near the place where the Matata Railway-station now stands. Te Arawa carried their wounded chief Tohi to the Pua-kowhai Stream, and he died there that evening. In revenge for his death his widow shot Te Aporotanga, a chief of the Whakatohea, who had been taken prisoner.

The pursuit ended at Matata. The invaders retreated in canoes to Whakatane along the Orini River, running parallel with the coast and connecting the Awa-a-te-Atua with the Whakatane. The Orini, then a fine deep waterway, is no longer navigable. About half the flotilla of canoes in which the Tai-Rawhiti warriors came had been left at Matata in readiness for return. The Ngati-Rangitihi, the present owners of Matata, give the names of some of the war-canoes: the "Tu-mata-uenga," a very large *waka-taua* belonging to Ngati-Porou; the "Uekaha," "Whanga-paraoa," "Tararo," and "Urunga-Kahawai." All the canoes were decorated in warlike fashion and bore carved figure-heads.

Te Kauru Moko, a venerable fighting-man of the Urewera or Tuhoe, of Te Rewarewa Village, Ruatoki, stated (January, 1921) that the Tuhoe and Ngai-Tama company of the Kingite contingent numbered sixty. Te Kauru and Netana Whakaari, of Waimana—both tattooed warriors of the almost extinct type—are two of the very few survivors of this war-party; both fought at Maketu and the Kaokaoroa. The late Tamaikowha, of Waimana, was also in the company; others were Hira Tauaki (Te Kauru's brother), Paora Whenuwhenu, Te Whakaunua, and Turoa Tuhua. The Urewera joined the contingent contrary to the counsel of their *tohunga*, Te Kaho (father of Te Tupara Kaho, of Ruatoki), who prophesied their defeat if they attacked the Arawa.

CHAPTER XLII.

THE GATE PA AND TE RANGA.

In January, 1864, the Government decided upon the despatch of a military force to Tauranga. The reason which prompted this measure was the knowledge that Tauranga was the route for the Kingites from the East Coast to the Waikato, that the Ngai-te-Rangi and other local tribes were hostile to the Government and had sent men to engage in the South Auckland fighting, that the principal native store of gunpowder was in rear of Tauranga, and that the district was an important source of supply of both food and munitions of war to the people of Waikato. Captain Jenkins, of H.M.S. "Miranda," was requested to institute a blockade of Tauranga in order to prevent traffic with the tribes of that part of the coast; and a body of troops commanded by Colonel Greer was landed at Te Papa, near the mission station on Tauranga Harbour. Two redoubts were built; one of these, the Monmouth Redoubt, stands on the Taumata-Kahawai cliff on the Tauranga waterfront. When the force was landed most of the Ngai-te-Rangi were away with Tamehana in the *pa* Te Tiki o te Ihingarangi, on the Upper Waikato, and were awaiting an attack there when the news arrived that their home-country had been invaded. Hurrying back, they began the erection of fortifications to withstand the British. The majority of the Ngai-te-Rangi selected a strong position at Waoku ("The Silent Woods"), on the edge of the great forest which extends from the hinterland of Tauranga towards Rotorua. The site was close to the Waimapu River, and a short distance to the east of the present Rotorua-Tauranga main road on the tableland overlooking the Bay of Plenty. Waoku was an ancient earthwork renovated and palisaded. Other sections of the tribe and the Piri-Rakau ("The People who Cling to the Bush") took up positions at Kaimai, Poripori, Wairoa, and Tawhiti-nui. The last-named place was a palisaded *pa* on a steep hill above the track from Te Puna, on the inner part of Tauranga, up to the forest at Whakamarama and Irihanga; the hill is immediately over the right-hand side of the present road going inland. This was the stronghold of the chief Te Moana-nui. The top of the hill was levelled and enclosed by a scarped rampart and a double timber stockade. Te Moana-nui, who had come from Matakana Island, had constructed the fort in the hope that the soldiers would come out and attack him, but his labour was for nothing. Besides about seventy Ngai-te-Rangi, there were thirty of the Koheriki at Tawhiti-nui; these were the roving warriors, with one or two women, who had fought the Forest Rangers in the Wairoa hills the previous year.

When the main stronghold at Waoku had been completed the chief Rawiri Tuaia (otherwise Puhirake), who afterwards fell at Te Ranga, wrote a letter to the British General at Tauranga, informing him that he and his people had built a *pa* and had made a road up to it from the harbour—the distance was ten or eleven miles—so that the soldiers would not be too weary to fight (" *kei ngenge te hoia* ") when they reached it. To this knightly challenge Rawiri, to his disappointment, received no reply. Becoming weary of waiting, Ngai-te-Rangi decided to move nearer to the troops and to take the aggressive. A *pa*

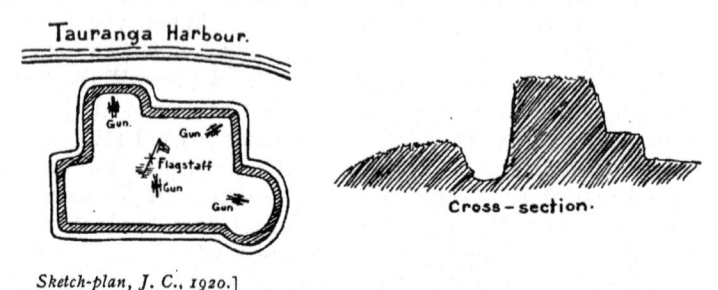

Sketch-plan, J. C., 1920.]

THE MONMOUTH REDOUBT, TAURANGA.

was fortified at Poteriwhi, on the Wairoa, and a letter equivalent to a challenge was also sent from there. The chiefs—among whom was Henare Taratoa (Ngati-Raukawa), who had been the teacher in charge of the mission school at Otaki—drew up a code of regulations for the conduct of the fighting. It was agreed that barbarous customs should not be practised, that the wounded should be spared, and the dead not mutilated; also that non-combatants or unarmed persons should not be harmed. These regulations were put into writing; the document was found by the troops a few weeks later in the trenches at Te Ranga.

As there was no sign of the British accepting the challenge to march inland, the Ngai-te-Rangi, after some of their advance skirmishers had exchanged shots with the soldiers near Te Papa, decided to move down closer to the troops. In April, 1864, they occupied and fortified a position on the Puke-hinahina ridge, two miles from the Tauranga Landing. The place was called " The Gate " by the Europeans at Tauranga, because on this spot, the crown of the ridge, there was a gateway through a post-and-rail fence and ditch and bank which ran across the hill from swamp to swamp. The fence was on the boundary-line between the European and Native land, and had originally been built by the Maoris to block the way against *pakeha* trespassers. The Church Mission authorities had then arranged with the Maoris that a gateway should be made where the track passed along the spur, so that carts could go in and out, and it was from the circumstance of Rawiri's fort being built at this spot that it came to be called the "Gate *Pa*."

The trench and bank of the fence-line were enlarged, and on the summit—where the little memorial church stands to-day, by the roadside—the Ngai-te-Rangi built their redoubt. The land sloped quickly on either side to the swamps that run up from the tidal arms of Tauranga Harbour, the Waimapu and the Waikareao. Timber was scarce there, and so the palisading was of the frailest—*manuka* stakes, *tupakihi*, and even *korari* or flax-sticks, with some posts and rails from a settler's stockyard and fences near the British camp. Trenches were dug and traversed against enfilading fire, underground *ruas* were made for shelter against shell-fire, and covered ways connected inner and outer trenches and rifle-pits. The main redoubt, in the form of a rough oblong, was on the highest part of the neck of land; on its left flank (the western side) the defences were continued by the construction of a smaller *pa*, which was not completed when the attack was delivered. The irregular line of fence along the whole front gave a fictitious appearance of strength to the position. The main *pa*, separated from the lower one by a ditch and parapet, was garrisoned by about two hundred warriors of Ngai-te-Rangi with a few men of the Piri-Rakau and other tribes. The small *pa* was occupied by the party of Koheriki, under Wi Koka, of Maraetai, who had been in Tawhiti-nui after leaving the Waikato. With them were about ten men of various tribes, chiefly Piri-Rakau. This wing of the Gate *Pa* was defended by not more than forty men, besides a brave young half-caste woman, Heni te Kiri-karamu (Heni Pore), already mentioned as having shared in the bush adventures of the Koheriki in the Wairoa Ranges; so that the total garrison of Puke-hina-hina did not exceed two hundred and fifty.

Women as well as men toiled in the building of the fort, but the women were sent safely away to the villages in rear, by Rawiri's order, before the fighting began. The only exception made was in the case of Heni te Kiri-karamu. She refused to leave her brother Neri, whom she had accompanied all through the war; moreover, she could use a gun and was recognized as a fighting-woman, so she was permitted to remain by her brother's side.

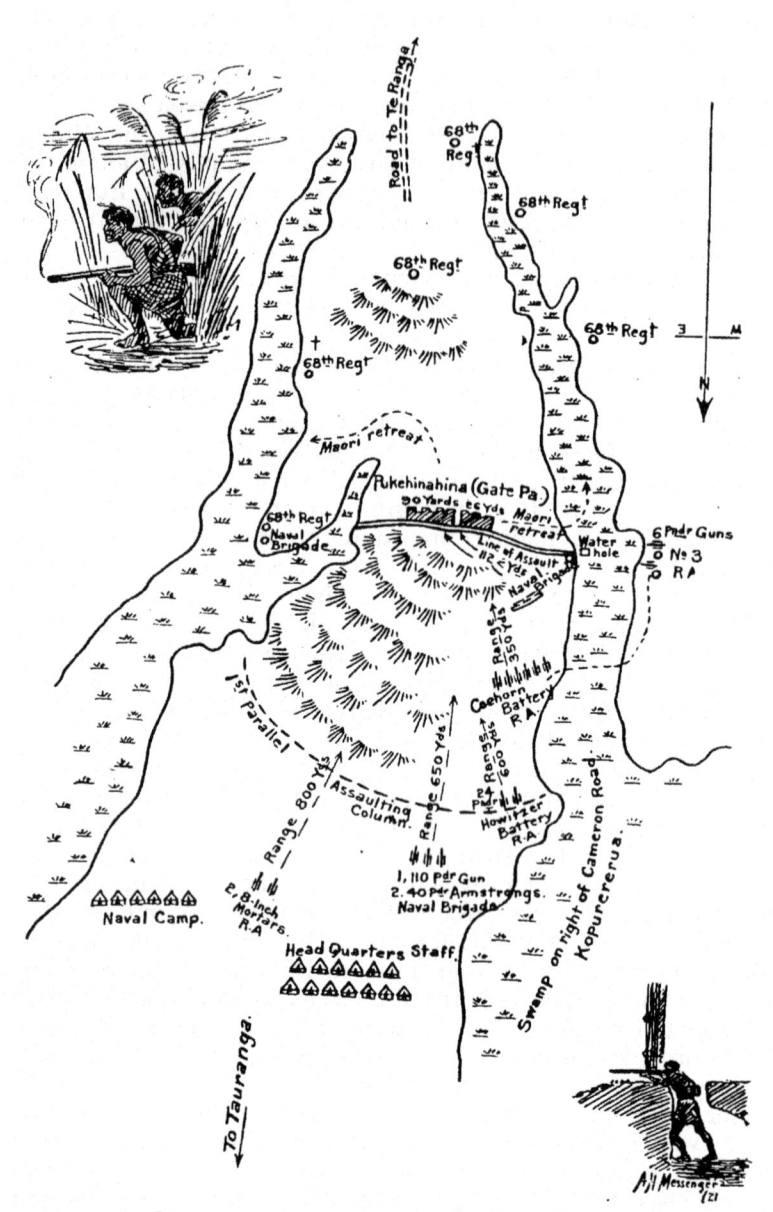

PLAN OF THE ATTACK ON THE GATE PA.
(29th April, 1864.)

A demand had been made by Colonel Greer that the Ngai-te-Rangi should cease their hostilities and give up their guns. To this demand Rawiri replied, "*E kore au e whakaae kia hoatu aku pu; engari ka aea atu koe a ka parakuhi au ki Te Papa*" ("I cannot consent to give up my guns, but if you so wish I shall take breakfast with you in Te Papa"). It was Rawiri's half-jocular way of announcing his intention of attacking the British camp.

The Maoris soon discovered the reason for the apparent reluctance of the British commander to attack. He had been awaiting reinforcements from Auckland. General Cameron arrived at Tauranga on the 21st April in H.M.S. "Esk," and established his headquarters at Te Papa. H.M.S. "Falcon," as well as the "Esk," brought reinforcements, and towards the end of April the General considered he had sufficient forces to march against the fortification challenging his front. On the 27th and 28th April General Cameron moved his troops and guns forward to Pukereia Hill, about 1,200 yards from the *pa*. On the night of the 28th Colonel Greer, with the 68th Regiment, numbering about seven hundred, moved across the swamp below the *pa* on the east side, and under cover of the darkness and rain took up a position well in rear of the native lines. A detachment of the Naval Brigade from the warships "Miranda," "Esk," and "Falcon," under Lieutenant Hotham (afterwards Admiral), joined the 68th; and the forces in rear were disposed so as to cut off the Maoris' retreat. In order to divert the natives' attention from the rear a feigned attack had been made on the front on the 28th.

The troops employed in the attack on the following day totalled about 1,650 officers and men, made up of a Naval Brigade of about 420, fifty Royal Artillery, 300 of the 43rd Regiment, and 700 of the 68th, besides 180 of a movable column consisting of detachments of the 12th, 14th, 40th, and 65th Regiments.

Soon after daybreak on the morning of the 29th the guns and mortars assembled at Pukereia opened fire on the entrenchment. The batteries were the heaviest used in the war of 1863–64 — extraordinarily heavy, indeed, when the really weak character of the defences is considered. The artillery employed consisted of a 110-pounder Armstrong gun, two 40-pounder and two 6-pounder Armstrongs, two 24-pounder howitzers, two 8-inch mortars, and six Coehorn mortars. The fire was directed chiefly against the left angle of the main redoubt, in order to make a breach for an assaulting-party. About noon a 6-pounder Armstrong was taken across an arm of the Kopurererua Swamp by means of laying down fascines and planks, and was hauled up to a position on the hill above. This enabled an enfilading fire to be delivered on the Maoris' left flank. The frail stockade soon began to vanish before the storm of projectiles, and the earth of the parapets was sent flying in showers. In rear of the main *pa* the Kingite flag was displayed on a tall flagstaff. Many shots were directed at it by the gunners, and some of the shells, passing over the fort, fell close to the 68th lines in the rear.

Rawiri strode fearlessly up and down the parapets encouraging his people. "*Kia u, kia u,*" he cried; "*kaore e tae mai te pakeha!*" ("Stand fast, stand fast; the white men will not reach us!") When the big guns opened fire on the *pa* he called, addressing the artillery," *Tena, tena, e mahi i to mahi!*" ("Go on, go on, with your work!"). To his tribesmen he cried reassuringly, in the height of the cannonade, "*Ko te manawa-rere, ko te manawa-rere, kia u, kia u!*" ("Trembling hearts, be firm, be firm!")

"The very first cannon-shot," narrated the warrior woman, Heni Pore, "killed two of our people. Before the shot was fired we had begun our morning service—we had prayer according to the ritual of the Church of England morning and night—and our lay reader, Hori, was in the act of pronouncing the final blessing when the shell was sent into us. I was standing by the side of the trench, with Hori on one side of me and another native minister named Iraihia te Patu-witi ('Elijah the Wheat-thresher') on the other side. Just below me in the trench crouched Timoti te Amopo, our old *tohunga;* he was not joining in the prayers, but was intently watching the big gun. Hori was uttering the final words of the prayer, '*Kia tau iho ki runga ki a tatou katoa*' (asking that the blessing of Christ might rest upon all of us), when suddenly old Timoti caught hold of my dress and pulled me down into the trench. Next moment the two men with whom I had been standing were killed by the shell from the big gun. Timoti had dragged me down instantly he saw the flash. Our chaplain, Hori, was terribly mutilated; he was unrecognizable. Iraihia te Patu-witi, too, was killed on the instant. But the shell did not burst on striking them. It went right into our *hangi*, about 10 yards in the rear, and the next moment we saw the potatoes we had scraped flying high in the air, all over the place. We heard the soldiers laughing and cheering at the sight. They had all been watching the effect of the first shot, and when they saw the potatoes flying in the air they thought it was white feathers that this bursting shell had scattered. Only by an instant had I escaped death.

"We did not pull trigger for some time after this," continued Heni. "When some of the infantry had advanced within range we all fired a volley together, at Rawiri's order '*Puhia.*' I fired several shots. It took some time to load, as the trench was not deep and we had to crouch down to ram home the charge, so that we should not be exposed."

At 4 o'clock in the afternoon the breach at the left angle of the main work was considered large enough for the entrance

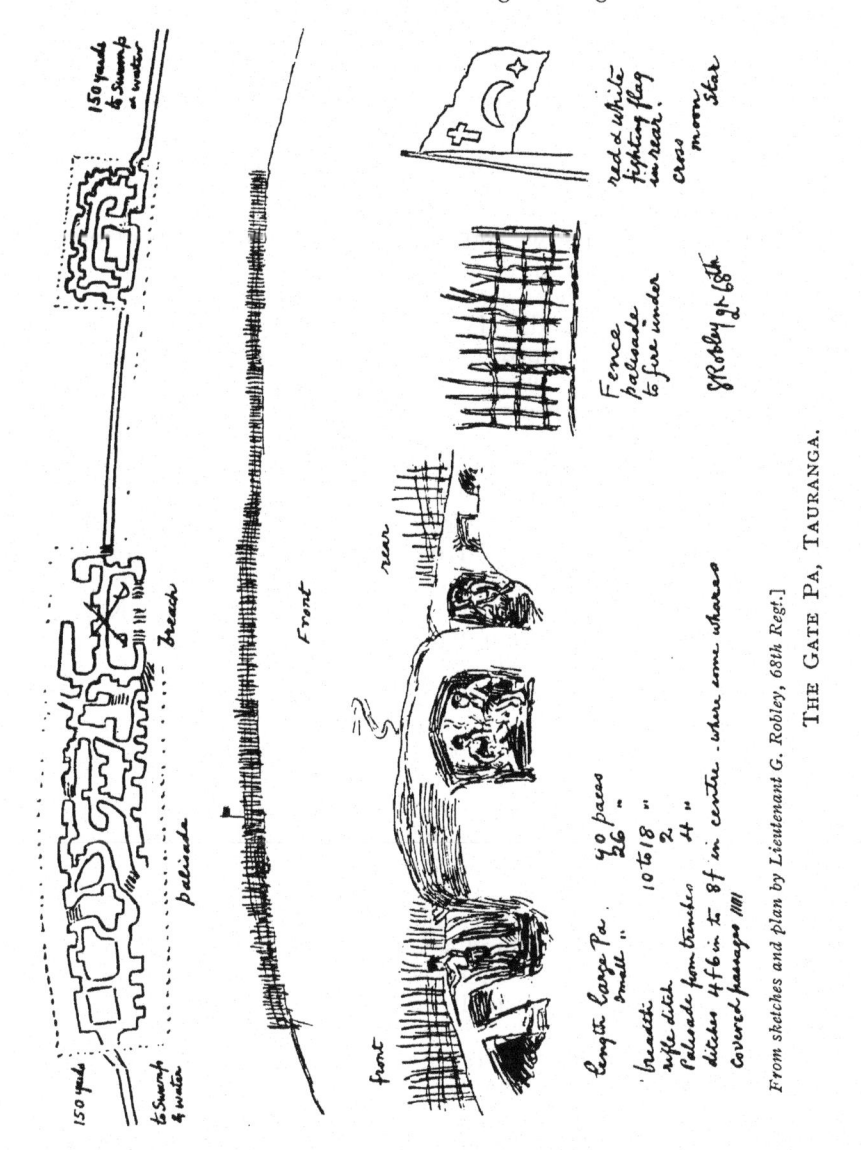

THE GATE PA, TAURANGA.

From sketches and plan by Lieutenant G. Robley, 68th Regt.

of a storming-party, and General Cameron ordered an assault. The storming-party consisted of 150 seamen and marines, under Commander Hay, of H.M.S. "Harrier," and an equal number of the 43rd Regiment, under Lieut.-Colonel H. G. Booth. The

14—N.Z. Wars.

stormers advanced four abreast—two sailors and two soldiers. Major Ryan's movable column was extended close to the front of the *pa* to keep down the fire from the rifle-pits, with orders to follow the assaulting column. The rest of the Naval Brigade and the 43rd Regiment, totalling about three hundred men, followed as a reserve. At the same time the 68th Regiment, warned by a rocket sent up as a signal for the assault, moved up closer to the rear of the *pa* and opened a heavy fire.

The venerable Heni now tells the story of the assault:—

"Some soldiers," she said, "attempted to storm our wing of the *pa*, while the bluejackets attacked the central redoubt. Colonel Booth was the officer who commanded the attack on our defences; of course we did not know who it was until long afterwards. The top rail of our fence had been smashed by the shells, and the officer leading came over this, and leaped the trench, sword in hand. He was thrusting at our men with his sword. We all jumped out of our trenches to meet the assault, and then there was a terrible combat hand to hand. Some of our men were firing, some were using their tomahawks, others the butt ends of their guns. My brother and I were side by side. Not many soldiers got into the section of trench where we fought. I did not club my gun, but jumped into the trench again and was loading when the troops were driven out, leaving their leader and several men lying wounded within our lines. The Maoris rushed out of the *pa* and fired upon the soldiers and bluejackets, who fell back in disorder. Wi Koka, leading us, was using a long-handled tomahawk. The officer, whom we afterwards learned was Colonel Booth, was felled by a young man named Piha, one of our Koheriki. When the Colonel fell, 8 or 10 yards in rear of our front trench, Piha stooped down over him and took the sword which the officer held out to him, and also took a watch from him. He afterwards said he wanted a watch or a ring as a trophy, and he intended to kill the Colonel, but before he could do so the order was given to man the trenches again.

"We had all gone outside the fence in the excitement of the battle, following the retreating soldiers, when we were recalled, and firing began again. I fired several shots after we re-entered the ditch. All this time there was a cloud of gunpowder-smoke over the *pa*, and a small drizzly rain began to fall. It seemed to be almost dark."

In the meantime the greater number of the storming-party had rushed cheering into the left angle of the main redoubt, and a desperate combat was waged. Navy cutlass met long-handled tomahawk—*tupara* was clubbed to counter bayonet and rifle. Skulls were cloven—Maoris were bayoneted—Ngai-te-Rangi tomahawks bit into *pakeha* limbs. The defenders, forced back by the first rush of the Naval Brigade, were temporarily dispossessed of the greater part of the *pa*, but at the rear they were driven back again by the heavy fire of the 68th Regiment, a fire which probably was fatal to some of the troops as well as the Maoris themselves.

This was the critical moment that decided the battle. The Maoris, driven back in the rear, met the sailors and soldiers, who were confused by the intricate character of the works with their crooked trenches and roofed-over pits. Many of the officers had been shot down in the first charge, and sailors and soldiers were crowded together, striking at their foes, but hampered by the restricted space and the maze of entrenchment. It was terrible work, but soon over. The stormers fell back in confusion before the bullets and the tomahawks of the garrison. The Naval reserves, under Captain Hamilton, of the "Esk," made an heroic effort to stay the panic, but the commander was shot on the top of the outer parapet when calling on his men to advance, and the whole force rushed down the glacis.

Commander Hay was mortally wounded, and nearly every other officer fell. Four captains of the 43rd lay close to each other just within the *pa*. Lieutenant Hill, of H.M.S. "Curaçoa" —the senior officer saved from the wreck of H.M.S. "Orpheus" at the Manukau in 1863—was shot when he had reached the centre of the fort. More than a hundred of the assaulting column were casualties, and the glacis and the interior of the *pa* were strewn with dead or dying. The Maoris suffered too, but not so severely.

The defenders of Puke-hinahina treated the wounded British with a humanity and chivalry that surprised their foes. With few exceptions, they did not despoil them of anything but their arms and such articles as naval officers' telescopes; they did not tomahawk them after they had fallen, and they gave water to the wounded lying in their lines. Heni te Kiri-karamu, a blend of Amazon and *vivandière*, was as compassionate as she was brave. It was she who under fire gave water to Colonel Booth, a deed that has wrongly been attributed to a man named Te Ipu. Asked for her narrative of this incident, Heni said:—

"I was in the firing-trench when I heard the wounded officer lying in our lines calling for water. There were other wounded soldiers distressed for want of water. When I heard these cries I could not resist them. The sight of the foe with their life-blood flowing from them seemed to elate some of our warriors, but I felt a great pity for them, and I remembered also a rule that had been made amongst us that if any person asked for any service to be performed the request must not be refused; it would be an *aitua* to ignore it—that is, neglect to comply would bring misfortune. So I rose up from the trench, slung

AFTER THE BATTLE.

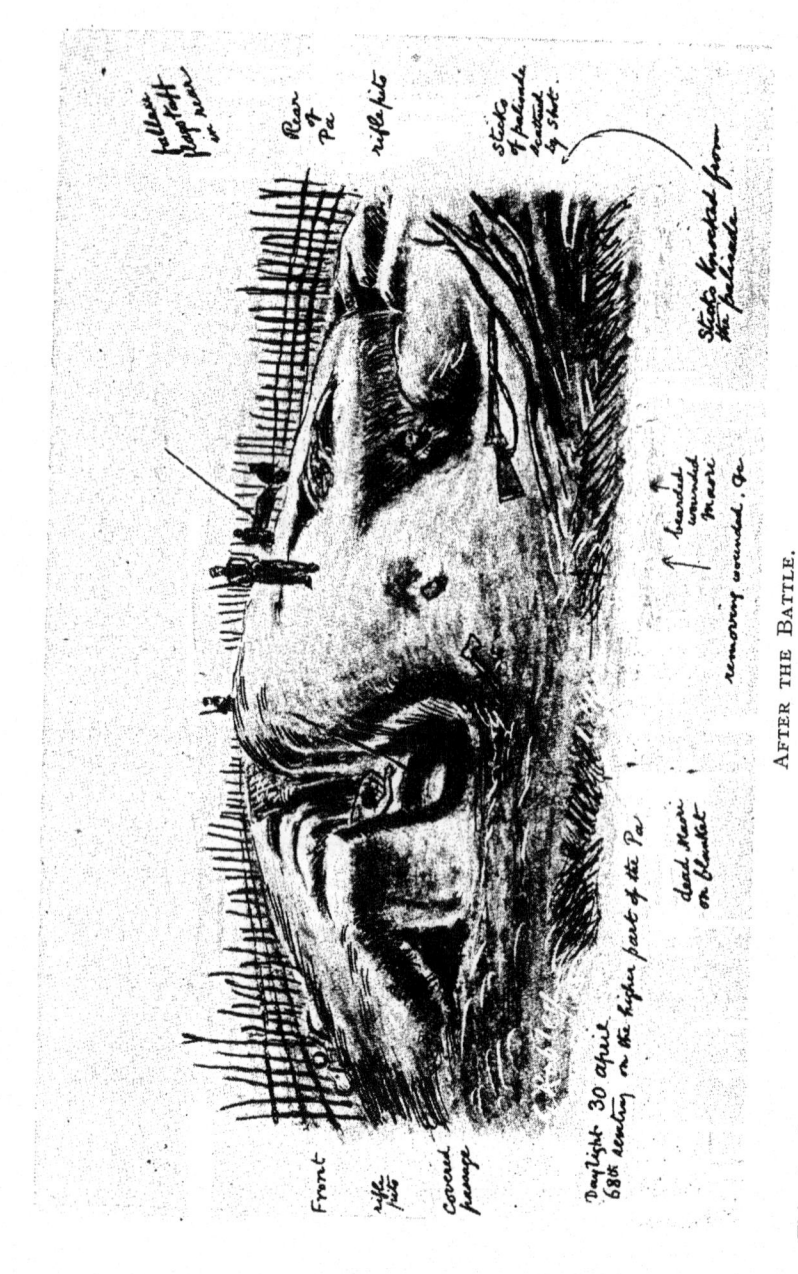

This sketch, by Lieutenant (afterwards Major-General) Gordon Robley, shows the interior of the Gate *Pa* on the morning of the 30th April, 1864, the day following the attack.

my gun, and was about to run back to the cooking-place where we kept our water when my brother asked me where I was going. I told him that I heard the dying men crying for water and I could not disobey the call. He said not a word, but stood with his gun-butt planted on the ground and his hands gripping the muzzle, and watched me earnestly while I ran to fetch the water. I had to go about 10 yards to the rear of the trench, and as our fence was almost demolished I was in view of the troops. I found that a small tin in which I had some water had been capsized, but that there was still the iron nail-can full. It was so heavy that I had to spill about half of it before I could conveniently carry it to the soldiers. I carried it in my arms to where the Colonel was lying. I did not know then that he was a colonel, but I could tell by his uniform that he was a senior officer. He was the nearest of the soldiers to me. I went down by his side, took his head on my knees, and said 'Here's water' in English. I poured some of the water in one hand which I held close to his lips so that he could drink. He said 'God bless you,' and drank again from my hand. I went to the three other soldiers and gave them water one by one in the same way. Then, placing the nail-can so that it would not spill, I ran back to the trench."*

Evening had now descended on the battlefield. The Koheriki discovered that Ngai-te-Rangi, after repulsing the bluejackets, had abandoned their *pa*, having exhausted their ammunition. The left-wing defenders concluded, therefore, that the wisest course for them also was to retire. Their position was a very weak one, and was sure to be stormed next day, as there were so few to hold it, and the artillery had so thoroughly battered the defences. So that night, under cover of the darkness, they took to the Kopurererua Swamp on their left. Before leaving, Heni gave another drink to the mortally wounded officer, and left the water-can by his side. As for Ngai-te-Rangi, they had retreated in good spirits, after collecting arms and accoutrements from the British dead and wounded. They broke into small parties and made their way skilfully through

---

* It was not until the year 1867, when Heni and her husband were keeping the Travellers' Rest Hotel at Maketu, that she learned the identity of the officer to whom she had given water. "Colonel St. John came to the hotel one day," said Heni, "and asked to see me. Seizing my hand he said, 'I did not know until lately that it was you who gave water to my dear friend Colonel Booth at the Gate *Pa*.' Then he told me that Colonel Booth, when dying in the hospital at Te Papa, informed the surgeon, Dr. Manley, that it was a Maori woman who spoke English that gave him water. Long after the war a friend sent me a picture by a New Zealand artist showing a man with a calabash carrying water to Colonel Booth. It amused me, for besides the mistake about the man there was no calabash, but an old iron nail-can."

15—N.Z. Wars.

the lines of the 68th. The soldiers fired on them, but the garrison escaped with only a few wounded. They travelled inland to the Waoku *pa*, and thence dispersed to their various stations along the edge of the forest; and the Koheriki, after many adventures, made their way inland to Poripori.

The British casualties numbered more than one-third of the total force composing the storming-party. Ten officers were killed or died from wounds, and four were wounded; of non-commissioned officers and privates twenty-one were killed and

HorI Ngatai, of Tauranga.

(Died 1912.)

Hori Ngatai, head of the Ngai-te-Rangi Tribe, was an excellent type of the Maori chief and warrior of the past generation. In 1863 he and some of his tribe fought at Meremere, on the Waikato River, and at Otau, Wairoa South. He was one of the defenders of the Gate *Pa*, and in 1901 described the battle to the writer of this History. In his later years Hori Ngatai worthily led his tribe in the farming industry at Whareroa, Tauranga Harbour. At one time he was the largest grower of wheat and maize at Tauranga.

seventy-six wounded; total killed and wounded, 111 officers and men.

The 43rd Regiment lost their colonel, four captains, and one lieutenant killed, and a lieutenant and two ensigns severely wounded. Among the killed were two brothers, Captain and

Lieutenant Glover. Nearly all the Naval Brigade officers were killed or wounded. The official return of officers killed and wounded was as follows :—

Naval Brigade : Killed—Captain Hamilton, H.M.S. "Esk"; Lieutenant Hill (late of "Orpheus"), H.M.S. "Curaçoa"; Mr. Watts, gunner H.M.S. "Miranda." Wounded—Commander Hay (abdomen, mortally), H.M.S. "Harrier"; Lieutenant Hammick (shoulder, severe), H.M.S. "Miranda"; Lieutenant Duff (back, two places, severe), H.M.S. "Esk."

43rd Regiment : Killed — Captain R. C. Glover (head) ; Captain C. R. Muir (or Mure) (tomahawk, right axilla) ; Captain R. T. Hamilton (head) ; Captain A. E. Utterton (neck) ; Lieutenant C. J. Langlands (chest). Wounded—Lieut.-Colonel Booth (spine and right arm, mortally) ; Lieutenant T. G. E. Glover (abdomen, mortally) ; Ensign W. Clark (right arm, severe) ; Ensign S. P. T. Nicholl (scalp, slight).

A bluejacket named Samuel Mitchell, captain of the foretop of H.M.S. "Harrier," was recommended for the Victoria Cross for carrying Commander Hay, who was mortally wounded, out of the *pa*.

The Maori losses in killed totalled about twenty-five, including the Ngai-te-Rangi chiefs Te Reweti, Eru Puhirake, Tikitu, Te Kani, Te Rangihau, and Te Wharepouri. Te Moana-nui received three gunshot-wounds. Te Ipu was another warrior badly wounded. Te Reweti received six or seven bullet-wounds and had his legs broken.

The Trenches at Te Ranga.

During May the troops, with Captain Pye's Colonial Defence Force Cavalry in advance, took possession of the Maoris' abandoned rifle-pits and settlements on the Wairoa Stream. A portion of the British force, with the warships (excepting the "Harrier") returned to Auckland. The Ngai-te-Rangi meanwhile had received reinforcements from Rotorua, including some of the Ngati-Rangiwewehi, of Puhirua and Awahou villages—a sept of the Arawa who declined to fall in line with the rest of the tribe and espouse the British cause—and also a party of fifty warriors of the Ngati-Hinekura and Ngati-Tamatea-tutahi *hapus* of Ngati-Pikiao, from Rotoiti. In addition, there was a war-party of Ngati-Porou, chiefly the Whanau-ia-Hinerupe *hapu*, from Pukemaire, in the Waiapu Valley, East Cape. These determined warriors were headed by Hoera te Mataatai. In June the Kingites resolved to force another trial of strength with the Queen's troops, and a position was taken up on the prolongation of the Puke-hinahina ridge, about three miles inland from the Gate *Pa*. At this place, Te Ranga, the natives entrenched themselves, but were observed by a British reconnoitring-party before they had completed the fortifications. The main track

424 NEW ZEALAND WARS.

From a drawing by Brigadier-General Carey, in "Illustrated London News," 1864.]

TAURANGA IN 1864,

Showing the camp of the 43rd and 68th Regiments at Te Papa.

inland to Oropi passed along this long leading ridge—the present road from Tauranga via Pye's *Pa* follows the same route—and Ngai-te-Rangi selected the narrowest part for their entrenchments. On either side of this strategic highway to the interior the ground fell steeply to undulating partly wooded valleys and swamps with watercourses; the descent on the east, the natives' right flank, was very abrupt. Across this narrow neck the Kingites constructed their line of trench, with some flanking rifle-pits on the right front on the edge of the gully. The ridge-top was level of surface. The advance from the coast was along a gentle inclined plane.

On the 21st June a strong reconnoitring column, under Colonel Greer, advancing along the leading ridge from the Gate *Pa*, found the Maoris hard at work on their entrenchments. They were not given time to complete the formidable *pa* contemplated. Colonel Greer decided to attack at once. He had a force of about six hundred men, composed of detachments of the 43rd Regiment, under Major Synge, the 68th, under Major Shuttleworth, and the 1st Waikato Militia, under Captain Moore. Sending back to the camp for reinforcements and an Armstrong gun, the British commander threw out skirmishers and engaged the native outposts, then opened a heavy fire on the defenders of the trenches. The 43rd and a portion of the 68th were sent out on either side, and kept up a flanking fire. After about two hours of this fighting from cover the gun and the infantry reinforcements arrived in support. Colonel Greer then ordered an assault. At the bugle-sound of the "Charge" the 43rd, 68th, and 1st Waikatos advanced cheering, and in a very few minutes had cleared the trenches at the point of the bayonet. Colonel Greer in his report said they carried the rifle-pits "in the most dashing manner." They charged over the level glacis under a very heavy fire from the Kingite double-barrel guns, but the casualties were comparatively small, as most of the Maoris fired too high. The Ngai-te-Rangi and their allies fought like old heroes. They stood up to meet the bayonet charge unflinchingly, and as they had no time to reload they used gun-butt and tomahawk with desperate bravery. There were many hand-to-hand encounters. Even after being bayoneted some of the Maoris felled their foemen with their tomahawks. But the Kingite valour was of no avail before that rush with the bayonet. Scores of warriors went down under the steel, and the survivors broke for the cover of the gullies and swamps in the rear. The Colonial Defence Force Cavalry followed them for several miles, but the country was difficult for mounted work.

The British casualties in this short and sharp affair, the final battle of the campaign, were thirteen privates of the 43rd and 68th killed, and six officers and thirty-three non-commissioned officers and privates wounded. The 43rd and their comrades exacted a terrible vengeance for their defeat at the Gate *Pa*. Quite 120 Maoris were killed, more than half of them with the

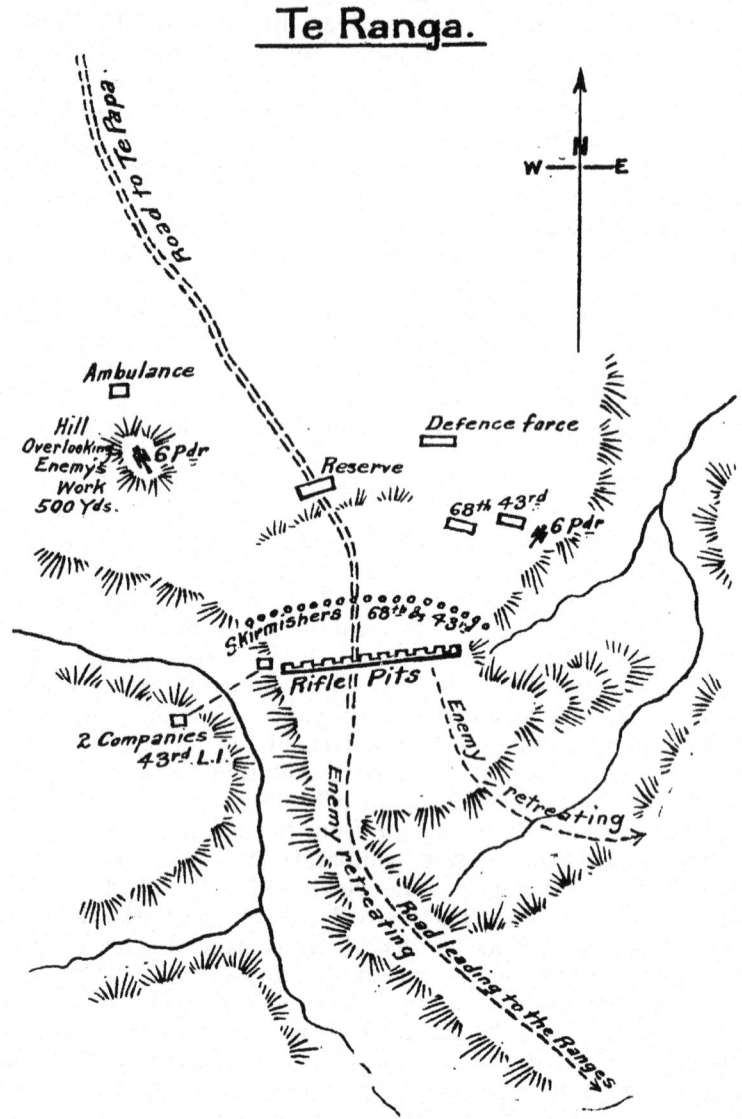

Te Ranga.

PLAN OF THE ATTACK ON TE RANGA ENTRENCHMENTS.
(21st June, 1864.)

bayonet; the rest were shot as they fell back gallantly fighting. Rawiri Puhirake, the commander at the Gate *Pa*, and Henare Taratoa, the Otaki mission teacher who had helped to frame the chivalrous fighting code, were among the killed. On Henare's body was found the "order of the day" for combat, beginning with a prayer and ending with the words in Maori, from Romans xii, 20 : " If thine enemy hunger, feed him ; if he thirst, give him to drink." The small Ngati-Porou contingent resisted to the death; thirty of the party were killed. The contingent of fifty of Ngati-Pikiao from the Lake Rotoiti settlements fell almost to a man. The Ngati-Rangiwewehi war-party also suffered very severely, and their losses at Te Ranga that day greatly influenced the survivors of the clan towards Pai-marire

From a photo about 1860.]

HENARE TARATOA.

(Killed at Te Ranga.)

when that fanatic faith reached the lakes country and the East Coast.

Two British soldiers were recommended for the Victoria Cross for their valour in the charge at Te Ranga. One was Captain Smith, of the 43rd, who led the right of the advance and received two wounds; the other was Sergeant Murray, of the 68th, who killed a Maori about to tomahawk a corporal who had just run him through with his bayonet.

A number of the Maori wounded died in hospital at Te Papa. The natives killed on the field were laid out in three

428   NEW ZEALAND WARS.

[*From a sketch by Major-General Gordon Robley, 1864.*]

SURRENDER OF THE NGAI-TE-RANGI TRIBE.

Soon after the defeat of the Kingite tribes at Te Ranga the greater number of the Ngai-te-Rangi came in and made submission to the British authorities at Te Papa, Tauranga, and handed in their arms. The peace pact was loyally observed by all but a few of Ngai-te-Rangi who joined the Piri-rakau Hauhaus in the fighting at Irihanga, Whakamarama, and elsewhere in 1867.

long rows—thirty in one row, thirty-three in another, and thirty-four in another. They were buried in the rifle-pits, their self-dug graves. Others were buried where they fell when retreating. Several years later the remains of the gallant patriot Rawiri Puhirake were reinterred in the military cemetery at Tauranga, by the side of his adversary Lieut.-Colonel Booth, killed at the Gate *Pa*. This tribute to an heroic and knightly foe was a measure of the general admiration exhibited by the British for their Ngai-te-Rangi antagonists. The Tauranga tribes surrendered soon after Te Ranga, and the friendliest relations were established between the fighters of the two races, who esteemed each other for the courage and the humanity which had distinguished the whole conduct of the brief campaign.

NOTES.

Possibly it was the finding of the Maori "order of the day" on Henare Taratoa's body that gave rise to the report, so widely published, that it was he who gave water to Lieut.-Colonel Booth and other wounded soldiers on the repulse of the British attack on the Gate *Pa*. Heni Pore says she was not aware at that time of the code framed by Taratoa and his fellow-chiefs. In the private chapel of the Bishop's palace in Lichfield, England, there is a painted window (placed there by the first Bishop Selwyn) commemorating the Gate *Pa* incident attributed to Henare Taratoa. There is no doubt of Henare's chivalry and high-mindedness, but it is Heni Pore who rightly deserves the credit of this specific deed of humanity in the lines at Pukehinahina. The episode offers an inspiring historical subject for some of our New Zealand artists.

The present main road from Tauranga to Rotorua cuts through the centre of the Gate *Pa* works, at a distance of two miles from the town; and the road inland via Pye's *Pa*—the most direct route to Oropi and Rotorua—also traverses the centre of the entrenchments at Te Ranga. A little memorial church stands by the roadside on the spot once occupied by the trenches of Ngai-te-Rangi at the Gate *Pa*, but there is nothing to inform the passer-by as to the site of the defences. On the crown of the Pukehinahina Hill behind the church the lines of the British redoubt erected in 1864 on the remains of the Maori *pa* are still well marked. The trench and fence on the west side of the road, above the Kopurererua Swamp, indicate the position of the left wing held by the small Koheriki party.

At Te Ranga, alongside the road, there are the remains of the trenches in which more than a hundred Maoris were buried. The road passes through the levelled lines; on each hand, but chiefly on the left, going inland, are the depressions indicating the rifle-pits and ditches of the works. In a paddock on the edge of the sudden descent to the valley, a few yards east of the road, there are trenches overgrown with gorse and fern; these formed the Maori right flank. A Maori monument is to be erected to mark the sacred spot where so many gallant warriors fell.

END OF VOLUME I.

APPENDICES.

SUPPLEMENTARY NOTES TO CHAPTERS.
(Chapter I.)
EARLY MILITARY OPERATIONS IN NEW ZEALAND.

THE first occasion on which British forces came into conflict with Maori warriors (leaving out of consideration Captain Cook's trifling encounters) was the punitive expedition to the Taranaki coast in 1834, when H.M.S. "Alligator" and the schooner "Isabella," from Sydney, landed bodies of sailors and soldiers who had been sent to rescue Mrs. Guard and her two children captured when the barque "Harriet" was wrecked near Cape Egmont. The troops employed (besides the sailors) were sixty-five men of the 50th Regiment, under Captain Johnson. On the 8th October the forces landed on the beach near Waimate *pa*, on the south side of the Kapuni River, and fired heavily on the Maoris after securing the remaining child, little Jack Guard. A British flag of truce was flying at the time, but the troops got out of hand. After the sharp skirmishing the force escaladed the evacuated hill-fort Waimate, which had been shelled on the 1st October, and also captured the *pa* Orangi-tuapeka, on the northern side of the Kapuni. On the 11th October both fortified villages were destroyed.

The first British troops stationed in New Zealand were 100 men of the 80th Regiment, under Major Bunbury, who arrived at Auckland from Sydney in 1840.

In 1842, as the result of an outbreak of war between the Ngai-te-Rangi and Arawa Tribes in the Bay of Plenty—an aftermath, by a curious chain of circumstances, of Taraia's cannibal raid on Ongare, Whanake's *pa* on Katikati Harbour—a military expedition was despatched from Auckland to Tauranga. Two traders' boats had been seized, and as one of these was retained by the Arawa, of Maketu, it was proposed to attack that *pa*. Major Bunbury took fifty of his men, and was given three guns from H.M.S. "Tortoise," a store-ship loading *kauri* spars at the Great Barrier. The Government brig "Victoria" landed the small force at the entrance to Tauranga Harbour, and Bunbury encamped at Hopu-kiore, a short distance east of Mount Maunganui. Several weeks were spent there quietly, and then the expedition was withdrawn, after serving as a kind of buffer between the two tribes, which presently made peace. Lieutenant Bennett, R.E., had shortly before this examined and reported on a number of the Maori fortified positions at and around Tauranga.

(Chapter IV.)
THE FALL OF KORORAREKA.

The authorities in Kororareka had timely warning of Heke's intended attack, but failed to profit by it. On the evening of the 10th March Mr. Gilbert Mair came across from Wahapu to Kororareka in his boat and warned the Police Magistrate (Mr. Beckham) that Heke intended attacking the town and the flagstaff next morning with four or five divisions. Mr. Mair's information was based upon an announcement made by Heke himself; the Ngapuhi warriors had been assembling near Mair's place at Wahapu for three or four days previously. Heke invariably let his intentions be known, and invariably carried them out. Archdeacon Williams wrote to the Magistrate on the same day, saying, "I understand that the natives intend to make their attack in four divisions." In spite of these warnings, however, the surprise of the flagstaff blockhouse was complete.

(Chapter IX.)
The Capture of Rua-pekapeka.

It is said that the principal damage to the smashed carronade (sketch, p. 75) mounted by Kawiti in Rua-pekapeka *pa* was caused many years after the war by some Europeans who amused themselves by exploding a charge of blasting-powder in it.

(Chapter X.)
The New Zealand Company's Purchases, Wellington.

In the Land Claims Court held at Wellington in 1842 by Mr. Spain, the Imperial Government's Commissioner, Colonel Wakefield was asked, "Was it explained to the natives before they signed the deed that they were selling their *pas*, burying-grounds, and cultivated lands contained within the boundaries specified in the deed?"

The answer was: "The expression made use of was that they were selling all the land within those boundaries, but that reserves would be made for them; there was no special mention made as to their *pas*, burial-grounds, and cultivated lands."

Mr. Spain, in his report on the Port Nicholson lands (1st March, 1845), criticized the manner in which the deed had been interpreted to the Maoris by Richard Barrett. Spain asked Barrett to give exactly the terms in which he had explained to the natives the deed of purchase by the Company. He did so in Maori, which was translated literally into English by the Court interpreter, as follows:—

"Listen, natives, all the people of Port Nicholson. This is a paper respecting the purchase of land of yours. This paper has the names of all the places of Port Nicholson. Understand, this is a good book. Listen, the whole of you natives to write your names in this book; and the names of the places are Tararua [continuing on to the other side of Port Nicholson, to the name Parangarahu]. This is a book of the names of the channels and the woods, and the whole of them to write in this book, people and children, the land to 'Wideawake.' When people arrive from England it will show you your part, the whole of you."

Barrett was afterwards asked, "Did you tell the natives who signed the deed that one-tenth of the land described should be reserved for the use of themselves and their families, or simply that the Europeans should have one portion of the land and the natives the other portion?" His answer was, "No, I did not tell them that they would get one-tenth; I said they were to get a certain portion of the land described, without describing what that portion was."

"It appears to me," wrote Mr. Spain, "that this interpretation in explanation was not calculated to explain to the natives who were parties to the purchase-deed a correct idea of what lands that instrument purported to convey, or of the nature or extent of the reserves that had been made for their benefit, and this will in a great measure account for the very determined manner in which the natives generally in the district opposed the occupation of the lands by the Europeans, and denied the sale to Colonel Wakefield from the earliest period to the arrival of the settlers."

The Karori Settlement, Wellington.

The following is an extract from a letter written by Judge H. S. Chapman, Wellington, 24th July, 1846, to his father in England:—

"The attack on the camp at the Hutt produced a good deal of alarm among the settlers, even in the town and elsewhere, and for several days even our quite neighbourhood [Karori] was agitated. A body of thirty-two Militia was enrolled; twelve armed police were sent up, and other preparations made to prevent surprise and repel attack. This was something, though not so well done as it might have been. Some of the settlers went into town, but we did not see any reason for so doing until 26th May, when I received an especial warning from Moturoa, a friendly chief of the Ngati-Awa, and from Hemi, another of the same tribe, that I had better go into town, as it had certainly been determined in Rangihaeata's *pa* to attack Karori. I have since learned that this was true—that it was discussed whether the attacks should be confined to the Hutt or be extended elsewhere, and Rangihaeata said it should be at Karori. I believe his policy was to send out parties of ten or twelve to plunder and murder in different directions, but I believe he has been restrained by the weakness of his own force, by the preparations everywhere made, and by the opposition of his own followers. This last may be attributed to native custom being in favour of attacks on the Hutt, where he had a real quarrel and a real claim for satisfaction (*utu*), whereas he has no such claim elsewhere. Rauparaha claimed the merit of this, and I think it not unlikely that he may have used his influence in that direction, but I believe the chief opposition was within the *pa* Wai-taingi-nui [Paua-taha-nui]. I know for certain that there is an old chief of the Ngati-Toa called Te Ra-ka-herea who joined his relation Rangihaeata from what the Natives called *whakama*—" cause (to be) white," or shame—that is, because all his relations being with Rangi, he felt *whakama* at not being with them ; but being at the same time not ill-disposed towards the *pakehas*, he has acted as a bridle on Rangi's angry passions.

" Karori is certainly the least likely place for an attack. It is far from Rangi's *pa*—the military station is between it and Karori in one direction, and other difficulties intervene ; still, I thought a diversion might be made here simultaneously with an attack on the Hutt. Then, all the settlers rely on me, and as I could not be sure that we were secure I could not feel justified in lulling the people into a feeling of security which might be fallacious. I therefore told all the settlers to send the women and children into town, which was done, and we followed in the evening."

A party of sailors from H.M.S. " Calliope " went out to Karori to protect the property of Judge Chapman and other settlers.

(Chapter XII.)

FORT PAREMATA, PORIRUA.

The stone barracks, two-storeyed, at Paremata, near the entrance to Porirua Harbour, were built 1846–47, and were enclosed in a stockade extending to the waterfront. The earthquakes of 1848 and 1855 reduced the building to a ruinous condition. It originally had one or more small cannon mounted for a time on its turrets or flanking works. The remains of the lower walls are to be seen from the railway-line at the Paremata Bridge over the entrance to Paua-taha-nui Inlet.

(Chapter XIV.)

THE NAME " WANGANUI."

" Whanganui," meaning the great bay or estuary, referring to the mouth of the river, is the correct spelling of the name usually now written " Wanganui." An alternative traditional meaning is " the place of long-waiting," in allusion to the necessity of waiting for low tide before crossing at the mouth. The " h " has been dropped in common usage, and it has therefore been deemed best to follow in this History the modern spelling in respect of the town and the river. The original form " Whanganui," however, has been retained when referring to the Maori tribes of the district.

(Chapter XVI.)

THE MAORI KING MOVEMENT.

Bishop G. A. Selwyn strongly sympathized with the Maori aspirations for self-government, which he considered were an indication of a desire for a better kind of government than that which they had. He thought the Maoris' desires might have been directed into lawful channels. " I never knew or read of any people," he told a Committee of the House of Representatives in 1863, " so entirely desirous of law as the New-Zealanders." In 1860 Selwyn had sent Governor Gore Browne a memorandum in which he made the following important suggestions embodying a large measure of home rule for the Maoris :—

" If the central district of the northern Island, including Waikato, Taupo, Rotorua, Opotiki, Waiapu, and Poverty Bay, were formed into one or more provinces, a simple system of elective and representative government, under immediate sanction of the Governor, might probably be brought into operation. The form of government, as in the Swiss cantons, need not be in all parts exactly the same, but might be adapted to the wishes and customs of particular tribes, provided that in all cases two fundamental points were adhered to—that the chief magistrates and councillors should be recommended by the tribe and confirmed by the Governor, and that all regulations made by them should require the Governor's assent. It would probably be found possible to bring these chief magistrates together in a general council, and many regulations made at such a meeting and assented to by the Governor might be held to be binding upon all the tribes. This system ought to rest at first upon voluntary compact, and rather to be offered as a boon than enforced by authority, because while the native people are thirsting for better government they are not without fear of oppression. The tone of some of the English newspapers has given them sufficient reason to expect the usual fate of a race assumed to be inferior."

Selwyn, reviewing this proposal after three years, considered that such a scheme of government might either have absorbed the King movement or have allowed it to remain standing by itself in the midst of other and better systems carried on under the direction of the Government. He thought the Maori could have been moulded easily into any system that would elevate the race and tend to union and social amalgamation with the Europeans. It was most essential that there should be tribunals for land ; without them no system of government would be useful.

Sir George Grey accepted some of Selwyn's ideas, and on his last visit to Ngaruawahia before the war, when he met the principal Kingite chiefs, with the exception of Tawhiao and Rewi, propounded a scheme of self-government in a last effort to reconcile the two races. Grey summarized the proposals in these words in a despatch some years after the war (27th October, 1869) to Earl Granville, Secretary of State for the Colonies :—

" Whilst large bodies of troops were in the country, and before the war commenced, I paid a visit to the Waikato tribes, who I believed were resolved upon a formidable outbreak. The whole of their principal chiefs met me, with the exception of the Maori King, who was ill ; and I, to those chiefs, with the full consent of my responsible advisers, offered to constitute all the Waikato and Ngati-Maniapoto country a separate province, which would have the right of electing its own Superintendent, its own Legislature, and of choosing its own Executive Government—and, in fact, would have had practically the same powers and rights as any State of the United States has now. There could hardly have been a more ample and complete recognition of Maori authority, as the Waikato tribes would within their own district—a very large one—have had the exclusive control and management of their own affairs. This offer was, however, after full discussion and consideration, refused, on the ground they would accept no offer that did not involve an absolute recognition of the Maori King and his and their entire independence from the Crown of England—terms which no subject had power to grant, and which could not have been granted without creating worse evils than those which their refusal involved."

THE CHOOSING OF THE MAORI KING.

The following is an account from native sources describing the efforts of the Maori kingmakers to find a chief willing to take the office of head of the confederation of tribes. It differs in some details from and amplifies the narrative in Chapter XVI; it is interesting also for its picturesque Maori idioms and proverbial expressions.

Tamehana te Rauparaha, after his voyage to England, pondered over the question of the good government of the Maori people, and formed the belief that they would be benefited by the setting-up of a King. He suggested to his cousin, Matene te Whiwhi, that they should search for a King for the tribes. This was in 1851-52. They went to the Whanganui and made their proposal to the chief Te Anaua, but he was unwilling to take the kingship, and said, " Inland yonder is Ruapehu the mountain; there is Turoa the man." So the delegates went up the river and placed their request before Pehi Turoa, the high chief of the Upper Whanganui tribes. Turoa in his turn indicated the *ariki* of the Ngati-Tuwharetoa Tribe, of Taupo, by quoting the proverbial saying, " *Ko Tongariro te Maunga, ko Taupo te Moana, ko Te Heuheu te Tangata*" (" Tongariro is the Mountain, Taupo is the Sea, Te Heuheu is the Man "). Tamehana and Matene therefore travelled to the south end of Lake Taupo and interviewed Te Heuheu Iwikau. He, too, declined, saying it was impossible for him to be King; he had only a small tribe. He suggested the great East Coast chief Te Kani-a-Takirau as a suitable King. The request was made to Te Kani, who replied to the purport that he did not want any foreign titles; he was *ariki* in his own domains.

Next the offer was made to Te Amohau, of the Arawa, but the chief Moko-nui-a-rangi of that tribe objected, saying, " If Te Amohau is a king, then I am a king too."

The delegates had also been to Taranaki, and had met with a refusal from Te Hanataua, chief of Ngati-Ruanui. So they were in a dilemma; no one wanted to be King.

At length (1856) a large meeting was held at Taupo, and was attended by representatives of all the tribes. Matene te Whiwhi in an oration unfolded his final proposal in the eloquent and figurative manner of the Maori. " I look far over the sea to the south," he said, " and what do I see ? Mountains covered with snow and ice. I turn and gaze across the land to the east and what do I behold but cabbage-trees ? [An allusion to the Kaingaroa Plain.] I turn my eyes to the belly of the Fish of Maui [Taupo]; I see nought but the little *kokopu* fish and the crayfish that walks backwards *(te koura hoki whakamuri)*. I turn to the west and look over the forests to Taranaki. I see there but broken ropes *(taura motu-motu)*. [Meaning, the tribes of that district were suffering from wars and disunion.] I look far northward; I see there a leaking house. Now," declared Matene, making his point and climax, " I turn my eyes to Waikato. I behold Waikato Taniwha-rau, Waikato of whose river it is said, ' *He piko he taniwha; he piko he taniwha* ' (' Waikato of a hundred dragons; Waikato whose every bend holds a water monster—*i.e.*, a strong and numerous tribe, with many great chiefs'). Yonder is the man who should be King of the Maori people."

Such was the manner in which Matene directed the attention of the tribes to Potatau te Wherowhero, the warrior chief of Waikato, and soon thereafter Potatau was chosen as King.

At the great ceremonial meeting at Ngaruawahia (1858) for the purpose of installing Potatau as King, Iwikau te Heuheu and Wiremu Tamehana Tarapipipi te Waharoa were the inducting high chiefs. The solemn rite of making the old warrior King of the Maori *Kotahitanga* took this form:—

Iwikau said: "Potatau, this day I create you King of the Maori people. You and Queen Victoria shall be bound together to be one *(paiheretia kia kotahi)*. The religion of Christ shall be the mantle of your protection; the law shall be the *whariki* mat for your feet, for ever and ever onward" *(ake, ake tonu atu)*.

"*Ae*," replied Potatau. "Yes, I agree, for ever and ever onward." And the aged warrior King continued: "*Kotahi te kohao o te ngira e kuhuna ai te miro ma, te miro pango, te miro whero*" ("There is but one eye of the needle, through which the white, the black, and the red threads must pass").

This declaration was succeeded by the anointing after the Scriptural manner. Wiremu Tamehana poured the oil on Potatau's head, and all the people bowed their heads three times in obeisance at the call, "*Whakahonare ki te Kingi*" ("Do honour to the King").

This narrative attests the altruistic aims of the kingmakers. They sought a head to bind the tribes together for the national betterment, in amity with the white Queen, and Potatau himself was anxious to continue his long friendship with the *pakeha* people.

(Chapter XVII.)

THE WAITARA PURCHASE.

Sir George Grey, Governor, in his despatches to the Secretary of State for the Colonies, strongly criticized the methods of a previous Administration in forcibly dispossessing Wiremu Kingi and other owners of the disputed Pekapeka Block, Waitara, and detailed the reasons for the renunciation of the attempted purchase. Writing on the 24th April, 1863, he said: "My settled conviction is that the natives of the Waitara are in the main right in their allegations regarding the Waitara purchase, and that it ought not to be gone on with. . . . It does not involve any new acquisition of territory for Her Majesty and the Empire." The Queen had no legal title to the land, and it seemed more than doubtful if such a title could ever be given to her; and the block had never been paid for. Teira Manuka had only received a deposit of £100, and this the Government decided to relinquish.

In further despatches and minutes the Governor said that Wiremu Kingi's own home at Te Kuikui *pa* and the homes of two hundred of his people were destroyed by the troops in 1860; the houses and the surrounding cultivations were burned. The Waitara owners thereupon retaliated by burning an exactly corresponding number of European settlers' houses.

"Ought Her Majesty," Sir George Grey asked in a memorandum, "to make such a purchase in which she gained for an inconsiderable sum a property worth much more, and acquired against their will and consent the homes of more than two hundred of her subjects, which they had occupied in peace and happiness for years, and who were not even accused of any crime against Her Majesty or her laws, but some of whom had, on the contrary, risked their lives in rendering her service in former wars?"

The Governor further showed that the forcible occupation of the Pekapeka Block in 1860 had convinced the Maoris that a new system of obtaining lands was to be established, and that they would all be despoiled like Waitara if they did not make general resistance. They became convinced that their destruction was decided upon, and thus there arose an almost universal belief that the struggle was one for house and home. Hence the wrong done the natives by the seizure of the Waitara land was the cause of other wars.

APPENDICES. 437

Chapter XXVI.
THE GOVERNMENT'S APPEAL TO THE NGATI-WHATUA TRIBE (1860).

A hitherto unchronicled incident in the early stages of the Government's quarrel with the Waikato tribes was the despatch of Mr. S. Percy Smith (afterwards Surveyor-General) to the Kaipara district in order to enlist the assistance of the Ngati-Whatua Tribe. Mr. Smith was well acquainted with these people, having been surveying in the Kaipara and Northern Wairoa districts in 1859-60. The following is an extract from his MS. journal of reminiscences (furnished by his son, Mr. M. Crompton Smith, Chief Draughtsman, Survey Department) :—

"At the time of my return to town (from survey work at the Kaipara) there was considerable anxiety in Auckland on account of the Waikato tribes, which, it had been reported, were about to make a descent on the city and drive the white people into the sea. Most of the troops were in Taranaki, and the forces to oppose such a raid were composed of the Volunteers and Militia, only partially trained. It was therefore decided to send for the Orakei and Kaipara people (Ngati-Whatua) to come to the defence of the city. As I knew the people well by this time, it was thought I was the best messenger to fetch them. On the 4th April, 1860, therefore, I received instructions to return to Kaipara with all possible speed and bring the people in at once. They were then assembled at Northern Wairoa, engaged in peacemaking with Nga-Puhi. An hour after receiving my instructions I was away up the Wai-te-mata with three Maoris on this business. We travelled on over the portage through the night, arriving at Kapoai, a native village on the upper Kaipara, at 3 a.m., and, as soon as the tide served, started down the river for the Wairoa. I remember we all fell asleep on the way, but there was only a slight breeze, so no harm befell us. When we arrived at Tauhara we found all the natives had gone on to Te Kopuru, some forty miles up the river, where I found them encamped, on the site of the present Kopuru sawmills. In addition to about four hundred Ngati-Whatua, there were some two hundred Nga-Puhi, and they had built a square of temporary huts and tents with a large open space in the centre for speeches and war-dances.

"As soon as I arrived I was seated on a stool in the centre of this square, where the letter from the Government was read and I had to explain the necessity for the Auckland tribes returning at once to assist in the defence of the city. But they did not appear in any hurry, and declared that they could not leave till they had concluded the peace with Nga-Puhi, all of which was very annoying to me, as I had to impress them to make all haste back. Otherwise this great meeting was very interesting to me, for it was held with all the formality of ancient times—long speeches, war-dances, and all kinds of old ceremonies, not the least interesting of which were the *hari-tuku-kai*, or songs and dances of the women and young men as they advanced into the square, bringing the baskets of food held in their hands above their heads. My tent was pitched in the square, and generally one of the chiefs sat with me to explain the meaning of the various speeches and ceremonies. It was not until the 11th that peace was made and we all left, the Nga-Puhi going up the river, and the rest of us down stream to Tauhara; and a very fine sight it was to see our flotilla of about thirty boats and several fine war-canoes under sail. We were detained there by bad weather until the 18th, for the crossing inside Kaipara Heads is only to be undertaken in fine weather; it is so dangerous a place owing to the heavy seas which get up. It was not till the 20th that we arrived in town, and then most of my relieving force had melted away. Luckily the Waikato tribes had changed their minds and gone home, and so ended my urgent trip to fetch help to Auckland.

"Had the necessity arisen there is no doubt the Ngati-Whatua Tribe would willingly have fought against their old enemies the Waikato. And.

moreover, this tribe felt a kind of responsibility for the safety of the *pakeha*, for after a great meeting at Okahu (Orakei, on Auckland Harbour) they had sent an emissary to the Bay of Islands, to Governor Hobson, inviting him to occupy their country on the Isthmus of Auckland, and form his seat of Government there. [This was in the beginning of 1841 ; the Auckland Settlement had already been established, but the seat of Government was still at the Bay of Islands.] It was not entirely an unselfish offer on their part, for the Tamaki Isthmus had been the constant highway of hostile war-parties both from north and south for ages past, and they thought that if they could get the white man to settle there these hostile incursions would cease, which in fact they did, for ever. In these raids Ngati-Whatua always suffered."

(Chapter XXVII.)
THE WELLINGTON DISTRICT AND DEFENCES (1863).

Just before the British troops crossed the Waikato border river, the Manga-tawhiri (July, 1863), a letter was sent by Taati te Waru and Porokoru Titipa, two of the leading chiefs of Upper Waikato (at Rangiaowhia and Te Awamutu), to the tribes in the southern parts of the Island inviting them to join in the general war against the Europeans. The tribes addressed were Ngati-Kahungunu, Te Atiawa, and Ngati-Raukawa, inhabiting the districts from the Wairarapa and Manawatu to Otaki and Waikanae ; the chiefs named included Ngairo, of the Wairarapa, and Wi Tako Ngatata, an erstwhile supporter of the Government, at Waikanae. The letter, which had been discussed at a meeting of the *runanga* in the Ngati-Maniapoto meeting-house " Hui-te-Rangiora," at Kihikihi, invited the southern Maoris to consider whether they should not follow Waikato's example and " sweep clean the fronts of your houses "—in other words, rise against the *pakeha*. The writers quoted Rewi's favourite war-song, which he either chanted or sent in writing on his Kingite recruiting missions, the ancient *ngeri* beginning " *Puhi kura, puhi kura, puhi kaka* " ("Red plumes, red plumes, plumes of the *kaka* "), and ending with an injunction to " grasp firm your weapons—strike." The " red plumes " were now interpreted as referring to the uniforms of the soldiers.

The call to arms excited sympathy among some of the Ngati-Kahungunu, and a critical situation existed in the Wairarapa until Dr. Featherston, Superintendent of the Province of Wellington, assisted by Major Gorton, commanding the Militia, took measures to arm the white residents. Volunteer Rifle Corps were quickly sworn in at Greytown, Carterton, and Masterton, and stockades were begun at Masterton and Carterton.

It had been reported that the Ngati-Kahungunu intended to march over the Rimutaka Range and attack the Hutt settlements. The prompt defence arrangements overawed the Kingite section of the Wairarapa natives. The Kingites had urged Wi Tako Ngatata, of Waikanae, to attack the settlement at Paua-taha-nui, but he gave information to the Government side, and declined to fall in with the war-party's scheme, although he was a sympathiser with the King movement. A detachment of mounted troops (Colonial Defence Force) was stationed at Paua-taha-nui.

The Upper Hutt had been provided with a fortified post in the beginning of 1861. This was a stockade and ditch, with a two-storeyed timber blockhouse forming one of the angle bastions. The stockade was constructed on McHardy's Clearing, between the present sites of Wallaceville and Trentham. The old blockhouse is still standing ; it is loopholed for rifle-fire, and made bullet-proof in the usual way with a filling of gravel between the outside wall and the lining. The blockhouse was garrisoned on occasions in the " sixties " by the Upper Hutt Militia, who were chiefly bushmen and sawmill workers. A similar defensive work was built, at the end of 1860' at the Lower Hutt, near the bridge, but was never required.

APPENDICES.

(Chapter XXVIII.)
THE NGATI-PAOA INVASION OF AUCKLAND.

Hori Ngakapa te Whanaunga (p. 249) was one of the leaders of the war-canoe expedition of the Ngati-Paoa Tribe to Auckland Town in 1851 in order to exact redress for the wrongful arrest of the chief Hoera, due to a mistake on the part of the police when he went to inquire into the arrest of a man named Ngawiki for theft. The Ngati-Paoa settlements were up in arms, and a fleet of five large canoes assembled at Te Huruhi, Waiheke Island. This fleet consisted of canoes from Pukorokoro (Miranda), Taupo (Sandspit), Waiari, Wharekawa, and Te Umu-puia (Te Wairoa). The crews were composed of the Tau-iwi, Pakahorahora, Ngati-Tai, and Ngati-Whanaunga, numbering two hundred and fifty to three hundred men. Te Puhata commanded the Ngati-Paoa *hapus*, whilst Ngati-Whanaunga were directed by young Hori Ngakapa in a great war-canoe called " Te Waikohaere." Haora Tipa came in command of the " Maramarua,' a decorated canoe manned by fifty paddlers. Another chief was Aperahama Pokai, of Pukorokoro. The flotilla, augmented by several Waiheke canoes, swept up into the Waitemata on the morning of the 23rd April, 1851, and the crews leaped ashore on the beach at Waipapa (Mechanics Bay) and performed a great war-dance preparatory to demanding redress for the insult to their chief (who was temporarily under the sacred ban of *tapu* when he was roughly handled by a native policeman). Warning, however, had reached Governor Grey, and the warriors found themselves faced by the local troops—the 58th Regiment, with four guns, and the Royal New Zealand Fencibles—who lined Constitution Hill and the Parnell slopes commanding the bay, while a British frigate, H.M.S. " Fly," dropped down the harbour and anchored off Waipapa, with her guns trained on the beached fleet of canoes.

After much angry argument the Maoris obeyed the Governor's ultimatum, and with heavy labour dragged their canoes to the water—it was now low tide—and paddled down the harbour for Orakei and their homes. Their chiefs later made formal submission to the Governor and presented him with several greenstone *meres*.

Mr. George Graham writes that this incident is spoken of among the Ngati-Paoa as " Te Toanga-roa" ("The Long Hauling"), in reference to the dragging of the canoes from high-water mark to low water over the mud-flats of Mechanics Bay.

THE ROYAL NEW ZEALAND FENCIBLES.

The corps known as the Royal New Zealand Fencibles, referred to in the foregoing note, was a body of veteran soldiers converted into military settlers, established through Governor Grey's efforts as a protection for the southern frontier of the Auckland Settlement. It consisted of discharged British soldiers, about three-fourths of them pensioners, and all men of approved character and physique. The corps was enrolled in England in 1847. The term of service in New Zealand was to be seven years (most of the soldiers became permanent settlers); the pay was 1s. 3d. per day in addition to any pension; free passages were granted to New Zealand for the soldiers and their wives and families; and on arrival in the colony each Fencible was given possession of a two-roomed cottage and an acre of land, already partly cleared and made ready for cultivation; he also received an advance for furniture and stock. The members of the corps were required to attend six days' drill in the spring and six in the autumn, and to attend church parade every Sunday, fully armed, for inspection. The Commandant (Major Kenny) was paid £600 per annum, and two captains £300; each officer was given a house and 50 acres of land. The discipline and drill of these old soldiers were excellent. The Fencibles included veterans of the wars in China and Afghanistan and the great battles in India, and several had served in the British Legion enlisted for the Carlist War in Spain in 1836. The settlements in which the pensioners were established were Onehunga, Otahuhu, Panmure, and Howick; these places were practically founded as villages by the Fencibles. Three companies were given land at Onehunga, three at Howick, one at Otahuhu, and one at Panmure. Not only did they form a strong wall of defence for Auckland on the south, covering the routes by the Tamaki River and Manukau Harbour, but they provided a much-needed source of labour for the farmers on the outskirts.

(Chapter XXIX.)

THE FOREST RANGERS AND THE BOWIE-KNIPE.

The knife with which Von Tempsky's (No. 2) Company of the Forest Rangers was armed, 1863–64 (pages 258–259), was somewhat after the pattern of the bowie-knife of Texan fame. Many stories have been related as to the origin of the knife, and it has often been accredited to Colonel James Bowie, a man of mark on the old Texas and Arkansas frontier, U.S.A. The facts, however, as related recently in the *Arkansas Gazette* centennial number (quoted in the *Adventure* Magazine) by the Hon. D. W. Jones, ex-Governor of the State of Arkansas, show that James Bowie was not the inventor, although he was the man who made the weapon famous. The first maker of this kind of knife was James Black, a blacksmith, gunsmith, and cutler in the frontier town of Washington, Arkansas. He was a most skilful maker of hunting-knives, and his weapons were celebrated for their fine temper. Black appears to have discovered by experiment the secret of Damascus steel. About 1831 James Bowie gave Black an order for a fighting-knife, and the artificer made one after his own matured taste in point of size and shape. Shortly afterwards Bowie was attacked by three desperadoes, all of whom he killed with the knife. Black thereafter was in great demand as a maker of " Bowie-knives."

Colonel J. M. Roberts, N.Z.C., of Rotorua, states that the knives were made in Auckland from a pattern supplied by Von Tempsky. They were rather roughly finished, but the steel was good. In shape the weapon was very like a sheep-shears blade; length of blade about 9 inches, width at the handle end about 2½ inches. The back for part of the length was about ¼ inch thick, and was gradually ground to a fine edge.

(Chapter XXXI.)

ESCAPE OF THE KOHERIKI FROM THE WAIROA RANGES.

The venerable Arawa half-caste woman Heni te Kiri-karamu (Heni Pore, or Jane Foley), of Rotorua, gave the writer the following narrative of the manner in which the small party of Koheriki with whom she fought in the war eluded the troops in the redoubts and camps forming a chain from the Thames Gulf to the Waikato River at the end of 1863:—

" After the surprise and defeat of some of our people by Jackson's Forest Rangers in the Upper Wairoa bush (14th December, 1863) we became very cautious in our movements, and anxious to make our way to the main body of the Kingites in the Waikato. The soldiers had camps and redoubts in the Wairoa Valley and along the western side of the ranges, from

Papakura southward, and a chain of military posts was established from Pukorokoro (the Miranda), on the Thames Gulf, across to the Waikato River. We were thus hemmed in on all sides. We camped for some time in a deep valley between the Mangatawhiri and the Mangatangi Streams, in the mountains south-east of the Wairoa. We were afraid even to light fires for cooking or to warm ourselves, and afraid, too, to shoot wild pigs or birds for food, lest the sound of the shots would bring the Rangers down on us. We scouted cautiously out to the edge of the forest in the upper valley of the Mangatawhiri, and there, peering through the trees, we saw the white tents and the sentry cordon of the troops barring our way. We were in a bad way now for food, and for three weeks we lived almost entirely on wild honey and cold water. Besides my mother and my children, my sister Hera (Sarah) was with me at this time; we had got her up from Taupo village (at the Sandspit) to help me with the children. One of the Piri-Rakau men (there were two or three with us) also assisted us in carrying the little ones through the forest.

"It was now decided that we should break through the chain of troops. Two of our best men were sent out to the open land as scouts, and they let us know the most propitious time for making our dash through and across the river ahead of us (the Mangatangi). There was a log bridge by which we hoped to cross, a place where the river was very deep; it consisted of two or three trees sawn down, squared, and thrown across the river. Our little rearguard—the two men who had gone out scouting, and who were instructed to cut down the bridge after we had passed—had a perilous post, but we were all in a most desperate position. Once we crossed the river, however, we would be safe. We made our escape in the night. The troops lit fires in the fern in order to deter us from passing through, but the smoke from these fires screened us and helped our safe passage. We passed so close to the tents that we could hear some of the soldiers playing an accordion and laughing and talking. [This was near the Surrey Redoubt.] After a very anxious time, during which we kept strict silence, we passed the sentry lines and crossed the river by the log bridge, which our axemen then chopped through. By this time it was daylight, and the white sentinel reported the track of our march. A force was immediately sent in pursuit of us; we could see dust rising and the bayonets shining in the sun. Some of the troops were mounted men. [The troops were Waikato Militia and C.D.F. Cavalry.] Their advance was stopped by the destruction of the bridge, and we were safe away for the Waikato country. We travelled southward a long way inland from the Waikato River, in the direction of the Piako. Soon after crossing the river we had to wade through a deep, boggy swamp, a very exhausting journey. At last we reached solid land on its south side, practically an island, and there we rested for a day or two recruiting our energies and revelling in the abundant supply of food—bush-pigeons, eels, pork, and potatoes.

"After a good rest," continued Heni, "we embarked in canoes, which we found on the shore of this island in the lagoon; it was the northern part of Lake Waikare. We crossed the lake, and continued our journey to the country of our friends the Ngati-Haua, William Thompson's tribe. We crossed over some low hills into the swampy valley of the Piako, and from there we went on to Matamata, on the Upper Thames, where Te Raihi, the Ngati-Haua Queenite chief, was living. He befriended us, and we had a rest, then he advised us to go on to Peria, close to the river. Peria was a large village, the great gathering-place of many Kingite tribes, from the Waikato valley and the Hauraki to Rotorua and as far away as the East Cape. All were there — Ngati-Haua, Ngati-Raukawa, Ngati-Rangiwewehi, of the Arawa nation, and Ngati-Porou from the East Cape. At Peria I met Pokai and Hori Ngakapa and their tribe the Ngati-Paoa. We made this our home for a season. We had fields of maize, wheat, and potatoes which grew abundantly, and we ground the wheat and maize into flour in steel hand-mills, and made bread and maize cakes, and we were supplied with plenty of other food—sheep, bullocks, and pigs. It was a land of abundance, Peria, in William Thompson's day. This was the summer of 1863–64. From Peria we all went farther inland again, carrying our arms and provisions, and joined the main body of Waikato in a very fine strong *pa* called Te Tiki o te Ihingarangi. It stood on a cliff-top above the Waikato River, on the left or western side of the river, between Pukerimu—then a camp of the soldiers—and the Maunga-tautari Ranges. It was strongly palisaded and trenched. It was an ancient fighting *pa*, which Waikato had greatly strengthened. When we abandoned it we crossed over to the eastern ranges, and thence to Okauia and Tauranga."

Operations on the Wairoa.

Lieut.-Colonel Arthur Morrow, V.D. (Staff, retired), supplies the following narrative of the expedition of the Auckland Rifle Volunteers to Wairoa South in 1863 :—

"It was on a raw, dreary morning in the early spring of 1863 that the detachments of the Auckland Rifle Volunteers intended to relieve the Militia garrison doing duty in the Galloway Redoubt in the Wairoa district embarked on the Government steamer 'Sandfly,' then commanded by Captain Marks. We landed at the farm owned by the late Captain Salmon, and made all possible speed by a bush track to the redoubt. The site on which the camp was situated commanded the bridge and approaches to the river some 300 or 400 yards distant to the east; farther on in that direction, on the other side of the river, was the stockade, a heavily timbered loopholed structure. Near-by was the store and district post-office. The ground on the north and west faces of the redoubt—an earthwork of rectangular shape, with salient angles, and later enclosed with a strong palisade—was covered with dense bush. The parish church stood a quarter of a mile to the north. The ground to the east and south had been cleared of bush and was under grass, whilst that to the south-eastward of the stockade still contained a good deal of standing timber faced by a thorn hedge. We took up the quarters allotted to us within the quadrangle in company with a detachment of the 65th Regiment, under Lieutenant Chevalier, later relieved by a detachment of the 18th (Royal Irish) Regiment, under Lieutenant Russell.

"On the afternoon of the 12th September we received the welcome intelligence through a friendly chief (Hori te Whetuki), called by the settlers 'Long George,' that the rebels had decided on attacking the camp in three days. On the morning of the 15th, when some of the men were playing cricket across the river, in the temporary company of a fatigue-party—told off to procure some slab timber for use in the redoubt—two shots were fired at them in quick succession from the hedge adjoining the bush, about 150 yards from the stockade. The cricketers and fatigue-party (who were unarmed) ran to the redoubt and stockade, from which the fire was quickly returned. The natives, however, not deeming it prudent to endeavour to carry the works by assault in the face of such a well-sustained rifle-fire, finally retired. The only casualty reported on our side was a slight arm-wound occasioned to Ensign Johnson by a spent ball. A young lad of Mr. Niccol's had a narrow escape, a ball having passed through his cap

"On the afternoon of the 17th we were again thrown into a state of excitement by the appearance of two travel-stained men of the mounted patrol, who galloped into camp with the news that a large party of natives was plundering the settlers' houses about three miles distant, and had exchanged some shots with the patrol. A detachment of twenty men from the stockade, under Lieutenant Steele, with thirty men from the redoubt, the whole under the command of Major W. C. Lyon, made a forced march to intercept the natives on their way to their settlement at Otau, a few miles up the river. Coming up with them in about an hour, our party opened fire, and, although the range was at first a long one, it had the effect of causing them to drop a considerable number of their packs containing loot. As they possessed an advantage over us in the direct route they were taking, we made a detour through a belt of bush and fallen timber, and came up with them at a closer range, when we commenced firing, killing three of their number. A deep stream, swollen by the recent rains, impeded us, and some of the men who wore greatcoats disappeared one after the other in the swollen torrent, and only managed to cross by great exertion. We succeeded at last in crossing, but our advance was finally checked by the Wairoa River, and we were obliged to content ourselves by extending in skirmishing order across the face of a hill commanding their village, and kept up a well-sustained fire on them, to which they replied vigorously by independent firing, as well as in volleys from numbers of men formed into large squares. There was very heavy firing, but we sustained no casualties. As it was now approaching dusk we retired, maintaining six paces intervals, as they had commenced an outflanking movement to cut us off.

"Our firing having been heard at the camp, we soon heard the bugle sounding the 'Advance' as a party of men of the 18th Regiment, under Lieutenant Russell, came to our relief. We now gave the natives a parting volley, and returned to camp. On the following morning a party of fifty men from our camp, with twenty Wairoa Rifles from the stockade, under Lieutenant Steele, left at 4 o'clock, arriving within 300 yards of the native village (Otau) shortly before daylight. We fired heavily into the *whares*, but as the river was still in flood we were unable to approach their position to a close range, and drew off without sustaining any casualties. On our way back to camp we buried the men killed on the previous evening. Later on in the day another expedition was organized, and twenty men of the 18th were despatched to occupy the position in front of the village, whilst Major Lyon, with seventy-five of all ranks, marched by a track on the other side of the river to take the settlement in the rear. We found, however, that the natives had gone. It was unfortunate that this course was not decided upon in the morning attack, when it would have assured success. We made a search through the village and secured much of the goods taken from the settlers (which we were enabled to return). The *whares* were riddled with bullets, and the profusion of blood-stains, both inside and out, testified to the native losses. We got several guns and tomahawks, and returned to camp.

"Matters now remained quiescent for a little time; then we ascertained that a large native force had assembled in the settlement of Urungaheuheu, some four miles distant across the river from our camp. An expedition was again organized, consisting of the 18th men with as many of the Rifle Volunteers as could be spared—having regard to the efficient protection of the redoubt. We arrived in the settlement early in the forenoon, only to find that the natives had made a hurried departure, leaving an old woman as the sole occupant. After a brief halt we pushed on again in the direction taken by the natives, and discovered that they were erecting a *pa* some miles distant in the ranges. Not being possessed of artillery or even sufficient supplies for such an expedition, we were obliged to return, picking up some fresh supplies for the camp in the way of pigs and poultry, in addition to which we recovered some watches and other valuables belonging to the settlers, together with guns and tomahawks. Our campaign was now brought to a close for the present, as we received orders to return to Auckland by the 'Sandfly,' under the command of Lieutenant Hunt (H.M.S. 'Harrier'). A relief detachment of Militia took our place in the redoubt."

(Chapter XXXII.)
The Titi Hill Fight, Mauku, 1863.

With reference to the late Volunteer Heywood Crispe's fast ride from Mauku to Drury for reinforcements (Titi Hill fight, 1863) (page 296), Mrs. Crispe, of "Te Mahoe," Mauku, states that her husband rode the distance (13½ miles) in less than an hour. "He had a powerful mount, and it was absolutely necessary to go full gallop at all times, as the Maoris often ambushed and fired at messengers on the route Mauku to Drury. On the morning of the Titi Hill fight, as there was a strong body of Maoris in the neighbourhood, it was important in more ways than one to secure immediate reinforcements, and with a good horse and rider there is no doubt that a record was put up."

(Chapter XXXVII.)
The Forest Rangers and a Scouting Expedition.

Shortly before the operations at Orakau (1864) some of the Forest Rangers distinguished themselves—though unofficially—by a daring expedition into the Maori country south of the Puniu River. They found camp life under Imperial control very irksome and slow after the freedom they had enjoyed in their active and useful campaigning, and parties of them relieved the comparative monotony by scouting along the frontier, occasionally skirmishing at long range with the Maoris. During March a small party from the two companies, under Lieutenants Roberts and Westrupp (Jackson and Von Tempsky were on leave), made an expedition from Kihikihi into the unknown enemy country across the Puniu. Keeping the Tokanui hills (the "Three Sisters") on their right, they penetrated a considerable distance to the south-east, and after crossing some streams (the Mangatu.u and Waikeria were two of these small rivers) they bivouacked on a wooded hill above the large settlement called Wharepapa, where there was a gathering of fugitives from the occupied country. The smoke was rising from the cooking *hangis* in the early morning as the Rangers descended the hill. The Maoris abandoned their breakfast and their village when the dreaded "Mirihia" ("Militia," as they distinguished the carbineers) came doubling down upon them, and retreated so speedily that Roberts and his comrades found it useless to follow them, and contented themselves with the captured pork and potatoes. It was not until long afterwards that Roberts ascertained the name of the village. This is one of the venturesome expedi ions of the Rangers which did not figure in despatches. In fact, it was not appreciated by the Imperial officers. When Roberts and Westrupp reported to the officer in command at Kihikihi Redoubt the result of their scouting enterprise he had them and their Rangers transferred to Te Awamutu Camp for their "wholly unauthorized ' zeal.

FOREST FIGHTING.

THE SKIRMISH AT THE BIG CLEARING, PATUMAHOE.

Major Von Tempsky, in his MS. journal (now in the Turnbull Library, Wellington), gave the following animated description of the first skirmish of the Mauku Forest Rifles and the Forest Rangers (8th September, 1863) :—

"We mustered about fifty men, including fifteen Mauku Rifles, under Lieutenant Lusk. From the Lower Mauku, where the stockade of the settlement was erected, the houses of the settlers straggle along a wooded ridge running south ; at about a mile and a half another ridge joins the former at a right angle, dotted with another set of settlers' houses, amongst them a little church with a white steeple, now made bullet-proof and garrisoned by settlers and Militia. At the eastern end of that settlement the native village of Patumahoe commences ; it had been abandoned long ago by the natives who had joined the cause of the fighting tribes. South of this about a mile or two lies the farm of Messrs. Lusk and Hill. We visited the house, and there at last we found fresh tracks. We followed them like sleuth-hounds. They led through the corner of a large paddock, then entered the bush by a well-beaten path. We were about a mile from the paddock when we heard three, four, five, six shots fired, evidently in the paddock. We turned and hastened back. It was reported from the rear that Maoris could be heard shouting to one another. Jackson and Lusk decided that the party should divide, a process I did not believe in but had to assent to. One party, under our ensign, Hay, and guided by Mr. Hill, were to look up the Maoris in our rear, as it was thought that there would be found the strongest number of enemies ; thirty men, all Forest Rangers, were allotted to that party. The remaining twenty, under Jackson, Lusk, and myself, proceeded towards the paddock.

"Cautiously we sallied from the bush, reconnoitring the paddock. We saw no enemy. At last we saw a beast lying dead, evidently. That sign at least was satisfactory. We rushed up to it, found it warm yet, and with six bullet-holes in it. We looked around ; nothing else was visible. The paddock was of great length, about half a mile square, covered with burnt stumps and logs. The settlers set to skinning the beast while it was warm, and I reflected on the probabilities of our case and kept the men from lumping together, as I did not believe in the apparent serenity of the bush.

"We had just scattered a bit when another shot was fired, towards the south-west corner of the paddock. There was no mistake in this ; there were the Maoris, and thus they intended to draw us on. We pleased them to a certain extent, but not exactly the way they wanted us to go—across the open paddock right on to the dense bush where the shot was fired. We made for the bush immediately opposite to us and followed its cover along the edge towards the direction of the shot. We knew that at every step now we might come upon the Maoris, and I can assure you we kept a sharp lookout all around us ; but we saw nothing ; nothing moved except what we moved.

"Thus we marched on. Where the deuce are the Maoris ? Down comes a volley with a vengeance. The powder-smoke is blown into our faces ; I rub my eyes—I can hardly see for the saltpetre-fumes in them. 'Give it to them, boys, right and left ! ' and away crack our carbines and rifles. Over the din, the clatter and spatter of shots, you can hear the high-pitched voice of a Maori chanting an incantation. Our carbines answer. Ah, you hear a change of key now—you hear those two or three fellows singing 'Miserere Domine'—and such a Miserere!—that one fellow in particular must have been hit in the spine, for his yells are abominable. Are none of our men hit? I cannot see one down yet—they are all behind the trees, and blazing away for the very life of them. What they can see, however, is an enigma to me, for all that I have seen, and see, are blue puffs of smoke from the green undergrowth. Once I saw a black head—had it on the bead of my revolver nearly, but it ducked. I have not fired a shot yet. Hang firing—I will try my old Mexican blade. A perfect labyrinth of fallen trees from the clearing, interlaced with a new green growth of creepers and old supplejack, is the accidental breastwork our friends have chosen as their fortress. I struggle into it, get hopelessly caught, and struggle out again. No advance that way, certainly. I join once more the skirmishers.

"Jackson has fallen in with a new idea. He has drawn five Rangers into the paddock behind some logs, and shouts to us to come to him. Of course it is a mistake; we remain where we are; but the Rangers commence blazing away, and we might get a friendly bullet by mistake, so we have to form in the paddock also, losing every chance of cutting off the retreat of the Maoris.

"There behind good cover, stumps and logs, a harmless exchange of shots is carried on for a while. Our thirty Rangers appear on our left wing, panting; they have found no Maoris, and, hearing our firing, have joined us.

"I urge a charge. Not yet. Very well. I can see nothing to fire at, so I lie behind my stump and look at Lusk, who is in the same predicament. I have a dog with me who won't go under cover, and gets hit in the head—only a graze though, as I found out afterwards.

"At last, while the fire of our opponents had grown slacker, for very good reasons, a party was sent from our right flank to cut them off. We were to charge when the cheer of this party was heard. We rushed with frantic valour into the bush. The bush was calmer than ever. We traverse and jump from tree to tree. Strange is this bush fighting—mysterious: blue smoke, green leaves, perhaps a black head: cries, defiant, soul-rending, you hear perhaps—yes, you can hear them talking next door to you, coolly, familiarly, but you see nothing—nothing tangible to grasp, to wrestle with.

"Our circumventive force still continued cheering in the depths of the wood, so that I began to think they had made a find of some of our game, but there they were dancing around a dozen extempore huts, the Maori encampment, revelling in retaken plunder and eating the Maori dinner cooking on the Maori fire. There was no sign of a body anywhere. Yet there could be no doubt that several of them must have been hit, judging from the painful climax of howls they set up after our first meeting at 20 yards, where several of our men on the left flank must have seen the backs of several Maoris lying behind the stumps. We now know that five were killed, and that one hundred Maoris were opposed to us, mostly Patumahoe natives then engaged in plundering and destroying settlers' property in the neighbourhood. I believe that after our first close encounter no one on our side made any hits excepting perhaps Jackson and Hay, as both of them were crack shots and don't fire at the smoke, as the general run of excited combatants do.

"We returned to Mauku laden with spoil and intoxicated with our victory. The Forest Rangers and Mauku Rifles had fleshed their arms at last, and that is no small matter with young soldiers. In casualties Alfred Speedy, son of Major Speedy, was shot through the cap, W. Worthington through the trousers, and Mr. Wheeler through the coat. This from a volley at 20 or 15 yards. Too much powder, ye Maoris!"

THE WRECK OF H.M.S. "ORPHEUS."

H.M.S. "Orpheus," a 21-gun steam-corvette, manned by a crew of 256 officers and men, was totally wrecked on the Manukau bar on the 7th February, 1863, when bound to Onehunga from Sydney to take up duty on the New Zealand Station.

The pilot-station at the heads showed the signal to take the bar, and the "Orpheus" came in under steam and sail before a good westerly breeze. The ship was carrying all plain sail, and her starboard foretopmast studding-sail was set. She was drawing 21 feet. She struck heavily on the western end of the middle bank, which afterwards was proved to have shifted three-quarters of a mile from where it was laid down on Drury's chart; the navigation officers of the "Orpheus," however, had also the "Niger" navigator's sailing-directions. The pilot-station watcher, seeing the ship running into danger, semaphored to her to stand more out to sea, but the warning signal was observed too late.

The ship struck twice, and the engines were ordered full speed astern, but the screw did not work; the way the ship had on sent her firmly into the sand.

The topsails were lowered, and the other sails were clewed up. Great seas were now breaking over the ship, and, after one boat had with difficulty got clear, the crew all took to the yards and rigging. The steamer "Wonga Wonga," bound south from Onehunga, went to the rescue, and approached the wreck as closely as she could. Some of the bluejackets, sliding down the foretopmast-stay, jumped into the sea and were picked up; others who attempted it were drowned.

The one boat which got clear took the news to the pilot-station, but it was night before the tragic story reached H.M.S. "Harrier," lying at Onehunga, twenty miles away, and by that time all was over.

The rollers breaking on the bar burst continually over the hull and lower masts. The yards and shrouds were thick with sailors despairingly looking for rescue. About 6 o'clock in the evening Commodore Burnett, who was in the mizzen-rigging, hailed the men, asked them to pray to God, and said he would be the last to leave the ship.

The mainmast was the first to go over the side. As it was falling the men clinging to the yards and rigging gave three heart-rending farewell cheers, which were answered by the men on the other masts, and next moment the gallant sailors were vainly struggling for their lives. The foremast soon followed, and then the mizzenmast gave way and crashed into the surf. The mizzentop fell on Commodore Burnett and partly stunned him, and he was drowned.

Out of the crew of 256 all told, only sixty-nine (including eight officers) were saved.

The bar which proved fatal to the beautiful corvette "Orpheus" and the greater number of her crew is called by the Maoris "Te Kupenga o Taramai-nuku" ("Tara's Fishing-net"), a reference to an ancestral chief whose name is associated with several places on the Auckland coast. Another native name for it is "Te Whare o te Atua" ("The Dwelling of the God"). The sandbanks are the northern remnant of a strip of low-lying land called Paorae, which anciently extended outside the present coast-line from the Manukau southward to Waikato Heads.

MILITIA DUTY IN THE WAIKATO WAR.

Redoubt-building and Escort Work.

The following are extracts from a diary kept (1863-64) by Captain James Stichbury, of Ponsonby, Auckland, when a private in the 1st Battalion of Auckland Militia; they are interesting for the glimpses they give of the tribulations and humours of the citizen soldier's life on active service:—

4th July, 1863.—Commenced drill, but being the first time made rather a mess of it. Continued drill every morning until the 9th, when we had a summons for actual service at 2s. 6d. per day. Drill every morning until the 18th, when we marched to Otahuhu in a very hot sun. We all thought it was a tremendous long walk with our sixty rounds of ammunition and rifle. Nothing to eat the first night.

21st July.—At 9 o'clock came off guard. At 10 marched from the camp to our destination, Papatoetoe, to build a redoubt. Reached it at 2 o'clock; took our tent and bread and raw meat with us. As soon as we had got our tents pitched—we had not time to dig the trenches round—it came on to rain. We had nothing to eat this night, for the rain would not let the fires burn; and, what made it worse, we had no blankets for two days after we arrived here. We had to lie on the wet ground with only our greatcoats and no fern. Dreadful night.

22nd July.—Very cold and miserable this morning, having to lie in the wet all night. Rain never ceased all day. Had to build some cook-houses as well as we could. Had no grog to-day, although we were entitled to it as soon as we started from Otahuhu. All the men were half-dead and laid up with the cold. Another night in our wet clothes and no fern.

23rd July.—Got served out to us a blanket and piece of oilskin, which came in very acceptable. Rain left off in the afternoon, which enabled us to get some of our things dry, and got some fern and had a comfortable night's rest.

24th July.—Served out with regimental clothes. They were forage cap with topknot, blue-serge shirt, trousers with red stripe down the side, blucher boots, short leggings; also tin plate, pannikin, knife, fork, spoon, haversack, &c. We get, per day, 1 gill of rum, 1 lb. of meat, 1¼ lb. of bread, ⅛ oz. of tea, ⅙ oz. of coffee, ⅓ oz. of sugar, and a grain of pepper and salt.

4th August.—At 9 o'clock fatigue parade. I was told off to work in the trenches. I got my shovel, but I did not do any work until I saw the captain; so I went up to him and told him I could not work in the trenches without my grog, for it is hard work digging on dry bread and hot coffee; besides, the grog is the only thing which keeps us alive this wet weather. [The diarist the previous day had been sentenced to "three days grog stopped" for absence without leave.]

5th August.—We have to get up an hour and a half before daylight. No matter what weather it is, there we have to stand, wet through and frozen with the cold, till we are dismissed. Have to clean our arms and belts. Had breakfast—very nice dry bread, as stale as a brick, and coffee without milk and very little sugar. After breakfast told off to dig in the trenches. Weather showery.

6th August.—We have to furnish our outer guards and picquets. The guard consists of a sergeant, a corporal, and nine men. The picquet consists of twenty-four men. They all go out of nights in the bush to look for Maoris, and their orders are to shoot every one they come across.

7th August.—Soldiering is very nice in dry weather, but in wet, and sleeping on the ground and under canvas, it is dreadful. Half the men in the camp are laid up with cold and rheumatism. I am on guard for four and twenty hours, and have rather a dismal post. We are stationed about half a mile from each other, and have two hours on and four hours off.

8th August.—The men that were confined last night [some of No. 5 Company had been put in the guard-tent for grumbling at their meat] were all let off with a reprimand. At 9 o'clock we were all paraded to have the Articles of War read to us on account of No. 5 Company's goings-on last night. As soon as we were marched into the hollow of the hill, so that we should be out of the wind, it came down to rain in torrents, and there we had to stand until the Colonel had done reading. He did not care, because he had an oilskin coat on, and we were in our blue shirts. After standing there in the rain for about twenty minutes we were dismissed, and away we went into our tents like a lot of drowned rats.

10th August.—At work in the bush to-day, under Lieutenant Tole, cutting trees down to make a new road to the Wairoa.

21st August.—(Papatoetoe.) Fine day. Told off for the trenches again. At a quarter to 9, as soon as we all got into bed nice and snug and the lights were out, two shots were fired by the sentry, and out we all went with only our pouch-belts on and our rifles. The order was given to load. We were all in such a hurry to get loaded that some put three cartridges in at once. Others left their ramrods in their rifles, and some went flying over the redoubt. Young B. and several others ran as hard as they could to Otahuhu, for they thought the Maoris were coming. A great many fired two or three shots each. As soon as it was a little quiet the Colonel and some other officers went to see if there was anybody about, and they found it was the grindstone that we were fighting.

22nd August.—Fine day. Everybody went to look at the poor grindstone, as they thought it would have been shattered to pieces. There was not a mark to be seen, although there were about a hundred shots fired at it. Went into the bush and found some bee-hives in the trees. Got two buckets of honey—quite a treat.

Second Expedition.

20th October, 1863.—Started from Albert Barracks, Auckland, at 2 p.m. Volunteer band played us as far as Parnell and then dropped off, and we went on. Arrived at Otahuhu Camp at 7 o'clock. Had no blankets, and nothing to eat.

21st October.—Got up at 7, and tried to get some meat for breakfast but could not. Had dry bread and a little drop of milk we managed to buy between us. Formed up at 9 to march to Drury. Very hot on the road, and dust very troublesome. Arrived at the camp at half-past 4 after a march of fifteen miles, with sixty rounds of ammunition, greatcoat, haversack full of different things, and rifle, weighing altogether about 30 lb.

24th October.—(Drury.) They have shifted us from where we first came to, and a dreadful place they have put us. When we were out before we built a splendid redoubt at Papatoetoe, the best and most comfortable in New Zealand. As soon as we got it finished we were sent to Auckland for a little while, and then sent to Drury—but I think a better name for it would be Dreary—to build another redoubt.

29th October. — Escort. Came back from Mauku; very miserable walking over the wet clay and a heavy load to carry, and forced to keep a sharp lookout.

30th October.—Forty men told off on engineers' fatigue to build a redoubt for the Artillery. The men all marched off the parade-ground, and when they got to the redoubt they all sat down and would not work, because this looks as if they bring us out to build redoubts for soldiers. (Saturday afternoon.) Went to the 18th (Royal Irish) camp and saw two men flogged for getting drunk. Sat in the tent singing songs until lights were out.

31st October (Sunday).—Dry bread and coffee for breakfast. Twenty-five men told off to unload cargo-boats of coal and flour. Seven of them [men who would not work] were tried and sentenced to seven days' pack-drill and grog stopped for the same period, and seven men were sent to the stockade at Otahuhu for seven days' hard labour and had their hair cut quite short. That is war-time. We must work on Sunday or go to prison.

1st November.—Warned for escort. After I got my breakfast one hundred men started at 7 from our camp, and some Regulars from the 18th camp. The distance is nine miles. The first redoubt we arrived at was Sheppard's Bush. We were strengthened there by forty men. The second redoubt was Martin's Farm. There we were strengthened by sixty men. Then we marched through the bush to our destination, called Williamson's Clearing Redoubt. Halted here for half an hour until the down convoy came, and off we started for Drury again. Reached our camp about 3 o'clock, very hungry and tired. Warned for commissariat fatigue for to-morrow to unload cargo-boats.

4th November.—(After coming off guard.) Sat in the tent on our pannikins, but could not lie down, for the floor was all in a flood and the rain coming through the tent. Not a wink of sleep all night. Went on my next relief. Thunder and lightning all night.

9th November.—Mud up to our knees and more than that. Have to lie in our tent in a frightful state, not being able to get dry fern, the weather being so unsettled. Went to see three soldiers belonging to the 18th Regiment flogged. In war-time they do not imprison them, because they cannot spare them.

14th November.—Escort started for the front at 7. Came back at 3, one man missing. Sergeant put under arrest for not looking after him and for reporting him present. We expect he straggled away from the main body and the natives have got him. Picquet sent out for him, but they came back without any signs of him.

21st November.—All the soldiers here are warned for the front, and we have to find all the duties until some more soldiers come to help us. The duties take about two hundred men every night. On regimental picquet to-night—that is, to go to the village and pick up the drunken men and bring them to camp.

26th November.—Hospital fatigue. Told off to build a house, but I wanted to get some of my clothes washed, so I would not go, and Ensign Hoben put me in the guard-room. I had to remain there until Sunday morning at 11 o'clock. Tried by Captain Britton, and he was going to give me a week in the stockade and to have my hair cut short. Then he asked the officers of my company what sort of character I had, and they gave me a good one, so he only gave me two days' pack-drill and grog stopped. I went as cook and got off.

28th November.—Fine day. A very strong escort up to Williamson's Clearing—about 120 horses, and 112 on the up and down convoy. The down convoy brought three corpses—a midshipman and two officers of the Army, and five wounded men (from Rangiriri).

30th November.—About a hundred Maoris came down from the Queen's Redoubt under an escort of four hundred soldiers; passed through here, and were taken on by a relief to Otahuhu.

APPENDICES.

2nd December.—No convoy to-day in consequence of the remainder of the Maori prisoners (from Rangiriri) coming down. There are about eighty under a very strong escort.

10th December.—(Orders for Otahuhu.) Got up at daylight, being half past 3. Got everything packed up and breakfast at 7. The dinner was cooked overnight ready for us. Struck the tents at 8. As soon as the bugle sounded down came all of them—all but one—and all the rest began hissing them that stopped in it. There were about thirty tents: all went down in a minute. Got all the tents and different things into the drays and the camp cleared. Then had to sit in the hot sun till the relief came. We waited until 1, and no relief, so we went on, after getting orders not to sing on the road as we did before. The Major [Tighe] is a regular old soldier and very strict. We got grog at 1—two glasses each. Formed up in close column, and then the word was given, " Form fours—Right—Left wheel—Quick march," and off we went in first-rate style. Very hot on the road. Reached the camp at Otahuhu at 4, like negroes with the dust, after a march of fifteen miles. No tea for us, as the men could not get it till 7. Had some sardines and bread, and went to bed in a hut full of fleas. Being tired, we were glad to sleep anywhere.

4th February, 1864.—(At Otahuhu Camp.) Got up at 5, gave our blankets up, had a wash and our breakfast, then tidied up our things ready for starting. At 9 o'clock we paraded, and shortly afterwards started for Drury. Rather hot and dusty on the road. Stopped at Burton's (Papatoetoe) to have a drink and a piece of lunch for twenty minutes; then we started again, and stopped at two springs, and then at Papakura to have a drink. We were pretty jolly on the road, singing all the way, and one or two of the men had concertinas and played some very lively tunes. On the road we marched too fast for the other companies, so the captain commanding put our company right behind. Then we would not march at all, so we dropped behind a long way, and he made us double. Then we dropped behind again, and when we marched into camp he gave us one hour's drill after walking sixteen miles with a load. We did it, but we all felt it very much. The commanding officer then was Captain Taylor, of No. 1 Company. After we had done drill we gave him three growls.

19th February. — Beautiful morning. At 7 started on convoy to Williamson's Clearing, escorting three Armstrong guns and about sixty carts loaded with ammunition, provisions, and other things. Very hot on the march, and the roads are being fresh metalled, and very miserable to walk on. Got to our destination at 12 and watered the horses, and then met the down convoy, about seventy carts, all empty. The officers would not let one of us ride. We all got into the carts, but were soon turned out again. (At night.) Large fires to be seen in the bush.

23rd February. — Got up at 5, cleaned my rifle and belts, had breakfast, and at 7 started for Williamson's Clearing. The day was beautifully fine, but the sun very hot. We were strengthened at every redoubt on the road, as usual. Got to the redoubt at Williamson's Clearing at 12. Was given charge of a prisoner belonging to the 18th Regiment (for Drury). He had fifty lashes and three months' hard labour.

LIST OF ENGAGEMENTS AND CASUALTIES (1845-64).

In the following chronological list of the principal engagements and skirmishes during the period ending with the Kingite wars, 1864, the Maori losses are in many cases only approximate. The natives whenever possible carried off their dead and wounded, and it was difficult to obtain exact information as to their losses. The Maori figures in numerous instances are probably an underestimate; the number of wounded is unknown.

Date.	Engagement.	British. Killed.	British. Wounded.	Maori. Killed.	Maori. Wounded.
1845.					
Mar. 11	Kororareka..	15	21	34	68
May 8	Puketutu (Omapere)..	14	40	30	50
June 30 / July 1	Ohaeawai ..	41	73	10	..
1846.					
Jan. 11	Rua-pekapeka	12	30	20	30
May 16	Boulcott's Farm (Hutt)	8	3	10	..
Aug. 6	Horokiri	3	8	..	..
1847.					
May 19	Wanganui ..	..	..	2	..
July 19	,,	3	11	3	10
1860.					
Mar. 17	Te Kohia (L pa), Waitara	2	2	..	..
Mar. 28	Waireka	2	12	50	..
June 27	Puke-ta-kauere	30	34	..	..
Sept. 7	Huirangi	1	2	..	..
Oct. 12	Kaihihi River positions	..	..	..	..
Nov. 6	Mahoetahi ..	4	17	50	60
Dec. 30	Mata-rikoriko	3	20	6	..
1861.					
Jan. 23	No. 3 Redoubt, Huirangi	5	11	50	40
Feb. 10	No. 7 Redoubt, Huirangi	2	28	..	..
Mar. 3	Brooklands (New Plymouth) ..	1	1	..	..
Mar. 5	Sap at Te Arei	1	4	..	..
Mar. 17	,,	1	..	..	..
1863.					
May 4	Wairau, Taranaki	9	..	..	..
June 4	Katikara, Taranaki ..	3	..	40	..
July 17	Koheroa, Waikato ..	1	12	30	..
	Martin's Farm, Great South Road	5	11	..	..
July 22	Kirikiri (Papakura) ..	2	4	..	..
July 24	Wairoa Road	1	..	..	..

APPENDICES.

LIST OF ENGAGEMENTS AND CASUALTIES (1845-64)—*continued*.

Date.	Engagement.	British. Killed.	British. Wounded.	Maori. Killed.	Maori. Wounded.
1863.					
Aug. 25	Williamson's Clearing (Pukewhau)	2	1	3	..
Sept. 2	Pokeno	..	..	..	..
Sept. 7	Camerontown (Lower Waikato)	8	1	7	20
Sept. 8	Kakaramea (Razorback)	..	..	1	..
	Hill's Clearing, Mauku	..	..	5	..
Sept. 14	Pukekohe East	3	8	40	..
	Burtt's Farm, Paerata	2	..	..	..
Sept. 15, 17, 18	Wairoa South stockade and Otau	..	..	8	..
Oct. 2	Allen's Hill, Taranaki	2	6	..	..
Oct. 23	Titi Hill, Mauku	8	4	20	..
Oct. 30	Meremere shelled	..	..	..	..
Nov. 20	Rangiriri	47	85	50	..
Dec. 14	Wairoa Ranges	..	..	8	..
1864.					
Feb. —	Waipa River (near Whatawhata)	1	..	..	..
Feb. 11	Waiari (Mangapiko)	6	5	40	30
Feb. 21	Rangiaowhia	5	3	12	..
Feb. 22	Hairini	3	15	25	..
Mar. 11	Kaitake	1	6	..	..
Mar. 24	,,	..	4	..	..
Mar. 31 April 1 April 2	Orakau	17	51	160	50
April —	Taurua (Rotoiti)	3*	4	20	..
April 21 to 26	Maketu	..	..	..	..
April 27	Kaokaoroa	1*	..	50	..
April 29	Gate *Pa*, Tauranga	31	80	20	..
June 21	Te Ranga	13	39	120	27
	Totals	313	653	924	383†

* Arawa.   † Incomplete; total unknown.

CORRECTIONS.

Page 326.—*For* "old sulphur-workings," Kawau Island, *read* "copper-workings."

Page 403. — Plan of Waiari, Mangapiko River: It is considered most probable that the bathing-place where the troops were attacked was at the northern end of the Waiari *pa* peninsula, instead of at the point shown on plan.

INDEX.

Ahumai at Orakau, 381, 383, 392, 393.
Akaroa blockhouses, 92.
Albert Barracks, Auckland, 238.
Alexandra Redoubt, 256.
Alexandra Township, 401, 402.
Allen, Bugler, 103, 105.
Arawa defeat East Coast tribes, 404–410.
Arei, Te, 196–197; approached by sap, 206–214.
Armitage, James, killed, 255.
Aro, Te, Wellington, defences at, 89.
Artillery, Maori, at Ohaeawai, 52, 63, 67; at Rua-pekapeka, 75, 78; at Meremere, 308–312; at Paterangi, 335, 336.
Artillery, Royal Field, arrives in New Zealand, 212–213.
Atkinson, Major, 155, 167, 168, 169, 173, 190, 222–223.
Auckland defences, 33, 236, 237, 238.
"Avon," gunboat, 300, 301, 310, 313.
Awamutu, Te, 230, 231, 232, 341–353, 369, 391, 392, 397, 399.

Barrett, Richard, 85, 432.
Bates, Colonel H. S., 201, 202, 328.
Bates, H. D., 202.
Beckham, Thomas, 19, 29.
"Bee," brig, 96.
Bell Block, Taranaki, 140, 141, 144, 160, 161, 162, 222.
Bell, Sir Dillon, 140, 236, 245.
Booth, Lieut.-Colonel, 417–423.
Boulcott's Farm, Hutt, 99, 101–107.
Bowie-knife, Forest Rangers', 258, 259, 440.
Bridge, Colonel Cyprian, 32, 45, 57, 59, 62, 64.
Brooke, Captain E., 324, 332.
Brooke, Lieutenant C. F., 183.
Bunbury, Major, 32, 431.
Burtt's Farm, Paerata, 275–280.
Busby, Mr., 4.
Bush Rangers, Taranaki, 218, 219, 222.

Cabbage Bay, 241, 242.
Calvert, Captain, 253.
Cameron, Lieut.-General, 215, 216, 219, 220, 242, 243, 253, 246, 310, 311, 312, 313, 378, 379.
Cambridge, Township of, 401, 402.
Carbine, Terry and Calisher, 258.
Carey, Lieut.-Colonel, 184, 185, 191, 313, 369.
"Castor," H.M.S., 70, 71, 81, 82, 83.
Casualties, list of, 452.
Cavalry charges in Maori wars, 350.
Chapman, Judge H. S., 89, 95, 432.

INDEX. 455

Chapman, Mr. Justice, 95, 142.
Churches fortified, 239, 240.
Cipher code, Maori, 235.
Clay Point, Wellington, 90.
Colvile, Major, 408.
Confiscation of Waikato, 399, 402.
Cowan, W. A., 357, 396.
Cracroft, Captain P., 157, 173, 174, 175.
Crispe, Heywood, 293, 296, 444.
Cudby, John, 92, 105.
Customs duties, first, 15.

Daldy, Captain W. C., 313, 316.
Davis, Rev. R., 36.
Deighton, Richard, 112-116.
Despard, Colonel, arrival of, 47.
Devon Road, New Plymouth, 155, 159, 195.
" Die-Hards " (57th Regiment), 211.
" Driver," H.M.S., 96, 97, 98, 99, 100, 113, 115, 116.
Drury, 215, 227, 240, 241, 242, 243, 249, 316, 317.

Easton, J. and G., 269, 272.
" Eclipse," H.M.S., 219, 221, 302, 306, 322.
" Elphinstone," H.E.I.C.S., 70, 71.
Engagements, list of, 452.
Epiha Tokohihi, 179, 189, 200.
" Esk," H.M.S., 306, 307, 313, 415.
Esk Redoubt, 314.

" Falcon," H.M.S., 408, 409, 415.
Fencibles, Royal New Zealand, 439.
First British march inland, 35.
First British troops in New Zealand, 431.
First engagement, Taranaki War, 159.
First engagement, Waikato War, 246.
First shots in Heke's War, 20.
First steamer on Waikato River, 300-301.
First steamship in New Zealand, 96, 97-98.
Fitzroy, Governor, 4, 16, 18, 19, 20, 31, 47, 70.
Flagstaff, Kororareka, first cut down, 17 ; again, 18, 20, 25.
" Fly," H.M.S., 439.
Forest Rangers formed, 258.
Fort Arthur, Nelson, 91.
Fort Britomart, Auckland, 32, 237, 238.
Fort Richmond, Lower Hutt, 92, 93, 96.
Fortresses, Maori and others compared, 52.
Free, W. H., 61, 62, 63, 65, 67, 68, 81, 169, 193.

Gage, John, 341, 369.
Galloway, Major-General, 237, 243.
Galloway Redoubt, Wairoa, 281, 282.
Gate *Pa*, Tauranga, 411-423 ; site of, 429.
Gilfillan, J. A., 132.
Gold, Colonel, arrives Taranaki, 157.
Gorst, Sir John, 227, 229, 230, 231, 232, 237, 245.
" Governor Grey," schooner, 136.
Grey, Sir George, 70, 78, 84, 98, 99, 109, 113, 115, 131, 136, 141, 149, 215, 216, 227, 228, 229, 230, 231, 326.

Hairini, Battle of, 347-351.
Hamilton, Captain J., R.N., 419.
Hamilton, Township of, founded, 401.
Hand-grenades used at Rangiriri, 324; at Orakau, 378, 379.
Harris, Major B., 274, 284.
Hauraki Tonganui, 382, 383.
Haurua *pa*, 398.
Hay, Commander, R.N., 419.
" Hazard," H.M.S., 18-31, 56.
Heaphy, Major C., V.C., 340.
Hector, C., 22, 28, 29.
Heke, Hone, his history, 13, 14, 15; raid on Kororareka, 16, 17; hoists American flag, 18-19; captures Flagstaff Hill, Kororareka, and cuts down mast for fourth time, 25; fighting at Omapere, 44; wounded, 47; taken to Tautoro, 53; at Rua-pekapeka, 80; his death, 84.
Heuheu, Iwikau te, 147, 148.
Heuheu, Horonuku te, 376.
Heuheu Tukino, 147.
Heuheu, Piripi te, 348, 359, 392, 393.
Hine-i-turama, killed at Orakau, 390, 391.
" Hokioi, Te," Maori newspaper, 230, 232.
Horokiri (Horokiwi), attack on, 123-127; site of, 127-129.
Huirangi, Waitara, 196-208.
" Hui-te-Rangiora," council-house, 179, 352.
Hulme, Lieut.-Colonel, 32, 35-36, 40-45.
Hursthouse, C. W., 154, 169, 170.
Hutt Valley land disputes and war, 85-108.

" Inflexible," H.M.S., 118, 134, 136, 137.
" Iris," H.M.S., 156, 185.

Jackson, Major W., 258, 259, 285, 289, 290, 298, 338, 378, 391.
Johns, William, 260, 286.

Kaihihi (Taranaki) forts taken, 187.
Kairau (Waitara) occupied, 196, 197.
Kaitake *pa* taken, 223, 224.
Kaokaoroa, Battle of, 409-410.
Katikara (Tataraimaka) stormed, 219-221.
Kawau Island, Maoris escape from, 326.
Kay, Andrew, 229, 232, 369.
Kereopa te Rau, 348, 350.
Kihikihi occupied, 352.
Kingi, Wiremu (Te Rangitaake), 113, 150-153.
Kiri-karamu, Ihaia te (Taranaki), 143, 152.
Kiri-karamu, Heni te (or Heni Pore), 252, 286; at Gate *Pa*, 413, 416, 418-421.
Kirikiri-roa (Hamilton), 351, 401.
Koheriki *hapu*, 252, 284, 287; at Gate *Pa*, 413.
Koheroa, engagement at, 246-248.
Kooti, Te, 5.
Kororareka, the beach at, 6-12; capture of, 23-31.
Kou, Rihara, 50, 55, 64, 80.

Land League, Maori, 140-144.
Last, Major, 100, 106, 109, 123-127.
Leslie, Colonel, 200, 385.
Lyon, Major, 281-283.

INDEX. 457

McDonnell, Thomas, 263, 264, 344, 345, 352, 408, 409.
McKenna, Ensign, V.C., 255, 256.
Macpherson, Major, 64.
Mahoetahi, Battle of, 188-195 ; lament for, 194.
Mair, Captain Gilbert, 35, 391, 407.
Mair, Gilbert, sen., 431.
Mair, Major W. G , 344, 345, 380-383, 390, 391, 397, 399, 402, 405.
Maketu, 404, 405, 408.
Mamaku, Topine te, 101-106, 135, 398.
Manawapou, 142.
Manga-tawhiri River, 229, 232, 242 ; crossed by troops, 245.
Maning, F. E., 38, 58.
Marsland Hill, 155, 157, 158.
Martin's Farm, ambush at, 248-250.
Mauku, church stockaded, 288 ; defence and engagements, 288-298
Meremere, 308-313.
Messenger, A. H., 143.
Messenger, Captain, 180, 182, 183.
Messenger, Colonel W. B., 160, 167, 172, 173, 190.
Messenger, E., killed, 199.
Messenger, Private W., wounded, 173.
" Miranda," H.M.S., 305, 313.
Miranda expedition, 313-314.
Morrow, Lieut.-Colonel A., 442.
Murray, Lieut.-Colonel, 167-176, 185.

Naval Brigade at New Plymouth, 157 ; at Puke-ta-kauere, 180 ; at Rangiriri, 319-324 ; at Gate *Pa*, 415.
Naval Volunteers, Auckland, 313-317.
Nelson, Major, 179-185.
Nene, Tamati Waka, 17, 18, 33, 34, 35 ; at Omapere, 36 ; at Ohaeawai, 58 ; at Rua-pekapeka, 71, 76, 80.
New Plymouth fortifications, 156, 157, 158, 176.
Ngakapa, Hori, 248, 249, 252, 439.
Ngaruawahia, 226, 327-329.
" Niger," H.M.S., 157, 173-176.
Nixon, Colonel M., 345.

Ohaeawai, attack on, 47-69.
Okaihau, 36, 38, 39.
Omapere, 33, 36.; fighting at, 37-46.
Omata Stockade (Taranaki), 162-164.
Onehunga, 315, 316, 317.
Onuku-kaitara, 178, 179, 180, 186, 197.
Orakau, Village of, 355-357 ; first expedition to, 358 ; fortified, 360-367 ; siege of *pa*, 369-397.
" Orpheus,' H.M.S., wrecked, 447.
Otau, engagement at, 282-283.

Paerata, Ahumai te, 381, 383, 392, 393.
Paerata, Hitiri te, 366, 386, 391.
Paerata, Hone Teri te, 366, 388.
Paerata, Te, 366.
Page, Lieutenant G. H., 101-105.
Papakura, defences at, 239.
Paparata, 262, 263, 264.
Papatoetoe Redoubt, 239, 448, 449.
Paratui *pa*, 398.

Patara te Tuhi, 225, 232, 233.
Paterangi, fortifications at, 328-337.
Patumahoe, fight at (Big Clearing), 289-292 ; origin of name, 298 ; Von Tempsky's account of fight, 445.
Paua-tahanui, operations at, 109-122.
Pekapeka Block, Waitara, 151, 436.
Pekehawani (Puniu River), 180.
Pene Taui, 34, 35, 48.
Perry, Sergeant, 266-275.
Phillpotts, Lieutenant G., at Kororareka, 28-31 ; killed at Ohaeawai, 57, 63, 68, 69.
" Pihoihoi, Te," 230, 231, 232.
Pikopiko, fortifications at, 328, 330, 334, 335.
Pitt, Colonel, 236.
Pitt, Major-General Dean-, 237.
Plimmerton, 114.
Pokai, R., 23, 29, 43, 44, 46.
Pokeno, 241, 242, 243, 254.
Pokiha Taranui (Major Fox), 407, 409.
Pomare, Bay of Islands chief, 15, 16, 22, 33.
Pomare, Sir Maui, 102, 108.
Porirua, operations at, 109-119.
Poroutawhao *Pa*, 130.
Potatau te Wherowhero, 147, 148, 225, 226, 227, 435, 436.
Pou-patate Huihi, 193 ; at Orakau, 378, 385, 386.
Pratt, Major-General, arrived, 185 ; his sap towards Te Arei, 206-213.
Pukekohe East, fight at church stockade, 265-275.
Puke-ta-kauere, engagement at, 178-184.
Puketutu *pa*, attack on, 36, 39-46.
Pukorokoro (Miranda), 313-314.
Puni, Te, 86, 106, 107.
Pye, Captain, 348, 350.

Ranga, Te, Battle of, 423-429.
Rangiaowhia invaded by British, 341-351.
Rangihaeata, Te, 86, 88, 100, 101, 102, 109-129 ; death of, 130.
Rangiriri, Battle of, 318-326.
Rauparaha, Tamehana te, 118, 145.
Rauparaha, Te, his capture, 113-119.
Raureti Paiaka, 179, 271, 274 ; at Orakau, 377-386.
Raureti, Te Huia, 179, 193, 194, 269, 271, 274, 334 ; at Orakau, 367-396.

Razorback Redoubt (Kakaramea) attacked, 254.
Rewi Maniapoto (Manga), 179-180, 200, 231, 232, 352, 354 ; at Orakau, 358-388.
Rhodes, H., Paterangi, 334, 340.
Rhodes's Clearing, Razorback, 243.
Ring, Captain, 248-251, 370.
Roberts, Colonel J. M., 259, 263, 369, 370, 371, 389, 391.
Robertson, Captain, R.N., 26.
Rore, Te, occupied by British, 329.
Rotoiti, Lake, fighting at, 405-408.
Roto-marama *pa*, 398.
Russell, Captain, 100.
Russell (Kororareka), 6-12 ; English church at, 27.
Rutland Stockade, Wanganui, 132-134.

INDEX.

"Sandfly," armed steamer, 304, 313, 408, 409.
Sap at Kaihihi River, 187; at Te Arei, 197, 206-214; at Orakau, 371-384, 396.
Scott, Captain Joseph, 269, 272, 273.
Selwyn, Bishop G. A., 30, 341, 434.
Smith, S. Percy, 143, 437.
Stanley, Captain, R.N., 110, 115, 116, 123.
Stichbury, Captain J., 448.

Taiamai, Bay of Islands, 34, 37, 68.
"Taiporohenui," council-house, 142.
Tai-Rawhiti tribes invade Arawa country, 404-410.
Tamehana, Wiremu, founds Maori kingdom, 146, 147, 148; makes peace with Brigadier-General Carey, 399.
Taranaki settlement, 140; type of settlers, 154-155; first shots in war, 159.
Taratoa, Henare, 412, 427.
Tawhiao, King, 227, 230.
Teira, Hori, 215, 216, 217, 218.
Tempsky, Von, joins Forest Rangers, 261-262; scouting at Paparata, 262-264; fight at Patumahoe, 289-292; at Paterangi, 329-330; at Waiari, 339-340; at Rangiaowhia, 341-346; at Orakau, 369-391.
Thorndon fortifications, Wellington, 89, 90.
Tiki-o-te-Ihingarangi, fortifications at, 329, 399.
Titi Hill fight, Mauku, 292-297.
Tupotahi at Orakau, 366-394.

Urewera Tribe, war-party at Hairini, 348; at Orakau, 358-394; contingent at Kaokaoroa, 410.

"Victoria," Government brig, 18, 22, 28, 96, 132.
"Victoria," Australian warship, 176-177.

Waiari, engagement at, 337-340.
Waikato, military road to, 242, 243; first engagement, 246; first steamer on river, 300-301; gunboat flotilla, 300-303; end of war, 398-402; confiscation of land, 402.
Waikato War, causes of, 225-235.
Waipa country invaded, 329.
Wairarapa defences, 438.
Waireka, Battle of, 166-176.
Waitara, attempted purchase of, 150-153; war begins at, 158; war ends, 214.
Wanganui, war at, 131-139.
Wellington settlements, land disputes and war of 1846, 85-130; defences of, 88-96.
Whakaari, Netana, 410.
Whaleships at Kororareka, 6-12.
Wharepapa, Forest Rangers' expedition to, 444.

By Authority: W. A. G. SKINNER, Government Printer, Wellington.—1922.
[1,000/7/21—10399